Llewellyn's Golden Dawn Series

Secrets of a Golden Dawn Temple

The Alchemy and Crafting of Magickal Implements

by

Chic Cicero
and
Sandra Tabatha Cicero

1992
Llewellyn Publications
St. Paul, Minnesota, U.S.A. 55164-0383

FIRST EDITION

Cover photo by Michael Yencho
Color plates and photos, diagrams and construction of all magical tools and implements by Chic Cicero and Sandra Tabatha Cicero

Library of Congress Cataloging-in-Publication Data

Cicero, Chic, 1936-
    Secrets of a Golden Dawn temple : the alchemy and crafting of magickal implements / by Chic Cicero and Sandra Tabatha Cicero
        p. cm. -- (Llewellyn's Golden Dawn series)
    Includes bibliographical references.
    ISBN 0-87542-150-4 : $19.95
    1. Hermetic Order of the Golden Dawn—Rituals.   I. Cicero, Sandra Tabatha, 1959- .   II. Title.   III. Series.
BF1623.R7C48 1992
135'.4--dc20

92-10006
CIP

Permissions:
    Drawings copyright © Adam P. Forrest
    Rituals, *The Golden Dawn,* copyright © Israel Regardie
    Meditation copyright © OZ

Llewellyn Publications
A Division of Llewellyn Worldwide, Ltd.
P.O. Box 64383, St. Paul, MN 55164-0383

An Act of Magick

The act of constructing a wand or other ritual object is an act of Magick. The Magician spends an extraordinary amount of time creating ritual objects, not because it is only through these objects that magick can rightly be performed, but because the act of creating is a magickal process of growth, one which initiates the development of Will in accordance with the Divine Intent or Purpose. This in turn contributes to the success of the ritual.

The construction of a ritual object should be treated like any other magical operation. It should focus all parts of the Magician's mind (intellect, creativity, imagination, spiritual self) into one purpose—to manifest an object which will be a receptacle for Higher Forces, in order that the Magician too can become a worthy receptacle of that which is Divine.

It is not necessary to create a perfect work of art. A person who works long and hard on a wand that looks crude will ultimately have more success than a person who purchases a ready-made wand that is flawless.

With this book, clear instructions are finally available on how to fabricate the wands and implements of the Golden Dawn, some of the most significant, profound and beautiful of all the ritual tools that have ever been produced in the Western Magickal Tradition. With the materials and tools available to the modern Magician, these instruments can be recreated with stunning accuracy and magnificence.

But this book is more—it also gives you access to the magickal techniques that can be applied to these implements. The various tools presented here each have a very specific symbology attached to them. Relying upon this symbology, we have created rituals uniquely designed for each particular implement, while remaining true to the teachings and magickal techniques of the Hermetic Order of the Golden Dawn.

Learning how to build objects and how to use the tools you construct is the transformational alchemy that will lead to your further spiritual development. It is this growth which is the true goal of ceremonial magic. Building the tools and working with them as described in this book will make a difference in your life. The tools you create will reinforce and enhance your own magickal abilities, and they will make every aspect of your life more magickal.

About the Authors

Chic Cicero was born in Buffalo, New York. He is a former jazz musician and a businessman. Chic has been a practicing Ceremonial Magician for the past 25 years. He was a close friend of Israel Regardie, and was one of the key people who helped Regardie resurrect a legitimate branch of the Hermetic Order of the Golden Dawn in the U.S. in the early 1980s.

Sandra Tabatha Cicero was born and raised in Soldiers Grove, Wisconsin. She graduated from the University of Wisconsin, Milwaukee with a Bachelor's Degree in the Fine Arts. After college she worked as a graphic artist and an entertainer. She spent five years working on the paintings for *The New Golden Dawn Ritual Tarot*.

Both Chic and Sandra are acknowledged adepts of the Hermetic Order of the Golden Dawn. They are active in the Magickal community as a whole, and are currently working on a number of books and Tarot decks.

To Write to the Authors

If you wish to contact the author or would like more information about this book, please write to the author in care of Llewellyn Worldwide and we will forward your request. Both the authors and publisher appreciate hearing from you and learning of your enjoyment of this book and how it has helped you. Llewellyn Worldwide cannot guarantee that every letter written to the authors can be answered, but all will be forwarded. Please write to:

THE LLEWELLYN NEW TIMES
P.O. Box 64383-150, St. Paul, MN 55164-0383, U.S.A.
Please enclose a self-addressed, stamped envelope for reply, or $1.00 to cover costs.
If outside U.S.A. enclose international postal reply coupons.

Free Catalog from Llewellyn

For more than 90 years, Llewellyn has brought its readers knowledge in the fields of metaphysics and human potential. Learn about the newest books in spiritual guidance, natural healing, astrology, occult philosophy and more. Enjoy book reviews, new age articles, a calendar of events, plus current advertised products and services. To get your free copy of the New Times, send your name and address to:

THE LLEWELLYN NEW TIMES
P.O. Box 64383-150, St. Paul, MN 55164-0383, U.S.A.

ABOUT LLEWELLYN'S GOLDEN DAWN SERIES

Just as, 100 years ago, the original Order of the Golden Dawn *initiated* a powerful rebirth of interest in The Western Esoteric Tradition that has lasted through this day, so do we expect this series of books of add new impetus to The Great Work itself among an ever broadening base of sincere students.

> *I further promise and swear that with the Divine Permission, I will from this day forward, apply myself to the Great Work— which is: to purify and exalt my Spiritual Nature so that with the Divine Aid I may at length attain to be more than human, and thus gradually raise and unite myself to my Higher and Divine Genius, and that in this event I will not abuse the great power entrusted to me.*

With this oath, the *Adeptus Minor* of the Inner Order committed his/herself to undertake, consciously and deliberately, that which was ordained as the birthright of all Humanity: TO BECOME MORE THAN HUMAN!

It is this that is the ultimate message of Esotericism: that evolution continues, and that the purpose of each life is to grow into the Image set for us by our Creator: to attain and reveal our own Divinity.

These books and tapes will themselves make more easily accessible the Spiritual Technology that is inherent in the Golden Dawn System. It is a system that allows for individual as well as group endeavor; a system that works within or without an organized lodge; a system that is based on universal principles that will be shown to be global in their impact today.

And practical. The works in this series will be practical in their applications and requirements for application. You need neither to travel to the Mountain Top nor obtain any tool other than your own Consciousness. No garment need you other than that of your own Imagination. No authority need you other than that of your own True Will.

Set forth, then, into The New Dawn—a New Start on the greatest adventure there is: to become One with the Divine Genius.

Also by Chic Cicero and Sandra Tabatha Cicero

The New Golden Dawn Ritual Tarot (deck)
The New Golden Dawn Ritual Tarot (book)

Forthcoming

Self-Initiation
Tarot Talismans
Scrying on the Tree of Life
Archangelic Magick
The Telesmatic Tarot
The Tarot of the Four Worlds
The Sumerian Tarot

CONTENTS

The Neophyte Hall – The Altar – A Meditation on the Altar – The Cross and Triangle – Meditation Ritual on the Cross and Triangle – The Banners of the East and West – The Banner Poles – A Meditation on the Banners – The Pillars – Portable Pillars – The Pillar Diagrams – Concerning the Vignettes – A Meditation on the Pillars – The Iset or Temple Throne – A Meditation on the Throne of the Stolistes – Implements of the Neophyte Officers – The Neophyte Officers and their Godforms – The Neophyte Office's Implements – The Consecration of a Tipharetic Talisman – The Hegemon's Wand – Ritual for Spiritual Development – The Sword of the Hiereus – The Supreme Banishing Ritual of the Pentagram – The Wand of the Kerus – An Invocation of Hermes-Thoth – The Cup of Stolistes – The Rite of Self-Consecration – The Sword of the Phylax – The Implements of the Dais Officers – The Dais Officers – The Imperator's Sword – The Praemonstrator's Wand – The Cancellarius' Wand – The Past Hierophant's Wand – The Lamens of the Seven Officers of the Neophyte Hall – The Collars – The Apparel of the Neophyte Officers – The Cloak or Tabard – The Tau Robe – A Meditation on the Tau Robe – A Simple Robe – The Nemyss – A Meditation/Ritual on the Nemyss – The Sash – Assumption of Godforms, a Guided Meditation – The Rite of Assumption to the Godform of Thmê

"I cannot now think symbols less than the greatest of all powers whether they are used consciously by the masters of magic, or half consciously by their successors, the poet, the musician, and the artist."

—W. B. Yeats (Frater D.E.D.I.)
Magic, 1901

DEDICATION

This book is dedicated to the true Initiates of the Hidden Knowledge who work tirelessly and silently for the completion of the Great Work, without thought of monetary profit or personal glory. Without their careful nurturing, the special Light that remains to this day known as the Hermetic Order of the Golden Dawn would have certainly been extinguished.

We remain especially grateful to G.H. Frater E Cinere Phoenix and G.H. Soror Monocris De Astris for their devoted and firm commitment to the high ideals and original goals of the Order.

We would also like to thank Carl and Sandra Weschcke for all that they have done to insure that the teachings of the Golden Dawn have been readily available to students across the world.

Above all, we warmly thank Francis Israel Regardie, who held out the lamp of the Hidden Knowledge for all of us.

ACKNOWLEDGEMENTS

It gives us great pleasure to acknowledge the many people who contributed in some way to the completion of this book:

Chris Monnastre for providing the Foreword; Adam Forrest for his contribution of original artwork for the Pillar diagrams, the Epilogue, much-needed corrections on the Coptic spellings and colorings of the various Godforms of the Neophyte Hall, as well as his invaluable advice; Isidora Forrest for her work on robes, collars and tabards, in addition to her photo of a stained glass Water Cup; Donald Michael Kraig for providing the Afterword; OZ for furnishing the meditation on the Assumption of Godforms in the Neophyte Hall; Ceil Thomas for providing the section describing the Banners; Bill Allen for his section on the Geomancy box along with a ritual for its consecration; V.H. Frater R.H.K. for his original Pillar designs; Anupassana and George Wilson who provided material on the nemyss and corrections for the Day/Night Houses of the planets in the section describing the Lotus Wand; V.H. Frater A.A.A. who provided corrections to the Divine names on the Elemental Weapons; and finally, Sior Chappell, Logan and Danaé Sullivan for simply being there for us throughout this long project.

Foreword

Magickal consecration is a spiritually sophisticated process of setting apart the mundane for sacred use. However, the consecration of magickal implements does not begin with the ceremonial process, but with ALL the preparations prior to a full Temple working, including finding the needed materials, crafting and painting the components of each tool, and doing research to ensure that the final product is as accurate as possible. An important feature of this book is that it presents instructions for the crafting of implements based not simply on the subjective judgments of the authors (though the final products can be quite beautiful), but upon hours of research to ensure that each implement is perfectly aligned with the Western Tradition.

Both the procedure and the spiritual benefits to be gained from the crafting of magickal implements were first taught to me by Israel Regardie, whom I often visited from 1981 to 1983, at his home in Sedona, Arizona. One weekend Regardie suggested that it might be a good time for me to obtain some experience in the making and consecration of talismans. Personal circumstances dictated that a Venus talisman would be the most appropriate focal point.

It took me approximately seven hours—an appropriate numerical correspondence to Venus—to locate the paints, papers and other materials, verify the correspondences, and then construct the talisman. While the actual ritual consecration was performed weeks later, in Los Angeles, in full Temple, and under supportive astrological influences, the consecration process actually began with the inception of the idea for the talisman and the hours of preparation preceding the formal work. This selection of this particular talisman, the attendant ritual and the prior preparation has, I might add, successfully influenced the past nine years of my life!

A noteworthy feature of this book is that it guides the student through the wonderfully and deeply spiritually significant adventure of the so-called "Outer Order."

All Outer Order work has for its goal the attainment of the Knowledge and Conversation of the Holy Guardian Angel, or Christ consciousness. C. J. Jung, in his autobiography *Memories, Dreams, Reflections*, wrote about similar experiences which occured to him at Bollingen, where his own unique dialogue with the unconscious demanded of him the crafting, building, painting and bringing to life in a five sensate world the symbols which flooded his experience at the time. He writes of finding a particular stone while in this process. "The first thing that occurred to me was a Latin verse by the alchemist Arnaldus de Villanova (died 1313). I chiseled this into stone; in translation it goes:

"Here stands the mean, uncomely stone,
'Tis very cheap in price!
The more it is despised by fools,
The more loved by the wise."

This book will surely provide inspiration to every reader who desires to undertake this process of magickal craftsmanship. The final caveat is not to become mired in the small steps of the journey, but to be ever aware of aspiring to that Knowledge and Conversation of which Regardie related to the hopeful completion of the Great Work.

With ever the highest goals in sight, the Grade Initiations will put you on paths of increasing inner challenges. What is contained within this book can do nothing but offer honest, sincere and a miraculous richness in the forward movement of each aspirant's quest toward the completion of the Great Work! This is not an inflated promise. This is a certainty.

—Chris Monnastre
Los Angeles, 1992

Introduction

Magick is a spiritual science. It is a technical system of training with a divine rather than mundane objective. The goal of Magick is to discipline and strengthen the Will and the Imagination. When you create something in your imagination, you are creating it in the subtle layers of the Astral. All of the machines, music, books, inventions and everyday objects that we use and take for granted began as blueprints in someone's mind. What was first imagined was then created. Bringing the Astral image of something into manifestation, be it an object, event, circumstance, or spiritual state of mind, has always been one of the goals of Magick. This is especially true when it comes to making magickal or ritual objects.

The act of constructing a wand or other ritual object should be considered an act of Magick. The Magician spends an extraordinary amount of time creating ritual objects, not because it is only through these precious objects that Magick can rightly be performed, but because the construction of these items is the catalyst for a magickal process of growth, one which initiates the development of Will in accordance with the Divine Intent or Purpose. Israel Regardie, founder of the modern incarnation of the Golden Dawn, emphasizes this point in regard to the fashioning of the Magician's wand. This same principle may be applied to all of the Magician's implements:

> "Since the Wand is the symbol of the Creative Will, its construction should be accompanied by a distinct exertion of that Will, and in this idea is the rational of many of the apparently far-fetched injunctions given by Theurgists in connection with the acquisition of suitable weapons. . .
>
> Were [Eliphas] Levi's advice to be followed, for instance, in connection with the Wand, then that instrument should be

fashioned from a a perfectly straight branch of the almon or hazel tree, cut without hacking or boggling with a single blow from the tree with a sharp knife before the sun rises, and at the season when the tree is about to blossom. It should be subjected to a process of meticulous preparation, stripping the branch of leaves and twigs, removing the bark, and neatly trimming the ends and smoothing down the knots, followed by other significant processes which can be ascertained by consulting Transcendental Magic. Underlying all these processes is the development of the Will. The Magician who has troubled himself to the extent of rising two or three times at midnight on behalf of his Wand and denied himself rest and sleep, will, by the very fact of his self-denial, have benefited considerable in Will. In such an instance, the Wand actually will be a dynamic symbol of the Creative Will, and it is such symbols and instruments as this which in Magic are required."*

The elaborate preparation undertaken by the Ceremonialist is necessary not for the performance of magick *per se*, but rather for the proper development of the mind and the Creative Will of the Magician. This in turn contributes to the success of the ritual:

"[Wands and other Elemental weapons] function as the visible embodiment of the Magician's own condition of soul and mind, without which they fail of effect as thaumaturgic symbols. If the Magician's mind, for instance, be not sharp and analytic, and if this quality of mind be not contributed to the making of the sword, how should the elemental spirits and the dog-faced demons obey his commands to get themselves gone from the circle of invocation? The chalice, too, as the symbol of the Intuition as well as of the divine Imagination, must likewise be fashioned in such a way and attended by high thoughts and great deeds as to embody some intuitional idea, either bearing on the exterior design or word of supreme significance, or exemplifying by the shape of the Cup alone a divine idea."**

Constructing a ceremonial wand focuses all parts of the Magician's mind (intellect, creativity, imagination, spiritual self) into one purpose—to manifest an object which will be a receptacle for Higher Forces, in order that the Magician too, can become a worthy receptacle of that which is Divine.

We have seen photographs of many elemental weapons constructed a century ago by some of the Golden Dawn's most promi-

---

* Israel Regardie. *The Tree of Life*, p. 117.
** Ibid, pp 117-8.

nent and brilliant members. Some of those implements seem very rough by our own standards, but achieving material perfection was never the point. What is important is that those members constructed their personal tools to the best of their abilities—putting their own Creative Wills into action. A Magician who works long and hard on a wand that looks crude will ultimately have more success than a person who purchases a ready-made wand that is flawless.*

In this book we have tried to make available clear instructions on how to fabricate the wands and implements of the Golden Dawn, some of the most significant, profound and beautiful of all the ritual tools that have ever been produced in the Western Magickal Tradition. With the materials and tools available to the modern Magician, these instruments can be recreated with stunning accuracy and magnificence. It is not our intention, however, to present merely a construction manual for the manufacture of magickal implements. Granted, the main purpose of this book is to show how to produce the various items which are vital to a properly equipped Golden Dawn Temple. But more than that, we wish to give the student access to magickal techniques which can be applied to those same implements, both in their construction, consecration, and their use.

The various wands and magickal tools presented here each have a very specific symbology attached to them. Relying upon this symbology, we have included old and new rituals uniquely designed for each particular implement. These rituals are of varying degrees of difficulty and intensity, requiring different levels of knowledge and ceremonial experience. Someone who has little magickal experience and who doesn't know the basics cannot be expected to jump headlong into a complex ceremony, and for this reason we have included in this introduction a guide to the rituals by grade. Whether the student is actively involved in Temple work or is progressing through self-initiation, he/she should have a basic idea of what level of magickal experience applies, and act accordingly. Furthermore, the construction of a ritual object should be treated like any other magickal operation, and thus it is important to keep in mind the high purposes for which the objects are being made. You should not try gluing wand sections together or cutting

---

* Israel Regardie gave his personal Elemental Tools, along with other implements, to one of our Order members. We have been fortunate to have the opportunity to document Regardie's tools via photography.—C.C.

out fabric for a robe if you are highly aggravated over something. The project can be put aside until things calm down.

OVERVIEW OF THE GOLDEN DAWN SYSTEM

The focus of the Hermetic Order of the Golden Dawn has always been to preserve and teach to its members the basic precepts of the Western Esoteric Tradition. The success of the Order in reaching this goal is indicated by the fact that the teachings and techniques of the Golden Dawn have been copied and imitated by many authors and magickal groups for decades. Because each and every item in a Golden Dawn Temple has complex symbolism associated with it, careful attention to detail should be applied when constructing such implements.

This book examines the techniques used to make implements within the Golden Dawn tradition for use in private magickal work. For the student who might not be thoroughly familiar with the Golden Dawn system of Magick, a brief overview of the Order and its grades are provided here:

The grades of the Golden Dawn correspond to the Sephiroth on the Qabalistic Tree of Life. These grades are divided into three separate groups known as the First, Second, and Third Orders. The list of the grades (from lowest to highest) is as follows:

Grade	Corresponding Sephirah	Element
Neophyte 0=0	———	———
Zelator 1=10	Malkuth	Earth
Theoricus 2=9	Yesod	Air
Practicus 3=8	Hod	Water
Philosophus 4=7	Netzach	Fire
Adeptus Minor 5=6	Tiphareth	———
Adeptus Major 6=5	Geburah	———
Adeptus Exemptus 7=4	Chesed	———
Magister Templi 8=3	Binah	———
Magus 9=2	Chokmah	———
Ipsissimus 10=1	Kether	———

The First Order consists of the grades from Neophyte through Philosophus. The grade of the Neophyte is a probationary period which is not assigned a sephirah on the Tree of Life. A person of this grade would be considered a member of the Order, but not yet an Initiate. The grades from Zelator through Philosophus are known as the Elemental grades, and are each attributed to one of the four elements (fire, water, air, earth). Advancement through the grades of the First Order is designed to expose the initiate to the four elemental principles of nature. But more importantly, the student learns to recognize and balance these four elements as part of his/her own psychological makeup. The keywords of the entire First Order could easily be rendered as "learn to balance."

Between the grades of the Philosophus and Adeptus Minor there is an additional initiation ceremony that is not assigned to a sephirah on the Tree of Life. The Portal is not properly a grade, but it is in fact a probationary period between the First and Second Orders. The Portal is attributed to the fifth element of Spirit which crowns and completes the other four elements. It is also a period of incubation; the initiate who has equilibrated the four elements within the psyche undergoes a symbolic interval of gestation before being "born" as an Adept of the Second Order.

The Second Order consists of grades from Adeptus Minor to Adeptus Exemptus. It is within the Second Order that the intitiate begins the practice of Ceremonial Magick. (This is because the First Order is primarily a school where the foundations of Magick are taught.) The Second Order guides and teaches the First Order, and is likewise guided and taught by the Third Order.

The Third Order, consisting of grades from the Magister Templi to Ipsissimus, is made up of non-physical beings who are guardians of the entire current represented by the Golden Dawn. It is not possible for a living Adept to attain these high grades since it entails crossing the Abyss.

The First and Second Orders are governed by three officers known as the Greatly Honored Chiefs. They are the Imperator, the Praemonstrator and the Cancellarius, who are assigned to the spheres of Geburah, Chesed and Tiphareth, respectively. More on the G.H. Chiefs of the Order will be discussed in the first chapter of this book.

OVERVIEW OF THIS BOOK

Chapter 1 contains the bulk of information necessary for the construction of a Golden Dawn Temple in the Outer Order. The rituals and meditations given range from simple meditations for the Neophyte, to the charging of a talisman for the Zelator Adeptus Minor.

Chapter 2 concentrates on the secondary props of the Outer Order Temple and the Admission Badges. This chapter is best described as a workbook within a book for the student who is advancing through the elemental grades of the Outer Order. Besides the practical information on making the Badges, various rituals and guided visualizations are given for each level or degree of the First Order from Zelator to Philosophus.

In chapter 3, the tools of the Portal grade are described, as well as the Enochian Tablets. The wands and some of the Second Order implements are examined in chapter 4.

The Adept's personal Temple implements are given in chapter 5. These include the Four Elemental Weapons as well as the Magick Sword, Lotus Wand and Rose Cross Lamen. The traditional consecration rituals for these implements are given here in a form that is easy to follow. In addition, new rituals using all of these tools are also provided.

We have also included a section on the fabrication of new, non-traditional implements which are based on rituals inspired by the Golden Dawn system of magick. These are given in chapter 6.

RITUALS BY GRADE

For the Neophyte: Regular performance of the Qabalistic Cross, the Lesser Banishing Ritual of the Pentagram, and the Adoration of the Lord of the Universe given in this introduction are recommended. Chapter 1 contains meditations on the Banners, the Pillars, and the Tau Robe, which are also suitable for the 0=0 grade.

Rituals for the Elemental grades are all in chapter 2. *For the Zelator:* An Invocation of the Element of Earth. *For the Theoricus:* A Journey on the 32nd Path of Tau, and an Invocation of the Element of Air. *For the Practicus:* A Journey on the 31st Path of Shin, A Journey on the 30th Path of Resh, and an Invocation of the Element of Water. *For the Philosophus:* A Journey on the 29th Path of Qoph, A Journey on the 28th Path of Tzaddi, A Journey on the 27th Path of Peh, and an Invocation of the Element of Fire.

Rituals for the Portal grades in chapter 1: The Rite of Self-Purification and the Rite of Self-Consecration; in chapter 3: the Meditation on the Portal Grade, the Rite of Self-Consecration through Sulphur, the Rite of Self-Purification through Salt, a Simple Meditation on the Portal Lamens, and the Purification of the Elements Within. (Note: Although traditionally the Supreme Invoking Ritual of the Pentagram is prescribed for the 5=6 grade, we believe that the student may begin to perform this ritual in the Portal grade, seeing that he/she has now been introduced to the Five Elements. Consequently, the Supreme Banishing Ritual of the Pentagram given in chapter 1 could also be performed. In both the SIRP and SBRP, the Portal initiate may substitute the LVX Signs with the Portal Signs.)

Rituals for the Adept Grades: The remaining advanced rituals in this book (including some which are described in this introduction and in chapters 1, 3, 4, 5, and 6) are intended for ceremonial use by the Magician who has attained at least the level of skills assigned to the Adeptus Minor grade.

COLOR

Color is extremely important to the Magician, because it is through the proper application of color (and symbols, and sound) that the the Ceremonialist is able to forge a magickal link with the Divine Intelligences. Thus color is of primary importance to the creation of virtually all of the implements discussed in this book. Because today pigments in paint are measured and standardized with a high degree of accuracy, students can paint their magickal tools and be fairly certain that they have achieved the correct hue necessary to make the colors "flash."

The names given to pigments have always been a source of confusion to students exploring the color scales of the Golden Dawn. In this book, you will not find such undescriptive titles as "Butterfly Blue" or "Ultra-violet." Here only the true or generic names of colors will be used.

Traditional Name	Generic Name
Scarlet	Red
Red Orange	Red-orange
Orange	Orange
Amber	Yellow-orange
Yellow	Yellow
Greenish Yellow	Yellow-green

Emerald	Green
Greenish Blue	Blue-green
Blue or Azure	Blue
Indigo	Blue-violet
Purple	Violet
Ultra-violet or Crimson	Red-violet

Since most of the implements are built from wood, any type of acrylic paint may be used to color them. However, since some brands do not have certain pigments required for making flashing colors, we recommend using Liquitex, Winsor & Newton, or Brera. The following list shows how the colors you will need are described by the major brands of acrylic paint:

Color	Liquitex	Winsor & Newton	Brera
Red	Naphthol Red Light	(same)	(same)
Orange	Cadmium Orange	(same)	(same)
Yellow	Cadmium Yellow Light	(same)	(same)
Green	Permanent Green Light	(same)	(same)
Blue	Brilliant Blue	(same)	Cyan Brilliant Blue
Blue-violet	Cobalt Blue	(same)	(same)
Violet	Prism Violet	(same)	Reddish Violet
Red-violet	Deep Magenta	Quinacridridone Violet	Deep Magenta

The colors listed above can be mixed to form red-orange, yellow-orange, yellow-green, and blue-green. You will need to purchase Titanium White, Mars Black, Iridescent Gold and Iridescent White.

Flashing Colors

Some items in this book are painted in what is referred to as "flashing colors." This means that certain implements are painted in complementary colors (two colors that are directly opposite each other on a color wheel). The pigment which covers the most area and portrays the overall color of the implement is known as the "ground" color. Symbols, names or sigils are then painted on the ground in the appropriate flashing color, which is known as the "charge" color. It is necessary with flashing colors to paint the ground color first. When this is dry, paint the symbols and names first in white, and let the paint dry completely before painting the desired "charge" color over it. If you paint a charge color directly over a ground color, the ground will often absorb the charge rendering it dull and lifeless, negating its flash. By painting the names and sigils in white and then painting the pigment over this, the charge colors retain their vitality and the flashing colors remain true to their name and power.*

The Color Scales

An elaborate color scale system was devised by the Golden Dawn to depict the Sephiroth in each of the Four Qabalistic Worlds. The Qabalah teaches that the Sephiroth were created by the path of the Flaming Sword, which resulted in Four Worlds or realms, each evolving from the one before it. As an outcome of this, each Sephirah has four levels of existence attributed to it. The Four Worlds and their corresponding color types are:

1) ATZILUTH—The World of Archetypes—the King Scale,
2) BRIAH—The World of Creation—The Queen Scale,
3) YETZIRAH—The Astral World—The Prince Scale,
4) ASSIAH—The Active World—The Princess Scale.

The color scales have additional associations with the formula of the Tetragrammaton or Four-lettered Name of God. This in turn has correspondences with the four elements: King Scale—Fire, Queen Scale—Water, Prince Scale—Air, and Princess Scale—Earth. The King and Queen Scales, the fundamental scales of masculine (active) and feminine (passive) energies, are of primary importance to the construction of the many elements in this book. By painting an implement with a passive Queen Scale color, the tool is rendered more open or receptive to the desired energies. On the other hand, if the King Scale color is used, the energy of the implement will be more outwardly forceful. On certain implements, both color scales will be represented to strike a balance between the active and the passive energies. To learn more about these color scales, we suggest

---

* Always use a good quality sealant on your magickal implements to protect the painted surface and to prevent discoloration. Clear lacquer finish is the best sealant. Polyurethane and varnish tend to dry and age with a brownish tint that could discolor your ritual tools. For the various wands of the Golden Dawn, where color is a top priority, discoloration is certainly not desirable.

xxiv > Secrets of a Golden Dawn Temple

that the reader consult the Fifth Knowledge Lecture in Regardie's *The Golden Dawn*, as well as our first book, *The New Golden Dawn Ritual Tarot*.

WORDS AS TOOLS

The Vibratory Formula

It is stated in the Neophyte ceremony that, "by names and images are all powers awakened and re-awakened." Words, like colors, are intangible tools of the Magician used to focus the mind on the energies desired. Like color, certain words or Names of Power, when properly vibrated or intoned, attract certain energies which are associated with them. A technique known as the *Vibratory Formula* is a method by which Divine names and words are spoken forcefully and with authority in a "vibration."

The Magician should first of all concentrate on the Divine White Brilliance of the Sephirah of Kether, all the while keeping the mind focused on the sphere of highest aspiration. The Practitioner should then concentrate his/her consciousness in the heart of the Tiphareth center, bringing down the white brilliance from Kether to the Sixth Sephirah. The letters of the name to be vibrated should then be formulated in white within the heart center. Then the name is slowly pronounced so that the sound vibrates throughout the entire body, and the Magician should imagine that the sound reaches into every corner of the universe. The Vibratory Formula of pronouncing names normally produces a slight sense of fatigue combined with exhilaration if performed correctly.

Pronunciation

The following section gives pronunciations of some essential words used in many of the rituals in this book. Some of these words are Hebrew, some Latin, some Greek, some Egyptian, and some Enochian. As a footnote on Enochian, there are primarily two methods of pronouncing Enochian words. S. L. MacGregor Mathers recommended that consonants should be followed by the vowel sound that is obtained in the corresponding Hebrew letter. For example, in the word EXARP the final letter "P" is pronounced "Peh" exactly like the Hebrew letter. Dr. W. W. Wescott taught a method of pronouncing words that stressed the English sound of the consonants. The letter "M," for example, would then be pronounced as "em," and the letter "S" would be "ess." A major exception to both these methods is the letter "Z," which is always pronounced "zoad." For the most part, the student must rely upon his/her intuition when it comes to Enochian, since there is no absolute consensus on the matter. It is best if these words and their meanings are committed to memory as they are prevalent throughout Golden Dawn rituals.

Pronunciations of Certain Words Used in Ritual

ADONAI (Ah-doh-nye*) Hebrew—"Lord."

ADONAI HA-ARETZ (Ah-doh-nye Hah-Ah-retz) Hebrew—"Lord of the Earth."

AGLA (Ah-gah-lah) Hebrew notaricon or acronym for "Atah Gibor Le-Olahm Adonai" which means "Thou art great forever, my Lord."

ARARITA (Ah-rah-ree-tah) Hebrew notaricon or acronym—"Achad Raysheethoh; Achad Resh Yechidathoh; Temurathoh Achod"—"One is His Beginning; One is His Individuality; His Permutation is One."

ATAH (Ah-tah) Hebrew—"Thou Art."

BITOM (Bay-ee-toh-em) Enochian Name for the Spirit of Fire.

EHEIEH (Eh-hey-yay) Hebrew—"I am."

ELOHIM (El-oh-heem) Hebrew—"Gods."

EMOR DIAL HECTEGA (Ee-mor Dee-ahl Heck-tay-gah) Enochian—The Three Great Secret Names of God born under the Banner of the North.

EMPEH ARSEL GAIOL (Em-pay Ar-sell Gah-ee-ohl) Enochian—The Three Great Secret Names of God born upon the Banners of the West.

EXARP (Ex-ar-pay) Enochian Name for the Spirit of Air.

HEKAS, HEKAS, ESTE, BEBELOI! (Hay-kahs, hay-kahs, es-stay bee-beh-loy!) Greek—Traditional proclamation that a ritual is about to start.

HCOMA (Hay-koh-mah) Enochian name for the Spirit of Water.

IAO (Ee-ah-oh) Supreme Deity of the Gnostics.

---

* Note: The last syllable rhymes with "high."

OIP TEAA PEDOCE (Oh-ee-pay Tay-ah-ah Pay-doh-kay) Enochian—The Three Great Secret Names of God born upon the Banners of the South.

ORO IBAH AOZPI (Or-oh Ee-bah-hay Ah-oh-zohd-pee) Enochian—The Three Great Secret Names of God born upon the Banners of the East.

I.N.R.I. (letters pronounced separately) Latin initials with many meanings.

KHABS AM PEKHT (Khobs ahm Peckt) Egyptian—"Light in Extension."

KONX OM PAX (Kohnx ohm Pahx) Greek—"Light in Extension."

LE-OLAHM, AMEN (lay-oh-lahm ah-men) Hebrew—"forever, unto the ages."

L.V.X. LVX (letters pronounced separately, pronounced together as "lukes") Latin—"Light."

MALKUTH (Mahl-kooth) Hebrew—"The Kingdom."

NANTA (En-ah-en-tah) Enochian—Name of the Spirit of Earth.

SHADDAI EL CHAI (Shah-dye El Chai) "Almighty Living God."

VE-GEBURAH (v'ge-boo-rah) also (v'ge-voo-rah) Hebrew—"and the power."

VE-GEDULAH (v'ge-doo-lah) Hebrew—"and the glory."

YEHESHUAH (Yeh-hay-shoo-ah) Hebrew—The Pentagrammaton or Five-lettered Name of God.

YEHOVASHAH (Yeh-ho-vah-shah) Hebrew—The Pentagrammaton.

YHVH (Yod-heh-vav-heh) Hebrew—the Tetragrammaton or Four-lettered Name of God.

YHVH ELOHIM (Yod-heh-vav-heh El-oh-heem) Hebrew—"The Lord God."

YHVH ELOAH VE-DAATH (Yod-heh-vav-heh El-oh-ah V'-Dah-aath) Hebrew—"Lord God of Knowledge."

Table of Planetary or Magickal Hours

	Sunday	Monday	Tuesday	Wednesday	Thursday	Friday	Saturday
Sunrise							
1st Hour	Sun	Moon	Mars	Mercury	Jupiter	Venus	Saturn
2nd Hour	Venus	Saturn	Sun	Moon	Mars	Mercury	Jupiter
3rd Hour	Mercury	Jupiter	Venus	Saturn	Sun	Moon	Mars
4th Hour	Moon	Mars	Mercury	Jupiter	Venus	Saturn	Sun
5th Hour	Saturn	Sun	Moon	Mars	Mercury	Jupiter	Venus
6th Hour	Jupiter	Venus	Saturn	Sun	Moon	Mars	Mercury
7th Hour	Mars	Mercury	Jupiter	Venus	Saturn	Sun	Moon
8th Hour	Sun	Moon	Mars	Mercury	Jupiter	Venus	Saturn
9th Hour	Venus	Saturn	Sun	Moon	Mars	Mercury	Jupiter
10th Hour	Mercury	Jupiter	Venus	Saturn	Sun	Moon	Mars
11th Hour	Moon	Mars	Mercury	Jupiter	Venus	Saturn	Sun
12th Hour	Saturn	Sun	Moon	Mars	Mercury	Jupiter	Venus

Table of Planetary or Magickal Hours

Sunset	Sunday	Monday	Tuesday	Wednesday	Thursday	Friday	Saturday
1st Hour	Jupiter	Venus	Saturn	Sun	Moon	Mars	Mercury
2nd Hour	Mars	Mercury	Jupiter	Venus	Saturn	Sun	Moon
3rd Hour	Sun	Moon	Mars	Mercury	Jupiter	Venus	Saturn
4th Hour	Venus	Saturn	Sun	Moon	Mars	Mercury	Jupiter
5th Hour	Mercury	Jupiter	Venus	Saturn	Sun	Moon	Mars
6th Hour	Moon	Mars	Mercury	Jupiter	Venus	Saturn	Sun
7th Hour	Saturn	Sun	Moon	Mars	Mercury	Jupiter	Venus
8th Hour	Jupiter	Venus	Saturn	Sun	Moon	Mars	Mercury
9th Hour	Mars	Mercury	Jupiter	Venus	Saturn	Sun	Moon
10th Hour	Sun	Moon	Mars	Mercury	Jupiter	Venus	Saturn
11th Hour	Venus	Saturn	Sun	Moon	Mars	Mercury	Jupiter
12th Hour	Mercury	Jupiter	Venus	Saturn	Sun	Moon	Mars

Comments

Magickal or Planetary Hours are not the same as regular daily hours. Divide the total time between sunrise and sunset by 12. This will give you the length of the Magickal Hours of the day. Dividing the time between sunset and sunrise by 12 will give you the length of the Planetary Hours of the night. The hours of the day and night will be of different lengths except on the Equinoxes.*

* Sunrise and sunset tables are given in *Llewellyn's Daily Planetary Guide.*

ESSENTIAL RITUALS, ADORATIONS AND EXERCISES

There are a few primary rituals or exercises that will need to be committed to memory in order to utilize them in the advanced rituals described in the later pages. Some of these rituals, such as the Qabalistic Cross, the Analysis of the Keyword and the Adoration to the Lord of the Universe, are used regularly as integral components of more complex rituals. Others, such as the Lesser Banishing Rituals of the Pentagram and the Hexagram, are separate rites of protection which are performed singularly for psychic defense, or at the beginning and closing of more complex ceremonies. The Supreme Invoking Ritual of the Pentagram is used at the commencement of many of the advanced rituals in this book to summon forth the Powers of the Elements. The Exercise of the Middle Pillar, which activates the equilibrating spheres of the Tree of Life within the Magician, is the foundation upon which many formulas of Magick, such as the Assumption of the Godforms, are built. This section is followed by a brief description of the various grade signs of the Order.

The Qabalistic Cross (QC)

Stand and face East. Imagine a brilliant white touching the top of your head. Reach up with the index finger or blade of a dagger to connect with the light and bring it to the forehead.

Touch the forehead and vibrate "ATAH" (Thou art).

Touch the breast and bring the dagger blade or index finger down until it covers the groin area, pointing down to the ground. Imagine the light descending from the forehead to the feet. Vibrate "MALKUTH" (the Kingdom).

Touch the right shoulder and visualize a point of light there. See the shaft of light running through the center of the body form a horizontal beam of light from your heart center that joins with the point of light at the right shoulder. Vibrate "VE-GEBURAH" (the Power).

Touch the left shoulder and visualize a point of light there. See the horizontal shaft of light extending from the heart center to join this point of light. Vibrate "VE-GEDULAH" (the Glory).

Imagine a completed cross of light running from head to feet and shoulder to shoulder.

Bring the hands outward, away from the body, and finally bring them together again, clasped on the breast as if praying. Vibrate "LE-OLAHM, AMEN" (Forever, unto the Ages).

The Lesser Banishing Ritual of the Pentagram (LBRP)

Stand and face East. Perform the Qabalistic Cross.

Facing East, use the index finger of the right hand or dagger point to trace a large Banishing Pentagram of Earth. Thrust the dagger tip or index finger through the center of the pentagram and vibrate "YHVH." (Keep the right arm extended throughout, never let it drop.)

Turn to the South and trace the same pentagram there. Charge the figure as before, intoning "ADONAI."

Turn to the West and trace the pentagram. Charge it with "EHEIEH."

Turn to the North and draw the pentagram, intoning "AGLA."

Begin here

Lesser Banishing Pentagram

Keep the arm extended. Turn to face the East. Extend both arms out in the form of a cross and say, "Before me RAPHAEL. Behind me GABRIEL. On my right hand MICHAEL. On my left hand URIEL. For about me flames the pentagram, and in the column shines the Six-rayed Star."

Repeat the Qabalistic Cross.

The Adoration to the Lord of the Universe

Face East. Say, "Holy art Thou, Lord of the Universe!" (Give the Projection Sign).

Say, "Holy art Thou, whom Nature hath not formed!" (Give

the Projection Sign).

Say, "Holy art Thou, the Vast and the Mighty One!" (Give the Projection Sign).

Say, "Lord of the Light, and of the Darkness!" (Give the Sign of Silence).

The L.V.X. Signs

Sign of Osiris Slain

Mourning of Isis

Apophis and Typhon

Sign of Osiris Risen

The Analysis of the Keyword

Extend your arms out in the shape of the Tau Cross. Say with feeling, "I.N.R.I." (Pronounce each letter.) "YOD NUN RESH YOD" (Yode-noon-raysh-yode). As the names of the Hebrew letters are pronounced, trace them in the air before you, from right to left.

Return to the stance of the Tau Cross saying, "The Sign of Osiris Slain."

Put your right arm straight up in the air from the shoulder. The left arm should be straight out from the left shoulder so that the position of the two arms together resemble the letter L. Hands are to be open flat with palms forward. Turn your head so that you are looking over your left arm. Say, "L, the Sign of the Mourning of Isis."

Raise the arms overhead to an angle of 60 degrees so that they form the letter V. Keep the arms straight and the palms facing forward. Throw the head back and say, "V, the Sign of Typhon and Apophis."

Cross the arms on the chest to form the letter X. Bow your head and say, "X, the Sign of Osiris Risen."

Say slowly and powerfully, "L.V.X." (Spell out each letter separately and give the sign of each as you do so.) Say "LUX" [lukes].

Remain in the Sign of Osiris Slain and say, "The Light . . ." (hold arms out in the Tau Cross position for a moment then recross them again on the chest)" . . . of the Cross."

Return to the Osiris Slain position and say,
"Virgo, Isis, mighty Mother,
Scorpio, Apophis, Destroyer,
Sol, Osiris, Slain and Risen,
Isis, Apophis, Osiris."

Through the previous oration, gradually raise the arms and lift the head upwards. Vibrate strongly, "IAO."

(Note: This is the end of the Analysis of the Keyword as performed in the Banishing Ritual of the Hexagram (BRH). However the Analysis of the Keyword is performed slightly different from this in the Rose Cross Ritual. In the RCR, the next step would be to vibrate the four names from the Tablet of Union [except when in the Vault] "EXARP. HCOMA. NANTA. BITOM." The final step would be to aspire toward the Light and bring it down through your head to your feet while saying, "Let the Divine Light Descend.")

EAST
Banishing Hexagram
of Fire

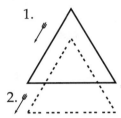

SOUTH
Banishing Hexagram
of Earth

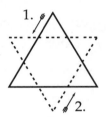

WEST
Banishing Hexagram
of Air

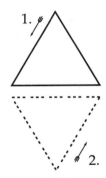

NORTH
Banishing Hexagram
of Water

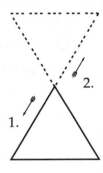

Hexagrams for the Lesser Banishing Ritual of the Hexagram

The Lesser Banishing Ritual of the Hexagram (BRH)

(This ritual uses the four lesser forms of the hexagram assigned to the quarters in accordance with the Zodiacal wheel.)

Face East and perform the Qabalistic Cross.

With right index finger or implement, trace the Banishing Hexagram of Fire toward the East. Thrust through the center of the figure and vibrate the word "ARARITA."

Move to the South and trace the Banishing Hexagram of Earth. Charge the center of the figure as before and vibrate

"ARARITA."

Move to the West and draw the Banishing Hexagram of Air. Energize it by thrusting through the center of the figure and vibrate as before, "ARARITA."

Go to the North and draw the Banishing Hexagram of Water. Thrust and intone as before, "ARARITA."

Return to the East and perform the Analysis of the Keyword.

The Supreme Invoking Ritual of the Pentagram (SIRP)

Stand and face east. Perform the Qabalistic Cross.

Facing east, trace a large Invoking Pentagram of Spirit Active. Thrust through the center of the pentagram and vibrate "EX-ARP." Trace the Spirit sigil in the center and intone, "EHEIEH." Give the LVX Signs. Then trace the Invoking Pentagram of Air and vibrate, "ORO IBAH AOZPI." Draw the sigil of Aquarius in the center of the pentagram and intone, "YHVH." Give the Sign of the Theoricus.

Turn to the South and trace a large Invoking Pentagram of Spirit Active. Thrust through the center of the pentagram and vibrate "BITOM." Trace the Spirit sigil in the center and intone, "EHEIEH." Give the LVX Signs. Then trace the Invoking Pentagram of Fire and vibrate, "OIP TEAA PEDOCE." Draw the sigil of Leo in the center of the pentagram and and intone, "ELOHIM." Give the Sign of the Philosophus.

Turn to the West and trace a large Invoking Pentagram of Spirit Passive. Thrust through the center of the pentagram and vibrate "HCOMA." Trace the Spirit sigil in the center and intone "AGLA." Give the LVX Signs. Then trace the Invoking Pentagram of Water and vibrate "EMPEH ARSEL GAIOL." Draw the sigil of the eagle in the center of the pentagram and intone, "Aleph Lamed, AL." Give the Sign of the Practicus.

Turn to the North and trace a large Invoking Pentagram of Spirit Passive. Thrust through the center of the pentagram and vibrate "NANTA." Trace the Spirit sigil in the center and

EAST

Invoking
Spirit
Active

SOUTH

Invoking
Spirit
Active

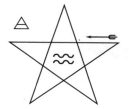

Invoking
Air

Invoking
Fire

WEST

Invoking
Spirit
Passive

NORTH

Invoking
Spirit
Passive

Invoking
Water

Invoking
Earth

**Invoking Spirit and Elemental Pentagrams for the
Supreme Invoking Ritual of the Pentagram**

intone, "AGLA." Give the LVX Signs. Then trace the Invoking Pentagram of Earth and vibrate, "EMOR DIAL HECTEGA." Draw the sigil of Taurus in the center of the pentagram and and intone, "ADONAI." Give the Sign of the Zelator.

Keep the arm extended. Turn to face the East. Extend both arms out in the form of a cross and say, "Before me, RAPHAEL. Behind me, GABRIEL. On my right hand, MICHAEL. On my left hand, URIEL. For about me flames the pentagram, and in the column shines the Six-rayed Star."

Repeat the Qabalistic Cross.

The Exercise of the Middle Pillar

(This exercise can be performed either standing, siting, or lying down.)

After a few minutes of relaxation, imagine a sphere of white light just above your head. Vibrate the name "EHEIEH" (I am). Keep vibrating this word until it is the only thought in your mind. Then imagine a shaft of light descending from your Kether center to your Daath center at the nape of the neck.

Form a sphere of light at the Daath center. Vibrate the name "YHVH ELOHIM" (the Lord God). Intone the name until it is your only thought.

Bring a shaft of light down from the Daath center to the Tiphareth center around your heart. Form a sphere of light there. Vibrate the name "YHVH ELOAH VE-DAATH" (Lord God of Knowledge) several times until it fills your consciousness.

See the shaft of light descending from Tiphareth into the Yesod center in the genital region. Imagine a sphere of light formed there. Intone the name "SHADDAI EL CHAI" (Almighty Living God) several times as before.

Visualize the shaft of light descending from Yesod into your Malkuth center at the feet and ankles. Vibrate the name "ADONAI HA ARETZ" (Lord of Earth) a number of times as before.

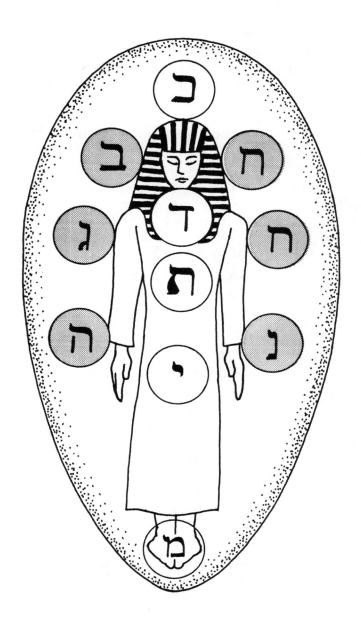

Visualization Points of the Exercise of the Middle Pillar

Imagine the Middle Pillar complete. Then circulate the light you have brought down through the Middle Pillar around the outside of your body to strengthen your aura. Using the cycles of breathing, bring the light up one side of the body and down the other, from Malkuth to Kether and back again. After performing this for a short period of time, imagine the ribbon of light rising up the front of your body and descending down your back.

Still employing rhythmic breathing, visualize the shaft of light rising up the Middle Pillar in the center of your body. When it reaches Kether, imagine a shower of light surrounding the outside of your body as it descends to Malkuth again. Circulate the light in this manner for some time. Then see the light rise again in a ribbon that spirals round the outside of your body.

Finally focus some of the energy back into your Tiphareth center, the seat of equilibrium and balance.

(Note: this simple exercise of the Middle Pillar is the basis for many complex formulas of Magick.)

The Grade Signs

The Neophyte Signs:

The Saluting Sign, also called the Sign of the Enterer, the Attacking Sign, and the Sign of Horus. Bring the arms up as if touching Kether, then bring the hands down to either side of the head at eye level (fingers extended, hands held flat with palms down). Then step forward with the left foot, at the same time thrust the arms directly forward, and sink the head till the eyes look exactly between the thumbs.

The Sign of Silence, also called the Sign of Protection and the Sign of Harpocrates. Bring the left foot back sharply, both heels together—beat the ground once with the left foot as it is placed beside the right. Bring the left hand to the mouth and touch the center of the lower lip with the left forefinger. Close the other fingers and thumb and drop the right hand to the side.

The Zelator Sign: Raise the right arm straight up in a forty-five degree angle from the body, hand held flat with the thumb facing toward the ceiling.

THE NEOPHYTE SIGNS

The Enterer Sign

The Sign of Silence

THE ELEMENTAL GRADE SIGNS

The Sign of Zelator

The Sign of Theoricus

The Sign of Practicus

The Sign of Philosophus

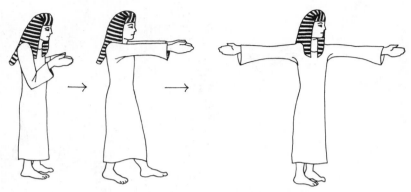

Portal: The Opening of the Veil

The Theoricus Sign: Bend both arms at the elbow. Keep the hands at the level of the head, palms upward as if supporting a great weight.

The Practicus Sign: Form a triangle apex downwards over the chest with both hands. Keep the elbows level with the shoulders.

The Philosophus Sign: Form a triangle apex upwards on the forehead with both hands, palms outward.

The Portal Signs: The Rending or Opening of the Veil. Clasp the hands together as if praying, then thrust them forward. Take a step forward with the left foot and separate the hands as if opening a curtain.

The Closing of the Veil: A complete reversal of the Opening Sign.

The L.V.X. Signs: See the description of these signs as given in the Analysis of the Keyword.

It is our hope that this book will supply the reader with the information needed to construct the various tools of the Golden Dawn, but we also wish to provide a strong foundation of magickal training for the working Magician. Regardie often stated that the Magician should "enflame thyself with prayer" in order to exalt the mind into an advanced state of spiritual attunement. We also suggest that students "envelop themselves with ritual" and employ the various tools in this book to help toward that end. (Many of these rituals were taken from Regardie's *The Golden Dawn*.)

Chic Cicero constructing a Wand

Part 1

The Outer Temple

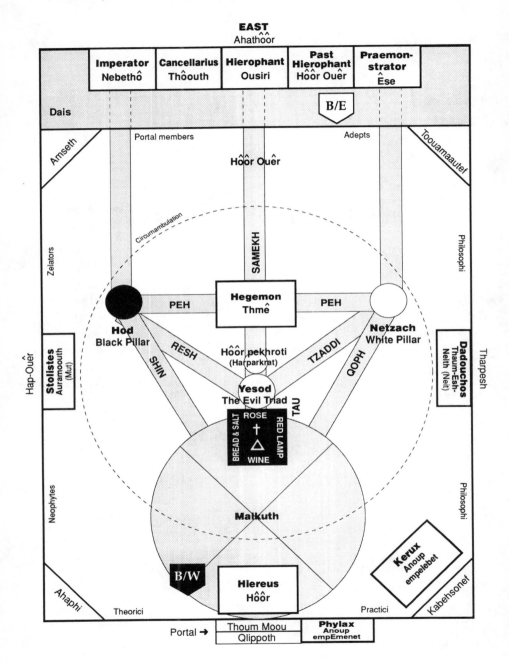

Temple Layout and Godforms of the Neophyte Hall

CHAPTER ONE

Implements of the Neophyte Grade

During the process of initiation, the Neophyte encounters a Temple filled with symbolism in the form of ritual implements and clothing worn by officers who are the living personifications of the Gods and Goddesses of Egypt—the initiators into the Higher Mysteries. The Hall of the Neophytes is the most important Temple arrangement in all of the Outer Order rituals. Its composition is based primarily upon the glyph of the Qabalistic Tree of Life. Within the Neophyte Ritual itself are hidden many formulae of Magick. The implements of the First Order are not present in the Hall merely for theatrics and effect, but rather they are the visible emblems of invisible forces within the Hall which are directed and orchestrated by the Hierophant and other Second Order members.

THE NEOPHYTE HALL

The ideal dimensions for the entire Temple should be approximately 20' by 16'. The Dais in the East should be about 4' in width, leaving the rest of the Temple a 16' x 16' square. Of course, ideal conditions are not always available; at times a spare room or basement must serve as the Neophyte Hall, making the dimensions of the Temple a non-negotiable issue. In the perfect Temple, the floor should be black or composed of black-and-white tiles. From the perspective of a new Neophyte undergoing initiation, who is hoodwinked and sees little of the actual Neophyte Ritual, the entire room could be painted black. However, the Temple is also used for Elemental grade ceremonies, so it would be perfectly acceptable for the four walls to be painted in the four Elemental colors: East—yellow,

West—blue, North—black. The ceiling could be white. (Our first Neophyte Hall in 1977 had the walls and the ceiling draped completely in white silk fabric which was gathered at a point directly over the central and invisible station of Hoor pe Khroti [Harparkrat].) Also, the Enochian Tablets, which are to be present in the Neophyte Hall but hidden from view, could be veiled with curtains in the appropriate Elemental colors. (Information on the Tablets is provided in Chapter 3.) If at all possible, the room should be soundproof. We have often found that soft music (such as Tibetan Bells) played faintly in the background (preferably on a tape deck with auto-reverse) can noticeably enhance the psychic receptivity of all ritual participants. The lighting should be as dim as possible, with candlelight coming from each of the four quarters: the veiled lights atop the Pillars, the red lamp upon the Altar, and the lamp of the Kerux. Ideally, these would be the only sources of light within the Hall. To the blindfolded candidate, who is groping in the darkness of the Outer World, the main source of illumination is the lamp of the Kerux, which flickers dimly one step ahead at all times. The general atmosphere of the entire Neophyte Hall is one of solemn stillness, a darkness which is pregnant with power and Hidden Light.

The Altar

Use and Symbolism

The Altar is a point of focus in the Neophyte Hall of the Golden Dawn. Its black, closed shape is enigmatic, for it is an emblem of Nature or the Material Universe, concealing the mysteries of all dimensions within, while revealing only the surface to the exterior senses. Its double cubical shape is derived from a passage taken from the Emerald Tablet of Hermes which reads, "The things that are below are a reflection of the things that are above." The Altar is black to symbolize the physical world in which we live...a world sometimes dark and obscure.

Placed in the eastern part of Malkuth (as far as the Temple is concerned), the Altar is the core of the Temple. It may be painted black, but to an adept its blackness will veil citrine on the east, olive on the south, russet on the north; the west side alone and the base will be black, while the summit is of a brilliant whiteness. All Divine Light brought into the Temple through the Hierophant and circulated by the officers is eventually grounded within the Altar. Once the ceremony is ended, the Supernal Light is withdrawn from the symbols upon the Altar so that it is not diminished by improper regard. In some ways the Altar, like the individual, is a physical vessel which temporarily conceals and contains the Spirit until it is withdrawn back into the Godhead.

The Altar is also an excellent container for ritual tools, candles, robes and other implements. The double-cubical design provides plenty of space inside while the sliding front gives it the smooth appearance of a Chinese box.

Materials Needed
>3/4" plywood (pine or birch) comes in 4'x 8' sheets. You will need 1-1/2 sheets.
>Yellow carpenter's glue
>1-1/2" brads
>Wood putty
>Black polyurethane or acrylic enamel

Tools Needed
>Table saw or circular saw
>Hammer
>Nail punch
>L-square
>Putty knife
>Sandpaper
>Large paint brush
>Yard stick or tape measure

Construction
1) Lay out the one and one half sheets of plywood. Measure out and label clearly all the sections of the altar (front, back, etc.) as in the diagram. (Front and back are each 20" x 38-1/2", Two sides are each 18-1/2" x 38-1/2", top and bottom are each 20" x 20", and the shelf is 18" x 18-1/2".)

2) Cut apart all sections with saw. Take one of the sections marked side and apply glue to one of the 38-1/2" edges. Keep this edge facing up.

3) Line up the long edge of the back section perpendicular to the glued side and nail the two sections together. (Note: the edge of the back section will still be visible, while the glued side edge should not be.)

4) Take the remaining side panel and apply glue to one edge as before. Nail this piece perpendicular to the remaining long edge of the Back as in the previous step. (You should now have three sections nailed to-

gether which form an inverted U-shape.)

5) Lift the unfinished altar upright. Three edges (of the back and two sides) should now face the ceiling. Apply glue to all three edges. Take the top section and place it flush against these three edges. Nail into place.

6) Turn the Altar upside-down and apply glue to the three edges as before. Nail the bottom panel flush against these three edges as in the previous step.

7) Lay the Altar on its side. Measure to find the exact center of the back (both inside and out). With a pencil and ruler, draw a line parallel to the top and bottom which marks the center. Also find the center of the side panels and mark them.

8) Take the shelf and apply glue to one 18-1/2" edge and both 18" edges. Slide the shelf inside the Altar with the glued 18-1/2" edge up against the center line drawn on the back. Make sure the shelf is straight. Nail the shelf into place from the outside (on all three sides).

9) The only remaining section is the front, which should fit snugly into place without hinges. It can be pulled out or pushed into place, giving the Altar a smooth, closed-cube appearance. (If too tight, the top and bottom edges may need some sanding.)

Finishing Steps

10) With nail punch and hammer, make sure no nail heads stick out from the wood. Fill any nail holes or cracks with wood putty and putty knife. Let dry.

11) Sand off excess putty or any other rough areas remaining on the surface of the Altar.

12) Paint the Altar completely inside and outside with black polyurethane or acrylic enamel. Allow to dry.

(Note: In the early Temples, the sides of the Altar were often painted with flat black paint, while the top alone was coated with a glossy black. This made clean-up of accidental spills easier.)

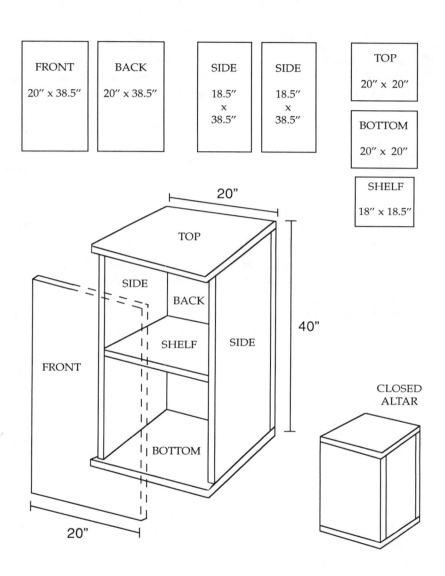

FRONT	BACK	SIDE	SIDE	TOP
20″ x 38.5″	20″ x 38.5″	18.5″ x 38.5″	18.5″ x 38.5″	20″ x 20″

BOTTOM

20″ x 20″

SHELF

18″ x 18.5″

The Altar

Ritual For Use

A Meditation On The Altar

Place the finished Altar just west of center in your Temple space. (The actual center of the Temple is the invisible station of Harpocrates.) The Adept should be dressed in Outer Order regalia.

Relax. Perform the Lesser Banishing Ritual of the Pentagram (LBRP).

Go to the west of the Altar and face east. Place your hands on the sides of the Altar.

Perform the Four-fold Breath: Breathe in to the count of four, hold the air in the lungs to the count of four, exhale to the count of four, and keep the lungs empty to the count of four.

Continue breathing in this manner as you begin the following visualization. Concentrate on a point as defined in mathematics. *The point is tiny speck, having a fixed position but no depth.* Realize that within this minute point is concealed the brilliance and power of the Divine which exists throughout nature, in all her aspects.

In your mind's eye, see the point expand into a circle which is divided into four sections colored respectively: citrine, olive, russet and black. The circle becomes a square that sits on top of the Altar before you. The square opens up at its center and the four sections break apart to cover the four sides of the Altar: citrine on the eastern side, olive on the south, russet on the north, and solid black on the west.

Visualize the top of the Altar start to glow until it is brilliant white . . . the white of the Divine Light reflected down upon the physical Altar—just as the Higher Self of the individual is a reflection of the Divine Self, cast into each person.

See a column of light descending upon the Altar and casting a halo of light around it. Release your hands from the sides of the Altar but remain in meditation with your eyes closed.

Imagine the Altar starting to rise off the floor. It floats upward as if seeking to join with the source of the light from above. It rises above your head, and you see the bottom of the Altar which is black, the color of Earth and the flashing color of Spirit.

Just as matter aspires toward Spirit, the Altar disappears into the white brilliance. The Spirit having descended into matter, the matter then ascends to join with Spirit. Contemplate these ideas for some length of time.

Then bring the Altar back into the Temple by vibrating the Divine names of the Middle Pillar Exercise: "EHEIEH, YHVH ELOHIM, YHVH ELOAH VE-DAATH, SHADDAI EL CHAI, ADONAI HA-ARETZ." As you intone each name, the Altar gradually descends until it has reached its original position. Place your hands back upon its sides.

When you are ready to end the meditation, perform the Lesser Banishing Ritual of the Pentagram (LBRP) and close the Temple.

THIS ENDS THE RITE

The Cross and Triangle

Use and Symbolism

Although many people think the symbol of the Golden Dawn is the Sun within a hexagram consisting of the two Triangles of Fire and Water, the true symbol of the Order is the red cross above the White Triangle. These emblems represent the Forces and manifestation of the Divine Light, concentrated in the White Triangle of the Supernals as the synthesis. The Red Cross of Tiphareth is placed above the White Triangle, not to dominate it, but to bring it down and manifest it into the Outer Order, as though the Slain and Resurrected One, having raised the symbol of self-sacrifice, had thus touched and brought into action, in physical matter, the Divine Triad of Light. The Cross and Triangle together represent Life and Light.

The Cross and Triangle act as the receptacles of the Divine Light which is attracted into the Temple by the Hierophant during the mystic circumambulation—symbolic of the rise of Light. These sublime symbols also play an important role in the Neophyte ceremony when the new candidate is asked to take an oath. They remain a focal point for projected energy throughout the ritual. Whenever the Neophyte Hall is set up for personal magickal work, such as charging a talisman, the Cross and Triangle should be upon the Altar, acting as nucleus for the ceremony and attracting the Divine Forces into manifestation.

Materials Needed

One 5" square piece of soft wood (pine, bass, or balsa), 1/2" thick

Gesso

Acrylic paints: white and red

Clear lacquer finish (spray or brush on)

Tools Needed

Scroll saw or coping saw

Electric drill with a bit that is wider than your saw blade

Sandpaper: medium and fine grained

Artist's paint brushes

Construction

1) With the saw, cut a 5" equilateral triangle out of the piece of wood. (All three angles should be 60°.)

2) With a pencil, draw another equilateral triangle on top of the one you have just cut out. This one should be smaller on all sides by 1/2".

3) Drill a hole inside the pencil line of the smaller, drawn triangle. (Remember, it is important to use a drill bit that is wider than your saw blade.) Try to drill the hole near one of the angled corners—not in the center of the triangle. This is because you will use the smaller triangular piece of wood to make the cross.

4) With your saw unplugged, detach the blade from the saw. Stick the blade through the hole you have drilled and re-attach the blade to the saw. Plug the saw back in and begin cutting exactly on the penciled lines until you have completely cut out the inner triangle.

5) Unplug the saw. Detach the blade from the saw and remove the pieces of wood. You should now have a 5" equilateral triangle that is 1/2" thick on all sides of its three component lines. (The hollow space in the center should be 3-1/4" all around.)

6) Take the solid piece of wood you have cut from the center of the Triangle. With a pencil and a ruler, a draw a Calvary cross of six squares, using 1/2" units of measure. (The shaft of the cross will be 1/2" wide and 2" long. The crossbeam will be 1/2" wide and 1-1/2" long. The crossbeam should start 1/2" below the top of the shaft.)

7) Re-attach the blade to the saw and plug the tool in. Cut the cross out of the wood.

Finishing Steps

8) Sand the entire surface of both the cross and the triangle.

9) With paint brush, cover both pieces with gesso. Let dry. Sand gessoed pieces until smooth.

10) Paint the triangle with acrylic white. Paint the cross with red. Let both pieces dry thoroughly, then apply a sealant for protection.

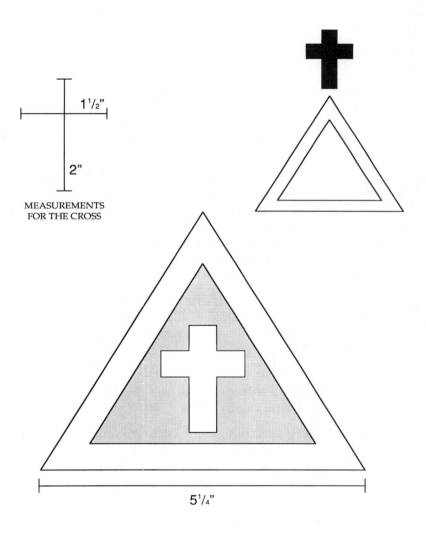

1½"

2"

MEASUREMENTS
FOR THE CROSS

5¼"

The Cross and Triangle

Ritual for Use

Meditation/Ritual on the Cross and Triangle

The Black Altar should be in the center of room (slightly closer to the west as before). Centered on top of the Altar should be the Red Cross above the White Triangle. The Adept should be dressed in Outer Order regalia.

Relax. Perform the LBRP.

Circumambulate the Temple clockwise three times, giving the Neophyte Signs when passing the East.

Go to the west of the Altar and face east. Place your hands on either side of the Cross and Triangle. Begin the Four-fold Breath exercise as given in the preceding Altar meditation.

Place your right hand on the Triangle and say, "There are two contending Forces and One eternally uniting them. And these Three have their Image in the three-fold Flame of our Being and in the three-fold wave of the sensual world. The Immortal Light, that Triune Light is that which moved in Darkness and formed the world out of Darkness." Visualize the Hebrew letter, Shin, in brilliant white, descending from above the Altar.

Give the Sign of the Rending of the Veil: Put your hands together in front of your chest as if praying. Thrust the clasped hands straight out in front of you and separate them as if parting a curtain. Take a step forward while in the position of a Tau Cross (arms straight out from shoulders.)

Imagine the white shin descending into the Triangle, which then glows brilliantly with Light.

Place your right hand upon the Red Cross and say, "In all cultures there is One who was unfolded in the Light. At his head is the rushing Wind, at his feet—the mighty Sea. On his right hand is the Sacred Flame, and on his left hand—the fertile Earth."

Stand in the position of the Tau Cross (Osiris Slain). Imagine a yellow rose entering the top arm of the Cross from the East. Into the right arm of the Cross, visualize a pyramid of Flame entering. From the West, see a chalice of water being absorbed into the bottom arm. On the northern side, see a paten of bread and salt enter the left arm.

Cross the arms upon the chest in the position of Osiris Risen. Bow your head.

Say, "After the Formless and the Void and the Darkness, then cometh the Knowledge of the Light. Khabs Am Pekht. Konx Om Pax. Light in Extension."

Remain in the Sign of Osiris Risen while contemplating the idea of the Divine Light being brought into physical manifestation. Vibrate "EHEIEH" four times using the Vibratory Formula of the Middle Pillar.

Imagine your Lower Will, centered in the Ruach (controlled by the sphere of Tiphareth) aspiring toward the Higher Will of the Neshamah. For only through submission of the Lower to the Higher, can the Divine Consciousness descend into the Human Self . . . The Supernal White Triangle of Light manifesting in the red Cross of Life.

After completing the meditation, perform the reverse circumambulation three times counterclockwise.

Perform the LBRP and declare the Temple duly closed.

THIS ENDS THE RITE

The Banners of the East and West

Contributed by Ceil Thomas

Use and Symbolism

The Banners are the duality of Light and Dark working from East to West, where the Pillars are duality of Light and Dark working from South to North, thus forming a cross within the Neophyte Temple. They are not only barriers or signposts for the Eastern and Western parts of the Hall, but they are also battery points for which the Light/energy can travel from one end of the Temple to the other and back again.

The Banner of the East is a representation of the Initiate being transformed into the Perfect Knowledge of Light. It is a symbol that can be used in meditation to help the student gain a greater understanding of what the Order is striving to teach. It is a symbol of the Dawning Sun.

The Banner of the East as it is described in the Portal Initiation:

"The field of the Banner of the East is White, the color of light and purity. As in the previous case, the Calvary Cross of six squares is the number of Tiphareth, the yellow Cross of Solar Gold, and the cubical stone, bearing in its center the sacred Tau of Life, and having bound together upon it the form of the macrocosmic Hexagram, the red Triangle of Fire and the blue Triangle of Water—the Ruach Elohim and the Waters of Creation." (It is the action of the Fire of the Spirit through the Waters of Creation under the harmony of the Golden Cross of the Reconciler.)

"Within the center of the Hexagram is a Tau-cross in white, to represent its action as a Triad; and the whole is placed on a white field representing the Ocean of Ain Soph Aur. The Banner is suspended from a gold colored bar by red cords, and the pole and base should be white. The base represents the purity of the foundation—the shaft, the Purified Will directed to the Higher. The golden cross-bar is that whereon the Manifest Law of Perfection rests; the Banner itself, the Perfect Law of the Universe, the red cords and tassels represent the Divine Self-renunciation, whose trials and sufferings form, as it were, the Ornament of the Completed Work."

This symbol can be also be likened to a shield that protects the student throughout the process of initiation from the Forces of negativity. A greater knowledge of the Banner of the East will begin to unfold through meditation and Order work.

The Banner of the West is partly explained in the Zelator Initiation:

"The White Triangle refers to the three Paths connecting Malkuth with the other Sephiroth; while the red cross is the Hidden Knowledge of the Divine Nature which is to be obtained through their aid. The Cross and Triangle together represent Life and Light."

It can also represent the possibility of rescuing the Evil; but it is the Cross of Tiphareth that is placed within the Triangle that represents the sacrifice that has to be made in order to reach the Higher. The Red Cross may be bordered in gold to represent the metal obtained in and through the Darkness of Putrefaction. The Banner of the West is on a black field representing Darkness or Ignorance of the Outer, the White Triangle is the Light shinning through the Darkness but which is not comprehended. The Banner of the West is a symbol of Twilight, the balance of Light and Darkness. The pole is black, also representing Darkness, but the cross bar is gold and the tassels red for the same reasons as given for the Banner of the East.

The Banner of the East always remains in the eastern portion of the Hall while the Banner of the West may move to many different positions. When the Banner of the West changes its position within the Hall, it does so in order to bar the way of the Initiate. It makes a new demand upon the Candidate and requires a new sacrifice in order for the Initiate to continue on the Path leading to the Higher.

It is preferable to always construct the banners in matching sets. These are tools that are always used together and should be created together. I always light a red candle and light incense before I begin working on any magickal tool. While lighting the candle and incense I connect with the energies of Fire and Air, the creative and intellectual aspects of the work at hand. I ask the powers that be to guide my hands in this creation and bring me knowledge and wisdom through this work. I ask that this tool be a proven, valid instrument in my endeavors toward the Great Work.

Materials Needed
 1/2 yard of white satin
 1/2 yard of black satin
 1/2 yard of gold (the new lamés work just fine)
 1/3 yard of red satin
 1/3 yard of blue satin
 1 yard of iron-on interfacing (medium weight)

10 red tassels (short or long)
24" or red cord
24" of black cord
1 roll of bonding web
Threads in the appropriate colors
3/4" dowels (2 pieces 16" long)
4 screw-eyes (big enough for the cord to go through)
Finial ends or wooden balls to fit the end of the dowel
Wood glue
Metallic gold paint
Fine sandpaper

Tools Needed

Sewing machine
Scissors
Needles and gold thread
Iron and ironing board
Measuring tape
Access to a copy machine that will enlarge the pattern pieces.

Construction

1) Enlarge the banner pattern so that it is 15" wide. Make several copies so that you can use them as patterns to cut out and also as placement guides.

2) Begin with the banner field: cut two pieces for each banner (two pieces of white and two of black). The banner fields should have a 1/2" seam allowance all around, making the finished banner 16" wide. Do not sew the banner fields together at this time.

3) Cut out all the triangles and crosses to use as patterns. Cut pieces of iron-on interfacing slightly larger than the triangles and the crosses.

4) Iron the largest triangle interfacing piece to the back of the white satin. Iron one of the smaller triangle pieces to the back of the blue satin and one to the back of the red satin. Iron the large cross piece and the middle-sized cross piece of interfacing to the back of the gold fabric. Next iron the smallest cross piece to the back of the red satin. Now iron the Tau Cross piece of interfacing to the back of the white satin.

5) Lay the pattern pieces for each triangle and cross onto the back of each piece of fabric and draw around each pattern piece, leaving a border of approximately 3/8". ·

6) Cut out the triangles and crosses, cutting the corners and cutting the central angles in as shown in the illustration. (This technique is dem-

THE BANNER OF THE EAST

Field – White
Large Cross–Gold
Upper Triangle–Red
Lower Triangle–Blue
Tau Cross–White

THE BANNER OF THE WEST

Field–Black
Triangle–White
Cross–Red
Outline of Cross–Gold

onstrated with the large white triangle from the Banner of the West. After you have completed it you can move on to the other triangles and crosses and follow the same technique.)

7) Lay the paper pattern piece on the back of the cutout of the large triangle. Iron the seam allowance over the pattern piece forming a fold line. Remove the paper pattern and cut a strip of bonding web long enough to fit between the seam allowance and the triangle.

8) Press the seam allowance to the triangle. Repeat for the other arms of the triangle, being sure to do the inside of the triangle as well.

9) Press the points carefully so that you end up with a perfect triangle. Repeat this process with the other two triangles and the crosses.

10) After all the triangles and crosses are pressed flat (making sure the seam allowances are turned under and glued with the bonding web), then place the large white triangle on the right side of one of the black field pieces.

11) Use one of the extra enlargements of the Banner of the West to position it correctly. The lower points of the triangle should follow the line that is formed with the angles running downwards to form the point of the banner.

12) Carefully pin the triangle in place and cut strips of bonding web for all three sides. Press the triangle in place, gluing it to the banner field piece. Next place the small gold cross within the triangle and follow the same procedure. Then glue the red cross on top of the gold cross and glue it down with bonding web.

13) Now that all the pieces are in place, stitch along all the edges to secure them to the field piece. This stitching will be seen on the banner so be sure to use the appropriate color thread with each item.

14) When you start to place the red and blue triangles on the Gold Cross on the Banner of the East, you must cut one of the triangles so that they interlock. There is a broken line on the blue triangle showing where it needs to be cut. Interweave the triangles pinning them in place as they move over each other.

15) After everything has been sewn to the front (of each separate banner) pin the back piece to the front, making sure the right sides (outsides) are facing each other. Be sure it is square and all the edges match.

16) Now stitch down one side, along the angle to the bottom point, up the other angle and then up the opposite side, making sure you leave a 1/2" seam allowance. Clip the corners and turn the banner inside out.

17) To make the corners square, take a pair of scissors and go inside the banner and push the corner seams outward. (Not too much that you push through, just enough to make them square.)

CONSTRUCTION TECHNIQUES OF THE BANNERS

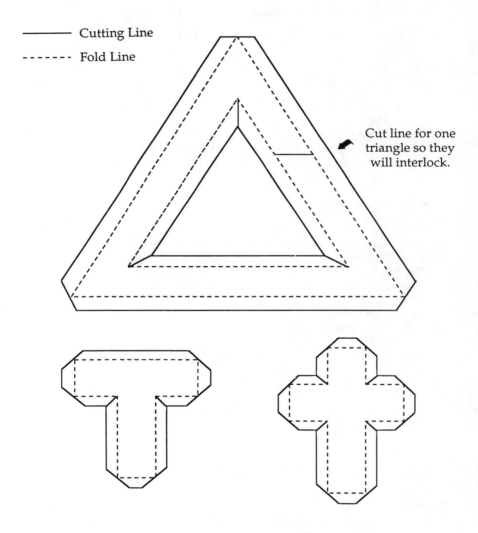

————— Cutting Line

- - - - - - Fold Line

Cut line for one triangle so they will interlock.

Pieces are cut from the wrong side of fabric that has iron-on interfacing pressed on. Lay pattern piece on top of interfacing and trace around it. Cut approximately 3/8" for seam allowance. Trim outside corners and clip inside corners. Press along fold lines.

18) Press the banner so that the seams are flat. Next, fold and press a 1/2" seam along the top. Stitch this seam flat.

19) Now you are ready to hand stitch the red tassels to each corner and the bottom point. To make the cross bars, sand the 16" long dowels smooth and attach the finials or 1" wooded balls to the ends.

20) Paint each cross bar with a metallic gold paint and let dry completely.

21) Place a screw-eye about 1/2" from the end of the dowel. Tie a knot in one end of the cord and thread it through one of screw-eyes. Thread the other end of the cord through the other screw-eye and tie a knot.

22) Apply these same techniques to construct the Banner of the East. You can attach the banners to the golden cross bars with gold thread. The black cord is used to hang the Banner of the West and the Red is for the Banner of the East. This forms a convenient suspension for the banners and makes it easy to remove them from the poles.

The Banner Poles

Materials Needed
> Two 1-1/4" thick dowel poles, approx. 67" in length
> Two 4" x 4" thick pieces of wood, 6 inches in length
> One piece of 3/4" plywood or pine, 16" long by 8" wide
> One piece of 3/4" plywood or pine, 12" long by 6" wide
> Two ornate wooden caps (found in builder's supply stores)
> Two metal screw-in hooks
> Yellow carpenter's glue
> Wood putty
> White latex paint
> Black latex paint
> Box of 2" brads

Tools Needed
> Table or circular saw
> Hammer
> Awl
> Electric drill with a flat 1-1/4" bit

Construction
1) Take the 16" x 8" piece of plywood and cut it in half with the saw so that you are left with two 8" x 8" pieces of wood. Put one of the pieces aside.

2) Take the 12" x 6" piece of plywood and cut it in half, leaving you with two 6" x 6" pieces of wood. Put one of the pieces aside. Apply glue to the 6" x 6" piece of wood and center it on top of the 8"x 8" piece.

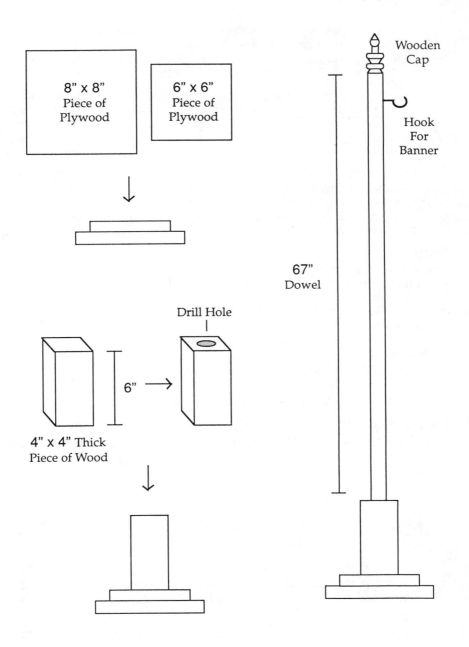

The Banner Pole

3) Take one of the 4" x 4" thick pieces of wood and drill a 1-1/4" wide hole into the center of one end. This hole should be at least 1-1/2" deep. Glue and center the undrilled end of the 4" x 4" onto the top of the 6" x 6" plywood. Nail all three pieces together from the bottom.

4) Take the wooden cap and glue it to one end of the dowel pole. (Note: these caps sometimes come with a small dowel sticking out of the bottom. If such is the case, drill an appropriate sized hole into one end of the dowel and then glue the cap into place.) Glue the other end of the dowel into the hole drilled into the 4" x 4". Allow the glue to dry.

5) About 6" down from the top of the cap, make a small hole in the shaft with an awl. Screw the metal hook into the hole. (The banner will be suspended from this hook.) You should now have one completed banner pole. With the remaining materials, make a second banner pole in the same manner as the first.

Finishing Steps

6) Paint one banner pole entirely white for the Banner of the East. The other pole used to support the Banner of the West should be painted completely black. (Note: it also is acceptable to paint the bottoms of the poles after the manner of the Pillars—with countercharged lotus petals.)

Ritual for Use

A Meditation on the Banners

For this meditation/ritual the Neophyte should wear the robe and headdress of the Outer Order in addition to the sash of the 0=0 grade. The Temple is to be arranged in accordance with the Neophyte Hall.

After a period of relaxation, perform the LBRP.

Circumambulate the Temple once (giving the Neophyte Signs when passing the east).

Go to the west of the Temple and face the Banner of the West. Contemplate its symbolism, taking mental note of everything connected with it including the Banner pole, tassels, etc. Give the Neophyte Signs at the Banner. Then close your eyes but retain the image of the Banner in your mind. Begin the following visualization:

———— ❋ ————

Behind your closed eye-lids you see nothing but blackness. It is the darkness of obliviousness, of the secular, mundane world which looks upon the manifest universe and sees only the outer surface of things. This is not the black color of the element of earth. It is the darkness of not knowing the Inner. This twilight is very deep and thick. This is truly the abode of Blindness and ignorance of the Higher. Instinctively, you give the Sign of the Enterer followed by the Sign of Silence. As you do so, a glimmer of light appears, far off in the blackness. It is a comforting point of illumination within the unobservant darkness . . . a focal point for you to cling to.

As you observe it, the light divides into three points which form a perfect triangle, the strongest shape in the universe. Even here, the reach of the Supernal Triad is extended. Even here in the evil which is ignorance, there is the possibility of rescue. The Divine Light does not forsake the darkness, for the whiteness of pure Spirit shines ever brighter because of the surrounding blackness. Even here in the darkness which is ignorance, there is hope. The three sides of the Triangle are like gleaming paths which lead out of the darkness to the dawning Light.

A solid red square forms in the center of the black field behind the Triangle. Before your mind's eye it unfolds into a cross. The unfolding of the square is a kind of self-renunciation of one form for another. This takes place within the White Triangle of Light as if to give sacrifice only unto the Higher, as an escape from the black abode of ignorance. Five drops of sacrificial blood are seen at the borders of the darkness, evidence of trial and suffering. Behind the unfolded square is a glory of gold, the perfect metal of the Alchemists, formed in and through the Darkness of Decay. It is the gold of Tiphareth which forms an aura around the red cross.

The scene before you is the difficult path traveled by an Initiate of the mysteries. Darkness and ignorance is all around. Courage, perseverance and self-sacrifice are needed to overcome obstacles which threaten the magician's progress in the Great Work. Yet the rewards for doing so are indeed great.

———— ❋ ————

When finished with the meditation, give the Neophyte Signs again toward the Banner of the West, then circumambulate the Temple once and stop in the East.

Face the Banner of the East and contemplate its symbolism. Notice every detail. Give the Neophyte Signs at the Banner. Close your eyes but retain the image in your mind. Begin the following visualization:

Behind your eyes is a field of absolute brilliance . . . a whiteness so intense that it too, seems blinding. This is the Ocean of infinite perfection, the boundless Light . . . the ultimate completion of the Great Work. At the edges of the white field are again the five familiar drops of blood, the price paid by the Initiate for ascension to the Perfect Knowledge of the Light.

The sacrificial red cross of the previous Banner has become large and fully enveloped by the golden aura. It is the cross of Solar Gold— the Reconciler in victory and harmony. It has passed through the night of darkness. It stands upon a foundation of purity, formed out of the refined Will to aspire unto the Highest.

Two triangles converge upon the golden Cross; the red Triangle of Fire and the blue Triangle of Water. Visualize the two triangles forming separately from above and below. They move to interlock firmly around the figure of the reconciling Cross. Like the element of Air, this Cross separates and equilibrates between these two opposing forces. The Cross is the child of these parental forces; the offspring of the Spirit of Fire and the Waters of Creation. It is that which binds them together.

Imagine the white Triangle of the Banner of the West in the center of the golden Solar Cross. See it turn into a white Tau Cross, the sacred Tau of Life, emphasizing the action of the Triad in this Banner.

This is the image of the Perfect Law of the Universe. You realize that many more such meditations will be necessary to unravel its mysteries. For the Banner of the East, although a truly beautiful symbol, is but a pale effigy compared to the true excellence of the Divine. All symbols and words are inadequate to describe such perfection.

When finished with the meditation, give the Neophyte Signs at the Banner. Circumambulate the Temple one time and return to the East.

Give the Adoration to the Lord of the Universe.

Perform the reverse circumambulation three times.

Perform the LBRP.

THIS ENDS THE RITE

The Pillars

Use and Symbolism

The two Pillars of the Neophyte Hall are referred to the "the Pillars of Hermes" of "Shu" and of "Solomon." In the Book of the Dead they are called "The Pillars of Shu," the "Pillars of the Gods of the Dawning Light," and also as "the Northern and the Southern Columns of the Gate of the Hall of Truth." The Pillars represent the two columns in the Temple of Solomon and the two great contending Forces of the manifest Universe.

The Black Pillar on the left (north) side of the Temple is called Boaz, and it represents the female or Yin principle. It is also known as the Pillar of Cloud and the negative polarity. The White Pillar on the right (south) side of the Temple is called Jachin, and it represents the male or Yang principle. It is known as the Pillar of Light and Fire and the positive polarity. Dion Fortune called the these columns the "Pillar of Force" (white) and the "Pillar of Form" (black).

In the ancient Egyptian texts, the Pillars are represented by the sacred gateway, the door to which the aspirant is brought when he has completed the negative confession. The archaic drawings on the one Pillar are painted in black upon a white ground, and those on the other in white upon a black ground, in order to express the interchange and reconciliation of opposing forces and the eternal balance of light and darkness which gives force to the visible universe.

The black cubical bases represent darkness and matter wherein the Spirit, the RUACH ELOHIM, began to formulate the Ineffable Name, that Name which the ancient Rabbis have said "rushes through the universe," that Name before which the Darkness rolls back at the birth of time. At the base of both Pillars rise the Lotus flowers, symbols of regeneration. (Note: These are to be painted just above the black cubical bases. The lotus on the White Pillar is painted black. Conversely, that on the Black Pillar is painted white.) The flaming red triangular capitals which crown the summit of the Pillars represent the Triune manifestation of the Spirit of Life, the Three Mothers of the Sepher Yetzirah, the Three Alchemical Principles of Nature, the Sulphur, the Mercury, and the Salt.

In Z-1, the Pillars are described as follows:

> "The Bases of the two Pillars are respectively in Netzach and Hod; the White Pillar being in Netzach and the Black Pillar in Hod. They represent the Two Pillars of Mercy and Severity. The bases are cubical and black to represent the Earth Element in Malkuth. The columns are respectively black and white to represent the manifestation of the Eternal Balance of the Scales of Justice. Upon them should be represented in counterchanged color any appropriate Egyptian designs, emblematic of the Soul.
>
> "The scarlet tetrahedronal capitals represent the Fire of Test and Trial; and between the Pillars is the porchway of the Region Immeasurable. The twin lights which burn upon their summits are "The Declarers of the Eternal Truth." The bases of the tetrahedra, being triangular, that on the white pillar points East, while that on the Black points West. They thus complete the Hexagram of Tiphareth—though separate, as it is fitting in "The Hall of the Dual Manifestation of Truth."

(Note: some authors have interpreted the foregoing passage to mean that the capitals are four-sided pyramids which are attached to a flat triangular base. What the passage really implies is that the capitals themselves are triangular; having three sides that form a pyramid . . . the fourth side is actually the basal side which the pyramid rests upon, as in the Admission Badge to the 31st Path of Shin in the grade of Practicus.)

Construction

Construction of the black and white columns or pillars used in the Neophyte Hall (and throughout all levels of the Order) have resulted in some of the most creative designs imaginable. The two pillars, which rest upon a square base and have a tetrahedron capital, can be built in a variety of ways.

One of the easiest ways to acquire a set of pillars is to use two heavy cardboard tubes which are found inside rolls of carpeting. (The local carpet store can usually provide these.) Two square wooden boxes can be made for the bases. Simply cut a circle into

The Pillars and Altar

the top of the box and slide the tube down into the base. The circle you cut should be only wide enough to slip the pillar securely into the box.

One Temple we know of uses massive wooden pillars that came from an old victorian-style house. Columns like this can be found in salvage yards and used by the enterprising Magician, so long as they are in good shape and not rotting away. (Be careful of rusty nails.) Once the old paint has been removed with solvent and any nail holes have been filled with wood putty, the columns can be set into wooden bases as described above and painted with black and white enamel. We must note that columns of this sort make the most impressive looking pillars that we have ever seen in any Temple.

Long, thick lengths of PVC pipe, which is used for plumbing and water drainage can also be made into pillars and set into wooden bases. One Initiate we are aware of was able to procure interlocking, plastic trash cans which, when placed one on top of the other, made perfectly smooth, slender pillars. The outside of these Pillars were then covered with self-adhesive black and white vinyl or contact paper.

Our own pillars were constructed from a ring of 2x4s which were glued together and cut into circular form on a large lathe. (Definitely not the easiest way to make pillars.) Nowadays a number of companies specialize in making artificial stone and marble pillars, stands, and other decorative items, which are molded from new light-weight materials that resemble the real article. Although they can be costly, they could save the magician time and work.

The two capitals which surmount the pillars are red tetrahedrons which can be fashioned out of cardboard. (See chapter 2 for the construction of a tetrahedron.) Ideally, the capitals should have some method of illumination from the inside, but this could result in a fire hazard, and as always, safety should come before symbolism. Our own pillars are surmounted by red stained-glass capitals. A small light bulb is held inside the top of each pillar by a metal bracket; the electrical cord runs down the hollow center of the pillar and out of a small hole drilled into the base. The lights to both pillars are connected to a rheostat so that the amount of light can be regulated and the heat it throws off kept to a minimum.

Portable Pillars
Contributed by Frater R.H.K.

A readily transportable and easily stored set of pillars can be made from cloth, which is then suspended from the ceiling or hung over any of a variety of portable supports, such as a microphone stand, or patio umbrella stand.

You'll first need to obtain four urethane rings, such as are used to form the foundation for a seasonal wreath. Be sure to use urethane foam rather than styrofoam. Although the styrofoam will work, it tends to crumble, and small white flakes will adhere to the cloth as well as spread themselves around your Temple space. The rings are available at most large craft stores and come in a variety of sizes.

The size ring you choose will determine the size of the columns. The height of the column should be proportional to the diameter of the ring; an aesthetic decision you will have to make. I have made 10' columns for use out of doors using 12" diameter rings and 8' columns for use indoors utilizing 10" rings. If you choose to set the columns on cube bases you may wish to use smaller rings, 8" or 6" for instance.

The cloth which is used for the column itself should be a stretch-knit synthetic material rather than a broadcloth cotton. This is important, as the stretching property of the knit cloth is necessary to wrap around the rings without folds or wrinkles.

The first step after obtaining the rings is to determine their inside circumference in order to know how wide to cut the material for the columns. Measure across the middle of the ring ... you are measuring how wide the hole is at its widest point. In order to find out how big around the hole is (its circumference), you will now need to multiply the measurement across by 3.14 or 3-1/7, depending on whether you use a metric ruler or a fractional one. The resulting number plus 1" is the width the cloth must be. Its length should be one foot longer than the desired column height.

To create the columns, fold the cloth in half lengthwise. Remember, if the cloth has a grain or facing side, you will need to determine which end is up and which side is the outside. The side of the cloth which will be the finished outside should be folded to the inside at this point. Sew a seam the length of the cloth 5/8" in from the cut edges thus creating a long tube. Please note that the resulting tube will now be slightly smaller than the hole in the foam ring.

Turn the tube right side out and insert one end into the foam collar such that about 6″ sticks through. Opening the tube up, fold the excess material outside the foam ring and wrap it around the foam, tucking the excess material under what is now the bottom outside edge of the column. The material may now be fastened on the inside with pins. If you have measured everything correctly, the material should stretch nicely over the ring, leaving a tight, round column end with no wrinkles.

You may note that the seam will show where it wraps around the foam, but this is unnoticeable if its edges are folded back neatly, or you may choose to do some more involved sewing in order for the seam at this point to be hidden . . . that's up to you.

Follow the same procedure for the other end of the column. At this point the column is ready to be suspended in some manner. Wire or string can be attached to the top ring and the column hung from the ceiling or a door way. Inspect the column to insure that the rings are inserted evenly and do not hang at a strange angle. The column should hang such that there are no wrinkles or folds; in fact, from even a short distance, the columns should look solid, as if made of wood. If it does not, you have done something wrong.

The cloth can be painted or silk-screened with appropriate decoration, or left plain. This is more easily accomplished before it is sewn together, but you must be careful to leave room for the seam allowance and the material to be folded under at each end.

The finished columns can be hung over any sort of support, such as a microphone stand, or supports such as those on which the Banners hang. Since the columns are hollow tubes, the supports can be inside them, and thus not visible when the columns are in use. A more portable stand can be created using a tripod of a telescope, or fishing poles. Outdoors, poles can be driven into the ground and the column slipped over these. The column bottoms can be attached to the ground for more stability. (Cloth columns originally created by Fr. RHK for use in large scale outdoor ritual.) Another fairly simple column design for those with some carpentry experience is a tapered square column. Its advantage is that one side may be hinged and the interior used as storage space for the taller wands and staffs. The flat sides are also very easy to either paint with appropriate designs or to attach placards, tablets, photocopies or the like, as needed. The disadvantage is that they are a bit heavy, but the weight can be offset with the addition of casters or wheels built into the base.

The finished column is made in three pieces: a cube base, the tall tapered middle section, and the capital. The suggested size is an 18" cube with 5' columns and a 6" capital, creating an over-all length of 7'. The cube bases are both painted black. One column will then be painted black, the other white, resulting in one entirely black structure and the other white standing upon a black base.

Cut four pieces of 1" x 12" shelving board the desired column length minus the size of the cube base as the separate column capital. In the case of our example, this length would be 5'. Taper each of these pieces by cutting a triangular slice from both sides so that you wind up with four boards five feet long, 11-1/4" wide at one end and 8-1/4" wide at the other.

These four pieces are then nailed together such that they create a square column . . . you will need to overlap each piece correctly to avoid one width being wider than the other. The resulting column when viewed from the end will be a square tube and the overlapping edges will form a Fylfot cross, which you might take pains to orient appropriately for the column you are creating.

The capital for the columns is an eight inch square with vertical corners, rather than tapered ones like the columns. Its top is a flat board, 11-1/4" by 11-1/4". Put together, the capital looks sort of like a mortar board hat, but set atop the tapering column it adds a finished proportion to the overall design. An improvement would be to use wide crown molding for the edges of the capital, which would present a curving flared effect, thus lending more to the image of the papyrus style columns of ancient Egypt.

The three pieces are then fastened together, creating an impressively large column which leaves little doubt which way the Path lies . . . just be careful moving these beacons, as their weight can pose somewhat of a challenge. (Squared papyrus columns were designed by Sor. Terra and built by Fra. RHK for the use of the Benu em-Phenu Har Temple in Tennessee.)

————— ✳ —————

The Pillar Diagrams (Vignettes)

In the original pillar diagrams of the Order in England, certain plates were left out of the vignettes from the Egyptian Book of Dead.

Regardie felt that this was because not all of the diagrams within those vignettes were essential to the Neophyte Hall as envisioned by Mathers. The original art work of the pillar diagrams in this book were supplied by Adam Forrest and based upon descriptions from those earlier Temples. However, as stated in Z-1, the Pillars can be illustrated with any appropriate Egyptian designs, emblematic of the Soul. Because of this, George Wilson, a very talented dual scholar of the Golden Dawn and of Egyptology, is preparing an entirely new translation of the 17th and 125th Formulae which will hopefully be published in the next few years. Mr. Wilson and Mr. Forrest are collaborating on a set of expanded vignettes to accompany this translation.

The Pillar Diagrams
Contributed by Adam Forrest
The Five Registers on the Black Pillar

For the Pillar Boaz, the Order employs the symbolism of the vignette accompanying the 125th Formulae of Coming Forth by Day. The 125th Formula is entitled "The Formula of Entering in the the Hall of Two Truths; A Paean to Osir, the Chief of Amentet. On the Black Pillar, the vignette is divided into five registers, which we shall call for the sake of this discussion B1 (the uppermost) through B5 (the lowest).

Register B1—Registers B1-B3 depict a dozen Deities who serve as witnesses to the Weighing of the Soul. In Register B1 are portrayed the first four of the twelve Gods: Sia, Hu, Hathor, and Hor (Horus).

The first two Deities occur most frequently as a pair. Sia and Hu are two Aspects of the creative Power of the High Gods. The name of Sia means "Mind" or "Thought," equivalent to the Platonic Greek Nous. In Heliopolis, He was the Mind of Re, the Source of Life. In Memphis, He was identified with the Heart of Ptah, the Creator. His intriguing name glyph, which He wears as a crown, has not yet been convincingly deciphered.

Register B2—The next four deities are in Register B2: Iset (Isis), Nebetho (Nephthys), Nuet, and Geb.

Iset and Nebetho are sisters, often referred to by many duel forms: e.g. the Yakhueti ("the Two Shining Ones") Indeed it is impossible to understand Nebetho, who had no separate cult of Her own, outside that relationship, for in truth She is an aspect of Her sister; She is the Dark Iset. In the Greek Magical Papyri, we even find the compound form Isenephthys (i.e., Isis-Nephthys).

Register B3—The last four of the Twelve Gods are illustrated in Register B3: Tefnut, Shu, Tum, Re-Hor-Akhuti. Re-Hor-Akhuti is the last of the Twelve. His name means "The Sun, Hor of the Two Horizons." (This is the deity Whom Thelemites know from Crowley's simulated Coptic as Ra-Hoor-Khuit.)

Register B4—depicts the most famous tableau in the Formulae of Coming Forth by Day, and probably in all of Egyptian iconography: the Weighing of the Heart, or the Judgement Scene.

The Initiate is separated into his many constituent parts. The tripartite monster with the head of a crocodile, the forequarters of a lion, and the hindquarters of a hippopotamus is named Ammut, literally "the Eater of the Dead." The candidate is finally either declared to be meekheru (Egyp., "Justified, Righteous"; lit., "True of Voice") or false. If false, his soul is devoured by the voracious Ammut.

Register B5—the Justified Initiate, his heart having been found true in the Scales of Meet, is led by Hor, son of Iset, the archetype of the Initiate in this World, into the presence of His Father, Osir, the archetype of the Adept in the Higher World.

Note that the Initiate is now unified. The Formula of Solve et Coagula is complete in him. Osir Onnofer (Egyp., "Osiris the Beautiful One"), the Tipharetic God of Rebirth and Adeptship, is enthroned in a royal Pavilion. The Pavilion is flanked by the two sacred Pillars, and its roof is topped with Disk-crowned Uraei, symbols of the Power of the God.

Osir Onnofer is depicted in a balanced triple Form. The two Goddesses, Nebetho and Iset, Who touch and support Him are Aspects of Himself, as surely as the Enthroned Form of the King. The Three Deities represent the Aspects of Osir Onnofer corresponding to the Adept Triad of Chesed, Gevurah, and Tiphareth. The three Implements which He bears represent the same Triad of Powers: the Nekhekh Scourge corresponds to Fire, Sulphur, and Nebetho; the Heka Crook to Water, Mercury, and Iset; and the Benu Phoenix Wand to Air, Salt, Osir, and the Middle Pillar.

B–1

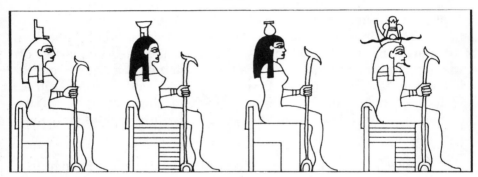

B–2

B–3

Golden Dawn Pillar Vignettes
Copyright © 1991 Adam Forrest

B–4

B–5

Golden Dawn Pillar Vignettes

The Four Sons of Hor are shown with the Lotus.

The sacred Wadjet Eye, symbol of (in this case) the omniscience of the God, brings Osir the feather of Meet, proof that the new Adept is truly in equilibrium.

The Adept is now identified with Osir the Beautiful, and is even entitled to add the sacred Name Osir to his own name.

The Vignette of the White Pillar

For the Pillar Jakhin, the Order employs the symbolism of the vignette accompanying the 17th Formula of the Formulae of Coming Forth by Day. The 17th Formula bears the lengthy title "The Beginning of the Exaltations (and) Enlightenments, Coming Forth into Shining Nuterkheret (the Divine Underworld), into Beautiful Amentet (the West, where the sun sets), Coming Forth by Day in All the Forms Which He Desireth, Playing Senet, Sitting in the Chamber, (and) Coming Forth as a Living Soul." On the White Pillar, the vignette is divided into twelve registers, which we shall call J1 (the uppermost) through J12 (the lowest).

Register J1—The hieroglyphic emblem of Amentet. The initiate in the seh hall. Senet is an ancient boardgame whose paradigm is the journey, unlike chess, whose paradigm is war. The Ba of the Initiate on a shrine. The Initiate in adoration before the Akoru (Sef and Duau).

Register J2—Iset and Nebetho in adoration on either side of a chest from which the head of Re arises.

Register J3—Initiate in adoration before Osir and the Benu. A small votive altar.

Register J4—Iset and Nebetho as two Hawks, and also as two uraeus cobras on two lotuses, flank the body of the Initiate. The Ba brings shen "infinity," to the Initiate. (Note: The lotuses were mistakenly identified by Brodie-Innes as axes.)

Register J5—The Initiate in adoration before two Gods. The first is Hah, with His hand stretched forth over the Eye of Hor. The second is Wadj-Wer, with His hands stretched out over two bodies of water.

Register J6—Pylon of Rosetau with seated God. Wadjet Eye over pylon. Muhweret.

Register J7—Four Sons of Hor flanking a shrine from which the head of Re rises.

Register J8—Hor Khant-Maati, Maa-Atefef; Kheribeqef; and Anup (Anubis).

Register J9—Seven Gods: Nedjhah-Nedjhah, Aqedqed, Khantihehef, Imi-Onnutef, Teshermaa, Besmaa-em-Qereh, and Anem-hur.

Register J10—Initiate in adoration before five ram-headed Deities: Re, Shu, Tefnut, Geb, Ba-Neb-Djedu.

Register J11—Before the sacred Ished (Gk. Persea) Tree, Re in the Form of Mau beheads Apop. Ahathoor, the Great Goddess.

Register J12—In the Boat of Eternity, with Djehoti forward and Hor aft, the Goddess Ahathoor, Khepri with the Divine Scarab of the Dawn overhead.

J–1

J–2

J–3

Golden Dawn Pillar Vignettes

J–4

J–5

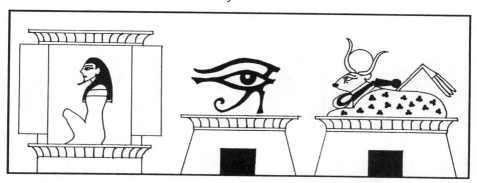

J–6

Golden Dawn Pillar Vignettes
Copyright © 1991 Adam Forrest

J–7

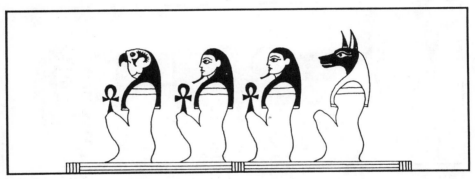

J–8

J–9

Golden Dawn Pillar Vignettes

J–10

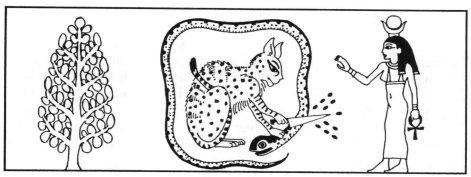

J–11

J–12

Golden Dawn Pillar Vignettes

Concerning the Vignettes
An excerpt from a paper by Mathers

The archaic illustrations are taken from vignettes of the 17th and 125th chapter of the Ritual of the Dead, the *Egyptian Book of the Per-em-Hru* or the "Book of Coming Forth into the Day," the oldest book in the world as yet discovered. The Recension of the Priests of ON is to be found in the walls of the pyramids of the Kings of the 5th and 6th Dynasties at Sakarah, the recension of the 11th and 12th Dynasties on the sarcophagi of that period, and the Theban recension of the 18th Dynasty and onward is found on papyri, both plain and illuminated. No satisfactory translation of these books is available, none having been yet attempted by a scholar having the qualifications of mystic as well as Egyptologist.

The Ritual of the Dead, generally speaking, is a collection of hymns and prayers in the form of a series of ceremonial Rituals to enable the man to unite himself with Osiris the Redeemer. After this union he is no longer called the man, but Osiris, with whom he is now symbolically identified. "That they also may be One of us," said Christ of the New Testament. "I am Osiris" said the purified and justified man, his soul luminous and washed from sin in the immortal and uncreated light, united to Osiris, and thereby justified, and the son of God; purified by suffering, strengthened by opposition, regenerate through self-sacrifice. Such is the subject of the great Egyptian Ritual.

The 17th Chapter of the Theban recension consists of a very ancient text with several commentaries, also extremely old, and some prayers, none of which come into the scheme of the original text. It has, together with the scheme of the original chapter, been very carefully translated for the purpose of this lecture by the V.H. Frater M.W.T (Blackden), and V.H. Soror S.S.D.D. (Farr) has made many valuable suggestions with regard to the interpretation. The Title and Preface of the 17th Chapter reads:

"Concerning the exaltation of the Glorified Ones, of Coming and Going forth in the Divine Domain, of the Genies of the Beautiful land of Amentet. Of Coming forth in the light of Day in any form desired, of Hearing the Forces of Nature by being enshrined as a living Bai."

And the rubric is:

"The united with Osiris shall recite it when he has entered the

Harbour. May glorious things be done thereby upon earth. May all the words of the Adepti be fulfilled."

Owing to the complex use of symbols, the ritual translation of the Chapter can only be understood by perpetual reference to the ancient Egyptian commentaries, and therefore the following paraphrase has been put together to convey to modern minds as nearly as possible the ideas conceived by the old Egyptians in this glorious triumphal song of the Soul of Man made one with Osiris, the Redeemer.

"I am TUM made One with all things.

"I have become NU. I am RA in his rising ruling by right of his Power. I am the Great God self-begotten, even NU, who pronounced His Names, and thus the Circle of the Gods was created.

"I am Yesterday and know the secret of Osiris, whose being is perpetually revered of RA. I have finished the work which was planned at the Beginning, I am the Spirit made manifest, and armed with two vast eagle's plumes. Isis and Nephthys are their names, made One with Osiris.

"I claim my inheritance. My sins have been uprooted and my passions overcome. I am Pure White. I dwell in Time. I live through Eternity, when Initiates make offering to the Everlasting Gods. I have passed along the Pathway. I know the Northern and the Southern Pillars, the two Columns at the Gateway of the Hall of Truth.

"Stretch unto me your hands, O ye Dwellers in the center. For I am transformed to a God in your midst. Made One with Osiris, I have filled the eye socket in the day of the morning when Good and Evil fought together.

"I have lifted up the cloud-veil in the Sky of the Storm. Till I saw RA born again from out the Great Waters. His strength is my strength, and my strength in His strength. Homage to you, Lords of Truth, chiefs who Osiris rules. Granting release from Sin, Followers of Ma where rest is Glorious. Whose Throne Anubis built in the day when Osiris said:

" 'Lo, a man wins his way to Amentet. I come before you, to drive away my faults. As ye did to the Seven Glorious Ones who follow their Lord Osiris. I am that Spirit of Earth and Sun.'

"Between the Two Pillars of Flame. I am RA when he fought beneath the Ashad Tree, destroying the enemies of the Ancient of Days. I am the Dweller in the Egg. I am he who turns in the Disc. I shine forth from the Horizon, as the gold from the mine. I float through the Pillars of SHU in the ether. Without a peer among the Gods. The Breath of my mouth is as a flame. I light upon the Earth with my glory. Eye cannot gaze on my darting beams, as they reach through the Heavens and lick up the Nile with tongues of flame. I am strong upon Earth with the strength of RA. I have come into Harbour as Osiris made perfect. Let priestly offerings be made to me as one in the train of the Ancient of Days. I brood as the Divine Spirit. I move in the firmness of my Strength. I undulate as the Waves that vibrate through Eternity. Osiris has been claimed with acclamation, and ordained to rule among the Gods. Enthroned in the Domain of Horus where the Spirit and the Body are united in the presence of the Ancient of Days. Blotted out are the sins of his body in passion. He has passed the Eternal Gate, and has received the New Year Feast with Incense, at the marriage of Earth with Heaven.

"TUM has built his Bridal Chamber. RURURET has founded his shrine. The Procession's completed. HORUS has purified, SET has consecrated, SHU made one with OSIRIS, has entered his heritage.

"As TUM he has entered the Kingdom to complete union with the Invisible. Thy Bride, O Osiris, is Isis, who mourned Thee when she found Thee slain. In Isis, thou art born again. From Nephthys is thy nourishment. They cleansed thee in thy Heavenly Birth. Youth waits upon thee, ardour is ready at thy hand. And their arms shall uphold thee for millions of years. Initiates surround Thee and Thine enemies are cast down. The Powers of Darkness are destroyed. The Companions of Thy Joys are with Thee. Thy Victories in the Battle await their reward in the Pillar. The Forces of Nature obey Thee. Thy Power is exceeding great, The Gods curse him that curseth Thee. Thine Aspirations are fulfilled. Thou are destroyed who barred Thy way."

The 125th Chapter is concerned with the entry of an Initiate into the Hall of the Two Columns of Justice, and commenced with a most beautiful and symbolic description of Death, as a journey from the barren wilderness of Earth, to the Glorious Land which lies beyond. The literal translation of the opening lines is as follows:

"I have come from afar to look upon thy beauties. My hands salute Thy Name of Justice. I have come from afar, where the Acacia Tree grew not. Where the tree thick with leaves is not born. Where there come not beams from herb or grass. I have entered the Place of Mystery. I have communed with Set. Sleep came upon me, I was wrapped therein, bowing down before the hidden things. I was ushered into the House of Osiris. I saw the marvels that were there. The Princes of the Gates in the Glory."

The illustrations in this chapter represent the Hall of Truth as seen through the open leaves of its door. The Hall is presided over by a God who holds his right hand over the cage of a hawk, and his left over the food of eternity. On each side of the God is a cornice crowned by a row of alternate feathers and Uraei symbolizing justice and fiery power. The door leaf which completes the right hand of a stall is called "Possessor of Truth controlling the Feet," while that on the left is "Possessor of strength binding the male and female animals." The 42 Judges of the Dead are represented as seated in a long row, and each of them has to be named, and the Sin over which he presided has been denied.

This chapter describes the introduction of the Initiate into the Hall of truth by Anubis, who, having questioned the aspirant, receives from him an account of his Initiation, and is satisfied by his right to enter. He states that he has been taken into the ante-chamber of the Temple and there stripped and blindfolded, he had to grope for the entrance of the Hall, and having found it, he was reclothed and anointed in the presence of the Initiated. He is then asked for the Passwords and demands that his Soul should be weighed in the Great Balance of the Hall of Truth, whereupon ANUBIS again interrogates him concerning the symbolism of the door of the Hall, and his answers being found correct, ANUBIS says: "Pass on, thou knowest it."

Among other things the Initiate states that he has been purified four times, the same number of times that the Neophyte is purified and consecrated in the ceremony of the Neophyte. He then makes the long Negative Confession, stating to each Judge in turn that he is innocent of that form of Sin over which he judges. Then he invokes the Judges to do him justice, and afterwards describes how he had washed in the washing place of the South, and rested in the North, in the place called "Son of the Deliverers" and he becomes the Dweller under the Olive Tree of Peace, and how he was given a tall flame of fire and a scepter of cloud which he preserved in the salting tank in which mummies were swathed. And he found there another scepter called "Giver of Breath" and with that he extinguished the flame and shattered the scepter of cloud, and made a lake of it. The

Initiate is then brought to the actual Pillars, and has to name them and their parts under the symbol of the Scales of a Balance. He also has to name the Guardian of the Gateway, who prevents his passage, and when all these are propitiated, the plea of the Hall itself cries out against his steps, saying "Because I am silent, because I am pure," and it must know that his aspirations are pure enough and high enough for him to be allowed to tread upon it. He is then allowed to announce to Thoth that he is clean from all evil, and has overcome the influence of the planets, and THOTH says to him: "Who is He whose Pylons are of Flame, whose walls of living Uraei, and the flames of whose House are streams of Water?" And the Initiate replies "Osiris!"

And it is immediately proclaimed: "Thy meat shall be from the Infinite, and thy drink from the Infinite. Thou art able to go forth to the sepulchral feasts on earth, for thou hast overcome."

Thus, these two chapters, which are represented by their illustrations upon the Pillars, represent the advance and purification of the Soul and its union with Osiris, the Redeemer, in the Golden Dawn of the Infinite Light, in which the Soul is transfigured, knows all, and can do all, for it is made One with the Eternal God.

KHABS AM PEKHT
KONX OM PAX
LIGHT IN EXTENSION

A Meditation on the Pillars

For this meditation/ritual the Neophyte should wear the robe and headdress of the Outer Order in addition to the sash of the 0=0 grade. The Temple is to be arranged in accordance with the Neophyte Hall.

After a period of relaxation, perform the LBRP.

Circumambulate the Temple thrice deosil (clockwise) giving the Neophyte Signs when passing the East.

Perform the Adoration to the Lord of the Universe.

Stand between the Pillars, with one hand touching each column. Close your eyes and begin breathing with the Four-fold Breath technique. Commence the following visualization:

———— ✳ ————

Imagine yourself standing between two enormous columns. The column on your right consists of pure flames. That on your left is comprised of swirling clouds. Feel the polarity of the two Pillars; one white, positive, male, active, and exhibiting the qualities of Force, the other black, negative, female, passive, and displaying the qualities of Form. Light and Dark. Mercy and Severity. Two total opposites which cannot exist one without the other.

Now see yourself as a third Pillar formed between these two great rivals. You are the Pillar of Mildness and Equilibrium that exists between the Light and Dark Pillars. You temper and balance their opposing energies. Your color is neutral grey, the blending of black and white. Your arbitration is what gives harmony and grace to the manifest universe.

———— ✳ ————

Continue this meditation for as long as you desire. Then perform the Reverse Circumambulation, three times widdershins (counterclockwise).

Again perform the Adoration to the Lord of the Universe.

Perform the LBRP. Declare the Temple duly closed.

THIS ENDS THE RITE

The Iset Or Temple Throne

Use and Symbolism

The Iset is one of our own contributions to the furnishings of a modern Golden Dawn Temple. Its design is based upon the traditional Egyptian throne seen in countless vignettes from the Book of the Dead.

In ancient times the throne represented the seat of Divinity. Homage was paid to the throne in the absence of any human occupant. When a king spoke to the people from horseback, he did so as a king; but when he spoke from the throne, his words were considered the utterances of God. The throne was regarded as a sacred

The Iset

Dwelling-place which not only housed the Divine Spirit, but also acted as a container for spiritual energy, localizing it at certain times and places.

The throne therefore partakes of the same symbolism as a chalice; a receptacle of Divine energies. It is thus a feminine symbol—the name "Iset" is taken from the name of Isis (Ese), the Egyptian goddess whose name means "throne." This signifies her role as supporter or upholder of the Universe. The Sphere of Binah on the Tree of Life also has allusions to the throne; one of Binah's titles is "Khorsia," meaning the throne, while the choir of angels associated with this Sephirah is the Aralim or "thrones." Binah is the reservoir of Divine energy from the paternal Chokmah; she stabilizes and regulates it, eventually giving it form.

In the Neophyte Hall of the Golden Dawn, each throne is a seat of a particular Godform, therefore each is a reservoir for the energies which are attributed to a specific deity. A properly trained Hierophant creates the astral shells of each particular godform in the Hall. Upon entering the Temple and taking his/her station, each officer "steps into" and animates the particular Godform and connects his/her Ruach with the Godform "shell" located at the Iset. At one point the Hierophant must leave his throne and take on a different Godform, while leaving the original deity in astral form seated upon the Dais. At certain times, if a Temple is short on officers, it becomes necessary for a member to take on dual roles, moving around the Temple as one Godform, while building up the other form at its throne.

The Iset should not be considered as just another piece of furniture. Its design is based upon that of a traditional Egyptian throne taken from ancient papyri, and it is intended to be a vessel for specific forces which are built up by the Hierophant and employed in Golden Dawn ritual. The Godform of each particular Iset can be built up through a meditation designed to invoke it.

Materials Needed
   One 4' x 4' sheet of 3/4" plywood
   12-13 feet of 1/4" screen molding
   Yellow carpenter's glue
   1-1/2" brads
   Smaller brads (#6) for molding
   Wood putty
   Black polyurethane or acrylic enamel

Tools Needed
- Table or circular saw
- Hack saw
- Mitre box or simple protractor
- Hammer
- Nail punch
- Putty knife
- Sandpaper
- Large paint brush
- Yard stick or tape measure

Construction

1) Take the sheet of plywood and measure and label clearly all sections of the Throne according to the diagram. (The back is 20" x 12", the front is 15" x 12", the top is 11" x 12", and two sides are each 15" x 10-1/2.") Cut all sections apart with the saw.

2) Take one side section and apply glue to one of the 15" edges. Keep this edge facing up. Take the front panel and line up one of its 15" edges perpendicular to the glued side edge. Nail the two pieces together. (Note: The edge of the front section should be visible, but not that of the side section.)

3) Take the remaining side panel and apply glue to one edge as before. Nail this piece perpendicular to the other 15" edge of the front as in the previous step. (Note: you should now have three sections nailed together which form the shape of an upside-down U.)

4) Place the Throne on its front, so that the U-shape is upright. The two long edges of both side sections should be facing the ceiling. Apply glue to these two edges. Take the back panel and place it lengthwise over the glued side edges so that the top of the back section overhangs the 15" length of the sides and front by 5". Nail into place.

5) Stand the Throne upright. Apply glue to the three flush edges of the front and two sides. (The back edge should be facing the ceiling, 5" above the glued edges.)

6) Take the top section and apply glue to one of its 12" edges. Place the top over the three glued edges of the front and sides, so that the glued 12" top edge is up against the back panel. Nail into place.

Finishing Steps

7) Take the screen molding and cut it with the hack saw into the following lengths: Two 20", two 15", two 11", and two 12-1/4" pieces.

8) With glue and small brads, attach molding to Throne to give a recessed look as in the diagram.

9) You should be left with two pieces of 12-3/4" molding. Take one piece

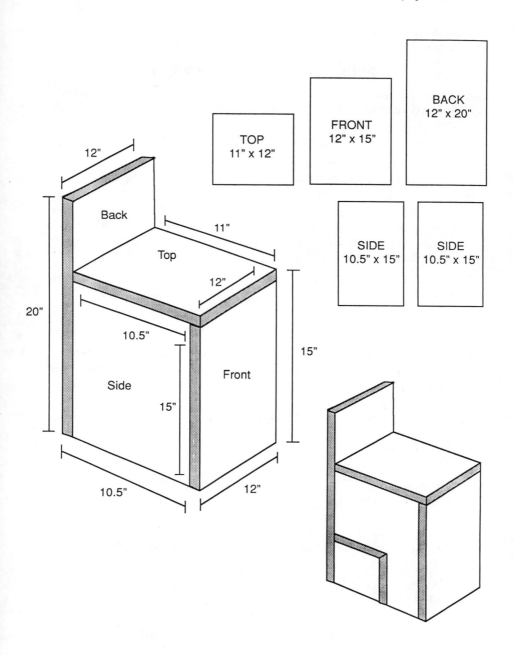

The Iset

and measure off 7". With either a mitre box or pencil and protractor, mark off and cut a 45 degree angle, so that you end up with two mitred pieces of molding (one 7" in length, and the other 5-3/4"). Glue and nail into place on the Throne as indicated by the diagram.

10) Use nail punch and hammer to make sure no nail heads stick out. Fill in nail holes and cracks with wood putty and putty knife. Allow to dry.

11) Sand off excess putty and rough areas. Paint the entire Throne with black polyurethane or acrylic enamel. Let dry.

Note: Not all Temple Isets need to be painted entirely black. In some cases, different officers will need Thrones which are specifically colored to represent their particular office. For the Hierophant—red with inlaid green, Hegemon—white with inlaid black, Hiereus—black with inlaid white. The rest of the Thrones are to be all black. Each Iset should be marked underneath so that they are always used by a specific officer.

Ritual for Use

Meditation on the Throne of the Stolistes

This meditation can be used by any Adept who holds the Station of Stolistes in order to supplement his/her knowledge and practical ceremonial experience. The Temple should be arranged in accordance with the Neophyte Hall. The seat of the Stolistes is in the North along with lamen and cup. Dress in the regalia of the Outer Order.

Relax. Perform the LBRP.

Vibrate "EHEIEH" four times using the Vibratory Formula. Give the LVX Signs. Face west. Close your eyes and begin the Four-fold Breath. Before you where the Altar would be, imagine a brilliant light beginning to manifest. As you breathe, visualize this light becoming brighter. The light pulsates with each division of the Four-fold Breath; as you breath in, the light becomes sheer ultimate brilliance. Upon holding the breath, the light turns to white brilliance, a color which is not as blinding as the first. It continues to whiten as you breathe out. At the empty hold, the white light becomes flecked with gold, as if the light were manifesting into physical form. See this light descending into your Kether center. By aspiration, your Ruach strives from Tiphareth to join this light.

Go clockwise to the North and face the Iset of Stolistes. Visualize a form developing in the light. It is feminine and glows with a bluish aura. You begin to make out her features. She has the straight nose and long dark hair of an Egyptian. She wears a blue tunic which reaches down to her feet. Her collar is banded orange, blue and orange. Her wristbands are also striped blue and orange. She holds in her hands a blue chalice and stands upon a pavement of black and white. Her throne is blue ornamented in orange. She is the Goddess of the Scales of the Balance at the Black Pillar. You hear her name, "Auramoouth," the Light shining through the Waters upon Earth." Picture her name in white within your heart center. Imagine also her sigil. Project a rose pink ray of thought from Tiphareth which animates the figure of the Goddess.

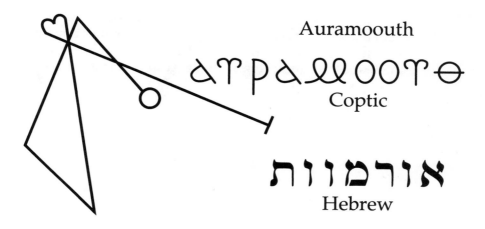

Auramoouth

ⲁⲧⲣⲁⲙⲟⲟⲧⲑ
Coptic

אורמוות
Hebrew

Auramoouth in Coptic and Hebrew with Sigil

Strive to visualize the form strongly. When this is accomplished, imagine the Goddess saluting with the LVX signs. You approach the Throne of Stolistes and sit down. As you do so, the form of the Goddess does likewise. Imagine the great form of the goddess around you like a glowing blue aura. All unbalanced thoughts and feelings are washed away. Feel her cool, purifying essence within you. Your hands are her hands. Through her, you have attained the cleansing embodiment of the seas, oceans, rivers, and rains. You feel the Divine Light acting through Water to purify and vitalize the Earth. Silently repeat her name within your mind and heart and invoke the qualities of cleansing water each time you do so. Ground the energy of the goddess by the Formula of the Middle Pillar, vibrating the Divine Hebrew names of Kether, Daath, Tiphareth, Yesod and Malkuth: EHEIEH, YHVH ELOHIM, YHVH ELOAH VE-DAATH, SHADDAI EL CHAI and ADONAI HA ARETZ.

After meditating for a while in this fashion, stand up, but leave the godform of Auramoouth seated upon the throne. Turn to face the figure and give the Projection Sign at the Iset, followed by the Sign of Silence. Finally, salute the figure with the LVX signs. Withdraw your thought-ray from the Godform back into your Tiphareth center. See the form of the goddess start to dissipate, but imagine her cleansing and purifying qualities remaining within the Iset. When the figure has totally vanished, end the meditation by returning to the east and performing the LBRP.

THIS ENDS THE RITE

IMPLEMENTS OF THE NEOPHYTE OFFICERS

The Neophyte Officers and Their Godforms*

Hierophant:

   Egyptian Osir, Coptic Ousiri, Graeco-Egyptian Osiris. Osiris in the Netherland. Expounder of the Mysteries in the Hall of the Dual Manifestation of the Goddess of Truth.

   The Hierophant is the Master of the Hall, seated in the East of the Temple, on the outer side of the Veil Paroketh, to rule the Temple under the Presidency of the Chiefs. There he fills the place of a Lord of the Paths of the Portal of the Vault of the Adepts, acting as Inductor to the Sacred Mysteries. The Hierophant must be of the 5=6 grade and a Zelator Adeptus Minor. His office is represented by two Godforms, the active and passive aspects of Osiris. Seated as Hierophant, he is clothed in the Godform of Osiris, who never moves from the Dais. When the Hierophant has to move from the Dais, he is covered by the form of Osiris in action—Hoor-Ouer, Horus the Elder, which is built up by the past Hierophant. If no one is seated as Past Hierophant, then Inner Order members help the Hierophant to formulate the second Godform. The insignia and symbols of the Hierophant are:

- The Throne of the East in the Path of Samekh, outside the Veil.
- The Mantle (Cloak or Tabard) of bright flame scarlet, bearing a white cross on the left breast.
- The Lamen suspended from a white collar.
- The Banner of the East.

Hiereus:

   Egyptian Hôr, Coptic Hôor, Graeco-Egyptian Hôros, Latinized Greek Horus. Horus in the Abode of Blindness unto and Ignorance of the Higher. Avenger of the Gods.

   The station of Hiereus is at the extreme west of the Temple and in the lowest point of Malkuth, where he is enthroned in its darkest part (in the quarter represented black in the Minutum Mundam Diagram). Representing a Terrible and Avenging God at the Con-

---

* The various Egyptian, Coptic, Graeco-Egyptian and Greek versions of the Godforms given here are from a paper entitled "The Godforms of the Visible Stations," by Adam P. Forrest.

fines of Matter, at the borders of the Qlippoth, he is enthroned upon Matter and robed in Darkness, and about his feet are Thunder and Lightning—the impact of the Paths of Shin and Qoph—Fire and Water, terminating respectively in the Russet and Olive quarters of Malkuth. There he is placed as a mighty and avenging Guardian to the Sacred Mysteries. The symbols and insignia of the Hiereus are:

- The Throne of the West in the Black of Malkuth, where it borders on the Kingdom of Shells.
- The Black Mantle of Darkness, bearing a white cross on the left breast.
- The Sword of Strength and Severity.
- The Lamen suspended from a scarlet collar.
- The Banner of the West.

The Hegemon:

Egyptian Mĕet, Coptic Thmĕ, Greek Themis. Before the Face of the Gods in the Place of the Threshold.

The station of Hegemon is between the two Pillars whose bases are in Netzach and Hod, at the intersection of the Paths Peh and Samekh, in the symbolic Gateway of Occult Science—as it were, at the Beam of Justice: at the point of intersection of the Lowest Reciprocal Path with that of Samekh, which forms a part of the Middle Pillar. She is placed there as the Guardian of the Threshold of the Entrance and the Preparer of the Way for the Enterer—therefore the Reconciler between Light and Darkness, and the Mediator between the Stations of Hierophant and Hiereus. The symbols and insignia of Hegemon are:

- The Mantle of pure whiteness, bearing on the left breast a red cross.
- The Mitre-headed Scepter.
- The Lamen suspended from a Black Collar.

Kerux (also spelled Keryx):

Egyptian Anup em Yebet, Coptic Anoup-empeIebet, Graeco-Egyptian Anoubis of the East, Latinized Greek Anubis. Watcher for the Gods.

The Kerux is the Herald, the Guardian and Watcher within the Temple, as the Sentinel is the Watcher without—and therefore is his charge the proper disposition of the furniture and stations of the

Temple. He is the Guardian of the Inner side of the Portal—the sleepless Watcher of the Gods and the Preparer of the Pathway to Divine Wisdom. He is also the Proclaimer. His peculiar ensigns of Office are:

- The Red Lamp to signify the Hidden Fire over which he watches.
- The Magic Staff of Power to represent a Ray of the Divine Light which kindles the Hidden Fire.
- Two Potions whereby to produce the effect of Blood.

Stolistes:

Egyptian Mut, Coptic Auramoouth, Graeco-Egyptian Mouthis. The Light Shining through the Waters upon Earth. Goddess of the Scale of Balance at the Black Pillar.

The Stolistes is stationed in the northern part of the Hall to the northwest of the Black Pillar whose base is in Hod, and is there as the Affirmer of the powers of Moisture, Water, reflected through the Tree into Hod. The Cup is the Receptacle of this, filled from Hod so as to transmit its forces into Malkuth, restoring and purifying the vital forces therein by Cold and Moisture. There is a connection between Auramoouth and the Aurim or Urim of the Hebrews. The Stolistes has the care of the Robes and Insignia of the Temple as symbolized by his cleansing and purification the purging away of the Evil of Malkuth by the Waters of Spirit.

Dadouchos:

Egyptian Neit, Coptic Thaum-Esh-Nèith, Graeco-Egyptian Neith. Perfection through Fire manifesting on Earth. Goddess of the Scale of Balance at the White Pillar.

The Dadouchos is stationed towards the midst of the southern part of the Hall, to the southwest of the White Pillar whose base is in Netzach and is there as the Affirmer of the Powers of Fire, reflecting down the Tree to Netzach. The censer is the Receptacle thereof—the transmitter of the Fires of Netzach to Malkuth, restoring and purifying the vital force therein by Heat and Dryness. There is a connection between Thaum-Esh-Neith and the Thummim of the Hebrews.

The Dadouchos has charge of all lights, fires and incense, as representing the purifying and purging of Malkuth by Fire and the Light of Spirit. The Stolistes and the Dadouchos together also purify the Temple, the Members and the Candidate by Water and by Fire.

Phylax (Sentinel):

Egyptian Opowet, Coptic Ophooui, Graeco-Egyptian Ophois; also Egyptian Anu em Ament, Coptic Anoup emp Emenet, Graeco-Egyptian Anoubis of the West, Latinized Greek Anubis.

The Watcher without. The Phylax sits outside of the Hall to guard its outer perimeter. He has a sword in his hand to keep out intruders.

Neophyte Officers' Implements

Hierophant's Wand

Use and Symbolism

The Hierophant's Wand is symbolically the most important wand in the Neophyte Hall and in all of the Halls of the Outer Order. Known as the "Scepter of Power," this wand, when wielded by a duly initiated and trained Hierophant, is a powerful implement used to open or close the Temple in any Grade of the First Order. The wand represents the forces of the Middle Pillar on the Tree of Life. This fact reaffirms the Golden Dawn's emphasis that equilibrated Forces (perfect balance of natural opposites) is the true source of Life and Light in the Universe. The implements of the two contending forces, the Hiereus' sword and the Hegemon's Wand, are also very powerful, but more limited in use. The Scepter of Power acts as a lightning rod which brings down the Light from the Kether beyond the veil, and fuses the energies of the Tree together into a mighty triad of Severity, Mercy, and That which reconciles between them. This is especially apparent in the Initiation Ceremony of the Neophyte, when a triad of these same forces are formed over the head of the candidate upon his/her reception into the Order.

The crown of the Hierophant's Wand naturally alludes to the Sephirah of Kether. (Note: the topmost ring next to the crown is not properly a gold band like the others. It acts as a buttress and support for the wand-head, giving it strength. This ring should be considered as part of the wand-head itself. It thus partakes of the same symbolism as the crown and Kether.) If six crown points are used,

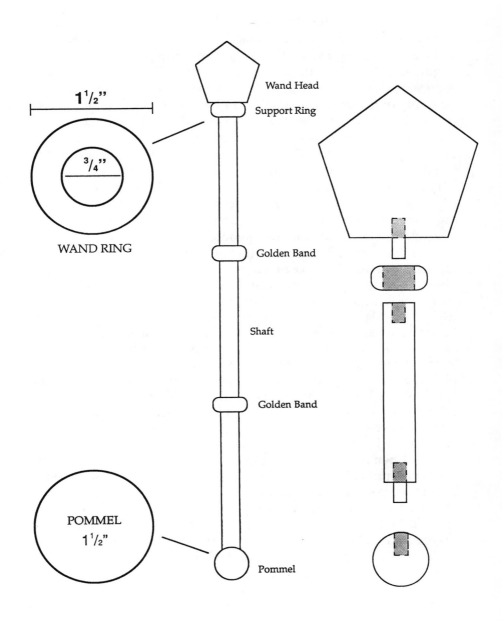

1 1/2"

3/4"

WAND RING

Wand Head

Support Ring

Golden Band

Shaft

Golden Band

POMMEL
1 1/2"

Pommel

Basic Wand Construction

the emphasis is on the Macrocosmic hexagram; if ten are used, the totality of the Tree of Life is stressed. The three golden bands in descending order represent Daath, Tiphareth and Yesod. The pommel or golden ball at the bottom of the wand refers to Malkuth. The shaft represents the descending Paths of Gimel, Samekh and Tau. The Hierophant normally wields the implement by the Path of Tau, the part of the shaft between the pommel and the third golden band. This symbolizes the active role he/she plays as a magnet for the Divine Light of Kether; attracting it through the Middle Pillar and bringing it into manifestation to Malkuth (the Temple or the Candidate.) A true Hierophant who holds the title of "Expounder of the Mysteries" knows that he/she is ultimately a channel for the Divine Light made worthy to do so through initiation, study, hard magickal work and dedication. Ego should not play any role here.

Besides actual initiations, the Hierophant's Wand can be used for many magickal purposes where the Force of Kether and the Middle Pillar is desired, so long as it is used with the respect worthy of such a sublime and powerful implement. The wand can certainly be used to Invoke or Banish the elements with great effect, and this is precisely what the Hierophant does with it in the Elemental grade ceremonies. (Note: In the original Order papers known as Z-1, there is a warning against misuse of the Hierophant's Wand. Many people have interpreted this to mean that the Scepter is never to be used to invoke the Elements in a ritual such as the SIRP. What Z-1 actually warns against is the use of the "Opening and Closing by Scepter" in a ritual where Elemental spirits have been invoked. This method is done by the Hierophant when time is short, by simply declaring the Temple open or closed by the power of the Scepter. Once again this method is not to be used when the Elements have been invoked ... the proper pentagrams MUST be drawn by the Hierophant in order to open or close the Hall correctly.)

The Scepter of Power (see previous page) can also be employed to consecrate other implements or talismans with the particular energies of the Spheres and Paths of the Middle Pillar.

Materials Needed
    One 3/4" thick dowel approx. 36" long
    A small piece of 3/4" pine wood
    A piece of soft wood (balsa or bass) 1/4" thick
    Two 1/4" wooden dowels or pegs 1" in length
    One 1-1/2" wooden ball

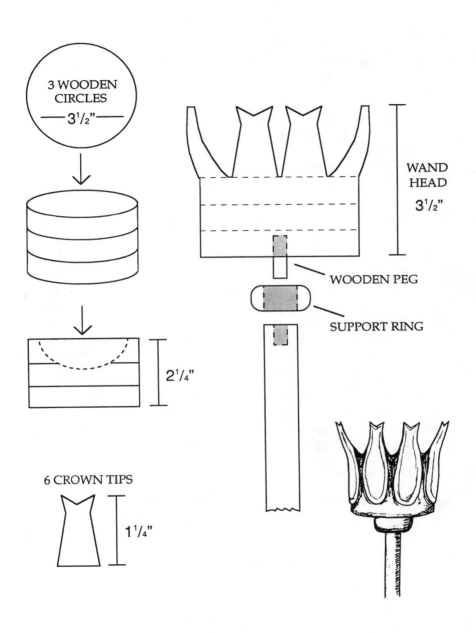

3 WOODEN CIRCLES

—3¹/₂"—

WAND HEAD

3¹/₂"

WOODEN PEG

SUPPORT RING

2¹/₄"

6 CROWN TIPS

1¹/₄"

The Hierophant's Wand

Yellow carpenter's glue
Gesso
Acrylic paints: red and iridescent gold
Clear lacquer finish (spray or brush on)
Ruler or yard stick

Tools Needed

Jigsaw or scroll saw
Electric drill with 1/4" and 3/4" bits
Sandpaper
Artist's paint brushes
Rotary power tool with gouging bit

Construction: The Crown

1) With the jigsaw, cut a total of eight 3-1/2" diameter circles out of the 1/4" thick piece of bass or balsa wood.

2) Glue all eight pieces together to make one solid circular piece of wood which is 2" in thickness and 3-1/2" in diameter.

3) With rotary power tool and gouging bit hollow out the top (flat) side of this circular piece of wood to form a concave or curved hollow space which is about 3/4" to 1" deep. Sand smooth.

4) From the remainder of the 1/4" thick wood, cut out 6 to 10 crown tips. Taper the upper ends of the crown tips with sandpaper to form points. Angle the bottom ends of the crown tips with sandpaper so that when glued to the main part of the crown, the tips will tilt outward slightly. Glue the tips around the edges of the top (hollowed-out) side of crown.

5) With rotary power tool grind and sand out curves on sides of crown for a sculptural effect as in diagram or leave the curved sides smooth. Drill a hole 1/2" deep and 1/4" wide in the center of the bottom side of the crown.

Construction: The Shaft, Rings And Pommel

6) Into the leftover piece of 3/4" thick pine wood, drill a 3/4" diameter hole. Around this hole, draw a 1-1/2" diameter circle. Cut this circle out of the wood using the scroll saw. Repeat this same process three more times, so that you end up with four donut-shaped rings of wood.

7) Take the 36" long dowel (shaft) and drill a hole 1/2" deep and 1/4" in diameter into one end of it. Do the same to the other end. Glue one of the 1" wooden pegs into one of the holes you have just drilled so that half of the peg is embedded into the end of the dowel and half of it sticks out. Do the same at the other end of the shaft.

8) Apply glue to the inside of all four rings. Slide one of the rings over

the top end of the shaft. Slide the remaining rings over the other end of the shaft and space all the rings evenly, approximately 9" apart, starting from the topmost ring. (Note: the rings should fit snugly. If they are too tight to slide into place, the inside hole may require some sanding.)

9) Take the 1-1/2" wooden ball (pommel) and with sandpaper form a flattened area about 3/4" wide. Into the center of this, drill a hole which is 1/2" deep and 1/4" in diameter. Pour some glue into the hole you have just drilled and attach the ball to the bottom end of the shaft, over the wooden peg.

10) Finish assembling the wand by pouring some glue into the hole at the bottom of the crown and attaching it to the top of the shaft, over the wooden peg. (Note: the crown should fit snugly, and butt up against the topmost ring.) Let the glue dry for a few hours.

Finishing Steps

11) Sand the entire surface of the scepter. With a paint brush, cover the wand with a coat of gesso. Allow time to dry.

12) Sand the painted surface (especially the shaft) lightly until smooth. Paint the entire crown and shaft of the wand with acrylic red. Allow to dry.

13) Paint the four rings and pommel with iridescent gold. Allow to dry. Paint or spray on a sealant such as clear lacquer to protect the painted wand. Allow to dry.

Ritual for Use

The Consecration of a Tipharetic Talisman

The Z.A.M. (Zelator Adeptus Minor) should dress in the regalia of the Second Order. Arrange the Temple in accordance with the Hall of the Neophytes. Outside the circle, wrapped in a black piece of cloth and bound three times with a black cord, should be a talisman you want charged with the energies of Tiphareth. (This could be a piece of jewelry, a solar gemstone or a piece of paper with symbols relating to Tiphareth drawn on it.) You will also need the Cross and Triangle, a sword, a chalice of water, a censer or stick of incense, and a piece of white cloth for wrapping the talisman at the end of the ceremony. The main implement in this ritual is the Hierophant's Wand.

After a period of relaxation and meditation, give five knocks with a dagger handle against the side of the Altar. Go to the northeast and proclaim, "HEKAS, HEKAS, ESTE BEBELOI!"

Perform the Lesser Banishing Ritual of the Pentagram (LBRP) and the Lesser Ritual of the Hexagram (BRH).

Perform the Supreme Invoking Ritual of the Pentagram (SIRP).

Go to the station of Stolistes (North) and take up the water cup. Starting in the East, trace a cross in the air with the cup. Sprinkle water thrice in the form of the Invoking Water Triangle. Do this at all quarters. Then circumambulate the Temple twice more while saying, "So therefore first, the priest who governeth the works of Fire must sprinkle with the lustral Waters of the loud, resounding Sea." Replace the cup.

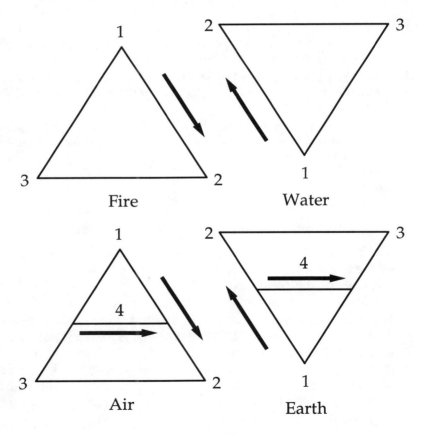

Fire/Water/Air/Earth Triangles

Go to the station of the Dadouchos (South) and take up the incense. Again go clockwise to the East, trace a cross and wave the incense thrice in the form of the Invoking Fire Triangle. Do this at all quarters. Then circumambulate the Temple twice more while saying, "And when after all the phantoms are banished, Thou shalt see that holy and formless Fire, that Fire which darts and flashes through the hidden depths of the Universe. Hear Thou, the voice of Fire!" Replace the incense.

Go to the west of the Altar and face east. Say, "The Holy Guardian Angel of (state Magickal name) under the authority of the Concealed One is in command of those beings who have been summoned to this ceremony. I charge all ye Archangels, Angels, Rulers, Kings, and elementals called to this place to witness and aid in this Rite. I call upon the Crown, EHEIEH, the One Source Most High, to look with favor upon me as I perform this ceremony. Grant me success in this, my search for the Hidden Wisdom and my aspiration towards the Light Divine. To the glory and completion of the Great Work. So mote it be."

Grasp the Hierophant's Wand just under the crown. Go to the east and perform the Qabalistic Cross. Then draw an Invoking Hexagram of the Supernals and visualize it in a golden light while intoning "ARARITA." In the center place the sigil of Saturn in brilliant white. Vibrate "YHVH ELOHIM." Then draw the letter Aleph also in brilliant white and intone the name of the letter. Go to the South and draw the same hexagram

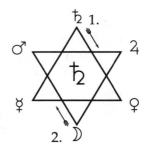

Invoking Hexagram of the Supernals

while vibrating the same names. Repeat this procedure in the West and North. Upon returning to the East, repeat the Analysis of the Keyword as given in the BRH.

Grasp the Hierophant's Wand by the middle ring (the Tiphareth ring). Go to the East. Trace in gold the six *Invoking Hexagrams of the Sun* in the air with the wand. Vibrate "ARARITA" while tracing each hexagram. In the center of each figure trace the orange sigil of Sol while intoning the name, "YHVH ELOAH VE-DAATH." Then draw the Hebrew letter

Resh also in orange and intone the name of the letter.

Say, "Thou majestic king and child! Sphere of Beauty and the Vision of the Harmony of things! Zoar Anpin, the Lesser Countenance! Tetragrammaton—God of Knowledge! Thou, upon whom the whole of Creation depends for unity and balance! The keys of the mysteries of death and resurrection are in Thy grasp! Sphere of Shemesh, the sun, and the realm of healing belong to Thee! The Cross, the Cube and the heart are Thine! Let a ray of Thy perfection descend and awaken within me the power to charge this talisman with the healing, equilibrating, and mystical energies of Tiphareth."

Visualize the Banner of the East surrounding you on all sides, enveloping you like a cloak.

Say, "In the Divine Name of YHVH ELOAH VE-DAATH, I command ye, O ye dwellers in the Invisible Realms, that ye fashion for me a magickal base in the Astral Light wherein I may invoke the Divine Forces to charge this talisman."

"Grant unto me the presence of RAPHAEL, the Great Archangel of the sphere of Tiphareth. Let the choir of angels known as the MELEKIM, the Kings, be present at this ceremony so that this talisman may be duly charged with all of the powers of the sixth Sephirah." Put the wand aside.

Place the black-wrapped talisman at the edge of the circle to the west. Push it into the circle with the tip of the sword. Say, "Creature of Talismans, enter thou within this sacred circle, that thou mayest become a worthy dwelling place for the Forces of Tiphareth."

Consecrate the talisman with Water and Fire. (Dip your fingers into the water and mark the talisman with a cross. Sprinkle thrice in the form of the Invoking Water Triangle. Wave the incense in the form of a cross and give an additional three waves in the form of the Invoking Fire Triangle.)

Say, "In the name of YHVH ELOAH VE-DAATH, I (give magickal name) proclaim that I have invoked ye in order to form a true and potent link between my human soul and the Light Divine. To this end I have brought into this circle a Talisman covered with a black veil and bound thrice with a cord, so that this creature of talismans shall not see the light nor move until it be duly consecrated unto me. I proclaim that this talisman SHALL be charged by the Archangel RAPHAEL, so that through its use, spiritual knowledge, harmony, and healing powers may be mine, Thus may I be better enabled to perform the Great Work."

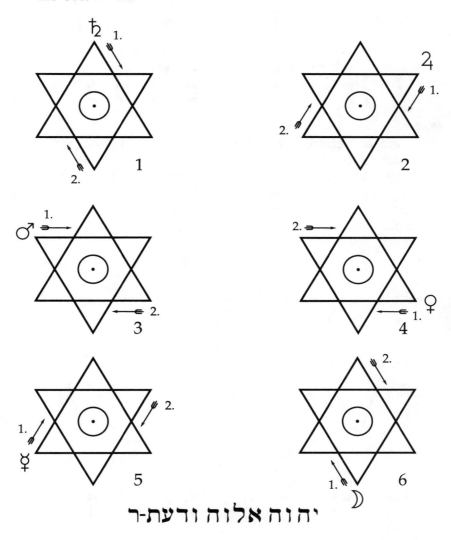

Six Invoking Hexagrams for Sol

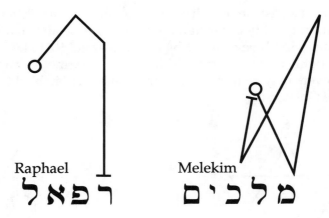

Raphael   Melekim

רפאל   מלכים

Place the talisman at the foot of the Altar and say, "I (magickal name), do solemnly pledge to consecrate this talisman in due ceremonial form. I further promise and swear to use it to obtain mystical experiences, conversation with my Higher Divine Genius, and cure illness. May the powers of Tiphareth, the sphere of Beauty, witness my pledge."

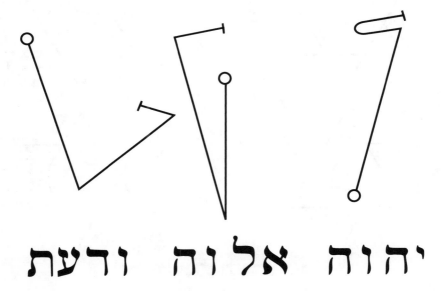

יהוה אלוה ודעת

YHVH ELOAH VE–DAATH

Place the talisman upon the white triangle on the Altar and stand west, facing the East. With sword in hand, trace over the talisman the sigils of YHVH ELOAH VE-DAATH and of RAPHAEL while intoning the their names. (Note: vibrate YHVH ELOAH VE-DAATH a total of twelve times according to the Vibratory Formula.) Then say,

"I invoke the Great Archangel of Tiphareth, RAPHAEL, the mighty healer of God! Lay Thy hand invisibly on this talisman and give it life. Anoint it, so that through its use I may traverse the path of the Mystic, to the glory of the ineffable name. I also invoke the choir of angels known as the MELEKIM, (intone and trace the sigil) the mighty Kings to aid me in this work of art. Descend I command Thee, Mighty archangel RAPHAEL to charge this talisman, that it may become a powerful tool consecrated to the work of the Magick of Light."

Lift the talisman in the left hand, smite it thrice with the sword, and raise both it and the sword aloft, stamping the foot three times. Then take the wrapped talisman to the North and say:

"The voice of the Exorcism said unto me, 'Let me shroud myself in darkness, peradventure thus shall I manifest myself in Light. I am the only being in an abyss of Darkness. From the Darkness come I forth ere my birth, from the silence of a primal sleep. And the Voice of Ages answered unto my soul, Creature of Talismans, the Light shineth in the darkness, but the darkness comprehendeth it not. Let the Mystic Circumambulation take place in the path of Darkness with symbolic light of Occult Science to lead the way."

Visualize the light of a lantern held by an angelic hand before you. Circumambulate the Temple once with the talisman and the sword, following the light. After going around once, stop in the south and lay the talisman on the ground. Bar it with the sword saying, "Unpurified and unconsecrated, Thou canst not enter the Gate of the West."

Purify the talisman with Water and consecrate with Fire as before. Lift it with the left hand, face the West and say, "Creature of Talismans, twice purified and twice consecrated, thou mayest approach the Gateway of the West."

Pass to the West with the talisman in the left hand. Partly unveil it, smite it once with the sword and say,

"Thou canst not pass from concealment unto manifestation, save by the virtue of the name ELOHIM. Before all things are the Chaos and the Darkness, and the gates of the Land of Night. I am He whose Name is Darkness. I am the Great One of the Paths of the Shades. I am the Exorcist in the midst of the Exorcism. Take on therefore manifestation without fear before me, for I am he/she in whom fear is Not."

Replace the veil over the talisman and carry it once more around the Circle. Then stop in the North, place the talisman on the floor and say: "Unpurified and unconsecrated, thou canst not enter the gate of the East." Purify and consecrate the talisman with Water and Fire as before. Lift it in the left hand and say, "Creature of Talismans, thrice purified and thrice consecrated, thou mayest approach the gateway of the East."

Go to the East and partly unveil the talisman. Strike it once with the sword and say, "Thou canst not pass from concealment unto manifestation save by the virtue of the name YHVH. After the formless and the Void and the Darkness, then cometh the knowledge of the Light. I am that Light which riseth in darkness. I am the Exorcist in the midst of the Exorcism. Take on therefore manifestation before me, for I am the wielder of the forces of the Balance. Creature of Talismans, long hast thou dwelt in darkness. Quit the night and seek the Day."

Take the talisman to the west of the Altar. Place it again on the white triangle. Hold the pommel of the sword immediately over it and say, "By all the Names, Powers, and rites already rehearsed, I conjure upon thee power and might irresistible. KHABS AM PEKHT. KONX OM PAX. LIGHT IN EXTENSION. As the Light hidden in darkness can manifest therefrom, so shalt thou become irresistible."

Put the sword aside and take up the Hierophant's Wand, grasping just below the crown. Go to the east of the Altar and face west. Repeat the following invocation:

"YHVH ELOAH VE-DAATH! Oh thou Tetragrammaton, God of knowledge, God made manifest in the realm of the Mind. Thee do I invoke! Thou art the fulcrum of the Universe. Thee do I invoke! Thou most beautiful child, king, son and god. Thee do

I invoke! Thou who art known as the Mediating Intelligence, because in Thee are multiplied the influences of the Emanations, causing that influence to flow into all the reservoirs of the blessings with which they themselves are united. Thee do I invoke! Thou whose virtue is Devotion to the Great Work. Thee do I invoke! Thou, whose experience is the Vision of the Harmony of things. Thee do I invoke! Thou spoke the Word and Osiris was torn to pieces. Thou spoke the Word and Osiris was resurrected unto a Greater Life. Thee do I invoke!"

Pause and contemplate.

Circumvent the Altar and take up the talisman. Put it on the floor to the east of the Altar in the place between the Pillars of the Neophyte Hall. Stand just east of the talisman and face west. Holding the wand by the middle ring, trace all six traditional Invoking Solar Hexagrams over the talisman (see illustration on page 65). Vibrate "ARARITA" while drawing the hexagram. Intone "YHVH ELOAH VE-DAATH" when tracing the sigil of Sol. Vibrate the name of "RESH" when drawing the letter in the center. Follow this procedure for all six hexagrams.

Then focus the entire force of the will, and project it at the talisman using the Sign of the Enterer at least three times or until you feel your energy begin to drain. When this happens, give the Sign of Silence at the end for protection. A light should be visualized flickering about the talisman. Return it to the white triangle upon the Altar. Purify and consecrate it again. Remove the black cord. Strike the talisman three times with the sword and proclaim, "By and in the name of YHVH ELOAH VE-DAATH, I invoke upon Thee the Power of Tiphareth!" Put aside the sword and take up the Hierophant's Wand by the middle ring. Trace over the talisman the sigils of YHVH ELOAH VE-DAATH, RAPHAEL and MELEKIM. (Vibrate the Divine Hebrew name of Tiphareth twelve times as before.)

Circumambulate the Temple thrice with the wand and the talisman. Then go to the position of the Hierophant in the east. Unveil the talisman, placing it back upon the ground in front of you. Still grasping the wand by the middle ring, contemplate the various attributes of the Sephirah of Tiphareth. Make the Sign of the Rending of the Veil and say, "Let the white brilliance of the Divine Spirit, reflected into the amber brilliance of the glorious Sun descend upon this talisman, to fill it with the splendor of Thy majesty, that for ever it may be unto me an aid to aspire to the Great Work."

Draw the Flaming Sword over the talisman. Take up the talisman and step between the Pillars. Formulate an astral Banner of the East enveloping itself around the talisman. Hold it on high and say, "Behold, all ye powers and forces I have invoked. Take witness that I have duly consecrated this talisman with the aid of RAPHAEL, Archangel of Tipha-reth, that it may aid me in the form of mystical experiences and visions, and also grant me the ability to heal others as well as myself. May it bring me balance and harmony.

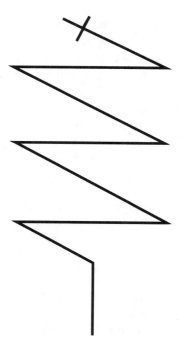

The Flaming Sword

And by the exaltation of my higher nature, may it assist me in my Path to the Light Divine."

Wrap the talisman in white silk or linen and place it upon the Altar. (Note: Never banish over a talisman, or when a talisman is uncovered.)

Go to the East and trace the six Banishing Solar Hexagrams there.

Perform the Reverse Circumambulation (counterclockwise three times). Feel the energy that you have carefully built up throughout the ceremony begin to dissipate.

Perform the LBRP.

Perform the BRH.

Say, "I now release any spirits that may have been imprisoned by this ceremony. Depart in peace to your abodes and habitations. Go with the sanction of YHVH ELOAH VE-DAATH and the blessings of YEHESHUAH YEHOVASHAH."

Knock five times as in the beginning.

Say, "I now declare this Temple duly closed. So mote it be!"

THE RITUAL IS ENDED

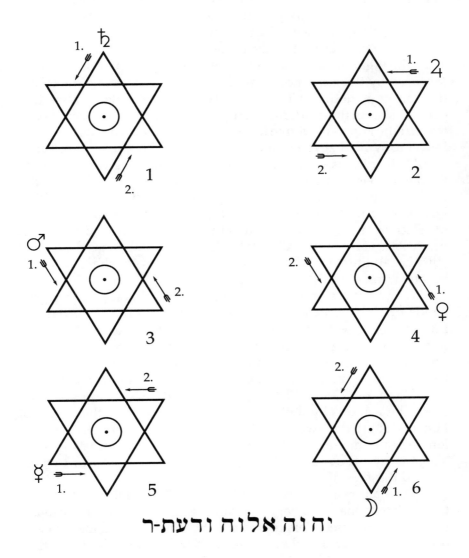

יהוה אלוה ודעת-ר

Six Banishing Hexagrams for Sol

The Hegemon's Wand

Use and Symbolism

The Mitre-headed Scepter is the distinctive ensign of the Office of Hegemon. In the hands of a skilled Initiate who holds the office of Hegemon, this wand is a powerful tool which attracts the Forces of the Pillar of Mercy (the White Pillar) on the Tree of Life. This imple- ment is the counterpart to the Sword of the Hiereus which repre- sents the Pillar of Severity. Known also as the "Scepter of Wisdom" it is used by the Hegemon at all times when conducting the candi- date throughout the Hall. This is because it represents the attraction of the Forces of the candidate's Higher Self which seek ever to aspire toward the Forces of Divine Mercy and Light. Outwardly, the wand is said to symbolize religion which guides and regulates life, but its occult meaning is far more complex than this. The wielder of the Scepter of Wisdom acts as the candidate's Higher Self which guides and protects him/her through the journey of initiation. The Mitre- head is split in two and not closed, to indicate the dual manifestation of Wisdom and Truth; and well as the two great contending Forces of Darkness and Light. Above all, this wand symbolizes the goal of spiritual attainment—the marriage of opposites which results in ul- timate union with the Eternal.

As in the case of the Hierophant's Wand, this scepter has gold bands or rings which represent certain Sephiroth on the Tree of Life—in this case, the spheres of the Right Hand Pillar of Mercy. The mitre-head, along with its supporting ring represents Chokmah. The bands then symbolize in descending order the spheres of Chesed and Netzach. The sections of the shaft allude to the Paths of Vav, Kaph and Qoph. The grip by which the Hegemon normally holds the wand is by the Path of Qoph (The Moon—the Forces of Flux and Reflux) between the last band and the pommel, which re- fers to Malkuth. The Shaft is red to represent the Primordial Fire of Yod energy—the first igniting spark of the Flaming Sword which formed the Tree of Life.

The split head of the mitre is gold and in some cases the two tips each terminate in a ball. The mitre is charged with a red calvary cross of six squares. This represents the Wisdom of Chokmah as a duplicated aspect of Kether, attracted by the symbol of self sacrifice.

The Scepter of Wisdom can be employed to invoke the Forces (Sephiroth and Paths) of the Pillar of Mercy. Once again, such an implement must be handled with respect for its power and that which it symbolizes. It can be used for the consecration of talismans with the specific energies of the White Pillar in the same manner that the Hierophant's Scepter can be utilized for charging talismans with the Forces of the Middle Pillar. One can also take advantage of the particular energies of the Hegemon's Wand which attract the Forces of Divine Mercy and Light. A ritual of this sort can greatly enhance spiritual development and eventually result in conversation with the Higher Self.

Materials Needed
   One 3/4" thick dowel approx. 36" long
   One 6" x 12" piece of 3/4" soft wood (pine, balsa or bass)
   One 1/4" wide strip of balsa or basswood (can be found in most
      hobby shops)
   Two 1/4" wooden dowels or pegs 1" in length
   One 1-1/2" wooden ball
   Carpenter's wood glue
   Gesso
   Acrylic paints: red and iridescent gold
   Clear lacquer finish (spray or brush on)

Tools Needed
   Jigsaw
   Electric drill with 1/4" and 3/4" bits
   Sandpaper
   Artist's paint brushes
   Rotary power tool with gouging bit

Construction: The Mitre-head
1)   With the jigsaw, cut out sections A and B from the 6" by 12" piece of wood as shown in the diagram. (Both pieces are exactly the same.)

2)   Lay section A flat on your table or work area. With a rotary power tool grind and sand down the curved edge of section A so that the curved part is thinnest at the very top of the mitre, while the ends of the curve at the widest part of the mitre are nearly their original width. (The result should be a piece of wood which at its widest point begins to taper down to a thin curved edge at its top.) Repeat this procedure on section B.

3)   Glue the ground-out sides of A and B together so that they lie one o top of the other. Viewed from the side, the top of the mitre-head should show a hollowed-out V-shape.

4)   Once the glue has dried, sand down the mitre so that it tapers gracefully, getting thicker toward the bottom.

5) Drill a hole 1/2"" deep and 1/4" wide in the center of the bottom side of the mitre-head.

Construction: The Shaft, Rings and Pommel

6) Into the left-over piece of 3/4" thick pine wood, drill a 3/4" diameter hole. Around this hole, draw a 1-1/2" diameter circle. Cut this circle out of the wood using the scroll saw. Repeat this same process three more times, so that you end up with four donut-shaped rings of wood.

7) Take the 36" long dowel (shaft) and drill a hole 1/2" deep and 1/4" in diameter into one end of it. Do the same to the other end. Glue one of the 1" wooden pegs into one of the holes you have just drilled so that half of the peg is embedded into the end of the dowel and half of it sticks out. Do the same at the other end of the shaft.

8) Apply glue to the inside of all three rings. Slide one of the rings over the top end of the shaft. Slide the remaining rings over the other end of the shaft and space all the rings evenly, approximately 11" apart, starting from the topmost ring. If the rings are too tight, sand inside the center hole. (Note: As with the preceding wand, the ring closest to the mitre-head acts as a support and partakes of its symbolism. The remaining two rings are the proper gold bands.)

9) Take the 1-1/2" wooden ball (pommel) and with sandpaper form a flattened area about 3/4" wide. Into the center of this, drill a hole which is 1/2" deep and 1/4" in diameter. Pour some glue into the hole you have just drilled and attach the ball to the bottom end of the shaft, over the wooden peg.

10) Finish assembling the wand by pouring some glue into the hole at the bottom of the mitre-head and attaching it to the top of the shaft, over the wooden peg. (The mitre-head should fit snugly against the support ring.) Let the glue dry.

Finishing Steps

11) Take the 1/4" strip of balsa wood and cut it into six pieces: two 1-3/4" in length, and four 1/2" in length.

12) On the front of the mitre-head, glue one larger and two smaller pieces of the wood so that they form the figure of a calvary cross. Let dry. Sand down to smooth the edges of the four arms of the cross. With the remaining strips of wood, repeat this figure on the back of the mitre-head.

13) Sand the entire surface of the scepter. With a paint brush, cover the wand with a coat of gesso. Allow to dry.

14) Sand the painted surface (especially the shaft) lightly until smooth. Paint the shaft and two crosses with acrylic red. Allow to dry.

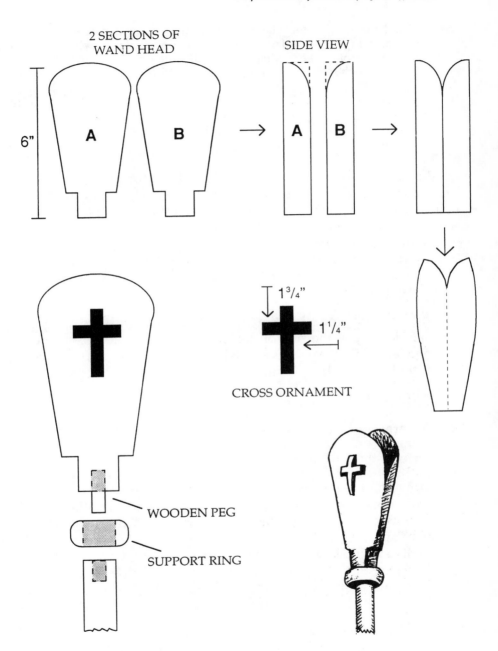

2 SECTIONS OF
WAND HEAD

SIDE VIEW

6"

A

B

A

B

1³/₄"

1¹/₄"

CROSS ORNAMENT

WOODEN PEG

SUPPORT RING

The Hegemon's Wand

15) Paint the rings, pommel and mitre-head (except for crosses) with iridescent gold. Allow to dry. Paint or spray on a sealant such as clear lacquer to protect the painted wand. Allow to dry.

Ritual for Use

Spiritual Development

Let the Z.A.M. be dressed in the regalia of the Second Order. Altar, Cross and Triangle are to be arranged as in the previous rituals. If you have completed the Pillars at the time of this ritual, place them east of the Altar as in the Neophyte ceremony. A black handled dagger should be used for Banishings. A cup of water and censer should be ready at the north and south of the Temple. Have a sword ready in the west. The main implement for this ritual will be the finished Hegemon's Wand.

> After a period of relaxation, give five knocks with the dagger handle against the side of the Altar. Go to the Northeast and proclaim, "HEKAS, HEKAS ESTE BEBELOI! Far, far from this sacred place be the profane!"
>
> Perform the LBRP.
>
> Perform the BRH.
>
> Perform the SIRP.
>
> Circumambulate the Temple three times sunwise and give the Projection Sign and the Sign of Silence when passing the East. Go west of the Altar and face east. Extend the arms in the form of a Tau Cross and say,
> "Holy art Thou, Lord of the Universe,"
> "Holy art Thou, whom Nature hath not formed,"
> "Holy art Thou, the Vast and the Mighty One,"
> "Lord of the Light and of the Darkness."
>
> Grasp the Scepter of Wisdom by the supporting ring just under the Mitre-head (Chokmah). Go to the East and perform the Qabalistic Cross. Then draw an Invoking Hexagram of the Supernals, visualizing it in a golden light while intoning

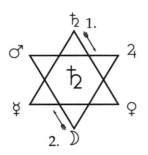

**Invoking Hexagram
of the Supernals**

"ARARITA." In the center of the figure, trace the sigil of Saturn in brilliant white. Vibrate "YHVH ELOHIM." Then draw the Hebrew letter Aleph also in brilliant white and intone the name of the letter.

Go to the South and draw the same hexagram while vibrating the same names. Repeat this procedure in the west and north. Upon returning to the East, repeat the Analysis of the Keyword as given in the BRH.

Go to the west of the Altar and face east. Begin with the Qabalistic Cross. Still grasping the supporting ring of the wand, trace an *Invoking Pentagram of Spirit Active* over the Altar while vibrating "EX-ARP." In the center, draw the Spirit sigil in brilliant white and vibrate "EHEIEH." Trace an Invoking Pentagram of Spirit Passive while intoning the name "HCOMA." While drawing the Spirit sigil in the center, vibrate "AGLA."

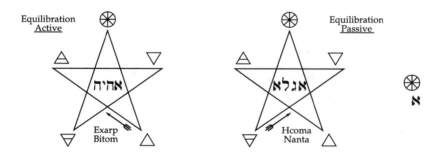

Draw an Invoking Pentagram of Spirit Passive while vibrating the name "NANTA." For the Spirit sigil in the center, vibrate "AGLA."

Draw an Invoking Pentagram of Spirit Active while vibrating "BITOM." For the Spirit sigil in the center, vibrate "EHEIEH." Give the LVX signs. Repeat the Qabalistic Cross.

Say, "Supernal Splendor which dwellest in the Light to which no mortal can approach, wherein is Mystery, and Depth un-

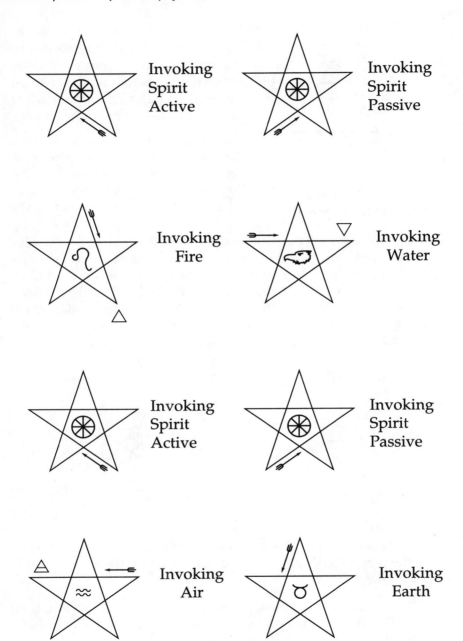

Spiritual Development Pentagrams

thinkable, I implore Thee who art known as YAH, the Illuminating Intelligence. Thou who art the Crown of Creation and the Splendor of Unity! Divine Duplication of the One! Thou who art called the Second Glory which is exalted above every head! AB! ABBA! Yod of Creation! Look upon me in this ceremony which I perform to Thine Honor and for my own Spiritual development. Grant thine aid unto the highest aspirations of my Soul, in thy Divine Name YAH, by which Thou dost reveal thyself as the initiator of Wisdom and the Divine Force which stimulates Creation.

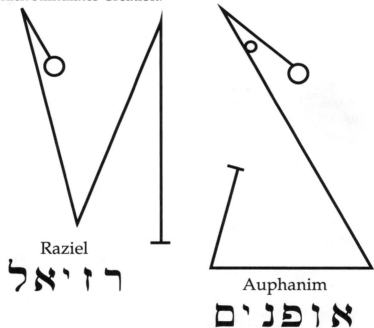

Raziel

רזיאל

Auphanim

אופנים

"I implore Thee to grant unto me the presence of Thy Archangel RAZIEL. (Trace the sigil of the Archangel while vibrating the name.) O RAZIEL, Thou Herald sent Forth from the Godhead! Thou whose Book of Sapphire holds the secrets of the Stars! I ask Thee to plant within me the seeds of Wisdom which will enable me to conquer the unbalanced aspects of myself, thus furthering my spiritual growth.

"O ye strong and mighty ones of the Sphere of Chokmah who are called AUPHANIM (trace sigil and vibrate the name) the Wheels who encircle the Universe ever cycling the destinies of men and women in accordance with their actions. Aid me with your power! Surround me with a veil of Wisdom, that in this chamber of the Divine Mystery, I may hear nothing that comes not from on high, and see naught that may distract my vision from the Glory of the eternal Crown. That I may behold only the holy vision that descends from that Divine Brilliance, the scintillation and coruscation of the Divine Glory. That Divine Brilliance, that Light which illuminates the universe, that Light which surpasseth the Glory of the Sun, beside which the Light of mortals is but Darkness. That in the closing of my physical senses to the vibrations of the outer and the lower, I may learn to awaken those spiritual facilities by which I may attain at length to the perfect union with the Divine."

Go to the North and take up the cup. Return with it to the west of the Altar and face east. Dip the two fingers of your right hand in the water and mark yourself on the forehead with a cross, followed by a triangle. Pause for a moment as you contemplate the water purifying your soul from all that is unbalanced and mundane.

Replace the cup. Go clockwise to the South and take up the incense. Return with it to the west of the Altar. Trace a cross in the air in front of your forehead, followed by a triangle. Pause and contemplate the fire of the incense consecrating your soul with a passion which burns for Union with the Divine. Replace the incense and have the sword in readiness near the Altar. Return to the west of the Altar.

Kneel and grasp the scepter by the first golden band (Chesed) so that the mitre-head is just in front of your forehead. Say, "Holy art Thou, Lord of the Universe! From Thine hands flow down all grace and blessing. Thou who rule equally over Light and Darkness! Oh God and Nature! Thou Self from nothing. In Thee I am Self, and exist in Thy Selfhood from Nothing. Live Thou in me and through Thy Divine Mercy which descends from the fourth Sephirah of Chesed, bring me unto that Self which is in Thee. I desire the attainment of Wisdom and conversation of my higher and Divine Genius, the True Magick and perfect happiness."

Rise and project an astral image of yourself to the east of the Altar. Physically hold the wand by the Chesed band while your astral form holds it by the path of Qoph. Turn and face your body. Place your left hand in the left hand of the Astral form. Vibrate both physically and astrally, "EHEIEH. EHEIEH. EHEIEH. EHEIEH" using the Vibratory Formula. Say, "Thou who dwellest in the boundless Light, in whom only is Being, who alone can say I AM, beginner of movement, bestower of Life! I aspire to reach that divine and only selfhood which is in Thee! Grant that I may be so enabled as to live by the absolute control and purification of my natural body and soul, so that having no other desire, I may become a worthy Temple for my Higher Genius. For the desire of Thy house, Oh Adonai, hath eaten me up, and I desire to be dissolved and be with Thee. May my human nature, becoming as the perfect Malkuth, the resplendent intelligence, be thus exalted and illuminated. Cause the Divine influx to descend and rend away the veils of darkness from my mortal vision, that I may know Thee, Adonai, as the only True Self."

Return to the physical body. Place the flat of the sword upon your neck and say, "So help me, the Lord of the Universe and my own higher Soul."

Holding the sword in the right hand, raise both arms on high. Aspire silently to the Light.

Put the sword aside and take up the scepter by the Chesed band. Pass to the North. Project your astral form to the throne of the Hierophant in the east, face your physical body and say, "The voice of my Undying and Secret Soul said unto me—'Let me enter the Path of Darkness and, peradventure, there shall I find the Light. I am the only Being in an Abyss of Darkness; from an Abyss of Darkness came I forth ere my birth, from the Silence of a Primal Sleep.' And the Voice of Ages answered to my Soul—'I am He who formulates in Darkness, the Light that shineth in Darkness, yet the Darkness comprehendeth it not.'"

Return to the physical body. Visualize a divine brilliance, forming a beautiful angelic figure, whose burning torch illuminates the surrounding darkness. Circumambulate the Temple once following the angel. As you do so, endeavor to draw the Divine Light within the vortex created by the circumambulation. Vibrate "YHVH ELOHIM." After the second passing of the East, vibrate "YAH."

Stop in the South and visualize yourself between two mighty pillars of
Fire and Cloud. Their bases are buried in black rolling clouds of chaos,
but their summits are lost in the brilliant Light which penetrates unto the
Divine Glory. Contemplate first the
Pillar of Mercy, followed by the Pillar
of Severity.

Pass to the West and say, "Before all
things were the Chaos and the Darkness and the Gates of the Land of
Night. Darkness is the name of the
Great One of the Paths of the Shades. I
banish the forces of darkness and
fear, for fear is failure and I am without fear and shall continue onward."

יה

Yah

Circumambulate the Temple again following the angel, then
stop in the north. Visualize the pillars of Fire and Cloud once
more. Vibrate "EHEIEH."

Pass to the East and say, "After the Formless and the Void and
the Darkness, then cometh the Knowledge of the Light. Thou
art the Light dawning in darkness, Oh vision of the Rising Sun.
Unbalanced Power is the ebbing away of Life. Unbalanced
Mercy is but weakness and the fading out of the Will. Unbalanced Severity is cruelty and the barrenness of Mind. Thou
dwellest in the place of the balance of Forces, where alone is
perfect justice."

Follow the Angel to the West of the Altar and face east. Grasp
the wand by the second golden band (Netzach) and kneel,
while at the same time projecting your astral form between the
pillars. Say, "Lord of the Universe, the Vast and the Mighty
One! Ruler of the Light and of the Darkness! Look with favor
upon my higher aspirations, and grant unto me that my Genius
may manifest unto me and in me and through me, with physical manifestation. KHABS AM PEKHT. KONX OM PAX.
LIGHT IN EXTENSION."

Return to your body. Rise and go to the east of the Altar, facing east. Still holding the wand by the Netzach band, say, "And now with passion and desire for spiritual ecstacy do I crush down the evil and the unbalanced beneath the universe in me. The Fire of Spirit hath given me Victory! My desire is for the everlasting and Divine Love which is eternal. May my Divine Genius manifest unto me physically, in me and by me! Thus may I forward the Great Work!"

Pass forward to stand between the pillars. Give the Projection Sign three times toward the east. (At each projection, visualize the veils of darkness being cast aside.) Follow with the Sign of Silence. Throw your arms back in the form of a Tau Cross, attracting the Higher Self from above. Imagine your Divine Genius as a beautiful white figure attracted to you by aspiration. Strive with all your will to exalt yourself unto the Genius.

Imagine a light before you in the east which takes on the shape of a colossal divine figure. Then visualize once again the Pillars of Fire and Cloud before you.

Circumambulate the Temple three times while saying, "I am the Sun in his rising, passed through the hour of cloud and of Night. I am Amoun the concealed One, the Opener of the Day. I am Osiris Onnophris, the Justified One, Lord of Life, triumphant over death. There is no part of me that is not of the Gods. I am the Preparer of the Pathway, the Rescuer unto the Light. Out of the Darkness, let the Light arise."

Stand between the Pillars again and face East. Grasp the wand by the pommel which represents Malkuth. Feel the total manifestation of the Divine Genius as it envelopes you. Exalt yourself in the likeness of a colossal Being, and endeavor to realize that this is the only True Self. Vibrate again "EHEIEH" four times, using the Vibratory Formula.

Say, "In the name and power of the Divine Spirit, I invoke Thee, Oh, my divine Genius that thou manifest Thyself to me and in me, to help me to purify my lower self, to teach me and assist me to unite myself unto thee in divine perfection, so that I also may be built into the living rock, a pillar of the Temple of Adonai."

After contemplating this say, "Thus at length have I been enabled to begin to comprehend the form of my higher self." At this time the aspirant may ask the Genius to make comprehensible what things may be necessary for his/her instruction or guidance. Take as much time as is needed.

Return to the west of the Altar and face East. Say, "And now in the Name and Power of the Divine Spirit, I invoke ye, ye Angels of the Watchtowers of the Universe and charge ye to guard this my mystic sphere. Keep far removed the evil and the unbalanced, that they penetrate not into my abode of the Mysteries. Keep my mind pure and free from the tendencies of fanaticism or spiritual pride. Inspire and sanctify me that I may enter into the center of my being, and there receive the illimitable Wisdom of the Light Divine."

When finished, perform the Reverse Circumambulation. Repeat the Adoration to the Lord of the Universe.

Hold the wand by the supporting ring under the mitre-head. Trace over the Altar the Banishing Pentagrams of Spirit Active and Spirit Passive. Give the Sign of the Closing of the Veil.

Perform the LBRP.

Perform the BRH.

Stand in the East and say, "I now release any spirits that may have been imprisoned by this ceremony. Depart in peace to your abodes and habitations. Go with the sanctions of YA, and of EL, and the blessings of YEHESHUAH YEHOVASHAH. I now declare this Temple duly closed. So mote it be!"

THE RITUAL IS ENDED

The Sword of the Hiereus

Use and Symbolism

The sword is primarily comprised of a blade and a guard; thus an emblem of conjunction. In fact during the Middle Ages, the Sword often took on the form of a cross. Traditionally, the sword is the proper instrument of a knight, who is the defender of the forces of light against the forces of darkness. Its essential symbolic meaning is of the ability to wound and defend—attributes of strength and sovereignty. There is also a curious relationship between the words "sword" and "word."

The Hiereus is the officer known as "The Avenger of the Gods." He guards the Temple from the Qlippoth or Evil Ones who dwell beneath Malkuth in the Kingdom of Shells. He represents a terrible avenging god at the confines of Matter, who is enthroned upon Matter and robed in Darkness. His Sword symbolizes the Forces of the Pillar of Severity: Binah is at its tip, Geburah is at the midsection of the blade, and Hod is represented by the brass guard. The two paths of Cheth and Mem are referred to the equal sections of the blade between Geburah and Binah, and between Geburah and Hod. The grip is red to represent the Path of Shin—alluding to Universe governed by the flaming force of Divine Severity. Malkuth, although not a part of the Pillar of Severity is represented by the black pommel, for as is the case with the other scepters of the Outer Order, all the Forces of the Tree of Life are grounded in Malkuth. The "Sword of Vengeance" is the name of this implement.

Because the Sword of the Hiereus is used to guard the Temple, its natural use other than in Golden Dawn ceremonies is for banishing and protection. At any time in the Hall of the Neophytes, the Hierophant may call upon the Hiereus to perform the Lesser Banishing Ritual of the Pentagram.

Construction

Any convenient sword can be employed for the sword of the Hiereus. The best sword to obtain for this purpose would be a military sword with a brass guard. The grip should be painted red and the pommel should be black. It is also quite feasible for one to make a sword from an iron bar and a wooden handle (to be painted in the aforementioned colors.) For this task we suggest the reader refer to the section on construction of the Magick Sword in chapter 5.

The following ritual can be performed in a room that is to become a permanent Temple space. It can also be performed often to clear a room that must be used out of necessity for both Temple and secular purposes. Whenever the need for clearing an area of unwanted energies arises, the Sword of Vengeance can be employed with much success.

Ritual for Use

The Supreme Banishing Ritual of the Pentagram (SBRP)

All that the Adept needs for this ritual is the sword and the ceremonial clothing of the Magician. (If you are banishing a room which is to be re-dedicated as a Temple space, clear the area of ALL objects and furniture.)

Face the East. With sword in hand, perform the Qabalistic Cross. (Be sure to hold the sword with point up throughout this part of the ritual.)

Trace with the tip of the sword in the air before you, the Banishing Pentagram of Spirit Active. Vibrate the name "EXARP." Draw the spirit sigil in the center and vibrate "EHEIEH." Give the LVX Signs. Then draw the Banishing Pentagram of Air and intone the name, "ORO IBAH AOZPI." Trace the sigil of Aquarius in the center and vibrate, "YHVH." Give the Sign of Theoricus. Then raise the hands above the head as if to touch Kether. Step forward with the left foot while simultaneously bringing the hands to eye-level and thrusting them forward in the Projection Sign. (This Sign is also known as the "Attacking Sign" and when used with the Sword of Vengeance, it is a potent gesture of Force and Will.) Then stamp the ground with the left foot and give the Sign of Silence (also called the "Sign of Protection") as a shield against all attack and protection from any reflux current of energy.

Go clockwise to the South and trace the Banishing Pentagram of Spirit Active while vibrating the name, "BITOM." Draw the Spirit sigil in the center and intone, "EHEIEH." Give the LVX Signs. Then trace the Banishing Pentagram of Fire. Vibrate "OIP TEAA PEDOCE." Draw the sigil of Leo in the center and vibrate "ELOHIM." Give the Sign of Fire. Then give the Projection Sign and the Sign of Silence.

EAST

Banishing
Spirit
Active

SOUTH

Banishing
Spirit
Active

Banishing
Air

Banishing
Fire

WEST

Banishing
Spirit
Passive

NORTH

Banishing
Spirit
Passive

Banishing
Water

Banishing
Earth

Banishing Spirit and Elemental Pentagrams for SBRP

Go to the West and trace the Banishing Pentagram of Spirit Passive while vibrating the name "HCOMA." Draw the sigil of Spirit in the center and intone, "AGLA." Give the LVX Signs. Trace the Banishing Pentagram of Water and intone the name, "EMPEH ARSEL GAIOL." Draw the sigil of the eagle in the center and vibrate, "Aleph Lamed, AL." Give the Sign of Practicus. Then give the Attacking Sign and the Sign of Protection.

Go to the North and trace the Banishing Pentagram of Spirit Passive while vibrating the name "NANTA." Draw the sigil of Spirit in the center and intone, "AGLA." Give the LVX Signs. Trace the Banishing Pentagram of Earth and vibrate the name, "EMOR DIAL HECTEGA." Trace the sigil of Taurus in the center and intone, "ADONAI." Give the Sign of Zelator. Then give the Projection Sign and the Sign of Silence.

Return to the East. Stand in the form of the Tau Cross and say, "Before me, RAPHAEL. Behind me, GABRIEL. On my right hand, MICHAEL. On my left hand, URIEL. For about me flames the Pentagram and in the column shines the Six-rayed Star!" (Visualize each Archangel when intoning the names.)

Repeat the Qabalistic Cross as in the beginning.

The ritual is ended and the room should be completely void of all previous energies. The process of building the Temple can now proceed.

SO MOTE IT BE

The Wand of the Kerux

Use and Symbolism
The Caduceus Wand of the Kerux is a most impressive and complex implement. It is the Wand of Hermes (also known as Thoth and Mercury), the god of Wisdom, Magick and communication. Legend has it that Hermes intervened in a fight between two serpents who then curled themselves around his wand. An even older version of this dates back to ancient Mesopotamia, where the intertwining serpents were a symbol of the god who cures all illnesses, a meaning which was absorbed into Greek culture and is still preserved in the medical emblems of today. (Raphael, the healer of God

and the Archangel of elemental Air also carries a caduceus.)

Like the other wands thus far described, the symbolism of the Caduceus is based upon the Tree of Life. The upper point of the Wand rests on Kether, and the wings stretch out to Chokmah and Binah, thus comprehending the three Supernal Sephiroth. The lower seven are embraced by the serpents whose heads fall on Chesed and Geburah. These are the twin serpents of Egypt and the currents of the Astral Light. In addition to this, the wings and the top of the wand form the Hebrew letter Shin, the symbol of Fire. The heads and upper halves of the serpents form the letter Aleph, while their tails enclose Mem, the symbol of Water—the Fire of Life above, the Waters of Creation below, and the Air as the Reconciler vibrating between Fire and Water.

The Rod of Hermes represents the balanced forces of Eternal Light working invisibly in the darkness. This wand is borne by the Kerux along with the Lamp of the Hidden Knowledge to lead the candidate who sees nothing. The Godform taken on by the Kerux is that of one of the Anubian Guards. (Anubis, God of the Underworld is considered a lower manifestation of Thoth.) The light he carries is the invisible Divine Force which guides the candidate, while the wand is that Power which directs the flow of the Divine current. The hidden energies of the wand may be revealed to the student through meditation.

The Caduceus Wand can be used in an invocation ritual of Hermes-Thoth to gain the magickal knowledge necessary to become the archetypal Magician. It could also be used to invoke the three ancient elements of Fire, Air and Water through the three Mother letters. Lastly, the wand could be employed in a healing ritual where the archangel Raphael would be invoked.

Materials Needed
   One 3/4" thick dowel approx. 31" long
   A one pound box of oven-hardening clay
   One 1/4" thick dowel 2-3/4" in length
   One 1-5/8" wooden ball
   One 3/4" thick dowel approx. 16-18" in length
   A 3/4" thick piece of soft wood approx. 14" in length and 4" wide
   Yellow carpenter's glue
   Wood putty
   Gesso
   A strong bonding glue such as epoxy
   A sheet of drawing paper at least 18" in length

Aluminum foil
Acrylic Paints: red, yellow, blue, white and black
Sealant; clear lacquer finish (spray or brush on)

Tools Needed
Jigsaw
Electric drill with 3/4" and 1/4" bits
Rotary power tool with gouging bit
Sandpaper
Artist's brushes
A cookie sheet used for baking

Construction: The Wings
1) With the jigsaw cut out two wing sections 7" long and approximately 4" wide as shown in the diagram.

2) With a pencil draw stylized feathers on both sides of both wings. Use the rotary power tool to gouge and grind the outline of the feathers, giving them a sculpted look. Sand the wings until they have a smooth 3-dimensional appearance.

3) At the part of each piece where the wing will be attached to the shaft of the wand, drill a hole that is 1/4" wide and 1" deep. (Be sure both wings are drilled identically.)

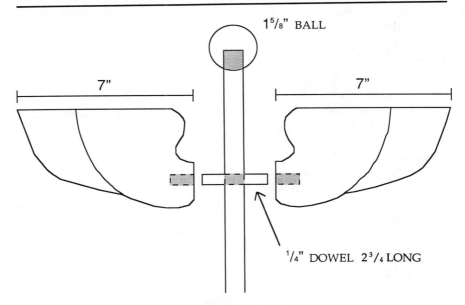

$1^5/_8$" BALL

7"   7"

$^1/_4$" DOWEL $2^3/_4$ LONG

Detail of Construction

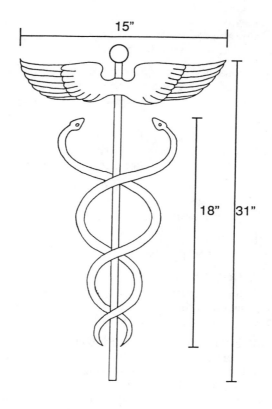

15"

18" 31"

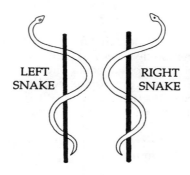

LEFT
SNAKE

RIGHT
SNAKE

The Wand of the Kerux

Construction: The Shaft

4) Take the wooden ball and drill a hole into it that is 3/4" wide and 3/4" deep. Pour glue into the hole. Put one end of the 31" long dowel in the hole drilled into the wooden ball. Press in firmly and let the glue dry.

5) Approximatelyy 3-3/4" down from the top of the ball, drill a 1/4" hole completely through the shaft. Pour some glue into this hole. Take the thin 2-3/4" long dowel and run it through the hole so that 1" of the 1/4" thick dowel sticks out on both sides of the shaft.

6) Pour glue in the holes previously drilled into both wing sections. Attach wings to the shaft by sliding them into place over the 1/4" dowel on either side of the shaft. Let the glue dry firmly.

7) Where wings connect to the shaft, apply wood putty to fill in gaps and give a smooth, continuous appearance. Do the same where the shaft joins to the ball. Let putty dry.

8) Sand the wand smooth and paint with gesso. Let dry. Sand the painted wand and put it aside.

Construction: The Serpents

9) On the sheet of drawing paper, draw the two serpents as you see them depicted in the diagram, 18" in length. The widest part of the figure (just below the heads) should be approximately 9".

10) Take some of the clay and knead it by hand until it is soft and pliable. Then roll out a long coil or rope of clay. The coil should be about 5/8" thick and taper down to the serpent's tail. Check to see if the coil is nearing the proper dimensions of the serpent by and placing it in position over your drawing. Add some clay to the thick end of the coil, to give the serpent a diamond-shaped head. The mouth and eyes of the snake can be drawn into the clay with a tooth pick or pin.

11) When you have one serpent that fits perfectly on your drawing, put it aside and get the cookie sheet and aluminum foil. Lay a piece of aluminum foil over the cookie sheet and wrap it firmly around the edges. Lay your drawing on top of the aluminum and with a pencil, trace the pattern of the two serpents. (When you remove your drawing, the serpent pattern should be imprinted into the aluminum foil.) At this point you will refer to the diagram showing the Right Snake and the Left Snake. We will begin with the Right Snake. Place the clay snake onto the aluminum foil in the position of the Right Snake.

12) Take the 16" long dowel and position it onto the aluminum foil where the shaft of the wand would be according to the pattern. The Right snake will touch this dowel in three places. The middle point where the serpent touches the dowel is the only one where the dowel is on top of the serpent. At the upper and lower points, drape the serpent on top of the dowel.

13) At the three points where serpent joins dowel, press the clay gently, so it will leave a slight indentation where the dowel touched it. (This will make it easier to attach the finished serpent to the real wand shaft later.)

14) Place the cookie sheet in the oven and follow the package directions for baking the clay. At this time, begin rolling out the second snake.

15) When baking time is over, take the cookie sheet out of the oven and let the serpent cool before you touch it. After the finished serpent has cooled, remove it from the dowel and aluminum foil and put it aside. Get the second snake and place it onto the foil in the position of the Left Snake. As before, the snake will touch the dowel in three places. But this time at the middle point, the serpent will be on top of the dowel, while at the top and bottom points, the dowel will be on top of the serpent. Once again press the clay gently so that the dowel will leave indentations. Bake the serpent as before.

Finishing Steps

16) Position the Right Snake into place on the winged shaft. Apply a strong glue such as epoxy to the three points where the serpent touches the shaft. Let dry. Position and glue the Left Snake into place on the wand. Let dry.

17) Paint the serpents with gesso. Allow to dry. Paint the top portion of the wand (which includes the ball and wings) with acrylic red. Paint the shaft yellow from the bottom of the wings to the second point where the serpents touch. Paint the remaining section of the shaft with brilliant blue. The Right Snake should be painted white, while the Left Snake is to be painted black. (Note: it is also acceptable to paint the serpents exactly as the shaft—yellow to the middle point and blue from the middle to the end of their tails.)

(The method given above is complicated. We have seen adequate Caduceus Wands cut completely out of foam-core board, a piece of styrofoam that is approximately 1/4" thick, covered on both sides with poster board. If the wand is not abused, it will hold up nicely.)

Ritual for Use

An Invocation of Hermes-Thoth

The Z.A.M. should be dressed in the regalia of the Second Order. Arrange the Temple in accordance with the Neophyte Hall; pillars east of the Altar, cup of water in the North, incense in the south. The Caduceus Wand of the Kerux should be placed in the Southwest.

Consult an ephemeris to determine the position of the planet Mercury. Find out what the Rising Sign is for the time of the working to discover what sign the planet is in. Another method of working is to consider Aries as the Rising Sign in the East of the Temple. The other signs fall in their natural order counterclockwise around the Temple as in a Zodiacal chart. Whatever sign the planet is in at the time of the ritual will determine its position in the Temple. (Note: for the best possible results perform this ritual on a Wednesday at the hour ascribed to Mercury. See the Chart of Planetary Hours in the introduction, pp xxvii-xxviii.)

Give five knocks against the side of the Altar with the hilt of a dagger. Go to the Northeast and say, "HEKAS, HEKAS, ESTE BEBELOI! PROCUL O PROCUL ESTE PROFANI!"

Perform the LBRP.

Perform the BRH.

Perform the SIRP.

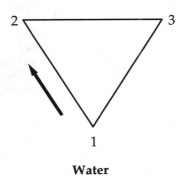

Water

Go to the North and pick up the chalice of Water. Go to the East and trace a cross in the air with the chalice. Sprinkle water thrice in the form of the Invoking Water Triangle. Do this in all four quarters. Upon returning to the east, hold the cup on high and circumambulate the Temple once slowly while saying, "The Rivers have raised, O Tetragrammaton! The Rivers have raised their sound. The Rivers keep raising their pounding. Above the sounds of the vast waters, the majestic breaking waves of the sea, AL is majestic in the Height!" Replace the chalice in the North.

Go to the South and pick up the incense. Go to the East and trace a cross in the air. Wave the incense thrice in the form of the Invoking Fire Triangle. Do this in all four quarters. Upon returning to the East, circumambulate the Temple once more while saying, "The Voice of Tetragrammaton draws out flames of

Fire. From the heavens, Tetragrammaton spoke, that we might hear and receive illumination. And upon the Earth, Tetragrammaton displayed unto us, his great Fire. The Words of the Elohim were heard in the Fire!"

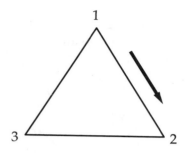

Fire

Circumambulate the Temple three times, saluting with the Neophyte Signs as you pass the East.

Go to the West of the Altar and face East. Perform the Adoration to the Lord of the Universe.

Take up the Caduceus Wand. Face the direction where the planet Mercury would appear in the sky at the time of the working. Trace the Invoking Hexagram of Mercury with the wand while vibrating "ARARITA." Draw the planetary sigil while intoning the name "ELOHIM TZABAOTH." Trace the Hebrew letter Tau while intoning the name of the letter.

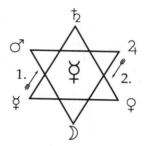

Invoking Hexagram of Mercury

Say, "I invoke ye, Oh Powers of Splendor! Thou who art known as the God of Hosts and the Absolute or Perfect Intelligence! Thou art the mean of the Primordial, which has no root by which it can cleave or rest, save in the hidden places of Gedulah, from which emanates thy proper essence. Thou who art the Glory and the Vision of Splendor. Look with favor upon my invocation of the God of Wisdom that I may receive an influx of occult knowledge and magickal proficiency, which will better enable me to understand the hidden mechanism of the Universe! Thus will I be enabled to rightly vibrate the Names of

Power! Thus may I more perfectly manifest the Rise of the Light Divine! Grant me an increase of Intellectual skills and Magickal abilities! Keep far removed from me the unbalancing effects of fanaticism, arrogance, and inflation of the ego! Hold me to that path of Hermes-Thoth, so that I too may walk as a messenger of the Gods, in the footsteps of the Magician!"

Go Sunwise to the East and perform the Qabalistic Cross. Then say, "Not unto my name but to Thine be ascribed the Kingdom, the Power and Glory everlasting, now and forever more, Amen." Vibrate "EHEIEH" four times using the Vibratory Formula in order to activate the Neshamah and attract the Divine Light. Give the LVX Signs.

Go to a point between the pillars and imagine a great figure of a god standing before you. He appears as a nude youth with a winged helmet and winged sandals. In his right hand he holds the Caduceus Wand. The wind blows through his hair as he hovers above the clouds.

Raise the Wand before you and say, "Lord of the Radiant Staff about which the two serpents are entwined! Exalted Herald of the Gods! Thee I invoke! Divine Messenger and Bringer of Dreams! Protector and Guide of Humanity! Thee I invoke! Swift Lord of Oracles! Giver of light to the mind! Patron of arts and sciences! Thee I invoke! Divine scribe and Lord of the sacred texts! Thou who art known as HERMES, the Lord of Magick! I invoke thee to enter this sacred place and grant unto me your Wisdom and Intellectual Powers. Thus may I at length comprehend the Hidden Forces which move through the Universe, so that I may be better enabled to complete the Great Work."

Throw your arms out in the form of a Tau Cross. Endeavor to visualize the form strongly and take note of any action or words given by the figure.

Say, "Thou Great One of Learning and Communication! Reveal unto me now, your more ancient form which was known in the land of Egypt. Come Thou before me as DJEHOTI! Come Thou before me as THOTH! Come Thou forth as the Ibis-headed One! I invoke Thee, Oh Master of Knowledge and Mighty One of the art of Magick! Come Thou forth I say!" Trace the letters of the name Thoth in the air. Also trace the sigil of Thoth.

Thoth

Give the Projection Sign to the East three times. Then give the Sign of Silence. The form of Hermes disappears into the mist. In his place you see before you a figure seated on a throne. Endeavor to visualize the form strongly: the white head of an Ibis with a black beak, a yellow and violet-striped nemyss, and reddish-brown limbs. His kilt is white and his overkilt is striped yellow and violet as are his wristbands. His collar is banded violet, yellow, violet. In one hand, he bears a yellow Djed wand, and in the other a yellow scribal pallet with brush-pens of the seven rainbow colors. His throne, which stands upon a white pavement is also yellow, bordered with violet.

Again throw the arms back in the position of the Tau Cross. Say, "Oh Thou Master of Speech Divine! The God enthroned upon the seat of Wisdom! Thou who measureth and numbereth the stars! Thrice Great One! Thee I invoke! Thou who art the Glowing Heart of RA! Thee I invoke! Thou who art the God of Equilibrium! Thee I invoke!

Thou who holdeth the Knowledge of the Universe yet protecteth it with the cunning of the dog-headed ape! Thee I invoke! Arbiter of Day and Night! Thee I invoke! Thou whose words are brought to life! Thee I invoke! I invoke THOTH in the presence of the Divine! Come Thou forth and aid me in this my search for Wisdom and Magickal Skill! Grant me the knowledge of the words that move the elements in obedience to the Will of the Eternal!" (Vibrate the name of THO-OOTH three times.) "BEHOLD! My Word is spoken!"

Make the sign of the Rending of the Veil. Vibrate "ELOHIM TZABAOTH" ten times using the Vibratory Formula. Visualize the god rising from the throne and standing in the same place and position as your own physical body, as if the larger Godform were superimposed over you. Feel a link between the form created and your Tiphareth center (the seat of the Ruach or reasoning mind.) A white ray of light from your Tiphareth center activates the figure of the god, bringing it to life. YOU are the creative spark that animates the form.

Say, "I am the giver of numbers and of medicine. I am the creator of astronomy and astrology. I am the father of all the sciences. I established the worship of the gods. I composed the hymns and prayers which men addressed to them. I am the author of every book. I am the creator of alphabets and hieroglyphs. I invented the laws and taught the priests and priestesses. If Thou wilt, call me be the names of THOTH, DJEHOTI, HERMES, MERCURY, NABU, ENKI, or ODIN, for I myself created these names.

"I am the heart and tongue and mind of Ra. I am the Will of God translated into Speech. I am the Speech of God translated into Action. I am MAA HKERU (Mah Ker-oo), He whose word is Just. My Word is called BREATH and my soul shall breathe for ever and ever. My Word is unseen, yet it liveth throughout the Universe. Learn my Word and it shall come to be.

"I am the Self-begotten One. I am he who recordeth the Weighing of the Soul and who assisteth the deceased in the Underworld. I pilot the Ship of Ra when he riseth in the East and when he seteth in the West. I spoke the Word and the Heavens were established. I spoke the Word and the Forces of Light and of Darkness were held in balance. I spoke the Word and the Will of Ra was carried out. I spoke the Word and enemies of Osiris were vanquished. I gave the Word to Isis and the dead Osiris was brought back amongst the living. I casteth the net of Ra and the Four Winds were captured.

"My Word is Knowledge. My Word is Vibration. My Word is Movement. My Word is Transformation! My Word opens the Gate of Ecstasy! Mighty is my Word! Hear now the Word of Djehoti! Hear now the Speech of Tho-ooth!"

Cross your arms over your chest. Pause and meditate upon the Godform of Thoth. Take note of any information the form has to offer you. Feel the strength of the connection between the God-form and yourself. Continue only after you feel that you have absorbed the information given to you.

Say, "The Speech in the Silence. The Words against the Son of Night. The voice of Thoth before the Universe in the presence of the eternal Gods. The Formulas of Knowledge. The Wisdom of Breath. The Radix of Vibration. The shaking of the Invisible. The Rolling Asunder of the Darkness. The Becoming Visible of Matter. The Piercing of the Coils of the Stooping Dragon. The Breaking Forth of the Light. All these are in the Knowledge of Tho-oth."

Thrust both arms forward in the Projection Sign. Still holding the wand, remain in this position and say, "At the Ending of the Night; At the Limits of the Light: Tho-oth stood before the Un-born Ones of Time!"

"Then was formulated the Universe. Then came forth the Gods thereof. The Aeons of the Bornless Beyond. Then was the Voice vibrated. Then was the Name declared."

"At the Threshold of the Entrance, between the Universe and the Infinite, in the Sign of the Enterer, stood Tho-oth, As before him were the Aeons proclaimed. In Breath did he vibrate them. In Symbols did he record them. For betwixt the Light and the Darkness did he stand!"

Take as much time as is needed for contemplation. Give the Sign of Silence. Withdraw the ray of light from the Godform back into your Tiphareth center. Imagine the Godform of Thoth leave you and return to his throne in the east.

Give the Signs of Osiris, Slain and Risen. Say, "I am endowed with Glory. I am endowed with Strength. I am filled with Might, and I am supplied with the books of Thoth. Behold me in the character of a scribe. Thou didst give me the command, and I have recorded what is right and true, and I do bring it unto thee each day."

Completely withdraw any remaining energy that you have cast out back into your Tiphareth center. Visualize the form of Thoth disappearing into the mists of the east. Give the Sign of the Closing of the Veil.

Perform the Reverse Circumambulation three times.

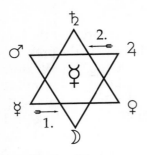

**Banishing Hexagram
of Mercury**

Go to the position in the Temple where you previously traced the Invoking Hexagram. In that same place, draw now the *Banishing Hexagram of Mercury*. Say, "In the Divine Name, ELOHIM TZABAOTH, I release the powers of Mercury and of Hod. I thank Thee for permitting me to enter thus far into the Sanctuary of Thy Mysteries." Give the LVX Signs.

Purify and consecrate the Temple with Water and Fire as in the beginning.

Perform the LBRP.

Perform the BRH.

Say, "I now release any spirits that may have been imprisoned by this ceremony. Depart in peace unto your abodes and habitations. Go with the sanction of ELOHIM TZABAOTH and the blessings of YEHESUAH YEHOVASHAH."

Give five knocks as in the beginning.

Say, "I now declare this Temple duly closed."

SO MOTE IT BE

The Cup of Stolistes

Use and Symbolism

Stolistes is stationed in the northern part of the Hall to the northwest of the Black Pillar whose base is in Hod. She is therefore the Affirmer of the Powers of Moisture and Water, reflected from Chesed into the Water Temple of Hod. Her cup is the receptacle of this, filled from Hod so as to transmit its forces into Malkuth, restoring and purifying the vital forces therein by Cold and Moisture. She is known as "The Light shining through the Waters upon Earth." With the cup of water, the Stolistes purifies the entire Temple including the members, with the Water of Spirit.

The Cup of Stolistes can be used to purify and purge any Temple or sacred space from the influences of the mundane. The water

The Banners

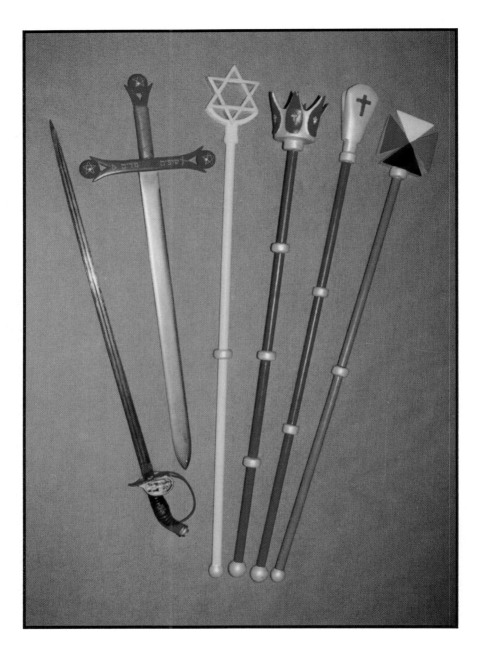

The Outer Order Wands

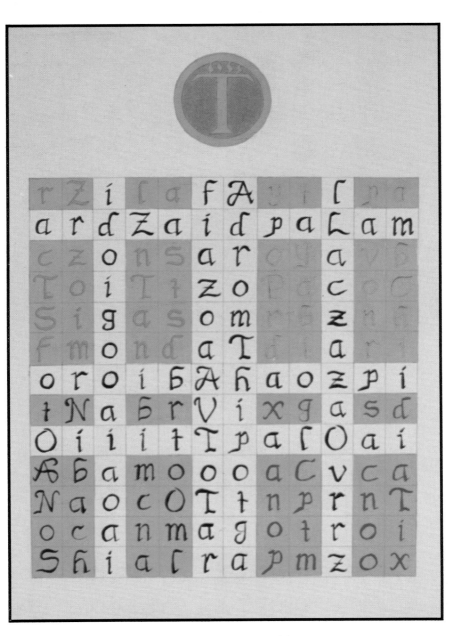

The Enochian Air Tablet

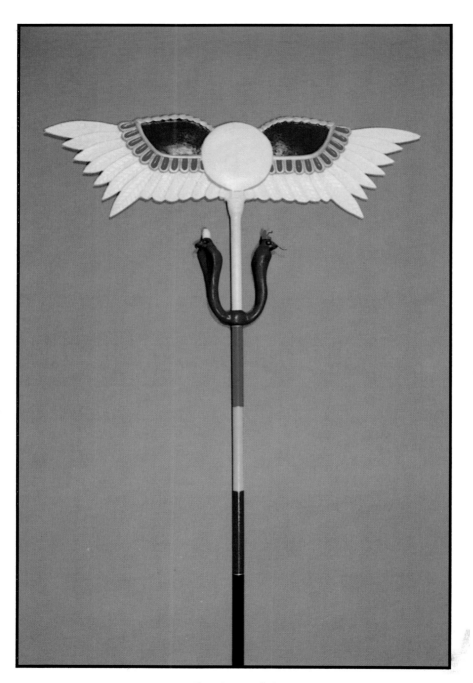

The Ur-uatchti
(Chief Adept's Wand)

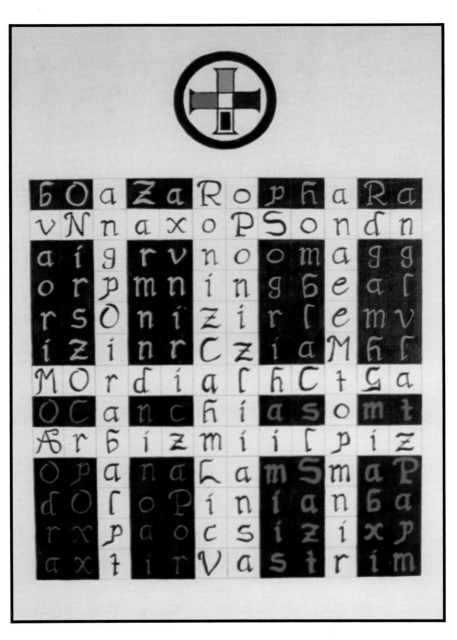

The Enochian Earth Tablet

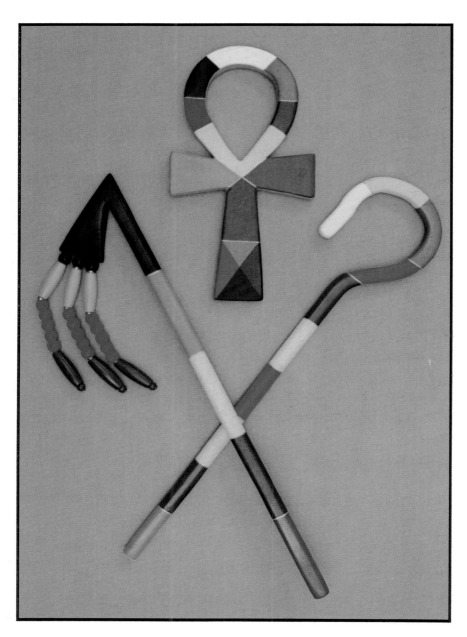

Crook, Scourge and Crux Ansata

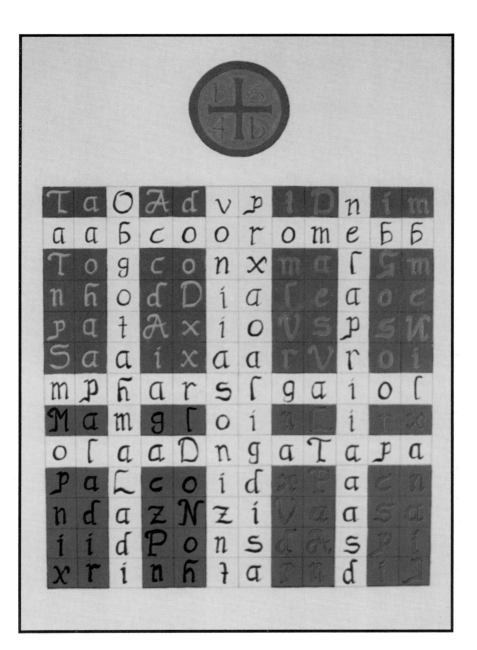

The Enochian Water Tablet

The Four Elemental Implements

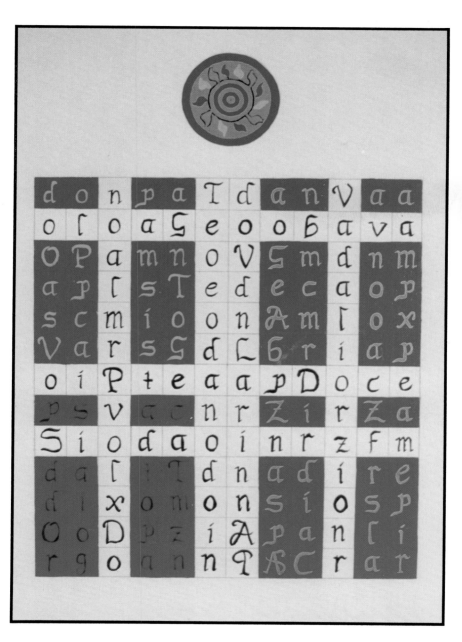

The Enochian Fire Tablet

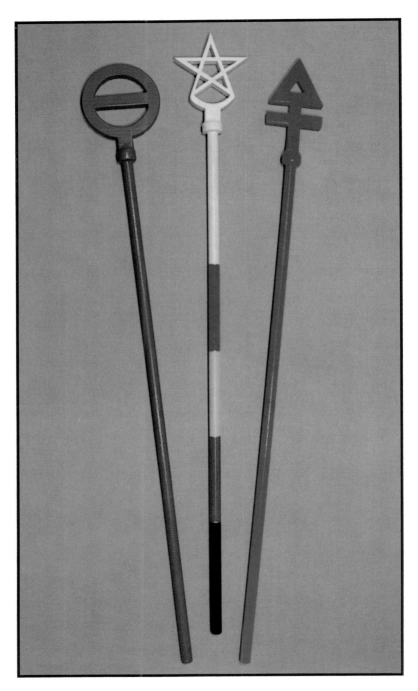

The Portal Wands

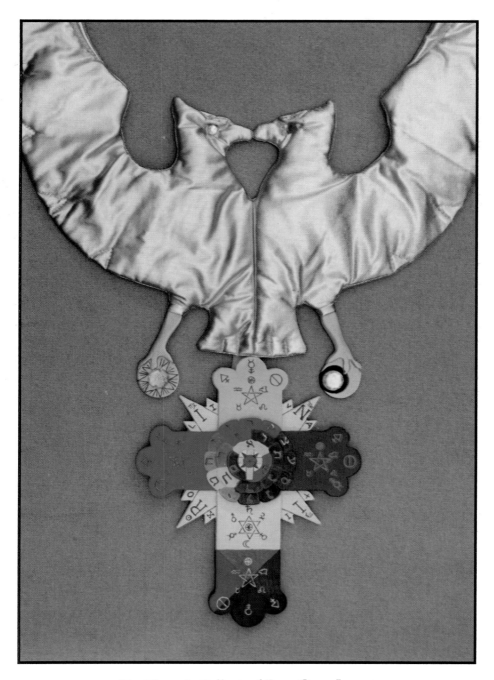

**The Phoenix Collar and Rose Cross Lamen
of the Chief Adept**

The Lamens

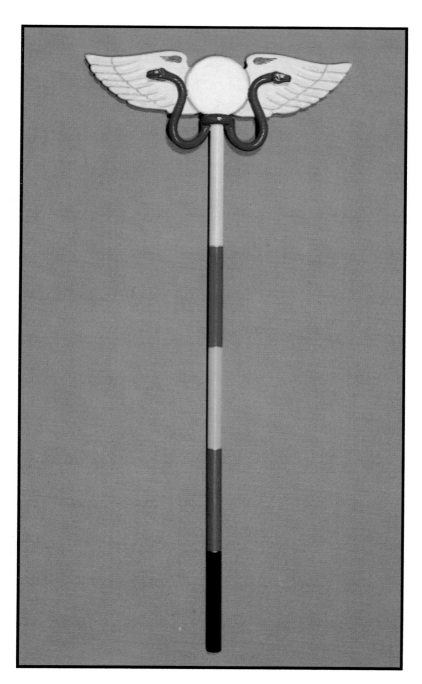

The Chief Adept's Wand

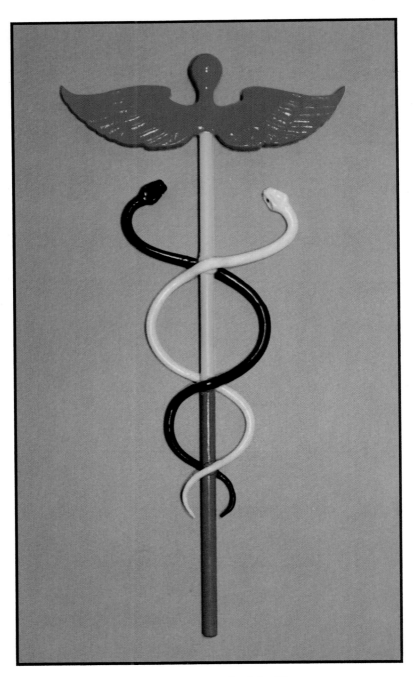

The Caduceus Wand of the Kerux

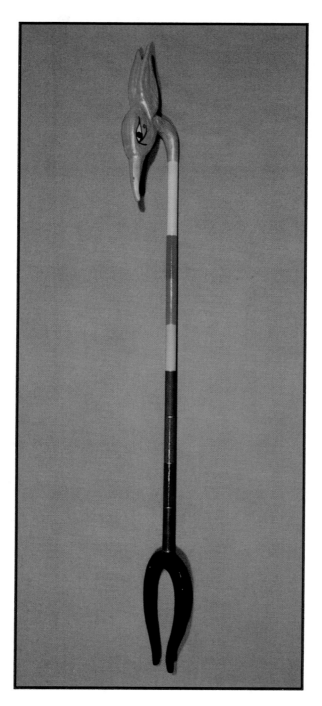

The Phoenix Wand

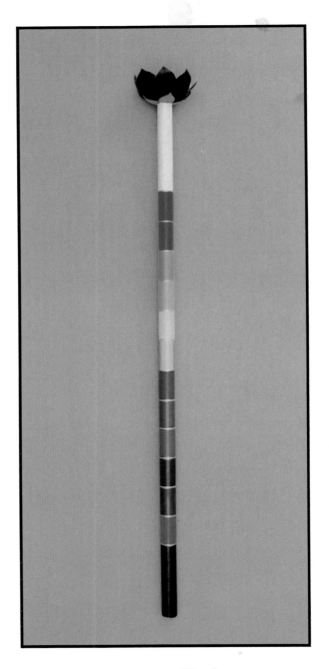

The Lotus Wand

contained therein can be charged and employed in a ritual of self-purification as well. Any water thus charged can be saved for use in later rites.

Construction

For the Cup of Stolistes, any brass chalice or metal goblet will suffice. However if the reader truly wishes to have an authentic Stolistes implement he/she should consult the section describing the Water Cup given in chapter 5. This cup can be painted in the colors of Blue and Orange, but without the sigils or Hebrew names.

Ritual for Use

The Rite of Self-Purification

The Magician of the Portal grade should be dressed in the regalia of the Outer Order with crossed sashes. The Cup of Stolistes should be 1/2 to 3/4 full of purified water. Place it in the northern part of the Temple at the station of Stolistes. Incense is to be placed at the station of the Dadouchos in the South. Stand east of the Altar and face the East as well.

Perform the LBRP.

Go deosil to the North and take up the cup. Return to the East and trace in the air (with the cup) a cross. Then dip your fingers in the water and sprinkle thrice toward the East, forming the three points of the Water Triangle. Walking deosil, repeat this in all four quarters.

Consecrate the Temple with Fire, starting in the East, using the Censer to trace the Cross and the Fire Triangle in all four quarters.

Stand at the North and face the Altar. Holding the cup in both hands, perform the Qabalistic Cross.

Visualize the Ace of Cups from the Tarot. See the blue chalice suspended above the clouds by a feminine angelic hand. Pure glistening water flows abundantly down from this cup. Within the brilliant spray of mist above the cup is traced the Hebrew letter Heh, the source of cleansing water.

Dip your fingers into the Cup and anoint the crown of your head (Kether) with the water in the form of the Cross and Triangle.

Vibrate the name "YECHIDAH" (Yeh-Khee-dah) as you do so. (Yechidah is the part of the Soul which is attributed to Kether...the true and Divine Self.) Imagine the water from your fingertips as the Sacred Water from the Ace of Cups—cleansing and purifying your sphere of sensation so that the Yechidah expresses itself more clearly to you. Concentrate on this image and vibrate the name "EHEIEH" four times—one for each letter of the name in Hebrew. Feel the power of the name (I am) within every cell of your body as you breathe forth the name of Eheieh.

Again dip your fingers into the cup and anoint yourself on the left temple with the Cross and Triangle. Vibrate the name "CHIAH" (Kh-ee-ah) as you do this. (Chiah is the part of the Soul which is attributed to Chokmah...the True Supernal Will.) Imagine again the symbol of the Ace of Cups purifying your aura in order for the Chiah to manifest itself more clearly. Intone the name of "EHEIEH" (I am) four times as before.

Anoint yourself on the right temple with water using the form of the Cross and Triangle. Vibrate the name "NESHAMAH" (Neh-shah-mah) as you do so. (Neshamah is the part of the Soul which is referred to Binah, but whose name is also extended over the other two Supernals as well. The Neshamah is the Divine Intuition and the Highest Aspiration of the Soul.) Visualize the chalice from the Ace of Cups pouring forth its purifying essence in order for the Neshamah to shine ever brighter within you (see Ace of Cups card in *The New Golden Dawn Ritual Tarot Deck*). Intone the name of "EHEIEH" four times as before.

Anoint yourself with the Cross and Triangle directly over your heart. Vibrate the name "RUACH" (Roo-ach) as you do so. (The Ruach is the Conscious Mind and reasoning powers attributed to the five Sephiroth below the Supernals. It is centered in Tiphareth.)

Imagine the Sacred Water from the Ace of Cups bathing your heart center and opening the conscious mind unto the Divine Self. Intone the name of "EHEIEH" four times using the Vibratory Formula as before. As you do this, the Ruach joins with the Neshamah, and thus heart, mind and Soul are united—opening a purified channel for the descent of the Divine into the Temple (your physical body) and the lowest aspects of the soul, the Nephesch and the G'uph.

Ace of Cups

Contemplate any information you may be given at this point in the ritual. Take as much time as you need.

When finished, withdraw the image of the Sacred Waters from your G'uph, Nephesch, Ruach, Neshamah, Chiah and Yechidah. See the Waters returning to the Ace of Cups, which disappears behind a veil of cloud. Yet imagine that a drop of the pure liquid remains within each soul-center that you have cleansed.

Give the Sign of Silence. Purify the Temple with water as in the beginning, starting in the East.

Return the Cup to the Station of Stolistes. Go to the East and perform the LBRP.

THE RITE IS ENDED

The Censer or Thurible of Dadouchos

Use and Symbolism

Dadouchos is stationed in the southern part of the Hall to the southwest of the White Pillar whose base is in Netzach. She is therefore the Affirmer of the Powers of Fire, reflected down from Geburah into Netzach. Her censer is the receptacle thereof—the transmitter of the Fires of Netzach into Malkuth, restoring and purifying the vital forces therein by Heat and Dryness. She is known as "Perfection through Fire manifesting on Earth." With the Thurible of Incense, the Stolistes consecrates the entire Temple including the members, with the Fire of Spirit.

The censer can be used to consecrate, vitalize and devote any Temple or sacred space to the workings of the Divine Spirit. In addition, the coals and incense contained therein can be charged and employed in a ritual of self-consecration. Any ashes thus charged can be saved and used in later rites.

Construction

For the censer of Dadouchos, any metal brazier used for holding hot coals and incense will suffice. The best possible censer for this purpose will be suspended from a chain like the brazier used in the Catholic Church. This will enable the Dadouchos to swing the implement freely when consecrating the Hall. However the choice of a censer may well depend on what is available. (At certain times we have been forced to use a simple stick of incense as the implement of Dadouchos when certain important officers experienced allergic reactions to too much smoke.) The most significant aspect of this implement is that it contains the spark of the Sacred Flame.

Ritual for Use

The Rite of Self-Consecration

Let the Adept be dressed in the regalia of the Outer Order. A burning coal should be placed within the censer. Add Frankincense. Place it in the Southern part of the Temple at the station of Dadouchos. The cup of water is to be placed in the North. Stand east of the Altar and face the east as well.

Perform the LBRP.

Purify the Temple with water, starting in the East, tracing the Cross and the Water Triangle.

Go deosil to the South and take up the censer. Return to the East and trace a cross in the air with the censer. Then swing the implement thrice toward the East, forming the three points of the Fire Triangle. Walking deosil, repeat this in all four quarters.

Stand at the South and face the Altar. Holding the chains of the censer in both hands, perform the Qabalistic Cross. (Be sure that you do not have too much incense burning at this point in the ritual so that you will not be overwhelmed by smoke.)

Visualize the Ace of Wands from the Tarot (see *New Golden Dawn Ritual Tarot Deck*, available from Llewellyn Publications). See the burning branch held by a masculine angel hand emerging from bright red clouds of Fire. The multi-colored points of flame ignite in all the colors of the Manifest Universe the first enlivening Fire of Spirit. Surrounding the wand on all sides like a halo are twenty-two green flaming Yods.

Hold the chains of the censer high in front of you and trace with it the form of the Cross and the Triangle of Fire. Vibrate the name "YECHIDAH" (Yeh-Khee-dah) as you do so. Imagine the Sacred Flame from the Ace of Wands—vitalizing and consecrating your sphere of sensation . . . dedicating it to the Force of the Light Divine. See one of the Hebrew Yods from the Ace of Wands descend into your Kether point... energizing the Yechidah, the Divine Self.

Concentrate on this image and vibrate the name "EHEIEH" four times (one for each letter of the name in Hebrew). Feel the power of the name (I am) within every cell of your body as you breathe forth the name of Eheieh.

Hold the censer on high and trace the Cross and Triangle slightly left of the first Cross and Triangle. Vibrate the name "CHIAH" (Kh-ee-ah) as you do this. Imagine again the symbol of the Ace of Wands sanctifying your aura in order for the Chiah (the True Supernal Will) to receive consecration. See another Hebrew Yod implant itself in the Chiah (Chokmah) sphere. Intone the name of "EHEIEH" (I am) four times as before.

Hold the censer on high and draw the Cross and Triangle slightly to the right of the first such figures. Vibrate the name "NESHAMAH" (Neh-shah-mah) as you do so. Visualize the torch from the Ace of Wands burning with a sacred passion to free the Divine within you... so that the Highest Aspirations of your Soul break through the barriers that the Lower Self has put into place. Visualize the Hebrew Hod being absorbed into the Neshamah at Binah. Intone the name of "EHEIEH" four times as before.

Hold the censer at heart level and trace the Cross and Triangle directly in front of the Tiphareth center. Vibrate the name "RUACH" (Roo-ach) as you do so. Imagine the Sacred Flame of the Ace of Wands burning away the blockage between all parts of the Self, opening the conscious mind unto the influence of the Divine. See another Hebrew Yod implanting itself in your Ruach. Intone the name of "EHEIEH" four times using the Vibratory Formula as before. As you do this, the Ruach joins with the Neshamah, and thus heart, mind, and Soul are united— opening a consecrated channel for the descent of the Divine into your Nephesch and even the G'uph; thus making your body a Temple devoted to the Divine Spirit of Life.

Contemplate any information you may be given at this point in the ritual. Take as much time as you need.

When finished, withdraw the image of the Sacred Flame from your G'uph, Nephesch, Ruach, and Neshamah. The Ace of Wands disappears behind a veil of cloud. Yet retain the Hebrew Yods, as Sparks of Divinity within each soul-center that you have dedicated to the Great Work.

Ace of Wands

Give the Sign of Silence. Purify and consecrate the Temple with Water and with Fire as in the beginning, starting in the East.

Return the censer to the Station of Dadouchos. Go to the East and perform the LBRP.

THE RITE IS ENDED

The Sword Of The Phylax (Sentinel)

Use and Symbolism

The Phylax is the guardian of the outside of the Temple. With sword in hand, he guards against intruders. The most effective use of the Sentinel's Sword outside of a full Order ceremony, would involve a simple Banishing Ritual.

Construction

Any convenient sword can be employed for the sword of the Phylax. As is the case with the Hiereus, the best sword to obtain would be a military sword with a brass guard. The grip should be painted black and the guard should be gold. One could also make a sword from an iron bar and a wooden handle (to be painted in the aforementioned colors.) Again we suggest that the reader refer to the section on construction of the Magick Sword in chapter 5.

Ritual for Use

See The Lesser Banishing Ritual of the Pentagram (LBRP).

THE IMPLEMENTS OF THE DAIS OFFICERS

The Dais Officers

The Dais officers consist of the Three Chiefs of the Outer Order, and the Past Hierophant. The proper seat of the Chiefs is beside the Hierophant, and if desired the Imperator and Cancellarius may be seated to the right and Praemonstrator and Immediate Past Hierophant to his left—the Cancellarius and Immediate Past Hierophant being nearest to the Hierophant on their respective sides. The Chiefs stand before the Veil in the East of the Temple as the Representatives of the Inner Order and therefore no meeting can be held without one of them. Preferably all Three Chiefs should be present (should a Chief be absent, it is well to have the station filled by an Adept). The other officers of the Temple exist only by their authority and permission.

The Three Chiefs are in the Temple and rule it, yet they are not comprehended in, nor understood by, the Outer Order. They represent, as it were, Veiled Divinities sending a form to sit before the Veil Paroketh, and like the Veils of Isis and Nephthys, they are impenetrable save to the Initiate. The synthesis of the Three Chiefs may be said to be in the form of Tho-oth Who cometh from behind the Veil at the point of its Rending. Yet separately, they may be thus referred:

The **Imperator**, from his relation to Geburah, may be referred to the Goddess Nephthys (Nebethô). Upon him the energy and stability of the Temple depend; and if he has sub-officers to assist him, they partake of his symbolism. His mantle is the flame scarlet Robe of Fire and Severity, and is thus the symbol of unflinching authority, compelling the obedience of the Temple to all commands issued by the Second Order. His lamen is similar to that of the Hierophant, of the same colors, but depending from a scarlet collar. He may bear a Sword similar to that of the Hiereus. His place in the Temple is at the extreme right of the Dais and at the Equinox he takes the Throne of Hierophant when that office is vacated.

The **Praemonstrator**, from his relation to Chesed, may be referred to the Goddess Isis (Ese). His duty is that of Teacher and Instructor of the Temple, always limited by his obligation to keep secret the Knowledge of the Second Order from the Outer Order. He superintends the working of the Outer Order, seeing that in it nothing be relaxed or profaned; and duly issues to the Temple any instruction regarding the Ritual received by him from the Greatly Honored Chiefs of the Second Order. He is therefore to the Temple the Reflector of the Wisdom beyond. His sub-officers partake of his symbolism. The Praemonstrator wears a mantle which is the bright blue Robe of Water, representing the reflection of the Wisdom and Knowledge of Chesed. He may wear a lamen like that of the Hierophant, but blue upon an orange field and depending from a collar of blue. He may bear a scepter surmounted by a Maltese Cross in the Elemental colors.

The **Cancellarius**, from his property of Recorder, may be referred to the God Thoth (Thôouth). Upon him depend the records of the Temple, the order of its working, the arrangement of its meetings and the circulation of its manuscripts. He is the Recorder and, more immediately than either of the preceding Chiefs, the Representative of the executive authority of the Second Order over the Outer. His duty is to see that in no case knowledge of a grade be given to a member who has not properly attained to it. He is the immediate circulator of all communications from the Second Order. His sub-officers partake of his symbolism. The Cancellarius' mantle is the yellow Robe of Air. The Cancellarius may wear a lamen like that of Hierophant, but of yellow on a purple field, and depending from a purple collar; and he may bear a scepter surmounted by a hexagram of amber and gold.

The **Past Hierophant**, who served as Hierophant for the previous six months before the Equinox, also sits upon the Dais and builds up the Godform of Hôôr Ouêr (Horus the Elder). He/she wears the Hierophant's mantle as well as a smaller version of that officer's lamen. As already stated, the Past Hierophant's Scepter is the same as the Hierophant's, depicting the affinity which exists between these two Dais Officers. (When the Hierophant moves off the Dais, he/she takes on the godform of Hôôr Ouêr built up by the Past Hierophant, who similarly assumes the Godform of Ousiri.)

The Scepters of the Chiefs should be of the same color as their mantles, with a gold band to represent Tiphareth, the first grade of the Inner Order. The Sword of Imperator should have a plain scarlet hilt, with gold or brass mountings, while the Scepter of Praemonstrator should be blue with a gold band.

Of all the implements in the Neophyte Hall, the weapons of the Dais Officers should be used only by the Chiefs of the Order or those Adepts who represent them. They are designed to bring the energies of the spheres of Geburah, Chesed, and Tiphareth into the Temple, grounding the current in Malkuth. However, a Magician would be well advised to set the wands in their proper stations in the East for all workings in the Neophyte Hall. A meditation on each of the Dais implements in turn will yield much valuable information concerning the workings of the Triad of the Order.

The Imperator's Sword

Use and Symbolism

The Imperator's Sword is a form of the Sword of Justice, a symbol assigned to the sphere of Geburah. This weapon implies governance and firmness; qualities necessary to the Chief who is symbolically seated in the Sphere of Severity. The sword is associated with fire and symbolizes purification. The steel of the sword alludes to toughness, and the all-conquering spirit. This implement is used to bring the energies of Nephthys into the Temple via the Black Pillar.

Construction

Any convenient sword can be employed for the sword of the Imperator. As is the case with the Hiereus, the best sword to acquire would be a military sword with a brass guard. The grip should be painted red and the guard should be yellow or gold. The Magician could also make a sword after the manner of the Adept's personal sword mentioned in chapter 5, to be painted in the colors given here.

The Praemonstrator's Wand

Use and Symbolism

The Maltese Cross which crowns the Wand of the Praemonstrator is described in the Portal Ritual thus:

"The Cross of Four Triangles called the Maltese Cross, is a symbol of the Four Elements in balanced disposition. It is here given in the colors of the King's Scale, and is also assigned to the Four Sephiroth ruling the Grades of the Outer-Earth to Malkuth, Air to Yesod, Water to Hod and Fire to Netzach.

"It is again, the Cross which heads the Praemonstrator's Wand, who represents the Sephirah Chesed, the Fourth Sephirah. Four is the number of Jupiter, whose Path unites Chesed to Netzach."

The Cross of Four Triangles (the Pyramidal Cross) represents the descent of the Divine and Angelic Forces into the pyramid symbol. This implement is used to bring the energies of Isis into the Temple via the White Pillar.

Materials Needed
    One 3/4" thick dowel approx. 36" long
    One 5" x 9" piece of 3/4" soft wood (pine, balsa or bass)
    Two 1/4" wooden dowels or pegs 1" in length
    One 1-1/2" wooden ball
    Yellow carpenter's glue
    Gesso
    Acrylic paints: red, yellow, blue, black, gold
    Clear lacquer finish (spray or brush on)

Tools Needed
    Scroll saw or jigsaw
    Electric drill with 1/4" and 3/4" bits
    Sandpaper (coarse, medium and fine)
    Artist's paint brushes (medium to large)

Construction: The Maltese Cross Head
1)   Draw a 5" by 5" square on the piece of soft wood. Cut off the excess wood. Draw the shape of the Maltese Cross unto the piece of wood. With the saw, cut out the cross, removing the excess (shaded) area shown in the diagram. Sand smooth.

2)   Drill a hole 1/2" deep and 1/4" wide in the center of the bottom side of the wand head.

Construction; The Shaft
3)   Into the leftover piece of 3/4" thick pine wood, drill a 3/4" diameter hole. Around this hole, draw a 1-1/2" diameter circle. Cut this circle out of the wood using the scroll saw. Repeat this same process once more, so that you end up with two donut-shaped rings of wood.

4)   Take the 36" long dowel (shaft) and drill a hole 1/2" deep and 1/4" in diameter into one end of it. Do the same to the other end. Glue one of the 1" wooden pegs into the hole you have just drilled, so that half of the peg is embedded into the end of the dowel and half of it sticks out.

5)   Apply glue to the inside of one of the wooden rings. Slide it over the top end of the shaft. (Note: If the ring is too tight, sand inside its center hole.) Apply glue to the other wooden ring and slide it over the opposite end of the shaft to a point about at center of the dowel (approximately 17" up).

6)   Pour some glue in the hole you drilled into the bottom end of the wand head and attach the Maltese Cross to the wand shaft. The head of the wand should fit snugly against the supporting ring.

7)   Take the 1-1/2" wooden ball and, using sandpaper, form a flattened area about 3/4" wide. Into the center of this, drill a hole which is 1/2"

deep and 1/4" in diameter.

8) Pour some glue into the hole you have just drilled and attach the ball to the bottom end of the shaft, over the wooden peg.

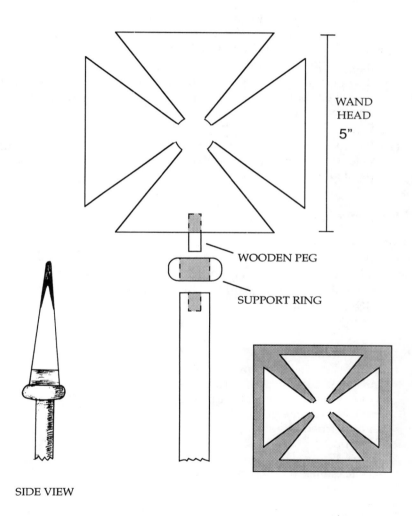

WAND HEAD 5"

WOODEN PEG

SUPPORT RING

SIDE VIEW

The Praemonstrator's Wand

Finishing Steps

9) Sand the entire surface of the scepter so that it is smooth. With a paint brush, cover the wand with a coat of gesso. Allow to dry.

10) Sand the painted surface (especially the shaft) lightly until smooth. Apply a second coat if needed. Paint the head of the wand as follows:

> Top Quarter: Yellow
> Right Quarter: Blue
> Left Quarter: Red
> Bottom Quarter: Black

(Note: Both sides of the Maltese Cross need to be painted; however the right and left quarters of both sides must be painted separately as described above. You can't simply paint all the way around each arm. The front and back of the wand head should therefore be separated by painting the side edges with gold.)

11) Paint the wand shaft completely blue. Paint the rings and pommel gold. Paint or spray on a sealant such as clear lacquer to protect the painted wand. Allow to dry.

The Cancellarius' Wand

Use and Symbolism

The hexagram which heads the wand of the Cancellarius is a symbol of perfection, of Tiphareth, and of the two great opposing forces in balanced equilibrium. This wand attracts the Divine Energie of Kether through the sphere of Tiphareth, bringing the energies of the Middle Pillar into the Temple.

Materials Needed

> One 3/4" thick dowel approx. 36" long
> One 7" x 9" piece of 3/4" thick soft wood (pine, balsa or bass)
> Two 1/4" wooden dowels or pegs 1" in length
> One 1-1/2" diameter wooden ball
> Yellow carpenter's glue
> Wood putty
> Gesso
> Acrylic paints: yellow, orange, gold
> Clear lacquer finish (spray or brush on)

Tools Needed

> Scroll saw or coping saw
> Electric drill with 1/4" and 3/4" bits
> Sandpaper (coarse, medium and fine)
> Artist's paint brushes (medium to large)

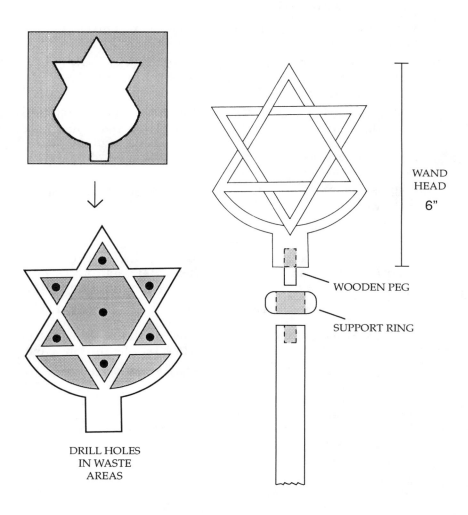

WAND
HEAD
6"

WOODEN PEG

SUPPORT RING

DRILL HOLES
IN WASTE
AREAS

The Cancellarius' Wand

Construction: The Hexagram Head
1) Draw the hexagram shown in the diagram with proper dimensions on the 7" x 9" piece of wood. (See diagram showing the degrees of the angles and size of the hexagram.)

2) With the saw, cut out the outer shape of the hexagram and its supporting crescent shape.

3) Drill nine holes, one inside each of the shaded (negative space) areas of the wand head. (Remember: it is important to use a drill bit that is wider than your saw blade.)

4) With your saw unplugged, detach the blade from the saw. Stick the blade through one of the holes you have drilled and re-attach the blade to the saw. Plug the saw back in and begin cutting out the shaded area of wood. Repeat this process for all nine drilled holes until all the waste area of wood has been cut out.

5) Drill a hole 1/2" deep and 1/4" wide in the center of the bottom side of the wand head.

Construction: The Shaft
6) Into the left-over piece of 3/4" thick pine wood, drill a 3/4" diameter hole. Around this hole, draw a 1-1/2" diameter circle. Cut this circle out of the wood using the scroll saw. Repeat this same process once more, so that you end up with four donut-shaped rings of wood.

7) Take the 36" long dowel (shaft) and drill a hole 1/2" deep and 1/4" in diameter into one end of it. Do the same to the other end. Glue one of the 1" wooden pegs into the hole you have just drilled so that half of the peg is embedded into the end of the dowel and half of it sticks out.

8) Apply glue to the inside of the rings. Slide one ring over the top end of the shaft to a point at the center of the dowel (approximately 17" down). (If the ring is too tight, sand inside its center hole.) The other ring is the support for the wand head. Pour some glue in the hole you drilled into the bottom end of the wand head and attach the hexagram to the wand shaft. Let dry.

9) Take the 1-1/2" wooden ball and using sandpaper, form a flattened area about 3/4" wide. Into the center of this, drill a hole which is 1/2" deep and 1/4" in diameter. Pour some glue into the hole you have just drilled and attach the ball to the bottom end of the shaft, over the wooden peg.

Finishing Steps
10) Sand the entire surface of the scepter so that it is smooth. With a paint brush, cover the wand with a coat of gesso. Allow to dry.

11) Sand the painted surface (especially the shaft) lightly until smooth. Apply a second coat if needed. Paint the wand as follows:

Shaft: Yellow
Ring and Pommel: Gold
Wand Head: Yellow

(Note: the interlaced triangles forming the hexagram should be differentiated somehow—either by painting gold lines to separate them, or by painting one triangle a slightly different shade of yellow (add some orange).)

12)   Paint or spray on a sealant such as clear lacquer to protect the painted wand. Allow to dry.

The Past Hierophant's Wand

The Past Hierophant's Wand is identical to that of the Hierophant.

(Corrected Coptic spellings for all Godforms in this chapter are taken from *The Godforms of the Visible Stations*, 1991, by Adam P. Forrest.)

THE LAMENS OF THE SEVEN OFFICERS
OF THE NEOPHYTE HALL

A lamen is a symbol worn by an officer in a Golden Dawn Temple. Lamens are important tools which help Initiates focus on their assigned offices and the Godforms they represent. Its energy is not unlike that of a talisman—built up by the group *egregore* and consecrated by initiates during numerous Order ceremonies and initiations. The lamens are usually placed at the Officers' stations before the ceremony, to be worn only after entering the Temple and taking on the Godform (previously built up by the Hierophant at the station). In a like manner, they should be removed before exiting the Temple at the closing. (For information concerning the lamens of the Dais Officers, see pp. 112-113 under the descriptions of individual officers.)

The lamens are worn suspended by collars which vary in color, according to the office. The collars of the Middle Pillar Officers are described below. The Lesser Officers wear lamens suspended from black collars. The designs are in white on a black field to show that they are Administrators of the Forces of Light acting through the Darkness, under the Presidency of the Superior Officers. (For instructions on how to make the collars, see pp. 128-130.)

Hierophant's Lamen: The lamen is partially explained in the Portal Ceremony thus: "The Hierophant's Lamen is a synthesis of Tiphareth, to which the Calvary Cross of six squares, forming the cube opened out, is fitly referred. The two colors, red and green, the most active and the most passive, whose conjunction points out the practical application of the knowledge of equilibrium, are symbolic of the reconciliation of the celestial essences of Fire and Water. For the reconciling yellow unites with blue in green, which is the complimentary color to red, and with red in orange which is the complimentary color to blue. The small inner circle placed upon the Cross alludes to the Rose that is conjoined therewith in the symbolism of the Rose and the Cross of our Order."

But in addition to this, it represents the blazing light of the Fire of the Sun bringing into being the green vegetation of the otherwise barren Earth. And also the power of self-sacrifice requisite in one who would essay to initiate into the Sacred Mysteries. So as the Scepter represents the Authority and Power of the Light, the lamen affirms the qualifications necessary to him who wields it, and therefore it is suspended from a white collar, to represent the Purity of the White Brilliance from Kether. Hence it should always be worn by the Hierophant.

The Hiereus' Lamen: This lamen is partially explained in the Portal thus: "The Outer Circle includes the four Sephiroth, Tiphareth, Netzach, Hod and Yesod, of which the first three mark the angles of the triangle inscribed within, while the connecting Paths: Nun, Ayin, and Peh form its sides. In the extreme center is the Path Samekh through which is the passage for the Rending of the Veil. It is therefore a fitting lamen for Hiereus as representing the connecting link between the First and Second Orders, while the white triangle established in the surrounding Darkness is circumscribed in its turn by the circle of Light."

In addition to this explanation, this lamen represents "The Light that shineth in Darkness though the Darkness comprehendeth it not." It affirms the possibility of the Redemption from Evil and even that of Evil itself, through self-sacrifice. It is suspended from a scarlet collar as representing its dependence on the Force of Divine Severity over-awing Evil. It is a symbol of tremendous strength and fortitude, and is a synthesis of the office of Hiereus as regards the Temple, as opposed to his office as regards the outer world. For these reasons it should always be worn by Hiereus.

The Hegemon's Lamen: The lamen is explained in part in the Grade of Philosophus thus: "The peculiar emblem of the Hegemon is the Calvary Cross of Six Squares within a Circle. This Cross embraces Tiphareth, Netzach, Hod and Yesod, and rests upon Malkuth. Also the Calvary Cross of Six Squares forms the cube and is thus referred to the Six Sephiroth of Microprosopus which are Chesed, Geburah, Tiphareth, Netzach, Hod and Yesod." In addition to this, it represents the black Calvary Cross of Suffering as the Initiator by Trial and Self-Abnegation, and the Opener of the Way into the Comprehension of the Forces of the Divine Light. It is therefore suspended from a black collar to show that Suffering is the Purgation of Evil.

The Kerux's Lamen: This lamen is thus explained in the Grade of Theoricus: "The Tree of Life and the Three Mother Letters are the Keys wherewith to unlock the Caduceus of Hermes. The upper point of the Wand rests on Kether and the Wings stretch out to Chokmah and Binah, thus comprehending the Three Supernal Sephiroth. The lower seven are embraced by the Serpents whose

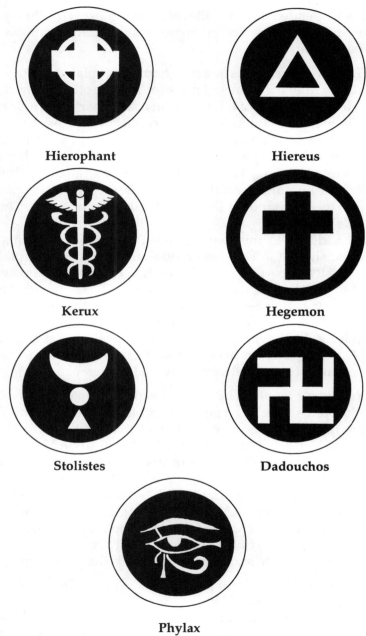

Hierophant

Hiereus

Kerux

Hegemon

Stolistes

Dadouchos

Phylax

The Outer Order Lamens

heads fall on Chesed and Geburah. They are the twin Serpents of Egypt and the currents of Astral Light. Furthermore, the Wings and top of the Wand form the letter Shin, the symbol of Fire; the Heads and the upper halves of the Serpents form Aleph, the symbol of Air as the Reconciler; while their tails enclose Mem, the symbol of Water—the Fire of Life above, the Waters of Creation below, and the Air symbol vibrating between them."

The Stolistes' Lamen: This lamen is thus explained in the Grade of Practicus: "The Cup of Stolistes partakes in part of the symbolism of the Laver of Brass and the Sea of Solomon. On the Tree of Life it embraces nine of the Sephiroth exclusive of Kether. Yesod and Malkuth form the triangle below, the former the apex, the latter the base. Like Caduceus, it further represents the three Elements of Water, Air, and Fire. The Crescent is the Water which is above the Firmament; the circle is the Firmament, and the triangle is the consuming Fire below, which is opposed to the Celestial Fire symbolized by the upper part of Caduceus."

The Dadouchos' Lamen: This lamen is thus explained in the Grade of Zelator: "The Hermetic Cross, which is also know as Fylfot, Hammer of Thor, and Swastika, is formed of 17 squares taken from a square of 25 lesser squares. These 17 fitly represent the Sun, the Four Elements, and the Twelve Signs of the Zodiac." In addition to this, the lamen has a more extended meaning. The Hermetic Cross, the Bolt of Whirling Flame, which is represented by the cross of Four Axes whose heads may be either double or single and turned in either direction, is a symbol of terrific strength, and represents the Fire of Spirit, cleaving its way in all directions throughout the Darkness of Matter. Therefore it is borne on the Lamen of Dadouchos, whose office is that of Purification and Consecration by Fire, and from it also may be drawn by meditation several formulae of strength.

The Phylax's Lamen: A eye drawn in Egyptian style is the symbol on the lamen of the Sentinel. This signifies his role as the Watcher Without. It is the All-Seeing Eye which guards the Temple. The "Divine Eye" of the Egyptians—a hieroglyphic called Wadjet often called the Eye of Horus, was referred to "He who feeds the sacred Fire or the intelligence of man" . . . in other words, Osiris. The Egyptians also defined the eye (the circle of the iris with the pupil as its center) as the "sun in the mouth" meaning the Creative Word. The Phylax can be seen in this light as extending the "word" of Osiris beyond the borders of the Temple, through the Divine Eye.

The lamens can be used by members of the Temple to develop their skills at assuming Godforms assigned to specific Officers. The meditation "Assumption of the Godforms" at the end of this chapter focuses on the various Godforms of the Neophyte Hall. Immediately after is a ritual describing how to use a lamen in the assumption of a godform.

Materials Needed
    One 20" x 10" piece of plywood that is 1/4" thick
    Wood putty
    Gesso
    Acrylic paints: black, white, red, green
    Sealant: such as clear lacquer finish

Tools Needed
    Electric jigsaw, scroll saw or coping saw
    Compass, pencil and straight edge
    File or rasp
    Artist's brushes—fine and medium sizes
    Sandpaper—medium and fine

Construction
    (Note: It is often possible to purchase pre-cut wooden disks at a craft store or hobby shop. These disks will save you time and labor but they must be of comparable size and thickness to the ones described below.)

1) Using the compass, draw seven 4" circles on the piece of wood. Cut out circles with saw. (You may want to cut out seven square pieces of wood with a circle drawn on each piece, using a jigsaw. A scroll saw can then be used to cut out each circle from the separate squares.)

2) If the circle of wood has jagged edges, file them smooth. Any gaps in the wood can be filled in with wood putty. Sand the wood until it is smooth. Paint entirely with gesso. Let dry. Sand. Apply another coat if needed.

3) Draw the specific design shown for all seven officers' lamens—one on each of the seven disks.

4) Each lamen has a "ground" color and a "charge" color. The ground, also called the "field" refers to that area which serves as a foundation, base or background. It is usually the largest area of color. The charge color is given to the sigil, "charging" the lamen with a specific symbol. In the officers' lamens, the charge color is also given to the outer

circle which surrounds the field. The individual lamens should be painted as follows:

> Hierophant: Ground—green, Charge—red
> Hegemon: Ground—white, Charge—black
> All Others: Ground—black, Charge—white

6) After all paint has dried, apply a coat of sealant for protection. (Note: An extra length of plywood may be purchased and cut out for the lamens of the Officers on the Dais. The four lamens are drawn exactly like the Hierophant's lamen but painted thus: Imperator—red on green, Praemonstrator—blue on orange, Cancellarius—yellow on violet, Past Hierophant—red on green [may be slightly smaller than the Hierophant's lamen]).

The Collars

Use and Symbolism

The primary symbolism of the collars has already been explained. The lamens worn by the Officers are suspended from collars which vary in color. Originally, the collar may have been merely a cord or a ribbon running through a hole in a "lip" created at the top of the lamen. Such a hole drilled or cut into the lamen diminishes the integrity of its symbolism. It is aesthetically unacceptable as well. An eye-hook screwed into the top of a lamen is a better solution, but the lamen may be easily flipped over when worn. Both of these problems are solved by the construction of a proper fabric collar as given here.

Materials Needed
> One yard of sturdy, non-stretch fabric in the desired color
> One yard of fusible interfacing
> Thread in the desired color
> A 1" wide piece of self-adhesive velcro that is 2" long
> A package of 1" wide velcro (not self-adhesive)

Tools Needed
> Sewing machine
> Scissors and pins
> Iron and ironing board

Construction
1) Cut out four identical collar shapes similar to the diagram; two front pieces and two back pieces. (The collar pattern is 15" long.) Cut out two pieces of the fusible interfacing identical to the collar shape.

2) Iron and fuse the interfacing to the wrong side of both front pieces. (Follow manufacturer's directions for fusing the interfacing.)

3) Stitch the two front pieces together at the "V" (at the bottom—see the diagram). Stitch the two back pieces together in the same fashion. Stitch the front to the back, leaving one end open so you can turn it. (Be sure to clip around the curves.)

4) Turn the collar right side out. Iron flat and hand stitch the remaining open ends of the collar closed. Sew the two corresponding pieces of velcro to the two ends just stitched. Stitch another velcro tab to the back of the collar at the "V."

5) Glue the corresponding velcro tab to the back of lamen. The lamen can now be attached to (or removed from) the collar at any time.

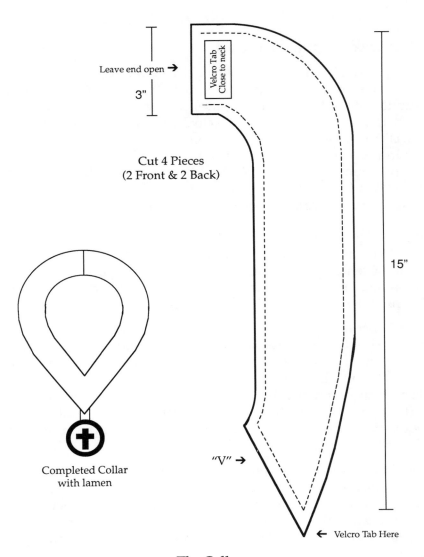

Leave end open →

3"

Velcro Tab
Close to neck

Cut 4 Pieces
(2 Front & 2 Back)

15"

Completed Collar
with lamen

"V" →

← Velcro Tab Here

The Collar

APPAREL OF THE NEOPHYTE OFFICERS

The Cloak (Mantle) or Tabard

The cloak or mantle is a sleeveless, loose-fitting garment worn over the robe. In the Outer Order, the Dais officers as well as the Middle Pillar officers wear mantles emblazoned with certain symbols. The traditional form of the cloak seems very fitting for northern climates. However, we have often discovered that in subtropical environments, a cloak worn over a robe can be stifling and unconducive to magickal work. We will therefore describe how to construct both the cloak and the tabard—an acceptable alternative based upon a garment worn by medieval knights over armor.

Use and Symbolism

Whether the cloak or the tabard is used, the symbolism remains essentially the same. The mantle or outer garment worn over the robe is a badge of authority. Its color and the color of the emblems attached to it signify energies specific to each officer.

The Imperator's Mantle: The proper mantle of Office of the Imperator is red—the flame scarlet Robe of Fire and Severity, as on him do the energy and stability of the Temple depend. His mantle is the symbol of unflinching Authority, compelling the obedience of the Temple to all commands issued by the Second Order; and upon the left breast thereof is the Cross and Triangle of the Golden Dawn, both white, presenting the purification of the Temple in the Outer Order by Fire.

The Praemonstrator's Mantle: The proper mantle of Office of the Praemonstrator is the bright blue Robe of Water, representing the reflection of the Wisdom and knowledge of Chesed. On her breast is the symbol of the Golden Dawn, the Cross and Triangle in white, representing the purification of the Outer Order by Water.

The Cancellarius' Mantle: The proper mantle of Office of the Cancellarius is the yellow Robe of Air. On his breast is the Cross and Triangle of the Golden Dawn in white, representing the purification of the Outer Order by Air.

The Hierophant's Mantle: The mantle of the Hierophant is bright red, representing the flaming energy of the Divine Light, shining into infinite Worlds. Upon the left breast is a White Cross to represent purification unto the Light, and this cross may be one of the following forms: Calvary, Pyramidal, Equilateral or Maltese. It is indifferent which of the Crosses be employed, seeing that each represents the operation of the Light through the Veil. (Note: The mantles of the three Middle Pillar officers should all bear the same style of cross, no matter which one is preferred. In the same manner, the Dais officers should all bear the Six-squared Cross and the Triangle—the symbol of the Hermetic Order of the Golden Dawn which they govern.)

The Hiereus' Mantle: The mantle of the Hiereus is the black robe of Darkness, threatening and terrible to the Outer, as concealing an avenging Force ever ready to break forth against the Evil Ones. On the left breast is a white Cross to represent the purification of Matter into the Light.

The Hegemon's Mantle: The mantle of the Hegemon is the robe of pure whiteness, representing the the spiritual purity which is required in the Aspirant to the Mysteries and without which qualification none can pass between the Eternal Pillars. It represents the Divine Light which is attracted thereby and brought to the aid of the Candidate. It symbolizes the Self-Sacrifice that is offered for another to aid him in the attainment of the Light. It also signifies the atonement of error, the Preparer of the Pathway unto the Divine. Upon the left Breast is a Cross, usually the Calvary form, of red to represent the energy of the Lower Will, purified and subjected to that which is Higher—and thus is the Office of Hegemon especially that of the Reconciler. The mantles are always to be worn by the main officers in any Hall of the Outer Order.

Construction
    The cloak can be constructed out of two yards of inexpensive non-stretch fabric in the appropriate color. This fabric should be 45" wide. Fold the material in half lengthwise, giving you 3' in the front and 3' in the back. At the center of the material cut out a circle for the neck. (A dinner plate makes an excellent pattern for a circle.) Cut a line straight down the front from the neck. Round off the corners and hem up all edges. Sew a cord to either side of the neck so that the wearer can tie a knot to secure the garment when in use. Symbols specific to each cloak may be cut out of felt or a similar material and glued to the left side of the cloak.
    For the Tabard, three yards of inexpensive non-stretch material

will be needed. Cut out a piece of fabric that is 100" long and 16" wide. Fold in half lengthwise, giving you 50" in the front and the back. At the center of the material, cut out a circle for the neck. Hem up all edges. Added symbols may be cut out and attached to the front of the tabard.

The Tau Robe

Use and Symbolism

A black robe is part of the required clothing for members of the Outer Order of the Golden Dawn. The Tau Cross, which looks like the letter T, is the preferred form of this robe. This also refers to the Hebrew Tau, the last letter of the Hebrew alphabet. It is likely that this symbol originated among the Egyptians from the image of the wide rack of a bull's horns and the vertical line of the animal's face (Taurus).

By wearing the black Tau robe, the members of the Outer Order of the Golden Dawn affirm that their journey up the grades and toward the Light is one that begins in darkness, the darkness and ignorance of the outer, secular world. Only when the Forces of the Black Pillar are rightly understood and balanced can the White Pillar be safely approached.

The robe should be worn whenever Temple work is to be done. As part of the Magician's total magickal environment, the wearing of the robe helps to focus the mind on the ritual work at hand, putting the Magician into a mystical state of consciousness which can only aid in the success of the ceremony.

Materials

Black material (such as cotton, silk, doeskin, or crepe) that is 48" wide
Black thread

Tools Needed

Measuring tape
Scissors and pins
Sewing machine
Iron and ironing board

Construction: Preparation of the Material

1) Measure yourself from your neck to the floor. This will be known as measurement "A." The material you buy should be twice the length of measurement "A," plus one yard.

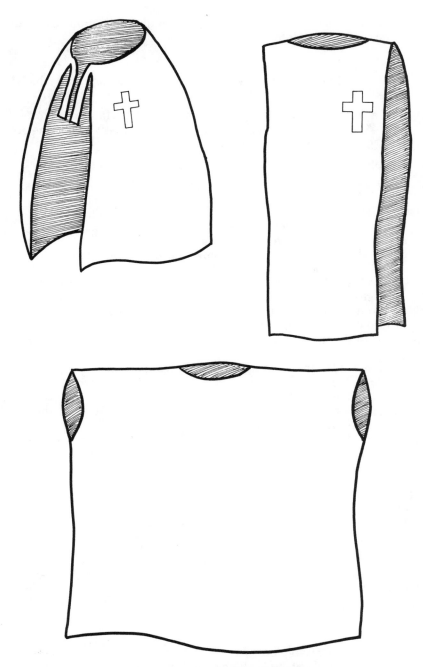

Cloak, Tabard, and Simple Robe.

2) Wash and dry the material in accordance with the manufacturer's directions. Iron the material if needed.

Preliminary Cutting

3) Lay the material out lengthwise with the right side (the side which is to be the outside of the robe) up.

4) Fold a section over so that you have a doubled surface equal to "A," plus 4". (Note: there will be a single layer of fabric left over at the bottom.) Check the length carefully.

5) Cut off the single layer and put it aside for the time being.

6) Make a second fold lengthwise.

Marking the Material

7) With the tape measure, mark the fabric as follows:
   a) 2" down from the top right hand corner.
   b) 14" down from the top right hand corner. (For a broad person, increase the measurement to 16".)
   c) From the last mark, draw a straight line across to the selvage edges.
   d) From the right hand fold, measure along the marked line a length equal to 1/2 of your chest circumference.
   e) From the upper right hand corner, mark 4" across the top of the fabric.
   f) Connect the marks to make the following lines:
      (1) A semi-circular curve connecting the two marks at the top of the right hand corner.
      (2) A diagonal line from the lower left hand corner of the material to the 1/2 chest measurement mark.
      (3) A line that curves up 2" from the 1/2 chest measurement mark and connects with the chest measurement line at the selvage edge.

Cutting the Material

8) Cut through all layers of material, cutting lines 1 and 2 of the diagram. Unfold the material so that it looks more like the finished robe.

9) Take the single layer of material that was put aside earlier. Fold it widthwise with the inside out so that the doubled length is 18". (For broad persons this measure will be 20".) Cut off the single layer that remains at the bottom and put it aside.

10) Cut the remaining doubled portion in half.

The Sleeves

11) Take one of the two pieces just cut, and place it with the fold on top, even with the fold at the top of the robe. Overlap the edges by 1" under the existing sleeve.

THE TAU ROBE

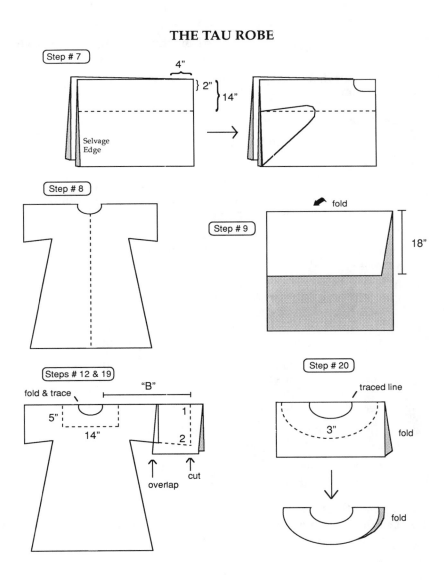

Tau Robe Construction

12) Measure from where your neck joins your shoulder, down the arm, to the tip of the middle finger. This is measurement "B."

13) Measure across the top of the robe from the right edge of the neck hole and mark off point "1" at a distance of measurement "B."

14) Draw a straight line down from the marked point "1" to point "2" in the diagram. From the corner of the robe sleeve draw a line to point "2."

15) Cut both lines which lead to point "2."

16) Do the other sleeve in the same manner.

Cutting the Facing

17) From the excess fabric, fold a piece of 10" x 14" material in half. Center the material up under the neck hole of the robe. Trace around the neck opening onto the fabric underneath.

18) Remove the marked piece of material and, using a tape measure, mark 3" away from the traced line in several places until you have a second curved line. Cut along both lines.

19) You should now have four pieces of fabric which are cut and ready to sew: the main part of the robe, two sleeves and the neck facing.

Sewing the Robe: The Neck Facing

20) Hem the outer edge of the neck facing 1/2" all around.

21) Lay the robe out flat, with the right side up. Pin the facing material around the robe's neck, placing the right sides of the fabric together. (Note: the hem of the fabric should be up.) Point the pins toward the center of the neck to make sewing over them easier.

22) Sew all around the neck, leaving a 5/8" seam. Clip all around the neck towards the seam, but take care not to cut the seam thread.

23) Turn the robe inside out. Pull the facing through the neck opening. Lay the robe out on its wrong side and tack.

Sewing the Sleeves

24) Lay the fabric out, wrong side up. Pin the right sides together (where sleeve extension meets the robe's sleeve. See the diagram). Sew along the dotted line, leaving 5/8" seam allowance. Iron the seams open.

25) Do the other arm the same way.

Sewing the Sides of the Robe

26) Fold the material over at the shoulders with the wrong side out. Pin under the arms and along the sides. Sew, leaving a 5/8" seam allowance. Clip under the arm seam, toward the seam, but be careful not to cut the seam thread.

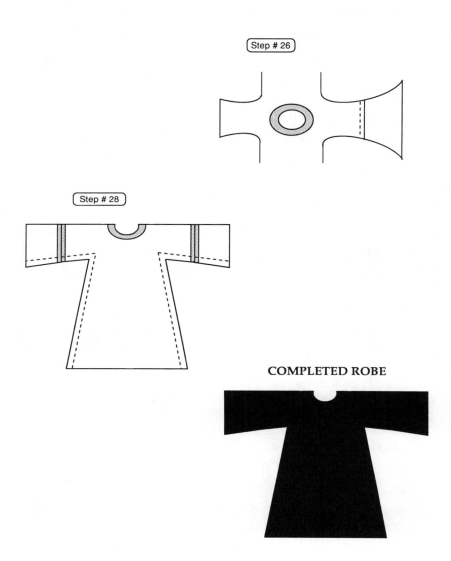

Step # 26

Step # 28

COMPLETED ROBE

Tau Robe Completion

Hemming

27) Hemming the sleeves: turn under 1/2" of the sleeve edge. Iron, pin and sew. Try the robe on and turn the sleeve under so that the robe meets the first knuckle. Iron, pin and sew.

28) Hemming the bottom: Turn the robe up 1/2". Iron, pin and sew. Try the robe on and turn up the bottom, so that the edge of the robe does not touch the floor. Pin, iron and sew.

Finishing Steps

29) Turn the robe right side out, try it on and check to make sure that it fits. Iron.

Ritual for Use

Meditation on the Tau Robe

For this brief meditation, the student will need only the robe, a white candle, a drawing of the Hebrew letter Tau, and a comfortable place to sit.

Take a ritual bath. First take a shower to clean off, and then fill up the bathtub with warm water. Add bath salts or perfumed oil to the water. For an added spiritual effect, white candles and incense may be employed in the bathroom.

Simply soak for a few minutes and let go of any negativity into the cleansing water. Then pull the plug and drain the water while remaining in the tub. Feel your doubts and worries siphon out with the water, leaving you feeling relaxed and energized. Then dry off and robe up.

Perform the LBRP.

Stand before the Hebrew letter Tau and stretch your arms out so that you resemble a T-cross. Fix the image of the Tau firmly in your mind before continuing.

Light the white candle and be seated in a comfortable position. Begin the Four-fold Breath. Breathe in to the count of four, Hold the air to the count of four, exhale to the count of four, and keep the lungs empty to the count of four. With each cycle of breathing, feel yourself slipping into a deeply meditative state.

Imagine yourself floating within a vast expanse of space—a galaxy of utter darkness. For the moment, you feel completely

alone in the universe, drifting through the void. Slowly, you become aware of a point of light, far away from you, across the solar system. The tiny beacon sends threads of warmth to touch
your skin, even at this great distance. Its radiance comforts you
and you realize that you are not alone in the universe—and you
never have been. You are not afraid, and you feel secure. With
each breath you WILL yourself closer to the light.

The darkness lessens as you advance. The light becomes a
glowing polygon within which is a candle-flame, cutting
through the blackness of space. You enter this unusual star to
bathe in its soothing heat. Upon closer inspection, you see that
the candle sits on a large stone covered by a golden cloth. It is an
unusual white candle with three wicks, each burning a separate
tongue of flame. The white-hot flames are surrounded by a single halo of light tinged with red. This is the Divine Light that
shines in and out of darkness, yet the darkness cannot comprehend it. The three-fold flame of the Eternal.

Silently you aspire toward the Light, affirming your desire for
the Knowledge of the Light and for the Completion of the Great
Work. Give the Neophyte Signs. The light glows ever brighter
with your desire for it. In your vision, stretch forth your hand
toward the candle-flame to receive the Light. A spark from the
candle manifests in the palm of your hand. Place the flame over
your heart and absorb it into your Tiphareth center, feeling the
soothing Light spread to every part of your body. Bask in this
Light for as long as you wish. When finished, return slowly to
normal consciousness.

Perform the LBRP. This ends the meditation.

A Simple Robe

The Tau robe may seem too complex for Magicians who lack
sewing skills. A square robe can be manufactured quickly and easily. Although it is not symbolically correct, the square robe is better
than no robe at all, and it does have a very spiritual feel to it.

You will need 2-1/2–3 yards of black material that is 65" wide.
Fold the material in half lengthwise. At the center of the fabric, cut a
circle for the neck. Slip the material over your head though the hole
just made and check the length of the robe, cut off any excess material. (The robe should almost touch the floor.)

Sew up the sides of the robe, but leave 12" open at the top of both sides for arm holes. Hem around these openings. Hem the bottom of the robe as well as the neck opening.

The Nemyss

Use and Symbolism

The nemyss or Egyptian Headdress is part of the traditional ceremonial garb of a Golden Dawn Magician. It is shown in many ancient papyri as either flowing down the back of the neck or gathered—ending in a "tail." We have chosen the gathered-style of nemyss as more truly representing the symbolism of Eternal Life, the Ankh, which the nemyss is based upon.

The ankh shape was supposedly based upon the form of a sandal-strap. The contour of the ankh also resembles a device used in ancient Egypt to measure the depth of the river Nile. Since the Egyptians depended heavily upon this river for food and agriculture, the Ankh-shape came to symbolize Life itself.

The Ankh-cross is a sacred symbol which alludes to the manifestation of the Divine Life Force. It also signifies the Divine Union of opposites; active and passive, male and female. The Ankh combines the masculine Tau shape with the feminine oval, alluding to the powers of generation. The shape of the Ankh expresses a profound idea; that of the circle of life spreading outwards from its origin and manifesting into the four elements. From another point of view, the circle of the Ankh alludes to the sun, the horizontal line to the sky, and the vertical line to the earth. As a microcosmic sign, the circle would represent the human head or reasoning powers (or the sun, which gives man life), the horizontal line his arms, and the upright line his body. The Ankh can also be interpreted as an early form of the emblem of Venus. In any case the Ankh, the sign of Divine Light and Life, is the most sacred and enduring symbol of the ancient Egyptians.

The shape of the Ankh is nearly the same as the symbol of Venus, the only planet whose sigil contains all the spheres of the Tree of Life. This, too, is symbolically very significant to the makeup of the nemyss. To wear an Ankh in the form of a headdress signifies the striving for Eternal Life which only spiritual attainment can bring. In the mysteries of Egypt, the initiate encountered all varieties of of actual and visualized dangers, holding above his head the Crux Ansata, before which the dark powers fled. In Hebrew tradition, the back of the head (Qoph) is covered so that symbolically no impure or unbalanced energies or thoughts may "slip in." By covering one's head with the sacred emblem of the Ankh, the Golden Dawn Magician puts him or herself in a magickal state of mind, and calls upon the Forces of Eternal Life and Light. But in addition to this, the initiate is covering the Supernal Sephiroth in his/her Sphere of Sensation for power and protection from all outside influences.

By wearing both the Tau robe and the nemyss together, the initiate truly becomes a complete and living symbol of the Ankh.

Materials Needed
2-1/2 yards of black-and-white striped material that is 65" wide
A package of fusible interfacing
A package of bonding web
Black or white thread
A package of polyester filling or similar stuffing material
A package of 1" wide elastic

Tools Needed
Sewing machine
Scissors and pins
Measuring tape
Straight edge and pencil
Iron and ironing board

Construction: Preliminary Cutting
1) After ironing, lay the material out, right side up. With straight edge and pencil, mark off a rectangle that is 36" long and 18" wide. To either end of the rectangle, draw two curved flaps (each 8" long and 6-1/2" wide). (Make sure that the stripes run parallel with the width as in the diagram. This is the "body" of the nemyss.) Cut out the body of the nemyss including the flaps as one large piece.

2) Mark off another rectangle on the fabric that is 36" long and 6" wide. This is the lining.

3) Mark off another rectangle that is 18" long and 6" wide. This is the tail. (Again, be sure that the stripes run parallel with the width.)

4) Cut out all three rectangles and put aside. Cut out two separate flaps as shown in the diagram.

Sewing and Fusing
5) Cut out a piece of fusible interfacing that is 6" wide and as long as the full length of the nemyss body (flap to flap). Lay the fusing side of the interfacing against the wrong side of the nemyss. Then following the

manufacturer's directions for fusible interfacing, iron the two pieces together.

6) Take the lining section and pin it to the interfaced edge of the nemyss body along the 36" length of the original rectangle. (Be sure that both pieces have the wrong side out.) Sew them together along this edge. Iron the seam open.

7) Place the nemyss right side up on your work area. Take one of the separate flaps and pin it to its counterpart on the nemyss body. (Note: While the nemyss body is right side up, the separate flap piece will be wrong side up.) Sew around all sides of the flap except for the width edge next to the main part of the nemyss body. Clip around the curved edge, taking care not to cut the seam thread.

8) Turn the flap right side out and iron. Then cut a piece of bonding web to fit inside the flap through the remaining open end. Iron the flap to fuse it to the nemyss body. Do the remaining flap the same way.

9) Then iron the hem of the lining open. Cut a piece of bonding web to fit between the nemyss body and the lining (inside of both). Iron and fuse into place.

10) Hem up the sides and bottom edge of the nemyss. The main body of the headdress is now complete.

Finishing Steps

11) Find the center of the nemyss along the top inside edge. Measure and mark off 6-1/2" on either side of the center. Sew a dart on either side of the center at these marks.

12) Cut a piece of elastic approximately 10" long. (The length of the headband may vary.) Sew the ends of the headband to the inside of the nemyss at the wide ends of the darts.

13) Fold the tail section in half lengthwise and iron it flat, wrong side out. Cut one edge at an angle as shown. This will be the end of the tail.

14) Sew the two long edges of the tail together, including the angled end. Then turn the tail right side out and stuff it with bulk polyester fiber or similar stuffing material.

15) Gather up the bottom edge of the nemyss in 1" pleats. Sew the tail to the nemyss in the center of the pleats.

THE NEMYSS

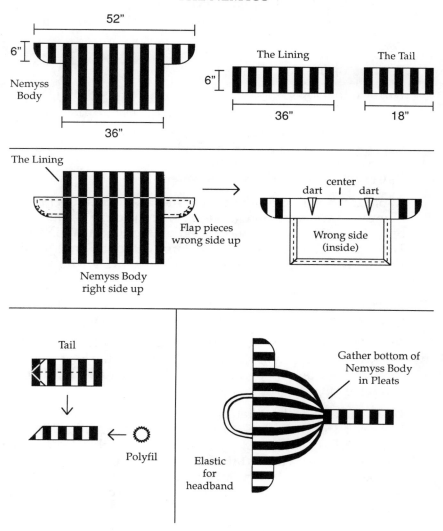

The Nemyss Construction Diagram

Ritual for Use

Meditation/Ritual on the Nemyss

Arrange the Temple in accordance to the Neophyte Hall. The Magician should take a ritual bath, then put on Tau Robe and nemyss.

Perform the LBRP.

Perform the BRH.

Perform the SIRP.

Take up the cup of water and purify the Temple by tracing a cross and sprinkling thrice in all quarters starting in the East. Say, "Seek thou the way of the Soul, whence or by what order, having served the body, to the same place from which thou didst flow down in the radiant waters."

Replace the cup and take up the incense and consecrate the Temple (trace cross and wave incense thrice in all quarters). Say, "Every way to the unfashioned soul stretch out the Reins of Fire. When thou seest a sacred Fire, without Form, shining flashingly through the depth of the world, Hear the voice of Fire."

Trace the Invoking Pentagrams of Spirit Active and Spirit Passive over the Altar and vibrate the appropriate names.

Replace incense and circumambulate the Temple thrice, saluting with the Neophyte Signs when passing to the East. Then go west of the Altar and perform the Adoration to the Lord of the Universe.

Go to the east of the Altar and stand between the Pillars with arms outstretched in the form of a Tau cross. Say, "I invoke Thee, Divine Spirit of Eternal Life! Thou art the Voice in the midst of Silence! Thou art the Light of Shore in the center of the tempest-swept sea! Thou art the Divine Union of Opposites, YHVH ELOHIM! SHEKINAH! The Presence of the Living is Here!"

Visualize a white Hebrew letter Shin surrounded by a halo above you. Vibrate the name "YHVH ELOHIM" a number of times while maintaining the image of the Shin. Imagine the Shin transforming into a glyph of the Tree of Life. It then changes first into a Venus symbol, then into a large white Ankh. Continue vibrating the name as the Ankh descends to cover your nemyss and enter the back of your head. Feel the revitalizing presence of Divine Light and Eternal Life pulsating throughout your being. Perceive its protective power keeping from you all outside energies. Visualize yourself as a life-sized Ankh: Your head and extended aura form the circle, your outstretched arms form the arms of the Ankh, while your body is the vertical shaft. You have invoked within yourself, the Eternal Sun, Sky and Earth. Contemplate the true meaning of Eternal Life.

Cross your arms in the Sign of Osiris Slain and say, "Khabs Am Pekht. Konx Om Pax. Light in Extension!" Continue to meditate for as long as you desire.

Purify and consecrate the Temple as before.

Perform the Reverse Circumambulation.

Perform the LBRP and the BRH.

Say, "I now release any spirits that may have been imprisoned by this ceremony. Depart in peace to your abodes and habitations. Go with the sanction of YHVH ELOHIM and the blessings of YEHESHUAH YEHOVASHAH! I now declare this Temple duly closed."

SO MOTE IT BE

The Sash

The Sash is a long band worn over one shoulder. It is to be constructed by the aspirant and embellished by him/her with symbols depicting the Initiate's current status or grade.*

The sash of the First Order is black, to represent the Black Pillar, to which the Outer Order is referred. The sash fits over the Initiate's left shoulder, running from the Chesed center to the Hod center (right hip). This also alludes to the watery and passive current of the Black Pillar.

---

* In Regardie's *The Golden Dawn,* the sash emblems for the Theoricus Grade are listed as being white, while those for the Practicus Grade are said to be purple. The numbers given for the Zelator Grade are shown as red. The reasons for this particular color scheme have never been made clear. In fact the only colors given in the old Order papers that appeared appropriate were those for the Philosophus Grade—green for the Sephirah of Netzach. Consequently, current Order members are encouraged to use the colors of the Sephiroth for all of the Elemental grades; violet for Yesod and the Theoricus Grade, orange for Hod and the Grade of Practicus. The numbers 1 and 10 of the Zelator grade should be white, the color that flashes against the four-colored Sephirah of Malkuth.

The sash of a Neophyte is solid black with a white triangle to symbolize light dawning in darkness. In the grades that follow additional emblems are added to the sash as shown in the diagram.

Construction

1) To construct the sash you will need 2-1/2 yards of sturdy black material cut into a long strip that is 10" wide. Fold the material in half widthwise (not lengthwise) making the sash 5" wide. Iron the material flat.

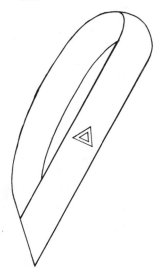

2) Sew the lengthwise edges of the sash together, wrong side out. Turn the sash right side out. Iron flat.

3) Place the sash over your left shoulder and adjust it so that it crosses over your right hip. Pin the sash here to hold it in position. Trim off the excess material so that the ends of the sash form a point at the bottom of the piece. Hem up the ends of the sash and sew them together as pinned.

4) For the white triangle, you may either glue on three strips of white ribbon or cut thin strips of white self-adhesive felt. (Additional grade symbols can be added employing these same materials, or by using fabric paint.)

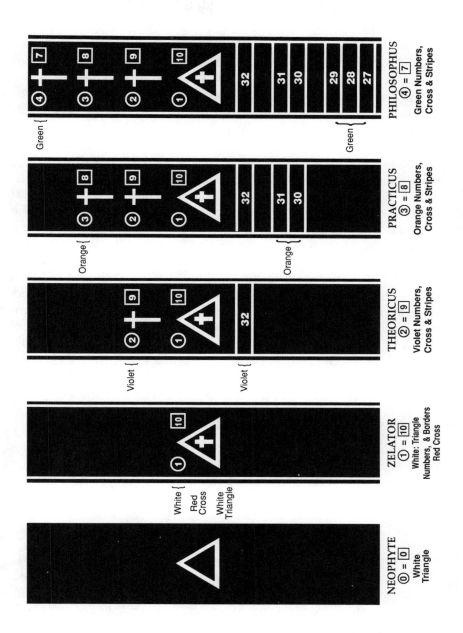

The Black Sash

Assumption of Godforms—A Guided Meditation

Copyright 1992 by OZ

This is a meditation designed to be used by a working group or Temple practicing the Golden Dawn system. It is especially effective utilized as a preparation for the Opening of the Hall of the Neophytes Ceremony. In this case, all members should be robed and seated within the Hall. A Narrator, or the Hierophant, may read the entire meditation aloud as all others participate through mental visualization. The meditation may be adapted for a more interactive use so that each Officer actually moves to the Altar during the meditation and there assumes his/her Godform. The Officers may also at this time recite the God's speech. The meditation may also be adapted for use by single or multiple individuals or non-ceremonial groups who wish to gain some sense of the energies available in a fully operative Golden Dawn Temple. If the mediation is not followed by an actual Temple working, the Godforms should be taken off and the meditation closed at the finish of the working. Instructions for this are given at the end of the meditation. It is also recommended that a banishing rite such as the Lesser Banishing Ritual of the Pentagram be used both before and after this working, especially if the meditation is performed outside a fully consecrated Temple Hall.

The Godform Meditation

Preparation: Let everyone who is to participate seat themselves comfortably, in a position that is easily maintained for the duration of the meditation. The Narrator begins:

Enter now a state of complete physical relaxation. Close your eyes. Let your breath become controlled and regular, yet fully relaxed. Inhale deeply and slowly. Exhale thoroughly and evenly. Focus your attention just on your breath. (Pause.) Bring your attention now fully within this space. Be aware of other members of the group, of the surroundings of this room. Be aware of your own inner consciousness, and how it expands to fill your aura both within and beyond the bounds of your body. Let your mind be relaxed yet fully alert. With each breath, let your body become more and more relaxed. Enter your own deep meditative state.

Let us now enter the Temple of Truth. The place gradually builds around us, rising as if materializing from the very ground beneath us. Watch as clouds of mist gather around us and rise into tall, steep flat walls, coming to a high ceiling. We are completely enclosed, surrounded on six sides—the earth beneath, the white ceiling above, and four walls around us of protective solid light. Look down now, and see that beneath our feet is a smooth floor of tiles, black and white, in alternating squares. Before us, in the center of this Temple, sits the double cubical Altar of the Universe, smooth and black. Upon it are the red rose, the red lamp, the chalice, and a dish of salt and bread. In the center are the red cross and white triangle, the symbols by which we enter this place. They glow in brilliant lightforms of a radiant red and a stunning white. On either side of the Altar are pillars. To our right, the White Pillar; to our left, the Black Pillar; each with a shaded red light at its summit. In the East there is only a veil, delicate and seemingly partially transparent. It moves slightly, as if there were a breeze in the room. All is silent.

We are alone in the Temple. The Great Gods await beyond our sensing. We come here today to bring these ancient beings to life in this sacred Hall. Nothing awaits now but the Great Work, which we must here begin. We prepare ourselves for the calling. Each of the Gods will come as we call to them, one at a time. Each Officer of the Hall will take on one of the representations. As the Officer steps into the form of the God, she or he then assumes the form of the Goddess or God. The human steps into the God from behind, first being sure to mentally ask permission from the God to carry the image. The relationship that is created between mortal and God is one of mutual cooperation. The assumption of the Godform is visualized by everyone in the Hall, as the usual form of the Officer is seen wearing the lightform of the God. The God allows her/his form to be animated by the Officer's body. The Officer take responsibility for carrying the God's image within the Hall but in no way is overpowered by the will of the Divine Being. The forms of the Gods are carried or worn by the human Officers in such a way that the God's own personalities may be expressed through words, actions and gestures via the Officer's bodies. The Officers maintain their own personal wills and full responsibility for carrying out the duties of the ceremony.

We stand in the west side of the Temple, looking to the veil in the East. The veil seems to part very slightly in the center as a brilliant point of light shines through. It is like a beam directly from the veil to the Altar. As the light passes over the Altar, it diffuses and spreads over us, creating a halo of warm light that surrounds and engulfs us. All eyes are on the point of light in the East. (Pause.) A shadow passes through the light as a figure appears from the darkness behind the veil. At first we see only a silhouette. Then we see that this is a very tall and impressive living being, and we begin to make out details of his appearance. He steps forward from the veil and we see that he is radiant, shining as only a being who is of the Gods may shine. As he stands momentarily still, we see clearly now the figure of Osiris. This is Osiris in the Netherland, the Expounder of the Mysteries in the Hall of the Dual Manifestation of the Goddess of Truth. His appearance is that of a Great God, stately and majestic. His face is a face of power and authority, which radiates in a warm reddish-brown, the skin tone of an Egyptian. He wears the tall white crown of the South, over a nemyss striped white and yellow. He looks at us with deep blue eyes, and from his chin hangs the royal Egyptian beard denoting judgement, which is gold tipped. He wears a collar in bands of red, blue, yellow, and black—and on his back is a bundle strapped across his chest by scarlet bands. His hands are free, and he wears wristbands banded yellow and white. He holds a white crown-headed scepter of the Hierophant.

Osiris steps forward, moving between the two pillars and to the East side of the Altar. Here he stands, majestically silent. The Hierophant of our Temple comes forward to the west of the Altar. Osiris and the Hierophant face one another across the Altar, and their eyes meet. The beam of light that travels from behind the veil seems to follow their gaze. The Hierophant of our Temple steps clockwise around the Altar and comes to stand behind the figure of Osiris. She stands now directly in the path of the beam of light which continues to shine through her and on to the West. She stops there a moment, then steps slowly into the image of Osiris from behind. As she does so, she begins to feel herself take on the form of his body, the colorings, his wrappings, garments and accoutrements. As the two beings merge we see what looks like a blending of their auras. It is like a sharing. She steps into him, like a figure donning a costume of light. It is her body and her form still, yet we see also the image of Osiris, his body of light animated now by the human form. We listen as Osiris speaks to us:

"I am Osiris, God of the Dead. I am He who is sacrificed and resurrected, he who eternally dies and is reborn. I journey the way of death to bring light back to the living world, and as such I preside and rule in this Hall of Dawning Light. I suffered my own death at the hand of my only brother, Typhon. It was by love, and through the magick of my twin sister-lovers, Isis and Nephthys, that I was brought back to life. As such I am living proof of the regenerative powers of these secret mysteries. I preside over the judgement of the souls in this Temple where my two sons, Horus and Anubis, stand guard. I watch over the work of these mysteries, and preside over the journeys of your souls. It is my wish to guide you in your search for the Wisdom of the returning Light."

The figure of Osiris moves to the East and is seated in a throne of black and white which appears now before the veil. Behind and above Osiris, the light still beams forth from the veil, to the Altar, and glowing into the West. Now another shadowy figure appears in the East and from the darkness steps out. The image makes his way from behind the throne of Osiris. As he moves forward into the Hall we see clearly the figure of Horus. He has the head of a great hawk, and he moves with great strength. This is Horus in the Abode of Blindness unto and Ignorance of the Higher, Avenger of the Gods. His face is that of a lively hawk—tawny and black with bright piercing black eyes. The beak is golden-hued and the throat is white. He wears the red crown of the North over a nemyss of black banded with red. His body is that of a human, and the skin a warm-reddish brown. His linen kilt is white, with an overkilt striped black and red. His pectoral collar is banded red, black, red. His wristbands are banded black and red. He carries the red-handled sword of the Hiereus. He moves forward between the Pillars and comes to stand at the east side of the Altar, surveying the surrounding with his sharp eyes. Our Hiereus comes forward to the west of the Altar and stands, meeting the gaze of Horus. Their eyes follow the path of the beam of light. The Hiereus then moves with the sun, clockwise, around the Altar to a place directly behind Horus and in line with the beam of light. After only a moment, he steps forward into the image of Horus and feels himself becoming one with the qualities and appearance of this great God. We watch as the two images merge, our Hiereus and Horus. (Pause.) Horus speaks:

"I am Horus. I am the son of the Great God Osiris and his sister-wife Isis, Goddess of Nature and Magick. I am the heir to the Throne of Osiris, because of my birth which came out of his death. From his lifeless body, thence I came into the womb of Isis, and from thence into this world as the opponent, successor, and avenger. I battle the evil Set-Typhon who slew my father, his brother. I give honor as well to my half-brother Anubis, who sacrificed one day of his own life that I might be born. The Immortal Gods have set me in the place of Justice, and I am the avenger of those who take what does not belong to them. I am the protector of this Temple. I guard the way from demons and darkness, and I face the fear which darkens the way. I come to aid you in this overcoming of your own darkness within."

Horus moves from behind the Altar to a black and red throne which now appears against the west wall of the hall. There he is seated, guarding.

We look now again to the point of light coming from the veil in the East. A tall, slender figure appears, moving from behind the throne of Osiris forward into the hall. This is the figure of a Goddess, tall, elegant and majestic. The figure is Maat, the Goddess of Ultimate Truth. She is a beautiful female figure, carrying an obvious dignity and presence of power. Her face and body are a natural Egyptian skin color, a rich, deep golden hue. She wears a yellow and violet nemyss, bound at the brow with a violet band from which rises, in front, a tall white feather. Her gown is of yellow linen, and her collar is banded red, yellow and blue. Her right wristband is banded yellow and blue, and her left wristband is banded yellow and red. She carries the Mitre-headed scepter of the Hegemon. She moves slowly and gracefully forward between the pillars and to the east side of the Altar. Our Hegemon now steps forward and stands West of the Altar. Maat's eyes and the Hegemon's eyes meet in the pathway of the beam of light. The Hegemon moves around the Altar, as the others have, standing directly behind the figure of Maat. He then steps forward into the image of Maat, taking her onto his body. He assumes the form, shape, image and countenance of this great Goddess. We see the merging of the two images, his and hers. As the two begin to be as one, Maat speaks:

"I am Maat, the Goddess of Ultimate Truth. My very name means Truth, Harmony, and Order, and I am the balance which existed before anything in the universe . . . before even the birth of the Gods. In my presence none remain unchallenged by the Gods, nor by their own heart. I weigh the hearts of all the dead and decree their Fates. I was before all things, for without truth there can be no Order, and without Order there can be no form. All things before and without Truth are naught but chaos. I have been called to this Temple to give Truth to its works. I take the place of the balance point within the Temple, and I show the way of balance towards the Light. I see what may not be seen by others. Be wary of my words as they come to you."

The figure of Maat steps back now, and is seated in a throne of yellow and violet which appears just between the pillars and a little forward. She holds her place along the line of the beams of light, which continues to shine through her and directly to the Altar. In the East, we see another figure emerge, almost stealthily. As he moves into view we see that it is the figure of Anubis. This is Anubis of the East, Watcher of the Gods. Anubis has the head of a black jackal, very alert, with pointed ears well pricked up. His nemyss is violet banded with yellow. Over his human body he wears a kilt striped yellow and violet. His pectoral collar is banded yellow, violet, yellow. His wristbands are banded violet and yellow. He carries a wand terminating in the winged solar disk and bound with two serpents. He also bears a yellow lamp whose flame burns in the form of a white yod. He wends his way around the figure of Maat, seated in the place of the Hegemon, and comes to stand at the east of the Altar. Our Kerux steps forward and stands at the Altar's west side where her eyes meet those of Anubis. The two lock gazes along the line of light, then the Kerux moves around the Altar and to the aligned place behind Anubis. She moves with careful deliberateness into the form of Anubis, assuming his shape and mannerisms as she does so. We watch her image enter his, and look on as another assumption takes place. A red gleam appears in Anubis' eye, as we hear him speak:

"I am Anubis. I am the Son of the Great God Osiris and his sister-lover Nephthys, the dark twin of Isis. Although the gentle Nephthys bore me of a union with the brother of her husband, Isis her sister took and raised me as her own. The Queen of Magick became my second Mother, and through her I learned the ways of the magick of the Gods. I am the heir to Osiris upon the Earth. Thus do I walk both upon the Earth and in the realms of the Gods, and I serve as messenger to Gods and mortals. I am the Walker between the Worlds, the guide and guardian of the many Ways. I come to this Temple to be also the messenger between the many worlds which lie within. I show the pathway from this world to other worlds, and lead the way for the journey of the soul. I shall guide all souls who seek themselves."

Anubis moves to a place in the southwest of the Hall and sits in a violet throne which appears there. He sits ready, alert to every motion and sound. We turn our attention back to the East where a softly-appearing figure seems to almost float from the veil into the Hall. As she moves forward from behind the throne, we see a most beautiful Goddess. It is Auramoouth. She is the Light shining through the Waters upon the Earth, and Goddess of the Scales of the Balance at the Black Pillar. Auramoouth is entirely human. Her face and body are a natural color. She wears a vulture headdress over a nemyss striped blue and orange. Her linen gown is blue, and her pectoral collar is banded orange, blue, orange. She bears a blue cup. Auramoouth moves forward, around Maat, and to the east of the Altar. Our Stolistes comes forward and stands facing her from the west of the Altar. His eyes and her eyes meet for a moment. The Stolistes then moves around the Altar and behind Auramoouth, standing directly between her and Maat. After a brief moment, the Stolistes steps forward and takes on the figure of Auramoouth, stepping into her image and her form. Auramoouth remains steady in our image, as his form becomes part of that image. Auramoouth speaks to us:

"I am Auramoouth of the Sky, beloved of Nuit, the Star Goddess. I am the waters through which the course of each day and journey of the soul must flow. Mine are the cow, the cat, and the lioness, all sacred creatures of the blood of life. I am the holder of the Cup of the Waters of Life, and I bring this power of the presence divine to this Temple. Special blessings I attend, and I may show the way of the heart of the waters to those who are able to feel."

Auramoouth moves now to her throne of blue and orange, which appears against the northern wall of the Hall. We look again to the place in the East from which the light radiates. Much as before, another figure appears. This time the image moves firmly and quickly into view and we see suddenly another Goddess. Her name is Thaum-Aesch-Niaeth, and she is also called Neith. She is Perfection through Fire manifesting on Earth, Goddess of the Scales of the Balance at the White Pillar. Neith appears as a human woman. Her face and body are natural. She wears a vulture headdress over a nemyss striped red and green. Her linen gown is red. Her pectoral collar is banded green, red, green. Her wristbands are banded red and green. She bears a red censer. Our Dadouchos moves forward to a place just west of the Altar and stands facing Neith. Their eyes share the radiant beam of light. Our Dadouchos now moves sunwise around the Altar and takes her position just behind Neith, in the correct alignment. She moves forward into the image of the Goddess, taking on her form and feeling herself merge into Neith. We see the transformation taking place. She speaks:

"I am Thaum-Aesch-Niaeth of the Sky, Goddess of War and Transformation. I warm the body and the heart, and I fire your passions. I am the Fire of the Southern winds, bringing the dry desert heat which consecrates through the energy of the spark of life. I bring the power of the Sacred Flame to bless this Temple. I show the sharp and quick lightning that is the way of illumination, and I burn in the desires of your souls for this Light. Do not mistake me, or my words."

Neith moves to her red and green throne, which appears against the southern wall of the Hall. We look again to the East. There appears another figure moving almost as a shadow moves, with perfect grace. Once again we see a figure of Anubis, but soon we can tell that this time the colorings are not the same. This is Anubis of the West. His head is that of a black jackal. His ornaments and dress are all entirely black and white. His nemyss is black, and his kilt is white with a black overkilt. His collar is banded black, white, black, and his wristbands are black. He bears a red sword. He makes his way to the eastern position of the Altar. Our Phylax then steps forward and faces Anubis, and their eyes meet. The Phylax (Sentinel) then steps around the Altar behind Anubis. He stands there a moment before moving forward and taking on the form of Anubis of the West. He steps into the image, and we watch as the sharing takes place. Anubis speaks to us:

"I am Anubis of the dark and the light. I am a reflection of Anubis of the East, the messenger-guardian of this Temple, as Nephthys, our Mother, is the reflection of Isis, the Mistress of magick. It is I who guard and guide the entering and leaving of all forces that pass to and from this sacred place. None may pass by me but those who carry the passwords gained from the journey of seeking this Light. These are the keys to the mysteries, and the keys to gaining entrance to the Higher Temple. I watch over the doorway. Here is your place of beginning, and it is by my way—showing that all who begin this path may first enter the place of Light."

Anubis of the West takes his place at the door to the Temple, upon a black and white throne, where he sits in readiness, at guard. The Gods now stand in residence in their proper positions. The Temple is complete. (Pause.) All eyes return to the East. We see there the point of light, continuing to shine in its brilliant radiance. The light comes from behind Osiris, originating just slightly above his head. The beam from the light comes to the Altar, and spreads out in a gleaming glow towards the West. As we watch, the Light in the East begins to take on a more golden hue, and the point begins to grow ever so slightly larger. We can see through the veil now, just dimly. The light seems to come from a distant horizon. Still somewhat hidden behind the veil, we see the first light of a rising morning sun. It is as though the veil covers a portal which opens onto a vista of landscape and morning light. It is the Dawn. There are wisps of clouds, now becoming tinted and radiant with the golden hue. We see pinks and ambers and lavenders which appear softly in the clouds showing vaguely through the veil. Yet the golden radiance shines brightly into our Temple, illuminating the room, the walls, the pillars and Altar. The golden light grows and warms and brightens everything around us. The beam of light expands and fills the Temple. We are bathed in the Light of radiance, the Light of Illumination, in the presence of the Beings of Light."

The Hierophant gives one knock. This is the knock which begins the Opening of the Hall of the Neophytes. The meditation proceeds directly into the ceremony.

Continuation of the Godforms

Once the Opening of the Hall is complete, the "work" of the Temple may include active participation of the Godforms. These beings may be allowed to speak, either through the Officers or to the Officers. Their assistance may be elicited, with permission, for magickal workings. Questions of relevance to the Temple may be put to them. It is always of greatest importance to treat these Gods with absolute honor and respect. Whatever assistance they provide should be accepted with great thanks.

Whenever a period occurs during which the contact of the Godforms grows weak or is diluted through distraction (such as during a re-arrangement of the Temple furniture or a discussion of mundane affairs) it is helpful to take a moment and allow the Officers to sit in silent meditation and re-establish the Godforms' images. This should be done prior to beginning any further magickal or Temple working.

In the case of an initiation, the new Candidate may be introduced to the Godform of Har-poor-kraat. This brief meditation may take place after the completion of the initiatory section of the ceremony and before the Closing of the Hall.

The Godform for the Neophyte

The Narrator or Hierophant should direct everyone to become relaxed and bring their attention to this work.

"Let us all assume our positions as Watchers and Guardians of this Sacred Hall. Let the forms of the Gods be re-established. Our new Soror(s)/Frater(s) sit(s) in the place of darkness. Let Har-poor-kraat be invoked from invisible presence. Turn your attention now to a place East of the Altar, at the feet of the Hegemon. There blooms a giant lotus blossom with petals of white. Seated upon the lotus is a young child, an infant God. He faces the East. His youthful face and body are a very light golden skin tone. He has deep, profound blue eyes. His hair is dark yet shines with a golden light, and a curl of hair, denoting youth, comes round his face on the right side. His collar is banded yellow and blue; his waist cloth is yellow and blue with a golden girdle, from which hangs a lion's tail. His wristbands are banded yellow and blue. The forefinger of his left hand rests upon his lips, in a childlike gesture of both innocence and silence. This is Har-poor-kraat, Harpocrates, God of Silence and Mystery, and a protector of the Neophyte. As the younger brother of Horus, and child of the Gods, he serves to protect our Temple and our new Soror(s)/Frater(s) with the purity and silence of his innocence. You may call him to you by placing your own left forefinger, now, upon your own lips. You may call him to you at any time you have need of him with this same gesture. May it always remind you of your vow of secrecy."

The Closing of the Hall

Immediately following the Har-poor-kraat meditation, or following a moment to re-establish the Godforms after a Temple working, the Hierophant gives the knock which begins the Closing of the Hall. At the end of the Closing, the Forms of the Gods may be released to remain with the Hall. As the Officers leave the Hall, the Godforms are left behind. Officers will step out of the images as they leave their robes and insignias and stations. Each Officer may independently visualize herself/himself stepping out from the back of the Godform, in reverse of the manner in which the Godform was assumed. The image of the God then becomes gradually invisible. If the interactive form of this meditation has been used, the Officers may wish to come to the Altar, in turn, and actually step out of their Godforms there. It is important to give a personal silent thanks to your own God as you release yourself. The Godforms should only be released in this manner into a fully consecrated Temple space that is used for no other types of workings. In all cases it should be understood that the Godforms are released to return to their own realms by their own will. Outside a fully consecrated Temple or in any space that will be used for other workings, the Godforms should be properly removed and a banishing should be performed.

Taking off the Godforms

This method may be used if a more formal removal is desired. This should always be used if you are using this meditation outside a regularly established Golden Dawn Temple. If the assumption of Godforms is not followed by the Opening and Closing of the Hall of the Neophytes Ceremony, a period of time should be permitted for working with these forms. Once the Godforms are established, a period of silent meditation may be used to allow each participant to experience the Godform and to communicate internally. It may be that with experience, the Godforms will wish to speak or otherwise express themselves to the participants. To close this working, the godforms should then be taken off as described here. The Narrator or Hierophant asks everyone to become quiet, and with eyes closed to return to a meditative and relaxed state.

The Temple of Truth is around us. The Gods are with us. Let us take a moment and allow what is here to become one with all that is within. (Pause.) Anubis of the West, the Watcher Without, comes from his place at the door and circumambulates to the position at the west of the Altar. Here he stands for a moment, facing the east. He then moves sunwise around the Altar and stands at its east side facing west. Here he remains, as our Phylax takes one full step backwards and out of the image of Anubis. The Phylax then continues sunwise the Altar and returns to the west. The Phylax and Anubis stand facing each other over the Altar. They speak to one another silently with their eyes. The Phylax gives the salute, the Sign of the Enterer and the Sign of Silence, to the east, then returns to his place within the Hall. Anubis fades slowly from our view.

Thaum-Aesch-Niaeth comes from the South to the west of the Altar. She faces the East. She then steps around to the east of the Altar and faces west. Our Dadouchos takes one step backwards, and leaves the image of Neith. The Dadouchos moves with the sun and returns to the west side of the Altar. Neith and our Dadouchos meet with their eyes. The Dadouchos gives the Saluting Signs, then returns to her place within the Hall. Neith slowly disappears.

Auramoouth comes around the Hall and to the west of the Altar. She faces the East, then moves to the Altar's eastern side, facing west. From out of her image steps our Stolistes. He moves around to the west of the Altar and stands a moment to meet the gaze of Auramoouth. He gives the signs. He then returns to his place in the Hall. The image of Auramoouth fades until we see her no more. Anubis of the East comes to the west of the Altar and stands facing east. He moves around and stands in the East facing west. Our Kerux steps back from his image, then around the Altar to face him. They look into one another's eyes. The Kerux gives the signs. As the Kerux returns to her place in the Hall, Anubis seems to grow dimmer and dimmer, then disappears.

The stately figure of Maat rises and moves to the place at the west of the Altar. Facing the East, she stands. Maat moves sunwise to the Altar's eastern side and faces west. She stands motionless as the being of our Hegemon steps backward and out of her image. He then comes around to face her across the Altar, and their eyes meet for a moment. He gives the Saluting Signs to the East. Our Hegemon returns and takes his place between the pillars as gradually Maat becomes invisible to our eyes. The hawk-headed Horus steps directly forward to the Altar's west and faces the East. He moves around to the East facing west, and our Hiereus steps out from his image. The Hiereus comes around to the west side again, and now Horus and our Hiereus look directly into each other's eyes. Their eyes remain locked as the Hiereus gives the signs, then steps backwards to his place. The image of Horus fades from our view.

Osiris now moves to the west of the Altar. He stands a moment, silent and still. As he faces the East, a sense of closure comes over us. (Pause.) Osiris then moves to the East of the Altar and stands facing West. Out from his image steps the Hierophant of our Temple, directly behind Osiris. She then returns, moving around to the West of the Altar and looking directly into the powerful eyes of Osiris. Our Hierophant gives the signs to the East. The Hierophant takes one step backwards before returning around the Hall to the place in the East. The image of Osiris lingers a moment, and as he fades from the view of our eyes, we give thanks to all these Goddesses and Gods for what we have shared. (Pause.)

The Temple around us becomes the room around us. We become fully aware of our own bodies as our attention turns to the rhythm of our own breath. We feel ourselves fully present in this time, and place. With our eyes still closed, we see the surroundings of this actual physical space clearly. As we open our eyes, we feel alert and alive. We retain the essence of the experience, aware that we have walked with the Gods."

(Thanks and acknowledgment is hereby given for quotations on the corrected colors from *The Godforms of the Visible Stations*, Copyright 1991, by Adam Forrest. Thanks also to Dolores Ashcroft Nowicki and the Servants of the Light for inspiration on the manners of assumption of Egyptian Godforms. —OZ)

(Note: The colors assigned to the Godforms in the above meditation are different from the ones described in Regardie's, *The Golden Dawn*, in a manuscript entitled "The Egyptian Godforms of the Neophyte Grade." This late manuscript was apparently written by a member of the Stella Matutina and was never a part of the original Z-Documents. The colors it assigns to the Godforms apply only to Enochian Chess, not to the actual godforms assumed by officers in the Neophyte Hall. This becomes apparent when one examines the colors attributed to the Godform of Nephthys, which are described by the manuscript in pigments related to the element of Earth. In the Neophyte Hall it is obvious that Nephthys corresponds the sphere of Geburah and should be colored accordingly. —CC & STC)

Ritual For Use

The Rite of Assumption to the Godform of Thmê (Maat)

For this rite, the Adept should be dressed in the robes of the Outer Order. The Temple should be arranged according to the Neophyte Hall. A sword or dagger should be on hand for banishing. The Hegemon's wand, cloak, collar, and lamen should be placed at the station between the Pillars. The Adept is to be seated in the West.

Take a few moments to relax and practice the Four-fold Breath technique.

Give five knocks and go the Northeast to proclaim "Astu! Pu tebu-na bet em khut!" (Behold, I have endowed a place with power!)

Perform the LBRP.

Go to the west of the Altar and perform the Adoration to the Lord of the Universe.

Perform the Analysis of the Keyword.

Stand west of the Hegemon's station and face the East. Perform the exercise of Middle Pillar, awakening the five centers of the Pillar of Mildness within you. (Vibrate the Divine names of the spheres a number of times while bringing down the Divine light: Kether—"EHEIEH," Daath—"YHVH ELOHIM," Tiphareth—"YHVH ELOAH VE-DAATH," Yesod—"SHAD-DAI EL CHAI," Malkuth—"ADONAI HA-ARETZ").

Once the Middle Pillar is completely formulated within your sphere of sensation, trace within your heart the Coptic letters of the name THMÊ in pure white. Then trace the letters and sigil of the name between the Pillars.

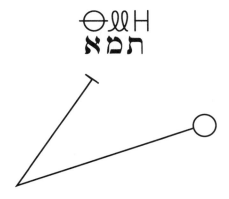

THME Forms

Bring the Divine Light down from your Kether center to your Tiphareth center, and as you do so give the Sign of the Enterer, at the same time vibrating the name "THMÊ" for as long as your exhalation of breath will last. At the end of the vibration give the Sign of Silence. Repeat this procedure of vibration a total of three times, once for every transliterated letter of the name (ThMA).

After the third vibration of the name, project a white ray of light from your Tiphareth center toward the throne between the Pillars and formulate the Godform of Thmê there: The Goddess Thmê stands between the Pillars. Her serene face is golden yellow, and her calm expression seems as though it could soothe even the hardest of hearts. Her nemyss is striped yellow and violet and is surmounted by a white Shu feather. Her linen gown is yellow, and her collar is banded with red, yellow and blue. Her right wristband is yellow and blue, while the her left wristband is yellow and red. She holds a Phoenix Wand, and her throne is yellow trimmed with violet upon a black and white pavement.

Continue projecting the white ray until the astral figure is well formulated. Then put on the cloak, collar and lamen of the Hegemon. Take up the Mitre-headed Scepter as well. Step into the Godform of Thmê that you have built up between the Pillars, facing West. Feel your mind and reasoning faculties (Ruach) empowering the shell of the astral Godform, breathing life into it. When you have felt this happen, proclaim, "Nuk nes! Netert en Maat!" (I am She! Goddess of Truth!)

Be seated, but remain in this Godform, contemplating its attributes and spiritual qualities, identifying them as your own. At times you may imagine two enormous wings attached to your arms which reach out to touch the Pillars beside you. After a pause, repeat the following:

"I am the daughter of Ra and the Lady of all the Gods and Goddesses. I stand with the God Thoth in the boat of Ra, the ship of the Sun. The scales and the feather belong to me. My feather is that which is weighed against the heart of the initiate in the Hall of Judgement. My name is Justice and my word is Truth. I am the goddess of all that is upright, genuine and steadfast. I am the eye of the storm and center of the wheel. Upon me resteth the balance of the Hall of the Mysteries. Upon me dependeth the equilibrium of the universe. None can pass between the Pillars whose heart is not Maat. When I cast my glance upon the Crown, I am Thma-Ae-st, Before the Face of the Gods in the Place of the Threshold. When I cast my glance to the right, I am Thma-aesh, the Fiery One of Severity. When I cast my glance to the left. I am Thma-ett, the Fluid One of Mercy. For I am the Maati, the dual goddesses of North and South."

Pause and contemplate. Then say the following:

"For the Soul of the Initiate cried out in anguish and in joy toward the Hidden Light. The soul stepped forward through blinding darkness in aspiration toward the Light. The Light glittered in the darkness, but was not comprehended thereby. Then the voice of the Guardian of the Threshold spake and said 'I am the Preparer of the Way between Light and Darkness. I am the Purity of the Light. I am the atonement of error. I am the self-sacrifice offered to another in a time of need. Take my hand and let thy heart, thy soul, and thy word be Maat."

Continue to meditate upon the Godform. Then stand and face the Altar.

Say, "Light and Darkness. East and West. Air and Water." (Give a knock.) "I am the Reconciler between them." Give the Neophyte Signs.

Say, "Heat and Cold. South and North. Fire and Earth." (Knock) "I am the Reconciler between them." Give the Neophyte Signs.

Say, "One Creator. One Preserver. One Destroyer. One Redeemer." (Knock) "One Reconciler between them." Give the Neophyte Signs.

Remain facing the Altar and say, "Holy art Thou, Who art in all things. If I climb up to Heaven, Thou art there and if I go down to Hell Thou art there also! If I take the Wings of the Mourning and flee unto the uttermost parts of the Sea, Even there shall Thy hand lead me and Thy right hand shall hold me. If I say, peradventure the Darkness shall cover me, even the Night shall be turned Light unto Thee!
        Thine is the AIR with its Movement!
        Thine is the FIRE with its Flashing Flame!
        Thine is the WATER with its Ebb and Flow!
        Thine is the EARTH with its enduring Stability!"

Imagine the yourself in the Godform of Thmê as the focal point of the Universe. Upon you, the harmony of the Cosmos depends. Once again, see the Divine Light descending through the Middle Pillar, from your Kether center to your Malkuth center.

Continue to meditate for as long as you desire. When finished, place the mantle, collar, lamen and wand of the Hegemon back upon the throne between the Pillars. Step out of the Godform of Thmê, which once again becomes inanimate. Withdraw the white ray from the Godform back into your Tiphareth center. Imagine the figure of the Goddess slowly begin to fade until it vanishes entirely.

Perform again the Adoration to the Lord of the Universe.

Perform the LBRP.

Give five knocks and declare the Temple duly closed.

THIS ENDS THE RITE

CHAPTER TWO

Implements of the Elemental Grades

The basic implements and furnishings of the Golden Dawn Temple have been thoroughly described in chapter 1. However, there are still some First Order tools that have not yet been covered. This is because these implements are not to be found in the Neophyte Hall, but in the four grades between the Neophyte and the Portal. In addition to this, while the basic props and Temple furnishings used throughout the Outer Order remain the same, the arrangement of the Temple, or Hall, varies with each grade. Sometimes within the ceremonies of a grade the Temple arrangement will change several times. During the Ceremony of the Philosophus, the Temple furnishings change position four times.

What we are primarily discussing here are the Halls of the Elemental Grades: Zelator, Theoricus, Practicus and Philosophus, including any additional props which need to be introduced. We will also be discussing the ten Admission Badges which are used in the Elemental grade ceremonies.

For additional information on the particular functions and the attributions of the Elemental grades, consult pp. 28-33 of Regardie's *The Golden Dawn*.

THE ELEMENTAL HALLS

As mentioned in chapter 1, the Neophtye Ritual is a preliminary ceremony that has hidden within it many magickal formulae and techniques. It is a ritual designed to awaken the candidate to the Divine Light. After several purifications and consecrations, the candidate is placed between the two Pillars, in the position of equilibrium and balance; on the path, so to speak, toward union with the Higher Self. The candidate has now been made aware of the Divine Light, but has yet to accomplish the task of Divine Union. This is done, in steps, through the Elemental Grades of the Outer Order.

The Elemental grades, which are the four grades of the First Order, represent an awareness of the elements within the psychological make-up of the candidate. These "inner elements" can be described as different divisions of the subconscious. The process undertaken by an Initiate advancing through the grades is truly an alchemical process, in which the psychic mechanism of the candidate undergoes a process of dissolution. During the ceremony of the Neophyte, the component elements are examined and purified through the Elemental grade ceremonies, and finally all the base constituents are consecrated and integrated back into the psyche of the Initiate. Thus aroused, the elemental portions of the mind become dedicated to Divine Union with the Higher Self, and ultimately to the completion of the Great Work. This process allows the initiate to bring unlimited energy and inspiration from the previously untapped subconscious depths into the realm of the conscious mind, where it can be employed for further spiritual growth.

Zelator Grade Ceremony

The first Elemental grade is that of Zelator, the grade which begins the alchemical metamorphosis of the candidate's psychic elements. The Zelator grade is attributed to the sphere of Malkuth, to the element of Earth, and to the Earthy part of the candidate's inner being. During the Zelator ceremony, the Earth spirits (Elementals) are invoked and the candidate is brought before three pathways: the Path of Evil, the Path of Good, and the Path of Balance. On the first two paths, the unprepared candidate is halted by Guardians and forced to turn back. The candidate finally attempts to traverse the Middle Path and is barred again by the Guardians of Good and Evil, but the Hierophant representing the Eternal and the Universal Soul intercedes and clears the path for safe passage. Access to the symbolic Temple of Solomon is granted to the aspirant, who personifies a priest of the Hebrew Mysteries entering the Tabernacle. The significance of certain symbols such as the seven-branched candlestick are explained to the candidate. At the end of the Zelator Ceremony, the Neophyte has become an initiate, and the element of earth has been firmly established in his/her psyche.

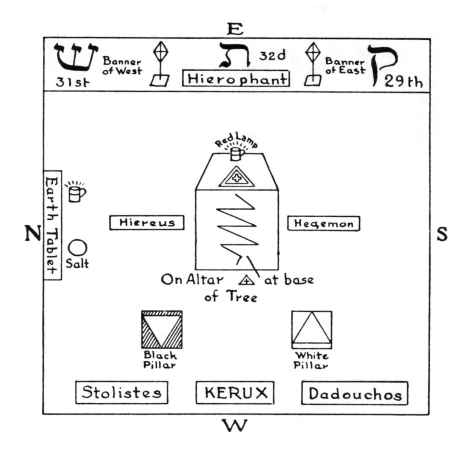

**Temple Layout for the Ceremony of the
Zelator 1 = 10 Grade**

Temple Set-up for the Zelator Hall

Here, the Altar occupies a position much farther east that its previous position in the Neophyte Hall. The pillars are moved well toward the west of the Temple. The officers in the Zelator Hall are six in number: Hierophant, Hiereus, Hegemon, Kerux, Stolistes, and Dadouchos. (The Sentinel remains outside the Hall.) During the first part of the ceremony, the stations of the six officers form a triangle, the symbol of Supernal creation and Divine Revelation. The lesser three officers compose the base, the Hiereus and Hegemon (representatives of the opposing light and darkness) are next, and the Hierophant, who personifies the higher powers, is located at the apex. This triangle, apex upwards, is also a triangle of Fire, which points to a relationship that exists between the letters Yod (Fire) and Heh Final (Earth) of the Tetragrammaton. (Keep in mind that the choir of angels attributed to Malkuth is known as the Ashim, or the "Souls of Fire." The Admission Badge of this grade, the Fylfot Cross, holds another clue to this mystery, because it is formed of 17 squares out of a square of 25 lesser squares. Twenty-five is also the number of squares attributed to the Kamea of Mars.) The initiation into the earthy Zelator grade and the sphere of Malkuth implies that a certain amount of Fire energy is involved. Since we have already shown that the Elemental grades allude to an alchemical process of analysis and dissolution within the aspirant, it is only natural that we find a fiery undercurrent pervading this first step on to the Tree of Life.

At the second point in the ritual, a cross is formed by five of the officers, the shaft of the cross is created by the three Chief officers in alignment with the Altar, while the Stolistes and Dadouchos compose the cross bar. This cross formation stresses the four elements as a balanced "whole" within the manifest universe, as well as the four sub-elements of Malkuth. The fact that it is composed of five officers and not six refers to the pentagram, the number of man—the microcosm, and the Initiate. But it also refers to the fifth element of Spirit, which surmounts and governs the other four.

Theoricus Grade Ceremony

The next grade ceremony is that of Theoricus, which is attributed to the sphere of Yesod, the element of air, and the Moon, the airy part of the Initiate's psyche. In this ceremony, the initiate encounters the four Kerubim, the angelic choir referred to Yesod. As the presidents of the elemental forces, the four Kerubim are each assigned one of the letters of the Divine Name YHVH. The Kerubim operate in and through the four elements in Yesod—the Astral Matrix upon which the manifest universe is formed. In the Theoricus Temple, the initiate learns that the Elemental Spirits are to be invoked through the power and the governance of the Kerubim and their Zodiacal symbols. Between the spheres of Malkuth and Yesod lies the 32nd Path of Tau, a journey through the subconscious which the aspirant must undertake.

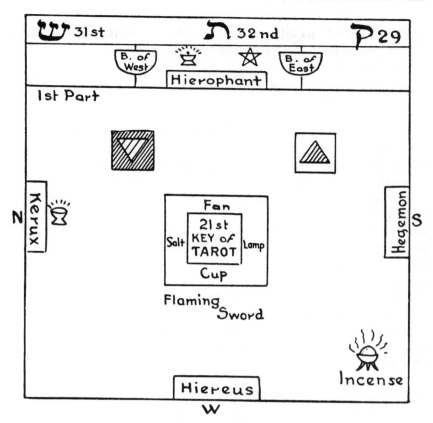

**Temple Layout for the Ceremony of the
2 = 9 Grade of Theoricus**

Temple Set-up for the Theoricus Hall

There are only four officers in the Theoricus Hall. (All of the offices of the Neophyte Hall are held by Initiates who have attained to a certain grade. Since the offices of Stolistes and Dadouchos can be held by someone holding the grade of Zelator, these officers no longer appear in the grades beyond the 1=10.) The stations are symmetrically positioned, East, West, North and South, with the pillars placed at the east end of the Altar. This balanced arrangement suggests the reconciling element of Air mediating between all opposing energies within the Hall, resulting in perfect equilibrium. The number four, with its correlation to Chesed (the first Sephirah of the manifestation below the Abyss) also alludes to the firm foundation or blueprint of the four elements inherent within the sphere of Yesod before they manifest in Malkuth.

Practicus Grade Ceremony

The third Elemental grade is that of Practicus, which is assigned to the Sephirah of Hod, the element of Water, the planet of Mercury, and the watery part of the Initiate's consciousness. During the ceremony, the aspirant is introduced to certain deities of the Samothracian Mysteries known as the Kabiri, "the Powerful." Three of the Kabiri, represented by the Three Middle Pillar officers; the Hierophant, the Hiereus, and the Hegemon , are known as Axieros, Axiokersos, and Axiokersa. In this ceremony, they also represent the various aspects of Fire. The aspirant portrays the fourth Kabir, Kasmillos, brother of the other three, who is killed and resurrected in another allegory of the process of spiritual alchemy. The two paths which lead the candidate to the watery sphere of Hod are in fact fiery (the 30th and the 31st paths of Resh and Shin). Water is nurturing and maternal, while Fire is productive and paternal; yet only from their union and perfect harmony can spiritual growth be attained. The two primary and parental elements of Fire and Water must always be held in balance. Thus in this ritual the Initiate's sphere of sensation symbolized by stagnant water is vitalized by the fiery and solar paths, so that it becomes a worthy vessel for the Divine Light. The waters of the intellect become a breeding ground for creativity and inspiration within the mind of the aspirant.

Temple Set-up for the Practicus Hall
As in the preceding ceremony, another officer is dropped from the ritual. (The office of Kerux, which can be held by an initiate of the Theoricus grade, is no longer required in the Practicus grade.) This leaves three officers who form an approximate equilateral triangle. The triangle, whose apex is again marked by the station of the Hierophant, refers to the Fire Triangle and the fiery nature of the 31st and the 30th Paths of Shin and Resh in relation to the Tree of Life Diagram (as well as the relationship between the Tree of Life and the layout of the Temple). For the later part of this ritual, when the Temple is arranged in Hod, the Hierophant takes up a temporary position west of the Altar, so that all three officers form the Water Triangle.

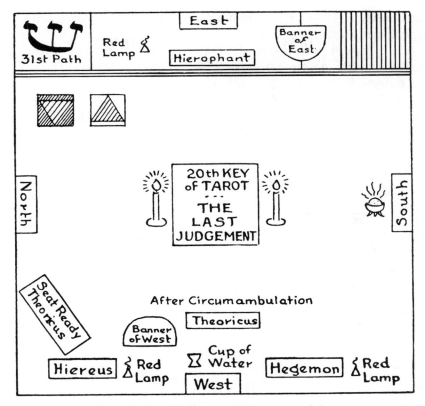

**Temple Layout for the Ceremony of the
3 = 8 Grade of Practicus**

Philosophus Grade Ceremony

The fourth Elemental grade, Philosophus, is attributed to the Sphere of Netzach, the element of Fire, the planet Venus, and the fiery part of the Initiate's pysche. In the Philosophus ceremony, the aspirant encounters various deities from the Egyptian pantheon who represent the various aspects of Water. Just as in the preceding ceremony of Practicus, the two primary elements of Fire and Water must always be equilibrated. Therefore two of the three Paths traversed by the candidate in this grade are watery (the 28th and the 29th Paths of Qoph and Tzaddi). The third route, the 27th Path of Peh, is a fiery path which joins Netzach to Hod on the Tree of Life. It is on this Path that the candidate realizes the price of spiritual stagnation and ignorance. On this difficult route, the candidate must rid him/herself of all that is base and low, retaining only that which is true and divine. It is also on this path that the aspirant becomes suddenly aware of personal conflicts in his her life, as well as various tests and trials of inner strength. This strenuous experience is one of the hallmarks of a successful initiation. As in alchemy, the process of analysis and dissolution must always precede assimilation. The task of Philosophus on the 27th Path is to examine and balance the energies of Fire and Water, Emotion and Intellect.

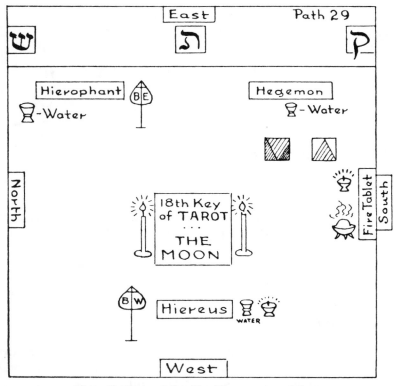

**Temple Layout for the Ceremony of the
4 = 7 Grade of Philosophus**

Temple Set-up for the Philosophus Hall

The same three officers appear as before. (The office of Hegemon for this particular ceremony must be held by someone who has attained to the grade of Philosophus; however in the Outer grade ceremonies he/she need only be a Practicus.) In the 4=7 ritual, the officers form the Water Triangle with the station of the Hiereus marking the apex in the West. This alludes to the watery nature of the 29th and 28th Paths of Qoph and Tzaddi, which the candidate traverses in this particular grade. The Pillars are in the Southeast, indicating the exact placement of the Paths on the Tree, as before.

In the fourth part of the ceremony, which marks the candidate's entrance into the 27th Path of Peh, all three officers are stationed in the East; the Hiereus and the Hegemon on either side of the Hierophant. This points out the direction of the 27th Path on the Tree of Life as a reciprocal Path—one which straddles all three columns on the Tree (the actual Temple Pillars are placed in the South). Finally, in the fifth segment of the ritual, the officers are positioned in the form of a Fire Triangle, the symbol of the fiery nature of the Sephirah Netzach, into which the aspirant has achieved entry.

THE ADMISSION BADGES OF
THE ELEMENTAL GRADES

An Admission Badge is something that is given to a candidate at his/her initiation to insure passage into the Temple. It can be a solid geometric object, a diagram, or a lamen of one of the officers. The candidate is usually unaware of the significance of a particular badge until its symbolism is described within the ritual by the Hierophant or another officer.

We have always felt that an Admission Badge should be solid, even if described as a simple diagram. For this reason, many of our badges are constructed in the manner of a lamen, and indeed a few of them are based upon the actual lamens of particular officers. Some Temples prefer to paint all of the badges white with black symbols, since traditionally the Outer Order members of the Golden Dawn were never taught the colors of the Minutum Mundum. This is not so out-of-step with the times as it may appear on the surface; we have many times found that some students, who have committed to memory the color scales of other Mystical/Magickal systems, become thoroughly confused when confronted with the King and Queen Scale colors of the Tree of Life. In these instances, the simple black and white badges are an aid to the student's ability to learn the correct symbolism without being bombarded by the advanced scales of color. However, we have chosen to incorporate the color scales into the badges, both for the richness of symbology as well as the beauty that the painted badges add to the ritual.

This chapter is almost a workbook in itself. Here we have provided rituals and guided visualizations for the Admission Badges of the Golden Dawn. These rites are designed for the student who is either working through the Outer Order of the Golden Dawn or is at a comparable level in his/her own personal Magickal work.

There are four Elemental invocation rituals included in this chapter, one for each of the Elemental grades. Since the Outer Order in one sense is contained within the sphere of Malkuth, the elements we are really discussing here are: Earth of Malkuth, Air of Malkuth, Water of Malkuth, and Fire of Malkuth. Thus there is only one basic Invoking Pentagram used in all four rituals—that of the Lesser Pentagram Ritual of the Outer Order, which only employs the Earth pentagram as opposed to the various pentagrams described in the SIRP of the Inner Order.

The Fylfot Cross

Use and Symbolism

The Fylfot Cross is the Admission Badge to 1=10 grade of Zelator. It is also called the Hermetic Cross, the Hammer of Thor, the Gammadion and the Swastika. It is formed of 17 squares out of a square of 25 lesser squares. These 17 represent the Sun, the Four Elements, and the Twelve Signs of the Zodiac.

The symbol of the Sun is at the center of the Cross at the point of stillness, while the Zodiacal Signs divided into the four Triplicities make up the arms of the Cross. The Cardinal Signs all begin at the center of the Cross, followed by the Fixed and Mutable Signs. The Arms terminate with the Elemental Symbols of each Triplicity. The whole Cross represents the center of the universe giving rise to the celestial Signs, which then formulate the elements of the physical world.

The Fylfot Cross, when painted black with white symbols, emphasizes the element of Earth, to which the Zelator Grade is assigned. When painted in the four colors of Malkuth, it underscores the Sephirah which is attributed to the Grade.

Since the Fylfot is originally formed out of 25 squares, this cross also has an affinity with Fire. (25 is the number of squares forming the Kamea or Magickal Square of Mars.) According to Cirlot, all the words for "cross" (crux, cruz, crowz, croaz, krois, krouz) have a common etymological basis in -ak, -ur, or -os, signifying the "light of the Great Fire." (This is also one reason why the lamen of the Dadouchos consists of this symbol.)

The Fylfot Cross is a symbol of an Equal-armed Cross with four arms appearing to rotate in the same direction, around a central axis. During the Iron Age, the Swastika represented the supreme deity. In the Middle Ages, the general interpretation of the figure was that it symbolized movement and the power of the sun. This Cross also signifies the action of the Origin upon the Universe.

In addition, the Fylfot is a symbol attributed to the first Sephirah, Kether. Here it represents the four latent (Primal) elements whose energies are united in Kether, activated by the Primum Mobile or First Whirlings. These energies are finally differentiated into the four base elements of Fire, Water, Air and Earth upon reaching the level of Malkuth on the Tree. The Fylfot Cross, given to the candidate in the Zelator grade, points out a close relationship that exists between Kether and Malkuth.

In addition to its employment in the 1=10 grade, the Fylfot Cross can used by the Zelator in a ritual/meditation on the elemental make-up of Malkuth.

Materials Needed
　　One 5" x 5" piece of pine or basswood that is 1/2" thick
　　Wood putty
　　Gesso
　　Liquitex acrylic paints: white, black, orange, violet, green
　　Sealant such as clear lacquer finish

Tools Needed
　　Scroll saw or jig saw
　　Pencil and straight edge
　　Artist's brushes
　　Sandpaper, medium and fine

Construction
　1) Take the 5" x 5" piece of wood and on one side, mark off five 1" squares (both vertically and horizontally). You will then have a piece of wood that has drawn on it a total of twenty-five 1" squares.

　2) With a pencil, shade in the appropriate squares as shown in the diagram. Cut out the shaded squares with the saw.

　3) Fill in any gaps with wood putty. Sand until smooth.

Finishing Steps
　4) Cover entirely with a coat of gesso. Let dry. Sand until smooth. Apply another coat if needed.

　5) The finished Cross may be painted in one of three ways:
　　a) White with black Zodiacal and elemental symbols.
　　b) Black with white Zodiacal and elemental symbols.
　　c) Divided into the four colors of Malkuth: Citrine—mixed from orange and green, Russet—mixed from orange and violet, Olive—mixed from green and violet, and Black. The Elemental and Zodiacal symbols are to be painted on one side of the Cross in white. Allow to dry.

　6) Spray or brush on a coat of sealant for protection. Let dry.

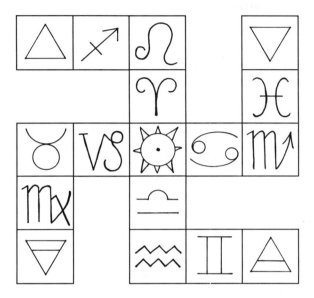

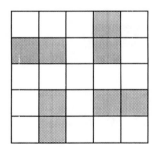

The Fylfot Cross

Ritual for Use

An Invocation of the Element of Earth and a Meditation on the Fylfot Cross for the Grade of Zelator

For this ritual the Zelator will need a black Outer Order robe, black and white striped nemyss, and the Outer Wand of Double Power (described in chapter 6). A black candle, a paten of bread and salt, and the finished Fylfot Cross should be placed on the Altar. The Temple is to be arranged in accordance with the Zelator Hall (as in the Second part of the initiation ceremony). Enter the Temple giving the Sign of the Zelator.

Relax for a few moments and perform the Four-fold Breath.

Go to the Northeast and say, "HEKAS, HEKAS, ESTE BEBELOI!"

With the black end of the wand, perform the Lesser Banishing Ritual of the Pentagram.

Say the following invocation: "Stoop not down into that darkly splendid world wherein continually lieth a faithless depth and Hades wrapped in gloom, delighting in unintelligible images, precipitous, winding, a black ever-rolling Abyss, ever espousing a body unluminous, formless and void."

Begin here

Lesser Invoking Pentagram

Go clockwise to the North. With the white end of the wand, trace the *Lesser Invoking Pentagram*. Thrust the wand through the center of the figure and vibrate, "AGLA!" Say, "In the Divine Name ADONAI HA-ARETZ, I open this Temple in the element of Earth. May the Archangel URIEL look with favor upon this ceremony! May the angel PHORLAKH and the ruler KERUB be also in attendance! I have gained admission to this Temple through the Badge of the Hermetic Cross. I am one who has received the Mystic Title of *Periclinus de Faustis* and the symbol of ARETZ. As a Wanderer in the Wilderness, I invoke the powers of Earth to bear witness to my spiritual endeavor. Grant me the knowledge of the element of Earth and the Active Realm, so that I may obtain Greater Understanding of Hidden Things and thereby advance in the Great Work."

Circumambulate the Temple three times, saluting with the Neophyte Signs when passing the East.

Go to the West and face east. Give the Adoration to the Lord of the Universe:

"Holy art Thou, Lord of the Universe!" (Projection Sign)
"Holy art Thou, Whom Nature hath not formed!"
   (Projection Sign)
"Holy art Thou, the Vast and the Mighty One!"
   (Projection Sign)
"Lord of the Light, and of the Darkness!" (Sign of Silence)

Go to the North and give the Zelator Sign.

Recite the Prayer of the Gnomes:

O Invisible King, Who, taking the Earth for Foundation, didst hollow its depths to fill them with Thy Almighty Power. Thou whose Name shaketh the Arches of the World. Thou who causest the Seven Metals to flow in the veins of the rocks, King of the Seven Lights, Rewarder of the subterranean Workers, lead us into the desirable Air and into the Realm of Splendor. We watch and we labor unceasingly, we seek and we hope, by the twelve stones of the Holy City, by the buried talismans, by the Axis of the Loadstone which passes through the center of the Earth—O Lord, O Lord, O Lord! Have pity upon those who suffer. Expand our hearts, unbind and upraise our minds, enlarge our natures.

   O Stability and Motion! O Darkness veiled in Brilliance! O Day clothed in Night! O Master who never dost withhold the wages of Thy Workmen! O Silver Whiteness—O Golden Splendor! O Crown of Living and Harmonious Diamond! Thou who wearest the Heavens on Thy Finger like a ring of Sapphire! Thou Who hidest beneath the Earth in the Kingdom of Gems, the marvelous Seed of the Stars! Live, reign, and be Thou the Eternal Dispenser of the Treasures whereof Thou hast made us the Wardens."

Give the Zelator Sign. Go to the west of the Altar. With the white end of the wand, trace the Invoking Earth Pentagram over the bread and salt. Place the wand aside.

Consume the bread and salt.

As you consume the Repast of Earth, meditate on the Fylfot Cross upon the Altar:

See within it an Equal-armed Greek Cross surrounded by the brilliant Whiteness of Kether. Imagine each arm of the Cross also in white. Within the pure Brilliance visualize the four letters of the Divine Name, YHVH in iridescent white flecked gold. Each letter attaches itself to one arm of the Cross. As each arm comes in contact with a Divine letter, it changes color. The Y-arm turns to red, the H-arm to blue, the V-arm becomes yellow and the H-final arm turns black.

Infused with the essence of the four Primordial Elements, the Cross begins to spin in one direction on its axis. The cross spins clockwise in the direction of Chesed. The speed of the rotation increases until the motion is swift. It is impossible to tell whether the Cross is moving or completely still. The colors become blurred—you can no longer distinguish them. The Cross develops into four axes joined at the handle, cleaving its way down the Tree of Life, following the Path of the Lightning Bolt.

When the whirling Cross finally reaches Malkuth, its velocity begins to decrease. The spinning motion gradually slows enough for you to see the symbol of the Sun at the still center of the figure. You now see that the colors of the arms have changed from the base elements in Kether to the Sub-elemental colors of Malkuth, showing the influence of all the Sephiroth as the energy of the Fylfot whirls its way down the Tree. Upon the arms of the Cross you see the Signs of the Zodiac as they first manifest in the physical Universe. From these Celestial Signs, the spinning of the Cross gives birth to the four elements of Fire, Water, Air and Earth as they materialize in the realm of Malkuth. The Zodiacal Signs spin in one direction, in accordance to the Celestial Wheel, while the elemental sigils seem to spin in the opposite direction, according to the YHVH formula.

The Cross comes to a complete rest in the Sephirah of inertia and stability. It is now as you see it on the Altar before you. However, you realize that the spinning and transforming action of the Fiery Fylfot could easily begin again, as Malkuth becomes the Kether of yet another Tree.

Take as much time as you need for the meditation.

Perform the Reverse Circumambulation.

Go to the East and say, "I now release any Spirits that may have been imprisoned by this ceremony. Depart in peace to your abodes and habitations. Go with the blessings of ADONAI HA ARETZ!"

Perform the LBRP with the black end of the wand.

Say, "I now declare this Temple duly closed." Exit with the Sign of the Zelator.

SO MOTE IT BE

The Solid Greek Cubical Cross

Use and Symbolism

The Solid Greek Cubical Cross is the Admission Badge for the path of Tau in the 2=9 grade of Theoricus. It is composed of 22 external squares which refer to the 22 letters that are placed thereon. The Cross is an emblem of the equilibrated and balanced forces of the Elements.

Upon the front of the Cross are the Hebrew letters which correspond to the four elements: Aleph-Air, Shin-Fire, Mem-Water, Tau-Earth. In the center is the letter, Resh, which is attributed to the Sun.

On the back side of the Cross are the letters that represent the remaining planets (minus Resh-Sol and Tau-Saturn): Beth-Mercury, Peh-Mars, Gimel-Moon, Daleth-Venus with Kaph-Jupiter (the Wheel) in the center.

The remaining three sides of the Aleph (Air) arm are painted with the letters corresponding to Libra, Aquarius and Gemini. The sides of the Shin (Fire) arm are covered by the letters which refer to Aries, Leo, and Sagittarius. The Mem (Water) arm includes the letters which are attributed to Cancer, Scorpio and Pisces. The sides of the Tau (Earth) arm include the letters corresponding to Capricorn, Taurus and Virgo.

The Cubical Cross combines the symbolism of the balanced elements with the 22 letters of the Hebrew alphabet to emphasize the eternal Forces which lay behind the base elements of the physical universe. In the 2=9 Ceremony it is stated that, "twenty-two are the letters of the Eternal Voice, in the Vault of Heaven; in the depth of the Earth; in the Abyss of Water; in the All-Presence of Fire. Heaven cannot speak their fullness—Earth cannot utter it. Yet hath the Creator bound them in all things. He hath mingled them in Water. He hath whirled them aloft in Fire. He hath distributed them through the planets. He hath assigned unto them the Twelve Constellations of the Universe." It is for this reason that the Cubical Cross is the symbol which admits the candidate to the 32nd Path of Tau, (from Malkuth to Yesod). It is called the Administrative Intelligence, which directs the Seven Planets in all their operations. Symbolically, this Path joins the Earth with the balanced powers of the seven planets (the Microprosopus portrayed by the Hexagram). It is the first Path leading out of the material state of Malkuth toward a comprehension of the Personality, formed by the Higher Self to function in a particular incarnation. On this Path, the Initiate encounters his/her own individual consciousness. This includes a descent into the subconscious with its hidden fears and self-made demons, as well as an ascent into a new Life of Higher Consciousness. In addition to its use in the 2=9 grade, the Solid Cubical Cross may be utilized by the Theoricus in a ritual/meditation on the 32nd Path.

Materials Needed
   One 1' length piece of 1-1/2" x 1-1/2" stock wood
   Wood putty
   Yellow carpenter's glue
   Gesso
   Acrylic paints: blue-violet, yellow and orange
   Clear lacquer finish

Tools Needed
   Table saw or hack saw
   Craft knife
   Sandpaper, all grades
   Artist's brushes

Construction
1) Take the piece of wood and mark off the following lengths: One 4-1/2" long piece, two 1-1/2" long pieces. Cut the marked sections apart with the saw.

2) Smooth each piece with sandpaper and fill in any gaps with wood putty.

3) Glue the two smaller pieces to the center of the length of the larger section, one on either side as shown in the diagram.

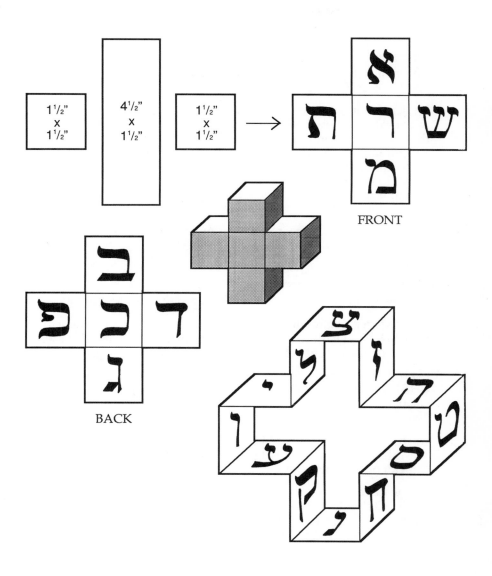

The Solid Greek Cubical Cross

4) After the glue has dried, take the knife and score both the front and back of the long section with two notched lines, so that the Cross has the illusion of being constructed from five separate 1-1/2" cubes.

Finishing Steps

5) Cover entirely with a coat of gesso. Let dry. Sand until smooth. Apply another coat if needed.

6) The Cross can be painted either white with black letters or blue-violet with orange-yellow letters (for the Path of Tau). On the front side of the Cross the Hebrew letters are to be arranged as follows:

    Top square: ALEPH
    Bottom square: MEM
    Middle square: RESH
    Right square: SHIN
    Left square: TAU

    On the back side of the Cross the following letters are to be painted:
    Top square: BETH
    Bottom square: GIMEL
    Middle square: KAPH
    Right square: DALETH
    Left square: PEH

    On the three remaining sides of the ALEPH-BETH arm, the letters LAMED, TZADDI and ZAYIN should be painted in that order—with Lamed on the left side of the Aleph, and Zayin to the right.

    On the three remaining sides of the MEM-GIMEL arm, the letters CHETH, NUN, and QOPH should be painted in the same way (with Cheth to the right of Mem, and Pisces on the left). (Note: The Kerubic Sign is always on the outermost side of the arm.)

    On the sides of the SHIN-PEH arm, the letters HEH, TETH and SAMEKH should be painted (with Heh on the side above Shin, and Samekh on the bottom side).

    On the three sides of the TAU-DALETH arm, the letters AYIN, VAV, and YOD should be painted (with Ayin on the bottom side, and Yod on the top, etc.). (Note: The letters should be painted so that at any given angle that the viewer is looking, all the letters on that side appear to be upright. Example: If the Cross is placed standing on its Mem-arm, the viewer looking straight down on the top of the Cross will see the letters Yod, Tzaddi and Heh all upright—the bottoms of all the letters toward the front side of the Cross. A view of the left side of this Cross in this position will reveal the letters Lamed, Vav and Qoph, one above the other, their bottoms all toward the Mem-arm.)

7) When all paint is dry, apply sealant for protection.

Ritual for Use

A Journey on the 32nd Path of Tau

For this ritual the Theoricus will need his Outer Order Robe and nemyss, the Outer Wand of Double Power, and the finished Cubical Cross. The Temple is to be arranged as in the Opening of the 2=9 Grade. Upon the Altar should be the Tarot trump of THE UNI-VERSE. A comfortable place to sit and meditate should be arranged west of the Altar. Enter the Temple with the Sign of Theoricus.

> After a period of relaxation has passed, go to the Northeast and say, "HEKAS, HEKAS, ESTE BEBELOI! Far from this sacred place be the profane!"

> Go to the East. With the black end of the wand, perform the Lesser Banishing Ritual of the Pentagram.

> Go the West of the Altar. With the white end of the wand of Double Power, trace a large letter TAU over the Tarot card. Visualize it in blue-violet (indigo). Intone the name of the letter twice. Give the Neophyte Signs toward the card. Put the wand aside, and take the Cubical Cross in your right hand.

> With all your powers of concentration, look upon the card and comprehend it, consider all its meaning and symbolism. Give the Sign of the Theoricus. At this point you may sit comfortably if you wish, but maintain a disassociation from the surrounding room. Behind the darkness of your closed eyelids, you begin to formulate the astral Temple of the Sephirah Malkuth, as the journey begins:

From the complete blackness, a dim light appears which permits you to take in your surroundings. You are in the midst of a great Temple with ten sides. The floor is divided into black and white tiles. The walls are built from large earthen bricks. Great oak columns support the ceiling which is pure rock crystal. In the southern side of the Temple is a great roaring hearth, whose fire warms the otherwise chill air within the Temple. Behind you in the West is a great fountain of sculpted marble in the shape of an eagle with a fish in its claws. . . water spouts from the mouth of both creatures. In the north part of the

Temple are two enormous stones used for grinding wheat. A black ox is harnessed to the ancient milling device, slowly turning it as it crushes the hulls of the grain. At the East of the Temple is a large brazier of burning incense. The scent of Dittany of Crete fills the Air. At the center of the Temple stands a black Altar carved from solid oak. It is covered by a cloth divided into the four colors of Malkuth: citrine, russet, olive, and black. The top of the Altar is white, and upon it is a bright burning flame.

Drawing nearer to the light, you intone the Divine name of this Temple, ADONAI HA ARETZ. The flame burns brightly as you do so. Next intone the name of the Archangel who governs the Forces of this sphere, SANDALPHON. Then vibrate the name of the angelic order who operate in Malkuth, the ASHIM, the Souls of Fire. Glowing embers dance around the central altar flame. Finally, you vibrate the name of the Temple itself, MALKUTH.

Within the swirling clouds of incense, a figure appears in the east. Appearing as a tall feminine form in robes of citrine, olive, russet and black is the Archangel, Sandalphon with dark hair and compassionate brown eyes. Instinctively, you give the sign of the Enterer. Sandalphon answers with the Sign of Silence. She speaks.

"You have entered the Immeasurable Region. This place is called THRAA, The Gate. It is the Gate of Justice, The Gate of Life and the Gate of Death. The Gate of Tears, and the Gate of Prayer. It is the Gate of the Garden of Eden and the Gate of the Daughter of the Mighty Ones. By what Sign have you entered herein?"

You answer by giving the Zelator Sign. She asks why you have come to this place. You hold up the Cubical Cross.

You face the Archangel across the light of the Altar, as you prepare for your journey into the 32nd Path. Finally, Sandalphon turns toward the east where is a great wooden door which had previously been obscured by the smoke from the incense. The Tarot card of The Universe hangs like a veil in front of it. Sandalphon traces a cross in the air with her hand and the veil parts. A large metal Tau is now clearly seen on the heavy oak door. The Archangel moves aside after showing the way. It is up to you to open the door. Undaunted, you approach it and give the Sign of the Theoricus. Holding out the Cubical Cross, you trace with it a large letter Tau. The door slowly opens.

Beyond the door, you enter a lush meadow ablaze with flowers. To the North are snow-capped mountains and cool running streams. To the South is a low-lying desert. Before you, in the East, the dawning sun is breaking over the low rolling hills. This is the path you have chosen. Sandalphon leads the way.

Time and space seen distorted as they often do on astral journeys. You pass by many fields, farms, and villages, covering vast distances in what seems like a very short interval. The breeze is cool against your skin, and a hint of storax is in the air.

The path you are on leads into the hill country which has less trees than did the grassy meadowland before it. The clay beneath your feet has given way to sandy soil. The air is warmer and there is no breeze here. The trail leads straight into a hillside where there is a cavern leading into the earth. On either side of the jagged stone opening is a column cut from solid rock. The base of each pillar is carved into the shape of a lotus flower, while the capital is sculpted into the form of a pomegranate. Before each column stands a gigantic muscular figure with the head of a beast. Their human bodies are covered by tunics, but the black fur and pointed features of jackals stick out beneath their nemysses. The figure on the left holds a large sword, while the figure on the right holds a staff entwined with serpents in one hand, and a red lantern in the other.

Sandalphon tells you to continue onward. This is as far as she will take you. As you approach the Anubian guards, they lunge forward with a growl, crossing their implements to block your advance. "Whence comest Thou?" they demand to know.

You respond by giving the Sign of the Zelator and saying, "I have entered the Immeasurable Region. I have passed through the Gate of Life and the Gate of Death. I seek to journey upon the path of Tau which leadeth between the Pillars from the Kingdom to the Foundation."

"In what Signs and Symbols do ye come?" they ask.

You answer by standing in the Sign of the Theoricus. "In the Divine name of SHADDAI EL CHAI; in the word MEM HEH and in this symbol of the Solid Greek Cubical Cross, which contains the Divine Number, twenty-two."

The twin guards step back. Anubis of the East with lantern and staff, turns to enter the cave. You give the Signs of the Neophyte and follow him in.

Just inside the entrance is a small antechamber with a black and white tiled floor. Four large winged statues stare at you without emotion. All have human bodies, but with different heads. One has the head of lion. Another has the head of an eagle. There is also a bull, and finally the winged form of a man. You pass by these silent sentinels holding the Cross high above you.

The light from outside of the cave soon fades as you descend deeper and deeper into the cave. Anubis leads silently on as the darkness closes in. The floor of the cave is rough, and you must feel the ground carefully with your feet to keep from stumbling. The ceiling presses in and you are forced to crouch at times. The path twists from one side to the other. At times you feel like you are climbing toward the surface again, only to follow your guide on another quick descent. Your sense of direction is gone—you quicken your pace to catch up to Anubis so that you won't get hopelessly lost. The light from his lantern makes strange and sinister shadows appear on the cavern walls. Voices from your past come to taunt you on this journey: school children calling you names, adults reprimanding you, peers telling you of your limitations. All the voices try to dissuade you from going deeper into the cave. "Go Back!" they warn. "You can't make it!" "It's too dangerous!" "You're too weak!" You know that the voices are merely echoes ... ghosts ... archetypes from your own mind that are uneasy at the prospect of being found out. You ignore them and press onward.

The dark journey through the twisted rock seems to take forever.

Finally, a dim light ahead is a welcome sight. Your guide leads you into a large chamber where the smell of burning oil from torches fills the room. The walls and floor are plain and seem to have been cut completely out of solid rock with simple tools. From a great dark hole in one wall of the room, a slow-moving stream of water fills a gutter carved out of the floor and flows to the opposite wall. There it flows under a huge stone door. A small number of beings are in the room with you. Apes with jeweled collars hold the ropes that are attached to the two sides of the great door. Many celestial beings with both human and animal heads can be seen bearing all kinds of food, incense, weapons, staffs, jewels, jars of perfume and more. There are also a few men and women in all manner of Egyptian dress ... some in fine silken clothes ... others in simple tunics. Everyone in the room appears to be waiting for something.

"This is the ARRIT," Anubis tells you,"the ante-chamber of the TAUT ... the Underworld. This is where I guide the souls of the dead. This too, is where the dead Sun-god RA enters the Underworld from the west ... for he is a dead god when the darkness of Night rules the sky. This is also AMENET, the Hidden Place. All assembled here wait for the coming of Ra. The souls of the dead hope to be permitted to enter the Sektet Boat of Ra . . . to travel in safety through the terrors of the Tuat . . . and finally be reborn with him at the Dawning Light of the Eastern sky. Behold, it is time!"

The anticipation of the assembly grows and is rewarded by the sight of two long lines of priests pulling heavy ropes. Finally the long prow of a boat enters the chamber from the dark hole in the wall. The boat, made from reeds, is light and slender. Thoth, the Ibis-headed God of Wisdom, stands at the bow to guide the vessel. At the center of the craft is a shrine where the Sun-god sits enthroned. He has the body of a man with the tawny head and piercing eyes of a hawk. A large solar disc crowns his nemyss, and he holds an ankh in one hand and a phoenix-headed staff in the other. The scarab, Khepera, surmounts the crown of the figure like a halo. But the god is old and has the pallor of death about him.

The god Horus stands at the rear of ship as an escort. At this marvelous sight, a roar of praise erupts from those assembled in the chamber.

At the center of the room, the boat stops and is boarded by the souls who have stood waiting for it. Anubis leads you to the craft. "You must continue your journey under the protection of Ra," he tells you. "I must return to give guidance to the dead. Have courage; the Tuat is filled with sights both wondrous and terrible. Fear nothing and your strength shall see you through."

From the boat, a hand is offered. You take it and climb aboard, giving a final farewell to Anubis, who is already on his way back to the surface—the light from his lamp bobs through the cavern tunnel. Finding a seat with the other passengers, you settle in for the ride. The apes you saw earlier pull on the ropes which open the great stone doors leading to the Tuat. Slowly the Sektet boat moves forward and enters the underworld.

The place called the Tuat is so enormous that it is difficult to tell whether it is enclosed under the earth or if it exists at some point in space beyond the earth. The stream has widened into a river in the middle of a valley, on either side of which is a mountain range. It is a noisy place inhabited by many creatures.

Monstrous beasts rummage about in the muddy shores. The souls of the dead are everywhere; milling around along the river bank, swimming alongside the boat. A few are permitted to climb on board, but others are turned away, because each soul must spend a certain amount of time in the underworld before re-entering the land of the Living.

The ship continues to travel through the twelve divisions of the Tuat, known as the twelve hours of the Night. Twin Pylons with serpent guardians mark each division. So many incredible sights appear that you can only sit and watch as Gods battle hostile spirits, evil serpents and crocodiles. There are great pits of fire that appear in the middle of the river. Hostile spirits harangue the dead who walk along the shore. There are also benevolent and helpful creatures whose bodies are formed from many different animals. At times it seems like many lesser gods appear from nowhere to pull the ship forward with serpents instead of ropes. Sacred animals such as bulls, winged cobras and baboons join in the processions through the Underworld. And at one point, the great goddess Isis appears on the boat to utter magickal words which repel the enemies of Ra.

At the sixth division of the Tuat, the Sektet boat stops at a great stone shrine topped with spear-heads. Inside, the god Osiris is seated upon the summit of a flight of nine steps. He wears a double crown and holds in one hand a scepter and in the other an ankh, the symbol of Life. Before him is a pair of scales and a company of lesser gods. The Sektet boat pauses in homage to the God who reigns over the Underworld—Osiris, he who judges the dead, the Lord of Life, triumphant over Death.

After leaving the shrine, the journey continues as before, until eventually, the Sektet boat reaches the eleventh division of the Tuat . . . and the eleventh hour of the night. At this point, great pits of fire—each attended by a goddess—appear ahead of the boat, and the battle between gods and demons becomes decidedly more intense. The voices from your past which had earlier harassed you in the cave return to bother you now at this crucial moment. But you have already won over them in the knowledge that they are merely programmed archetypes within your own psyche, which do not wish to lose their position of prominence within your mind. In this last-ditch effort to force you to feel weak, inane, and guilty, the voices are desperate in the attempt to make you fail to complete this voyage.

The god Horus takes command of the vessel and orders all the demons and enemies of Ra to be consumed in the blazing fires. The attendant goddesses see that it is done. At this point, you also will your own personal demons into the purging flames. The ghostly voices are silenced. A sense of great relief and calm overtakes you, as the Sektet boat glides into the Twelfth Hour of the Night.

Twelve gods, all loyal servants of Ra, now pull the ship, which is no longer sailing on the river, but through the belly of a sacred serpent. In this surprisingly tranquil division of the Tuat, you hear in a whisper, the serpent's name, "Ka-en-Ankh-neteru, the Life of the Gods." The circle of the Tuat is near its end, but there is utter darkness in the bowels of this serpent. There is also a feeling of nervous excitement among the souls aboard the vessel. The horrors of the Tuat are in the past now, and a great transformation is about to take place.

As the ship enters the throat of the serpent, the enormous jaws begin to open. Beyond them is the indigo of the night sky, speckled with stars. As the boat slides off the tongue of the animal, the stars and planets themselves erupt into a song of praise for the reborn Sun god. Twelve goddesses pull the ship into the sky. The sektet boat of the night is no more. It is now the Matet boat of Day sailing into the eastern part of the sky. Ra himself has transformed before your eyes; no longer pale and old, the god glows with the life of youth. His Solar disc lights up the countryside far below in all directions.

Of the fortunate souls who have traversed the terrors of the Tuat in Ra's ship, some are rewarded with a new birth upon the earth, while others remain in the sky journeying at will through the universe. You, too, feel reborn and strengthened with the dawning of the sun upon the skies over the earth. The grass is wet and glistening with morning dew. Humans and animals below are just beginning to stir from their sleep and go about their daily activities. You realize that your journey upon the path of Tau is nearing its end, but for the Sun god this journey is a nightly occurrence. Silently, you thank the god for helping you travel this path. The warmth of the sun lulls you into a restful meditation.

When you open your eyes again, you see that an entire day has passed while you meditated. The last rays of light are fading as Ra's boat enters the western sky. Under the earth, the ship again enters the dark Arrit, the antechamber to the Tuat. This is the end of your journey through the underworld. You realize that you will traverse this path again, perhaps many times. However, you know that the journey will be easier each time. As the boat glides into the chamber, you see the familiar form of Anubis, who reaches out his hand to help you down from the vessel. With a final prayer of thanks to Ra, you turn and follow the jackal-headed god through the winding tunnel to the cave entrance. Once you are outside the cave, Anubis joins his twin and stands guard at the threshold. You salute them both with the Sign of the Theoricus.

Sandalphon is waiting on the path which leads to Malkuth. Following her, you return to the Tenth Sephirah. The angel seals the great wooden door behind you after entering the Temple. The flame upon the Altar is a welcome sight after such an arduous adventure. The great fireplace, fountain and oaken walls are very familiar and comforting. Standing before the Altar, you partake of the sacred flame a few moments before leaving the Temple. Saying goodbye to Sandalphon, you salute with the Projection Sign. She answers with the Sign of Silence.

Bring your astral self back into your body and make yourself slowly aware of the physical room around you. Do not get up too quickly.

Perform the LBRP with the black end of the wand.

Say, "I now declare this Temple duly closed." Exit with the Sign of the Theoricus.

SO MOTE IT BE

The Caduceus Badge

Use and Symbolism

The Caduceus Admission Badge grants the candidate entry into the Temple of Yesod. It is an explicit representation of the same energies found hidden in the wand and lamen of the Kerux. On the front of the Badge, the Caduceus is shown against the glyph of the Tree of Life. On the reverse side, the staff is displayed with the Three Mother letters of the Hebrew alphabet. This symbolism has been thoroughly discussed in chapter 1. (See the Wand of the Kerux.) The Caduceus is also a symbol of precise symmetry. The winged sphere and intertwined serpents also suggest the tri-unity of heraldry (a shield between two supporters), always expressive of the idea of active equilibrium, of opposing forces balancing one another in such a way as to create a higher, static form. It is this equilibriating and reconciling aspect of the Caduceus which allies it to the element of Air.

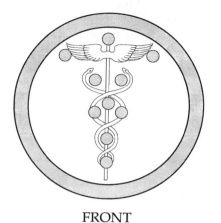
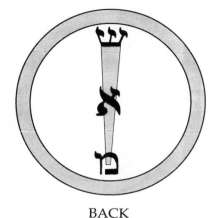

FRONT   BACK

The Caduceus Badge

If the Badge is painted primarily yellow, it emphasizes the element of Air, to which the grade of 2=9 is attributed. If the Badge is painted primarily violet, it underscores the Sephirah of Yesod, which is also assigned to the Theoricus grade.

Materials Needed
    A 5" x 5" piece of plywood that is 1/4" thick
    Wood putty
    Gesso
    Acrylic paints: yellow, violet, red, orange, green, blue,
        blue-violet, white, black, neutral grey
    Clear lacquer finish

Tools Needed
    Electric jigsaw or coping saw
    Compass, pencil and straight edge
    File or rasp
    Artist's brushes—fine and medium sizes
    Sandpaper—medium and fine

Construction
    (Note: Just as with the Officer's lamens in chapter 1, it may be possible to purchase pre-cut wooden disks at a craft store or hobby shop, so long as they are of comparable size and thickness.)

  1) Using the compass, draw a 4" circle on the piece of wood. Cut out the circle with the saw.

2) If the circle of wood has jagged edges, file them smooth. Any gaps in the wood can be filled in with wood putty. Sand the wood until it is smooth.

3) Paint entirely with gesso. Let dry. Sand. Apply another coat if needed.

Finishing Steps

4) The Badge may be painted in one of three ways:
   a) White with black diagrams
   b) Primarily yellow with violet diagrams
   c) Primarily violet with yellow diagrams

5) When the ground color is dry on both sides of the badge, the two different forms of the Caduceus may be drawn on it (one on either side). Both staffs should be primarily painted in the corresponding "flash" color of the "ground" color. If the base color of the badge is yellow, the Caduceus will be violet (or vice-versa).

6) On the drawing of the Caduceus encompassing the Tree of Life, the Sephiroth should be painted in their usual Queen Scale colors. (A thin white line should be painted around the spheres of Tiphareth and Yesod.)

7) On the reverse side of the Badge, the Hebrew letters should be painted as follows: SHIN-red, ALEPH-yellow, MEM-Blue. After all paint has dried, apply a sealant for protection.

Ritual for Use

An Invocation of the Element of Air and a Meditation on the Caduceus Badge for the Grade of Theoricus

For this ritual the Theoricus will need a black Outer Order robe, black and white striped nemyss, and the Outer Wand of Double Power (described in chapter 6). A yellow candle, a rose, and the finished Caduceus Badge should be placed on the Altar. The Temple is to be arranged in accordance with the Theoricus Hall (as in the Second part of the initiation ceremony). Enter the Temple with the Sign of Theoricus.

Relax for a few moments and perform the Four-fold Breath.

Go to the Northeast and say, "HEKAS, HEKAS, ESTE BEBELOI!"

With the black end of the wand, perform the Lesser Banishing Ritual of the Pentagram.

Say the following invocation: "Such a Fire existeth, extending through the rushings of Air. Or even a Fire formless, whence cometh the Image of a Voice. Or even a flashing Light, abounding, revolving, whirling forth, crying aloud."

Remain in the east. With the white end of the wand, trace the Lesser Invoking Pentagram. Thrust the wand through the center of the figure and vibrate, "YOD HEH VAV HEH!"

Say, "In the Divine Name SHADDAI EL CHAI, I open this Temple in the element of Air. May the Archangel RAPHAEL look with favor upon this ceremony! May the angel CHASSAN and the ruler ARIEL be also in attendance! I have gained admission to this Temple through the Badge of the Caduceus of Hermes. I am one who has received the Mystic Title of *Poraios De Rejectis* and the symbol of RUACH. I have been brought from among the Rejected. As a Lord/Lady of the 32nd Path, I invoke the powers of Air to bear witness to my spiritual endeavor. Grant me the knowledge of the element of Air and the Astral Realm, so that I may obtain Greater Understanding of Hidden Things and thereby advance in the Great Work."

Circumambulate the Temple three times, saluting with the Neophyte Signs when passing the East.

Go to the West and face east. Give the Adoration to the Lord of the Universe:

"Holy art Thou, Lord of the Universe!"
"Holy art Thou, Whom Nature hath not formed!"
"Holy art Thou, the Vast and the Mighty One!"
"Lord of the Light, and of the Darkness!"

Go to the East and give the Theoricus Sign.

Recite the Prayer of the Sylphs:

"Spirit of Life! Spirit of Wisdom! Whose breath giveth forth and withdraweth the form of all things:

Thou, before Whom the life of beings is but a shadow which changeth, and a vapor which passeth:

Thou, who breathest forth Thy Breath, and endless space is peopled:

Thou, drawest in Thy Breath, and all that cometh from Thee, returneth unto Thee! Ceaseless Motion, in Eternal stability, be Thou eternally blessed! We praise Thee and we bless Thee in the Changeless Empire of Created Light, of Shades, of Reflections, and of Images.

And we aspire without cessation unto Thy Immutable and Imperishable Brilliance. Let the Ray of Thy Intelligence and the warmth of Thy Love penetrate even unto us!

Then that which is volatile shall be fixed; the Shadow shall be a Body; the Spirit of Air shall be a soul; the Dream shall be a Thought. And no more shall we be swept away by the Tempest, but we shall hold the bridles of the Winged Steeds of Dawn. And we shall direct the course of the Evening Breeze to fly before Thee!

O Spirit of Spirits! O Eternal Soul of Souls! O Imperishable Breath of Life! O Creative Sigh! O Mouth which breathest forth and withdrawest the life of all beings, in the flux and reflux of Thine Eternal Word, which is the Divine Ocean of Movement and of Truth!"

Give the Theoricus Sign. Go to the west of the Altar. With the white end of the wand, trace the Lesser Invoking Pentagram over the rose. Place the wand aside.

Inhale the fragrance of the rose.

As you partake of the rose, meditate on the Caduceus Badge upon the Altar:

Contemplate the Tree of Life as it applies to the Caduceus. Visualize the Flaming Sword (acting under the forces of the Hidden Splendors) cutting through the three veils of negativity—forming as it does so, the ten Sephiroth. Imagine Kether lighting up brilliantly as the blade of the sword touches it. Then visualize the weapon creating the spheres of Chokmah and Binah. These emanations become two great wings which surround and support the topmost point of Kether. This is the Supernal Triad symbolized by the winged globe—an emblem of the aether or Heaven. Imagine the tip of the blade as it descends past the Supernals to touch the spheres of Chesed and Geburah, which become the heads of two serpents. The vipers turn inward and face one another with a stance of aggression. The two animals are rival powers, yet they are also mates. The combined powers of the Tree of Life hold the serpents in check, keeping them in a state of balance, for if either one of the animals were allowed free rein, the Tree would be poisoned and withered by the serpent's venom. The Flaming Sword continues its path downward, creating the rest of the Sephiroth: Tiphareth, Netzach, Hod, Yesod and Malkuth. These spheres form the bodies of the vipers, coiling about the staff of Hermes in a undulating sexual dance. This is not unlike the dance of the Kundalini; the manipulation of sexual energy resulting in a swift charge of energy rising up the central Pillar of Equilibrium. See the diagram as the Dance of Life: the shaft of the Eternal Triad implanting itself into manifestation—the opposing serpents rising in ecstasy to bring down the Divine Energy. It is the synthesis of the flux and reflux currents of Life and Light.

After meditating upon these images, turn the Badge over and contemplate the reverse side.

Visualize a vast field of white. Within this field, picture the Hebrew letter, Shin, in flaming red. This is the celestial Fire of the Heavens, whose burning embers were the first sparks of Life. Imagine a Triangle of Fire, apex upwards superimposed over the letter.

Below the Shin, imagine the letter, Mem, in brilliant blue, representing the Waters of Creation. It is the nurturing womb and the endless Sea where the first creatures of Earth were born. In your mind's eye, see a Water Triangle, apex downwards, form around the letter.

Between these two letters, a third appears; the letter, Aleph (Air), in bright yellow mediating between the other two. Visualize for a moment how the Hebrew letters actually resembling their symbolic counterparts on the Caduceus. The letter, Shin, easily transforms into the winged sphere at the top of the staff. The sinuous letter, Aleph, swiftly becomes the top half of the weaving serpents. The final letter, Mem, forms the two tails of the animals which enclose the sphere of Malkuth.

The reconciling Air of Aleph mediates between the opposing elements of Fire and Water, not by separating them, but by uniting them. Visualize the Fire and Water Triangles pulling together like magnets. Picture them sliding and interlocking over one another at the position of Aleph. The Reconciling Air provides the fulcrum upon which the opposing elements of Fire and Water can balance. This principle is very similar to that of the mating serpents from the previous side.

———— ✳ ————

Take as much time as you need for the meditation.

Perform the Reverse Circumambulation.

Go to the East and say, "I now release any Spirits that may have been imprisoned by this ceremony. Depart in peace to your abodes and habitations. Go with the blessings of SHADDAI EL CHAI!"

Perform the LBRP with the black end of the Wand.

Say, "I now declare this Temple duly closed." Exit with the Sign of Theoricus.

THE RITE IS ENDED

The Tetrahedron

Use and Symbolism

The Solid Triangle, Tetrahedron or Pyramid of Flame is the Admission Badge for the 31st Path of Shin in the 3=8 grade of Practicus. It is an appropriate hieroglyph of Fire, representing Simple Fire of Nature and the Latent or Hidden Fire. It is formed of four triangles, three visible and one concealed, which yet is the synthesis of the rest. The three visible triangles represent Solar Fire, Volcanic Fire, and Astral Fire, while the fourth and basal triangle represents latent heat-AUD. Active Fire is AUB, passive Fire is AUR, while the equilibrated name of Fire is ASCH.

The Sepher Yetzirah calls the 31st Path (from Malkuth to Hod) the Perpetual Intelligence; because it regulates the motions of the Sun and Moon in their proper order, each in an orbit convenient for it. For the Initiate traveling this Path, the key is "perpetual." This is the persistent regulation of the progress of the initiate's Personality toward the cosmic consciousness. The angelic powers, called forth by the student journeying upon the Tree, determine what aspects of the Initiate are unsuitable for his/her spiritual growth. These undesirable qualities are slowly burned away by the purging Fire of Shin. This permits the "Sun and Moon" of the Initiate (i.e. the positive and negative sides of the student) to work "each in their proper order."

In addition to its use in the 3=8 grade, the Tetrahedron may be used by the Practicus in a ritual/meditation on the 31st Path.

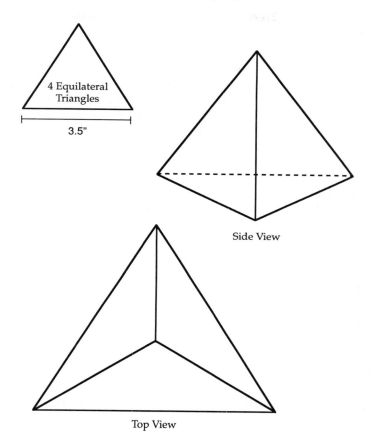

The Tetrahedron

Materials Needed

One 12" x 6" piece of heavy cardboard (such as matte board or poster board) that is approx. 1/8" thick.

White glue

Gesso

Acrylic paint: red

Clear lacquer finish

Tools Needed

Craft knife or matte-cutter

Medium artist's brush

Construction

1) Draw four equilateral triangles on the cardboard that are 3-1/2" long on each side.

2) Using the matte cutter or craft knife and straight edge, cut all the triangles out so that all of them have beveled edges. This means that you should adjust your cutting tool so that it slants and cuts the cardboard at an angle. The beveled edges should all slant toward the inside of each triangle, so that when you fit all the triangles together, the outside edges will fit precisely leaving a barely noticeable seam.

3) Glue all four triangles together so that they fit perfectly together into a four-side pyramid (including the bottom.) (Note: you may have to trim some of the triangles for this to happen.) Allow glue to dry thoroughly. Cover the pyramid entirely with gesso. Let dry. Add a second coat if needed.

4) The Tetrahedron can be painted in one of two ways:
   a) entirely white
   b) entirely red

5) When paint has dried, spray or brush on a coat of sealant to protect the paint.

Ritual for Use

A Journey on the 31st Path of Shin

For this ritual the Practicus will need his Outer Order Robe and nemyss, the Outer Wand of Double Power, and the finished Tetrahedron. The Temple is to be arranged as in the Opening of the 3=8 grade. Upon the Altar should be the Tarot Trump of JUDGEMENT. A comfortable place to sit and meditate should be arranged west of the Pillars. Enter with the Sign of the Practicus.

After a period of relaxation has passed, go to the Northeast and say, "HEKAS, HEKAS, ESTE BEBELOI! Far from this sacred place be the profane!"

Go to the East. With the black end of the wand, perform the Lesser Banishing Ritual of the Pentagram.

Go the West of the Altar. With the white end of the Wand of Double Power, trace a large letter SHIN over the Tarot card. Visualize it in Red. Intone the name of the letter thrice. Give the Neophyte Signs toward the card. Put the wand aside, and take the Tetrahedron in your right hand.

With all your powers of concentration, look upon the card and comprehend it, consider all its meaning and symbolism. Give the Sign of the Practicus. At this point you may sit comfortably if you wish, but maintain a disassociation from the surrounding room. Behind the darkness of your closed eyelids, you begin to formulate the astral Temple of the Sephirah Malkuth, as the journey begins:

Astrally, you give the Sign of the Zelator. Once again the ten-sided Temple of Malkuth formulates around you with its black-and-white tiled floor and rough-hewn oak walls. The sacred flame burns brightly upon the central Altar. The brazier of incense, fireplace, fountain, and mill stones are a familiar sight to you now.

You intone the Divine name of this Temple, ADONAI HA ARETZ, and call upon its Archangel, SANDALPHON, and the choir of angels, the ASHIM. Finally you vibrate the name of the Temple, MALKUTH.

From the clouds of incense in the East, Sandalphon appears. You salute her with the Sign of the Enterer, and she answers with the Sign of Silence. She speaks: "You have entered the Kingdom of Malkah, the Queen. What symbol do you bring to define what you seek?" You hold out the Pyramid of Flame.

Sandalphon leads you to a door in the Northeast part of the Temple. Before the door is a veil made from the Tarot trump of JUDGEMENT. The Archangel traces a Fire Triangle and the veil parts and vanishes. The door leading to the 31st Path is carved from pure fire opal and painted upon it is the Hebrew letter, Shin. Giving the Sign of Practicus, you then hold out the Solid Triangle and trace with it the letter, Shin. The door opens outward.

You and your guide step out onto the craggy side of a cliff. You can just make out the mountain tops which seem to rise above a valley below, whose subtleties are hidden to your view. Sandalphon leads you on a narrow descending path which seems more suited to the hooves of a mountain goat than to your feet.

By the time you reach the valley floor, it is mid-afternoon. The climate is moderate, but chill. Ahead, you hear a commotion—the sounds of people shouting and the bellowing of some great beast. This distraction causes you to step on a stinging nettle, but you ignore the pain. Sandalphon gestures for you to continue on the path without her.

Just over a hill, you discover the source of the disturbance. A primitive looking group of men have cornered a mammoth and driven it over the edge of a small ravine. The huge animal was carefully trapped by the hunters who used torches and dug-out pits of fire to maneuver the beast in the direction they wanted it to go . . . toward the ravine. Now, with the huge animal trapped, they kill it with heavy spears and rocks. When the mammoth is dead, the hunters give great shouts of joy which bring even more people onto the scene of the drama.

A woman and small boy who have come to help cut up the meat with stone knives notice you standing there. Puzzled, they approach. When they see the Pyramid of Flame in your hand, they smile and point to markings tattooed on the palms of their hands, which is that of a red triangle. This is the mark of the Tribe. They are the Clan of Fire.

With great efficiency, the animal is skinned, butchered, and hauled away to a nearby village. You follow, and appear to be accepted by these people and their strange and primitive ways. The main shelter of the encampment is an enormous cave, but a few simple lodges, made from mammoth bone and hide stand just a short distance from the cave entrance. From one of these shelters, a wise old medicine woman brings a bag of ointments and herbs to tend the wounds of some of the hunters. The entire village, women and children, young and old, help with the storing of meat and the curing of strips of hide. Chunks of meat are skewered to cook over several small fires around the camp. Everyone is hungry from all the work. Food including meat, flat bread, fruit and a spicy drink is passed around to all, including you. In the center of the village, and in front of the cavern entrance, burns a great bonfire. After they have eaten, the hunters are lead in, in a ceremony by an old shaman dressed in mammoth wool and a helmet carved from bone. They perform a sacred dance reenacting the hunt to thank the spirit of the mammoth for giving its life to feed the Clan. The celebration continues well into the evening. There is laughter around the fire, as well as talk of brave deeds, spirits, and gossip. The fire is the life of the village . . . it brings food, warmth, security, and protection to the tribe. It also brings them together as a human community, setting them apart from the animals in the valley.

Finally the festivity winds down and you feel the urge to press on with your journey. As you bid goodbye, some of the clan members give you small sacred objects: a lion carved from stone, a spearhead, and the tooth of a bear. You thank them and continue on the 31st Path.

The setting sun is hanging low in the sky behind you as you continue northeast of the valley. The land opens out into a wide sandy plateau with stunted trees and desert scrub. Off in the distance, you see the outline of a great pyramid against the evening sky. Two smaller pyramids loom on either side of the main one. Wanting to reach the structure before dark, you quicken your pace.

As you approach the great pyramid, its beauty becomes evident. Constructed from enormous red stones, many hieroglyphs and relief sculptures are carved into its surface. At the main entrance into the pyramid are two enormous goddesses enthroned before a pair of columns whose capitals end in carved lotus flowers. Both goddesses are lion-headed and bear a lotus staff in one hand and an ankh in the other. The goddess on the left wears a green tunic, while her twin is dressed in red. An uraeus sits atop the nemysses of both, surmounted by the Solar disc. As you draw near, the figures stand and bar your path with their staffs. They speak: "Thou canst not enter the Pyramid of Flame unless thou canst tell us our names."

"Thou art the sister goddesses of the West and East." You direct your answer to the figure in red. "Thou art Sekhet, lady of flame, beloved of Ptah. Thou art the fierce and scorching aspect of Fire, destroyer of the enemies of Ra, who consumes the wicked and the unbalanced." You turn toward the form in green. "Thou art the goddess Bast, the eye of Ra, whose name means "Fire." Thou art the power of the heat of the Sun as it warms the earth and causes the growth of plants and the bearing of seeds."

"In what Signs and Symbols do ye come?" they whisper.

Standing in the Sign of the Practicus you state, "In the Divine Name of ELOHIM TZABAOTH; in the name ELOAH, and in this symbol of the Pyramid of Flame."

The figures step back. The goddess Bast traces the Sigil of the Leo before you with her lotus staff. "In the Sign of the Lion," she says, "Thou art purified."

The goddess Sekhet traces the letter Shin before you. "In the letter of Initiation and of Judgement, Thou art consecrated. Pass Thou on."

Entering the pyramid, you give the Neophyte Signs. You step into a Great Hall with a black-and-white tiled floor. Two great Pillars, one black and one white, resembling the feet of two goddesses dominate the Hall. You recognize this chamber as the Hall of Dual Manifestation, the place of the Weighing of the Soul. You had to pass through its physical representation on earth when you were initiated as a Neophyte. Here you see it in its astral and original form. The scales of the goddess Maat are at the center of the Temple—their balance is tested and watched over by the jackal-headed Anubis. Thoth, the Ibis-headed god of wisdom, acts as a scribe, ready with stylus and clay tablet to record the judgement. A fierce-looking beast crouches menacingly behind Thoth—part hippopotamus, part leopard, and part crocodile. Forty-two lesser gods sit in silence on all sides of the room.

A goddess with a sistrum acts as your guide—the gentle sound of her implement is soothing. With the strength of conviction, you step forward and face the assembly of gods. You place the Tetrahedron upon the scales as a symbol of your heart and your deepest spiritual aspirations. The goddess Maat, governess of truth, places her feather in the scale also, weighing it against the purity of your heart. Anubis questions you with the determination of a prosecuting attorney. He asks you to describe all the symbols of the hall in detail. Luckily you are familiar with these symbols from your studies, and you satisfactorily answer all questions. The forty-two lesser gods each question you in turn:

"Hast thou given due thought to the body inhabited by thee?"

"Hast thou spoken unjustly in anger?"

"Hast thou been undiligent in work?"

"Hast Thou lived in the Light?"

"Hast Thou faced the mirror of Self?"

Their questions are hard, but you answer all of them truthfully to the best of your ability. At the end of their questioning, you are tired, but relieved, as if the negative confession had unburdened your soul. Thoth beckons you forward and asks one final question. "Who is He whose Pylons are of flame, whose walls of Living Uraei, and the flames of whose House are streams of Water?"

"Osiris!" you reply.

The God records your answer approvingly. "Pass on, thou knowest it," is his answer. The Hawk-headed god Horus, who has witnessed all of the proceedings, takes your hand in his, and leads you past the Devouring Beast, to a shrine in the Eastern part of the hall. He instructs you to kneel before an Altar in front of the shrine. There upon the Dais the God Osiris sits enthroned. He wears the tall white crown of the south flanked by two plumes. From his chin hangs the royal beard of authority and judgement, and he holds the Scourge of Severity, the Crook of Mercy and the Phoenix Wand. The Children of Horus are at his feet and the Goddesses of the two Pillars, Isis and Nephthys, stand behind him.

Upon the Altar before the god, you place the bear's tooth and the spearhead from the clan as an offering to the god of Judgment. He reaches out and touches the crown of your head with the Phoenix wand. The god speaks: "Thy meat shall be from the Infinite, and Thy drink from the Infinite. Thou art able to go forth to the initiatory feasts on earth, for thou hast overcome."

A lion-headed goddess, Tharpesh, bids you to rise and follow her. She leads you to a chamber where a statue of Ptah, the Creator God, stands with an iron knife in one hand and a hammer in the other. Ptah, the greatest of the old gods, is known as the architect of the Universe; patron of craftsmen, metalsmiths, and workmen. Next to the statue is a triangular portal whose edges are ringed with flames. The goddess gestures for you to enter the portal. Giving the Sign of the Practicus, you do so.

The heat of the flames are all around you. You no longer seem to be walking forward. Instead you are rising upward, like smoke. Sweating from the hot blast of air, your black robe is incinerated, but you feel no pain as this baptism of Fire continues. There is no fear, only the desire to rise like a phoenix into a new state of being through the initiating power of Fire. The sounds of a trumpet are heard somewhere above you.

Suddenly the roaring flames propel you upward though a square opening in the rocks above. There is no time to react. Naked, you rise to find yourself standing leg-high in a black stone tomb which juts out of the bare earth. Before you is a cool, placid lake covered by a layer of mist and steam. Above the mist is a truly glorious vision, the Archangel of Fire, Michael, surrounded by a fireball of red, orange, and green flames. His wings are sheer and translucent; formed from white-hot vapors at the center of the flame. Threads of Fire weave up and down his bare skin, disturbing not a single hair. The golden disc of Sol sits atop his dark-haired crown; and he blows a long summoning note upon a trumpet from which hangs a banner of white with a central red cross. Behind the figure is a rainbow formed from living creatures. The Seraphim, fiery serpents coruscate in a blazing stream within the bow of promise. The entire horizon beyond this vision is ignited with burning Yods. At the point where the flames meet the waters of the lake, great clouds of steam are formed.

As if this sight were not enough, you notice a movement to your left. A swarthy masculine figure rises from the dark earth in a halo of Fire. This is Samael—ruler of volcanic Fire—erupting from the belly of the earth. To your right, a female form breaks forth from the waters. She is Anael, ruler of the Astral Light. Her etheric twin rises at her side. You realize that you are in the presence of the three living powers of Fire: Solar, Volcanic and Astral . . . the three tongues of flame. Within you is the Hidden Fire, waiting to be ignited by a spark. Instinctively, you raise your arms in the Sign of Theoricus and the element of the Redeemer. As you do so, three fiery Yods from the crown of Michael come together, forming a flaming letter Shin, which drifts downwards. It is absorbed into your heart center. Another letter Shin is formed which hovers over the top of your head where it turns brilliant white. A feeling of calm elation overtakes you. You truly feel that you have become a part of something which is greater than yourself. From this day forward, you will strive to become more than human, and rise from the ashes of your old self.

An Adoration escapes from your lips, "There is no part of me that is not of the Gods!"

After a moment of contemplation, you silently thank the beings of flame. Turning, you step out of the tomb and are surprised to see the smiling face of Sandalphon. She carries a velvet black robe to replace the one that you sacrificed on the Path of Fire. With tenderness, she helps you into it.

The journey back is swift. It is now morning, and the dawning sun forms a magnificent backdrop for the three pyramids in the desert. In the valley at the mountain foothills, the Clan of Fire is just starting to stir. Smoke drifts upward from many cooking pits.

The treacherous path leading up the side of the cliff is the same, but your adventure has left you as nimble as an Alpine sheep. With no exertion, you are soon at the opal door at the Temple of Malkuth. Once inside, Sandalphon seals the portal.

Standing at the Altar flame, you feel totally rejuvenated. In fact you feel so strengthened that you are quite willing to rush headlong on to the 30th Path. Sandalphon persuades you otherwise. Bidding her farewell, you salute with the Neophyte Sign. She in turn gives the answering Sign.

———— ✳ ————

At this point bring your astral body back to the physical Temple around you. Do not rush.

Perform the LBRP with the black end of the wand.

Declare the Temple duly closed. Exit with the Sign of Practicus.

SO MOTE IT BE

The Solar Greek Cross of 13 Squares

Use and Symbolism

The Solar Greek Cross is the Admission Badge to the Path of Resh in the 3=8 grade of Practicus. It is formed of 13 squares which fitly refer to the Sun's motion through the Zodiac. The Celestial Signs are further arranged in the arms of the Cross according to the Four Elements with the Sun in the center and representing that luminary as the center of the whole figure.

The Thirtieth Path of Resh is called the Collecting Intelligence, because from it the Astrologers deduce the judgement of the Stars, and of the Celestial Signs, and the perfections of their science according to the rules of their resolutions. It is therefore the reflection of the Sphere of Sun and the Path connecting Yesod with Hod, Foundation with Splendor.

This Path, which connects the sphere of Yesod to that of Hod, is described as the "Collecting Intelligence" because it governs many integral factors in the make-up of the individual personality ... specifically, the Signs of the Zodiac, which are vessels of planetary influence. A person's Sun Sign is central to both his/her present and past incarnations. The 30th Path signifies a collecting of knowledge on every level. On this Path, the "collected" parts of the student's personality are given an infusion of the Sun's intellectual qualities of warmth and Light. Here the student also begins to perceive the Higher forces which have formed his/her own personality.

In addition to its role as Admission Badge in the Initiation ceremony of the Practicus Grade, the Solar Greek Cross can be employed by the Practicus in a ritual/meditation on the 30th Path.

Materials Needed

One 5-1/4" x 5-1/4" piece of pine or basswood that is 1/2" or 3/4" thick
Wood putty
Gesso

Acrylic paints: orange, blue
Clear lacquer finish

Tools Needed
Scroll saw or jig saw
Artist's brushes
Sandpaper, medium and fine

Construction
1) Take the 5-1/4" square piece of wood and on one side, mark off (both vertically and horizontally) a series of 3/4" squares. You will then have a piece of wood that has drawn on it a total of 49 squares.

2) With a pencil, shade in the appropriate squares as shown in the diagram. Cut out the shaded squares with the saw.

3) Fill in any gaps with wood putty. Sand until smooth.

Finishing Steps
4) Cover entirely with a coat of gesso. Let dry. Sand until smooth. Apply another coat if needed.

5) The finished Cross can be painted in one of two ways:
a) White with black sigils
b) orange with blue sigils

6) Spray or brush on a coat of sealant for protection. Let dry.

Ritual for Use

A Journey on the 30th Path of Resh

For this ritual the Practicus will need his Outer Order robe and nemyss, the Outer Wand of Double Power (see Chapter 6), and the finished Solar Greek Cross. The Temple is to be arranged as in the Second Part of the 3=8 Grade. Upon the Altar should be the Tarot trump of THE SUN. A comfortable place to sit and meditate should be arranged west of the Pillars. Enter the Temple with the Sign of the Practicus.

After a period of relaxation has passed, go to the Northeast and say, "HEKAS, HEKAS, ESTE BEBELOI! Far from this sacred place be the profane!"

Go to the East. With the black end of the wand, perform the Lesser Banishing Ritual of the Pentagram.

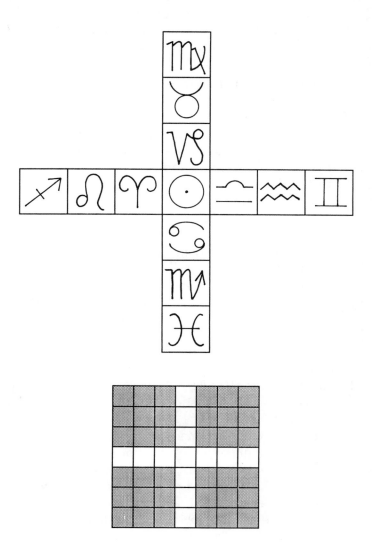

The Greek Cross of 13 Squares

Go to the west of the Altar. With the white end of the Wand of Double Power, trace a large letter RESH over the tarot card. Visualize it in orange. Intone the name of the letter thrice. Give the Neophyte Signs toward the card. Put the wand aside, and take the Greek Cross in your right hand.

With all your powers of concentration, look upon the card and comprehend it, consider all its meaning and symbolism. Give the Sign of the Practicus. At this point you may sit comfortably if you wish, but maintain a disassociation from the surrounding room. Behind the darkness of your closed eyelids, you begin to formulate the astral Temple of the Sephirah Malkuth, as the journey begins:

Astrally, you give the Sign of the Zelator. The now familiar Temple of Malkuth formulates around you. The central flame burns brightly with a renewed passion upon the central Altar.

As before you intone the names which call forth the inhabitants of this Temple, ADONAI HA ARETZ, SANDALPHON, ASHIM, and finally, MALKUTH. Sandalphon appears as in your previous journeys and you exchange the usual Signs. This time you hold up the Solar Cross for the Archangel to see. She takes you swiftly through the portal of Tau directly in the east of the Temple. Within a short time you are at the entrance to the Temple of Yesod. You enter without Sandalphon, giving the Neophyte Signs.

Nine walls form the inner chamber which is a rich violet color. The figure of an enneangle or nine-sided polygon graces the floor. In each of the nine corners of the room, a brazier of incense hangs, scenting the room with the smell of jasmine. Around the ceiling are depicted the various phases of the moon inlaid with quartz and ebony. The central Altar is surrounded by four large statues, each with four faces: that of a man, a lion, an eagle, and a bull. The Altar itself is cast in silver and covered with a velvet indigo cloth. The Temple flame burns from a silver bowl supported by three crescents.

The feel of this Temple is quite different from that of Malkuth. No sensations of security or solidity are evoked here. There is an ethereal quality to everything here. You almost feel as if your hand would pass right through the kerubic statues if you tried to touch them. There is also a sense of excitement akin to sexual awareness. This Temple is the dwelling place of the serpent power or kundalini. You can feel its power tingling certain nerves along your spine—stirred slightly by your entrance into Yesod.

With a sense of exhilaration, you vibrate the Divine name of this sphere, SHADDAI EL CHAI. You then call upon the Archangel GABRIEL for guidance, and the order of Angels known as the KERUBIM. Finally, you intone the name of the Temple itself, YESOD.

From the jasmine mists, the Archangel starts to formulate. Taking on a material form before you, Gabriel is dressed in robes of blue trimmed with orange. His features are breathtaking . . . a fine oval-shaped face framed by shoulder-length dark brown hair. His green eyes are large and sensual. The wings from his shoulders are very large and white. Somehow, you get the feeling that Gabriel could have just as easily appeared as a beautiful young girl . . . so slight and delicate is his appearance. He speaks:

"Behold around you, the Vision of the Machinery of the Universe. You have entered the Treasure House of Images and the sphere of Maya, Illusion. By what Sign hast thou entered into the Mirror of the Cosmos?

You answer by giving the Sign of the Theoricus.

"Why have you come to the house of the Almighty Living One?" he inquires. You hold up the Greek Solar Cross.

Satisfied, Gabriel takes you to the central Altar where he anoints you with a perfumed oil and gestures to a pair of violet leather sandals on the floor in front of the altar. He instructs you to wear these sandals on every path leading from the sphere of Yesod, that you may always tread upon a firm foundation in your journeys. The Archangel then takes you to a curtain in the northeast upon which is depicted the Tarot card of THE SUN. He traces the sigil of Sol and the veil parts, revealing a door carved from crysoleth. Upon the door is the Hebrew letter Resh in orange. Stepping forward, you hold up the Solar Cross and trace with it the letter Resh. The door opens and you and your guide start out on the 30th Path.

It is noon and the sun is at its zenith overhead. The ground you are walking along is rich and fertile . . . black soil that is perfect for most vegetation. Heliotrope and sunflowers abound. Groves of laurel trees cover the low rolling hills. A cool stream, full of fish meanders its way along the path. As a group of butterflies chase each other from flower to flower, you wonder if any place on earth could be more perfect than this.

Gabriel sets a steady pace that covers much ground. Eventually, you come upon a clearing where a drama is about to take place. The Sun god, Ra, is sitting upon the ground clutching the bleeding heel of his foot. A deadly viper, caught in the act, slithers away from the scene of the crime. The god is enraged with pain . . . his bellowing frightens all creatures within earshot. As the venom starts to work, the color drains from the deity's face and limbs. The solar disc on his headdress dims. Crying out against his impending death, Ra calls for Isis to heal his wound.

The great goddess appears quickly, for it was she who created the poisonous serpent . . . fashioning the creature from dust and Ra's own spittle. Isis is compassionate but firm. She will not heal Ra until he reveals unto her his most hidden name. The god is reluctant to do so, for it would mean that Isis would have power over him. Ra is proud and stubborn. At last when the fingers of death begin to steal the life away from him, he whispers his secret name to her.

Great Isis, skilled in the arts of magick, then utters the Words of Power taught to her by Thoth. As soon as the words are spoken, the poison is driven out of the body of Ra, and the color of life returns to him. With the help of the Ibis-headed one, Isis now possesses the words of power as well as the knowledge of how to pronounce and vibrate them. In this skirmish, the great Sun god has been outwitted by the lady of the Moon through intellect.

Gabriel gestures that it is time to move on. You continue on the Path of Resh until at length you come to a great city of shining stone buildings at the edge of the sea. On a 400-foot cliff overlooking the ocean is one of the Seven Wonders of the World, the great stone Pharos, the 100-foot tall lighthouse which guides ships into the port of Alexandria, the great cosmopolitan city which is the apex of knowledge and education in the ancient world.

The city was built according to a strict geometric design, with public buildings of marble, a huge gymnasium, and even an artificial hill dedicated to the god Pan. Walking along the the city's main street which is over 3 miles long and 100 feet wide, you are impressed by the people and their culture, which is neither Greek nor Egyptian, but contains the best of both. At the center of the city is a plaza dominated by two adjoining buildings; great columned structures set high atop marble steps. You and your guide enter the first building, the museum of Alexandria founded by Ptolemy. It is the first university and scientific institute in history.

There are many chambers to explore. In one room, the dissection of bodies provides anatomic studies for a group learning the art of medicine. Other rooms are set aside for zoological and botanical collections. You pass by a chamber where the Hellenistic mathematician Euclid is teaching his axioms of geometry to a number of students. In another room the astronomer Aristarchus is espousing the conclusion that the sun, not the earth is the center of our universe. There are are many studio chambers for artists, scientists and craftsmen.

Gabriel then leads you to the huge library where uncounted numbers of scrolls and tablets of clay, stone, and even wax tablets of writing are carefully stored and studied by historians, poets, astronomers and scholars from all over the ancient world. It was here that writing was for the first time divided into "books," these being determined by the length of the papyrus. A bronze statue of Hermes stands at the center of the great hall. The ceiling is covered by a circular fresco depicting a reproduction of the famous Zodiac of Dendera. There are many tables where the intellectuals of Alexandria are busy copying manuscripts of Greek literature. One of the books you see lying upon a table is Ptolemy's *Syntaxis*, an ancient book of maps which carefully explains the motions of the sun, moon and planets, giving a celestial latitude and longitude for each of them. The Emerald Tablet, and the Divine Pymander as well as the forty other works of Hermes Trismegistus can be found here.

Your guide leads you through a maze of books to a chamber deep within the library walls. At this point Gabriel tells you to continue on without him. The door into the chamber is guarded by a seated figure completely shrouded from head to foot in an unimpressive looking old cloak. A grizzled hand poking out of the robe grasps a staff adorned with carved serpents. Another hand is raised to stop you from entering. "In what Signs and symbols do you come?" the form croaks.

You answer by giving the Sign of the Practicus. "In the Divine name of ELOHIM TZABAOTH; in the word ELOAH and in this symbol of the Solar Greek Cross which refers to the Sun in the twelve Signs of the Zodiac."

"Thou canst not enter the Temple of the Logos unless thou canst tell me my name," the form replies.

"Thou art Tahuti, Lord of Divine Words. Thoth, the self-created counter of the stars and measurer of Earth art Thou. Hermes, the Thrice Great...God of writing, science and Magick."

The cloak and the illusion of age is suddenly cast aside to reveal the God of knowledge in his Greek persona with winged helmet and sandals. His skin is bronze and his youthful eyes sparkle with mischief. He seems delighted at the quickness of your response, but his only reply is to give the Sign of Silence as he opens the door for you. You step out into the bright sunlight.

Before you is a hill with a stone wall at its summit. The mound is divided into two halves; one side of earth, and one of water—the two receptive elements. The stones which comprise the wall are carved with various Zodiacal and astrological sigils. A pair of children are playing joyfully on the knoll. The young boy tumbles in the grass while the girl splashes him with water. In the sky above them is the sun, a huge and brilliant orange disc. It is surrounded by 12 rays, half of which are waved and feminine, and half of which are salient and masculine. Seven Hebrew Yods falling from either side of the disc contain within them the sigils of the planets of the ancients. In the center of the sun are the suggestions of a face, but without a mouth. The head of this solar being stirs feelings of awareness and recognition within you. You know that the countenance before you is the emissary of a Higher Mind, greater than anything you have yet encountered. Longing for an opportunity to have conversation with this Higher Consciousness, you give the Sign of the Practicus, the receptive cup.

A white yod begins to formulate where the Solar mouth would be. It floats down toward you and is absorbed into the crown of your head. The first link of inner communication is established between you and the Divine Teacher. It is a warm and loving feeling of spirituality that you simply cannot describe. No words can do it justice. No human can adequately recount it to another. No tongue can own it.

You salute with the Sign of Silence and a gesture of thanks. Before leaving this idyllic scene, you stop to play a momentary game of tag with the children, who both run laughing into the water, splashing at you. In turning, you see Gabriel, amused by your behavior. It is time to be heading back.

The mid-afternoon sun is hot during the trek back, and you are thankful that Gabriel came to get you when he did, before you ended up with a nasty burn. Some animal bones bleached white by the side of the road testify to the potential destructiveness of the Solar energy if not balanced by cool weather and rainfall.

Soon you are at the Temple of Yesod where you return the violet sandals to the foot of the Altar. The cool air of the chamber is refreshing after such a hot journey. The Archangel then guides you back to the Temple of Malkuth. Sandalphon closes the portal behind you. She goes to the fountain in the West and returns with a wooden chalice of water for you to drink from. Finally, bidding her farewell, you salute with the Projection Sign. She in turn gives the Sign of Silence.

At this point bring your astral body back to the physical Temple around you. Do not hurry.

Perform the LBRP with the black end of the wand.

Declare the Temple duly closed. Exit with the Sign of the Practicus.

THE RITE IS ENDED

The Cup of Stolistes Admission Badge

Use and Symbolism

The Cup of Stolistes Badge grants the candidate entry into the Water Temple of Hod. It is an explicit representation of the same energies found within the lamen and implement of the Stolistes. This Badge partakes in part of the symbolism of the Laver of Moses and the Sea of Solomon.

On the Tree of life, it embraces nine of the Sephiroth, exclusive of Kether. Yesod and Malkuth form the triangle below, the former the apex, the latter the base. Like the Caduceus, it further represents the Three Elements of Water, Air, and Fire. The Crescent is the Water which is above the Firmament, the Circle is the Firmament, and the Triangle the consuming Fire below, which is opposed to the Celestial Fire symbolized by the upper part of the Caduceus. The Cup is a symbol of spiritual receptiveness.

If the Badge is painted primarily blue, it emphasizes the element of Water, to which the grade of 3=8 is attributed. If the Badge is painted primarily orange, it underscores the Sephirah of Hod, which is also assigned to the Practicus grade.

Materials Needed

A 5" x 5" piece of plywood that is 1/4" thick
Wood putty
Gesso
Acrylic paints: yellow, violet, red, orange, green, blue,

blue-violet, white, black, neutral gray
Clear lacquer finish

Tools Needed
Electric jigsaw or coping saw
Compass, pencil and straight edge
File or rasp
Artist's brushes—fine and medium sizes
Sandpaper

Construction
(Note: Follow instructions 1-3 given for the Caduceus Badge.)

Finishing Steps
4) The Badge may be painted in one of three ways:
   a) White with black outline
   b) Primarily blue with an orange chalice
   c) Primarily orange with a blue chalice

5) On the drawing of the Stolistes Cup encompassing the Tree of Life, the Sephiroth can be painted in their usual Queen Scale colors. (A thin white line should be painted around the spheres of Chesed and Hod.)

6) After all paint has dried, apply a sealant for protection.

Ritual for Use

An Invocation of the Element of Water and a Meditation on the Cup of Stolistes Badge for the Grade of Practicus

For this ritual the Practicus will need a black Outer Order robe, black and white striped nemyss, and the Outer Wand of Double Power (described in chapter 6). A blue candle, a cup of wine, and the Admission Badge should be placed on the Altar. The Temple is to be arranged in accordance with the Practicus Hall (as in the Third part of the initiation ceremony). Enter the Temple with the Sign of the Practicus.

Relax for a few moments and perform the Four-fold Breath.

Go to the Northeast and say, "HEKAS, HEKAS, ESTE BEBELOI!"

With the black end of the wand, perform the Lesser Banishing Ritual of the Pentagram.

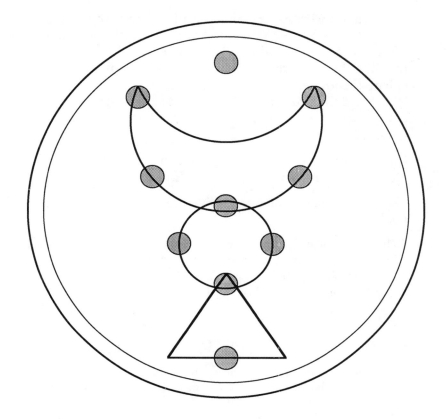

The Cup of Stolistes Badge

Say the following invocation: "So therefore first the Priest who governs the works of Fire must sprinkle with the Lustral Waters of the loud resounding sea."

Go clockwise to the West. With the white end of the wand, trace the Lesser Invoking Pentagram. Thrust the wand through the center of the figure and vibrate, "EHEIEH!"

Say, "In the Divine Name ELOHIM TZABAOTH, I open this Temple in the element of Water. May the Archangel GABRIEL look with favor upon this ceremony! May the angel TALIAHAD and the ruler THARSIS be also in attendance! I have gained admission to this Temple through the Badge of the Cup of Stolistes. I am one who has received the Mystic Title of Monocris de Astris and the symbol of MAYIM. As a Unicorn of the Stars I invoke the powers of Water to bear witness to my spiritual endeavor. Grant me the knowledge of the element of Water and the Creative Realm, so that I may obtain Greater Understanding of Hidden Things and thereby advance in the Great Work."

Circumambulate the Temple three times, saluting with the Neophyte Signs when passing the East.

Go to the West and face east. Give the Adoration to the Lord of the Universe:

"Holy art Thou, Lord of the Universe!"
"Holy art Thou, Whom Nature hath not formed!"
"Holy art Thou, the Vast and the Mighty One!"
"Lord of the Light, and of the Darkness!"

Go to the West and give the Practicus Sign.

Recite the Prayer of the Undines:

"Terrible King of the Sea, Thou who holdest the Keys of the Cataracts of Heaven, and who enclosest the subterranean Waters in the cavernous hollows of Earth. King of the Deluge and the Rains of Spring. Thou who openest the sources of the rivers and of the fountains; Thou who commandest moisture which is, as it were, the Blood of the Earth, to become the sap of the plants. We adore Thee and we invoke Thee. Speak Thou unto us, Thy Mobile and changeful creatures, in the Great Tempests, and we shall tremble before Thee. Speak to us also in the murmur of the limpid Waters, and we shall desire Thy love. O Vastness! Wherein all the rivers of Being seek to lose themselves—which renew themselves ever in Thee! O Thou Ocean of Infinite Perfection! O Height which reflectest Thyself in the Depth! O Depth which exhaltest into the Height! Lead us into the true life, through intelligence, through love! Lead us into immortality through sacrifice, that we may be found worthy to offer one day unto Thee, the Water, the Blood and Tears, for Remission of Sins! Amen."

Give the Practicus Sign. Go to the west of the Altar. With the white end of the Wand, trace the Lesser Invoking Pentagram over the cup of wine. Place the wand aside.

Drink the wine.

As you partake of the element, meditate on the Cup of Stolistes Badge upon the Altar:

Visualize the sphere of Kether emanating all energy to the rest of the Tree. The nine other Sephiroth are vessels of the Divine energy from beyond the Crown. The five Spheres from Chokmah to Tiphareth form the crescent which alludes to the Waters of Creation above the Firmament of Heaven. Five is a receptive number that gathers Form and transmits Force. The Crescent shown here represents the Cauldron of Life, receiving the creative energies of the Sephiroth contained therein.

Tiphareth is the point where the Crescent of the Waters meets the Circle of the Firmament. Four Spheres, from Tiphareth to Yesod are included here. The circle is a symbol of unity and wholeness. Combined with the number four, it becomes a symbol of great balance and stability. Here, the Divine energy received from the fertile cauldron is equilibrated through the Circle of Air; the centrifuge of the Heavens. The energies contained herein are balanced and strengthened to withstand the act of manifestation.

Yesod is the point of connection between the Circle of the Firmament and the Triangle of Fire, formed by two Sephiroth—Yesod and Malkuth. The number two alludes to the Fire of Chokmah as well as the Yod-Fire Force. Here, however, the Fire is purging and consuming, rather than the Celestial Fire which is the first spark of Life. The energy at this level is tempered and shaped, like the blade of a sword, into a instrument worthy of manifestation.

Imagine in your mind's eye, the Divine energy from the Crown of Kether radiating down into the Crescent-shaped cup where it is mingled with the fluid energies of the opposing Pillars of Severity and Mercy. Through Tiphareth, this energy is circulated through the Air of Equilibrium and Foundation. Finally, it passes through the womb of Fire—the Foundry of Manifestation.

Take as much time as you need for the meditation.

Perform the Reverse Circumambulation.

Go to the East and say, "I now release any Spirits that may have been imprisoned by this ceremony. Depart in peace to your abodes and habitations. Go with the blessings of ELOHIM TZABAOTH!"

Perform the LBRP with the black end of the wand.

Say, "I now declare this Temple duly closed." Exit with the Sign of the Practicus.

SO MOTE IT BE

The Calvary Cross of 12 Squares

Use and Symbolism

The Calvary Cross of 12 Squares is the Admission Badge to the Path of Qoph in the 4=7 grade of Philosophus. It is formed of twelve squares which fitly represent the Zodiac which embraces the Waters of Nu as the ancient Egyptians called the Heavens, the Waters which are above the Firmament. It also alludes to the Eternal River of Eden, divided into four heads which find their correlations in the four triplicities of the Zodiac.

The Great River is called Naher, which flows out of Eden, namely from the Supernal Triad. At Daath, it is divided into four heads. The first river is called Pison, the river of Fire, which flows into Geburah. Second is the River Gihon, the river of the Waters which flow into Chesed. The third is Hiddekel, the river of Air, flowing into Tiphareth, and the fourth, which receives the virtues of the other three, is Phrath (Euphrates), which flows down upon the Earth.

Cancer, the Cardinal Sign of Water is placed at the junction of the Cross (and of the four rivers). All the Cardinal and Mutable Signs are shown in alternating positions on the central shaft of the Cross, while the cross bar is composed of the Kerubic Signs.

The 29th Path of Qoph (from Malkuth to Netzach) is called the Corporeal Intelligence, because it forms the very body which is so formed beneath the whole Order of the Worlds and the increment of them. It is therefore a reflection of the Watery Sign of Pisces and the Path connecting the material universe as depicted in Malkuth with the Pillar of Mercy and the side of Chesed, through the

Sephirah Netzach, and through it do the Waters of Chesed flow down.

Case describes the "Collecting Intelligence" as "body consciousness" representing that stage of incarnation in which the physical body is organized into a form that the soul may inhabit. This Path is definitely concerned with the acts of reproduction and physical evolution. In addition, this is also a path of the Lower astral, where the student must face and overcome the phantoms and illusions reflected from the material plane. This probationary path of Water is also sexual; full of passions, reflexes and instincts. On this sometimes harsh path, the initiate learns not to fear the dark, but to accept it as the counterpart of the Light; examine it carefully and wait for the Sun to rise again.

In addition to its role as Admission Badge in the Initiation ceremony of the Philosophus Grade, the Calvary Cross of 12 Squares may be employed by the Philosophus in a ritual/meditation on the 29th Path.

Materials Needed
 One 6" x 3-3/4" piece of pine or basswood that is 1/2" or 3/4" thick
 Wood putty
 Gesso
 Acrylic paints: red-violet, yellow, green
 Clear lacquer finish

Tools Needed
 Scroll saw or jig saw
 Artist's brushes
 Sandpaper, medium and fine

Construction:
1) Take the piece of wood and on one side, mark off (both vertically and horizontally) a series of 3/4" squares. You will then have a piece of wood that has drawn on it a total of 40 squares.

2) With a pencil, shade in the appropriate squares as shown in the diagram. Cut out the shaded squares with the saw.

3) Fill in any gaps with wood putty. Sand until smooth.

Finishing Steps
4) Cover entirely with a coat of gesso. Let dry. Sand until smooth. Apply another coat if needed.

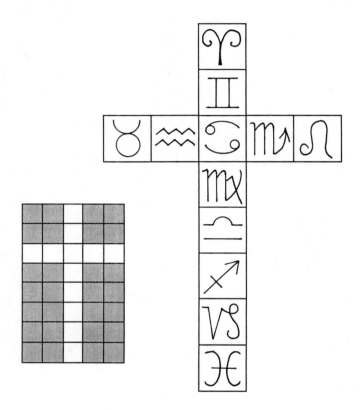

The Calvary Cross of 12 Squares

5) The finished Cross can be painted in one of two ways:
   a) White with black sigils
   b) Red-violet with yellow-green sigils

6) Spray or brush on a coat of sealant for protection. Let dry.

Ritual for Use

A Journey on the 29th Path of Qoph

For this ritual the Philosophus will need his Outer Order Robe and nemyss, the Outer Wand of Double Power (see Chapter 6), and the finished Cross. The Temple is to be arranged as in the Opening of the 4=7 grade. Upon the Altar should be the Tarot trump of THE MOON. A comfortable place to sit and meditate should be arranged west of the Pillars. Enter the Temple with the Sign of Philosophus.

> After a period of relaxation has passed, go to the Northeast and say, "HEKAS, HEKAS, ESTE BEBELOI! Far from this sacred place be the profane!"

> Go to the East. With the black end of the wand, perform the Lesser Banishing Ritual of the Pentagram.

> Go the West of the Altar. With the white end of the Wand of Double Power, trace a large letter Qoph over the tarot card. Visualize it in Red-violet. Intone the name of the letter thrice. Give the Neophyte Signs toward the card. Put the wand aside, and take the Calvary Cross in your right hand.

> With all your powers of concentration, look upon the card and comprehend it, consider all its meaning and symbolism. Give the Sign of the Philosophus. At this point you may sit comfortably if you wish, but maintain a disassociation from the surrounding room. Behind the darkness of your closed eyelids, you begin to formulate the astral Temple of the Sephirah Malkuth, as the journey begins:

Astrally, you give the Sign of the Zelator. The now familiar Temple of Malkuth formulates around you. The central flame burns brightly with a renewed passion upon the central Altar.

As before, you intone the names which call forth the inhabitants of this Temple, ADONAI HA ARETZ, SANDALPHON, ASHIM, and finally, MALKUTH. Sandalphon appears as in your previous journeys and you exchange the usual Signs. She asks "Why have you come to the bridal chamber of Kalah in the realm of the Active World?" This time you hold up the Calvary Cross of 12 Squares for the Archangel to see. She leads you to a curtain in the southeast of the Temple upon which is painted the Tarot card of THE MOON. She traces the symbol of Pisces and the veil fades into mist. In its place is a door carved from Mother of Pearl upon which is the Hebrew letter Qoph in red-violet. Giving the Sign of the Philosophus, you hold out the Cross and trace the letter Qoph before the door, which dissolves.

A great sea stretches before you, blanketed by a thick fog. You are uncertain how to cross this expanse of water until you notice a white shape rising from the deep. A large scallop shell breaks the surface of the water at your feet. You step down into it and sit down. Sandalphon is not coming with you, but she gives you a talisman carved from cuttlebone. On one side of it is the symbol of two fish joined by a rope— the Sigil of Pisces. On the other side is the representation of a crayfish. Bidding the Archangel farewell, you set out upon your journey, drifting across the waters. The Temple of Malkuth is soon lost from sight in the mist.

The water gently rocks the shell as you glide along. Not being able to see in any direction, you look down and are amazed at the variety of life just under the surface of the waters. Your sight seems greatly intensified; you see unicellular life forms such as protozoans or single-celled animals, feeding on microscopic food particles and reproducing by cell division. They are eaten by larger multi-celled creatures which are in turn devoured by small jellyfish and crustaceans. Fish hungrily snap up these tasty invertebrates. It is all quite fascinating to you. Nearby the fin of a dolphin cuts through the surface. The animal seems to be following you, or perhaps it is leading your unusual vessel.

Ahead of you, the mist parts and you see land. As you glide toward the shore, you see two great stone towers. The portal onto dry land is guarded by the twin Anubian Guards whom you have seen before on the 32nd Path. You stand and face them as your craft pulls into shore. Just as before, they cross their weapons and bar your approach with a snarl. "In what Signs and Symbols do ye come?" they demand.

Standing in the Sign of the Philosophus you state, "In the Divine

Name of YHVH TZABAOTH; in the word KAPH CHETH, and in the symbol of the Calvary Cross of 12 Squares." The figures step back and allow you to pass. You give the Sign of the Enterer followed by the Sign of Silence and enter the realm of Qoph.

The path leads though a thick, humid jungle of scale-covered trees, giant cycads, huge ferns, and dense thickets of horsetails or scouring rushes. Strange animal sounds can be heard intermittently through the forest. A small yet colorful feathered animal with claws and teeth glides through the treetops, catching a huge dragonfly in mid-flight. In a clearing ahead, you see two large animals locked in mortal combat. A large carnosaur kicks at the belly of a smaller crested plant-eater with deadly clawed feet. The wounded animal bellows in pain as the final blows are inflicted. The victor hungrily tears meat from the not-quite-dead victim, and turns its bloodied head to inspect you with a cold, dull eye. Hunger brings its attention back to the meal at hand. Relieved, you continue though the forest.

Farther up the trail you nearly stumble into a pit of tar. A giant, lumbering, haired beast has already expired in the black pool. It body is torn at by a pack of wolves who snap at one another over the possession of choice bits of flesh. Some of the animals have themselves become mired in the tar. The fearful cries of the unfortunates who lay exhausted in the pool are ignored by the rest of the hungry pack.

The jungle opens out into a swamp which makes travel difficult and precarious. It is dark and eerie in this place. Vapors from rotting vegetation rise to the surface of the fetid waters and cause strange phosphorescent lights and movements. It is easy to see why bogs of this type were thought to be haunted by the spirits of the dead. The swamp gases play about you, forming phantom shapes and faces against the dark canopy of the trees. In the middle of the marsh stands a large black stone carved into the shape of some terrifying ancient deity. From the scattered bones around the stone, you deduce that humans were once sacrificed here to avoid the wrath of an angry god who might withhold food animals and plants from hungry tribes. The ghosts of the sacrificed seem to linger here in the iridescent gasses. Without fear, but nonetheless anxious to leave this dreadful place, you press on.

Eventually, the swamp feeds into a river, and the ground on either side of it becomes more firm. The Path leads along the river bank amid tall rushes and cattails.

Feeling that you are being watched, you turn toward the river and see the unnerving form of a large crocodile eyeing you curiously. This is the Water God, Sebek, whom the Egyptians worshiped and feared. On the shore near him is an altar upon which a goat has been sacrificed and offered, to persuade the god not to wander about the canals of Egypt searching for hapless victims.

For the moment, he is appeased. You are thankful when the road finally leads away from the river.

Beyond the marshlands, the trail takes you up a hill at the top of which is a lion with two heads, one at either end of its body. The menacing beast sits squarely in your path. "Thou canst not enter the realm of Nature and witness the act of Creation unless thou canst tell us our names," the heads warn.

"Thou art the god SEF and the god TUAU. Thou art the twin Gods of Yesterday and Tomorrow."

"In what Signs and Symbols do ye come?" they ask.

You answer with the Sign of the Philosophus and say, "In the Divine name YHVH TZABAOTH, in the word KAPH CHETH, and in this symbol of the Four Rivers." You hold out the Calvary Cross. The creature steps out of your way and you continue up the hill.

At the summit, you look out over a barren landscape. This was the world that existed before the present one. This was the Aeon of time when god begot god, before the stars were positioned. This was the time when Tem, the god of the Setting Sun, produced from his own body by masturbation, his two children; Shu, the god of Air, and Tefnut, the goddess of the rains. From the mating of these two gods came the births of Nut and Geb.

The form of Nut fills the sky above you. Her skin is dark and bespangled with stars. Her arms project over her head and legs are straight with feet together. She is goddess of the starry heavens, mistress and mother of the gods, and coverer of the sky. Upon her head is a vase of water, for she is the water of the firmament, and the starry ocean above.

Her consort Geb, the green god of Earth, lays upon the dry and barren ground, propped up on one elbow. With one arm he reaches toward his heavenly lover, who comes to him. The goddess bends her great body into a semicircle which covers the reclining form of the earth god. Sky and Earth become locked in an intimate and passionate embrace which seems to last indefinitely.

Ra, the mighty Sun god, is angered by this great coupling. How will the Solar boat be carried across the sky if the Heavens are eternally mating with the earth? He orders their father, Shu, to separate the amorous pair. The Air god does so, stepping between the lovers and lifting Nut off of Geb. Her body then forms the arch of the heavens, her arms and legs become the four pillars of the sky and the cardinal points. The raising up of Nut from the embrace of Geb is the first act of creation; earth is now separate from the waters above it. The sun is now set between the earth and the sky by the reconciling element of Air. The sky, now pregnant, is able to give birth to Osiris, Isis, and other gods and goddesses. Overhead, you witness the process of birth, as the Constellations and planets are produced from the belly of Nut. The fertile Geb is enabled to cover the earth with trees, plants, animals and humans. The landscape before you, barren before the great mating, springs to new life with herbs, grains and wildflowers. Before your very eyes, the vegetation thrives and produces fruit.

The path leads on toward a Temple surrounded by a colonnade of lotus-topped pillars. The Temple itself is built from bricks of pure emerald overgrown with vines. The surrounding courtyard is lush with all manner of plants and wildflowers. A large disc-shaped brazier in front of the building contains a roaring fire.

A tap on your shoulder causes you to turn around. A short and stout being with a huge bearded face, large ears and shaggy hair sticks his tongue out and throws an armful of flowers at you. The god, Bes, dressed in animal skins and wearing a tiara of feathers, lets out a huge belly laugh at his jest. He is the god of joy, pleasure and amusement. He welcomes you to the courtyard with a comic dance which is deliberately clumsy, and you cannot help but laugh at his antics. In the dance, he humorously mimics your journey through the prehistoric jungle and the fetid swamp . . . snapping at your backside like Sebek the crocodile. At the end of his dance, the god takes a seat and begins to play a soft melody on a harp, for the goddess of Nature is about to make her appearance.

The beauty of Hathor, the Lady of love, music and dance, captivates you as she descends the steps of the Temple. The dark skin of her breasts and arms is soft and all-inviting. Her full lips and high cheek bones are accentuated by the slender curve of her neck. She wears a green half-tunic and the crown of cow's horns surmounted by the Solar disc. She is known as the great power of Nature which is perpetually conceiving and creating, rearing and nurturing all things great and small. She is the mother of her father and the daughter of her son. A train of attendant gods follow her every move, for she is known as the mother of every god and goddess. Plants bear seeds in every patch of earth where her foot has touched. Antelope drop their young at her passing.

Within an instant, the goddess transforms into a great cow. The child Horus comes forth to suckle from her. When he has had his fill, Hathor changes again, into her previous form, but with the head of a cow. Horus falls asleep in the lap of his nursemaid. She gestures at a small shrine in one corner of the garden, indicating that you should investigate.

Upon closer inspection, you notice two nude figures before the door of the grotto. On one side is Min, the god of the Moon and the bestower of fertility in men. His strong body testifies to his sexual powers. The other figure is Qetesh, a moon goddess whose voluptuousness and powers of love relate her to Hathor. A dish of lettuce, considered to be an aphrodisiac by the Egyptians, is placed in offering before each of the figures. You approach and present the signs of a Philosophus and the symbol of the Cross, but in order to enter the shrine, you must honor one of the lunar deities with a kiss.

Past the entrance into the building it is dark. Before you is a still pool of water. Beyond that is a hill with two forbidding towers. Two black dogs snap and bay at the ghostly face of the Moon, hanging low in the darkening sky. The lunar energies have stirred the wild animal passions within them. A lowly crayfish starts up the path of evolution which leads between the two higher animal forms. The creature must thread its way carefully through the terrors of the night, that it may live to see the glory of the morning sun. You realize that this is also the path of the initiate, who must face the demons in the back of his/her mind ... illusions created in the race consciousness as well as personal illusions and phobias. Like the crayfish, the Initiate must be prepared to move up the path of evolution. Although the journey is fraught with unpleasantness, the end result is growth and beauty.

You leave the shrine of the moon and walk down into the garden of Hathor. She is again as you saw her in the beginning with human features. Beside her is Sandalphon, ready to accompany you on the journey back. You bid farewell to the company of gods and return down the path to the river. Swiftly you pass the fetid swamp and the ancient jungle. The twin Anubis guards watch motionlessly from the shore as you and the Archangel sail away on the white scallop across the expanse of the sea. The Temple of Malkuth soon appears in the ocean mist. You enter and take a few moments to warm yourself by the hearth as Sandalphon seals the portal of Qoph.

After standing awhile at the Altar to take in its spiritual fire, you salute the Archangel with the Projection Sign. She in turn gives the Sign of Silence.

At this point bring your astral body back to the physical Temple around you. Do not hurry.

Perform the LBRP with the black end of the wand.

Declare the Temple duly closed. Exit with the Sign of the Philosophus.

THE RITE IS ENDED

The Pyramid of the Four Elements

Use and Symbolism

The Pyramid of the Four Elements is the Admission Badge for the 28th Path of Tzaddi in the 4=7 grade of Philosophus. On the four triangles are the Hebrew names of the four Elements: ASCH—Fire, MAYIM—Water, RUACH—Air, and ARETZ—Earth. On the apex is the word ETH, composed of the first and last letters of the Hebrew alphabet and implying essence or Spirit. The square base represents the Material Universe and on it is the word OLAM meaning "World."

The word "pyramid" is derived from a root word which means "fire," signifying that it is the symbolic representation of the one Divine Flame. A pyramid can easily be likened to the "Mountain of God," which was believed to stand in the center of the earth. The four sides of the pyramid are triangular to represent the three-fold aspect of the Divine enthroned within every aspect of the four-fold universe. The square base is a reminder that the structure is firmly based on the immutable laws of nature. The truncated pyramid shows the essence of the Divine firmly planted at the top of the design. It, too, is a square to indicate that the four-fold model of the cosmos begins with the Tetragrammaton.

The Sepher Yetzirah calls the 28th Path the Natural Intelligence; because through it is consummated and perfected the Nature of every existing thing beneath the Sun. It is therefore a reflection of the Airy Sign Aquarius, the Water-bearer, unto which is attributed the Countenance of Man, the ADAM who restored the world. For the Initiate, the Path that runs between Yesod and Netzach represents the hope of rebuilding the Garden of Eden by the deliberate changing of consciousness through the act of mediation; a combination of knowledge and imagination. Case describes meditation as "an unbroken flow of knowledge in a particular object." The fish-hook of Tzaddi is cast into the ocean of subconscious mentality to catch a bit of Divine truth. It is a period of inner quest and search. The process of meditation is both the procedure and the goal of spiritual attainment, for the act itself results in a change of energy from one form to another. The student on this Upper Astral path is exploring the very basic mysteries behind creation, life and death. However, the Initiate on the 28th path must take care not to become bewitched by the glamours and illusions which start in the sphere of Yesod. This is the path of the hopes, dreams and visions of mankind infused with the fertile life-force of Netzach. The way back to Eden is to function in accordance with the Universal Will.

In addition to its use in the 4=7 grade, the Pyramid of the Elements may be used by the Philosophus in a ritual/meditation on the 28th Path.

Materials Needed
> One 12" sq. piece of heavy cardboard (such as matte board or poster board) that is approx. 1/8" thick.
> White glue
> Gesso
> Acrylic paint: violet, yellow
> Clear lacquer finish

Tools Needed
> Craft knife or matte-cutter
> Medium artists' brush

Construction
1) Draw four equilateral triangles on the cardboard that are 3-1/4" long on each side.

2) Draw out one 3-1/4" square that will be the bottom of the pyramid. Draw a smaller version for the top that is 1/2" square.

3) Using the matte-cutter or knife and straight edge, cut the four triangles and the two squares so that all of them have beveled edges that slant toward the inside of each piece.

4) Cut 1/2" off the top angle of all four triangles. (This will give the pyramid its "truncated" look.)

5) Glue all four triangles together so that they fit perfectly together unto the base square. Glue the base and the top to the triangles so that they also fit perfectly together. (Note: you may have to trim some of the triangles for this to happen.) Allow glue to dry thoroughly.

6) Cover the pyramid entirely with gesso. Let dry. Add a second coat if needed.

7) The Truncated Pyramid can be painted in one of two ways:
a) entirely white with black letters
b) entirely violet with yellow letters

8) When paint has dried, spray or brush on a coat of sealant to protect the paint.

(Note: The pyramid, based upon a drawing in the Fifth Knowledge Lecture of Regardie's, *The Golden Dawn*, is shown formed from a single piece of cardboard that can be folded into the pyramid shape. In actual practice, however, we have never found this method of construction adequate given the proportions seen in the drawing. If the triangles in that diagram are extended into equilateral triangles, it could work.)

Ritual for Use

A Journey on the 28th Path of Tzaddi

For this ritual the Philosophus will need his Outer Order robe and nemyss, the Outer Wand of Double Power, and the finished Pyramid. The Temple is to be arranged as in the second part of the 4=7 grade. Upon the Altar should be the Tarot trump of THE STAR. A comfortable place to sit and meditate should be arranged west of the Pillars. Enter the Temple with the Sign of the Philosophus.

> After a period of relaxation has passed, go to the Northeast and say, "HEKAS, HEKAS, ESTE BEBELOI! Far from this sacred place be the profane!"

> Go to the East. With the black end of the wand, perform the Lesser Banishing Ritual of the Pentagram.

> Go the West of the Altar. With the white end of the Wand of Double Power, trace a large letter Tzaddi over the Tarot card. Visualize it in violet. Intone the name of the letter thrice. Give the Neophyte Signs toward the card. Put the wand aside, and take the Pyramid in your right hand.

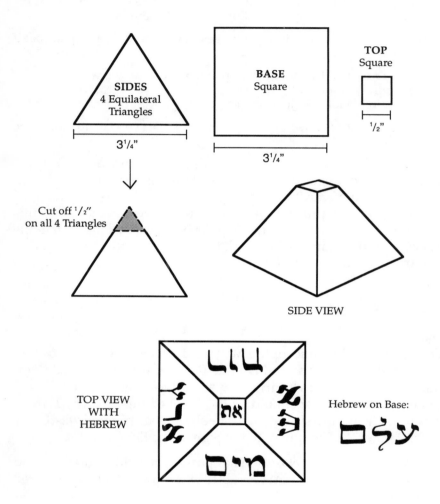

The Pyramid of the Four Elements

With all your powers of concentration, look upon the card and comprehend it, consider all its meaning and symbolism. Give the Sign of the Philosophus. At this point you may sit comfortably if you wish, but maintain a disassociation from the surrounding room. Behind the darkness of your closed eyelids, you begin to formulate the astral Temple of the Sephirah Malkuth as the journey begins:

Astrally, you give the Sign of the Zelator. The now familiar Temple of Malkuth formulates around you. The Altar flame lends its comforting warmth to the chamber.

As before, you intone the names which call forth the inhabitants of this Temple, ADONAI HA ARETZ, SANDALPHON, ASHIM, and finally, MALKUTH. Sandalphon appears as she has in all your previous journeys and you exchange the usual Signs. You hold up the Truncated Pyramid for her to see, and she takes you quickly through the eastern portal of Tau. Soon you are at the entrance to the Temple of Yesod. You enter without the Archangel, giving the Neophyte Signs.

The nine violet walls of the chamber, along with the enneangle carved into the floor, is a sight which never fails to heighten your sense of awareness. The thick sent of jasmine hangs in the air, bringing with it the tingling sensation of the Kundalini along the nerves of your spine. The phases of the moon, carved in quartz and ebony, seem to float eerily in the ceiling above the incense. The four kerubic statues around the silver altar and its central flame again bring a etheric feeling of awe and timelessness.

As before, you vibrate the Divine name of SHADDAI EL CHAI, the Archangel GABRIEL, the order of the KERUBIM, and finally, the name of the Temple itself, YESOD.

The beautiful Gabriel takes shape in the clouds of incense. The same dark hair, green eyes and fine-boned features are there, but this time, the robes of blue and orange cover a female form . . . the Archangel has chosen to emphasize her feminine aspects. She speaks:

"Behold around you, the realm of Foundation—the Sphere of the art of Magick. You have entered the current of the Astral Light. By what Sign hast thou entered into the Temple of Flux and Reflux?"

You answer by giving the Sign of the Theoricus.

"Why have you come to the chamber of change and alteration?" she asks. You hold up the Pyramid of the Four Elements.

The Archangel anoints you with perfume as you again step into the sandals of a Firm Foundation which provide you a better footing in the Astral Plane. Gabriel then takes you to a curtain in the southeast upon which is depicted the Tarot card of THE STAR. She traces the sigil of Aquarius and the veil evaporates, disclosing a door of glass, upon which is a panel of violet stained glass shaped in the form of the letter Tzaddi. Before it, you hold up the Pyramid and trace the letter of the fish-hook. The door opens and the journey on the 28th Path of The Star begins.

The scenery along this trail is the most lush and beautiful of any you have yet encountered. Not only is the sight of it beautiful, but the whole atmosphere of the landscape is one of overwhelming peace and promise. It is ideal . . . the perfect Garden of Eden. Gabriel walks swiftly, but you are in no hurry and pause frequently to admire some singularly lovely flower or butterfly, or listen to a songbird. The guide stops often to let you catch up to her.

The path ahead leads between two olive trees where a single figure stands guard with no weapon at all. He is not nearly as menacing as the portal guardians of other paths have been. Nevertheless, he blocks your entrance.

"Thou canst not enter the Garden of Perfected Nature, unless thou canst tell me my name," he states.

"SAA, god of feeling and intelligence is Thy name. Thou art the god that causes men and women to perceive, to feel, to understand and to become wise through experience," you reply.

"In what Signs and Symbols do ye come?"

Giving the Sign of Philosophus you answer, "In the Divine name YHVH TZABAOTH, in the word KAPH CHETH and in this symbol of the Pyramid of the Four Elements."

The god traces the sigil of Aquarius in the air before you and lets you pass, but not without a word of warning. "Respect the garden for its beauty, but also for its thorns which are felt but rarely seen." With that enigmatic word of caution, you continue up the path. Gabriel indicates that this is as far as she will take you.

In the main part of this paradise, there is a cool spring of pure running water which trickles through a grove of lilacs. Unhurried, you sit down on a large rock which overhangs the stream. A long blade of grass provides you with something to hold between your teeth. You lazily chew the stem, tasting the strong green fluid. The water beside the stone reflects your face back at you.

After a short while you notice three large yellow butterflies carrying a lily between them. They hover close enough for you to smell the sweet odor of the flower. "Come closer," they whisper, "Come and drink the nectar of the Garden of Paradise. Live here with us in eternal happiness!" The smell of the honey-liquid within the flower is intoxicating and inviting. You can imagine how sweet it would taste. But something holds you back. You are suddenly aware of the sandals of Yesod on your feet. The thought of the Firm Foundation suddenly thrusts itself into your mind. If you drink the fluid, you could become immortal and live in the Garden of Eden forever. But at what price? This way to immortality seems too easy. What good is it to become immortal if you have not yet learned the lessons of this incarnation? It is very tempting, but in the end, you refuse to drink.

Turning away, you glance down into the stream beneath your feet. To your surprise, the face that is reflected back at you is not your own. The triangular head and toothy grin of Sebek, the crocodile, has stealthily glided into position below you. Instinctively, you give the Attacking Sign at him, followed by the Sign of Silence. The scaly head disappears under the water.

The sound of laughter makes you look up. The butterflies have become sylphs who are amused that you almost fell for their illusion. The flower that they hold is a carnivorous pitcher plant. In a cloud of fairy dust, they vanish.

The glamour gone, you stand up and realize that you almost did not complete this journey. Much time has passed, it is late evening. Luckily, the Moon is high and full, with no clouds to obscure the light it provides. Looking around for the trail, you spot it and continue up the 28th path, this time with more respect and fewer misconceptions.

The road winds through thick vegetation and eventually into a grassy meadow. There stands a great and beautiful goddess with long, golden hair and milky skin. She is nude save for the symbol of the seven-pointed star at her brow. In each hand she grasps a vase, one grey and one black. Water from both vases pour out upon the ground at her feet, forming the headwaters of a great river. She is Isis, the mighty goddess. But she is also Hathor, and Nephthys, the dark-skinned beauty. In fact she is all goddesses, but perhaps she is best described by the title AIMA ELOHIM, the great Supernal Mother. The vases contain the essences of Chokmah and Binah, respectively, pouring out upon the earth to restore the decimated garden of Eden. A large heptagonal star surrounded by fourteen secondary rays sits in the sky above her head. This is the dog star, Sirius, as well as SEPT or SOTHIS, the Star of Hathor, which is known as the second sun in heaven. The seven planets of the ancients appear as smaller stars which encircle the Sept star like a halo.

To the right (Geburah) side of the figure is the Tree of the knowledge of Good and Evil, which symbolizes the mixed state of the human condition after the expulsion from the Garden of eternal happiness; pleasure and pain, love and anger, harmony and disorder. An Ibis, the bird of Thoth, perches itself on the forbidding tree as if to emphasize that only through the will power of the Magician can the garden be restored—through the proper use of knowledge in accordance with the Universal Will.

To the left (Chesed) side of the figure is the Tree of Life, the map which humankind may follow to reconstruct the Garden of Eden within the Personality of each individual through meditation and spiritual intuition.

You give the Sign and Words of a Philosophus, hold out the Truncated pyramid, and ask for guidance and inspiration from the Great goddess. She says nothing and scarcely seems to notice you, but continues to pour water into the river. For a brief moment you are perplexed, but decide to take a different approach. Seating yourself in the grass at the edge of the river, you begin to focus on the large star in the sky. You concentrate on the number of rays, seven primary plus 14 secondary—a total of 21. Closing your eyes, you begin to mentally intone the Divine name of Kether, EHEIEH, meditating only upon the quiet vibration of the name, and shutting out all else.

After vibrating the name for a period of time, the voice of goddess enters your mind. You listen as she speaks:

"Dost thou imagine that thou hast come to this place of thine own accord searching for Wisdom? Nothing is farther from the Truth. I have sought THEE out. I have brought thee here as a fish on the hook of Tzaddi cast into the shadowy ocean to bring thee into the Light. I seek thee as a bride seeks the groom. I seek thee as a reflection of mine own face in a mirror.

I am the gate which looks out upon the world and back in at myself. I lead humanity from falsity into Truth—from the separateness of the Outer into the wholeness and holiness of the Inner. This I work through INNER vision and hearing. The eyes and ears of the body are concerned only with the veneer of reality. The senses of the soul perceive far more that is Truth. The seeds of Truth and Wisdom are sown in silence and grow in silence and mystery. Not in confusion and noise is the work of Nature perfected, but in the calm meditation that seeks out thine own true self. Here shalt thou find me reflected. Herein lies the return to the Garden. Herein also is the universe resolved into its ultimate elements under the presidency of the Divine ETH."

When the goddess is done speaking, you open your eyes. She stands there as before, pouring out the essence of the Supernals into the river. As the water from the vases mix with that of the river, quartz crystals are formed, as though energy is transforming from a fluid into a solid form. This metamorphosis of energy reminds you of your own transformation—from a secular individual into an Initiate of the Hermetic Mysteries.

The vision of the star re-enters your thoughts. You are reminded of the story of Lucifer, not the devil of the Dark Ages, but the beautiful angel whose name means "Light Bearer" identified with the planet Venus—the Morning and Evening Star. Venus, the physical chakra of the Sephirah, Netzach, hangs in the sky with the other stars.

You sit on the river bank a long time, basking in the rays of starlight, filled with inspiration and creativity. The stars multiply into a galaxy. Each constellation presents itself to you, one after another. Soon the fingers of morning begin to grasp the eastern edge of the sky, pushing the stars ever higher above the horizon. As dawn breaks over the Garden, you know it is time to leave.

Backtracking the way you came, you soon arrive at the twin olive trees guarded by the god Saa. Gabriel is there waiting for you. Together you return to the Temple of Yesod where you replace the violet sandals at the foot of the Altar. She then guides you back to the Temple of Malkuth. Sandalphon seems particularly pleased to see you after this journey and welcomes you with an embrace worthy of an Archangel. She then closes the portal of Tzaddi. As always you take a few moments of silent communion over the Altar flame with Sandalphon. After this journey, such moments of silence seem pregnant with conversation. Finally, bidding her farewell, you salute with the Projection Sign. She in turn gives the Sign of Silence.

At this point bring your astral body back to the physical Temple around you. Do not hurry.

Perform the LBRP with the black end of the wand.

Declare the Temple duly closed.

SO MOTE IT BE

The Calvary Cross of 10 Squares

Use and Symbolism

The Calvary Cross of 10 Squares is the Admission Badge to the Path of Peh in the 4=7 grade of Practicus. It is formed of 10 squares which fitly represents the 10 Sephiroth in balanced disposition, before which the Formless and the Void rolled back. It is also the opened out form of the Double Cube and of the Altar of Incense. (The Altar of incense before the Veil of the Holy of Holies, was overlaid with Gold to represent the highest degree of purity.) This alludes to the path of Peh as a vehicle of purification . . . where the microcosm of man (represented by the ten Sephiroth) learns to separate the pure from the impure . . . to become a perfect mirror of the Greater Tree, the Microcosm of the Universe.

The Sepher Yetzirah calls the 27th Path the "Exciting Intelligence" because by it is created the Intellect of all created Beings under the Highest Heaven. It is therefore a reflection of the sphere of Mars, and the Reciprocal Path connecting Netzach with Hod, Victory with Splendor. It is the lowermost of the Reciprocal Paths, straddling all three Pillars on the Tree. To the initiate, this is one of the most difficult Paths on the Tree because it involves the sudden and complete destruction (or purification) of old "realities." However, the destruction of the Tower is followed by a process of rebuilding which balances the eternal conflict within all humans—the battle between intellect (Hod) and desire (Netzach). The balance between logic and emotion must be accomplished before any real spiritual progress can take place. The Tower of old beliefs, prejudices and habits, formed by parents, teachers, institutions and peers, must be blasted and re-examined. Some remnants of the Tower may then be re-integrated, others discarded. It is up to the initiate to decide.

In addition to its role as Admission Badge in the Initiation ceremony of the Philosophus grade, the Calvary Cross of 10 Squares may be employed by the Philosophus in a ritual/meditation on the 27th Path.

Materials Needed

One 4-1/2" x 3-3/4" piece of pine or basswood that is 1/2" or 3/4" thick
Wood putty
Gesso
Acrylic paints: red, green
Clear lacquer finish

Tools Needed
> Scroll saw or jig saw
> Artist's brushes
> Sandpaper, medium and fine

Construction
1) Take the piece of wood and on one side, mark off (both vertically and horizontally) a series of 3/4" squares. You will then have a piece of wood that has drawn on it a total of 30 squares.

2) With a pencil, shade in the appropriate squares as shown in the diagram. Cut out the shaded squares with the saw.

3) Fill in any gaps with wood putty. Sand until smooth.

Finishing Steps
4) Cover entirely with a coat of gesso. Let dry. Sand until smooth. Apply another coat if needed.

5) The finished Cross can be painted in one of two ways:
   a) White with black sigils
   b) Red with green sigils

6) Spray or brush on a coat of sealant for protection. Let dry.

Ritual for Use

A Journey on the 27th Path of Peh

For this ritual the Philosophus will need his Outer Order Robe and nemyss, the Outer Wand of Double Power, and the finished Cross. The Temple is to be arranged as in the Third part of the 4=7 Grade. Upon the Altar should be the Tarot trump of THE TOWER. A comfortable place to sit and meditate should be arranged west of the Pillars. Enter the Temple with the Sign of the Philosophus.

> After a period of relaxation has passed, go to the Northeast and say, "HEKAS, HEKAS, ESTE BEBELOI! Far from this sacred place be the profane!"

> Go to the East. With the black end of the wand, perform the Lesser Banishing Ritual of the Pentagram.

		1. כתר		
3. בינה	5. גבורה	6. תפארת	4. חסד	2. חכמה
		7. נצח		
		8. הוד		
		9. יסוד		
		10. מלכות		

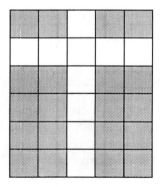

The Calvary Cross of 10 Squares

Go to the west of the Altar. With the white end of the wand of Double Power, trace a large letter Peh over the Tarot card. Visualize it in Red. Intone the name of the letter twice. Give the Neophyte Signs toward the card. Put the wand aside, and take the Calvary Cross in your right hand.

With all your powers of concentration, look upon the card and comprehend it, consider all its meaning and symbolism. Give the Sign of the Philosophus. At this point you may sit comfortably if you wish, but maintain a disassociation from the surrounding room. Behind the darkness of your closed eyelids, you begin to formulate the astral Temple of the Sephirah Malkuth, as the journey begins:

Astrally, you give the Sign of the Zelator. The ten-sided chamber of Malkuth appears around you.

As on previous journeys, you intone the names which call forth the inhabitants of this Temple, ADONAI HA ARETZ, SANDALPHON, ASHIM, and finally, MALKUTH. Sandalphon comes forth and you exchange the usual Signs. When she asks why you have come this time, you hold up the Calvary Cross of 10 Squares for her to see. Swiftly, the Archangel leads you through the portal of Shin in the northeast of the Temple and up the 31st Path to the Temple of Hod. Leaving Sandalphon, you enter the Water Temple giving the Neophyte Signs.

A great, eight-sided room surrounds you. The walls are draped in curtains of orange silk and the floor is covered with glittering fire opals. The scent of storax is heavy in the air. In each corner of the room is a statue of the God of Knowledge, given various names and appearances throughout history: Tahuti-Thoth, Enki, Hermes, Mercury, Nabu, Turms, Odin and Cilans. A statue of a hermaphrodite, Hapi, god of the Nile occupies a small shrine in one part of the Temple. The ceiling above you is dominated by a large blue sigil of Mercury. Within the circle of the sigil is the image of a cup. Your attention is drawn to the center of the room where eight alternating columns of Water and Fire enclose a small inner sanctuary. There is a blue Altar in the middle of this sacred chamber, covered by an apron, upon which is a disc of opal containing the Temple flame. In addition, there is a chalice of water and the Book of Knowledge with the figure of an octogram gracing its cover.

To announce your presence in the Temple and call forth its inhabitants, you vibrate the Divine name ELOHIM TZABAOTH and the name of the Archangel, MICHAEL. You then call upon the order of angels known as the BENI ELOHIM. Finally, you intone the name of the Temple itself, HOD.

Almost immediately, the great flaming being of Michael appears, just as you remember him from the Path of Shin; clothed in a fireball of red and orange flames with fingers of flame running the entire length of his body. His vaporous wings form a halo of pure heat around his head, and he carries a large sword, for he is the Prince of Light and the Leader of the Heavenly Hosts.

He speaks:

"Behold the Vision of Splendour and the reflection of Mercy! By what Sign does thou enter herein?"

You answer by giving the Sign of the Practicus.

"Why hast thou come to this Temple of the Perfect and Absolute Intelligence?"

You hold up the Calvary Cross of 10 Squares for the Archangel to see. Satisfied, he changes into a form that is easier for you to approach. The halo of flames vanishes and in its place is a suit of armour, Roman in design, which makes Michael look more like a winged human warrior than a being of living flame. His sword has become a long spear.

The Archangel takes you to the right side of the chamber and draws back a portion of the orange drapery to reveal another curtain with the image of THE TOWER painted upon it. He traces the symbol of Mars and the veil fades into mist. In its place is a door carved from ruby, upon which is the Hebrew letter Peh. Giving the Sign of the Philosophus, you hold out the Cross and trace the form of the letter Peh before the door, which dissolves. Together, you and your guide start down the path.

It is sunrise, and the Solar disc is just beginning to mark its ascent to your left. You pass low rolling hills dotted with grazing sheep. The grazing is sparse, however, because the land is similar to a high plains desert with meager amounts of rainfall. Joshua trees, cactus and desert scrub seem to be norm here, and the arid odor of pepper is in the air.

Eventually, the landscape begins to change, becoming more rocky and mountainous. Even the hardy desert scrub seems unable to get a foothold between the impartial granite slabs of this harsh place. Devoid of even the most durable of Nature's flora, the region looks as though it might just as well be a martian landscape. The trail seems treacherous, full of potholes and sharp, loose stones that cause you to misstep often. Michael says not a word as he walks effortlessly in front of you, but his protective presence is reassuring.

Just ahead of you, behind a craggy hillside, a wonderous image presents itself to your eyes—a great crown which sparkles with many jewels. As you get closer, you see before you an enormously high stone tower with the shining crown at its summit. The mighty fortress looks impenetrable and there are no windows. The path you are traveling leads straight to the entrance of the structure, where two well-worn battering rams have ended their days of combat only to be implanted in the ground as columns—their carved horns and ram-faces chipped and broken in many places. Before these crude pillars two figures hold watch over the entrance. Michael sends you on ahead. From here on you must face whatever awaits you alone, and act upon your own decisions. As you near the Tower, you begin to make out the features of the two guardians.

The form on the right has a muscular body covered by a red tunic. The piercing eyes of a hawk glare at you from under a nemyss surmounted by the double crown of Egypt. In one hand the swarthy being holds a club, and in the other an iron-tipped spear.

The left-hand figure is feminine, also dark in limb, who holds a lotus staff and an ankh. She too wears a tunic of red linen.

At your approach, the figures cross their implements, spear to staff, and block your advance. "Thou canst not enter the Tower of the Vibration of the Word unless thou canst tell us our names," they command.

You turn to the hawk-headed figure and say, "Thou art HORUS, god of battles, Slayer of Set and the enemies of Ra. HERU the Piecer, Son of the Sun." To the left-hand figure you answer, "Thou art NEPHTHYS, sister of Isis, lady of the invisible, dark goddess of death and life."

"In what Signs and Symbols do ye come?" They question.

Your answer is given in the Sign of the Philosophus. "In the Divine name ELOHIM TZABAOTH. In the word KAPH CHETH. And in this symbol of the Sephirotic Cross."

The figures step back and allow you to pass. A solid oak door stands in your way. You project at it with the Attacking Sign and it opens inward. Giving the Sign of Silence, you enter.

Once inside the damp, musky building, you feel a bit closed-in.

The Tower has been badly neglected and is in need of repair. Cobwebs and dust are everywhere. The floor-boards are rotten and crumble under your weight. Before you is a stone staircase that looks as though it leads to the crown of the tower. Perhaps there is something of value in this dingy old Tower that you need to explore. With renewed confidence you begin the ascent to the top. The stairs are slippery with mold, so you must watch your step. As you climb, you pass armaments of all kinds: cannons, gunpowder, shields, lances, broadswords and more. Apparently, the Tower has been under siege for some time, but it is well-fortified and armed to the teeth.

Nearing the top of the fortress, you hear sounds of music, dancing and laughter. Who, you wonder, could call such a place as this home? Your Will and curiosity drives you forward. Thrusting open a crumbling door at the top of the stairs, you gaze out onto a richly dressed group of nobles in silken robes and jeweled headpieces. They sit atop the crown of the tower under the shade a raised cloth. They are bloated and immobile from sheer gluttony. A few undernourished servants in rags do their best to minister to the needs and amusements of the group; playing flutes, dancing, and bringing food. The only reward of these attendants is disregard at best. The more unfortunate servants receive a kick or a fist. The wealthy barons and dukes argue with one another over luxurious trinkets which fall unnoticed to the floor when some new bauble grabs their attention. In front of this opulent group are enormous quantities of food and drink, so much food in fact that some of it appears to be spoiling. Yet tethered to a stone away from the food is a small monkey weak from hunger, with nothing to eat. The pitiful animal, kept only for amusement, has obviously been forgotten like the other court toys. This makes you angry. How dare these people be so neglectful and selfish?

Your presence has startled them. They stare at you with absolute astonishment. It is as if they have never seen anyone besides themselves in their domain. They seem to consider you an intruder. Frightened, they sound an alarm. From the door behind you and another opening behind the nobles, armored guards come running with raised swords. What you wouldn't give to have Michael by your side now!

Before any hands are able to grasp you, there is another sudden commotion. The aristocrats are now frantic because the sun has abruptly disappeared behind a great black cloud. Without warning there is a huge explosion of light and stone. A great bolt of lightning has struck the Tower! At the same moment, you hear a roaring vibration of sound as if all the angelic choirs above the Firmament suddenly opened their mouths and uttered the true name of Tetragrammaton. Within an instant there are no longer bricks beneath your feet and you are sailing through the air. For a moment you are certain that this must be the end of your journey. As you fall, you yell out, "ADONAI! I am free from the bonds of Darkness!"

Hands are suddenly there to grasp you. Michael, hearing your cry of willing sacrifice, has taken wing to keep you from falling into the void and sharing the fate of the Dukes of Edom. For the Lords of Chaos there is no rescue. From the Archangel's strong arms you watch as the nobles and the Tower's crown are swept away in the darkness—into the waiting mouth of Moloch . . . and the nothingness from whence they came. Fascinated, you can do nothing but watch. A voice enters your mind, and you listen quietly as you learned to do on the Path of Tzaddi:

"I am the Logos and the mouth that uttereth it. I beget life and I consume life. I am the Alpha and the Omega. All things which I create return unto me. Do not be mislead by this apparent demolition, for I destroy only to rebuild into a greater design. The soul of humankind evolves from this destruction; always growing and fading, changing yet living. Through this destruction is the soul preserved, that it may at length become One with the Source.

"Let those who would be free from the bonds of darkness learn to separate the spiritual from the material. Temper the Water of the Intellect with the Fire of Emotion. The Fire of Spirit moves and descends into the Fire of Form. Those who feel this Divine Fire within their souls shall ascend to live eternally within the new Tower which I alone shall build. The Logos shall be my building stone and the vibration of the Word shall be my mortar."

You are lying on the ground, but you did not feel the landing. Michael is standing above you smiling. The Archangel offers you his hand and pulls you to your feet. Remembering everything that has happened, you stare at the Tower in amazement.

The mighty crown which surmounted the structure has been utterly destroyed. Not one of its bricks remain. The entire upper portion of masonry has been knocked away. Three gaping holes have been blown into the wall revealing that the fire inside the fortress rages on. The openings resemble three blazing roses.

Squeezing your shoulder in a gesture of affection, Michael informs you that you have done well on this difficult test. What you rebuild out of the ashes of the Tower struck by Lightning will be far greater than anything you can now imagine. It is up to you to create a better, more balanced structure; discarding pieces of the old Tower which are obsolete, while keeping those pieces which are usable. The new Tower of the personality must be built in the image of the Higher Design, using knowledge and compassion, never the one without the other. But for the moment you must return to the Temple of Hod.

The landscape becomes less rugged and the road widens as you leave the desolate region of the old Tower. The desert vegetation returns to view. You feel revitalized by having survived the ordeal of the Tower. Michael walks beside you now, as if he is more confident of your own abilities.

A noise off to the right brings your attention to an apple tree beside the path that you had not noticed earlier. The monkey from the Tower sits amid the branches, happily munching on a piece of fruit. It is as if the ape of Thoth has been nourished by the blasting of the old fortress.

Once again you find yourself back at the Water Temple. You are reluctant to leave this place of learning, but you know that what you have accomplished today will take time to fully comprehend. Michael takes you down the path of Shin to the Temple of Malkuth. As you say goodbye to the Archangel, he transforms back into his true flaming appearance . . . the Light of God in the center of the ball of flame.

Sandalphon quickly seals the portal of the 31st Path behind you. She fetches a chalice to give you a long cool from the fountain. The Ashim are quite noticeable in the Temple after your journey on the Path of Peh. They resemble Yods of flame dancing above the Altar. You enjoy their company awhile before leaving. Finally, you bid goodbye to the inhabitants of the Temple and salute with the Projection Sign. Sandalphon gives the Sign of Silence.

At this point bring your astral body back to the physical Temple around you. Do not hurry.

Perform the LBRP with the black end of the wand.

Declare the Temple duly closed. Exit with the Sign of the Philosophus.

SO MOTE IT BE

The Cross of the Hegemon's Badge

Use and Symbolism

The Cross of the Hegemon's Badge grants the candidate entry into the Grade of Philosophus. The Calvary Cross of Six Squares embraces Tiphareth, Netzach, Hod and Yesod, and rests upon Malkuth. Also, the Calvary Cross of Six Squares is the opened-out form of the Cube, and is thus referred to the Six Sephiroth of Microprosopus which are Chesed, Geburah, Tiphareth, Netzach, Hod and Yesod.

This badge is given to the Philosophus to emphasize the balance that must be attained in the 4=7 grade between Water and Fire, emotions and intellect. The Calvary Cross of Six Squares underscores the reconciling sphere of Tiphareth tempering and equilibriated between the opposing energies which meet head-to-head in this harsh grade.

If the Badge is painted primarily red, it emphasizes the element of Fire, to which the grade of 4=7 is attributed. If the Badge is painted primarily green, it underscores the Sephirah of Netzach, which is also assigned to the Philosophus grade.

Materials Needed
   A 5" x 5" piece of plywood that is 1/4" thick
   Wood putty
   Gesso
   Acrylic paints: red, green
   Clear lacquer finish

Tools Needed
   * Electric jigsaw or coping saw
   * Compass, pencil and straight edge
   * File or rasp
   * Artist's brushes—fine and medium sizes
   * Sandpaper—medium and fine

Construction
   (Note: Follow instructions 1–3 given in this chapter for the Caduceus Badge.)

Finishing Steps
   4) The Badge may be painted in one of three ways:
       a) Black outer circle and cross against white field and white circles (for the Sephiroth)

    b) Red outer circle and cross with green inner field
    c) Green outer circle and cross with red inner field

5) The Sephiroth can be painted in their usual Queen Scale colors if so desired. After all paint has dried, apply a sealant for protection.

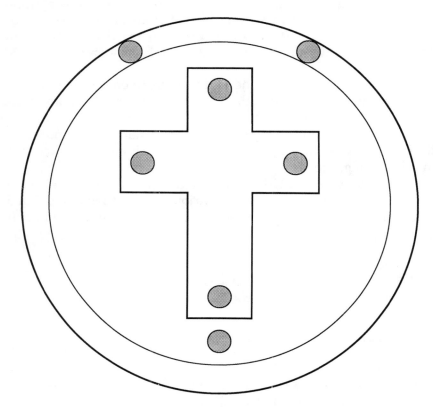

The Cross of the Hegemon's Badge

Ritual for Use

An Invocation of the Element of Fire
and a Meditation on the Cross of the Hegemon's Badge
for the Grade of Philosophus

For this ritual the Philosophus will need a black Outer Order robe, black and white striped nemyss, and the Outer Wand of Double Power (see chapter 6). A red candle and the Admission Badge should be placed on the Altar. The Temple is to be arranged in accordance with the Philosophus Hall (as in the final part of the initiation ceremony). Enter the Temple with the Sign of the Philosophus.

Relax for a few moments and perform the Four-fold Breath.

Go to the Northeast and say, "HEKAS, HEKAS, ESTE BEBELOI!"

With the black end of the wand, perform the Lesser Banishing Ritual of the Pentagram.

Say the following invocation: "And when after all the phantoms are banished, thou shalt see that holy and formless Fire, that Fire which darts and flashes through the hidden depths of the universe. Hear thou, the Voice of Fire!"

Go clockwise to the West. With the white end of the wand, trace the Lesser Invoking Pentagram. Thrust the wand through the center of the figure and vibrate, "ADONAI!"

Say, "In the Divine Name YHVH TZABAOTH, I open this Temple in the element of Fire. May the Archangel MICHAEL look with favor upon this ceremony! May the Angel ARAL and the ruler SERAPH be also in attendance! I have gained admission to this Temple through the Cross of the Hegemon's Badge. I am one who has received the Mystic Title of *Pharos Illuminans* and the symbols of ASCH and PHRATH. As an Illuminating Tower of Light I invoke the powers of Fire to bear witness to my spiritual endeavor. Grant me the knowledge of the element of Fire and the Divine Realm, so that I may obtain Greater Understanding of Hidden Things and thereby advance in the Great Work."

Circumambulate the Temple three times, saluting with the Neophyte Signs when passing the East.

Go to the West and face east. Give the Adoration to the Lord of the Universe:

"Holy art Thou, Lord of the Universe!"
"Holy art Thou, Whom Nature hath not formed!"
"Holy art Thou, the Vast and the Mighty One!"
"Lord of the Light, and of the Darkness!"

Go to the South and give the Philosophus Sign.

Recite the Prayer of the Salamanders:

Immortal, Eternal, Ineffable and Uncreated Father of all, borne upon the Chariot of Worlds which ever roll in ceaseless motion. Ruler over the Ethereal Vastness where the Throne of Thy Power is raised, from the summit of which Thine Eyes behold all and Thy Pure and Holy Ears hear all—help us, Thy children, whom Thou hast loved since the birth of the Ages of Time! Thy Majesty, Golden, Vast and Eternal, shineth above the Heaven of Stars. Above them art Thou exalted.

"O Thou Flashing Fire, there Thou illuminatest all things with Thine Insupportable Glory, whence flow the Ceaseless Streams of Splendour which nourisheth Thine Infinite Spirit. This Infinite Spirit nourisheth all and maketh that inexhaustible Treasure of Generation which ever encompasseth Thee— replete with the numberless forms wherewith Thou hast filled it from the Beginning.

From this Spirit arise those most holy kings who are around Thy Throne and who compose Thy Court.

O Universal Father, One and Alone! Father alike of Immortals and Mortals. Thou hast specially created Powers similar unto Thy Thought Eternal and unto Thy Venerable Essence. Thou hast established them above the Angels who announce Thy Will to the world.

Lastly, Thou hast created us as a third Order in our Elemental Empire.

There our continual exercise is to praise and to adore Thy Desires: there we ceaselessly burn with Eternal Aspirations unto Thee, O Father! O Mother of Mothers! O Archetype Eternal of Maternity and Love! O Son, the Flower of all Sons! Form of all Forms! Soul, Spirit, Harmony and Numeral of all things! Amen!

Give the Philosophus sign. Go to the west of the Altar. With the white end of the wand, trace the Lesser Invoking Pentagram over the red candle. Place the wand aside.

Take a few moments to feel the heat of candle flame.

As you partake of the element, meditate on the Admission Badge upon the Altar:

Visualize the throne of the Hegemon situated between two great Pillars—one of Fire and one of Cloud. The essence of these Pillars are summed up in the spheres of Chesed and Geburah. The opposing energies of Mercy and Severity are held in equilibrium by the station of the Hegemon, who sits at the point of junction between the 27th and 25th paths. Upon her lamen is the symbol of the double cube, identical to the Altar of the mysteries. Imagine the cube opening out into the Six-squared Calvary Cross, the Cross of perfect balance and order. Its summit is Tiphareth, its base is Yesod. The right and left arms of the Cross are Netzach and Hod. The Cross sits on top of the sphere of Malkuth, tempering the different energies of the Tree before letting them filter down into the 10th Sephirah.

The six squares of the Cross also refer to the Six spheres which form Microprosopus, also called Zauir Anpin, the Son of the Supernal Father and Mother. Visualize the form of the Reconciling Son placed over the Six-squared Cross in order to restore the Sephirotic system after the Fall of Eden: his head rests in Tiphareth, the seat of beauty and ultimate balance. His hands separate the opposing spheres of Netzach and Hod, his feet are firmly planted in the foundation of Yesod. Above his shoulders are the rival spheres of Chesed and Geburah. In the midst of such extremes, he remains the calm central point . . . the eye in the center of the storm.

This is the position the Philosophus must maintain. Encircled on either side by Fire and Water, intellect and emotion, the initiate of the 4=7 degree must strive to be the calm central point of balance, and like the Hegemon, he/she must maintain the balance of the surrounding universe. Only in this way can the Garden of Eden be restored in the soul of the Initiate.

Take as much time as you need for the meditation.

Perform the Reverse Circumambulation.

Go to the East and say, "I now release any Spirits that may have been imprisoned by this ceremony. Depart in peace to your abodes and habitations. Go with the blessings of YHVH TZABAOTH!"

Perform the LBRP with the black end of the Wand.

Say, "I now declare this Temple duly closed." Exit with the Sign of the Philosophus.

THE RITE IS ENDED

Part 2

The Portal

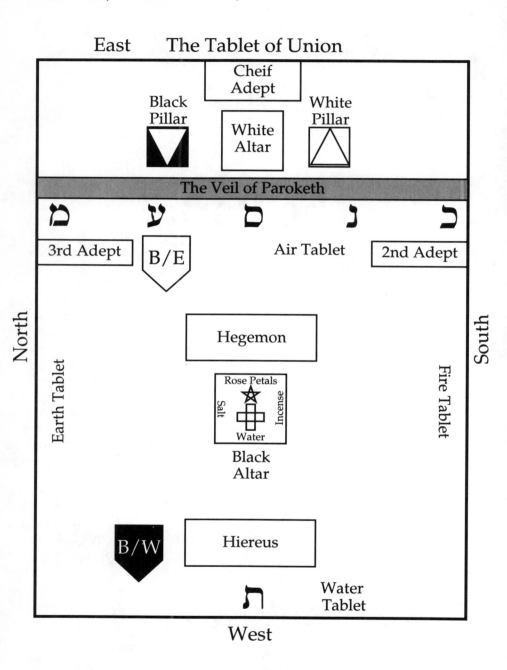

East   The Tablet of Union

The Portal Hall

CHAPTER THREE

Implements of the Portal Grade

The Portal Grade of the Golden Dawn is an intermediary stage between the First and Second Orders (the Golden Dawn and the R.R. et A.C.). The Portal Initiate is in a unique position of not belonging to either Order. He/she has completed the curriculum of the Golden Dawn after leaving the Philosophus grade, but is not yet a member of the R.R. et A.C. The candidate is thus in a period of probation to determine his/her possibilities of admittance to the Second Order, for it is truly a separate Order from that of the Golden Dawn.

Admission to the Second Order requires that the candidate aspire to create a sense of inner balance within, not merely strive to attain the title of a high degree in order to flaunt the Ego. Advancement to the Portal grade does not guarantee admission to the Second Order. As it states in the Portal Ceremony: "Admission further can be earned no more by excellence in intellectual learning alone, though that also is required of you. In token that all true knowledge cometh of grace, not upon demand..."

Whereas the entire Outer Order represents what in the strict interpretation of the Golden Dawn calls the "First Degree," the Portal is referred to the "Second Degree." (An initiation into the R.R. et A.C. would be the "Third Degree.") This is also the first time throughout all the initiations that the candidate is formally presented with the White Pillar. Until now the Initiate has been working with the Black Pillar which represents the Outer Order, as stated several times in the Portal Ritual:

> ...take in your right hand the Banner of the West and place your left hand in that of the Very Honored 3rd Adept, who is the living Symbol of the Black Pillar which ruleth in the Outer Order...

A primary theme in the Portal Ceremony is the candidate's coming out of Darkness and into the Light. Only after the darkness of the Black Pillar (i.e., the Initiate's lower personality symbolized by the Elemental grades of the Outer Order) has been explored and dealt with can the White Pillar be safely approached:

> Having traversed the Path of Tau, the darkness of the Astral Plane and of the Black Pillar, stand firm in Yesod, that the Black Pillar may become the White...
>
> ... Stretch out your hand to touch the Black Pillar, the Pillar of the First Degree, wherein all was as yet in the darkness of the Path Tau. This was a period of restriction and of groping, as was shown by the black sash, the Sign of the First Degree. Among its symbols were the Cross, upon which meditate, the mysteries of growth and change may become revealed.
>
> Stretch out now your right hand to touch the White Pillar, the Pillar of the Second Degree, wherein is the Fire of the Path Samekh. Its token in our Order, is the White Sash.

The White Sash is given to the Portal Initiate as a token of his/her attainment to the Second Degree. The Portal Sash is completely white, with no numbers or decorations of any kind, and it fits over the candidate's right shoulder instead of the left shoulder. (Follow the instructions given in chapter 1 on the making of a sash.) Just as the Black sash alluded to the Watery current of the Black Pillar, the white sash leads from Geburah to Netzach (right shoulder to left hip), indicating the Fiery current of the White Pillar.

In the Portal grade there is a curious mixture of both Outer Order Officers and Inner Order Adepts. The Hiereus and the Hegemon of the Outer Order are in charge of the Secondary Elements of Earth and Air, while the 2nd and 3rd Adepts of the Inner Order are in charge of the Primary Elements of Fire and Water. However, the Portal Grade is especially referred to the fifth element of Spirit or ETH (embodied by the Chief Adept) which crowns the four Elemental grades of the Outer Order just as the Spirit point crowns the Pentagram. This grade in particular is concerned with the process of inner alchemy—of separating and examining the parts of one's own psychological and spiritual workings—in order to balance and merge them again into a more unified whole which makes true spiritual attainment possible.

This chapter contains instructions on how to construct the Temple props and the wands and lamens which are unique to this grade and found nowhere else in either the First or Second Orders.

We have included all of the Enochian Tablets here, for although they are introduced to the candidate one by one in each of the four grades of the Outer Order, they are not presented as a unified system of Magick under the presidency of the Tablet of Union (Spirit) until the Portal grade. (The tablets are present in the Outer Order Hall, but they are, for the most part, behind veils until required for specific grade ceremonies.)

THE TEMPLE PROPS OF THE PORTAL GRADE

In the Portal Hall, the Chief Adept sits in the eastern-most part of the Temple behind the White Altar. Above his/her throne is placed the Tablet of Union. Flanking the White Altar are the two Pillars. This entire portion of the Hall is concealed behind the Veil of Paroketh, a physical curtain that represents an etheric boundary which lies before the Sephirah of Tiphareth on the Path of Samekh leading from Yesod. Just west of the Veil are placed the Hebrew letters Mem, Ayin, Samekh, Nun, and Kaph—corresponding to further Paths on the Tree of Life. The Second and Third Adepts are seated in the Southeast and the Northeast respectively. The Black Altar is located just west of the center of the Hall. The Hegemon sits east of the Altar, and the Hiereus is stationed in the West. The Enochian Tablets are placed in their respective quarters: Air—East, Fire—South, Water—West, and Earth—North.

The Veil of Paroketh

Use and Symbolism

The Veil of Paroketh, in addition to being an actual physical prop in the Portal Hall, is a symbol of an astral veil that exists on the glyph of the Tree of Life. It is described in the Portal grade as the Veil of the Tabernacle, before the Holy of Holies: the Inner Sanctum of the Temple. The Veil is a demarcator which separates the four lowest Sephiroth on the Tree of Life from the rest of the Tree. Situated on the 25th Path of Samekh, the Veil is the boundary between Tiphareth, the seat of the Higher Self, and the 7th, 8th, and 9th Spheres which make up the Triad of the lower Personality. To truly "Rend the Veil" means to evolve beyond the needs and wants of the lower personality and take a conscious step toward union with the

Higher Self. This conscious act of aspiration implies both a willingness to become a true Initiate of the mysteries, as well as the willingness to undergo the sacrifice that is necessary to achieve this goal. For Paroketh is also described as the Veil of the Four Elements of the Body of Man (i.e. humanity), which was offered upon the Cross for the service of man. The Veil is that which divides the apparent "separateness" of the world below from the "wholeness" of the world above, through self-sacrifice or self-denial. (Perhaps a more appropriate term would be "limit-denial.") The four separate elements which make up the personality of the Initiate must be purified by an infusion of Spirit before the domain of the Higher Self can be approached in any way. Only in this manner, can the Initiate become greater than sum of his or her parts.

The Hebrew letters which make up the word Paroketh are Peh, Resh, Kaph, and Tau; four letters which have additional correspondences to the four elements in the Portal Ceremony. Beyond the Veil of the Four Elements lies the Fifth Element—Spirit.

The Veil of Paroketh is also the symbol of the division that exists between the First and Second Orders.

Materials
    Two 7′ long 2″ x 4″ boards
    One 6′ long 2″ x 4″ board
    One 4′ long 2″ x 4″ board
    Two 6′ long 1″ x 2″ boards
    2″ nails
    2-1/2″ nails
    Adjustable curtain rod and attachments
    Two 65″ x 90″ pieces of fabric (may be either white, gold or violet)—
      (2 bed sheets in any of the above colors may be used)
    Sheer fabric 65″ x 90″ (may also be either white, gold or violet)
    Flat latex paint in the same color as the chosen fabric

Tools Needed
    Table saw, mitre saw or circular saw (or hand saw and mitre box)
    Hammer
    Sewing machine
    Scissors

Construction
1)   Take the two 7′ long 2″ x 4″s and nail them to either end of the 6′ long 2″ x 4″ as shown in the diagram. Take one of the 1″ x 2″s and cut off two 18″ lengths from it.

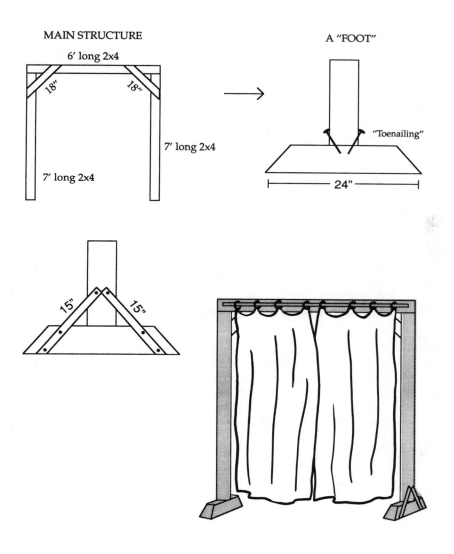

MAIN STRUCTURE

6' long 2x4

18"   18"

7' long 2x4

7' long 2x4

A "FOOT"

"Toenailing"

24"

15"   15"

The Veil of Paroketh

2) Using a mitre saw or a hand saw and a mitre box, mitre all four ends (of the 18" pieces) so that they are all angled at 45 degrees.

3) Nail the two 18" lengths to the 2" x 4"s, to act as corner braces as shown in the diagram.

4) Take the 4' long 2" x 4" and cut it in half. (These pieces are to be the "feet" which support the whole structure.) Mitre all four ends of the feet as before—(optional).

5) Nail one of the "feet" perpendicular to the remaining (bottom) end of one of the 7' long boards. Do this by "toe-nailing." (Using the longer 2-1/2" nails, pound the nails at an angle through the sides of the 7' board into the "foot.")

6) Cut the remaining 1" x 2" board into four 15" lengths. Miter one end of all four boards.

7) Nail all of these 15" long boards to the outside of the structure to act as braces for the feet. (One pair per foot as shown in the diagram. The mitred ends will be closest to the floor.)

Finishing Steps

8) Paint the entire structure with latex paint in one of the colors described above. Allow to dry.

9) Using screws or nails, attach the adjustable curtain rod to the 7' length of the top board.

10) Attach the fabric to the rod as you would a normal curtain. (The Sheer material goes over the heavier fabric on the front side.) You may wish to sew a large hem in the top of the material and thread the curtain rod through it, or simply push the round drapery pins directly through the fabric and hang them on the rod. Trim off any excess material and hem up the bottom.

Ritual for Use

See the ceremony entitled "Purification of the Elements Within" (pp. 295–301).

The White Altar

Use and Symbolism

This Altar is used by the Chief Adept behind the Veil of Paroketh. It is a reflection of the Black Altar of the Outer Order, but on a higher plane of working. Follow the instructions given in chapter 1 on the construction of the Double Cubical Altar, but use white paint instead of black.

Rituals for Use

See the rituals entitled: "The Supreme Convocation of the Watchtowers and The Purification of the Elements Within" (pp. 295–301 and 312–322).

A Guided Visualization for the Portal Grade
(Based on the Rite of the Pentagram and the Five Paths)

After taking a ritual bath and performing a rite of relaxation, put on the regalia of the First Order and the crossed black and white sashes. Two candles, one black and the other white, should be placed upon the Altar, north and south respectively. If possible, an Adept or another Portal member should read the following visualization to you after performing the LBRP. If another person is not available, familiarize yourself with the meditation before hand, and guide yourself along this journey. Enter the Hall giving the Portal Signs:

Close your eyes and continue breathing in the exercise of the Four-fold Breath. See yourself leaving your personal Temple behind. The room slowly fades from your view.

Imagine yourself standing in a great arched stone doorway. Before you is a magnificent Temple with marble pillars, an immense stone Altar, black-and-white tiled floor, an assembly of Egyptian gods and goddesses and Kerubic guardians. Anubis. Horus. Thmê. Osiris. This a place you are very familiar and comfortable with. It is the Hall of the Goddess, Thmê, the Hall of Two Truths. This is where your admission into the mysteries first took place, and your journey on the path of initiation began. For many months you have worked in this Temple, learning its secrets and studying its foundation. Now it is time to journey beyond the confines of this Temple and explore what lies ahead. Near the doorway in which you are standing there is one enormous Black Pillar. Figures and hieroglyphs are carved into its smooth obsidian surface. A red, stained-glass pyramid burns brightly upon its summit. You reach out your hand to touch this pillar, the symbol of the Temple you are leaving behind. You know that once you leave this Temple, the touch of the black pillar will never feel the same as it does now. The assembly of gods seem curiously elated at your parting, as if they understand more about your impending journey than you do. Saluting them with the Signs of a Neophyte, you turn and step out of the archway into a mist-covered landscape.

This is the strangest terrain you have ever encountered. It is neither day nor night. There are no trees nor plants of any kind, no rocks or hills. There is little of anything except a grey haze and fog-enshrouded ground. This is a complete detachment from anything you have yet experienced.

You look around for a guide, for caution tells you not to proceed until one appears. You withdraw for a while into a quiet meditation, imagining yourself as the child-god, Harpocrates, seated upon a Lotus flower. At length you are aroused from this meditation by a unimpressive figure in a simple brown robe. You test the authenticity of the guide by vibrating the Divine name of EHEIEH. You then exchange the Neophyte Signs. Your guide then leads you into the mist.

You continue walking for some time, uncertain of your direction, or if a path even exists under your feet. If only there were something, some marker or symbol, to give you a clue as to where you are going. But again there is nothing. You might be walking in a circle, for all you know. It is as though you and your guide exist is a state of limbo.

You ask the guide where you are going. He indicates that at this point in your spiritual development, it is up to you to decide where your path truly lies. You must find a way out of the fog. Taking the advice of your guide, you reach into yourself to find the knowledge you accumulated as an Initiate. This knowledge will aid you now. But knowledge is not enough, you must begin to put that knowledge to wise and practical use. You are not even certain of the direction you are facing, therefore you close your eyes and ask for the guidance of the Divine Light. Behind the darkness of your closed eyelids, you see an angelic hand appear, a flaming Yod held in its palm. Turning your body until the hand is directly in front of you, you then open your eyes. You now know what direction is east.

You invoke the four elements, saying the proper words and saluting each quarter with the Sign of the Rending of the Veil. As you salute the north, mountains, hills and lush forests appear around you. As you salute the east, a cool gust of wind rushes over you and clouds begin to form. As you open the Veil toward the West, vast oceans and pristine rivers are created. As you make the Sign toward the South, a bolt of lightning strikes a tree, starting a small brush fire that clears away dead vegetation.

A rich landscape has been formed around you where once there was nothing. You pause a moment to perform the Qabalistic Cross. Your guide gives a nod of approval. The two of you continue on in the direction of the eastern wind. A wheel appears off in the sky ahead, but you are too far away to see it clearly.

It is not long before a dreadful sight appears on the right hand side of the path you are traveling. In a field is a skeleton swinging a scythe back and forth, cutting the long stems of wild grass. Beneath its bony feet are human body parts protruding from the earth, which are nourishing the fresh vegetation. The skeleton stops swinging his implement and gives you a long, eye-less stare. A deadly scorpion picks over the bones for food, and a poisonous serpent curls around the scrawny legs of the reaper. Off in the distance beyond the figure is the colossal form of Typhon, spewing smoke and ash from his mouth like some infernal volcano.

This is the image of transformation, which most people fear intensely. It is a frightening image because many individuals fear change of any kind. Change is, however, a natural occurrence in the cycle of the universe. Change of consciousness is necessary for spiritual evolution. You notice a white eagle soaring above the head of the skeleton, a symbol of purity and transmutation. You give the Sign of the Enterer at the figure. It answers with the Sign of Silence. You and your guide proceed along the eastern path.

The landscape continues as before, unchanged in its richness. Far ahead of you, there appears to be a large tree in the shape of the letter Tau. A figure is hanging from it, but you are too far away to see any details.

To the left of the path another strange sight is evident. A hairy creature with a goat's head, huge bat-like wings and clawed feet stands on top of a cubical of black stone. To the rock are chained two smaller horned creatures who dance and mimic the larger being. The great demon spits and laughs at you as it flaps its leathery wings and rocks back and forth upon the Altar, trampling protective pentagrams underfoot. The figure hurdles a stream of obscenities at you and tells you to return from whence you came.

However, you are aware of the irony of this situation. The figure of the Devil is a conglomerate of various animal parts put together as an illusion to mislead you; a creation built up from humanity's own fears and corruption and which serves as a scapegoat for all evil acts committed by human beings. This illusion, like all illusions placed as obstacles to your spiritual growth, must be dealt with, exposed, and seen for what it truly is, or else you will remain like the two smaller creatures, held in bondage by their own misconceptions. The greater sight of the inner vision is called for. The figure of the Devil does not alarm you, in fact it provokes you into laughter.

The apparition of the Devil vanishes without a trace. Off in the forest beyond, you see the figure of gentle Pan, Greek God of nature, much maligned by Christianity which turned the peace-loving god into a monster. Pan is grateful that you have shattered the false illusionary form of the devil. With a flick of his goat's tail, he smiles and slips quietly into the woods. Soon after, you hear the sweet sound of music from his hollow-reed pipes.

Continuing on in the direction of the East, you and your guide eventually find yourselves in the middle of a great valley where a clear river divides the land. A mighty volcano spews ash into the distant sky, but even that impressive sight cannot draw your eyes away from the gigantic form of an Angel who straddles the river, one foot resting on dry land, and the other foot in the water. The eyes of the Angel are closed, and you get the impression that she does not need eyes to see you. Soft reddish hair frames her face and falls in long locks against her blue robe. Her wings are like two prismatic crescents which rise vapor-like into the air beyond. A single golden square adorns her azure garment, and the brilliant orb of the sun graces her brow. In her slender hands she holds two vases, one containing water, and the other containing fire. She mixes the two primal elements together, creating steam and liquid gold.

The Angel then releases the two vases which remain floating in the air, completely unsupported. The mixing of the elements continues as before; the Fire and Water now form an infinity sign as they flow from one vessel into the other. Her hands free, the Angel makes the Sign of the Philosophus. Without warning, a fierce lion appears from behind a bush, ready to spring at you. Somehow you realize that what is about to occur is necessary, and you resist the urge to banish. The great cat lunges at you and knocks you off your feet. The beast delivers a painful bite to your left hip then simply walks away and begins licking its paw. The sting of the wound is intense. The sight of blood on your hand causes you to enter a trance-like state:

Flames are all around you, engulfing your entire body. The pain of the wound increases as you feel the purging Fire burning away the impurities of your personality . . . all the untruths, jealousies, cruelties and injustices you have ever committed against others and against your own higher self. All these evils are brought to the surface like a boil. They arise out of your skin to surround your body like the foul smoke of a rubbish-fire. The stench of your own naked evils is enough to gag you, and you feel suddenly exposed and ashamed.

The Angel then makes the Sign of the Practicus, forming a cup over her heart with her hands. As she does so, you become aware of a pure white eagle flying low, skimming across the surface of the river. As you lay exhausted on the ground, the great bird circles above you and finally lands, sinking its sharp talons into your right hip.

The pain is almost a relief. A sudden rainstorm appears. Heavy drops of water wash over your face and into your mouth. The foul black cloud is washed away without a trace by the redeeming rain. The bird of prey is not at all bothered by the downpour. It regards you with stern eyes, but it seems to be saying, "mercy . . . forgiveness . . . peace."

The rain stops as suddenly as it began and the bird takes flight. The sun appears from behind a cloud and its rays form the most perfect rainbow you have ever seen in the east. A wondrous feeling of freedom overtakes you. You feel healed and rejuvenated. Standing up to face the Angel, you reach down to touch with both hands, the wounds left by the kerubic creatures. Holding out your hands toward the Angel, you notice that your hands are not bloodied. In the palm of one hand is a small tongue of flame and in the other is a handful of water.

The Angel makes the Sign of the Equated Cross over you. Bringing both hands together over your heart, you absorb the equilibrated elements into your Tiphareth center, and a rush of white brilliance reverberates throughout all the spheres and paths of your inner Middle Pillar.

The Angel begins to fade from view, transforming into glistening drops of mist which hang in the air and catch the sun's rays to form flowing prismatic shapes. The shimmering forms gather together into a thin wisp of a veil which extends before you in the east. Your guide, whom you had all but forgotten, takes you by the arm and places you in front of this etheric curtain. Giving the Sign of the Rending of the Veil, you part the curtain.

An immense White Pillar, counterpart to the Black Pillar that you saw earlier looms before you, stretching very nearly to the sky. Its white marble surface is fully etched with sacred scenes and symbols. Its red pyramid capital is almost lost to view in the clouds. You approach this Pillar and touch it, just as you embraced its black twin. An inner part of you rejoices at this union. For a long time you remain, in communion with the energies of the Pillar of Light.

At length it is time to end this journey. Your guide takes you back along the path, past Pan's forest and the figure of Death swinging his scythe. Finally, you come to the door of the familiar Temple in the west. You exchange the Signs of the Opening and the Closing of the Veil with your companion and bid him farewell. Then, giving the Neophyte Signs, you enter the Hall of Dual Manifestation.

The assembly of gods and goddesses seems elated to see you. The Temple is the same, but you feel different . . . changed somehow. It is as though you have reached a different level or plateau in your spiritual development, and your perspective is no longer the same as it had been. You spend a brief period of time at the Altar flame before deciding to end the meditation.

Finally, you see your own physical Temple room and see yourself seated within it. Bring your consciousness slowly back into your physical body, sensing the room around you. After adjusting yourself to your surroundings, you may bring the visualization to its completion.

At the end of the meditation, you may write down any impressions or experiences in a magickal diary before closing with the LBRP. Give the Sign of the Closing of the Veil when finished.

THE IMPLEMENTS OF THE
PORTAL GRADE OFFICERS

The Third Adept's Wand

Use and Symbolism

The Salt-headed Wand is the scepter of the Third Adept in the Portal Temple of the Order. The Third Adept in this particular ceremony always represents the feminine qualities of moisture and receptability. There is valid speculation within the Order as to the correctness of the symbolism concerning this particular wand—whether or not the symbol of Mercury should actually replace the Salt symbol as the wand-head. However we shall not enter into this discussion here. What we have provided is a description of the Third Adept's wand as portrayed in the original Order documents.

Of the Three Alchemic essentials, salt is the physical vehicle of manifestation for the other two. (The phrase "Salt of the Earth" takes on new meaning in this regard.) Sulphur characterizes each thing in a particular way—Mercury gives animation—but Salt provides the matrix. Salt is the receptive body—the material substance. Salt is in a continual state of evolution; taking on a new body as the old body is steadily cast away. This is a process of purification which arises out of separation. To cleanse is purification, but the work of purification is more than a degree of cleansing. That which is pure is freed from that which is impure. The purification of Salt in all of its triune parts: the body, soul and spirit, is an important step in the initiate's spiritual evolution.

The symbol of Salt on the Tree of Life embraces all the Sephiroth but Malkuth, and is as it were, the Reconciler between the Sulphur and Mercury. The horizontal dividing line in the sigil implies the precept of Hermes, "as above so below."

Materials Needed

One 3/4" thick dowel approx. 36" long
One 6" x 6" piece of 3/4" soft wood (pine, balsa or bass)
One 1/4" wooden dowel or peg 1" in length
Yellow carpenter's glue
Gesso
Acrylic paint: blue
Clear lacquer finish (spray or brush on)

Tools Needed

Scroll saw or coping saw
Electric drill with 1/4" and 3/4" bits
Sandpaper (coarse, medium and fine)
Artist's paint brushes (medium to large)

Construction: The Head

1) Draw the sigil of Salt shown in the diagram with proper dimensions on the 6" x 6" piece of wood. With the saw, cut out the outer shape of the symbol.

2) Drill two holes insidE the shaded half-circle shaded areas of the wand head. (Remember: it is important to use a drill bit that is wider than your saw blade.)

3) With your saw unplugged, detach the blade from the saw. Stick the blade through one of the holes you have drilled and re-attach the blade to the saw. Plug the saw back in and cut out the shaded area of wood.

4) Drill a hole 1/2" deep and 1/4" wide in the center of the bottom side of the wand head.

Construction: The Shaft

5) Into the left-over piece of 3/4" thick pine wood, drill a 3/4" diameter hole. Around this hole, draw a 1-1/2" diameter circle. Cut this circle out of the wood using the scroll saw. You will end up with a donut-shaped ring of wood.

6) Take the 36" long dowel (shaft) and drill a hole 1/2" deep and 1/4" in diameter into one end of it. Glue the 1" wooden peg into the hole you have just drilled so that half of the peg is embedded into the end of the dowel and half of it sticks out.

7) Apply glue to the inside of the ring. Slide it over the top end of the shaft. (If the ring is too tight, sand inside its center hole.)

8) Pour some glue into the hole you drilled into the bottom end of the wand head and attach the pentagram to the wand shaft. The head of the wand should fit snugly against the supporting ring. (Note: You may wish to add a middle band and a pommel to the wand for aesthetic purposes.)

Finishing Steps

9) Sand the entire surface of the scepter so that it is smooth. With a paint brush, cover the wand with a coat of gesso. Allow to dry.

10) Sand the painted surface (especially the shaft) lightly until smooth. Apply a second coat if needed.

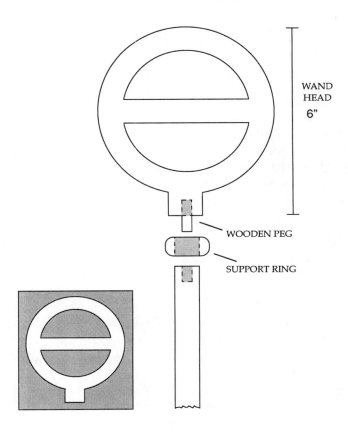

WAND
HEAD
6"

WOODEN PEG

SUPPORT RING

Third Adept's Wand in the Portal

11) Paint the wand entirely blue. Paint or spray on a sealant to protect the painted wand. Allow to dry.

Ritual for Use

The Rite of Self-Purification Through Salt

For this ceremony the Magician of the Portal should be dressed in the attire of the Outer Order, with crossed black and white sashes. The Temple should be arranged in accordance with the opening of the Portal grade. A dagger or sword for banishing should be at hand. Upon the Altar should be a rose, paten of salt, cup of water, and incense; as well as a small cauldron with burning charcoal. The magician should also have the finished Salt-headed wand. Enter the Hall giving the Portal Signs.

After a few moments of meditation, give five knocks and go clockwise to the Northeast. Proclaim, "HEKAS! HEKAS! ESTE BEBELOI!"

Perform either the LBRP or the SBRP.

Take up the incense upon the Altar. Starting in the East, trace a cross in the air. Wave the incense thrice in the form of the Invoking Fire Triangle. Do this in all quarters. Then circumambulate the Temple once more while saying, "Every way to the unfashioned soul stretch out the Reins of Fire. When thou seest a sacred Fire, without Form, shining flashingly through the depth of the world, Hear the voice of Fire." Replace the incense.

Take up the cup of water and go to the East. Trace a cross and the Invoking Water Triangle there. Repeat this in all quarters. Circumambulate the Temple once more and say, "Seek thou the way of the Soul, whence or by what order, having served the body, to the same place from which thou didst flow down in the radiant waters." Replace the cup.

Perform the mystic circumambulation around the Temple thrice, saluting with the Neophyte Signs when passing the east.

Go west of the Altar and face east. Perform the Adoration to the Lord of the Universe.

Perform the SIRP, saluting each quarter with the Sign of the

Rending of the Veil.

Take up the Salt-headed wand and go to the east of the Altar, facing the veil. With the wand, trace a large symbol of Salt and intone the name "YHVH ELOHIM" nine times using the vibratory formula. Visualize strongly the sigil in blue, surrounded by a halo of orange. Pronounce the Hebrew name of salt: "MELACH." Do this in all four quarters.

Return to the west of the Altar and face east. Give the Sign of the Rending of the Veil. Touch the head of the wand to the dish of salt. Then trace the sigil of salt upon your forehead with the top of the wand and vibrate "EHEIEH" three times, (for the triune aspects of alchemic salt). Then say, "ACHAD! And of the one Mind, the intelligible Mind. For the Mind is not without the intelligible; it exists not without it."

Again touch the wand tip to the salt and trace with it the symbol of salt on your left temple. Vibrate "YAH" three times while endeavouring to visualize the sigil. Say, "All things have issued from that one Fire. For the Creator perfected all things, and delivered them over to the second Mind, which the whole Race of humanity call the First."

Touch the wand again to the salt and trace the sigil of salt on your right temple. Vibrate "YHVH ELOHIM" thrice. Then say, "What the Mind speaks, it speaks by understanding. Power is with them, Mind is from Her. And there appeared the Triad, Virtue and Wisdom. And multiscient Verity. This way floweth the shape of the Triad, being pre-existent. Not the first Essence but they are measured. For thou must conceive that all things serve these three Principles. The first course is sacred, but in the middle. Another the aerial; which cherished the Earth in Fire. And Fountain of Fountains, and of all Fountains. The Matrix containing all things. Thence abundantly springs forth the generation of multivarious Matter."

Repeat this procedure and mark the left shoulder with the salt sigil. Intone the name "AL" three times. Then say, "Ideas being many ascend into the Lucid Worlds. Springing into them, and which there are three Tops. Beneath them lies the Chief of Immortals. Principles which have understood the intelligible works of the Creator. Disclosed them in sensible Works as in Bodies; being as it were, the ferry-man betwixt the Creator and Matter. And producing manifest Images of unmanifest things. And inscribing unmanifest things in the manifest frame of the world."

Mark the right shoulder with the sigil and vibrate the name, "ELOHIM GIBOR" thrice. Say, "For out of him spring all Implacable Thunders of the entirely-lucid strength of Father-begotten Hecate, and he who begirds the flower of Fire, and the Strong spirit of the Poles fiery above. He gave to his Intellectuals that they should guard the Tops. Mingling the power of his own strength in the Intellectuals. O how the world hath intellectual guides inflexible! Because she is the Operatrix, because she is the Dispensatrix of Life-giving Fire. Because also it fills the Life-producing bosom of Hecate. And instills in the Intellectuals the enlivning strength of potent Fire. They are the guardians of the works of the Eternal."

Touch the top of the wand in the salt and mark the sigil over the heart. Intone the name of "YHVH ELOAH VE-DAATH" three times. Then say, "For the soul being a bright fire, by the power of the Creator remains Immortal, and is Mistress of Life; and possesseth many complexions of the cavities of the world: For it is in imitation of the mind; but that which is born hath something of the Body. The channels being intermixed, she performs the works of incorruptible Spirit. For the Eternal did put the Mind in the Soul, and the soul in the body."

Trace a horizontal line across the body, just below the heart.

Touch the wand to salt again, marking the left hip with the sigil: Vibrate the name of "YHVH TZABAOTH" thrice. Say, "Of us the Creator of Gods and humans imposed, abundantly animating Light, Fire, Aether, Worlds. For natural works co-exist with the Intellectual Light of the Creator, for the soul which adorn'd the great Heaven, and adorning with the Creator. But her horns are fixed above, but about the shoulders of the Goddess, immense Nature is exalted. Again tireless Nature commands the Worlds and Works."

Repeat the process and mark the right hip with the sigil. Intone the name of "ELOHIM TZABAOTH" thrice. Then say, "From the Mind of the Eternal came omniform ideas; and flying out of one Fountain they sprang forth; for, from the Creator was the Counsel and end, by which they are connected to the Eternal, by alternate life from several vehicles. But they were divided, being by Intellectual Fire distributed; for the King did set before the multiform World and intellectual incorruptible pattern; this print through the World he promoting, of whose form according to which the World appeared beautified with all kinds of ideas, of which there is one fountain, out of which came rushing forth others distributed, being broken about the Bodies of the World, which through the vast recesses, like swarms, are carried roundabout every way."

Repeat the process and mark the groin with the sigil. Vibrate the name of "SHADDAI EL CHAI" three times. Then say, "The maker who operating alone framed the world. And there was another bulk of Fire, by itself operating all things that the body of the World might be perfected and not seem membranous. The whole World of Fire, and Water, and Earth, and all-nourishing Aether, the unexpressible and expressible Watchwords of the World. One life by another from the distributed channels passing from above to the opposite part, through the center of the Earth."

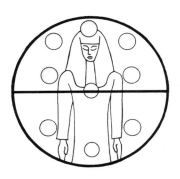

The Sigil of Salt on the Human Figure

Remain west of the Altar. Sprinkle salt into the burning cauldron. With the wand, trace the sigil of salt over the cauldron. Pronounce again the Hebrew name of the element: "MELACH." Give the Sign of the Rending of the Veil. Visualize the symbol of salt superimposed over your body, stretching from Kether to Yesod. Feel the receptivity of the passive alchemic principle as it provides a material body for the spiritual Sulphur and Mercury to enliven. Imagine yourself cleansed through the this process. Your purified body becomes a Temple for the Divine Spirit to dwell within. After contemplating this for a some time, say the following:

"True, without falsehood, certain and most true, that which is above is as that which is below, and that which is below is as that which is above, for the performance of the miracles of the One Thing. And as all are from One, by the mediation of one, so all things have their birth from this One Thing by adaptation. The Sun is its father, the Moon its mother, the Wind carries it in its belly, its nurse is the Earth. This is the Father of all perfection, or consummation of the whole world. Its power is integrating, if it be turned into earth. Thou shalt separate the earth from the fire, the subtle from the gross, with great ingenuity. It ascends from earth to heaven and descends again to earth. So thou hast the glory of the whole world."

Visualize an astral Banner of East enveloping you like a cloak, sealing the rite of purification with the protective Light of the Divine. Intone "EHEIEH" four times using the Vibratory Formula. Perform the Qabalistic Cross.

When finished, give the Sign of the Closing of the Veil.

Perform the Reverse Circumambulation.

Perform the LBRP or the SBRP.

Say, "I now release any beings which may have been imprisoned by this ceremony. Go in peace to your abodes and habitations with the blessings of YHVH ELOHIM!"

Give five knocks as in the beginning.

Say, "I now declare this Temple duly closed."

SO MOTE IT BE!

The Second Adept's Wand

Use and Symbolism

The Sulphur-headed Wand is the scepter of the Second Adept in the Portal Temple of the Order. The Second Adept in this Ceremony (as well as in the higher ceremonies of the Inner Order) always represents the qualities of heat and the active male principle. That is why the most fiery of the three alchemic principles is attributed this particular officer.

Sulphur is that which gathers together and fashions all that is of the Earth. The nature of Sulphur is both tangible and intangible.

Within its tangible aspect it is an oil and is to be found in all substances. Its intangible aspect is that of consciousness—to be found in all substances in varying degrees. Sulphur corresponds to the Superconsciousness or the Cosmic Consciousness.

Cirlot describes Sulphur as follows: "Symbolic of the desire for positive action, and of vital heat. In the complex symbolism of alchemy, sulphur represents one of the stages of the evolution of matter (and of the psyche). According to René Alleau, the various stages, from the lowest to the highest, can be classified as follows: PRIOR ELEMENTS, denoting the inherent possibilities of the cosmos, or of man; PRIME MATTER, or the elementary organization of inherent possibilities, equivalent perhaps to the unconscious, or the instincts; MERCURY, or the first purification, feelings, imagination, the dominant female principle; SULPHUR, or more profound purification, reason and intuition, the male principle; and the Great Work, or transcendence."

The symbol of Sulphur on the Tree of Life does not touch the four lower Sephiroth. The Cross terminates in Tiphareth, whereby, as it were, the Supernal Triangle is to be grasped, and Tiphareth is the purified human being.

The Sulphur-headed wand could be used by the Magician in a work of inner alchemy; that is, as part of a consecration rite designed to elevate the individual mind toward the cosmic consciousness. This is a process of self-evolution which uses the heat and activity of alchemic sulphur to expand ones spiritual awareness.

Materials Needed
  One 3/4" thick dowel approx. 36" long
  One 7" x 4" piece of 3/4" soft wood (pine, balsa or bass)
  One 1/4" wooden dowel or peg 1" in length
  Yellow carpenter's glue
  Gesso
  Acrylic paint: red
  Clear lacquer finish (spray or brush on)

Tools Needed
  Scroll saw or coping saw
  Electric drill with 1/4" and 3/4" bits
  Sandpaper (coarse, medium and fine)
  Artist's paint brushes (medium to large)

Construction: The Head
1) Draw the sigil of Sulphur shown in the diagram with proper dimensions on the 7" x 4" piece of wood. With the saw, cut out the outer shape of the symbol.

2) Drill one hole inside the central shaded area of the triangular section of the wand head. (Remember: it is important to use a drill bit that is wider than your saw blade.)

3) With your saw unplugged, detach the blade from the saw. Stick the blade through one of the holes you have drilled and re-attach the blade to the saw. Plug the saw back in and cut out the shaded area of wood.

4) Drill a hole 1/2" deep and 1/4" wide in the center of the bottom side of the wand head.

Construction: The Shaft
    (Note: Follow steps 5-8 as given for the construction of the Third Adept's Wand in this chapter.)

Finishing Steps
9) Sand the entire surface of the scepter so that it is smooth. With a paint brush, cover the wand with a coat of gesso. Allow to dry.

10) Sand the painted surface (especially the shaft) lightly until smooth. Apply a second coat if needed.

11) Paint the wand entirely red. Paint or spray on a sealant to protect the painted wand. Allow to dry.

Ritual for Use

The Rite of Self-Consecration Through Sulphur

For this ceremony the Magician of the Portal should be dressed in the attire of the Outer Order, with crossed black and white sashes. The Temple should be arranged in accordance with the opening of the Portal grade. A dagger or sword for banishing should be at hand. Upon the Altar should be a rose, paten of salt, cup of water, and incense; as well as a dish of anointing oil and a small cauldron of burning charcoal. The Magician should also have the finished Sulphur Wand. Enter the Hall giving the Portal Signs.

After a few moments of meditation, give five knocks and go clockwise to the Northeast. Proclaim, "HEKAS! HEKAS! ESTE BEBELOI!"

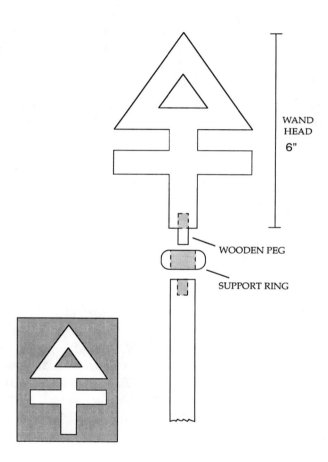

WAND
HEAD
6"

WOODEN PEG

SUPPORT RING

The Second Adept's Wand in the Portal.

Perform either the LBRP or the SBRP.

Take up the incense upon the Altar. Starting in the East, trace a cross in the air. Wave the incense thrice in the form of the Invoking Fire Triangle. Do this in all quarters. Then circumambulate the Temple once more while saying, "Every way to the unfashioned soul stretch out the Reins of Fire. When thou seest a sacred Fire, without Form, shining flashingly through the depth of the world, hear the voice of Fire." Replace the incense.

Take up the cup of water and go to the East. Trace a cross and the Invoking Water Triangle there. Repeat this in all quarters. Circumambulate the Temple once more and say, "Seek thou the way of the Soul, whence or by what order, having served the body, to the same place from which thou didst flow down in the radiant waters." Replace the cup.

Perform the mystic circumambulation around the Temple thrice, saluting with the Neophyte Signs when passing the East.

Go west of the Altar and face east. Perform the Adoration to the Lord of the Universe.

Perform the SIRP, saluting each quarter with the Sign of the Rending of the Veil.

Take up the Sulphur-headed Wand and go to the east of the Altar, facing the Veil. With the wand, trace a large symbol of sulphur and intone the name "YAH" twice using the Vibratory Formula. Visualize strongly the sigil in red, surrounded by a halo of green. Pronounce the Hebrew name for Sulphur: "GAPHRITH." Do this in all four quarters.

Return to the west of the Altar and face east. Give the Sign of the Rending of the Veil. Dip the point of the wand into the dish of anointing oil (not too much). Then trace the sigil of sulphur upon your forehead with the tip of the wand and vibrate "EHEIEH" three times, (for the triune aspects of alchemic sulphur). Then say, "Where the Parental Monad is."

Again dip the wand tip into the oil and trace with it the symbol of Sulphur on your left temple. Vibrate "YAH" three times while endeavouring to visualize the sigil. Say, "The Monad is enlarged, which generates two. For the Dyad sits by him, and glitters with Intellectual Sections."

Dip the wand again into the oil and trace the sigil of Sulphur on your right temple. Vibrate "YHVH ELOHIM" thrice. Then say, "For in the whole World shineth the Triad, over which the Monad rules. This Order is the beginning of all section. For the mind of the Creator said that all things be cut into three. Whose Will assented, and all things were divided. For the mind of the Eternal Creator said into three, governing all things by mind."

Repeat this procedure and mark the left shoulder with the Sulphur sigil. Intone the name "AL" three times. Then say, "For the Paternal self-begotten Mind understanding his work sowed in all the fiery bond of Love, that all things might continue loving forever. Neither those things which are intellectually context in the light of the Father in all things. That being the Elements of the World they might persist in Love."

Mark the right shoulder with the sigil and vibrate the name "ELOHIM GIBOR" thrice. Say, "Every way to the unfashioned soul stretch the Reins of Fire. The Fire-glowing cognition hath the first Rank. For the Mortal approaching to the Fire, shall have Light from God. For to the slow Mortal the Gods are swift. The Furies are stranglers of men. The burgeons, even of ill Matter, are profitable good. Let Hope nourish thee in the Fiery Angelic region."

Sigil of Sulphur

Dip the point of the wand in the oil and mark the sigil of Sulphur over the heart. Intone the name of "YHVH ELOAH VE-DAATH" three times. Then say, "It behooves thee to hasten to the Light, and to the beams of the Eternal; from whence was sent to thee a soul clothed with much Mind. These things the Creator conceived, and so the mortal was animated, for the parental Mind sowed symbols in souls; replenishing the Soul with profound Love. The Soul of Man will in a manner clasp God to herself; having nothing mortal, she is wholly inebriated from God: for she boasts Harmony, in which the mortal Body exists."

Remain west of the Altar. Burn some incense in the cauldron. With the wand, trace the sigil of Sulphur over the cauldron. Again pronounce the name of the element: "GAPHRITH." Give the Sign of the Rending of the Veil. Visualize the sigil of Sulphur superimposed over your body, stretching from Kether to Tiphareth. Imagine yourself consecrated through the act of devotion. Feel the heat of the active alchemic principle unfolding in manifold and distinctive ways which bring you ever closer to the Godhead which is One with all things. You begin to touch upon a greater consciousness than you have ever known. Continue this meditation for as long as you like.

Visualize an astral Banner of the East enveloping you as a cloak, sealing the act of consecration with the protective Light of the Divine. Intone "EHEIEH" four times, employing the Vibratory Formula. Perform the Qabalistic Cross.

When finished, give the Sign of the Closing of the Veil.

Perform the Reverse Circumambulation.

Perform the LBRP or the SBRP.

Say, "I now release any beings which may have been imprisoned by this ceremony. Go in peace to your abodes and habitations with the blessings of YAH!"

Give five knocks as in the beginning.

Say, "I now declare this Temple duly closed"

SO MOTE IT BE

The Chief Adept's Wand

Use and Symbolism

The Pentagram-headed wand is the scepter of the Chief Adept in the Portal Temple of the Order. The pentagram represents the four elements of nature crowned by the fifth—Spirit. As far back as the days of the Egyptians, the five-pointed star has signified "rising upward towards the point of origin." In the Portal Ceremony, it is wielded by the Chief Adept to instill these ideas deeply with in the psyche of the candidate, who in this ritual symbolically receives the fifth and final element.

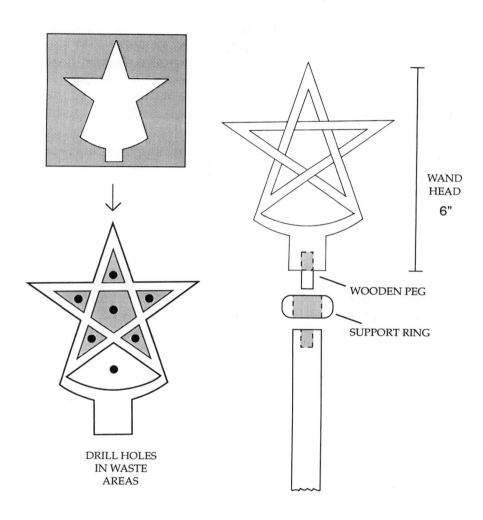

WAND
HEAD

6"

WOODEN PEG

SUPPORT RING

DRILL HOLES
IN WASTE
AREAS

The Chief Adept's Wand in the Portal.

The shaft of the scepter is also painted in the five elemental colors of the pentagram: SPIRIT—white (the longest section on the wand), FIRE—red, AIR—yellow, WATER—blue, and EARTH—black.

The Pentagram-headed Scepter can be employed to invoke any or all of the Five Elements including Spirit. An Adept could certainly use this wand in a ritual where the Enochian tablets (including the Tablet of Union) are also present. (A ritual for use of this wand is given after the section describing the construction of the Elemental Tablets.)

Materials Needed
   One 3/4" thick dowel approx. 36" long
   One 6-1/2" x 6" piece of 3/4" soft wood (pine, balsa or bass)
   One 1/4" wooden dowel or peg 1" in length
   Yellow carpenter's glue
   Gesso
   Acrylic paints: red, yellow, blue, black, white
   Clear lacquer finish (spray or brush on)

Tools Needed
   Scroll saw or coping saw
   Electric drill with 1/4" and 3/4" bits
   Sandpaper (course, medium and fine)
   Artist's paint brushes (medium to large)

Construction: The Pentagram Head
   (Note: Follow steps 5-8 as given for the construction of the Third Adept's Wand in this Chapter.)

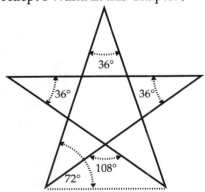

Pentagram Diagram

1) Draw the pentagram shown in the diagram with proper dimensions on the 6-1/2" x 6" piece of wood. (See diagram showing the degrees of the angles and size of the pentagram.) With the saw, cut out the outer shape of the pentagram.

2) Drill seven holes, one inside each of the shaded (negative space) areas of the wand head. (Remember: it is important to use a drill bit that is wider than your saw blade.)

3) With your saw unplugged, detach the blade from the saw. Stick the blade through one of the holes you have drilled and reattach the blade to the saw. Plug the saw back in and begin cutting out the shaded area of wood. Repeat this process for all seven drilled holes until all the waste area of wood has been cut out.

4) Drill a hole 1/2" deep and 1/4" wide in the center of the bottom side of the wand head.

Finishing Steps

9) Sand the entire surface of the scepter so that it is smooth. With a paint brush, cover the wand with a coat of gesso. Allow to dry.

10) Sand the painted surface (especially the shaft) lightly until smooth. Apply a second coat if needed.

11) Mark the shaft with a pencil into five sections: the top section under the wand head will be 10" in length. (This includes the support ring. The next three sections will all be 6" in length. The final section will be 8" in length.

12) Paint the head of the wand and the first section white. Paint the second section red. Paint the third section yellow. Paint the fourth section blue. Paint the last section black. Paint or spray on a sealant such as clear lacquer to protect the painted wand. Allow to dry.

THE PORTAL OFFICER'S LAMENS

The lamens belonging to the officers in the Portal differ from those lamens attributed to the same officers in the First Order. The reason for this is that the Portal Hall is the first Temple yet encountered where all the Officer's lamens have changed. Even the Hiereus and the Hegemon, the only Officers remaining from the Outer Order, wear emblems completely different from the ones they wore in the Neophyte Hall. In fact all of the officers in the Portal, with the exception of the Chief Adept, wear symbols that are unique to this particular Hall. The Second and Third Adepts wear lamens which symbolize their specific Elemental affiliation. The Hiereus and the Hegemon both wear lamens that are adorned with Hexagrams—references to the Macrocosm and to the Perfected Human Being.

The *Hegemon's Lamen* in the Portal Hall reveals her important duties as the keeper of the balance within the Temple. The lamen depicts the opposing Triangles of Fire and Water conjoined and in perfect equilibrium...the Macrocosmic Hexagram. This lamen is not unlike a simplified version of the Banner of the East (minus the central crosses), showing her importance in bringing the candidate throughout all the grades to the Antechamber of the Light of L.V.X. In the Portal Ritual, she is also the Officer who performs all of the workings of Elemental Air (once the Chief Adept has invoked all of the Elements). She shows therefore that Air is the Reconciler between the Forces of Fire and Water, and that only through perfect balance of these two extremes is the Portal to the Light traversed.

The *Hiereus' Lamen* in the Portal is identical to one of the diagrams shown to the candidate in this grade: "Below, is shown the Occult Symbol of Malkuth, the Tenth Sephirah. It is in four parts, corresponding to the Maltese Cross. They are Fire of Earth, Water of Earth, Air of Earth, Earth of Earth, as indicated by the Symbol. They correspond to the four grade of the First Order, which in one sense, quitteth not Malkuth, being the Grades of the four lowest Sephiroth of Malkuth in Assiah. Upon them is surcharged a white Hexagram in a circle. The 6 and the 4 make 10, the number of Malkuth on the Tree." (Note: this is also one reason why the Earth Pentacle of the Z.A.M. is based upon this design.) "The Hexagram is also the Sign of the Macrocosm—of Tiphareth, and of the Six Upper Sephiroth, wherefore it is white—Spirit ruling over matter. Six is a perfect number, for its whole equals the sum of its parts ... Remember that the whole number of Malkuth is 496—which again is a perfect number. Malkuth must then be equated and perfected by the 6 ruling the 4: and the link between 6 and 4 is the number of the Pentagram."

The Hiereus is the Officer who sits in the lowest point of Malkuth in the Hall at the border of the Qlippotic Realm, enthroned upon matter and robed in Darkness. In the Portal, he is the Officer in charge of the workings of Elemental Earth. His lamen in this grade primarily shows that Spirit must always govern matter (represented by the four sub-elements). If Spirit does not crown matter, the result is chaos and evil, symbolized by the Qlippoth.

The *Third Adept's Lamen* portrays the Forces of Water, and she thus oversees all the workings of Water in the Portal grade. Her lamen is painted in the Flashing Colors of Elemental Water. She represents the Powers of the Black (Feminine) Pillar in this grade. The lamen shows a octogram in the center of which is a water cup drawn in the style of the Stolistes Badge. The octogram is formed from two squares superimposed one over the other at an angle. It thus refers not only to the Sphere of Hod, but also to that of Chesed (i.e. the two watery Sephiroth).

The *Second Adept's Lamen* depicts the Powers of Fire, and he is in charge of all the workings of Fire in the Portal grade. He represents the Powers of the White (Masculine) Pillar in the Portal Ceremony. His lamen is painted in the Flashing Colors of Elemental Fire. Upon it are shown an upright Fire Triangle within a Pentagram. The Pentagram refers to the Sphere of Geburah, the fiery Sephirah.

The *Chief Adept's Lamen* differs from the others in that it is in the shape of the Rose Cross, which more properly belongs to the Second Order. This Lamen is worn by the Chief Adept in the Portal grade to give the candidate a glimpse of the symbolism of the Second Order. Because it is not like the other Portal Lamens, its use and symbolism is discussed separately and in greater detail below elsewhere in this chapter.

The lamens are hung from collars in the specific Elemental colors. Although these lamens officially occur only in the Portal Ceremony, they may be utilized by an Adept in any ceremony invoking Elemental energies. A Magician of the Portal grade should use them in a ritual/meditation designed to visually explore their colors and symbolism.

Materials Needed
> One 12" x 12" piece of plywood that is 1/4" thick
> Wood putty
> Gesso
> Acrylic paints: black, white, red, green, blue, orange, violet
> Clear lacquer finish

Tools Needed
> Electric jigsaw, scroll saw or coping saw
> Compass, pencil and straight edge
> A protractor
> File or rasp
> Artist's brushes—fine and medium sizes
> Sandpaper—medium and fine

Construction
> (As noted in chapter 1, pre-cut wooden disks may be purchased at a craft store or hobby shop.)

1) Using the compass, draw four 4" circles on the piece of wood. Cut out circles with saw.

2) If the circle of wood has jagged edges, file them smooth. Any gaps in the wood can be filled in with wood putty. Sand the wood until it is smooth.

3) Paint entirely with gesso. Let dry. Sand. Apply another coat if needed.

THE THIRD ADEPT

THE SECOND ADEPT

THE HIEREUS

THE HEGEMON

The Portal Lamens.

The Hegemon's Lamen

1) This lamen requires that you draw a perfect hexagram within a circle. This is done as follows: Find the center hole created by the compass point and draw a second, smaller circle 1/2" inside the edge of the disk.

2) Lightly draw a cross from the center of the circle which divides it into four equal portions.

3) Divide the circle into six equal parts beginning at the intersection of the top of the circle and the vertical line of the cross.

4) Draw lines which connect these points, forming the hexagram. Draw a second set of lines approx. 1/4" inside the first, giving the hexagram its thickness.

5) The lamen is to be painted as follows: The Fire Triangle is red, the Water Triangle is blue. (Be sure to make the triangles interlock.) They are painted against a white "ground." Apply sealant for protection.

The Hiereus' Lamen

1) See the directions given above for drawing a hexagram within a circle.

2) The hexagram is to be painted white against a ground composed of the four colors of Malkuth surrounded by a white outer circle. (Note: This lamen looks identical to the Earth Pentacle of the Zelator Adeptus Minor, except for the absence of sigils and Divine names around the white outer edge. See chapter 5.) The inner "ground" is a circular section divided into the colors of: citrine (top quarter), russet (left quarter), olive (right quarter) and black (bottom quarter). When paint is dry, apply sealant.

The Third Adept's Lamen

1) On this lamen, an octogram is to be drawn: Find the center hole created by the compass point and draw a second, smaller circle 1/2" inside the edge of the disk.

2) Lightly draw a cross from the center of the circle which divides it into four equal portions. Connect the points of the cross to form a square.

3) Find the center of each side of the square and draw a second cross from the center of the circle to the edge of the outer circle.

4) Connect the points of the cross to form a second square, which overlaps the first. Both squares together form the octogram.

5) A cup shaped like that of Stolistes is to be drawn in the center of the

lamen.

6) The octogram is to be painted completely orange. The cup and the small ground area behind the octogram should be painted blue. The outer circle should also be painted orange.

The Second Adept's Lamen

1) This lamen requires that you draw a perfect pentagram within a circle. This is done as follows:

2) Find the center hole created by the compass point and draw a second, smaller circle 1/2" inside the edge of the disk. Draw one line through the center point to the circle just drawn.

3) Using a protractor, draw two lines from the top point of the first line to the edge of the circle. These two lines should be at an angle of 18 degrees on either side of the original line. (The same lines will form a 36 degree angle with each other.)

4) From the bottom points of the two lines, draw two more lines, both at angles of 36 degrees from the first pair of lines. Connect the remaining ends of the last pair of lines, forming the pentagram.

5) Paint the pentagram entirely, filling in its form with green paint. A red Fire Triangle should be painted at the center of the figure. The ground area behind the pentagram should also be painted red. The outer circle should be green. When all paint is dry, apply sealant for protection.

Ritual for Use

A Meditation on the Portal Lamens

The Temple is to be arranged in accordance with the Opening of the Portal Ceremony.

For this meditation, the Magician of the Portal grade will need to be dressed in the regalia of the Outer Order (black robe, black and white nemyss, red sandals). The two crossed sashes are also to be worn. On the Altar should be: East—rose petals, South—a red candle, West—water cup, and North—platter of salt. The Portal lamens should be placed next to one of the Elemental Tablets: Hegemon—East, 2nd Adept—South, Hiereus—North, and 3rd Adept—West.

Before the commencement of the ceremony, the magician should take a ritual bath, perform a rite of relaxation, or both.

Enter the Temple giving the Sign of the Rending of the Veil.

Perform the LBRP.

Go to the North and trace a cross over the lamen of the Hiereus. Hold the lamen high and circumambulate the Temple once vibrating "ADONAI HA ARETZ." Return to the North and trace an Invoking Spirit Passive and an Invoking Earth Pentagram over the lamen. Vibrate "ADONAI" four times. Take a few moments to study the lamen carefully. Then put it down and Give the Sign of the Rending of the Veil over the lamen as if standing upon it. Close your eyes and visualize the lamen in your mind: See the colored arrows of the Maltese cross coming together and changing from the pure elemental colors to the earthy tones of Malkuth. See the white circle of spirit both containing and supporting the 10th Sphere. Then imagine the gleaming hexagram of Light—the Ruach Elohim and the Waters of Creation—breathing life into matter through the mating of Fire and Water. Continue this meditation for as long as you like before moving on, giving the Sign of the Closing of the Veil.

Go to the East and trace a cross over the lamen of the Hegemon. Hold the lamen high and circumambulate the Temple once vibrating "SHADDAI EL CHAI." Return to the East and trace an Invoking Spirit Active and an Invoking Air Pentagram over the lamen. Vibrate "YOD HEH VAV HEH" four times. Take a few moments to study the lamen carefully. Then put it down and give the Sign of the Rending of the Veil over the lamen as if standing upon it. Close your eyes and visualize the lamen in your mind: See the Fire Triangle and the Water Triangle separate and part from one another, apexes facing opposite directions. Feel the magnetism of the Middle Way which causes these two rivals to pull together and interlock firmly. From this intercourse, a third element is born—Air, the Reconciler—the first-born son of the marriage of the Father and Mother. Continue meditating on these ideas for a period of time before giving the Sign of the Closing of the Veil.

Go to the West and trace a cross over the lamen of the 3rd Adept. Hold the lamen high and circumambulate the Temple once vibrating "ELOHIM TZABAOTH." Return to the West and trace an Invoking Spirit Passive and an Invoking Water Pentagram over the lamen. Vibrate "AL" twice. Take a few moments to study the lamen carefully. Then put it down and Give the Sign of the Rending of the Veil over the lamen as if standing upon it. Close your eyes and visualize the lamen in your mind: Imagine the blue square of Chesed. See the square duplicate itself, resulting in an octogram. As the polygon changes form, it also changes color from blue to orange. The blue circle of the mighty Waters surrounds the shape, like an ocean encircling an island. On the center of this eight-sided Altar a blue chalice sits, containing all the Higher Forces of the Tree of Life in its receptive crescent-shaped bowl. Continue meditating on these ideas for a period of time before giving the Sign of the Closing of the Veil.

Go to the South and trace a cross over the lamen of the 2nd Adept. Hold the lamen high and circumambulate the Temple once vibrating "YOD HEH VAV HEH TZABAOTH." Return to the West and trace an Invoking Spirit Active and an Invoking Fire Pentagram over the lamen. Vibrate "ELOHIM" four times. Take a few moments to study the lamen carefully. Then put it down and Give the Sign of the Rending of the Veil over the lamen as if standing upon it. Close your eyes and visualize the lamen in your mind: Imagine a vast ocean of green, the most passive and receptive color. Within this fertile sea, a solid red Triangle appears, like a fiery sperm encountering the womb. A large green Pentagram appears around the red triangle—a symbol both of Fire and of Spirit, for Spirit must always guide the Power of Fire, whether it be in the form of a consecrating Flame or the Purging Fire of Geburah. Continue meditating on these ideas for a period of time before giving the Sign of the Closing of the Veil.

Go to the West of the Altar and meditate for a few moments on the fifth element of ETH, in the form of a white Hebrew letter Shin, and the sigil of the Spirit Wheel. Trace both Active and Passive Spirit Pentagrams.

Go to the East and perform the LBRP.

Give the Sign of the Closing of the Veil before leaving the Temple.

IT IS FINISHED

The Chief Adept's Lamen

Use and Symbolism

This Outer Form of the Rose Cross lamen is revealed to the candidate, as described in the Portal Ceremony, as a symbol which unites the numbers 4, 5, and 6. (The four arms of the cross—six the number of Tiphareth, to which the Rose Cross is attributed, and the five elements represented by the four arms of the cross plus the circle of Spirit.)

The Cross is a complex symbol whose main meanings include that of "conjunction" of opposing forces. The Cross represents the mystic center of the Cosmos . . . the place of junction for the Forces of the Universe. Consequently, the Cross affirms the primary relationship between the two worlds of the celestial and the earth-bound (Spirit and Matter). It represents the Spirit or Divine Light, brought into the physical world of manifestation—Life (the human body) symbolized by the four elements which are the components of Life.

The rose is primarily a symbol of completion, total achievement and perfection. It also alludes to the mystic center, and the heart. The rose is a yonic symbol associated with regeneration, productivity and purity. Because the flower unfolds when it blossoms, it is a worthy symbol of spiritual growth. To the Greeks it was a symbol of sunrise. The rose is the sacred flower of Venus, goddess of love, attributed to the 7th Sephirah. (Seven is described as the most blessed of all the numbers . . . and it is also the number assigned to the act of initiation into the mysteries.)

The Cross and Rose together refer to the synthesis of all these ideas. The red rose also alludes to the compassion and sacrifice of the Slain and Resurrected One. The Golden Cross alludes to the spiritual gold concealed within human nature.

This type of lamen can also be worn in general ritual work by a Neophyte Adeptus Minor (N.A.M.) who has not yet constructed a personal Rose Cross lamen as described in chapter 5.

Materials Needed

One 6" square piece of pine, bass or plywood that is 1/2" or 3/8" thick
One small piece of 1/8" thick basswood
Yellow carpenter's glue
Wood putty
Gesso
Acrylic paints: red, white, iridescent gold
Sealant

Tools Needed

> Scroll saw
> Craft knife with wood carving blade
> Sandpaper, medium and fine grade
> Artist's brushes—medium to very fine

Construction

1) Trace the Cross portion of the Lamen onto the 6" sq. piece of pine or plywood. Trace the four glories separately on the 1/8" basswood. Trace the circle for the rose on the 1/8" basswood.

2) Cut out all sections of the Lamen.

3) Paint the front and sides of the Cross with iridescent gold paint. Paint the back of the cross and the four glories white. Let dry.

4) Glue the four glories to the cross at the junction of the arms. Let dry. Fill in any gaps with wood putty. Sand, apply a coat of gesso and allow to dry. Sand lightly and add another coat if needed. Put the cross aside for the moment.

5) Trace three rows of petals onto the circular rose section. (Be sure to draw the small rose cross in the center of the rose as well.) Using a knife with carving blade, gouge out a slight depression in the center of each rose petal. When finished the rose section should have a 3-dimensional look.

6) Cover the front part of the rose with a coat of gesso. When gesso is dry, paint the front of the rose red. Let dry.

7) Apply glue to the back of the rose and attach to the Cross. Paint the small center Cross gold. The small circle behind the Cross is to remain white. If desired, outline all the petals of the rose (including the red 5-petaled rose in the center) with a thin line of black. The small glories behind the 5-petaled rose should be green. When dry, cover with a coat of sealant for protection.

Ritual for Use

See the ritual entitled: "The Supreme Convocation of the Watchtowers" (pp. 312–322).

The Portal Chief Adept's Lamen.

Admission Badge of the Portal—
The Greek Cross of Five Squares

Use and Symbolism

The Greek Cross of Five Squares is the Admission Badge to the Ritual of the Cross and the four Elements in the Portal grade. It symbolizes the equated forces of the Four Elements ruled by the fifth Element of ETH or Spirit. In addition, the number five alludes to the powers of the Pentagram; this Cross could well be described as a Pentagram in the shape of a Cross.

It is also described in the Portal Ceremony as: "a Cross of corrosion, corruption, disintegration and death. Therefore doth it fall in the Paths of Death and the Devil, unless in Hod, the Glory triumpheth over matter and the Corruptible putteth on Incorruption, thus attaining unto the beauty of Tiphareth; unless in Netzach, Death is swallowed up in Victory and the Transformer becometh the Transmuter into Pure Alchemic Gold. 'Except ye be born of Water and the Spirit, ye cannot enter the Kingdom of God.'"

This refers to some very basic alchemic principles. In the science of alchemy, purification arises out of separation, out of the various processes that transpire during the work with separation. Dissolution, also known as separation, is a form of decomposition—a breaking up. This is a crucial part of alchemic purification. That which is not essential is separated from that which is. That which is pure is freed from the impure. There is a natural and hidden fire within humanity that brings forth a cleansing process through heat, putrefaction and distillation—until the Pure Essence is revealed. Only that which has endured the Trial by Fire has been purified. Only that which complies with the Trial of devotion and love is pure.

This Cross is given to the candidate as a symbol of his/her various component "parts." The candidate symbolically examines and scrutinizes the separate parts, which represents the act of decomposition—a necessary step to purification. The different elements must be carefully equilibrated—any imbalance must be sacrificed. (Although we are discussing symbolic ritual acts, these processes must also occur in the psyche of the individual.) Until the Initiate has prepared the psyche through separation and purification, he/she cannot receive the ETH, the philosophical Mercury (Spirit), whereby through knowledge and understanding the lesser is transmuted into the greater. Only then can the true and indissolvible Stone of the Wise, be found within as a source of strength and inspiration.

Materials Needed

> One 10" by 10" piece of 1/8" thick masonite
> Gesso
> One yard of gold chain (approx. 1/8" thickness)
> Two small brass eye-rings
> Acrylic paint: white, black, red, blue, yellow
> Sealant

Tools Needed

> Jigsaw or scroll saw
> Electric drill with 1/8" bit
> Needle-nose pliers
> Wire cutters
> Sandpaper—all grades
> Artist's brushes—medium

Construction

1) Measure out a cross on the masonite that consists of five 3" x 3" squares. The total size of the cross will be 9" x 9". Draw a semi-circular "lip" which sticks out about 5/8" from the top square of the cross.

2) With the saw, cut out the cross (including the lip) in one piece as shown in the diagram.

3) Using a 1/8" bit, drill a hole into the center of the lip.

4) Sand the edges of the cross smooth. Cover the cross on both sides with gesso. Let dry.

Finishing Steps

5) On the smooth side of the masonite, lightly draw four lines which separate the five squares of the cross. Paint the squares thus:

> Top Square (including lip)—yellow
> Right Square—red
> Left Square—black
> Bottom Square—blue
> Middle Square—white

6) When paint is dry, apply sealant for protection.

7) Using wire cutters, cut off a 3" section of gold chain and stick it through the hole in the lip.

8) Take one of the small brass eye-rings and open it with the needle-nose pliers. Slip both ends of the 3" chain over the opened ends of the eye-ring. Close the eye ring back up again. You will now have a small

closed length of chain attached to the cross.

9) Cut about 3″ off the remaining length of chain, leaving a 30″ piece. Run this piece through the chain attached to the cross.

10) Take the other eye-ring and attach both ends of the long chain to it as before. The chain is now complete and able to be hung around the neck like a lamen.

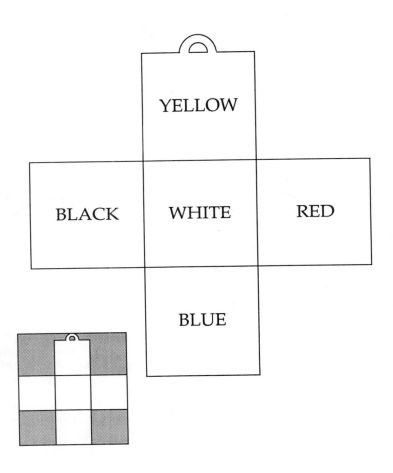

The Greek Cross of 5 Squares

Ritual for Use

Purification of the Elements Within

For this ceremony, the Magician of the Portal grade should be clothed in the robes and headdress of the Outer Order, and wearing the crossed sashes. The Temple should be arranged according to the Opening of the Portal Grade with the Veil of Paroketh in the East. On the Black Altar should be a rose, a red candle, a cup of water, and a dish of salt. Also on the Black Altar should be the Cross and Triangle, and the Tablet of Union (over which hangs a small pentacle). On the White Altar behind the veil, should be a container of powdered incense, and a small cauldron of burning charcoal; surrounded by a fresh rose, a red candle, cup of wine, and a paten of bread and salt. Close at hand should be the Greek Cross of Five Squares. The veil should be closed. Enter the Hall giving the Portal Signs.

After a period of relaxation, go to the Northeast and proclaim: "HEKAS! HEKAS! ESTE BEBELOI!"

Perform the LBRP.

Place the Greek Cross of Five Squares around your neck.

Go clockwise to the North of the Black Altar and take up the salt. Trace a Cross toward the Tablet of the North. Hold the salt high and say: "Before the mountains themselves had been settled down, ahead of the hills, I was brought forth as with labor pains when as yet the Creator had not made the earth and the open spaces and the first part of the dust masses of the productive land." Trace an Invoking Earth Triangle toward the Tablet.

Circumambulate the Temple once with the salt while vibrating the names, "ADONAI HA ARETZ. EMOR DIAL HECTAGA. URIEL. IC ZOD HE CHAL." Return to the North and trace the Invoking Spirit Passive Pentagram along with the Invoking Pentagram of Earth before the Tablet. Give the Sign of Zelator. Replace the salt on the northern side of the Black Altar.

Go the East and take up the rose. Trace with it a Cross in front of the Tablet of Air. Hold the rose on high and say: "The Light is brilliant in the skies, when a wind itself has passed by and proceeded to cleanse the hearts of humanity. Where, now, is the way by which the Light distributes itself, and the east wind scatters about upon the earth?" With the rose trace an Invoking Air Triangle toward the Tablet.

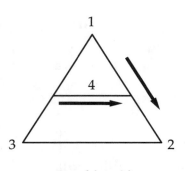

Invoking Air Triangle

Circumambulate the Temple once with the rose, while intoning the names: "SHADDAI EL CHAI. RAPHAEL. ORO IBAH AOZPI. BATAIVAH." Return to the east and trace the Invoking Spirit Active Pentagram and the Pentagram of Air before the Tablet. Give the Theoricus Sign. Return the rose to the eastern side of the Black Altar.

Go to the West and take up the cup of water. Trace with it a Cross in front of the western Tablet. Hold the cup high and say: "The Rivers have raised, O Tetragrammaton! The Rivers have raised their sound. The Rivers keep raising their pounding. Above the sounds of the vast waters, the majestic breaking waves of the sea, AL is majestic in the Height!" Trace an Invoking Water Triangle in front of the Tablet.

Circumambulate the Temple with the cup, vibrating the names: "ELOHIM TZABAOTH. GABRIEL. EMPEH ARSEL GAIOL. RAAGIOSEL." Return to the West and trace the Invoking Spirit Passive Pentagram and the Invoking Pentagram of Water. Give the Practicus Sign. Replace the cup on the western side of the Black Altar.

Go clockwise to the South and take up the candle. Trace with it a Cross before the Fire Tablet. Hold the candle high and say: "The Voice of Tetragrammaton draws out flames of Fire. From the heavens, Tetragrammaton spoke that we might hear and receive illumination. And upon the Earth, Tetragrammaton displayed unto us his great Fire. The Words of the Elohim were heard in the Fire." Trace an Invoking Spirit Active Pentagram and Invoking Fire Triangle in front of the Tablet.

Circumambulate the Temple with the candle, vibrating the names: "YOD HEH VAV HEH TZABAOTH. MICHAEL. OIP TEAA PEDOCE. EDELPERNA." Return to the South and trace an Invoking Pentagram of Fire in front of the Tablet. Give the Philosophus Sign. Replace the candle on the southern side of the Black Altar.

Go to the west of the Altar and face east. With the index finger, draw a cross over the Tablet of Union. Say, "Were I to take the wings of the dawn, that I might reside in the most remote sea, There, also, your own hand would lead me, and your right hand lay hold of me. Surely it is the Spirit in all humanity and the breath of the Almighty that gives them understanding." Trace an Invoking Fire Triangle over the Tablet, followed by an Invoking Water Triangle. Again trace the figure of a cross.

Circumambulate the Temple once intoning the names: "EX-ARP. HCOMA. NANTA. BITOM." Return to the West of the Altar and describe with your index finger the Invoking Pentagrams of Spirit, Active and Passive. Give the Sign of the Rending of the Veil.

Take the Greek Cross from around your neck and place it in the center of the Altar. Place the salt upon the black arm of the cross, the rose upon the yellow arm, the cup over the blue arm, and place the candle on the red arm. Take the pentacle that is hanging over the center of the Altar and lay it for a few moments on the white central square of the Cross. As you do so, imagine the various elements of your body split apart in equal portions. Imagine a brilliant flaming white letter SHIN descending to infuse the separate parts of your being with the cleansing energy of the Divine Spirit. The current of Power washes over you like a fiery liquid, purging you of all impurity and imbalance. Feel yourself dissolved in a process of separation designed to extract the pure spiritual essence within you. Contemplate this for a short period of time before continuing.

Replace the pentacle. Again hang the Greek Cross about your neck. Circumambulate the Temple thrice, giving the Neophyte Signs when passing the East.

Go to the west of the Altar and face east. Perform the Following

Adoration:

▽ "Holy art Thou, whose Word hath established all things!" (Projection Sign)

△ "Holy art Thou, of whom all Nature is the Image!" (Projection Sign)

▽ "Holy art Thou, Whom Nature hath not formed!" (Projection Sign)

△ "Holy art Thou, that art stronger than all power!" (Projection Sign)

⊕ "O thou unspeakable, unutterable, to be praised with silence!" (Sign of Silence)

Go the east. Say, "In the word Paroketh, the Veil of the Tabernacle before the Holy of Holies, and in the power of the Cross and the Pentagram, I claim to behold the Portal of the Vault of the Adepti." Give the Sign of the Rending of the Veil, parting the curtain of Paroketh as you do so.

Before you on the White Altar burns a charcoal in a small cauldron, surrounded by a rose, candle, wine and bread/salt. Reach out both hands to touch the white and black pillars for a moment, balancing yourself in the path of Samekh. Say the following prayer:

For Osiris On-Nophris, who is found perfect before the Gods, had said: These are the elements of my Body, perfected through Suffering, Glorified through Trial. For the scent of the dying Rose is as the Repressed Sigh of my suffering; And the flamered Fire as the Energy of mine undaunted Will; And the Cup of Wine is the pouring out of the Blood of my heart; Sacrificed unto Regeneration, unto the Newer Life; And the Bread and Salt are as the foundations of my Body, which I destroy in order that they may be renewed.

For I am Osiris Triumphant, even Osiris On-Nophris, the Justified. I am He who is clothed with the Body of Flesh, yet in whom is the Spirit of the Great Gods. I am the Lord of Life, triumphant over death. Those who partaketh with me shall arise with me.

I am the manifester in matter of those whose abode is in the Invisible. I am purified; I stand upon the Universe. I am its Reconciler with the Eternal Gods; I am the Perfector of Matter: And without me the Universe is not.

With your index finger, trace a Cross over the bread and salt and say, "In the name of ADONAI HA ARETZ and the word

ARETZ, do I offer myself upon the Altar of Spirit." Sprinkle some salt into the burning cauldron. Give the Sign of Zelator.

Draw a Cross over the Rose and say, "In the name of SHADDAI EL CHAI, and the word RUACH, do I offer myself upon the Altar of Spirit." Take a petal from the rose and place it in the cauldron. Give the Sign of Theoricus.

Trace a Cross over the cup of wine and say, "In the name of ELOHIM TZABAOTH, and the word MAYIM, do I offer myself upon the Altar of Spirit." Sprinkle some drops of wine into the cauldron. Give the Sign of Practicus.

Draw a Cross over the red candle and say, "In the name of YOD HEH VAV HEH TZABAOTH, and the word ASCH, do I offer myself upon the Altar of Spirit." Pour a small amount of wax from the candle into the cauldron. Give the Sign of Philosophus.

Stand in the position of the Tau Cross and say, "From the center outwards, so moveth the point as it traceth the line and the Cross. Equated and equilibrated lie here the Four Elements of the body of Osiris slain. May the corrosive Cross return upon itself, from without inward from the Four Quarters to the Center, and become by sacrifice and transmutation, an offering acceptable, a body glorified."

Trace a Cross over the cauldron and say, "In the name of EHEIEH, and in the word ETH do I aspire toward the Eternal Brilliance. Khabs Am Pekht. Konx Om Pax. Light in Extension." Place some incense into the cauldron. Give the Sign of the Rending of the Veil. Remain in this position for a short time, contemplating once again the glory of the purification into the Alchemic Gold.

Give the Sign of the Enterer. Say, "I invite you to inhale with me the perfume of this Rose, as a symbol of Air." Pick up the rose and inhale its fragrance. Return it to the Altar.

Say, "To feel with me the warmth of this sacred Fire." Spread your hands over the candle.

Say, "To eat with me this Bread and Salt as types of Earth." Dip the bread into the salt and eat it.

Say, "To drink with me this Wine, the consecrated emblem of Elemental Water." Trace a cross in the Air with the chalice before drinking the wine. When finished, invert the cup.

Use your hands to spread the cloud of incense over your face and head and say, "To partake together of the Essence of All."

Feel the disjoined elements of your body begin to come together once again into a unified whole. They have been separated, distilled, cleansed and purified through devotion and sacrifice. Imagine all impurities purged from your body and soul. This fills you with a Divine ecstacy as you are impregnated with Spirit. You realize that from this day forward, little by little, your mortal body will shed its earthly elements for the Eternal ETH, gradually becoming a Temple of the Holy Spirit. When you are finished with this meditation, give the Sign of Silence.

Give the Sign of the Closing of the Veil, closing the curtain of Paroketh as you do so. Perform the Qabalistic Cross.

Perform the Reverse Circumambulation thrice.

Go to the north of the Black Altar and take up the salt located there. Turn toward the Earth Tablet and trace the Banishing Pentagram of Earth. Give the Zelator Sign. Return the salt to the Altar.

Go to the East and take up the rose from the Black Altar. Turn toward the Air Tablet and draw the Banishing Pentagram of Air. Give the Theoricus Sign. Replace the rose.

Go to the west of the Altar and take up the cup of water. Turn toward the Water Tablet and draw the Banishing Pentagram of Water. Give the Practicus Sign. Replace the cup.

Go to the South and take up the red candle from the Black Altar. Turn toward the Fire Tablet and trace the Banishing Pentagram of Fire. Give the Philosophus Sign. Replace the candle.

Go to the west of the Black Altar and face east. With your index finger, trace the two Banishing Pentagrams of Spirit, Active and Passive. Give the Sign of the Closing of the Veil.

Go to the east of the Temple and say, "I now release any Spirits that may have been imprisoned by this ceremony. Go in peace to your abodes and habitations with the blessings of YOD HEH SHIN VAV HEH."

Peform the LBRP.

Say, "I now declare this Temple duly closed."

THE RITE IS ENDED

The Pentagram Arrangement of the Enochian Tablets

ENOCHIAN (ANGELIC) TABLETS

The Enochian Tablets, which include the four Elemental Tablets along with the Tablet of Union, originated from a system of Magick that was developed from the ceremonial skrying of Dr. John Dee and Edward Kelly. Beginning in 1582, the Elizabethan Magician and his seer continued to uncover the Enochian system over a period of seven years. The two men accumulated a great quantity of work, including an entire language with its own unique alphabet and syntax. This language, known as the "Secret Angelic Language," became known as Enochian because supposedly it was the

Angelic language revealed to Enoch by the Angel Ave. The structure of the Enochian system was based upon a cipher of numerological and set permutations of elements arranged on a grid of letters (the Tablets). From these Tablets were derived the names of various elemental powers, Angels, beings and spiritual dominions known as Aethyrs.

It was not until MacGregor Mathers incorporated it into the Golden Dawn curriculum 300 years later that the Enochian scheme of Magick became a truly effective and powerful system. Enochian is the unifying system of Magick that underlies much of the practical work of the Golden Dawn within the Higher Grades. It combines Qabalah, tarot, geomancy and astrology as well as elemental, planetary and astral work into a unified and comprehensive system. In fact, the Enochian system is so all-encompassing that we will not attempt to describe it in full detail here. We strongly suggest that the reader study the section dealing with Enochian in Regardie's book *The Golden Dawn* for more information on the subject.

The Enochian Tablets are four in number, each referring to one of the elements: Earth, Air, Fire, and Water. In addition to these four, there is another smaller Tablet, which is called the Tablet of Union, referring to the fifth Element of Ether or Spirit. It is a small Tablet of twenty squares, five letters wide and four deep. The first Line, EX-ARP, is attributed to Air. HCOMA, the second line, is assigned to Water. NANTA, the third line alludes to Earth. Finally, the fourth line BITOM is attributed to Fire. The function of the Tablet, as its name implies, is to unite and bind together the four Elemental Tablets. For purposes of study, the four Elemental Tablets (or Watchtowers) are arranged as are the elements in the Pentagram, although the order is not immediately apparent:

To each Tablet are referred innumerable attributions, the principal elementary ones being those of color. Certain squares on each Tablet were painted in the color of the Element, according to the King Scale, whilst others were left wholly or partly white. Thus in each Tablet there are four principal types of square:

- The Great Cross of 36 Squares, lettered in black on white, stretching through the entire Tablet.

- The Sephirotic Calvary Crosses, lettered also in black on white, in the four corners of each Tablet.

The Tablet of Air

r	Z	i	l	a	f	A	y	t	l	p	a
a	r	d	Z	a	i	d	p	a	L	a	m
c	z	o	n	s	a	r	o	Y	a	v	b
T	o	i	T	t	z	o	P	a	c	o	C
S	i	g	a	s	o	m	r	b	z	n	h
f	m	o	n	d	a	T	d	i	a	r	i
o	r	o	i	b	A	h	a	o	z	p	i
t	N	a	b	r	V	i	x	g	a	s	d
O	i	i	i	t	T	p	a	l	O	a	i
A	b	a	m	o	o	o	a	C	v	c	a
N	a	o	c	O	T	t	n	p	r	n	T
o	c	a	n	m	a	g	o	t	r	o	i
S	h	i	a	l	r	a	p	m	z	o	x

The Tablet of Water

T	a	O	A	d	v	p	t	D	n	i	m
a	a	b	c	o	o	r	o	m	e	b	b
T	o	g	c	o	n	x	m	a	l	G	m
n	h	o	d	D	i	a	l	e	a	o	c
p	a	t	A	x	i	o	V	s	P	s	И
S	a	a	i	x	a	a	r	V	r	o	i
m	p	h	a	r	s	l	g	a	i	o	l
M	a	m	g	l	o	i	n	L	i	r	x
o	l	a	a	D	n	g	a	T	a	p	a
p	a	L	c	o	i	d	x	P	a	c	n
n	d	a	z	N	z	i	V	a	a	s	a
i	i	d	P	o	n	s	d	A	s	p	i
x	r	i	n	h	t	a	r	n	d	i	J

The Tablet of Earth

b	O	a	Z	a	R	o	p	h	a	R	a
v	N	n	a	x	o	P	S	o	n	d	n
a	i	g	r	v	n	o	o	m	a	g	g
o	r	p	m	n	i	n	g	b	e	a	l
r	s	O	n	i	z	i	r	l	e	m	v
i	z	i	n	r	C	z	i	a	M	h	l
M	O	r	d	i	a	l	h	C	t	G	a
O	C	a	n	c	h	i	a	s	o	m	t
A	r	b	i	z	m	i	i	l	p	i	z
O	p	a	n	a	L	a	m	S	m	a	P
d	O	l	o	P	i	n	i	a	n	b	a
r	x	p	a	o	c	s	i	z	i	x	p
a	x	t	i	r	V	a	s	t	r	i	m

The Tablet of Fire

d	o	n	p	a	T	d	a	n	V	a	a
o	l	o	a	G	e	o	o	b	a	v	a
O	P	a	m	n	o	V	G	m	d	n	m
a	p	l	s	T	e	d	e	c	a	o	p
s	c	m	i	o	o	n	A	m	l	o	x
V	a	r	s	G	d	L	b	r	i	a	p
o	i	P	t	e	a	a	p	D	o	c	e
p	s	v	a	c	n	r	Z	i	r	Z	a
S	i	o	d	a	o	i	n	r	z	f	m
d	a	l	t	T	d	n	a	d	i	r	e
d	i	x	o	m	o	n	s	i	o	s	p
O	o	D	p	z	i	A	P	a	n	l	i
r	g	o	a	n	n	ꟼ	A	C	r	a	r

- The Kerubic Squares, which are always in the elemental color of the Tablet, and are the four squares immediately above each Sephirotic Cross.

- The Servient Squares, always in the elemental color of the Tablet, consist of the 16 squares of each lesser angle beneath each Sephirotic Cross.

The most important item on each Angelic Tablet is the Great Cross whose shaft descends from top to bottom and whose bar crosses the Tablet in the center. This Cross comprises 36 squares, and has a double vertical line which is called *Linea Dei Patris Filiique*, the Line of God the Father and the Son, and *Linea Spiritus Sancti*, the Line of the Holy Spirit, crossing this horizontally, and containing one rank of letters. The *Linea Spiritus Sancti* is always the seventh line or rank of letters from the top, while the two vertical columns of the *Linea Dei Patris Filique* are always the sixth and seventh columns counting from either right or left. The Great Cross is the mechanism which divides the Tablet . . . it separates and binds together the four sub-elements or Lesser Angles, as they are called, from the one another.

From this Great Cross, various Angelic and Divine Names are produced, which are of supreme importance. First of all there are the "Three Great Secret Holy Names of God" which are found in the *Linea Spiritus Sancti*. This line comprises twelve letters, which are divided into names of three, four, and five letters reading from left to right. Thus in the Air Tablet, you will find ORO IBAH AOZPI; in the Water Tablet: MPH ARSL GAIOL; in the Earth Tablet: MOR DIAL HCTGA, and in the Fire TABLET: OIP TEAA PDOCE.

These Three Secret Holy Names of God are the major names of the Tablets. These names are conceived to be borne as ensigns upon the Banners of the Great King of each quarter. The Name of the Great King is always a name of eight letters and comprises a spiral or whirl in the center of the Great Cross. The King is a very powerful force, and since it initiates the whirl it is to be invoked with due care.

The next series of important names obtained from the Great Cross are the Six Seniors. Their names begin from the sixth and seventh squares of the *Linea Spiritus Sancti*, including these squares, and read OUTWARDS along the three lines of the Great Cross to the edge of the Tablet. Each is a name of seven letters. The Eight-lettered Name of the King, and the six Names of the Seniors, are invoked by means of the Hexagram. They are attributed to the sun and planets, and are on a different and higher plane than the elemental names.

In the center of each Lesser Angle will be seen a Cross of Ten Squares. This is called the Sephirotic Calvary Cross. From the letters of this Cross are taken two divine names which call forth and control the Angels and spirits of the Lesser Angle, and their names are used in a preliminary invocation when working magically with a square of a lesser angle. From the vertical line of Sephirotic Cross, reading from above downwards, comes a Deity Name of six letters (known as the Angel of Call). From the cross-bar, reading from left to right, comes a Deity name of five letters (the Angel of Command). These deities are invoked using the Pentagram and their names must always be read in the directions described above.

We now come to the colored squares grouped above and below the Sephirotic Cross in each of the four angles. The most important are the four above the cross-bar of the Sephirotic Cross—called the Kerubic Squares. From these four squares are derived four names of four letters each. Thus, for the top rank of the Airy Angle of the Fire Tablet, we have DO(N)PA which gives us: DOPA, OPAD, PADO, ADOP. (Note: the white square in the center belongs to the Sephirotic Cross and is not included in the names derived from the Kerubic Squares.) These four names, the names of the four Kerubic Angels of the Lesser Angle, rule the servient squares below the Sephirotic Cross, and of the four, the first is the most powerful as the others are derived therefrom. By prefixing to these four names a letter from the appropriate line of the Tablet of Union, we obtain even more powerful names, archangelic in character. Thus for the Kerubic Rank of the Air Lesser Angle of the Fire Tablet (used as our example), the letter "B" of the word "BITOM" on the Tablet of Union is prefixed. This produces BDOPA, BOPAD, BPADO and BADOP.

The rule is that the first letter of the appropriate line of the Tablet of Union is prefixed only to the names formed from the Kerubic Squares. As an example of this method applied to the remaining servient squares, we find:

"I" is added to the 16 servient squares of the angle of AIR.
"T" is added to the 16 servient squares of the angle of WATER.
"O" is added to the 16 servient squares of the angle of EARTH.
"M" is added to the 16 servient squares of the angle of FIRE.

Thus BITOM will be used entirely on the Fire Tablet, and is never used on the other three Tablets. The first letter applies to the Kerubic Squares of each of the four Lesser Angles, whilst the remaining four letters apply to the 16 servient squares of those angles as shown above. (Thus in the Air Lesser Angle of the Fire Tablet, the 16 servient squares will yield a total of 16 Angelic names. The letter "I" can be prefixed to all of them: IOPMN, IPMNO, IMNOP, INOPM, etc.)

The ritual for the consecration of the Four Elemental Weapons gives excellent examples of the archangelic names formed from the Kerubic Squares by the addition of letters from the Tablet of Union.

The reader should note that the Elemental Tablets presented in this book are in accord with the final version revealed to Dee and Kelly by the Archangel Raphael on April 20, 1587, and not those described in the Stella Matutina manuscripts. (The main difference is that we have avoided the use of "double letter" squares.)

Again the student would be well-advised to seek out further information on this subject.

The Four Elemental Tablets

Materials Needed
> 3/4" plywood (pine or birch) which comes in 4' by 8' sheets. You will need 1/2 of a sheet.
> Wood putty
> Gesso
> Acrylic paints: white, black, red, yellow, blue, green, orange, violet
> Sealant

Tools Needed
> Table saw or circular saw
> Sandpaper—course, medium and fine
> Artist's brushes—coarse, medium and fine
> Compass

Construction
1) Lay out the half sheet of plywood. Measure off four sections of wood that are 20" x 16". Cut apart all sections with saw.

2) Fill in any gaps with wood putty. Sand all edges smooth. Coat entirely (front, sides and back) with gesso. Let dry.

3) Take one of the tablets and draw a 12" x 13" square on its front side.

(Note: This square is to be 5" from the top edge and 2" from the sides and bottom.)

4) Mark off the 12" x 13" figure completely into 1" squares. (There will be a total of 156 square inches.)

5) At the top of the tablet where there is a 5" wide white area, find the center and draw a 3" circle using a compass. (Center it between the top edge and the squared-off region.)

Finishing Steps

6) The tablets are to be painted in the King scale color of the each particular element. The shaded areas shown in each Elemental Tablet diagram are as follows:

> Fire Tablet: red.
> Water Tablet: blue.
> Air Tablet: yellow
> Earth Tablet: black.

7) The white areas (excluding the borders) will remain white with black letters in all four tablets.

8) Each tablet is divided into four "quarters" which are attributed to the four elements. Thus on every tablet; the bottom right quarter is attributed to Fire, the top right quarter is assigned to Water, the top left quarter is Air, and the bottom left quarter is Earth. The letters on the colored areas of each tablet are to be painted as follows:

FIRE TABLET

1.
Lesser angle
of AIR
Yellow letters
on Red.

2.
Lesser Angle
of WATER
Blue letters
on Red.

3.
Lesser Angle
of EARTH
Black Letters
on Red.

4.
Lesser Angle
of FIRE
Green Letters
on Red.

WATER TABLET

1.
Lesser angle
of AIR
Yellow letters
on Blue.

2.
Lesser Angle
of WATER
Orange letters
on Blue.

3.
Lesser Angle
of EARTH
Black Letters
on Blue.

4.
Lesser Angle
of FIRE
Red Letters
on Blue.

AIR TABLET

1.
Lesser angle
of AIR
Violet letters
on Yellow.

2.
Lesser Angle
of WATER
Blue letters
on Yellow.

3.
Lesser Angle
of EARTH
Black Letters
on Yellow.

4.
Lesser Angle
of FIRE
Red Letters
on Yellow.

EARTH TABLET

1.
Lesser angle
of AIR
Yellow letters
on Black.

2.
Lesser Angle
of WATER
Blue letters
on Black.

3.
Lesser Angle
of EARTH
White Letters
on Black.

4.
Lesser Angle
of FIRE
Red Letters
on Black.

9) All 1" lettered squares should be separated from one another with a thin black line. (Note: This can be painted with acrylic paint, but one needs a steady hand and patience to do it. Another effective way is to use a straight edge and a ballpoint pen with permanent non-running black ink.)

10) The Sigils of the Angelic Tablets are to be painted in the upper circle according to the diagram:

AIR—a symbol of a T with four Yods above it.
WATER—a Cross Potent, having two letters b.b., a figure 4 and a figure 6 in the angles thereof.

EARTH—a simple Cross potent in the four colors of Malkuth.
FIRE—a circle with twelve rays.

11)   When all tablets are painted, apply a coat of sealant.

12)   A hook or wire can be attached to the back of each tablet, so that they
       may be hung on the four walls of the Temple. If the walls of the Tem-
       ple are not conducive to hanging objects, Tablet stands similar to the
       Banner poles can be constructed and painted in the appropriate ele-
       mental colors.

The Tablet of Union

(For use and symbolism, see pp. 302-303, under "Enochian
Tablets.")

Materials Needed
       3/4" pine or birch plywood (use the left-over piece from the Elemental
          tablets)
       Wood putty
       Gesso
       Acrylic paints: white, black, red, yellow, blue
       One square piece of white felt material
       Fabric glue
       Sealant: clear lacquer finish

Tools Needed
       Table saw or circular saw
       Sandpaper—coarse, medium and fine
       Artist's brushes—coarse, medium and fine
       Scissors

Construction
   1)   Measure off a piece of wood that is 7" x 6." Cut out with saw.

   2)   Fill in any gaps with wood putty. Sand all edges smooth. Coat en-
         tirely (front, sides and back) with gesso. Let dry. Coat front and sides
         with white paint.

   3)   On one side of the piece, draw a 5" x 4" square. There will be a 1"
         white border all around the square. Mark off the 5" x 4" figure com-
         pletely into 1" squares. (There will be a total of 20 square inches.)

Finishing Steps
   4)   Take the white felt material and cut out a 7" x 6" square piece. Glue
         the felt to the back side of the Tablet. (This will keep it from scratching

the Altar.) Pile a few heavy books on the top side of the Tablet to insure that the felt is well secured to the wood. Allow to dry.

5) Paint the appropriate letters into the squares as shown in the diagram: Top line—EXARP in yellow letters, 2nd line—HCOMA in blue letters, 3rd line—NANTA in black letters, and for the last line—BITOM in red.

6) All 1' lettered squares should be separated from one another with a thin black line. When all paint is dry, apply sealant.

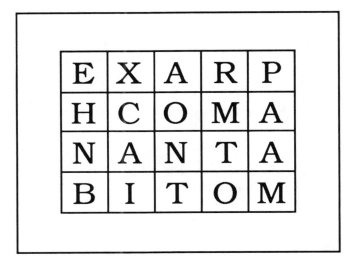

The Tablet of Union

Ritual for Use

Supreme Convocation of the Watchtowers

This ceremony is intended to be used much like Regardie's Opening by Watchtower, as a preliminary rite to other work such as the consecration of a talisman, a rite of healing, etc. The following ritual is more complex than Regardie's and is intended for high magickal workings requiring prior knowledge and practice of Enochian magick. (Note: For English translations of the Enochian passages in this ritual, refer to chapter 5.)

The Temple is to be arranged in accordance with the Portal grade; the four Elemental Tablets on their appropriate walls. The

Adept is to be dressed in the regalia of the Inner Order (white robe, yellow-and-white striped nemyss, yellow sash) but wearing the Lamen of the Red Rose and Golden Cross (Chief Adept's Lamen in the Portal). The White Altar is to be used in place of the Black Altar of the Outer Hall. Upon it should be a rose, candle, cup of water, and salt in their respective quarters. In the center of these should be placed the Tablet of Union. A sword should be used for banishing. The Adept should also have the Pentagram-headed Scepter (Chief Adept's Portal Wand) on hand for invoking. Enter the Hall giving the Portal Signs.

After a period of relaxation, give five knocks.

Go to the Northeast and say, "HEKAS! HEKAS! ESTE BEBELOI! PROCUL O PROCUL ESTE PROFANI! Far, far from this sacred place be the profane!"

Perform with the sword either the LBRP or the SBRP.

Perform the BRH.

Put the sword aside. Take up the candle from the Altar in your left hand. With your right hand, grasp the red band of the Pentagram wand. Turn toward the South. With the wand, trace an Invoking Triangle of Fire in front of the Elemental Tablet. Circumambulate around the Temple slowly and say, "The Voice of Tetragrammaton draws out flames of Fire. From the heavens, Tetragrammaton spoke, that we might hear and receive illumination. And upon the Earth Tetragrammaton, displayed unto us, his great Fire. The Words of YHVH were heard in the Fire."

Return to the South and place the candle there. Trace a cross, followed by the Invoking Fire Triangle. Still holding the wand by the red band, draw a large circle in front of the Tablet. Draw an Invoking Pentagram of Spirit Active. Vibrate "BITOM" while tracing the pentagram and "EHEIEH" while tracing the Spirit sigil. Give the LVX Signs. Then trace the Invoking Pentagram of Fire vibrating "OIP TEAA PEDOCE." Intone "ELOHIM" as you draw the sigil of Leo in the center. Give the Sign of Philosophus.

Say, "In the Names and Letters of the Great Southern Quadrangle, revealed unto Enoch by the Great Angel, AVE, I invoke ye,

Spirits of Fire, guardians of the Watchtower of the South!"

Trace the Six Invoking Solar Hexagrams in front of the Tablet. After the last hexagram is completed, trace the sigil of the Whirl directly in front of the center of the Tablet. Vibrate the name of the Enochian King, "In the name of EDELPERNA, (Ay-del-per-nah) Great King of the South, Spirits of Fire, adore your Creator!"

Recite the Sixth Enochian Key:

Gah S Diu Chis Em Micalzo Pil-Zin Sobam El Harg Mir Babalon Od obloc Samvelg Dlugar Malprg Ar Caosgi Od A C A M Canal Sobol Zar F Bliard Caosgi Od Chisa Netaab Od Miam Ta Viv Od D Darsar Solpeth Bi-En B-Ri-Ta Od Zacam G-Micalza Sobol Ath Trian Lu-Ia He Od Ecrin Mad Qaa-On."

Phonetic: (Gah-hay Ess Dee-oo Kah-hee-sah Ay-em, Mee-kahl-zoad-oh Peel-zoad-ee-noo; Soh-bah-may El Har-jee Meer Bah-bah-loh-noo Oh-dah Oh-bloh-kah Sahm-vay-lan-jee: Dah-loo-gar Mah-lah-peer-jee Ah-ray Kah-ohs-jee, Oh-dah Ah Kah Ah Em Kah-nahl So-bo-loh Zoad-ah-ray Eff Blee-ahr-dah Kah-ohs-jee, Oh-dah Kah-hee-say Nay-tah-ah-bay Oh-dah Mee-ah may Tay-ah Vee-ee-vah Oh-dah Dah. Dahr-sahr Sohl-pet-hay Bee-ay-noo. Bay-ree-tah Oh-dah Zoad-ah-kah-may Jee-mee-kah-el-zoad-ah So-boh-lah Aht-hay Tre-ah-noo Loo-ee-ah Hay Oh-dah Ay-kree-noo Mah-dah Kah-ah-noo.)

Trace a Cross in front of the Tablet and say: "In the name of ELOHIM, Spirits of Fire, adore your Creator!"

Go to the west of the Altar. Take up the cup of water in your left hand. With your right hand, grasp the blue band of the Pentagram wand. Turn toward the West. With the wand, trace an Invoking Triangle of Water in front of the Elemental Tablet. Circumambulate around the Temple slowly and say, "The Rivers have raised, O Tetragrammaton! The Rivers have raised their sound. The Rivers keep raising their pounding. Above the sounds of vast waters, the majestic breaking waves of the sea, YHVH is majestic in the Height!"

Return to the West and place the cup there. Trace a cross, followed by the Invoking Water Triangle. Still holding the wand by the blue band, draw a large circle in front of the Tablet. Draw an Invoking Pentagram of Spirit Passive. Vibrate "HCOMA" while tracing the pentagram and "AGLA" while tracing the Spirit sigil. Give the LVX Signs. Then trace the Invoking Pentagram of Water vibrating "EMPEH ARSEL GAIOL." Intone "Aleph Lamed, AL" as you draw the sigil of the Eagle in the center. Give the Sign of Practicus.

Say, "In the Names and Letters of the Great Western Quadrangle, revealed unto Enoch by the Great Angel, AVE, I invoke ye, Spirits of Water, guardians of the Watchtower of the West!"

Trace the six Invoking Solar hexagrams in front of the Tablet. After the last hexagram is completed, trace the sigil of the Whirl directly in front of the center of the Tablet. Vibrate the name of the Enochian King, "In the name of RAAGIOSEL, (Ra-ah-gee-oh-sel) Great King of the West, Spirits of Water, adore your Creator!"

Recite the Fourth Enochian Key:

"Othil Lusdi Babage Od Dorpha Gohol G-Chis-Ge Avavago Cormp P D Ds Sonf Vi-Vi-Iv Casarmi Oali MAPM Sobam Ag Cormpo Crp L Casarmg Cro-Od-Zi Chis Od Vgeg Ds T Capimali Chis Capimaom Od Lonshin Chis Ta L-O CLA Torzu Nor-Quasahi Od F Caosga: Bagle Zire Mad Ds I Od Apila. Do-O-A-Ip Qaal Zacar Od Zamran Obelisong Rest-El Aaf Nor-Molap."

Phonetic: (Oh-thee-lah Loos-dee Bah-bah-jee Oh-dah Dor-pay-hah Goh-hoh-lah: Jee-kah-hees-jee Ah-vah-vah-goh Kohr-em-pay Pay-Dah Dah-ess Son-noof Vee-vee-ee-vah Kas-ahrm-ee Oh-al-lee Em-Ah-Pay-Em Soh-bah-mah Ah-gee-Kohr-em-poh Kah-ar-pay El: Kah-sarm-jee Kroh-oh-dah-zoad-ee Kah-hee-sah Oh-dah Lon-shee-noo Kah-hee-sah Tay-ah Elo-oh Kay-El-Ah. Tor-zoad-oo Nohr-kwah-sah-hee, Oh-dah Eff Kah-ohs-gah; Bah-glay Zoad-ee-ray Mah-dah Dah-ess Ee Oh-dah Ah-pee-lah. Doo-ah-ee-pay Kah-ah-lah, Zoad-a Kar-ah Oh-dah Zoad-ah-mer-ah-noo Oh-bay-lee-son-jee, Ray-stel-ah Ah-ah-eff Nohr-moh-lah-pay.)

Trace a Cross in front of the Tablet and say: "In the name of AL, Spirits of Water, adore your Creator!"

Go to the East of the Altar. Take up the rose in your left hand. With your right hand, grasp the yellow band of the Pentagram wand. Turn toward the East. With the wand, trace an Invoking Triangle of Air in front of the Elemental Tablet. Circumambulate around the Temple slowly and say,

"The Light is brilliant in the skies, when a wind itself has passed by and proceeded to cleanse the hearts of humanity. Where, now, is the way by which the Light distributes itself, and the east wind scatters about upon the earth?"

Return to the East and place the rose there. Trace a cross, followed by the Invoking Air Triangle. Still holding the wand by the yellow band, draw a large circle in front of the Tablet. Draw an Invoking Pentagram of Spirit Active. Vibrate "EXARP" while tracing the pentagram and "EHEIEH" while tracing the Spirit sigil. Give the LVX Signs. Then trace the Invoking Pentagram of Air vibrating "ORO IBAH AOZPI." Intone "YOD HEH VAV HEH" as you draw the sigil of the Aquarius in the center. Give the Sign of Theoricus.

Say, "In the Names and Letters of the Great Eastern Quadrangle, revealed unto Enoch by the Great Angel, AVE, I invoke ye, Spirits of Air, guardians of the Watchtower of the East!"

Trace the Six Invoking Solar Hexagrams in front of the Tablet. After the last hexagram is completed, trace the sigil of the Whirl directly in front of the center of the Tablet. Vibrate the name of the Enochian King, "In the name of BATAIVAH (Bah-tah-ee-vah), Great King of the East, Spirits of Air, adore your Creator!"

Recite the Third Enochian Key:

"Micma Goho Mad Zir Comselha Zien Biah Os Londah. Norz Chis Othil Gigipah Vnd-L Chis ta Pu-Im Q Mospleh Teloch Qui-I-N Toltorg Chis I Chis-Ge In Ozien Ds T Brgdo Od Torzul. I Li E Ol Balzarg Od Aala Thiln Os Netaab Dluga Vonsarg Lonsa Cap-Mi-Ali Vors CLA Homil Cocasb Fafen Izizop Od Miinoag De Gnetaab Vaun Na-Na-E-El Panpir Malpirg Pild Caosg Noan Vnalah Balt Od Vaoan. Do-O-I-A p Mad Goholor Gohus Amiran Micma Iehusoz Ca-Cacom Od Do-O-A-In Noar Mica-Olz A-Ai-Om Casarmg Gohia Zacar Vniglag Od Im-Va-Mar Pugo Plapli Ananael Qa-A-An."

Phonetic: (Meek-mah! Goh-hoh Mah-dah. Zoad-ee-ray Kohm-sel-hah Zoad-ee-ay-noo Bee-ah-hay Oh-ess Lon-doh-hah. Nohr-zoad Kah-hee-sah Oh-thee-lah Jee-jee-pay-hay, Oon-dah-lah Kah-hee-sah Tah Poo-eem Kwo-Mohs-play Tay-lohk-hay, kwee-ee-noo Tohl-tor-jee, Kah-hees Ee Kah-hees-jee Ee-noo Oh-zoad-ee-ay-noo, Day-ess Tay Bray-jee-dah Oh-dah Tor-zoad-oo-lah. Ee-Lee Ay Oh-Lah Bahl-zoad-ahr-jee Oh-dah Ah-ah-lah, Tay-heel-noo Oh-ess Nay-tah-ah-bay, Dah-loo-gahr Vohn-sar-jee Lohn-sah Cah-pee-mee-ah-lee Vor-sah Cah El Ah, Hoh-meel Koh-kahs-bay; Fah-fay-noo Ee-zoad-ee-zoad-oh-pay Oh Dah Mee-ee-noh-ah-jee Day Jee-nay-tah-ah-bah Vah-oo-noo Nah-nah-ay-el; Pahn-peer-Mahl-peer-jee Pee-el-dah Kah-ohs-gah. Noh-ah-noo Oo-nah-lah Bal-tah Oh-dah Vay-oh-ah-noo. Doo-oh-ee-ah-pay Mah-dah, Go-hoh-lor Goh-hoos Ah-mee-rah-noo. Meek-mah Yeh-hoo-soh-zoad Kah-kah-coh-mah Oh-dah Doh-oh-ah-ee-noo Noh-ahr Mee-kah-ohl-zoad Ah-ah-ee-oh-mah, Kah-sarm-jee Go-hee-ah; Zoad-dah-kah-ray Oo-nee-glah-jee Oh-dah Eem-vah-mar Poo-joh, Plah-plee Ah-nah-nah-el Kah-ah-noo.)

Trace a Cross in front of the Tablet and say: "In the name of YOD HEH VAV HEH, Spirits of Air, adore your Creator!"

Go clockwise to the north of the Altar. Take up the dish of salt in your left hand. With your right hand, grasp the black band of the Pentagram wand. Turn toward the North. With the wand, trace an Invoking Triangle of Earth in front of the Elemental Tablet. Circumambulate around the Temple slowly and say, "The heavens are declaring the glory of Adonai; and the work of his hands the expanse is telling. One day after another causes speech to bubble forth, and one night after another shows forth knowledge. There is no speech, and there are no words. Into all the earth their measuring line has gone out, and to the extremity of the productive land their utterances. Praise Adonai, all you mountains and hills! "

Return to the North and place the salt there. Trace a cross, followed by the Invoking Earth Triangle. Still holding the wand by the black band, draw a large circle in front of the Tablet. Draw an Invoking Pentagram of Spirit Passive. Vibrate "NANTA" while tracing the pentagram, and "AGLA" while tracing the Spirit sigil. Give the LVX Signs. Then

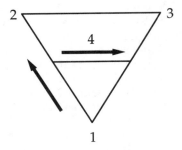

**Invoking Triangle
of Earth**

trace the Invoking Pentagram of Earth vibrating "EMOR DIAL HECTEGA." Intone "ADONAI" as you draw the sigil of Taurus in the center. Give the Sign of Zelator.

Say, "In the Names and Letters of the Great Northern Quadrangle, revealed unto Enoch by the Great Angel, AVE, I invoke ye, Spirits of Earth, guardians of the Watchtower of the East!"

Sigil of the Whirl

Trace the six Invoking Solar Hexagrams in front of the Tablet. After the last hexagram is completed, trace the sigil of the Whirl directly in front of the center of the Tablet. Vibrate the name of the Enochian King, "In the name of IC ZOD HEH CHAL (Ick-Zoad-heh-hal), Great King of the North, Spirits of Earth, adore your Creator!"

Recite the Fifth Enochian Key:

Sapah Zimmi D U-I-V Od Noas Ta Qanis Adroch Dorphal Caosg Od Faonts Piripsol Ta Blior. Casarm A-M-Ipzi Nazarth AF Od Dlugar Zizop Zlida Caosgi Tol Torgi: Od Z Chis E Siasch L Ta-Vi-U Od Iaod Thild Ds Hubar P E O A L Soba Cormfa Chis Ta La Vls Od Q Cocasb. Eca Niis Od Darbs Qaas F Etharzi Od Bliora. Ia-Ial Ed-Nas Cicles. Bagle? Ge-Iad I L."

Phonetic: (Sah-pah-hay Zoad-ee-mee-ee Doo-ee-vay Oh-dah Noh-ahs Tay-ah Kah-nees Ah-droh-kay, Dor-pay-hal Kah-ohs-gah Oh-dah Fah-ohn-tay-ess Pee-reep-sol Tay-ah Blee-ohr. Kah-sar-may Ah-mee-eep-zoad-ee Nah-zoad-arth Ah-eff Oh-dah Dah-loo-gahr Zoad-ee-zoad-oh-pay Zoad-lee-dah Kah-ohs-jee Toh Tor-jee: Oh-dah Zoad Kah-hee-sah Ay See-ahs-kay Ayl Tah vee-oo Od-dah Ee-ah-oh-dah Tay-heel-dah Dah-ess Hoo-bar Pay Ay Oh Ah El, Soh-bah Kohr-em-fah Kah-hee-sah Tay-ah El-ah Vah-less Oh-dah Koh Koh-kahs-bay. Ay-kah Nee-ee-sah Oh-dah Dahr-bay-ess Kah-ah-sah Eff Ay-thar-zoad-ee Oh-dah Blee-ohr-ah. Ee-ah-ee-al-el Ehd-nahs Kee-klay-sah. Bah-glay? Jee-ee-ah-dah Ee-el.)

Trace a Cross in front of the Tablet and say: "In the name of ADONAI, Spirits of Earth, adore your Creator!"

Go clockwise to the west of the Altar and face east. Grasp the wand by the white band. Trace a circle over the Tablet of Union. Then trace the Invoking Pentagram of Spirit Active, and intone the names: "EXARP" and "EHEIEH." Trace the Invoking Pentagram of Spirit Passive, and vibrate the names: "HCOMA" and "AGLA." Draw the same pentagram again, and intone the names: "NANTA" and "AGLA." Trace the Invoking Pentagram of Spirit Active and vibrate the names: "BITOM" and "EHEIEH." Give the LVX Signs.

Then say, "In the names and letters of the mystical Tablet of Union; that which binds together all the elements under the Eternal Essence, I invoke ye, O Divine Forces of the Spirit of Life."

Make the sign of the Rending of the Veil. (Visualize the Veil parting as you step through it.)

Remain west of the Altar, holding the white portion of the Pentagram Wand. Trace a circle over the Tablet of Union as you repeat the First Enochian Key:

Ol Sonuf Vorsag Goho Iad Balt. Lonsh Claz Vonpho Sobra Z-Ol Ror I Ta Nazps Od Graa Ta Malprg Ds Hol-Q Qaa Nothoa Zimz Od Commah Ta Nobloh Zien Soba Thil Gnonp Prge Aldi Ds Vrbs Oboleh G Rsam: Casarm Ohorela Taba Pir Ds Zonrensg Cab Erm Iadnah Pilah Farzm Znrza Adna Gono Iadpil Ds Hom Od Toh Saba Ipam Lu Ipamis Ds Loholo Vep Zomd Poamal Od Bogpa Aai Ta Piap Piamol Od Vaoan. Zacare Eca Od Zamran: Odo Cicle Qaa. Zorge Lap Zirdo Noco Mad Hoath Iaida."

Phonetic: (Oh-el Soh-noof Vay-oh-air-sah-jee Goh-hoh Ee-ah-dah Bal-tah, El-on-shee Kahl-zoad Von-pay-hoh: Soh-bay-rah Zoad-oh-lah Roh-ray Ee Tah Nan-zoad-pay-ess, Oh-dah Jee-rah-ah Tah Mahl-peer-jee: Dah-ess Hoh-el-koh Kah-ah No-thoh-ah Zoad-ee-mah-zoad Oh-dah Koh-mah-mah-kay Tah Noh-bloh-hay Zoad-ee-ay-noo So-bah Tah-hee-lah jee-noh-noo-pay Peer-jee Ahl-dee Dah-ess Ur-bass Oh-boh-lay Jee Rah-sah-may: Cahs-ar-may Oh-hor-ray-lah Tah-bah Peer Dah-es Zoad-oh-noo-ray-noo-sah-jee Kah-bah Air-may Ee-ad-nah. Pee-lah-hay Far-zoad-mee Zoad-noo-ray-zoad-ah Ahd-nah Goh-noh Ee-ah-dah-pee-el Oh-dah Vay-oh-ah-noo. Zoad-a-kah-ray Ay-kah Oh-dah Zoad-a-mer-ah-noo. Oh-dah Kee-clay Kah-ah. Zoad-or-jee Lah-pay Zoad-ee-ray-doh Noh-koh Mah-dah, Hoh-ah-tah-hay Ee-ah-ee-dah.)

Say, "I invoke ye, ye Angelic guardians of the stellar Realms! Ye whose abode lies beyond the domain of the Visible Kingdom!

Just as Ye are the stewards of the gates of the Universe, be ye also the defenders of this Magick Circle of Art! Protect this consecrated Temple from the profane and the unbalanced! Grant unto me the Strength, the Will and the Knowledge to perform this ceremony aright, that I might not degrade this sacred sphere. Grant unto me the Wings of Dawn! Let me prove myself to be a worthy vessel for the mysteries of the Eternal Spirit! Anoint me with the pure white Brilliance of the Light Divine!"

Go to the Northeast and say: "And Humanity was made of Life and Light into Soul and Mind; of Life the Soul, of Light the Mind. Let the Sun arise and empower the lamp of the Inner Sun through the vortex of the Light!"

Still grasping the Pentagram wand by the white part, circumambulate the Temple thrice following the course of the Sun. Give the Neophyte Signs when passing the East.

Go to the west of the Altar and face east. Perform the Following Adoration:

▽ "Holy art Thou, whose Word hath established all things!" (Projection Sign)

△ "Holy art Thou, of whom all Nature is the Image!" (Projection Sign)

▽ "Holy art Thou, Whom Nature hath not formed!" (Projection)

△ "Holy art Thou, that art stronger than all power!" (Projection Sign)

⊕ "O thou unspeakable, unutterable, to be praised with silence!" (Sign of Silence)

Repeat the following:

"I am He, the Bornless Spirit, having Sight in the Feet, Strong and the Immortal Fire. I am He, the Truth. I am He, who hate that evil should be wrought in the world. I am He that lighteneth and thundereth. I am He, whose mouth ever flameth. I am He from whom is the shower of the Life of Earth. I am He, the Begetter and Manifester unto the Light. I am He, the Grace of the World. The Heart Girt with a Serpent is my Name.

"Come thou forth and follow me, and make all spirits subject unto me, so that every spirit of the firmament and of the ether, upon the earth and under the earth, on dry land and in the water, of whirling air and of rushing fire, and every spell and scourge of God the Vast One, may be made obedient unto me. IAO SABAO. Such are the Words."

Remain west of the Altar. The Elemental beings have now been fully evoked. Say: "The Holy Guardian Angel of (state your magickal name) is in command of those beings that are commanded thereby. All ye beings have been here assembled for the purpose of..." (State here your intention for doing the ritual, in clear words and with firm resolve. The purpose of the ceremony may be for a separate ritual working within the opening rite given here, such as the consecration of a talisman, an invocation of a specific godform, a healing ceremony, a rite of protection, or some other magickal working.)

After the purpose of the ritual has been accomplished, by whatever spiritual exercise you choose to do, sit quietly facing the east, attempting to feel the presence of the spirit around and within you. Then return to the west of the Altar, facing East. Give thanks in your own words or in the following prayer:

"Unto Thee, sole wise, sole eternal and sole merciful One, be the praise and the glory for ever. Who hath permitted me, who now standeth humbly before Thee, to enter thus far into the sanctuary of Thy mysteries. Not unto me, but unto Thy name be the glory.
"Let the influence of Thy Divine Ones descend upon my head, and teach me the value of self-sacrifice, so that I shrink not in the hour of trial, but that thus my name may be written on high, and my Genius may stand in the presence of the Holy Ones—in that hour when the Son of Man is invoked before the Lord of Spirits and His name in the presence of the Ancient of Days."

When completely finished with the ritual working, perform the Reverse Circumambulation thrice.

Grasp the wand by the red section and go to the South. Draw a circle. Trace six Banishing Solar Hexagrams in front of the Elemental Tablet. Then trace the Banishing Pentagrams of Spirit Active and of Fire, vibrating the appropriate words and giving the appropriate signs. Place the candle back upon the Altar.

Hold the wand by the blue section and go to the West, facing the Tablet and draw a circle. Then trace the Banishing Solar Hexagrams and the Banishing Pentagrams of Spirit Passive and of

Water, with words and signs. Place the cup upon the Altar.

Hold the wand by the yellow part and go to the East. Trace a circle in front of the Tablet. Then draw the Banishing Solar Hexagrams and the Banishing Pentagrams of Spirit Active and of Air, with words and signs. Return the rose upon the eastern side of the Altar.

Grasp the wand by the black section and go to the North. Draw a circle in front of the Tablet. Trace the six Banishing Hexagrams. Then trace the Banishing Pentagrams of Spirit Passive and of Earth, with words and signs. Return the dish of salt to its place upon the Altar.

Go to the west of the Altar, facing east. Hold the wand by the white section and trace a circle over the Tablet of Union. Trace all four Banishing Spirit Pentagrams, vibrating: "EXARP—EHEIEH," "HCOMA—AGLA," "NANTA—AGLA," "BITOM—EHEIEH." Give the LVX Signs.

Say, "I now release any Spirits that may have been imprisoned by this ceremony. Depart in peace to your abodes and habitations, but be ready to come when ye are called. Go with the blessings of YEHESHUAH YEHOVASHAH." (draw the sigil of the Cross and the Circle)

Give the Sign of the Closing of the Veil.

Perform the LBRP or the SBRP.

Perform the BRH.

Say, "I now declare this Temple duly closed."

THE RITE IS ENDED

Part 3

The Inner Temple

CHAPTER FOUR

R.R. et A.C.

The Second Order of the Golden Dawn is really not a part of the Golden Dawn. It is the *Ordo Roseae Rubae et Aureae Crucis*—the Order of the Red Rose and Golden Cross. This Order, quite distinct from the Golden Dawn, is comprised of Adepts who have attained grades ranging from 5=6, 6=5, to 7=4. The higher grades of 8=3, 9=2, and 10=1 are ascribed to the invisible Third Order and cannot be attained by living persons (although some may claim to hold these high degrees honorarily). To use Regardie's words, "it is impossible for the ordinary individual to understand those (grades) above the grade of Adeptus Minor, and individuals who lay claim openly to such exalted grades, by that very act place a gigantic question mark against the validity of their attainment."*

It is the duty of the R.R. et A.C. to govern and teach the First Order of the Golden Dawn. The work of ceremonial magick begins upon the Initiate's entrance into the Second or Inner Order. The Golden Dawn is strictly a teaching Order, but the R.R. et A.C. is where the practical applications of magick truly commence. It is in the Second Order that the Initiate learns to construct and consecrate magickal tools and perform rituals of high magick.

The Second Order is essentially rooted in the spirit of Rosicrucianism, a spiritual philosophy founded upon the life of Christian Rosencruetz, also known as C.R.C., the supposed founder of the Brotherhood of the Rose Cross. This secretive order of initiates and adepts who studied alchemy, qabalah, astrology, magick and Christian mysticism, surfaced in Europe around 1614. MacGregor Mathers firmly established the ideals of Rosicrucianism into the

---

* Israel Regardie, *The Golden Dawn* (St. Paul, MN: Llewellyn Publications, 1982), p 30.

R.R. et A.C. by 1892, after he finished the elaborate initiation ceremony into the Adeptus Minor Grade. Based upon the legend of
Christian Rosencruetz, it involves the discovery of his tomb—the
Vault of the Adepti. This chamber is the primary Temple of the Second Order, and no one can be admitted to the R.R. et A.C. without it.
No individual can claim to be of a high degree in the Order who has
not taken an actual Adeptus Minor initiation performed in a physical Vault by a qualified initiator. This chamber is highly charged
once every year during the festival of Corpus Christi Day, the one
day of the year when the Consecration of the Vault of the Adepti is
performed. Corpus Christi means, of course, "the Body of Christ."
This Catholic feast day, held in honor of the Eucharist, falls on a different day each year, owing to the fact that it is celebrated a certain
number of days after Easter. This tradition, carried on by the Second
Order, was undoubtedly started by the early Rosicrucians who referred to it secretively as "Day C." Although some have suggested
that the Consecration of the Vault of the Adepti marks the date of
the summer solstice, the traditional date of the Ceremony is determined by the feast day of Corpus Christi, which can fall anywhere
from the end of May to the end of June. In fact, the Order does not
observe the solstices, only the equinoxes; the times when day and
night are equal in length, alluding once more to the Middle Pillar
and the balanced disposition of opposing forces.

The Officers of the Second Order Temple wear lamens identical to those worn by the Chief Adept in the Portal grade, except that
they are suspended by a yellow collar. The Chief Adept wears a
large Rose Cross Lamen analogous to that described in chapter 5,
but suspended from a collar in the shape of a double-headed phoenix. (The collar can be cut from leather and painted, or cut out of fabric and filled with a layer of polyester fiber or similar padding.)

The ritual clothing of an Adept of the Second Order is a white
Tau robe, yellow slippers/sandals, and a yellow and white striped
nemyss. The Inner Order sash has been described in early papers as
white and in later papers as yellow*. As an Initiate is advanced to the
higher grades of the Second Order, the sash is ornamented with appropriate symbols.

In the following pages, the ritual implements of the Second Order, especially the wands, will be examined. We begin this chapter
with a guided visualization for the Initiate of the Inner Mysteries.

---

* It is probable that what seems to be described as two different sashes is in fact one sash that
is white trimmed with yellow.

A Guided Alchemical Journey for the Adept
Based on the Legend of Christian Rosencruetz

After taking a ritual bath and performing a rite of relaxation, put on the regalia of the Second Order and light a single white candle on the Altar of your Temple. If possible, another Adept similarly prepared should read the following visualization quietly to you after performing the LBRP. If another Adept is not available, familiarize yourself with the passage beforehand and guide yourself along this journey. Give the LVX Signs when entering the Temple:

Close your eyes and continue breathing as in the exercise of the Four-fold Breath. See yourself leaving your personal Temple behind. The room slowly fades from your view.

Imagine yourself in a dark and dank place beneath the ground. The only sound is the clanking of heavy chains. You realize that you are in a dungeon and you are not alone. Other unfortunate ones are here with you. Some are bewailing their fate, but others are calm and patient. You can see none of their faces clearly.

Suddenly a rope is lowered into the dungeon from above. You and a couple of your companions pull yourselves out to freedom but most of the prisoners do not seem to be aware of the rope. You call to them to grasp the rope, but they do not hear you and continue to languish in the cell below. For the moment you cannot help them. A figure in a simple white robe is responsible for lowering the rope into the prison. You exchange the Neophyte Signs as well as the 5=6 Signs. You have found a true guide.

Once above the dungeon, you are overjoyed by the glorious light of the sun, which warms the dampness out of your robes. A splendorous view of Nature is before you, rolling grassy hills and lush forests. The scent of lilac is in the air. In a satchel at your side are your provisions; bread, salt, and water, enough to sustain you on a long journey. Confidently, you and your guide start out on an adventure, stopping only to pick some roses to adorn your sash. The events of the next seven days are remarkable and enigmatic.

Along the path, you encounter many wondrous sights, unusual birds and trees, beautiful maidens, knights, and castles. You journey across many miles of hills, rocks and plains. Finally you come upon a truly marvelous palace and are welcomed to enter. The palace is utterly enormous; a labyrinth where one can wander for years without exploring all of its remarkable rooms, cellars, staircases, paintings, and strange astronomical instruments. The palace is fully inhabited by angels, musicians, warriors, pages, and beautiful maidens. It is here that your guide informs you that a Royal Wedding is to take place and that you are one of many guests of honor.

In a huge banquet hall you meet other adepts who are both the invited and uninvited witnesses of the marriage. At the table, you are modest and reserved, still wondering why you, of all people, should be invited to such an exclusive event. Others in the hall scoff at you loudly and obnoxiously. It seems that all manner of people have come to this wedding; true adepts and impostors sit side by side. The ones making the most noise seem to be the ones most unworthy of being here. Over the din of the guests, a woman's voice is heard. This voice declares that all present will be judged on the following day to prevent the admission of unworthy persons to the wedding.

As the morning arrives, the word of the maiden comes true. All the guests are weighed on a scale against seven stones, and most of them are dismissed according to their merits. Some impostors can not even move the scale. They are stripped of their robes and driven away with scourges. A few kingly adepts who are unable to attain proficiency are dismissed honorably and given a drink of forgetfulness to spare them undue torment. A few of the scoffers are beheaded.

As you step into the scale, you are judged to be worthy. Afterwards, you are taken with a few other adepts to a garden filled with spectacular creatures; a lion swinging a shining sword. A unicorn, white and majestic, emerges from a dark grove of trees and kneels before its audience. The lion suddenly breaks its sword into two pieces and hurls them into a fountain. The beast rears angrily until a white dove carrying an olive branch drops a piece of it in the lion's mouth. After eating the branch, the lion becomes calm again and the unicorn returns to its placid grove. At length a maiden appears to lead you down a winding stone staircase. At the bottom of the stairs you are given a crown of laurel and robes embroidered with the Golden Sun and the Silver Moon. Soon after, you are presented to the King and Queen.

Within the Great Hall, a comedy is enacted before the whole assembly—a play which portrays the adventures of the Golden King and the Silvery Queen.

In the play, Putrefaction is the Dark King who leads the princess away into his kingdom. She is rescued, but surrenders voluntarily to her captor. Once more the Golden King frees her from the Dark Lord, and once again she falls prey to the monster, who has her whipped. She is condemned to die by poison, which does not kill her, but afflicts her with leprosy. The imprisoned girl refuses to see the Golden King's emissaries. Defiled and sick, her royal honors stolen from her, she submits to her tormentor. After a great battle, she is rescued against her will and restored to splendor by the Golden King.

At the end of the play, the assembly breaks into a joyous song, for the time of the wedding is near. A pompous celebration begins. Then, just as suddenly, a bizarre turn of events takes place. A drink called the Draught of Silence is offered to all and consumed by the family of the Bride and Groom. The entire royal family is willingly beheaded in the banquet hall and a day of mourning follows this most peculiar of all weddings you have ever witnessed.

A group of alchemists are locked in a tower where they work feverishly to resurrect the King and the Queen through their art. You also aid in this task, as your guide looks on. At length the alchemists produce a golden phoenix whose egg is cut by a diamond. The bird feeds upon the blood of the executed family. Its blood in turn slowly resuscitates the murdered King and Queen who are carried into the royal bed chamber to consummate the mystical wedding. You are graciously thanked by the King and Queen for your part in this wedding. The warden of the court presents you with a necklace bearing a golden stone, which he places about your neck.

Your guide informs you that the allegory you have witnessed before you is but a brief summary of an actual alchemical process, during which the female and male principles are joined together. It is yet another form of the Hieros Gamos, the Divine Marriage, the joining of the Fire and Water Triangles which form the hexagram, the symbol of perfection and purity.

After grasping the knowledge imparted to you at the Wedding of Silver and Gold, you and your companion leave the Palace and continue on your journey. You feel as though you have witnessed something extraordinarily special, and you are still left with a sense of modesty and awe.

You travel on for some time, experiencing nothing else of note until at length a high mountain appears off in the distance ahead of you. As you approach the mountain, you can see that its base is surrounded by an imposing brick wall. A fleet-footed rabbit scurries along the path before you. A blindfolded person is slowing feeling his way along the wall. Another is groping on hands and knees in an attempt to locate the path. The only entrance through the wall is marked by two pillars behind which is a stone arch. The figure of a naked old man is seated upon an old tree-trunk within the archway, acting as a guardian. Your guide bids you to continue on without him.

As you advance, the old man bars the way. He asks you to explain why you have come to this particular mountain. You state humbly that you have witnessed the marriage of Gold and Silver and are seeking further knowledge and spiritual growth in order to continue the Great Work. The Guardian of the Threshold asks you additional questions about the Tree of Life, which you answer honestly to the best of your ability. Finally he is satisfied. He explains that in order to enter the mountain, one must be humble. The purity of your heart is more important than the knowledge you have accumulated. Had you come to this mountain in an arrogant manner boasting of your knowledge, you would have become like the others, blindfolded and groping for the entrance. The guardian points out two creatures just within the entrance. To the left is a rabbit, ready to run at any given moment. To the right is a hen sitting on a nest of eggs. Taking your last adventure as a clue, you realize that these are two images of alchemical processes. The rabbit is a symbol of the active and swift method of proceeding in the alchemical operation of inner transmutation; while the brooding hen represents the slow and patient method. Both methods should be mastered by the Initiate. After passing this test, the old guardian moves aside and permits you to enter.

The path leading into the peak twists and turns like a great serpent, around jutting rocks and stunted mountain trees. It is dark inside the summit. Around one pile of rocks you suddenly come upon a horrible dragon with many heads, who spits fire at you. It sits squarely in the center of the road blocking your progress. You are unarmed and cannot think of a way to battle this primal beast, but you resolve not to turn back. Perhaps it is not necessary to fight the animal. Gathering courage, you stamp your foot thrice and give the LVX Signs. The dragon withdraws with no further incident, stepping off the road and permitting you to pass by.

Once you are past the beast, the passage leads you out into the open air of a plateau at the center of the mountain. With a sense of pride and accomplishment, you step confidently out onto the plateau, but as you so do, a great lion springs onto the rock and roars threateningly at you. You realize that after passing the dragon, you let your ego get carried away with you. This was unwise, for there are still more difficult tests ahead. You remember the wound you received from a lion in an earlier journey. After re-examining your own motives, you stand in the Sign of Osiris Slain to await the verdict of the lion.

The beast regards your attitude, then quietly moves off the rock, and begins to clean his fur with his tongue in a contented feline manner. Once the lion is off the path, you notice a stone tower beyond the plateau. Above its central door are perched two birds, a crow and an eagle, the two parts of the soul; the black bird of the subconscious and the white eagle of spirit. Both birds represent different aspects of the self as well as the Black and White Pillars you are already familiar with. Both of these facets of experience with must be integrated for true spiritual growth to occur.

Before entering the citadel, you notice a strange sight—to the left, the figures of the sun and moon are being washed and purified in a wooden tub. To the right is a furnace into which a glass container has been placed in the process of distillation. You now understand that purification and distillation are alchemical processes which act to cleanse both the outer and inner parts of the soul respectively.

You enter the tower and find yourself in the inner sanctum of the mountain. From the top of the tower, an old man plants a live tree into the wash basin below. The living essence of the purified sun and moon rises through the roots, trunk and branches of the tree to bear fruit in the forms of a heptagon and a glass container of pure liquid. From the other side of the tower, a tree without leaves grows above the furnace of distillation below. It bears fruit in the form of three stars.

You begin to climb the rugged peak of the mountain, pulling yourself up the jagged rocks with your bare hands. It is not an easy climb. Your hands and feet accumulate more than a few cuts and bruises along the way. At one point the rocks supporting you fall away, and you pull yourself up only by sheer determination. Finally you arrive at a small dwelling perched nearly at the tip of the summit. Wearily you enter the building and find within it a pure white, seven-sided room. On the ceiling is painted the symbol of a dove. In the center of this room is a circular altar. Upon the altar is a chalice of pure liquid. You drink the fluid and feel the fatigue quickly leave your body. A sense of spiritual calm overtakes you and you know that you are in the House of the Holy Spirit high atop the Mountain of Initiation. Out of a great window you look down upon the wonders of the world from a new spiritual perspective. Nothing in the universe seems exactly as it was before you began this great journey. The created world is filled with a purpose and essence you hadn't really noticed before. The vantage point you have attained is spectacular. Although you have reached a new plateau within your spiritual progression, you have in fact become reborn as a Neophyte on another level. This is not the time to rest and admire your achievements.

You turn your attention from the fields below to the tip of the mountain still above you. Upon the very summit is an orb surmounted by the symbol of vitriol and a cross. Vitriol is the acidic essence which penetrates to the core of the material substance. You are aware of a voice saying to you: "*Visita Interiora Terrae Rectificando Invenies Occultum Lapidem*—Visit the interior of the Earth, and by purifying, there discover the hidden stone."

The image of a shining crown appears above the orb, providing you a glimpse of the completion of the Great Work which you hope to someday attain. But for the moment this vision is enough.

Your journey is finished for now and you must return. Quickly you descend the mountain, passing the figures of the lion, the dragon and the Guardian of the Threshold. You leave the mountain behind and begin the journey home, rejoined by your guide. Eventually you pass the palace of the King and Queen who are playing a game of chess. You pass the unusual birds, trees and animals encounters earlier. You even pass by the dungeon in the ground where you were once held prisoner. That place has no part of you now. You bid farewell to your guide by exchanging the grade signs. At length you see your own familiar Temple and see yourself seated within it. Bring your consciousness slowly back into your physical body, sensing the room around you. After adjusting yourself to your surroundings, you may bring the visualization to its completion.

At the end of the meditation, you may record in your magical diary any impressions or experiences before closing with the LBRP. Give the LVX Signs before leaving the Temple.

IMPLEMENTS OF THE SECOND ORDER

The Chief Adept's Wand: The Ur-uatchti

Use and Symbolism

The Ur-uatchti is one of the most powerful and beautiful of all the wands of the Second Order. Outwardly, the Chief Adept's Wand is similar in appearance to that of the Kerux in the Outer Order. However, the symbolism of the Ur-uatchti includes the energies behind the Caduceus wand and much more. The Chief Adept describes the Wand in the Adeptus Minor Ceremony thus:

> My Wand is surmounted by the Winged Globe, around which the twin Serpents of Egypt twine. It symbolizes the equilibrated force of the Spirit and the Four Elements beneath the everlasting wings of the Holy One.

This wand is therefore an extension of the Chief Adept's Wand in the Portal, in which the forces of the four elements are crowned and governed by the fifth element of Spirit. In this case the linear form of Spirit (the Pentagram) has been exchanged for the image of the winged globe, a dazzling visual symbol which captures the true essence of Spirit in a manner which speaks to us on a higher level.

The winged globe is one of the most widespread of ancient symbols. It is an emblem of the sun and the heavens. In Egyptian texts the Ur-uatchti is associated with Horus, the warrior and a protector god: "From the height of heaven he was able to see his father's enemies, and he chased them in the form of a great winged disk." The text continues, "Finally, Horus and his companions went back to Nubia, to the town of Shashertet, where he destroyed the rebels of Uauat, and their ablest soldiers. When this was done Horus changed himself once more into the form of the winged sun-disk with uraei, and took with him the goddesses Nekhebet and Uatchit in the form of two serpents, that they might consume with fire any rebels who still remained. When the gods who were in his boat saw this they said, 'Great indeed is that which Horus hath done by means of his double snake diadem; he hath smitten the enemy who were afraid of him!' And Horus said, 'Henceforth let the double snake diadem of Heru-Behutet be called Ur-uatchti' and it was so. After these things Horus journeyed on in his ship, or boat, and arrived at Apollinopolis Magna (Edfu) and Thoth decreed that he should be called the 'Light-giver, who cometh forth from the horizon.' Hereupon Horus commanded Thoth that the winged sun-disk with uraei should be brought into every sanctuary of all the gods of the lands of the South and of the North, and in Amentet, in order that they might drive away evil from therein. Then Thoth made figures of the winged sun-disk with uraei, and distributed them among the Temples, and sanctuaries, and places wherein there were any gods, and this is what is meant by the winged disks with uraei which are seen over the entrances of the courts of the Temples of all the gods and goddesses of Egypt. The snake goddess on the right hand side of the disk is Nekhebet, and that on the left is Uatchti."

According to Manly Hall, the Ur-uatchti is emblematic of the three persons of the Egyptian Trinity . . . that the wings, serpents and solar orb are the insignia of Ammon, Ra and Osiris. Ammon, one of the oldest of the Creator gods in the Egyptian pantheon, is attributed to the Sephirah of Chesed, the Sphere symbolically occupied by the Chief Adept. The winged disk also represents matter in a state of sublimation and transfiguration. The wings indicate movement or flight—Spirit in motion. The two serpents allude to the harmony of opposing forces. The colors on the staff refer to the four elements of Fire, Air, Water and Earth.

The Chief Adept uses the Ur-uatchti in the Inner Order to bring the forces of Spirit and Light (L.V.X.) into the Temple. The large wand pictured in this book was the one used by Israel Regardie to consecrate the Vault of the Adepti at the Georgia Temple in 1982 (see color plate). Based on a diagram of the wand shown in Crowley's *Equinox*, the wand is a full 26" from wing tip to wing tip. (This lead Regardie to complain that the wand was simply "too damn big.") In response, a smaller, more manageable wand was constructed using the dimensions given here. The Ur-uatchti can be used in any ritual where the Invocation of Spirit is needed. Because of its affinity with the sphere of Chesed, the Ur-uatchti can be employed whenever the energies of Mercy are needed. It can also be used to invoke or banish the forces of the Elements (or those of the Three Mother Letters) with great effect. The protective powers of this wand can be utilized whenever strength and defense is called for.

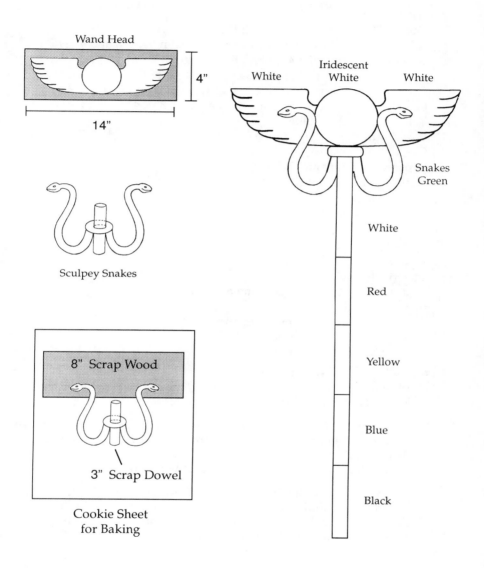

Wand Head

4"

14"

Sculpey Snakes

8" Scrap Wood

3" Scrap Dowel

Cookie Sheet
for Baking

White

Iridescent
White

White

Snakes
Green

White

Red

Yellow

Blue

Black

The Ur-Uatchti

Materials Needed
>   One 3/4" thick dowel approx. 29" long
>   A 3/4" thick piece of soft wood approx. 14" in length and 4" wide
>   A one-pound box of oven-hardening clay
>   One 1/4" thick dowel or wooden peg 1" in length
>   One 3/4" thick scrap piece of dowel approx. 3" in length
>   One 3/4" thick piece of scrap wood approx. 8" x 4"
>   Yellow carpenter's glue
>   Wood putty
>   Gesso
>   A strong bonding glue such as epoxy
>   Acrylic paints: red, yellow, blue, green, gold, white iridescent white
>   and black
>   Sealant: clear lacquer finish

Tools Needed
>   Jigsaw
>   Electric drill with 1/4" bit
>   Rotary power tool with gouging and carving bits
>   Sandpaper (all grades)
>   Artist's brushes (large medium and fine)
>   A cookie sheet used for baking

Construction: The Winged Globe

1)   With the jigsaw, cut out the winged globe as one piece from the 14" length of wood as shown in the diagram.

2)   With a pencil draw stylized feathers on both sides of both wings. Use the rotary tool to gouge and grind the outline of the feathers, giving them a sculpted look. Sand the wings until they have a smooth 3-dimensional appearance. Fill in any gaps with wood putty.

3)   Find the center of the bottom edge, where the winged globe will be joined to the wand shaft. There drill a hole that is 1/4" wide and 1/2" deep. Also drill the same size hole into one end of the 29" long dowel. This will be the top end of the shaft.

The Serpents

4)   Take some clay and knead it by hand until it is soft and pliable. Then roll out a 14" long coil or rope of clay. The coil should be no thicker than 1/2". Add some extra clay to both ends of the coil, and shape them into two diamond-shaped serpent heads. (You now have a clay snake with two heads, one at either end.) The mouth and eyes of the snakes can be drawn into the clay with a tooth pick or pin. Cut the two-headed snake in half.

5) Roll out another 1/2" thick coil of clay and shape into a perfect ring that fits over the 3" long piece of scrap dowel. Attach the two serpents firmly to the underside of the clay ring as shown in the diagram.

6) Take the 8" long piece of scrap wood and drape the upper halves of the serpents over it in the position they would occupy if draped over the actual head of the wand. Place the entire assembly (snakes, dowel and wood) onto a cookie sheet and follow the package directions for baking the clay. When baking time is over, take the cookie sheet out of the oven and let the serpents cool before you touch them.

Finishing Steps

7) Apply a strong epoxy to the inside of the serpent ring. Slide the serpent ring over the top end of the 29" dowel.

8) Pour some glue in the hole drilled into the top end of the shaft. Slide the 1/4" dowel or wooden peg into the hole firmly, so that half of it sticks out of the end of the shaft. Let dry.

9) Pour glue in the hole drilled into the bottom of the wand head, and slide over the wooden peg sticking out of the top of the shaft. Allow to dry.

10) Sand the wand smooth, especially the shaft. Paint the entire wand with gesso. Allow to dry. Sand the coated wand lightly. Apply a second coat if needed.

11) Paint the winged globe entirely white, but use gold paint to accent the carved lines of the feathers. A coat of iridescent white may be added to the sphere of the globe itself to distinguish it from the wings. Paint the serpents green.

12) With a pencil, mark the shaft of the wand into five sections below the serpent ring. The topmost section will be 6-1/2" in length, while the remaining four will be 5-1/2" long. Of these, the long top portion is to be painted white. The next section will be red. The third section will be blue, and the final part will be black.

13) After the painted wand has dried completely, apply a coat of sealant for protection.

Ritual for Use

The Supreme Invocation of ETH

For this ritual, the Z.A.M. should be dressed in the regalia of the Inner Order. The Hall should be arranged according to the opening of the Portal Ceremony; the Enochian Tablets should be in the appropriate quarters, and the Tablet of Union should be upon the White

Altar (which is substituted for the black.) On hand should be a sword for banishing as well as the newly finished Ur-uatchti. (Note: English translations of the Enochian Keys used here are given in chapter 5.) Give the LVX Signs upon entering the Temple.

After a few moments of relaxation, give five knocks. Go to the Northeast and say, "HEKAS! HEKAS! ESTE BEBELOI!"

Perform the LBRP.

Perform the BRH.

Perform the SIRP.

Take up the Ur-uatchti by the white portion. Trace with the wand-head the figure of a circle over the Tablet of Union. Draw the four Invoking Pentagrams of Spirit Active and Passive. (Vibrate the appropriate names: "EXARP, EHEIEH." "HCOMA, AGLA." "NANTA, AGLA." and "BITOM, EHEIEH.") Give the LVX Signs.

Repeat the First Enochian Key:

"Ol Sonuf Vorsag Goho Iad Balt. Lonsh Claz Vonpho Sobra Z-Ol Ror I Ta Nazps Od Graa Ta Malprg Ds Hol-Q Qaa Nothoa Zimz Od Commah Ta Nobloh Zien Soba Thil Gnonp Prge Aldi Ds Vrbs Oboleh G Rsam: Casarm Ohorela Taba Pir Ds Zonrensg Cab Erm Iadnah Pilah Farzm Znrza Adna Gono Iadpil Ds Hom Od Toh Saba Ipam Lu Ipamis Ds Loholo Vep Zomd Poamal Od Bogpa Aai Ta Piap Piamol Od Vaoan. Zacare Eca Od Zamran: Odo Cicle Qaa. Zorge Lap Zirdo Noco Mad Hoath Iaida."

Phonetic: (Oh-el Soh-noof Vay-oh-air-sah-jee Goh-hoh Ee-ah-dah Bal-tah, El-on-shee Kahl-zoad Von-pay-hoh: Soh-bay-rah Zoad-oh-lah Roh-ray Ee Tah Nan-zoad-pay-ess, Oh-dah Jee-rah-ah Tah Mahl-peer-jee: Dah-ess Hoh-el-koh Kah-ah No-thoh-ah Zoad-ee-mah-zoad Oh-dah Koh-mah-mah-kay Tah Noh-bloh-hay Zoad-ee-ay-noo So-bah Tah-hee-lah jee-noh-noo-pay Peer-jee Ahl-dee Dah-ess Ur-bass Oh-boh-lay Jee Rah-sah-may: Cahs-ar-may Oh-hor-ray-lah Tah-bah Peer Dah-es Zoad-oh-noo-ray-noo-sah-jee Kah-bah Air-may Ee-ad-nah. Pee-lah-hay Far-zoad-mee Zoad-noo-ray-zoad-ah Ahd-nah Goh-noh Ee-ah-dah-pee-el Oh-dah Vay-oh-ah-noo. Zoad-a-kah-ray Ay-kah Oh-dah Zoad-a-mer-ah-noo. Oh-dah Kee-clay Kah-ah. Zoad-or-jee Lah-pay Zoad-ee-ray-doh Noh-koh Mah-dah, Hoh-ah-tah-hay Ee-ah-ee-dah.)

Say, "I invoke Ye, Ye Angelic guardians of the Stellar Realms! Ye whose abode lies beyond the domain of the Visible Kingdom! Just as Ye are the stewards of the gates of the Universe, be Ye also the defenders of this Magick Circle of Art! Protect this consecrated Temple from the profane and the unbalanced! Grant unto me the Strength, the Will and the Knowledge to perform this ceremony aright, that I might not degrade this sacred sphere. Grant unto me the Wings of Dawn! Let me prove myself to be a worthy vessel for the mysteries of the Eternal Spirit! Anoint me with the pure white Brilliance of the Light Divine!"

Circumambulate the Temple thrice, saluting with the Neophyte Signs when passing the East.

Go to the west of the altar and face east. Perform the Adoration to the Lord of the Universe.

Hold the wand by the yellow band. Trace a circle over the first letter "E" in the first line of the Tablet of Union as you repeat the Second Enochian Key:

"Adgt V Paah Zong Om Faaip Sald Vi-I-V-L Sobam Ial-Prg I-Za-Zaz Pi-Adph: Casarma Abramg Ta Talho Paracleda Q Ta Lorslq Turbs Ooge Baltoh. Givi Chis Lusd Orri Od Micalp Chis Bia Ozongon. Lap Noan Trof Cors Ta Ge O Q Manin Ia-Idon. Torzu Gohe L Zacar Eca C Noqod. Zamran Micalzo Od Ozazm Vrelp Lap Zir Io-Iad."

(Ahd-gee-tay Vah-pah-hay Zoad-oh-noo-jee Oh-mah Fah-ah-ee-pay, Vee-ee-vee-el Soh-bah-may Ee-ahl-peer-jee Ee-zoad-ah-zoad-ah-zoad Pee-ahd-pay-hay: Cah-sar-mah Ah-brahn-jee Tah-hoh Para-clay-dah, Koh-Tah Lor-es-sel-koh Toor-bay-ess Oh-oh-jee Bal-toh-hah. Jee-vee Kah-hee-sah Loos-dah Ohr-ree Oh-dah Mee-cal-pah Kah-hees-ah Bee-ah Oh-zoad-oh-noo-goh-noo. Lah-pay Noh-ah-noo Tro-eff Cor-say Tah Jee Oh Koh Mah-nee-no Ee-ah-ee-doh-noo. Tohr-zoad-oo Goh-hay El. Zoad-ah-kah-ray Ay-kah Kah Noh-Kwoh-dah. Zoad-ah-mer-ah-noo. Me-kah-el-zoad-oh Oh-dah Oh-zoad-ah-zoad-may Vod-rel-pay, Lah-pay Zoad-ee-ray Ee-oh Ee-ah-dah.)

Give the Sign of Theoricus, followed by the LVX Signs.

Grasp the wand by the blue band and trace with it a circle over the first letter "H" of the second line on the Tablet of Union. Repeat the Second Enochian Key as before. When finished give the Sign of Practicus followed by the LVX Signs.

Grasp the wand by the black portion. Trace a circle over the first letter "N" of the third line on the Tablet of Union. Repeat the

Second Enochian Key as before. When finished, give the Sign of Zelator followed by the LVX Signs.

Grasp the wand by the red band and trace with it a circle over the letter "B" of the fourth line of the Tablet of Union. Repeat the Second Enochian Key as before. When finished give the Sign of Philosophus followed by the LVX Signs.

Go to the east of the Temple, facing the closed veil of Paroketh. With both hands, raise the Ur-uatchti high above your head. Vibrate the names, "ETH EHEIEH" six times, employing the Vibratory Formula of the Middle Pillar.

Give the Sign of the Rending of the Veil, physically parting the curtain of Paroketh as you do so. Visualize in the East the dazzling image of the dawning sun. In the center of this, imagine the Banner of the East. Repeat the following prayer:

"Homage to thee, O Ra, at thy beauteous rising. Thou risest, thou shinest at the Dawn. The Company of the Immortals praise thee at sunrise and at sunset, when as thy morning boat meeteth thy evening boat with fair winds, thou sailest over the heights of heaven with a gladdened heart.

"O thou Only One, O thou Perfect One, O thou who art Eternal, who art never weak, whom no power can abase, O thou splendor of the noon-day Sun, over the things which appertain to thy sphere none hath dominion at all. And therefore I make homage to thee.

"All hail Horus! All hail Tum! All hail Khephra! Thou great Hawk, who by thy beauteous face make all men to rejoice, thou renewest thy youth, and dost set thyself in yesterday's place. O divine youth, self-created, self-anointed, thou art the Lord of heaven and earth, and didst create beings celestial and beings terrestrial. O thou heir of eternity, everlasting Ruler, self-sustained, as thou risest thy gracious rays are upon all faces and abide in every heart. Live thou in me, and I in thee, O thou Golden Hawk of the Sun!"

Hold the wand by the white portion and perform the Qabalistic Cross.

Stand in the form of a pentagram (arms apart like the position of the Tau Cross, and legs wide apart). Visualize yourself standing between the Pillars, formulated as a black Egg of Akasa. From the dark center of the Egg (Tiphareth) extends upwards into the heights an astral semblance of the Ur-uatchti. As each of the following words are vibrated, let this scepter shoot higher and higher towards the Kether of the Universe. The visualization should be of the formation of an astral Middle Pillar down the center of which the Divine White Brilliance may descend.

Establish the Invoking Pentagram of Spirit Active over your physical body as follows: Vibrate the names "EXARP, EHEIEH" and "BITOM, EHEIEH." See a brilliant white flaming letter SHIN appear over your left foot. Silently vibrate the name "ELOHIM." The Shin moves diagonally across your body, coming to rest over your right hand, as you mentally vibrate "YOD HEH VAV HEH." The white Shin moves straight across your body to your left hand as you silently intone "Aleph Lamed, AL." The Shin again crosses your body diagonally, coming to rest over your right foot as you mentally vibrate "ADONAI." The Shin then ascends to the crown of your head. Loudly vibrate the word "ETH." Then see the Shin descend back down to your left foot. Imagine the Shin appearing next at your Tiphareth center, tracing there the sigil of the Spirit wheel. Vibrate loudly "EHEIEH" four times using the Vibratory Formula. (Imagine the astral form of the Ur-uatchti grow taller from your Tiphareth center.)

Establish the Invoking Pentagram of Spirit Passive over your physical body as follows: Vibrate the names "HCOMA, AGLA" and "NANTA, AGLA." See a brilliant white flaming letter SHIN appear over your right foot. Silently vibrate the name "ADONAI." The Shin moves diagonally across your body, coming to rest over your left hand, as you mentally vibrate "Aleph Lamed, AL." The white Shin moves straight across your body to your right hand as you silently intone "YOD HEH VAV HEH." The Shin again crosses your body diagonally, coming to rest over your left foot as you mentally vibrate "ELOHIM." The Shin then ascends to the crown of your head. Loudly vibrate the word "ETH." Then see the Shin descend back down to your right foot. Imagine the Shin appearing again at your Tiphareth center, tracing there the sigil of the Spirit wheel. Vibrate loudly "AGLA" four times using the Vibratory Formula.

Imagine the astral form of the Ur-uatchti grow ever taller from your Tiphareth center reaching toward the Universal Kether. See clearly the Divine White Brilliance, formulated as a flaming angelic figure descending upon the black egg.

Say, "Come thou, in the Power of the Light. Come thou in the Light of Wisdom. Come thou in the Mercy of the Light. The Light hath healing in its wings."

Visualize the angelic figure transforming into a white dove, then finally into a white flaming Shin. See the Shin enter the winged disk which then glows brilliantly with the Power of the Divine. Give the LVX Signs in Silence. Say,

"I am the Resurrection and the Life. They that believeth in Me, though they were dead, yet shall they live. And whosoever liveth and believeth in Me, shall never die. I am the First and I am the Last. I am He that liveth and was dead, and behold, I am alive for evermore, and hold the Keys of Hell and Death. For I know that my Redeemer liveth and that he shall stand at the latter day upon the Earth. I am the Way, the Truth, and the Life, No one cometh unto the Creator but by Me. I am the Purified. I have passed through the Gates of Darkness unto the Light. I have fought upon Earth for good, and have now finished my work. I have entered into the invisible.

"I am the Sun in its rising, passed though the hour of cloud and night. I am Amoun, the Concealed One, the Opener of the Day. I am Osiris Onnophris, the Justified One, Lord of Life triumphant over death. There is no part of me that is not of the gods. I am the preparer of the Pathway, the Rescuer unto the Light."

After this prayer, circumambulate the Temple three times, and then intone the name of "ETH" and visualize the flashing descent of the Supernal Light down the astral shaft of the Uruatchi. Imagine the twin serpents of Egypt praising the Eternal One as the Light enters them. The colored bands of the Three Mother Letters become especially vibrant as the Light descends. Finally the Light penetrates into your Tiphareth center, and the Black Egg surrounding you gradually becomes illuminated, until it changes into white.

Bring your feet together. With your arms still outstretched, say, "The Sign of Osiris Slain."

Keep the left arm out, but raise the right arm above your head. Turn your head to look over the left shoulder. Say, "L, the Sign of the Mourning of Isis."

Raise both arms high and say, "V, the Sign of Apophis and Typhon."

Cross the arms over the chest and say, "X, the Sign of Osiris Risen."

**Pentagram over the human figure for
Supreme Invocation of ETH**

Give the three letter Signs again, saying as you perform them, "L. V. X., LVX." Pause and give the Sign of Osiris Slain saying, "The Light..." Recross arms over the chest ."...of the Cross."

Say, "Let the White Brilliance of the Divine Spirit Descend." See and feel the white Egg surrounding you glow with the radiance of the Divine Eth. Maintain the image as long as you desire, then withdraw the shaft of the astral Ur-uatchti back into your heart center.

Say quietly, "Be my mind open to the Higher. Be my heart a center of the Light. Be my body a Temple of the Rosy Cross." Perform the Qabalistic Cross.

Give the Sign of the Closing of the Veil, physically closing the curtain of Paroketh as you do so.

Perform the Reverse Circumambulation. Trace the Banishing Pentagrams of Spirit Active and Spirit Passive over the Tablet of Union.

Perform the SBRP.

Perform the BRH.

Say, "I now set free any spirits that may have been imprisoned by this ceremony. Go in peace to your abodes and habitations with the blessings of YEHESHUAH YEHOVASHAH." Trace the Rose Cross toward the East.

Give five knocks as in the beginning.

Say, "I now declare this Temple duly closed." Give the LVX Signs when leaving the Temple.

THE RITE IS ENDED

The Second Adept's Wand: The Phoenix Wand

Use and Symbolism

The Phoenix is a mythical bird about the size of an eagle. The ancient Egyptians worshiped the phoenix which they called the bennu, a heron-like bird. This bird was supposed to have created itself, and to have come into existence from out of the fire which burned on top of the sacred Persea Tree of Heliopolis. The bennu was essentially a solar bird, and was a symbol of the dawning sun and of the dead sun-god, Osiris, to whom the animal was sacred, and from whose heart it sprang. The bennu represented the birth of the sun each morning from the dead sun of yesterday. In addition it became the symbol of the resurrection of mankind, because humanity's spiritual essence was believed to spring forth from the dead physical body. The bennu was thought to be a holy bird that made its appearance once every 500 years. According to Herodotus, the plumage of the phoenix was partly golden and partly red. At the back of its head the phoenix had a peculiar tuft of feathers.

Clement, in the first century A.D., describes the phoenix thus:

> There is a certain bird which is called a phoenix. This is the only one of its kind and lives five hundred years. And when the time of its dissolution draws near that it must die, it builds itself a nest of frankincense, and myrrh, and other spices, into which, when the time is fulfilled, it enters and dies. But as the flesh decays a certain kind of worm is produced, which being nourished by the juices of the dead bird, brings forth feathers. Then, when it has acquired strength, it takes up that nest in which are the bones of its parent, and bearing these it passes from the land of Arabia into Egypt, to the city called Heliopolis. And in open day, flying in the sight of all men, it places them on the altar of the Sun, and having done this, hastens back to its former abode.

Another source says that when the phoenix' death was near, it would make a nest of sweet-smelling woods and resins, which it would expose to the sun's rays until it burnt itself to ashes in the fire. A second phoenix would arise from the marrow of its bones.

Every legend about the bird alludes to periodic destruction and re-creation. To the ancient mystics, the phoenix was an appropriate symbol of the immortal human soul which rises triumphantly from the deceased physical body. In Christian symbolism it signifies the victory of eternal Life over Death. Medieval Hermetists considered the bird to be a symbol of alchemical transmutation. In alchemy, the phoenix corresponds to the color red, to the regeneration of universal life and to the completion of a process.

The Phoenix Staff or Wand contains all of these ideas. It also represents the Sulphur or the Active Masculine (Solar) Principle embodied by the Second Adept who symbolically occupies the position of Geburah. The wand ends in two prongs which in ancient times had a very practical (as well as Geburic) function; a person walking would sometimes come across a poisonous serpent which could be pinned to the ground with the double-ended staff. Besides the act of saving one from a nasty death, the Phoenix Wand thus represented the triumph of the sun-god Ra over the evil serpent Apep.

In the ceremony of the Adeptus Minor, the Second Adept describes his wand as follows: "Mine is a Wand terminating in the symbol of the Binary, and surmounted by the Tau Cross of Life, or the head of the Phoenix, sacred to Osiris. The Seven colors of the Rainbow between Light and Darkness are attributed to the Planets. It symbolizes Rebirth and Resurrection from Death."

The wand is used in the 5=6 Ceremony to bring into action the powers of Life and the vital heat of existence. The shape of the phoenix head suggests a hook, which locks into place over the Ur-uatchti and the Lotus Wand at crucial moments in the ritual.

The Phoenix Wand is a very powerful implement that can be used by an Adept whenever the fiery powers of Geburah are called for. It can also be used to invoke, charge or banish the Forces of the seven planets. The fiery nature of this wand gives special strength and authority to any magickal operation undertaken. The following ritual is a Consecration of a Lunar Talisman, used to enhance one's clairvoyant abilities by inducing dreams and visions.

Materials Needed
    One 3/4" thick dowel approx. 30" long
    A 1-1/2" thick piece of soft wood (pine or bass) approx. 12" in length
        and 5" wide
    One 3/4" thick piece of soft wood approx. 9" x 5"
    Two 1/4" thick dowels or wooden pegs 1" in length
    Yellow carpenter's glue
    Wood putty
    Gesso
    Acrylic paints: gold, white, red, orange, yellow, green, blue, blue-violet,
        violet, and black
    Sealant: clear lacquer finish

Tools Needed
    Jigsaw
    Electric drill with 1/4" bit
    Rotary power tool with gouging and carving bits
    Sandpaper (all grades)
    Artist's brushes (large, medium and fine)

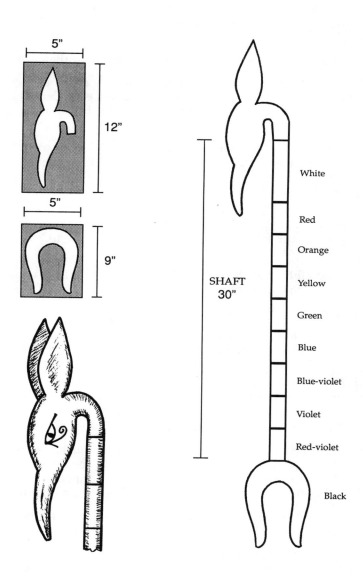

5"

12"

5"

9"

SHAFT
30"

White

Red

Orange

Yellow

Green

Blue

Blue-violet

Violet

Red-violet

Black

The Phoenix Wand

Construction: The Head of the Phoenix

1) Trace the basic shape of the Phoenix head unto the 1-1/2" thick piece of wood. (Note: draw the neck of bird slightly wider than the 3/4" width of the shaft.) Cut out the shape with the saw.

2) Make a cut about 4" into the piece of wood that divides the "ears or crests" of the phoenix into two as shown in the diagram.

3) Use the rotary tool to "flesh out" the true shape of the animal by rounding its neck and tapering its beak and ears. Generally soften all the rough edges. (Feathers may be implied by carving lines into the face.) Any gaps can be filled with wood putty.

4) Drill a hole 1/4" wide and 1/2" deep into the end of the bird's neck where the head of the wand will be joined to the shaft.

Construction: The Double-ended Shaft

5) Take the 3/4" thick piece of wood (9" x 5") and trace on it the shape of a horseshoe which will be the "foot" of the wand. (Be sure that the top curve of the foot is the thickest part (about 1-1/2"). Cut out the shape with the saw.

6) Sand all the rough edges smooth. Drill a hole 1/4" wide and 1/2" deep into the top of the horseshoe shaped foot.

7) Drill the same size hole into both ends of the 30" long dowel shaft.

8) Pour glue into both holes just drilled into the shaft. Attach the two 1/4" thick wooden pegs firmly into the glued holes. Allow to dry.

Finishing Steps

9) Pour glue into the holes drilled into both the wand head and the wand foot. Attach these two pieces to the dowel shaft by slipping them over the exposed ends of the wood pegs. Allow to dry.

10) Sand the neck of the Phoenix down until it matches the size of the shaft. Use wood putty to fill in any gaps. (The point of junction between the neck and the shaft should be unnoticeable.) Any gaps where the foot meets the shaft should be filled with putty as well.

11) Cover the wand completely with gesso. Let dry. Sand the shaft lightly and apply a second coat if needed.

12) With a pencil, mark the shaft of the wand from the neck to the foot into 8 sections. (The topmost section will be the longest—approximately 5-1/2". The remaining seven sections will be about 3-1/2" long.)

13) Paint the head and neck of the phoenix gold. Give it Egyptian style eyes using black and white paint.

14) Paint the long top section below the neck white. The remaining sections are painted thus in descending order: red, orange, yellow, green, blue, blue-violet, and violet. The foot is to be painted black.

15) After all paint has dried, apply a coat of sealant to the wand for protection.

Ritual for Use

Consecration of a Lunar Talisman

This Ritual would be best performed during the day and hour of Luna (see the Table of Planetary Hours, pp. xxvii–xxviii). (Remember that the Moon in increase is favorable for magickal working; likewise, the Moon in decrease is unfavorable.) The Z.A.M. should be dressed in the regalia of the Second Order. Arrange the Temple in accordance with the Neophyte Hall. Outside the Temple, wrapped in a black piece of cloth and bound three times with a black cord, should be a talisman you want charged with the energies of Luna. (This could be a piece of jewelry, a Lunar gemstone or a piece of paper covered with symbols which relate to the Moon.) Upon the Altar should be the Cross and Triangle, Tablet of Union, a chalice of water, and a censer or stick of incense. A sword for banishing should be close at hand. The position of Luna should be determined for the time of the ritual, and a symbol of the planet should be placed on the floor or hung on the wall corresponding to the direction noted. The Adept should wear, in addition to the Rose Cross lamen, a seal of Luna in the proper colors. You will also need a white cloth to wrap the talisman in after consecration. The main implement employed in this ceremony will be the newly finished Phoenix Wand.

After a period of relaxation and meditation, give five knocks. Then go to the Northeast and proclaim, "HEKAS! HEKAS! ESTE BEBELOI!"

Perform with the sword the LBRP.

Perform the BRH.

Take up the chalice of water. Starting in the East, purify the Temple in all quarters by tracing the Cross and the Invoking Water Triangle. Say, "All the fountains of the great deep were broken up . . . and the rain was upon the earth." Replace the cup.

Take up the incense. Consecrate the room with Fire in all quarters, starting in the East, tracing the Cross and Invoking Fire Triangle. Say, "The Voice of Tetragrammaton draws out Flames of Fire." Replace the incense.

Take the Phoenix Wand by the white portion and circum-ambulate the Temple three times deosil, saluting with the Neo-phyte Signs when passing the East. Then stand west of the Altar facing East and perform the Adoration to the Lord of the Universe.

Go to the East and perform the complete Supreme Invoking Ritual of the Pentagram (SIRP). Hold the white portion of the wand when performing the Qabalistic Cross. When invoking the elements, grasp the colored band of the planet that rules the Kerubic Sign of each specific element, while tracing the pentagram with the head of the Phoenix:

AIR—the blue-violet band of Saturn, co-ruler of the Sign Aquarius.

FIRE—the orange band of Sol, ruler of the Sign Leo.

WATER—the red band of Mars, co-ruler of Scorpio.

EARTH—the green band of Venus, ruler of Taurus. Finish with the Qabalistic Cross, holding the white portion of the wand.

Go to the west of the Altar and face east. Say, "The Holy Guardian Angel of (state magickal name) under the authority of the Concealed One is in command of those beings who have been summoned to this ceremony. I charge all ye Archangels, Angels, Rulers, Kings, and Elementals called to this place to witness and aid in this Rite. I call upon the Crown, EHEIEH, the One Source Most High, to look with favor upon me as I perform this ceremony. Grant me success in this, my search for the Hidden Wisdom and my aspiration towards the Light Divine. To the glory and completion of the Great Work. So mote it be."

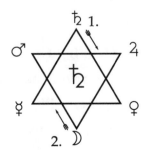

Still grasping the Phoenix Wand by the white portion, go to the east and perform the Qabalistic Cross. Then draw an Invoking Hexagram of the Supernals and

Invoking Hexagram of the Supernals

visualize it in a golden light while intoning "ARARITA." In the center of the figure place the sigil of Saturn in brilliant white. Vibrate "YHVH ELOHIM." Then draw the letter Aleph also in brilliant white and intone the name of the letter. Trace the same figures and name of the letter. Trace the same figures and intone the same names in the South, West, and North. Upon returning to the East, repeat the Analysis of the Keyword as given in the BRH.

Vibrate the name "EHEIEH" four times using the Vibratory Formula of the Middle Pillar. Say, "The changing God; Eternal, Infinite. Young and Old, of a spiral form. And another fountainous, who guides the Empyreal Heaven." Endeavor strongly to feel the Divine Presence. Then give the LVX Signs.

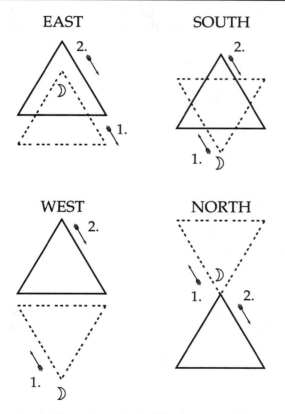

Four Lesser Invoking Hexagrams of Luna

Hold the Phoenix Wand high, grasping the white portion with both hands. Say, "For the Creator congregated seven firmaments of the world. Circumscribing Heaven in a round figure, he fixed a great company of inerratic Stars, and he constituted a Septenary of erratic Animals. Placing Earth in the middle, and Water in the middle of the Earth. The Air above these. He fixed a great company of inerratic stars, to be carried not by laborious and troublesome tension, but by a settlement which hath not error. He constituted them six; casting into the midst the Fire of the Sun, suspending their disorder in well-ordered Zones.

For the Goddess brings forth the great sun, and the bright Moon. O Aether, Son, Spirit, Guides of the Moon and of the Air, and of the Solar Circles, and of the monthly clashings, and of the Aerial recesses. The Melody of the Aether, and of the passages of the Sun, and Moon, and of the Air; and the wide Air, and the Lunar Course, and the Pole of the Sun. Collecting it, and receiving the Melody of the Aether, and of the Sun, and of the Moon, and of all that are contained in the Air. Fire, the derivation of Fire, and the Dispenser of Fire; His hair pointed is seen by his native Light; Hence comes Saturn. The Sun Assessor beholding the pure Pole; and the Aetherial Course, and the vast motion of the Moon, and the Aerial fluxions, and the great Sun, and the bright Moon."

Perform the Lesser Invoking Hexagram Ritual of Luna, commencing with the Qabalistic Cross. (Hold white band.) Then trace the four Lesser Hexagrams of Luna (four forms) in their respective Quarters, while holding the blue (Luna) band of the wand and tracing with the Phoenix head. Intone "ARARITA" as each figure is traced. Follow this with the Analysis of the Keyword.

Grasp the Phoenix Wand by the blue band and turn to face the direction where you have determined Luna be at the time of the working. In front of the Luna sigil, trace a large golden Greater Invoking Hexagram of Luna. Vibrate the name "ARARITA" while drawing the Hexagram. Intone "SHADDAI EL CHAI" when tracing the Moon sigil (in blue) at the center. Trace the Hebrew letter "ALEPH" also in blue and intone the name of the letter.

Say, "Thou Throne of the Almighty and Living One! Sphere of strength and foundation! Splendorous Vision of the Machinery of the Universe! Thou who wears as a diadem the crescent horns of LEVANAH carved from pearl and moonstone! Ninth in number! Purifier of the Divine Emanations; Thou who proves and corrects the designing of their representations, disposing the unity with which they are designed without diminution or division. The keys of the mysteries of regeneration are in Thy grasp! The Astral Light is Thy abode! SHADDAI EL CHAI! Let a ray of Thy perfection descend upon me, to awaken within my being that which shall prove a channel for the working of Thine abundant power. May this Lunar talisman which I am about to consecrate be a focus of thy light so that it may awaken within my soul a clear inner vision and enhanced psychic abilities."

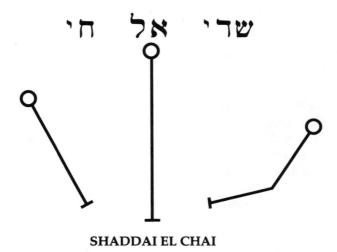

SHADDAI EL CHAI

Trace the Sigil and letters of SHADDAI EL CHAI (ShDI ALHI) in the Air with the wand. Then trace the sigil and the letters over your heart. Vibrate the name seven times using the Vibratory Formula.

Astrally formulate four Pillars surrounding you. Then visualize clearly a large Banner of the East. After the image is firmly within your mind, see it enveloping you as a cloak.

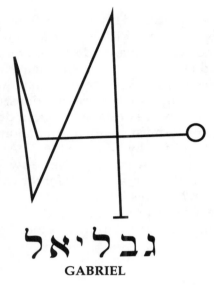

גבליאל

GABRIEL

Say, "In the Divine Name of SHADDAI EL CHAI, I command ye, O ye dwellers in the Invisible realms, that ye fashion for me a magickal base in the Astral Light wherein I may invoke the Divine Forces to charge this talisman. Grant unto me the presence of GABRIEL, the Great Archangel of the sphere of Yesod." (Hold the wand by the blue band. Trace the Greater Invoking Hexagram of Luna and in it the Sigil of Gabriel. Vibrate the name strongly.)

Say "O ye Strong Ones of Yesod, I conjure ye by the name of the Almighty One, and by the name of Gabriel, whose throne and seat ye are. KERUBIM! Come to me now! Be present at this ceremony and fill this sphere with your magick power!" (Trace the sigil of the Kerubim and intone the name.)

כרובים

KERUBIM

Command unto me the presence of GABRIEL, the Angel of Levanah, and her intelligences, MALKAH BE-TARSHISIM VE-AD RUACHOTH SCHECHALIM, (Mal-kah Bay-Tar-shee-sim Vay-ahd Roo-ach-oth Shay-chal-im) Queen of the Chrysolites and the Eternal Spirits of the Lions, that they may consecrate this most powerful symbol. I conjure ye potently to make manifest your presence within my soul that this Lunar talisman may be charged. Come forth, all ye powers and forces of the realm of Yesod, obey ye now in the name of SHADDAI EL CHAI, the divine ruler of your kingdom, and GABRIEL, your Archangel, and the mighty Kerubim!"

Put the wand aside. Place the black-wrapped talisman at the edge of the circle to the west. Push it into the circle with the tip of the sword. Say, "Creature of Talismans, enter thou within this sacred circle, that thou mayest become a worthy dwelling place for the Forces of LEVANAH."

Consecrate the talisman with Water and Fire. (Dip your fingers into the water and mark the talisman with a cross. Sprinkle thrice in the form of the Invoking Water Triangle. Wave the incense in the form of a cross and give an additional three waves in the form of the Invoking Fire Triangle.)

Say, "In the name of SHADDAI EL CHAI, I, (give magickal name), proclaim that I have invoked ye in order to form a true and potent link between my human soul and the Light Divine. To this end I have brought into this circle a Talisman covered with a black veil and bound thrice with a cord, so that this creature of talismans shall not see the light nor move until it be duly consecrated unto me. I proclaim that this talisman SHALL be charged by the Archangel GABRIEL, so that through its use, I may increase my powers of clairvoyance and psychic awareness, so that I may be better enabled to perform the Great Work."

Place the talisman at the foot of the Altar and say, "I, (magickal name), do solemnly pledge to consecrate this talisman in due ceremonial form. I further promise and swear to use it to obtain only pure and clear mystical visions and insights. May the powers of Yesod, the sphere of Foundation, witness my pledge."

Place the talisman upon the white triangle on the Altar and stand west, facing the East. With sword in hand, trace over the talisman the sigils of SHADDAI EL CHAI and of GABRIEL while intoning their names. (Note: vibrate SHADDAI EL CHAI a total of seven times according to the Vibratory Formula.) Then say, "I invoke the Great Angel of Yesod and Luna, GABRIEL, the Strong One of God! Lay Thy hand invisibly on this talisman and give it life. Anoint it, so that through its use I may increase my powers of psychic awareness and tread the path of the Seer, to the glory of Thine ineffable name. I also invoke the choir of angels known as the KERUBIM (intone and trace the sigil), the Strong Ones, that they may bind into this talisman the firm and sturdy Foundation of Yesod, which gives stability to the sphere of LEVANAH. O ye Mighty Ones of Yesod, assist me in this my invocation of the Lunar powers! I command ye to send hither the Intelligence of all Intelligences of the Moon, MALKAH BE-TARSHISIM VE-AD RUACHOTH SCHECHALIM, that she concentrate and bind into this talisman life and power. O ye divine Forces of Yesod, manifest yourselves through this Lunar Intelligence, to insure that this talisman give forth to me only true and correct psychic impressions in the form of dreams and visions; NOT the false and distorted images that abound in the Akashic Record.* Descend I command Thee, Mighty archangel GABRIEL to charge this talisman aright, that it may become a powerful tool consecrated to the work of the Magick of Light."

Lift the talisman in the left hand, smite it thrice with the sword, and raise both it and the sword aloft, stamping the foot three times. Then take the talisman to the North and say:

The voice of the Exorcism said unto me, "Let me shroud myself in darkness, peradventure thus shall I manifest myself in Light. I am the only being in an abyss of Darkness. From the Darkness came I forth ere my birth, from the silence of a primal sleep. And the Voice of Ages answered unto my soul, Creature of Talismans, the Light shineth in the Darkness, but the darkness comprehendeth it not. Let the Mystic Circumambulation take place in the path of Darkness with the symbolic light of Occult Science to lead the way."

Visualize the light of a lantern held by an angelic hand before you. Circumambulate the Temple once with the talisman and the sword, following the light. After going around once, stop in the south and lay the talisman on the ground. Bar it with the sword, saying, "Unpurified and unconsecrated, Thou canst not enter the Gate of the West."

---

* The Akashic Record is contained in the lowest level of the astral World of Yesod. It is a realm of images, dreams and fears of humanity built up from the beginning of time. The Akashic Record is created from both the history of the races and from the mental acts of each individual.

Purify the talisman with Water and consecrate with Fire as before. Lift it with the left hand, face the West and say, "Creature of Talismans, twice purified and twice consecrated, thou mayest approach the Gateway of the West."

Pass to the West with the talisman in the left hand. Partly unveil it, smite it once with the sword and say, "Thou canst not pass from concealment unto manifestation, save by the virtue of the name 'ELOHIM.' Before all things are the Chaos and the Darkness, and the gates of the Land of Night. I am He whose Name is Darkness. I am the Great One of the Paths of the Shades. I am the Exorcist in the midst of the Exorcism. Take on therefore manifestation without fear before me, for I am he in whom fear is not."

Replace the veil over the talisman and carry it once more around the Circle. Then stop in the North, place the talisman on the floor and say: "Unpurified and unconsecrated, thou canst not enter the Gate of the East." Purify and consecrate the talisman with Water and Fire as before. Lift it in the left hand and say, "Creature of Talismans, thrice purified and thrice consecrated, thou mayest approach the Gateway of the East."

Go to the East and partly unveil the talisman. Strike it once with the sword and say, "Thou canst not pass from concealment unto manifestation save by the virtue of the name YHVH. After the formless and the Void and the Darkness, then cometh the knowledge of the Light. I am that Light which riseth in darkness. I am the Exorcist in the midst of the Exorcism. Take on therefore manifestation before me, for I am the wielder of the forces of the Balance. Creature of Talismans, long hast thou dwelt in darkness. Quit the night and seek the Day."

Take the talisman to the west of the Altar. Place it again on the white triangle. Hold the pommel of the sword immediately over it and say, "By all the Names, Powers, and rites already rehearsed, I conjure upon thee power and might irresistible. KHABS AM PEKHT. KONX ON PAX. LIGHT IN EXTENSION. As the Light hidden in darkness can manifest therefrom, so shalt thou become irresistible."

Put aside the sword and take up the Phoenix wand by the white portion. Remain west of the Altar facing east. Repeat the following invocation:

SHADDAI EL CHAI! Oh thou Almighty and Living One! Supreme Lord of Life! Life-giver and Life-Creator! Thee do I invoke! Thou who activates the final manifestation of Form in the physical realm. Thee do I invoke! Thou Vision of the Inner Workings of the Universe. Thee do I invoke! Thou receptive Chalice that receives and purifies the influence of all the Emanations. Thee do I invoke! Thou whose image is that of a beautiful naked man, very strong. Thee do I invoke! Thou Mirror of Tiphareth, reflecting back the solar Light through the Luminary of the Moon. Thee do I invoke! Throne of the Aether of the Wise, the Akashic Light, the realm of both mind and matter. Thee do I invoke! SHADDAI EL CHAI! (Vibrate powerfully seven times, employing the Vibratory Formula.) I INVOKE THEE! Administer your divine guidance over these proceedings to insure that this Lunar talisman be properly charged. Grant unto me that through its use, my powers of perception may be increased. May it aid me to comprehend visions that are occult in nature. Thus may my clairvoyant abilities be expanded and my inner sight elevated. Thus will I be better equipped to perform the works of divination, astral travel, and Godform assumption. SHADDAI EL CHAI! I also ask that you instill within this talisman the power to resist the false and deceptive images that reside in the Sphere of Illusion known as Maya. Grant that this Lunar talisman provide me only with true impressions, reflected from Tiphareth and ultimately from the Crown on high. I invoke thee, exalt my soul to the feet of thy glory. Hear me and manifest in splendor to one who aspires to the Light of the Hidden Wisdom.

Circumvent the Altar and take up the talisman. Put it on the floor to the east of the Altar in the place between the Pillars of the Neophyte Hall. Stand just east of the talisman and face west. Holding the Phoenix Wand by the blue band, trace the Invoking Hexagram of Luna over the talisman. Vibrate "ARARITA" while drawing the hexagram. Intone "SHADDAI EL CHAI" when tracing the sigil of the Moon. Finally vibrate the name of "ALEPH" when drawing the letter in the center.

Greater Invoking Hexagram of Luna

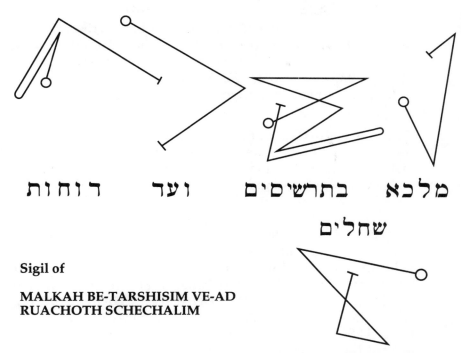

רוחות   ועד   בתרשיסים   מלכא

שחלים

Sigil of

**MALKAH BE-TARSHISIM VE-AD
RUACHOTH SCHECHALIM**

Intone the following names and trace their corresponding sigils over the talisman: "GABRIEL. KERUBIM. LE-VANAH. MAL-KAH BE-TARSHISIM VE-AD RUACHOTH SCHE-CHALIM."

לבנה

LEVANNAH

Say, "I invoke into this talisman the Forces and Powers of LEVANAH, the blue and silver crescent of the Moon. Thou bright lady of the night, Queen of dreams and visions, thee I invoke! Ruler of the Lunar tides and the currents of Flux and Reflux. Etheric partner of the Earth. Moonstone bride and mother who art the mirror of contemplation. Thou art a Goddess known by many names: ISIS. DIANA. ARTEMIS. SELENE. HECATE. UMA. Shining One of the silver bow and the veil! Beautiful art thou in thy fullness! By seed and by root, and by bud and leaf, and by flower and fruit of my entire being, do I invoke thee! Bestow upon this talisman your powers of foresight and intuition. May the perfume of thy essence anoint this Lunar talisman so that through its use my precognitive abilities may be increased. Thus may I be better able to comprehend the Hidden Nature of the Universe."

Focus the entire force of the will, and project it at the talisman using the Sign of the Enterer at least three times, or until you feel your energy begin to drain. When this happens, give the Sign of Silence at the end for protection. A light should be visualized flickering about the talisman. Return it to the white triangle upon the Altar. Purify and consecrate it again. Remove the black cord. Strike the talisman three times again with the sword and proclaim, "By and in the name of SHADDAI EL CHAI, I invoke upon thee the power of LEVANAH!" Put aside the sword and take up the Phoenix Wand by the blue band. Trace over the talisman the sigils of SHADDAI EL CHAI, GABRIEL, KERUBIM and MALKAH BE-TARSHISIM VE-AD RUACHOTH SCHECHALIM." (Vibrate the Divine Hebrew Name of Yesod seven times as before.)

Circumambulate the Temple thrice with the wand and the talisman. Then go to the position of the Hierophant in the East. Unveil the talisman, placing it back upon the ground in front of you. Still grasping the wand by the blue band, contemplate the various attributes of Luna. Make the Sign of the Rending of the Veil and say, "Let the white brilliance of the Divine Spirit, reflected through the silvery blue mirror of Levanah descend upon this talisman, to fill it with the splendor of Thy majesty, that for ever it may be unto me an aid to aspire to the Great Work."

Hold the wand by the white portion and draw the Flaming Sword over the talisman. Take up the talisman and step between the Pillars. Formulate an astral banner of the East enveloping itself around the talisman. Hold it on high and say, "Behold, all ye powers and forces I have invoked. Take witness that I have duly consecrated this talisman with the aid of GABRIEL, great archangel of Yesod and Levanah, that it may aid and improve my psychic abilities. May it provide me with a sure footing whenever I tread the paths of the Astral Realm, giving me the ability to discern between the true and the untrue. And by the exaltation of my higher nature, may it assist me in my path to the Light Divine."

Wrap the talisman in white silk or linen and place it upon the Altar. (Note: Never banish over a talisman or when it is unwrapped.)

Grasp the Phoenix Wand with both hands by the white portion and raise it on high. Say, "Not unto my name, O Adonai, but to Thine be ascribed the Kingdom, the Power and the Glory, now and forever more! Amen!" Give the LVX Signs.

Purify and consecrate the Temple with Water and Fire as in the beginning.

Perform the Reverse Circumambulation three times widdershins. Feel the energy that you have carefully built up throughout the ceremony begin to dissipate. Perform again the Adoration to the Lord of the Universe.

Perform the Lesser Banishing Hexagram Ritual of Luna, commencing with the Qabalistic Cross. (Hold white band.) Then trace the four Lesser Hexagrams of Luna (four forms) in their respective Quarters, while holding the blue (Luna) band of the wand and pointing with the black end. Intone "ARARITA" as each figure is traced. Follow this with the Analysis of the Keyword.

Greater Banishing Hexagram of Luna

Return to the position of Luna in the Temple. Hold the wand by the blue band and trace with the black end. Draw the Greater Banishing Hexagram of Luna in that direction, vibrating the "ARARITA," "SHADDAI EL CHAI" and "ALEPH."

Perform the Supreme Banishing Ritual of the Pentagram (SBRP). Hold the white band of the wand when giving the Qabalistic Cross and the Archangelic names. Trace the Banishing Pentagrams while grasping the appropriate colored bands (as in the SIRP at the beginning of the ceremony.) But be sure to point with the black end of the wand for Banishing.

Perform the LBRP.

Perform the BRH.

Say, "I now release any spirits that may have been imprisoned by this ceremony. Depart in peace to your abodes and habitations. Go with the sanction of SHADDAI EL CHAI and the blessings of YEHESHUAH YEHOVASHAH."

Knock five times as in the beginning.

Say, "I now declare this Temple duly closed."

SO MOTE IT BE

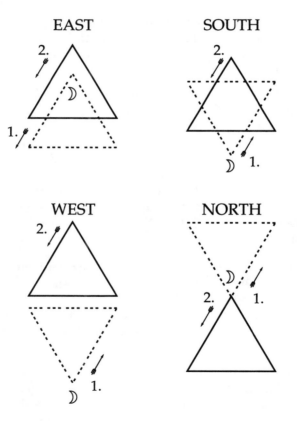

Four Lesser Banishing Hexagrams of LUNA

The Third Adept's Wand: The Lotus Wand

This wand is identical to that used by the Adept in almost all personal magickal workings. In the Second Order ceremonies, it is the official wand used by the 3rd Adept, who personifies the powers of Tiphareth. It symbolizes the development of Creation. The Lotus Wand represents Love, while the Phoenix Wand and the Ur-uatchi represent Life and Light. Instructions on how to make a conventional Lotus Wand are given in chapter 5; however, the Lotus Wand of the Third Adept should have a longer shaft than that of a conventional Lotus Wand because in ritual it is used in conjunction with the other wands of the main Officers and should be of similar length.)

SECONDARY IMPLEMENTS
OF THE R.R. et A.C.

The Crux Ansata: The Ankh Wand

Use and Symbolism

The symbolic meaning of the Ankh has already been explained at length in the section of chapter 1 which describes the nemyss. Of primary importance here is the fact that the ankh is a form of the symbol of Venus, the planet whose wall is the door into the Vault of the Adepti (i.e. the Second Order). It is thus the symbolic "Key" into the Temple of the Inner Order, the "Key of Life" and another form of the Rose and Cross. Venus is the only planet whose sigil embraces all of the Sephiroth on the Tree of Life. Therefore the wand is painted to represent the force of the ten Sephiroth in nature, divided into a Hexad and a Tetrad. The oval embraces the first six Sephiroth, and the Tau Cross contains the lower four, answering to the four elements.

The three main Adepts in the 5=6 Ceremony, the 3nd, 2rd and Chief Adept, use their Crux Ansatas to infuse the candidate with the Light of LVX, causing the Higher Self to descend into his/her Ruach by awakening the Sephiroth of the Middle Pillar in the candidate's Aura. The Crux Ansata can also be used by a Magician to charge his/her own Sphere of Sensation with the forces of the Middle Pillar. The "Key of Life" is a potent tool for unlocking centers of energy within the Adept: creating a pathway for the natural influx of Divine Light.

Materials Needed

    One 3/4" thick piece of soft wood (pine or bass) 14" long and 7" wide
    Wood putty
    Gesso
    Acrylic paints: white, grey, black, blue, red, yellow, green, orange, violet, gold
    Sealant: clear lacquer finish

Tools Needed

    Jigsaw
    Electric drill with a bit that is at least 3/4"
    Sandpaper (all grades)
    Artist's brushes (medium and fine)

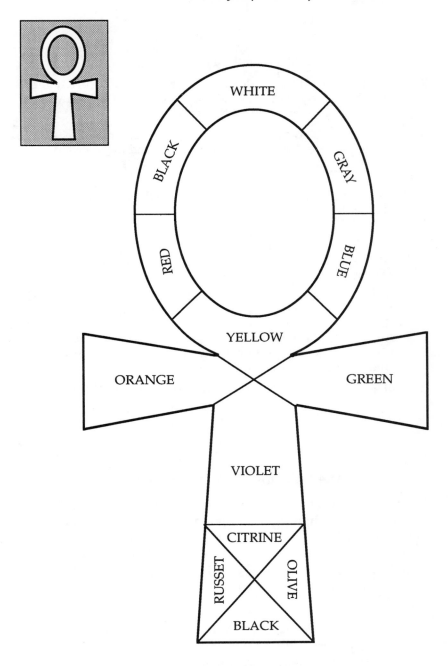

The Crux Ansata

Construction

1) Trace the pattern of the ankh onto the piece of wood. Cut out the outside edge of the ankh with the jigsaw.

2) Into the center of the shaded (waste) area of wood drill a hole or series of holes large enough to enable the blade of the jigsaw to move unobstructed in the center of this area.

3) Place the saw blade into the hole and cut out the waste area of wood, leaving the true shape of the ankh intact. Sand the ankh smooth.

Finishing Steps

4) Cover the wand entirely with gesso and allow to dry. Sand lightly. Add another coat if needed.

5) Using a pencil and ruler, divide the ankh into ten sections which represent the ten Sephiroth on the Tree of Life. (Note: the bottom section will be subdivided into the four colors of Malkuth.) Mark both sides of the ankh in this manner.

6) Refer to the diagram when painting the wand. Both sides should look identical and must be separated. (Note: You cannot simply paint the sides of the wand all the way around with a given color. This would result in one side of the ankh being painted incorrectly with the Tree of Life in a distorted position. Paint the outside and inside edge of the wand with gold to prevent this.)

7) After all paint has dried, apply a coat of sealant to the ankh for protection.

Ritual for Use

The Opening of the Spheres by Key

This ritual is based upon the exercise of the Middle Pillar. This practice is a means of aligning the personality with the Inner self, unifying all levels of consciousness. It acts to open all the spheres of the Middle Pillar, resulting in an unobstructed channgel for the Divine Light. To perform it the Adept should be dressed in the regalia of the Inner Order. The finished Crux Ansata is the only implement required.

After a few moments of relaxation, stand in the east of the Temple facing west, holding the Crux Ansata. Take some time to establish the exercise of the Four-fold Breath.

Give the LVX Signs.

Hold the wand by the white band of Kether. Raise the bottom of the Crux so that its Malkuth section touches the crown of your head. Give a half-turn of the wand slowly, mimicking the motion of a key opening a lock. Imagine a bright sphere of white light forming there. Vibrate the divine name "EHEIEH" (I am) a number of times until it is the only thing that exists in your conscious mind. Once you have accomplished that, pause to contemplate the sphere of Kether—the Crown; its attributes and spiritual qualities. This meditation performed, vibrate the same number of times the name of the Archangel "METATRON," whose name means "near Thy throne." Pause to contemplate the angelic form.

Bring the bottom of the Crux to the base of your throat (since it would be difficult to touch the nape of your neck). Turn the wand slowly 90 degrees again, activating the "Opening by Key." Visualize a shaft of light which descends from Kether to form a sphere of grey-white light at the base of your throat. Vibrate the Divine name "YHVH ELOHIM" (the Lord God) a number of times until it fills your consciousness. Meditate on the spiritual qualities of Daath-Knowledge. (Note: There is no archangel attributed to Daath, because it is not a proper Sephirah. Since Daath reflects the image of the Supernals—especially Binah—across the Abyss, the archangel "TZAPH-KIEL," whose name means "Beholder of God," may be vibrated here.)

Touch the bottom of the Ankh to your heart area and activate the Opening of the Sphere by Key. Visualize a shaft of light descending from Daath to Tiphareth, the sphere of beauty and harmony, forming a bright yellow sphere of light there. Vibrate the Divine name "YHVH ELOAH VE-DAATH" a number of times and contemplate "Tetragrammaton, God of Knowledge," as well as the spiritual and planetary qualities of the Sephirah. Then vibrate the archangelic name of "RAPHAEL" the same number of times. Pause and meditate on the angel whose name means "Healer of God."

Touch the Ankh to the groin, the moon center of Yesod, and activate the Key. Imagine the shaft of Light descending from Tiphareth to form a violet sphere of light at Yesod, the Foundation. Intone a number of times the name of "SHADDAI EL

CHAI," then pause and contemplate the "Almighty Living One." Then vibrate the name of "GABRIEL," and meditate on the angelic form of the "Strong One of God."

Point the Crux toward your feet and turn the Key. Imagine the shaft of light descending from Yesod into Malkuth forming a sphere of citrine, russet, olive, and black. Vibrate the divine name "ADONAI HA ARETZ" a number of times and contemplate the "Lord of Earth" as well as the spiritual qualities of the Kingdom. Then intone the name of the archangel "SANDALPHON" an equal number of times. Pause to consider the angelic figure whose name signifies "the Lord of the Extent of Height."

Pause and visualize the entire Middle Pillar of light which you have activated within your Sphere of Sensation.

Relax and circulate the energy with breathing. As you inhale, bring a ribbon of the light from Malkuth, up the left side of your body to Kether. When you exhale, see the ribbon of light going down the right side of your body from Kether to Malkuth.

After you have circulated the energy thus for a short period of time, inhale, bringing the ribbon of light up the front of the body from Malkuth to Kether. Exhale, and see the ribbon down the back of the body from Kether to Malkuth.

After a short length of time, change the circulation of energy again. Inhale, and imagine the shaft of light ascending the Middle Pillar in the center of your body. When the light reaches Kether, exhale and imagine a shower of brilliant white light surrounding you on all sides, which gathers up again at Malkuth.

After all these methods of circulation have been accomplished, see the light spiraling upward from feet to head, wrapping you like a mummy in bandages of pure light.

Finally center the energy in Tiphareth, the seat of balance. Release any excess energy; let it return to Kether.

End the rite by giving the LVX Signs.

(Note: After practicing this for many months, the Adept should employ the Opening of the Spheres by Key to formulate not only the

Middle Pillar, but the Sephiroth of the two side Pillars as well, using the method given here.) Below are the names attributed to each of the Spheres on the Tree of Life and the appropriate area of the body to which they correspond:

TREE OF LIFE

Sphere	Divine name	Archangel	Body area	Color
1. Kether	Eheieh	Metatron	Crown	White
2. Chokmah	Yah	Raziel	Left Temple	Grey
3. Binah	Yhvh Elohim	Tzaphkiel	Right Temple	Black
daath	Yhvh Elohim	Tzaphkiel	Nape of Neck	White-grey
4. Chesed	Al	Tzadkiel	Left Shoulder	Blue
5. Geburah	Elohim Gibor	Kamael	Right Shoulder	Red
6. Tiphareth	Yhvh Eloah Ve-daath	Raphael	Heart	Yellow
7. Netzach	Yhvh Tzabaoth	Hanael	Left Hip	Green
8. Hod	Elohim Tzabaoth	Michael	Right Hip	Orange
9. Yesod	Shaddai El Chai	Gabriel	Groin	Violet
10. Malkuth	Adonai Ha Aretz	Sandal-phon	Feet	Four colors

The Crook and Scourge

Use and Symbolism

The Crook and the Scourge symbolize the opposing concepts of Mercy and Severity. They are the additional implements of the Chief Adept when he/she is in the Godform of Osiris within the tomb. In ancient texts, the Phoenix staff, the scepter (crook) and the flail or whip were the three symbols of authority held by Osiris. The Crook or hooked staff is symbolic of the Mercy of Chesed and the White Pillar. In Christian symbolism, it is a pastoral attribute—the implement of a shepherd—and a symbol of faith. The hook stands for divine power, communication and connection. Its suggestive spiral shape also implies creative power. In the symbolism of the R.R. et A.C., the Crook is painted in the colors of the Minutum Mundum. It is divided into the colors symbolic of Kether, Aleph, Chokmah, Taurus, Chesed, Leo, Aries, Tiphareth, Capricorn and Hod.

The implement thus starts in the Supernal realm leading from Kether to Chokmah via the 11th Path (The Fool) and down to Chesed, the seat of Mercy from the 16th Path (The Hierophant) ending at length in the watery sphere of Hod.

The Scourge or Flail is symbolic of Severity and of the Black Pillar. It too is painted in accordance with the Minutum Mundum. It is separated into the colors of Netzach, Scorpio, Tiphareth, Gemini, Binah, Cancer, Geburah and Mem. The implement symbolically starts in the Fire of Netzach, and crosses the Crook of Mercy. The top of the scourge reaches the sphere of Binah before the flailed ends descend to Geburah and the 23rd Path of the Hanged Man.

The Crook of Mercy must be held in the right hand and the Scourge of Severity in the left hand. The arms should then be crossed upon the chest and the two implements will be in the proper position to represent the Pillars of Mercy and Severity in the Adept's Sphere of Sensation. According to the Adeptus Minor Ceremony, these tools are emblems of Eternal Opposing Forces between which the entire equilibrium of the Universe depends. The reconciliation of these Forces is the Key of Life (The Rose and Cross, as well as the Crux Ansata) and whose separation is evil and death.The Crook and Scourge may be employed by an Adept in a ceremony to balance and equilibrate the Forces of Mercy and Severity within him/her inner self. They may also be used in a ritual/meditation invoking the godform of Osiris.

Materials Needed

One 3/4" thick piece of soft wood that is 24" long and 12" wide

Eighteen 1/2" diameter round wooden beads

Three 3/8" diameter round wooden beads

Six 2" long cylindrical wooden beads (All of these beads can be found in most stores which sell hobby and craft supplies)

Nine 1/4" diameter metal beads

Three 6mm metal bead caps (Should be bigger than the hole which runs through the 3/8" wooden beads)

Three small eye screws

Roll of strong but thin wire

Wood putty

Gesso

Acrylic paint: white, yellow, grey, orange, red, blue, blue-violet, green and black

Sealant: clear lacquer finish

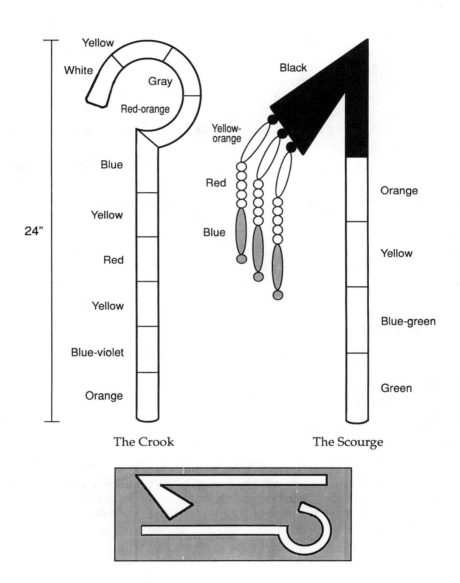

The Crook and Scourge

Tools Needed
   Jigsaw
   Soldering gun (with solder)
   Wire cutters
   Sandpaper (all grades)
   Artist's brushes (medium)

Construction: The Crook
1) On the piece of wood, draw out the basic shapes of both the Crook and the Scourge.

2) Cut out the form of the Crook with the jigsaw. Put the remaining piece of wood with the Scourge drawn on it aside.

3) Sand until smooth. Apply a coat of gesso and allow to dry. Sand lightly. Apply another coat if needed.

4) With a pencil, mark off the Crook into ten roughly even sections. Starting with the curved end of the Crook, paint the sections in descending order as follows:

1. White	5. Blue	9. Blue-violet
2. Yellow	6. Yellow	10. Orange
3. Grey	7. Red	
4. Red-orange	8. Yellow	

5) After all paint has dried, apply a sealant for protection.

Construction: The Scourge
1) Cut out the basic shape of the Scourge from the wood.

2) Sand the Scourge until smooth. Cover entirely with gesso and allow to dry. Sand lightly. Apply another coat if needed.

3) Apply a coat of gesso to all of the wooden beads. Allow to dry.

4) With a pencil, mark off the Scourge into five roughly even sections. (The "axe-like" shape of the head will be the longest section.) Paint the sections starting with the "axe" in descending order as follows:

1. Black	4. Blue-green
2. Orange	5. Green
3. Yellow	

5) Paint three of the 1/2" round wooden beads black. Paint the fifteen remaining 1/2" round beads red. Paint three of the 2" long beads yellow-orange. Paint the remaining three 2" beads blue. Paint the three 3/8" round beads blue.

Finishing Steps

6) Attach the three eye screws into the end of the "axe head" at even intervals.

7) From the roll of wire, cut off three 16" lengths of wire. Take one of the pieces of wire and run through one of the eye-screws attached to the Scourge. Fold the wire so that it is doubled. (The folded wire will be stronger but its length will now be 8".)

8) String the following number of beads in this order onto the doubled strand of wire: One black bead, one small metal bead, one long yellow-orange bead, one small metal bead, five red beads, one small metal bead, one long blue bead, one small blue bead.

9) Attach the small metal bead cap firmly to the two ends of wire sticking out from the last bead. Trim off any excess wire. Use a soldering gun to secure the wire to the bead cap. Attach two more strands of beads to the Scourge in the same manner.

10) After all parts of the Scourge have been assembled, apply a coat of sealant to protect the paint.

Ritual for Use

The Rite of Assumption to the Godform of Osiris

For this rite, the Adept should be dressed in the regalia of the Second Order. The Temple should be arranged according to the Portal of the Vault of the Adepti. A seat should be placed in the East and the finished Crook and Scourge should be placed upon it. A sword should be on hand for banishing. The Chief Adept's Wand should be placed in the East. The Adept is to be seated in the West. Give the LVX Signs upon entering the Temple.

Take a few moments to relax and practice the Four-fold Breath technique.

Give five knocks and go the Northeast to proclaim "Astu! Pu tebu-na bet em khut!" (Behold, I have endowed a place with power!)

Perform the LBRP.

Take up the Ur-uatchti by the white portion. Go to the west of the Altar and perform the Adoration to the Lord of the Universe.

Perform the Analysis of the Keyword.

Stand and face the East. Perform the exercise of Middle Pillar, awakening the five centers of the Pillar of Mildness within you. (Vibrate the Divine names of the spheres a number of times while bringing down the Divine light: Kether— "EHEIEH" Daath— "YHVH ELOHIM" Tiphareth —"YHVH ELOAH VE-DAATH" Yesod—"SHADDAI EL CHAI" Malkuth— "ADONAI HA-ARETZ")

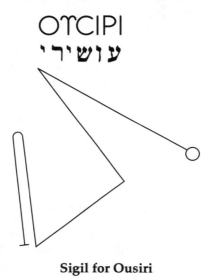

ОГСІРІ

עושירי

Sigil for Ousiri

Once the Middle Pillar is completely formulated within your sphere of sensation, trace within your heart the Coptic letters of the name OUSIRI (Osiris in Coptic) in pure white. Then trace with the wand the letters and sigil of the name toward the East.

Bring the Divine Light down from your Kether center to your Tiphareth center, and as you do so give the Sign of the Enterer, at the same time vibrating the name "OUSIRI" for as long as your exhalation of breath will last. At the end of the vibration give the Sign of Silence. Repeat this procedure of vibration a total of six times, once for every letter of the name.

After the sixth vibration of the name, project a white ray of light from your Tiphareth toward the throne in the east and formulate the Godform of Osiris there: The figure wears a yellow and white striped nemyss surmounted by the white Stenu Crown of the Upper Regions. His skin is reddish brown. From his chin hangs the royal beard of authority and judgement. He is wrapped entirely in white mummy cloth, except for his head and hands. His collar is banded white, red, blue, yellow and black. His wristbands are banded yellow and white. He holds in his right hand a white Djed Wand. His throne is white decorated with yellow, which stands upon a white pavement. (The lower part of his body is mummified, alluding to the material body of man, but the upper half is liberated, referring to the living spirit of humanity.)

Continue projecting the white ray until the astral figure is well formulated. Then put the Ur-uatchti aside. Take up the Crook and Scourge (crossing them over your chest) and step into the godform of Osiris that you have built up in the East, facing west. Feel your mind and reasoning faculties (Ruach) empowering the shell of the astral Godform, breathing life into it. When you have felt this happen, proclaim, "Nuk As-ar Unnefer!" (I am Osiris Onnophris!)

Be seated, but remain in this Godform, contemplating its attributes and spiritual qualities, identifying them as your own. After a pause, repeat the following: "I am the Prince in the field. My soul doth breath for ever and ever and my form is made anew with life upon earth. I am the lord of everlastingness, passing through millions of years in the course of mine existence. My name is made to endure. In the tomb I have lain only to again draw forth breath. I am renewed. The God Ptah hast opened my mouth. My word is Maat. Those who have lain in death, rise up to look upon me, and their hearts are at peace. I maketh mortals to be born again, renewed in their youth. I have received the Crook and the Whip. When I turn my face upon Amentet, the earth shinest as with refined copper. I am crowned even as Ra himself. His disk is my disk. His rays of light are my rays of light. His risings are my risings. His throne is my throne. His knowledge is my knowledge. Behold, my face shineth before Ra and my soul liveth before Amoun."

Pause and contemplate. Then say the following: "I am the Resurrection and the Life. He that believeth in Me, though he were dead, yet shall he live. And whosoever liveth and believeth in me shall never die. I am the first and I am the last. I am he that liveth but was dead, and behold I am alive for ever more, and hold the Keys of Hell and Death. For I know that my Redeemer liveth and that he shall stand at the latter day upon the earth. I am the Way, the Truth and the Life. No one cometh unto the Creator but by me. I am purified. I have passed through the Gates of Darkness unto Light. I have fought upon earth for good. I have finished my work. I have entered into the invisible.

I am the Sun in his rising. I have passed through the hour of Cloud and Night. I am Amoun, the Concealed One, the Opener of the Day. I am Osiris Onnophris, the Justified One. I am the Lord of Life, triumphant over Death. There is no part of me that is not of the Gods. I am the Preparer of the Pathway, the Rescuer unto the Light! Out of the Darkness, let the light arise!"

Stand and face the East. Still holding the Crook and Scourge, perform the Analysis of the Keyword.

Say, "I am the Reconciler with the Ineffable. I am the Dweller of the Invisible. Let the White Brilliance of the Divine Spirit descend." Once again, see the Divine Light descend through the Middle Pillar, from your Kether center to your Malkuth center.

Continue to meditate for a short length of time. When finished, place the Crook and Scourge back upon the eastern throne, stepping out of the godform of Osiris, which once again becomes inanimate. Withdraw the white ray from the godform back into your Tiphareth center. Imagine the figure of Osiris slowly begin to fade until it vanishes entirely.

Perform again the Adoration to the Lord of the Universe. Give the LVX Signs.

Perform the LBRP.

Give five knocks and declare the Temple duly closed.

THIS ENDS THE RITE

The Cross of Victory

Use and Symbolism

The Cross of Victory is a decidedly Rosicrucian implement. Within this cross, the pagan origins of the symbol along with its layers of Christian embellishment are joined in an implement which celebrates the more universal truths behind both philosophies. In Christian symbolism, the cross has a two-fold significance. First, it is the symbol of the death of the Redeemer; secondly, it is the symbol of humility, patience and the burden of life. (It is interesting to note that the emblem can be considered both a symbol of life and of death.)

To the ancients, who deeply considered the astronomical aspect of religion, the cross was a likely symbol of the equinoxes and the solstices, the four times when the Sun was symbolically "cruci-fied" by crossing the line of the ecliptic.* In most cultures, the Sun also symbolized a divinity who died every night only to be reborn each morning (like RA, the Egyptian Sun God). In fact most of the various dying-god myths center around a solar deity who dies and is resurrected.

The shape of the cross suggests the human body, pointing to the mortal side of the immortal Solar deity. The Cross also suggests the four elements as stated earlier. The Rose of 25 petals is composed of the five elements of Spirit, Fire, Water, Air, and Earth, divided into their sub-elements: Spirit of Spirit, Spirit of Fire, Air of Earth, etc. It is the Pentagrammaton or Five-lettered Name of God. The number 25 also alludes to the path of Temperance (Samekh) which leads from Yesod to Tiphareth on the Tree of Life.

The Cross of Victory is a symbol of strength. It alludes to the ultimate goal of an Initiate of the mysteries: to understand the na-ture of the Divine by analyzing the elements and sub-elements that comprise the manifest universe—"for as above, so below." The Rose transfixed upon the Cross of Victory is multicolored, but the cross itself is painted black. The Black Cross is a Cross of Suffering, be-cause the path of an Initiate is not an easy one—many tests and trials are to be encountered and overcome. The Black Cross also refers to putrification, an alchemical process that is necessary to extract the pure gold (essence) from the corruptible matter. This "gold" or di-vine essence is expressed in the unfolding Rose of Creation, which is also the dawning light of the Sun of Tiphareth.

Materials Needed

    One 7/8" x 1/2" piece of basswood that is 12" long (model strut found in the model airplane section of most hobby shops).
    One 1/4" thick piece of basswood that is 3-1/2" wide x 9" long
    One 1/8" thick piece of balsa wood that 3" wide by 3" wide
    One piece of black felt
    Yellow carpenter's glue
    Wood putty

---

* "In Herschel's groundplan of the universe in human form . . . our Solar system is located at the heart of the Divine Man of the skies. Hence, the catastrophe in our solar system, by which the ecliptic was sundered from the celestial equator, was a rapture or piercing of the heart of the Divine Man. The ecliptic and equator no longer coinciding, they formed a cross upon which the Divine Man was transfixed in space. This idea was familiar to the Hindus and to Plato." Manly P. Hall, *The Secret Teachings of All Ages* (Los Angeles, CA: The Philosophical Research Society, Inc., 1977), color plate 181, text accompanying illustration.

Acrylic paints: black, white, grey, yellow, blue, violet, orange,
   red, green
Sealant: clear lacquer finish

Tools Needed
   Scroll saw
   Small hammer
   Sandpaper (medium and fine grained)
   Artist's brushes (medium and fine)
   Craft knife with carving blade

Construction: The Platform
1)   Take the 9" piece of bass wood and cut it into 3 pieces; one that is
     3-1/2" square, one that is 3" square, and one 2-1/2" square piece.
     Sand the edges of all three pieces smooth.

2)   Glue all three pieces together, one upon the other, forming three tiled
     steps. Allow to dry.

3)   Find the center of the smallest (topmost) piece of wood. On it draw a
     rectangle 7/8" long by 12" wide. Cut out this rectangle using the
     knife. Cut entirely through the topmost piece of wood, and remove
     the rectangle (waste wood).

Construction: The Cross
4)   Take the 7/8" thick piece of basswood (12" long) and cut it into two
     pieces; one that is 7-3/4" long and the other 4-1/4" long. Sand the
     ends of both pieces smooth.

5)   Take the longer piece (the shaft) and mark it with two pencil lines;
     one that is 1-3/4" down from the top end, and the other 7/8" down
     from the first line.

6)   Using the scroll saw, make two cuts at the drawn lines half way into
     the wood. Use the knife to remove the section of wood that exists be-
     tween the two cut lines. (Note: You will be left with a piece of wood
     that resembles a timber from a log cabin—with a gouged out area for
     another log to fit into.)

7)   Take the shorter 4-1/4" piece (the crossbar) and pencil in two lines—
     both 1-5/8" from their respective ends. Cut these lines half way into
     the wood as before. Use the knife to again remove the wood between
     the lines, leaving a gouged out area.

8)   Slide the two pieces of wood together at the gouged-out areas of both,
     forming a perfect calvary cross. (Check to see if the pieces fit. If the
     pieces are too tight, sand them until they fit. If they are too loose, the
     gaps can be filled later with wood putty.) Glue the two sections of the
     cross together.

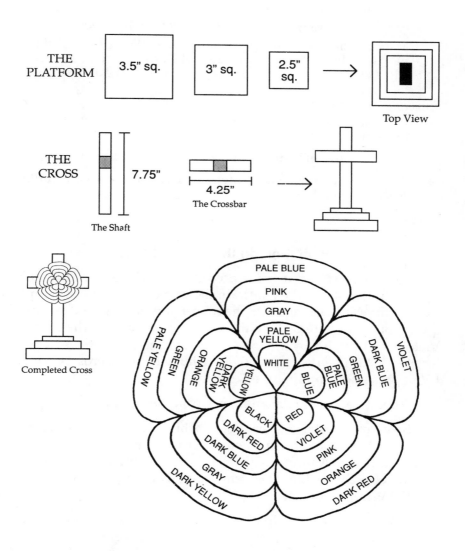

THE
PLATFORM

3.5" sq.

3" sq.

2.5"
sq.

Top View

THE
CROSS

7.75"

The Shaft

4.25"

The Crossbar

Completed Cross

The Cross of Victory

The Rose of 25 Petals

9)   Take the 1/8" thick piece of balsa wood and draw a 2-3/4" circle on it. Cut the circle out. Sand the outer edge of the circle smooth.

10) Mark the circle off into five equal sections. Where the pencil lines meet the edge of the circle, make a slight indentation (to indicate the edges of five rose petals). Use the knife to incise the drawn lines.

Finishing Steps

11) Glue the cross into the hole carved into the platform. Glue the rose to the front of the cross where the shaft joins the crossbar.

13) Paint the Cross of Victory entirely with a coat of gesso. Allow to dry.

14) Paint the Cross and the platform black.Paint the Rose according to the diagram.*

Ritual for Use

A Meditation on the Cross of Victory

The Temple is to be arranged in accordance with the Portal Temple. A chair or Iset should be placed in the western part of the Temple, close to the Altar, facing east. The robe, nemyss, sash, and lamen of an Adept are required. Upon the black altar should be the Cross of Victory surrounded by the rose, red candle, cup of water, and platter of salt. A small pentacle should be hung over the cross. Give the LVX Signs upon entering the Temple.

After a period of relaxation, perform the LBRP.

Stand in the Sign of Osiris Risen, while performing the exercise of the Four-fold Breath. Then, when you are calm and collected, perform the Analysis of the Keyword, ending with the phrase, "Let the Divine Light Descend" as you endeavor to bring down the White Brilliance.

Give the Sign of Osiris Slain. remain in this position as you state: "I invoke Thee, the great avenging Angel HUA, in the divine name IAO, that Thou mayest invisibly place Thy hand upon my head in attestation of my Obligation."

At this point, remain in the Sign of Osiris Slain as you recite the

---

* If desired, an image of the Resurrected One can be attached to the front of the Cross: not the bloodied and suffering Christ of the Catholics, but Christ the King, strong, calm and ascended.

Obligation of the Adeptus Minor from the 5=6 Ceremony in Regardie's *The Golden Dawn*. (Note: If you are a solitary Magician, not affiliated with the Order, a similar magickal obligation, such as that found in Donald Kraig's book *Modern Magick*, can be substituted.)

Take up the Cross of Victory and raise it high above your head. Say, "There are Three that bear witness in Heaven; the Father, the Word, and the Holy Spirit, and these Three are One. There are Three that bear witness on Earth; the Spirit, Water, and the Blood, and these Three agree in One. Except ye be born of Water and the Spirit, ye cannot enter the Kingdom of Heaven. If ye be crucified with the Christos, ye shall also reign with Him."

Replace the Cross upon the Altar, but remain standing just west of it. Pause to contemplate the various meanings behind the symbol of the Cross of Victory before you. Examine closely the colors an the rose, becoming familiar with them. When you have fixed the symbol of the Cross of Victory firmly in your mind, close your eyes and sit quietly with your arms folded in the Sign of Osiris Risen. Continue to meditate as follows:

Visualize the Tree of Life with all of its Sephiroth and connecting paths. Imagine the colors vividly. Then picture the figure of a great goddess at the summit of the Tree, AIMA ELOHIM, the Supernal Mother who represents all of the Three Supernals combined. She wears a gleaming crown of twelve stars, one for each sign of the Zodiac. Her robe is ornamented with the brilliant globe of the Sun. The Crescent Moon is under her feet. This goddess is the shining image of divinity and her face is full of beauty, grace and compassion. From her Supernal feet flows a mighty river, the great NAHER, the never failing waters. Naher contains the Waters of Life, clear as crystal, proceeding from the Throne, on either side of the Tree, bringing forth all manner of fruit in great abundance. This river flows downward to the area of Daath, where it divides into four new rivers:

> PISON—the river of Fire, flowing into Geburah where there isGold.
> GIHON—the Waters of Mercy, flowing into Chesed.
> HIDDIKEL—the river of Air, flowing into Tiphareth
> PHRATH—the river of Earth, flowing into Malkuth.

The rivers combined feed the Garden of Eden, the Tree of Life, and all of Creation in its primal splendor. The rivers form a Cross and on it the great archetypal Adam is extended. His head and body are positioned at Tiphareth, while his sturdy arms stretch out to Geburah and Gedulah (Chesed), the Spheres of Severity and Mercy. In Malkuth stands the great goddess Eve, who supports the entire Tree of Life by holding up its two mighty opposing Pillars of Light and Darkness. She stands in the realm of matter, sustaining the universe by completing and solidifying the Tree. Beneath her kingdom is a Dragon, coiled in sleep. This mighty and terrible beast has seven heads and ten horns, the Seven Infernal Palaces and the Ten Averse Sephiroth. It is the inverted and evil Tree which mirrors the Tree of Life. The abode of the Dragon is the kingdom of shells, cast-off forms and shadows that lies directly below Malkuth.

At the feet of the goddess Eve grows another Tree, the Tree of the Knowledge of Good and of Evil, which is between the Tree of Life and the Kingdom of Shells. Half of the branches of this Tree reach upwards to the seven lower Sephiroth, but also downwards to the seven Infernal Palaces. This is because knowledge is a double-edged sword—the same knowledge that gave humanity the power to think and capture the element of Fire for cooking, warmth, and energy also gave us the knowledge of gunpowder and nuclear weapons.

Just as in the story of Prometheus who stole the Divine Fire from Heaven assisted by Pallas Athene, the Goddess of Wisdom, the archetypal Eve reached down to partake of the fruit of knowledge. This can be considered the first act of Free Will, by which primitive humanity took a step forward in physical evolution from the almost animal level. In doing so, she changed the destiny of the human race forever, because a thinking animal had no place in the Garden of Paradise.

As Eve reached down to grasp knowledge for humanity, she left the two mighty Pillars unsupported. The Sephirotic Tree was shattered. Once knowledge was attained, the great Red Dragon was awakened and set lose. Adam and Eve could no longer remain like the other creatures in the forest, motivated by instinct alone. They now had the ability to think, make tools and use knowledge whether for good or ill...only their Free Will could decide which. Together they fell from the garden.

The coiled Dragon enveloped Malkuth, and its heads rose into the seven lower Sephiroth, even up to Daath at the feet of the great goddess AIMA ELOHIM. The four rivers of Eden were set upon. The beast grew an eighth head, and from this mouth of Leviathan, the Piercing and Crooked Serpent, came forth the Infernal Waters into Daath, threatening the Supernals themselves. On each head of the beast was engraved one of the names of the Lords of Chaos.

Then YHVH ELOHIM placed the Four Letters of the NAME, the Kerubim (guardians of the Gates of Eden), and the Flaming Sword between the devastated Garden and the Supernal Eden, protecting it from the Red Dragon. The mighty Kerubim fought back the serpent and a great chasm was formed to mark the battlefield, cutting off the Supernal Garden from the lower branches of the Tree of Life. Thick dark clouds obscured the Garden and hid it from humanity's sight.

Although this separation was necessary to keep the abuses of human knowledge from affecting the Garden of Paradise, ELOHIM did not wish for this separation to be a permanent barrier. Seekers of the Garden could find it again through hard spiritual work, such as tempering the different parts of the personality (cleansing the four rivers of Eden). For is said that "TETRAGRAMMATON placed Kerubim at the East of the Garden of Eden and a Flaming Sword which turned every way to keep the Path of the Tree of Life, for He has created Nature that Man being cast out of Eden may not fall into the Void. He has bound Man with the Stars as with a chain. He allures him with scattered fragments of the Divine Body in bird and beast and flower, and he laments over him in the wind and in the sea and in the birds. When the times are ended, He will call the Kerubim from the East of the Garden, and all shall be consumed and become Infinite and Holy."

And it is necessary that Adam should rise again to restore the Sephirotic System, and thus, as Adam had been spread on the Cross of the Four Rivers, so the new Adam should be crucified on the Infernal Rivers of the four-armed Cross of Death.

Imagine the Cross of Death as a large black wooden calvary cross. It is the cross of suffering and sacrifice. From the top of Cross is a plaque that reads I.N.R.I. Outwardly, you know that this usually interpreted as "Jesus of Nazareth, King of the Jews." But inwardly, you understand that these letters have many hidden meanings. To the Alchemists it meant "Igne Natura Renovatur Integra"—the whole of Nature is renewed by Fire. The letters also stand for the Hebrew initials of the four ancient elements. But it especially suggests the formula of IAO—Isis, Apophis and Osiris—the formula which is the key to restoring the Tree and reclaiming the Garden of Eden.

Now visualize the Rose of Creation blooming from the center of the Black Cross of Purification. It is the 25-petaled Rose of the Elements which unfolds in the name of the Pentagrammaton, the five-lettered name of Yeheshuah. The flower grows like the fresh vegetation in the tarot card of Death upon the dried wood of the Blackened Cross. From the center of the Rose you see a human form developing. It is a kingly and majestic form that is crucified on the Cross and the Rose. This is not an image of suffering as you might expect, but is instead a vision of vigor and victory. The form is clothed in golden and white robes. His arms extend in strength toward the spheres of Geburah and Gedulah. You may know the form as the Magickal Image of Tiphareth, as the second Adam, as Osiris, or as Christ the King. The figure can also be called Tammuz, Apollo or Buddha.

He is the symbolic prototype of the perfected Solar Deity, who suffered through earthy experience, was glorified through trial, was killed, and rose again to renew all things.

Visualize yourself stepping into the Godform crucified upon the Cross of Victory. At your right hand is Geburah and at your left is Chesed. The Rose of Samekh is behind you, tempering all elements and sub-elements within you. It soothes you and gives you strength. Recite in your mind the Obligation you gave at the beginning of this rite. If you would like to add anything personal to the Obligation, feel free to so.

After recalling the Oath, endeavor to feel the blade of some invisible dagger marking a cross upon your forehead, feet, right hand, left hand, and heart in succession.

Then imagine if you would, the Kerubim drawing back the clouds of darkness to offer you a glimpse of the Supernal Garden. See the four rivers of Paradise restored to their original state. A bridge is formed across the great chasm. You cannot yet traverse this abyss, but information may be sent across it to you. Above the chasm visualize the great goddess AIMA ELOHIM crowned with a renewed aura of splendor. Pause and reflect upon any information or images communicated to you, for reward of the Resurrected One is ultimately the Divine Union—the Hieros Gamos.

Continue the mediation for as long as you wish. Then go to the East and perform the Analysis of the Keyword.

Perform the LBRP.

Declare the Temple closed.

SO MOTE IT BE

THE VAULT OF THE ADEPTI

Kerubic Guardian Plaques

Use and Symbolism

According to Cirlot, the "cherubim" (Kirubi or Kherebu) which stood at the entrance to Assyrian Temples were nothing less than gigantic pentacles placed there by the priests as keepers of the threshold—a function which in China was fulfilled by griffins and dragons. The Egyptian Kerub, a creature with many wings and eyes, was a symbol of vigilance.

The Old Testament describes the Kerubim as they appeared to Ezekiel, surrounding the Merkabah or Chariot of God: "And out of the midst of it there was the likeness of four living creatures, and this is how they looked: they had the likeness of earthling man. And each one had four faces and each had four wings ... And as four the likeness of their faces, the four of them had a man's face with a lion's face to the right, and the four of them had a bull's face on the left; the four of them also had an eagle's face ... there was one wheel beside the living creatures, by the four faces of each ... And their appearance and their structure were just as when a wheel proved to be in the midst of a wheel." (Ezekiel 1: 4-10).

The symbolism of the Kerubim can be found elsewhere in the Scriptures. When the twelve tribes of Israel encamped in the wilderness, the banners of Judah (the lion), Reuben (the man), Dan (the Eagle) and Ephraim (the bull) were placed to mark the four corners of the camp. And in Christian symbolism four of the Apostles became associated with the Kerubim: Mark—the Lion, Luke—the Ox, John—the Eagle, and Matthew—the Man.

The Persians had a tradition that four brilliant stars, known as the "Four Royal Stars," marked the four cardinal points. (These stars were found in four constellations of the Zodiac, which at that time marked the four seasons.)

These bright Royal Stars were:

Regulus—in Leo, Aldebaran—in Taurus, Antares—in Scorpius, and Fomalhaut, in the Southern Fish (very closely situated to the constellation of Aquarius). These four stars were celebrated throughout Asia. The brilliant star in the constellation of the Eagle, Altair, has been suggested as the fourth Royal Star instead of Fomalhaut. Thus as in the vision of Ezekiel, the constellations of the Lion,

Ox, Man and Eagle stood in ancient times as the upholders of the Firmament and the Pillars of heaven. Like sentinels, they seemed to guard the four quarters of the sky. In the four Royal Stars, the four great Decans, or Gods who ruled the Signs, were believed to dwell.

Kerubic Guardian Plaque

The Kerubim ultimately constitute the mystical glyph of the completeness of divine wisdom. They are the guardians of the four rivers which flow down the Tree of Life from the Creator. The Kerubim are the Living Powers of Tetragrammaton on the material plane and the Presidents of the Four Elements. They operate through the Fixed or Kerubic Signs of the Zodiac and are thus symbolized:

Symbols of the Kerubim

Tetragrammaton letter	Element	Animal Sign	Symbol
VAV	AIR	MAN	AQUARIUS
YOD	FIRE	LION	LEO
HEH FINAL	EARTH	BULL	TAURUS
HEH	WATER	EAGLE	SCORPIO

The Kerubic Guardian Plaques are used to guard the Vault of the Adepti. They are described in the Adeptus Minor Ritual thus:

> Before the Door of the Tomb, as symbolic Guardians, are the Elemental Tablets, and the Kerubic Emblems, even as before the mystical Gate of Eden stood the watchful Kerubim, and the sword of flame. These Kerubic Emblems be the powers of the Angles of the Tablets. The Circle represents the four Angles of the Tablets bound together in each Tablet through the operation of the all-pervading Spirit, while the Cross within forms with its spokes the Wheels of Ezekiel's Vision; and therefore are the Cross and Circle white to represent the purity of the Divine Spirit. And inasmuch as we do not find the Elements unmixed, but each bound together with each—so that in Air we find not only that which is subtle and tenuous, but also the qualities of heat, moisture, and dryness, bound together in that all-wandering Element; and furthermore also that in Fire, Water and Earth we find that same mixture of Nature—therefore the Four Elements are bound to each Kerubic Emblem countercharged with the color of the Element wherein they operate; even as in the Vision of Ezekiel each Kerub had four faces and four wings. Forget not therefore that the Tablets and the Kerubim are the Guardians of the Tomb of the Adepti.

The Kerubic plaques could be constructed by an Adept and used in conjunction with the Enochian Tablets; each plaque placed in one of the four quarters over its corresponding Elemental Tablet. (Note: The plaques are not to be used in any Hall of the First Order, but may be employed in the Adept's personal Temple.)

A Magician may wish to make one Kerubic plaque for personal use, but not all four. If this is the case, the singular plaque should be painted as follows:

Circle and Cross—WHITE
Background of Lion—RED   Lion—GREEN
Background of Eagle—BLUE   Eagle—ORANGE
Background of Man—YELLOW   Man—VIOLET
Background of Bull—BLACK   Bull—WHITE

The singular Kerubic plaque can be placed on the outside entrance to the Magician's personal Temple. Positioned thus, it can serve to guard the Temple room from all unwanted influences. The following ritual is included for those who wish to use the single plaque.

Materials Needed
One 1/2" thick piece of plywood that is approx. 7" wide x 28" long
One 1/4" x 1/4" thick piece of balsa wood (model airplane strut—can be found in most hobby shops) You will need four 10" long strips (a total of 40")
One 1/4" thick piece of balsa wood that is 7" wide x 28" long
Yellow carpenter's glue
Wood putty
Gesso
Acrylic paints: white, black, yellow, violet, blue, orange, red, green
Sealant: clear lacquer finish

Tools Needed
Scroll saw
Electric drill
Sandpaper (all grades)
Artist's brushes (medium and fine)

Construction: A Single Plaque
1) Draw a 6" circle on the piece of 1/2" plywood. Cut out with the scroll saw. Put the wood aside. Draw a 6" circle on the 1/4" piece of balsa wood. Cut out.

2) Trace a smaller circle 1/2" inside the one just cut out. Drill a hole in the center of this smaller circle, using a drill bit that is wider than your saw blade.

3) Unplug the saw. Detach the blade from the saw and stick it through the hole just drilled. Re-attach the saw blade and plug the saw back in. Cut out the inside of the circle (which is waste area) leaving only the 6" diameter outer rim intact. (Note: Don't mutilate the waste area too badly ... the Kerubic heads will be drawn on this piece.)

4) Glue the 6" balsa rim to the 6" plywood circle. Allow to dry. Sand the outer part of both circles smooth. Fill in any gaps with wood putty.

5) Take one of the 10" long pieces of balsa wood (model strut) and cut it in half. Take one of the resulting 5" pieces and cut it into two pieces which are 2-3/8". Glue these three pieces of balsa wood into the center of the plywood circle, forming a perfect equal-armed cross. Where the balsa rim meets each arm of the cross, fill in gaps with wood putty. (Note: You will now have a plaque that is three dimensional—the four quarters of the piece are lower than the rim and the cross.)

6) Take the leftover balsa wood circle and draw the heads of the four Kerubim on it. Cut them out with the scroll saw. (Note: Balsa wood is very soft and the heads can easily be shaped and contoured using sandpaper.)

7) Glue the Kerubic heads to the plywood circle; one to the center of each quarter as shown. When all glue has dried, cover the plaque entirely with a coat of gesso. Allow to dry.

Finishing Steps
8) Paint the outer edge of the circle, the rim and the cross white. (Note: If a full set of plaques are desired rather than the singular one, construct three more plaques identical to the one just finished.) On the individual plaques, the Kerubim must be painted slightly different:

AIR PLAQUE
Background Color—YELLOW
Lion—RED
Eagle—BLUE
Man—VIOLET
Bull—BLACK

WATER PLAQUE
Background Color—BLUE
Lion—RED
Eagle—ORANGE
Man—YELLOW
Bull—BLACK

EARTH PLAQUE
Background Color—BLACK
Lion—RED
Eagle—BLUE
Man—YELLOW
Bull—WHITE

FIRE PLAQUE
Background Color—RED
Lion—GREEN
Eagle—BLUE
Man—YELLOW
Bull—BLACK

9) Facial detail may be added to all four heads. After all paint has dried, apply sealant for protection.

Ritual for Use

Charging the Guardians of the Temple

For this rite the Adept will need to prepare ahead of time a means by which to fasten the plaque to the outer door of his/her personal Temple. (A hook or glued strips of velcro will suffice.) Upon the Altar should be the Cross and Triangle, incense, a rose, red candle, cup of water, and platter of salt. The Lotus Wand and a sword or dagger for Banishing should be close at hand. Place the Kerubic plaque on the center of the Altar. Give the LVX Signs upon entering the Temple.

> After a few moments of relaxation, give five knocks to announce the commencement of the ritual.
>
> Go to the Northeast and proclaim, "HEKAS! HEKAS! ESTE BEBELOI!"
>
> Perform the LBRP.
>
> Perform the BRH.
>
> Take up the cup of water and go to the East. Trace with it the Cross and the Invoking Triangle of Water in all quarters. Then say, "And I heard the sound of their wings, a sound like that of the vast waters, like the sound of the Almighty One." Replace the cup.
>
> Take up the incense and go to the East. Trace with it the Cross and the Invoking Triangle of Fire in all quarters. Then say, "And as for the likeness of the living creatures, their appearance was like burning coals of Fire. Something appearing like torches was moving back and forth between the living creatures, and the fire was bright, and out of the fire there was lightning going forth." Replace the incense.
>
> Perform the Mystic Circumambulation, three times deosil giving the Neophyte Signs when passing the East.
>
> Perform the Adoration to the Lord of the Universe.
>
> Perform with the Lotus Wand the SIRP.
>
> Return to the west of the Altar and face east. Take up the red candle in the left hand and the Lotus Wand in the right. Trace a

circle over the Lion Kerub of the plaque. Hold the Lotus Wand by the yellow band of Leo and trace the Invoking Pentagram of Spirit Active over the lion, intoning the words "BITOM" and "EHEIEH." Give the LVX Signs. Then trace the Invoking Pentagram of Fire over the Lion. Vibrate, "OIP TEAA PEDOCE." Draw the sigil of Leo and intone "ELOHIM." Give the Philosophus Sign.

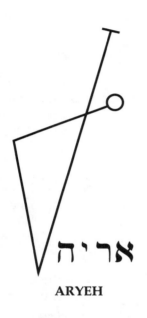

ARYEH

Vibrate the Kerubic name of "ARYEH" and trace its sigil over the Lion. Say "Strong and formidable Lord of Fire! ARYEH! Thou who ruleth the Sickle of Stars! Sole house of the Sun! ARYEH! Judah, thou art he whom thy brethren shall praise: thy hand shall be in the neck of thine enemies. Judah is a Lion's whelp! ARYEH! The Lion flames. There the Sun's course runs hottest. Empty of grain the arid fields appear when first the Sun into the Lion enters."

Trace a Cross over the Lion and say, "In the name of the head of the Lion and the powers of ASCH, I charge thee to guard this Temple and the mystic sphere contained within from all mundane and profane forces. Keep far removed the evil and the unbalanced. PROTEGE HOC TEMPLUM!"

Replace the candle and take up the cup in the left hand. Hold the Lotus Wand by the blue-green band of Scorpio. Trace a circle over the Eagle Kerub of the plaque. Then trace the Invoking Pentagram of Spirit Passive over the eagle, intoning the words, "HCOMA" and "AGLA." Give the LVX Signs. Draw the Invoking Pentagram of Water over the Eagle. Vibrate, "EMPEH ARSEL GAIOL." Then trace the sigil of the Eagle and intone "Aleph Lamed, AL." Give the Sign of Practicus.

Vibrate the Kerubic name of "NESHER" and trace its sigil over the Eagle. Say "There is a place above where Scorpio bent, in tail and arms surrounds a vast extent. In a wide circuit of the heavens he shines, and fills the place of two celestial signs. NESHER! Lofty Eagle born from the sting of the scorpion. Dan shall be a serpent by the way, an adder in the path. NESHER! Lord of the Waters of transformation! Only when Sol is your house can the iron be turned to gold!"

נ ש ר

NESHER

Trace a Cross over the Eagle and say, "In the name of the head of the Eagle and the powers of MAYIM, I charge thee to guard this Temple and the mystic sphere contained within from all mundane and profane forces. Keep far removed the evil and the unbalanced. PROTEGE HOC TEMPLUM!"

Replace the cup and take up the rose in the left hand. Hold the Lotus Wand by the violet band of Aquarius. Trace a circle over the Man Kerub of the plaque. Then trace the Invoking Pentagram of Spirit Active over the Man, intoning the names, "EXARP" and "EHEIEH." Give the LVX Signs. Draw the Invoking Pentagram of Air over the Man. Vibrate, "ORO IBAH AOZPI." Then trace the sigil of Aquarius and intone "YOD HEH VAV HEH." Give the Sign of Theoricus.

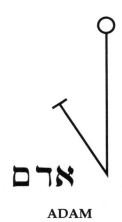

Vibrate the Kerubic name of "ADAM" and trace its sigil over the Man. Say, "While by the Horse's head the Water-Pourer spreads his right hand. Thou ridest upon the winged steeds of Dawn. ADAM! Bril-

א ד ם

ADAM

liant Lord of Air! Mighty One of the Eastern Wind! Reuben, thou art the firstborn, the might, and the beginning of strength, the excellency of dignity and the excellency of power. Emblem of the tribe of Reuben! ADAM! Great indeed are thy powers of thought."

Trace a Cross over the Man and say, "In the name of the head of the Man and the powers of RUACH, I charge thee to guard this Temple and the mystic sphere contained within from all mundane and profane forces. Keep far removed the evil and the unbalanced. PROTEGE HOC TEMPLUM!"

Replace the rose and take up the platter of salt in the left hand. Hold the Lotus Wand by the red-orange band of Taurus. Trace a circle over the Bull Kerub of the plaque. Then trace the Invoking Pentagram of Spirit Passive over the Bull, intoning the names, "NANTA" and "AGLA." Give the LVX Signs. Draw the Invoking Pentagram of Earth over the Bull. Vibrate, "EMOR DIAL HECTEGA." Then trace the sigil of Taurus and intone "ADONAI." Give the Sign of Zelator.

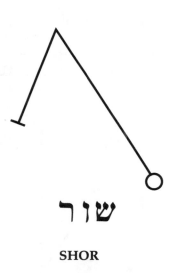

SHOR

Vibrate the Kerubic name of "SHOR" and trace its sigil over the Bull. Say, "Zephyr is wandering here with gentle sound, the first fresh fragrance of the Spring to seek: The milk-white steer, whose budding horns are crowned with flowery garlands, is kneeling on the ground. SHOR! Mighty Bull of Light! Sturdy Lord of Earth! Thou art Apis, Bull of the Nile. Ephraim, his glory is like the firstling of a bullock, and his horns are like the horns of unicorns. SHOR! Thou who plows the Furrow of Heaven! Thy hoof-prints are embedded in the earth!"

Trace a Cross over the Bull and say, "In the name of the head of the Bull and the powers of ARETZ, I charge thee to guard this Temple and the mystic sphere contained within from all mundane and profane forces. Keep far removed the evil and the unbalanced. PROTEGE HOC TEMPLUM!"

Replace the salt. Grasp the Lotus Wand by the white portion and trace a circle over the outer rim of the Kerubic plaque. Trace the Invoking Pentagrams of Spirit Active Spirit Passive vibrating the appropriate words; "EXARP—EHEIEH . . . . HCOMA—AGLA . . . . NANTA—AGLA . . . . BITOM—EHEIEH." (Be sure to trace the spirit wheel in the exact size of the plaque itself.) Give the LVX Signs.

Say, "I, (give magickal name), charge ye wardens of the Four Elements under the presidency of Spirit to act as sentinels of this sacred Temple. Be ye watchful guardians against all hostile and unwanted forces or beings. PROTEGITE HOC TEMPLUM! Keep this sphere pure and holy, so that I may enter in, undisturbed, and perform aright the works of the Magick of Light."

Give the Projection Sign at the Plaque five times. At the end give the Sign of Silence for Protection.

Give five knocks against the side of the Altar to seal the charge and announce that the Guardians have been appointed to their task.

Take up the Kerubic plaque from the Altar and attach it to the outer door of the Temple room.

Return to the east of the Temple and perform the Adoration to the Lord of the Universe.

Purify the Temple with Water and Fire as in the beginning.

Perform the Reverse Circumambulation, three times widdershins.

Say, "I now release any spirits that may have been imprisoned by this ceremony. Depart in peace to your abodes and habitations. Go with the blessings of YEHESHUAH YEHOVASHAH!"

Give five knocks.

Say, "I now declare this Temple duly closed."

THE RITE IS ENDED

A Description of the Vault of the Adepti

The Vault of the Adepti is the powerful ritual chamber of the R.R. et A.C. It is the crowning jewel of all ritual implements in the Western Magickal Tradition. No initiation into the Second Order is valid without it. The description of this chamber along with its contents make up some of the most vital portions of the *Fama Fraternitatis* (printed 1614), one of the three most famous Rosicrucian Manifestos.

In the *Fama*, the allegory of Christian Rosencreutz, his life and works are recounted, as well as the all important portrayal of C.R.C.'s burial chamber. It was this description that MacGregor Mathers brilliantly built upon in his creation of the Vault of the Adepti. The unnamed writer of the Fama recounts the story of the discovery of the tomb of the founder of the Rosicrucian Fraternity:

"In 1603, Brother N.N. became head of the inner circle of the Order. A year later, he thought to alter something of his building, to make it more fit. In such renewing he lighted upon the Memorial Table, which was cast of brass, and containeth the names of the Brethern, with some few other things. This he would transfer to a more fitting vault. In this table stuck a great nail, somewhat strong, so that when it was with force withdrawn, it took with it an indifferent big stone out of the thin wall or plastering of the hidden door, upon which was written in great letters:

POST CXX ANNOS PATEBO
(After 120 years I will return)

with the year of the Lord under it.

"Therefore we gave God thanks, and let it rest that same night, because first we would overlook our ROTA.

"In the morning following we opened the door, and there appeared to our sight a vault of seven sides and seven corners, every side five feet broad, and the height of eight feet. Although the Sun never shined in this vault, it was enlightened with another Sun, which had learned this from the Sun, and was situated in the upper part of the center of the ceiling. In the midst, instead of a tombstone, was a round altar, covered with a plate of brass, and thereon this engraven: A.C.R.C. *Hoc universi compendium unius mihi sepulchrum feci.* (I have made this sepulcher a single compendium of the universe.) Round about the first circle or brim stood:

Jesus mihi omnia
(Jesus is all things to me.)

"In the middle were four figures, inclosed in circles, whose circumscription were:
1. *Nequaquam Vacuum* (Nowhere a Void.)
2. *Libertas Evangelii* (The Liberty of the Gospels.)
3. *Dei Gloria Intacta* (The Untouchable Glory of God.)
4. *Legis Jugum* (The Yoke of the Law.)

"This is all clear and bright, as also the seventh side and the two heptagons. This vault we parted in three parts, the upper part or ceiling, the wall or side, the ground or floor. Of the upper part you shall understand no more at this time but that it was divided according to the seven sides in the triangle which was in the bright center. Every side or wall is parted into ten squares, every one with their several figures and sentences. The bottom again is parted in the triangle, but because therein described the power and rule of the Inferior Governors, we leave to manifest the same, for fear of the abuse of the evil and ungodly world. Every side or wall had a door for a chest, wherein there lay diverse things, that if it should happen, after many hundred years, the Fraternity should come to nothing, they might by this only vault be restored again.

"Now, as we had not yet seen the dead body of our careful and wise Father, we therefore moved the altar aside; then we lifted up a strong plate of brass, and found a fair and worthy body, whole and unconsumed. In his hand he held a parchment called T, the which next unto the Bible is our greatest treasure, which ought not to be delivered unto the censure of the world."

Under the genius of a Magician such as Mathers, this fragment of Rosicrucian knowledge become elucidated in the Ritual of the Adeptus Minor (as published in Regardie's *The Golden Dawn*): "Upon more closely examining the Door of the Tomb, you will perceive, even as Frater N.N. and those with him did perceive, that beneath the CXX in the inscription were placed the characters IX thus:

POST CXX ANNOS PATEBO
IX

being equivalent to Post Annos Lux Crucis Patebo—At the end of 120 years, I, the Light of the Cross, will disclose myself. For the letters forming LVX are made from the dismembered and conjoined angles of the Cross; and 120 is the product of the numbers from 1 to 5, multiplied in regular progression, which number five is symbolized in the Cross with four extremities and one center point.On the following morning, Frater N.N. and his companions forced open the door and there appeared to their sight a Tomb of Seven Sides and Seven Corners. Every side was five feet broad, and eight feet high, even as the same is faithfully represented before you. Although in the Tomb the Sun does not shine, it is lit by the symbolic Rose of our Order in the center of the first heptagonal ceiling. In the midst of the Tomb stands a circular Altar with these devices and descriptions on it:

A.G.R.C.—*Ad Gloriam Roseae Crucis.*
A.C.R.G.—*Ad Crucis Rosae Gloriam.*
Hoc Universal Compendium Unius Mihi Sepulchrum Feci -
Unto the Glory of the Rose Cross I have constructed
this Tomb for myself as a Compendium of the
Universal Unity.

"With the next circle is written:

Yeheshua Mihi Omnia—
Yeheshua is all things to me.

"In the center are four figures of the Kerubim (colored appropriately) enclosed within circles surrounded by the following four inscriptions and each distinguished by one of the following four inscriptions and each distinguished by one of the letters of the Tetragrammaton:

Yod—Lion—Nequaquam Vacuum—Nowhere a Void.
Heh—Eagle—Libertas Evangelii—Liberty of the Gospel.
Vau—Man—Dei Intacta Gloria—Unsullied Glory of God.
Heh (f)—Ox—Legis Jugum—Yoke of the Law.

and in the midst of all is Shin, the Letter of the Spirit forming thus the Divine Name Yeheshua, from the Tetragrammaton."

The complex scope of the symbolism of the Vault is further described later in the ritual of the 5=6: "It is divided into three parts—the Ceiling which is white; the Heptagonal Walls of seven Rainbow colors, and the Floor whose prevailing hue is black; thus showing the powers of the Heptad between the Light and the Darkness.

"On the ceiling is a triangle enclosing a Rose of 22 petals, within a Heptangle reflected from the Seven Angles of the Wall. The Triangle represents the Three Supernal Sephiroth; the Heptagram, the Lower Seven; the Rose represents the 22 paths of the Serpent of Wisdom.The Floor has upon it also the Symbol of a Triangle enclosed within a Heptagram, bearing the titles of the Averse and Evil Sephiroth of the Qlippoth, the Great Red Dragon of Seven Heads, and the inverted and evil triangle. And thus in the tomb of the Adepti do we tread down the Evil Powers of the Red Dragon and so tread thou upon the evil powers of thy nature. For there is traced within the evil Triangle the rescuing Symbol of the Golden Cross united to the Red Rose of Seven times Seven Petals. As it is written 'He descendeth into Hell'."

But the whiteness above shines the brighter for the Blackness which is beneath, and thus mayest thou comprehend that the evil helpeth forward the Good. And between the Light and the Darkness vibrate the colors of the Rainbow, whose crossed and reflected rays under the Planetary Presidency are shewn forth in these Seven Walls. Remember that thou hast entered by the door of the planet Venus, whose symbol includes the whole Ten Sephiroth of the Tree of Life. Each Wall of the Tomb is said mystically to be in breadth five feet and in height eight feet, thus yielding forty squares, of which ten are marked and salient, representing the Ten Sephiroth in the form of the Tree of Life, acting throughout the Planet. The remaining squares represent the Kerubim and the Eternal Spirit, the Three Alchemic Principles, the Three Elements, the Seven Planets, and the Twelve Signs, all operating in and differentiating the rays of each planet. Note that in all, the Central square alone remains white and unchanged, representing the changeless Essence of the Divine Spirit, thus developing all from the One, through the many under the governance of One.

The colors of the varying squares may be either represented by the color of the Planet and the color of the Force therein mixed together, or by these colors being placed in juxtaposition (not the preferred or most accurate method) or in any other convenient manner;

but the foundation of them all is the Minutum Mundum diagram (see Regardie's *Golden Dawn*, p. 233).

Concerning the symbolism of the coffin of C.R.C. and the diagrams on its surface are described as follows: The lower half of the lid—"Behold the image of the Justified One, crucified on the Infernal Rivers of Daath, and thus rescuing Malkuth from the folds of the Red Dragon." The upper half of the lid—"And being turned, I saw Seven Golden Light-bearers, and in the midst of the Lightbearers, One like unto the Ben Adam, clothed with a garment down to the feet, and girt with a Golden Girdle. His head and his hair were white as snow, and his eyes as flaming fire; His feet like unto fine brass, as if they burned in a furnace. And his voice as the sound of many waters. And He had in his right hand Seven Stars, and out of his mouth went the Sword of Flame, and his countenance was as the Sun in His Strength." (The diagram of this Biblical passage is based on a woodcut by Albrecht Durer.)

The remainder of the Pastos: "The head of the Pastos is white, charged with a golden Greek Cross and Red Rose of 49 Petals. The foot is black with a white Calvary Cross and Circle placed upon a pedestal of Two Steps. On the sides are depicted the 22 Colors of the Paths, between Light and Darkness."

V.H. Frater S.A. (Wescott) had this to add about the Pastos: "The Pastos which stands under the Circular Altar has no bottom but a hinged lid which can be turned back during the Second Point of the 5=6 Ceremony. The inner surface bears the colors of the Forces. Both the inner and the outer lid of the right side are in the positive scale of colors. To the left, they are in the negative Scale of colors. The head is white inside and out. Outside it bears the Red Rose of 49 petals on a Golden Greek Cross. Inside the 10 colors of the Masculine scale on the Sephiroth in the Tree of Life. The foot is black inside and out. Outside there is a Calvary Cross on three steps with a circle. Inside the 10 children colors in the Sephiroth on the Tree."

The Symbolism of the Seven Sides
By G.H. Frater N.O.M.

The following is a paper by Wescott, originally published in Regardie's *The Golden Dawn*, reprinted here in its entirety because of its excellent analysis of the symbolism of the Vault Walls.

Among those characteristics which are truly necessary in the pursuit of magickal knowledge and power, there is hardly any one more essential than thoroughness. And there is no failing more common in modern life than superficiality.

There are many who, even in this grade which has been gained by serious study, after being charmed and instructed by the first view of the Vault of Christian Rosencruetz, have made no attempt to study it as a new theme. There are many who have attained many ceremonial admissions and yet no nothing of the emblematic arrangement of the forty squares upon each side.

Some of you do not even know that Venus is, in an astrological sense, misplaced among the sides, and not two in five have been able to tell me why this is so, or what is the basis of the arrangement of the seven colors and forces. Many have told me which element out of the four is missing, and others have told me that the sign Leo occurs twice, but very few can tell me why the two forms of Leo are in different colors in each case, and only a few can tell me without hesitation which Three Sephiroth have no planet attached.

And yet even in the 1=10 grade you are told you must analyze and comprehend that Light or Knowledge, and not only take it on personal authority. Let us then be Adepti in fact, and not only on the surface; let our investigations be more than skin deep. That only which you can demonstrate is really known to you, and that only which is comprehended can fructify and become spiritual progress as distinguished from intellectual gain. Unless you can perceive with the soul as well as see with the eye your progress is but seeming, and you will continue to wander in the wilds of the unhappy.

Let your maxim be *Multum non Multa*—Much rather than many things. And tremble lest the Master find you wanting in those things you allow it to be supposed that you have become proficient in. Hypocrisy does not become the laity; it is a fatal flaw in the character of the occultist. You know it is not only the teacher in this Hall before whom you may be humiliated, but before your higher and divine Genius who can in no wise be deceived by outward seeming, but judgeth you by the heart, in that your spiritual heart is but the reflection of his brightness and the image of Tiphareth, and Tiphareth the reflection of the crowned Wisdom of Kether, and the concealed One.

There are but a couple of pages in the 5=6 Ritual which refer to the symbolism of the seven sides of the Vault. Read them over care-

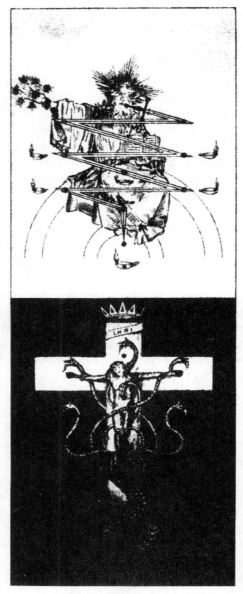

The Lid of the Pastos
The Golden Dawn © Israel Regardie

The Side of the Pastos

White							
	Vermilion		Yellow			Blue	
Scarlet	Red-Orange	Orange	Yellow	Greenish-Yellow	Yellowish-Green	Green	Blue
							Green-Blue

The Wall of the Vault

White	
Scarlet	Red
Red-Orange	
Orange	Orange
Amber	
Greenish-Yellow	Yellow
Yellowish-Green	
Emerald	Green
Green-Blue	
Blue	Blue
Indigo	Indigo
Violet	Purple
Crimson	
	Black

fully, and then let us study these things together. First, the seven sides as a group, and then the 40 squares that are on each side.

The seven sides are all alike in size and shape and subdivision, and the forty squares on each side bear the same symbols. But the coloring is varied in the extreme, no two sides are alike in tint, and none of the squares are identical in color excepting the single central upper square of each wall, that square bearing the Wheel of Spirit. The seven walls are under the planetary presidency, one side to each planet. The subsidiary squares represent the coloring of the combined forces of the planet; the symbol of each square is represented by the ground color, while the symbol is in the color contrasted or complementary to that of the ground.

Now these planetary sides are found to be in a special order, neither astronomical nor astrological. The common order of the succession of the planets is that defined by their relative distances from Earth; putting the Sun, however, in the Earth's place in the series— thus: Saturn, Jupiter, Mars, Sun, Venus, Mercury, Moon. Saturn is farthest from the Earth, and the Earth is between Mars and Venus. Beginning with Saturn in the case of the Walls of the Vault, the order is Saturn, Jupiter, Mars, Sun, Mercury, Venus, Moon. Here Mercury and Venus are transposed.

But there is something more than this. For Saturn, the farthest off, is neither the door nor the East, nor anywhere else that is obviously intended. For it is the corner between the South and the Southwest sides. Nor is it Luna, at the other end of the scale, in any notable position on the old lines.

There is, then, a new key to their order to be found and used, and such as are very intuitive see it at a glance. The planets are in the order of the Rainbow colors, and in colors because this Adeptus Minor grade is the especial exponent of colors. You Adepti are in the Path of the Chamelion—Hodos Chamelionis. If now you take the planetary colors and affix the planets and arrange them in the order of the solar spectrum and then bend up the series into a ring and make the chain into a Heptagram, and turn the whole about until you get the two ends of the series to meet at the Eastern point, you will have this mysterium:

Violet—Jupiter.	Indigo—Saturn.	Blue—Moon.
Green—Venus.	Yellow—Mercury.	Orange—Sun.
Red—Mars.		

Science teaches, and has rediscovered a great truth, that however valuable the seven colors of the prism may be, there are rays invisible and so not demonstrated here by space. Beyond the red end of the spectrum begins the violet, and these have a great chemical or Yetsiratic force. These forces, ever present and unseen, are represented by the Chief Adept standing erect at the Eastern angle, the most powerful person in the group, and delegate of the Chiefs of the Second Order, and through them of the Mystic Third Order. He it is who has, symbolically, at any rate, passed from death unto life, and holds the Keys of all the creeds. And he it is who may place in our hands the Keys of the locked palace of the King if we are able to make our knocking heard. Representing the East, coming from the East, he faces the Western world, bringing intuition with him; before him lies the symbolic body of our Master C.R.C., our grand exemplar and founder—or at other times, the empty Pastos, from which he has arisen, the Chief Adept.

He has Mars and Geburah at his right hand, and Jupiter and Gedulah at his left hand. He faces Venus in the West, the Evening Star, which represents the entry of the Candidate who has toiled all day until the evening. At even he enters the Western door of the planet Venus, that sole planet unto whose symbol alone all the Sephiroth are conformed. At "evening time there shall be light," the light of mixed colors. So the newly admitted Adept comes in contact with the totality of the planetary forces for the first time. A great opportunity opens before him; let him see well that he use it worthily. He enters through the green side of the vault. Green is the color of growth; let him see that he grows.

Upon each side of the vault are forty squares, five vertical series and eight horizontal, the whole being symbolically 5' x 8'. Now the published and printed *Fama Fraternatitas* says these forty feet were divided into ten squares. If you are mathematicians you would know that ten similar squares could not alone be placed in such and area and yet fill it. Ten squares alone to fill a rectangle could only be placed in an area of the shape 5' x 6'. Hence in the *Fama*, ten squares are a blind which we know to represent "Ten squares are marked and salient"—they are the Sephiroth.

Besides the Ten Sephiroth, there are the following: There are the four Kerubim, Three Alchemical Principles, Three Elements, Seven Planets, Twelve Zodiacal Signs, One Wheel of the Spirit—

The Ceiling of the Vault

The Floor of the Vault

The Circular Altar

**The Rose and Cross
at the Head of Pastos**
(49 Petals)

The Foot of the Pastos

thus 40 in all. The Spirit wheel is on every side and always in the center, and is always depicted unchanged in black upon white.

Upon the sides there are always the four Kerubic emblems—Zodiacal, yet different, for the Eagle replaces Scorpio. (Scorpio has three forms, the Scorpion, the Eagle, and the Snake for the evil aspect.) These Kerubim represent the letters of the name YHVH, and note that they are always arranged in the Hebrew order of the letters. Yod for the Lion, Heh for the Eagle, Vau for the Man, Heh final for the Ox, the Tauric Earth.

Note that these four Zodiacal signs are not in their own colors, but as symbols of the elements have elementary colors. As Zodiacal signs, then, they are found to be compounds of the Elemental and Planetary colors; but they are here as Kerubic emblems compounded of the Elemental color and the Planetary color of the side.

The Three Principles are composed of the color of the Principles, and the color of the Planet of any particular wall. Mercury being fundamentally blue, Sulphur red, and Salt yellow.

The Three Elementals have fundamentally the usual three colors, Fire red, Water blue, Air yellow. Note that Earth is missing.

The Seven planets have their colors as are often stated, and note that each of the seven is set beside its appropriate Sephirah, so that there are three Sephiroth which have no Planet: Kether, Chokmah, and Malkuth.

The four Zodiacal Signs are the lower portion of the sides of the vertical column. The central one has none of the twelve; they are allotted between the four remaining columns. Further note that they are only three ranks, the 5th, 7th, and 8th; none are in the 6th rank from above.

This arrangement then shows: Four Triplicities and three Quaternaries. Observe well the arrangement; it is complex but not confused.

1. Kerubic Fixed. Shining Rank.
2. Cardinal Fiery. Solar Rank.
3. Common (mutable) Airy. Subtle Rank.

From above down, or in columns these are: Earthy Signs. Airy Signs. Watery Signs. Fiery Signs.

Rank 5. The Kerubic line shows the signs in the order of Tetragrammaton read in Hebrew.

Israel Regardie in the Vault of the Adepti

Rank 7. The cardinal line shows the signs from the right in order of astronomical sequence of the solar course; vernal equinox, summer solstice, autumnal equinox, winter solstice.

Rank 8. The common line shows the Signs again in a different position. Here the earliest in the year is Gemini on the left of Mem, and passing left to Virgo, you then go round to extreme right to Sagittarius, pass centerwards to Pisces close to Malkuth. The coloring of each square is dual—a ground color, and the color of the emblem. The ground color is a compound of the color of the Planet of the side tinting the color of the Force to which the Square is allotted.

Each side has the Square of its own planet in its own unmixed color, and with this exception all the colored grounds are compound. The emblem color is always complimentary to the ground color.

The ritual of the Adeptus Minor gives the definite colors of each planet and sign which are to be used in this system. There are other allotments of color to each of these symbols and forces, but these are retained as mysteries yet to be evolved and revealed when you have become familiar with the present simple and elementary system.

All of the preceding information concerning the Vault, though it barely scratches the surface, should be more than enough to show the utter complexity and marvelous ingenuity that went into its creation. A complete analysis of the construction methods, symbolism, and use of the Vault would require reams of information that would make this book impossibly long. There is also the danger of misusing such a powerful ritual chamber where Banishings are forbidden. The possibility for disaster is great if a person unwittingly invokes some unwanted energy into this highly consecrated space and cannot get rid of it unless he/she completely clears the chamber by banishing—rendering it a magickal void. (We are even aware of one person who wishes to construct an eleven-sided Vault—obviously the perfect place to invoke the Qlippoth!) Therefore we will not go into detail about the construction of a Vault, but we will share a few insights brought about through experience. It is likely that some of the Vaults from the early days of the Order were painted on large sheets of canvas, intended to be more or less portable. Moina

Mathers (*Vestigia Nulla Retrorsum*) was responsible for painting the elaborate designs of the Vault at Isis-Urania in London (and possibly another at Ahathoor in Paris). Moina's preferred technique was a combination of oil paint and collage on canvas. It is possible that the walls of some Vaults were done in this manner.

When the Golden Dawn was revived in the United States in the early 1980's, it was decided that a more sturdy Vault was called for. This involved the construction of a room out of wood and plaster, not only ensuring that the angles of the heptagon would be absolutely correct, but also that the room would be a virtual sound-chamber; blocking out all outside noises while at the same time enhancing all spoken vibrations. When Regardie consecrated this Vault on Corpus Christi, June 26, 1982 and initiated two people into the grade of 5=6, he ensured that a valid initiatory branch of the original Order was established. The old house containing the Vault was altered to ensure that its inner chamber could not be discovered by accident. The parlor was completely sealed off from the rest of the house, as if the room never existed. Entrance to the chamber was gained only through a small door cut into the back wall of a closet, which lead to the antechamber or portal of the Vault.*

A small door was constructed in the Venus wall of the Vault to be the main entrance into the Tomb. The Solar wall of the Vault was in fact a huge door that swung open into what remained of the hidden parlor. Both of these doors were made to appear invisible to anyone inside the chamber. A small coffin was purchased at a local funeral parlor and painted in the appropriate colors to serve as the Pastos of C.R.C., i.e., the Chief Adept. (This later proved to be too heavy and awkward and has since been replaced by a pastos which is light and easily transported by a single person.)

The building of a Vault in such a manner is obviously a feat of carpentry that the average Magician studying on his/her own is not likely to undertake. However a single vault wall can be reproduced in miniature for study and meditation. This diminutive wall has proven to be an effective tool for Adepts who do not have consistent access to a proper vault. (Note: The colors on the miniature are the pure colors of the symbols, unmixed with Planetary colors.)

---

* As a note of interest, a reproduction of a painting entitled "A Man in Armor," by Rembrandt, hung on the outside door of this closet. That same weekend that Regardie consecrated the Vault, it was discovered in a book called *A Christian Rosenkreutz Anthology* that this same painting was said to represent none other than Christian Rosenkreutz himself.

The Miniature Vault Wall

Materials Needed

A piece of wood, canvas board or masonite that is 10" x 16"

Gesso

Acrylic paints: red, orange, yellow, green, blue, blue-violet, violet, red-violet, black, white

Clear lacquer finish

Tools Needed

Straight edge

Artist's brushes (various sizes)

Construction

1) Cover the board with a coat of gesso and allow to dry.

2) Mark the surface of the board off into 2" squares (five squares wide and eight squares high—a total of 40).

3) Trace the symbols onto the board according to the diagram. Paint the symbols as follows:

SQUARES	GROUND COLOR	CHARGE COLOR
Spirit	White	Black
Kerubic:		
Leo	Red	Green
Scorpio	Blue	Orange
Aquarius	Yellow	Violet
Taurus	Black	White
Sephiroth:		
Kether	White	Black
Chokmah	Grey	Pale Grey
Binah	Black	White
Chesed	Blue	Orange
Geburah	Red	Green
Tiphareth	Yellow	Violet
Netzach	Green	Red
Hod	Orange	Blue
Yesod	Violet	Yellow
Malkuth	Four Colors*	White

---

* Citrine, Russet, Black, Olive

Elements:

Fire	Red	Green
Water	Blue	Orange
Air	Yellow	Violet

Alchemic Principles:

Sulphur	Pale red (pink)	Dark Green
Mercury	Pale yellow	Dark violet
Salt	Pale Blue	Dark Orange

Planets:

Saturn	Blue-violet	Yellow-orange
Jupiter	Violet	Yellow
Mars	Red	Green
Sol	Orange	Blue
Venus	Green	Red
Mercury	Yellow	Violet
Luna	Blue	Orange

Zodiacal Signs:

Aries	Red	Green
Taurus	Red-orange	Blue-green
Gemini	Orange	Blue
Cancer	Yellow-orange	Blue-violet
Leo	Yellow	Violet
Virgo	Yellow-green	Red-violet
Libra	Green	Red
Scorpio	Blue-green	Red-orange
Sagittarius	Blue	Orange
Capricorn	Blue-violet	Yellow-orange
Aquarius	Violet	Yellow
Pisces	Red-violet	Yellow-green

5) After all paint has dried, cover with a coat of clear lacquer for protection.

Ritual for Use

A Meditation on the Miniature Vault Wall

Place a chair or Iset in the eastern part of your Temple facing west. Position the miniature wall so that when you are seated, it is at eye level. The wall should be no more than an arm's length away from you. The robe, nemyss, sash, and lamen of an Adept are required. A Lotus Wand (see chapter 5) is also needed.

After a period of relaxation, perform the LBRP.

Stand in the Sign of Osiris Risen, while performing the exercise of the Four-fold Breath. Then, when you are calm and collected, perform the Analysis of the Keyword, ending with the phrase, "Let the Divine Light Descend" as you endeavor to bring down the White Brilliance.

Be seated and meditate upon the miniature wall before you. At first simply note the pattern of the squares—try to feel or see the play of colors as they pass from square to square.

Close your eyes and await any messages that may be communicated to you concerning what you have observed.

After this you may wish to invoke one particular square on the wall by tracing its corresponding pentagram/hexagram over the exact square and vibrating the appropriate Divine Name. (Use the hexagram to invoke planetary squares, but use the pentagram to invoke the Elemental, Kerubic, or Zodiacal squares.)

After invoking the square, gaze at it intently, exactly as you would study a Tattwa symbol, attempting to implant the symbol firmly in your mind. Continue to vibrate the Divine Name associated with the square until it becomes a portal into which you may enter for the purpose of scrying. When this happens, close your eyes and let the astral scene unfold before you. (Note: Consult Regardie's *Golden Dawn* for further information concerning Scrying—in particular the section entitled "Of Skrying and Traveling in the Spirit-Vision" by V.H. Soror V.N.R.)

When you have finished all scrying and meditation, use the appropriate Banishings. (Although one should never banish in an actual Vault, the Miniature Wall can be treated much like an Enochian Tablet, to be invoked or banished when necessary.)

Again perform the Analysis of the Keyword.

Perform the LBRP.

THIS ENDS THE MEDITATION

CHAPTER FIVE

The Adept's Personal Temple

For a proper magickal working in the tradition of the Golden Dawn, the Adept will need many of the items mentioned in the preceding chapters. These include: the Banners of the East and West, the Pillars, the Cross and Triangle, an Iset, the Enochian tablets, the Altars (black or white depending upon the working), and the censer. It is a matter of tradition to have an oil lamp burning above the Altar as a sign of the radiant presence of the Divine. This lamp can be very basic, consisting of little more than a container filled with oil and a wick. Also needed are the white Tau robe, yellow sash, and the yellow-and-white striped nemyss which are the ritual garb of the Second Order. All of these items make up the core of the Adept's personal Temple, where the Magician does his/her personal and most powerful ritual work—outside of and apart from group Temple work.

In the Golden Dawn system, the Neophyte Adeptus Minor can only become a fully trained initiating Hierophant by undertaking a prescribed curriculum of study. A series of tests must be passed before the Neophyte Adept can claim the title of Zelator Adeptus Minor (Z.A.M.), the lowest grade which may hold the office of Hierophant. Included within this work is the construction and consecration of the Elemental Weapons or Implements. These implements are specialized tools for gaining access to and working with the spirits of the four elements. The Adept must also construct a Lotus Wand, which is to be carried at all Second Order functions, along with the Rose Cross Lamen, the personal emblem of both the Adept, and the Order to which he/she belongs. In addition, a personal Magickal Sword is needed.

To obtain real force implanted in any magickal weapon by consecration, the Adept is required to be healthy, pure, strong in mind, free from anxiety, and apart from disturbances. He or she is required to have mastered the details of the ceremony and to be familiar with the proper pentagrams and other symbols.

The Lotus Wand

Use and Symbolism

The Lotus Wand is for general use in magickal working. It is carried by the Z.A.M. at all meetings of the Second Order at which he has the right to be present. It is to be made by the Adept unassisted, and to be consecrated by him/her alone. It is to be untouched by any other person, and kept wrapped in white silk of linen, free from external influences other than his/her own on the human plane.

The ten upper and inner petals refer to the purity of the ten Sephiroth. The middle eight refer to the counter-charged natural and spiritual forces of Air and Fire. The lowest and outer eight refer to the powers of Earth and Water. The center and amber portion refers to the Spiritual Sun, while the outer calyx of four orange sepals shows the action of the Sun upon the life of things by differentiation.

As a general rule, the white end of the Wand is used to invoke and the black end to banish. The white end may be used to banish by tracing a banishing symbol against an evil and opposing force which has resisted other efforts. By this is meant that by whatever band you are holding the Wand, whether white for spiritual things, by black for mundane, by blue for Sagittarius, or by red for the fiery triplicity, you are, when invoking, to direct the white extremity to the quarter desired. When banishing, point the black end to that quarter.

The Wand is never to be inverted, so that when very material forces are concerned, the black end may be the most suitable for invocation, but with the greatest caution.

In working on the plane of the Zodiac, hold the Wand by the portion you refer to between the thumb and two fingers.

If a planetary working be required, hold the Wand by the portion representing the day or night House of the Planet, or else by the Sign in which the Planet is at the time.

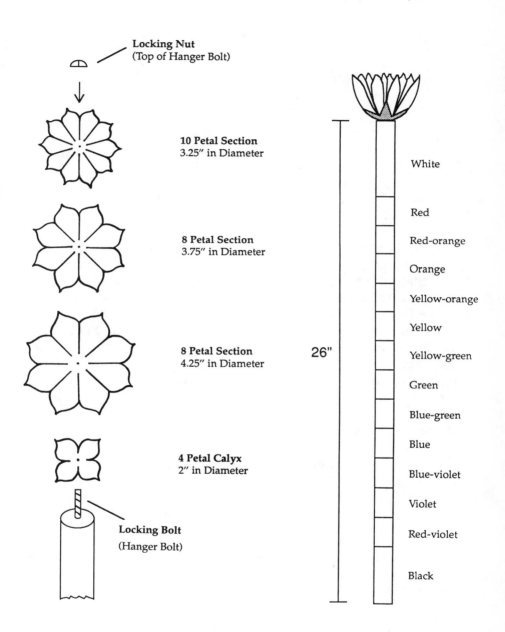

Locking Nut
(Top of Hanger Bolt)

10 Petal Section
3.25" in Diameter

8 Petal Section
3.75" in Diameter

8 Petal Section
4.25" in Diameter

4 Petal Calyx
2" in Diameter

Locking Bolt
(Hanger Bolt)

26"

White

Red

Red-orange

Orange

Yellow-orange

Yellow

Yellow-green

Green

Blue-green

Blue

Blue-violet

Violet

Red-violet

Black

The Lotus Wand

SATURN:	Day House—Aquarius
	Night House—Capricorn*
JUPITER:	Day House—Sagittarius
	Night House—Pisces
MARS:	Day House—Aries
	Night House—Scorpio
VENUS:	Day House—Libra
	Night House—Taurus
MERCURY:	Day House—Gemini
	Night House—Virgo
SOL:	In Leo only
LUNA:	In Cancer only

For example, if Venus is the planet referred to, use in the day Libra, and in the night Taurus.

Should the working be with the elements, one of the Signs of the Triplicity of the Elements should be held according to the nature of the Element you are intending to invoke. (*Fire Triplicity:* Aries, Leo, Sagittarius. *Water Triplicity:* Cancer, Scorpio, Pisces. *Air Triplicity:* Gemini, Libra, Aquarius. *Earth Triplicity:* Taurus, Virgo, Capricorn.) Bear in mind that the Kerubic Emblem is the most powerful action of the Element in the Triplicity.

Hold the Wand by the white portion for all Divine and Spiritual Matters or for the Sephirotic influences, and for the process of rising in the planes. Hold the black part only for material and mundane matters.

The Lotus Flower (sacred to Isis) is not to be touched in working, but in Sephirotic and Spiritual Things, the Flower is to be inclined towards the forehead; and to rise in the Planes, the orange colored center is to be fully directed to the forehead.

Materials Needed

One 3/4" dowel anywhere from 24"–40" in length. (The shorter length works better in ritual.) The wand we will describe here has a shaft length of 26."

One square foot of copper or tin sheet metal

One brass lock nut—also called a Hanger Bolt (a plain brass screw may be substituted)

Cider vinegar

---

* In Regardie's *The Golden Dawn*, the Zodiacal Signs given for the Day House and Night House of Saturn were mistakenly transposed. Here they are listed correctly.

Gesso
Acrylic paints: red, orange, yellow, green, blue, blue-violet, violet,
    red-violet, black, white
Sealant: clear lacquer finish

Tools Needed
    Electric drill
    Tin snips or metal shears
    A small vise
    Artist's brushes
    Emery cloth
    File
    Pliers
    One index card

Construction: The Flower
1)   With a pencil, draw out the four sections of the Lotus flower as shown
      on the sheet metal. The Largest section (8 petals) should be approx.
      4-1/2" in diameter. The second largest (8 petals) should be approxi-
      mately 4" across. The 10-petaled section should be about 3-1/2"
      across. The small, four-sepaled calyx is only 2" in diameter.

2)   Cut out the four pieces of the Lotus Flower and file the edges so that
      they are smooth. Wash the pieces with cider vinegar. Rough-up the
      surface of the metal on both sides of all sections with emery cloth to
      enable the paint to stick to it.

3)   Drill a hole in the center of each section of the flower. (Use a drill bit
      that is the same size as the shaft of the lock-nut or screw used to hold
      the assemblage together.)

4)   Using the pliers, bend the pieces so that they turn inward slightly,
      like an opening flower. Cover each petal with a piece of cloth first, to
      avoid marking the metal.

5)   Cover both sides of all sections with a white primer coat. Let dry.

6)   Paint the 10-petaled piece white on both sides. Paint the two 8-pet-
      aled pieces white on one side (inside) and olive on the other (outside).
      Olive is created from mixing green with violet. The Calyx is orange
      on both sides. (Note: Acrylic paint is theoretically not supposed to
      stick to metal, but if the pieces have been thoroughly washed with ci-
      der vinegar, then rubbed with emery cloth, you should have no diffi-
      culty, although it will take at least three coats of paint. We have cre-
      ated numerous Lotus Wands in this manner and have never experi-
      enced a problem.)

7)   On the olive-colored outside of the large 8-petaled piece, paint a pat-
      tern of five veins in black on each petal. Spray or brush on sealant for
      protection. Let dry.

Construction: The Shaft

8) Drill a hole in one end of the dowel which is to be the top. (Use a bit that matches the size of the shaft of the Lock nut or screw that will hold the assemblage together.)

9) Cover the dowel with a coat of gesso. Let dry and sand. Repeat if necessary.

10) Measure down 4-1/2" from the top of the dowel. Mark with a pencil. Pencil in twelve more marks going down the shaft from the first measurement at intervals of 1-1/2". The measurement from the last pencil mark to the end of the Wand will be 3-1/2".

11) Using an index card as a straight edge by wrapping it around the dowel at the place of the first pencil mark, draw a line completely around the shaft. Do this at all penciled measurements leading down the dowel.

12) Paint each section of the dowel as shown in the diagram using the acrylic paints listed.* Let paint dry completely. Spray or brush on sealant for protection. Let dry.

Finishing Steps

13) Assemble all the pieces of the Lotus as follows: The 10-petaled piece is placed inside the smaller of the two 8-petaled pieces. This is in turn placed inside the large 8-petaled piece. The calyx is placed under the others, between the larger petaled section and the top of the shaft.

14) Attach the screw portion of the brass lock nut into the hole drilled in the top of the shaft. Place the assembled Lotus Flower over the end of the screw; the threaded top of the screw should stick out from the end of the shaft. Place the lock nut over the exposed end of the screw and turn until it locks into place. The Lotus should now be firmly attached to the Wand. (The advantage in using a brass lock nut as opposed to a regular brass screw is that it looks like the center of a flower, rather than the head of a screw.)

---

* Some authors have mistakenly listed the color of the Leo (Teth) band as lemon yellow or greenish-yellow. The true color for this band is pure yellow as given on a standard color wheel. This is also true for the Teth Petal on the Rose Cross Lamen.

Ritual for Use

Consecration of the Lotus Wand

The Adept will need: a private Temple space, a Black Altar, the Cross and Triangle, incense, a rose, a chalice of water, a candle, salt on a platter, an astrological figure of the heavens for the time of the working (as per the instructions given in the Invocation of Hermes-Thoth in chapter 1), a set of astrological symbolic drawings to be placed around the room in accordance with the figure of the heavens, the new Lotus Wand, and white linen or silk for wrapping. The Adept should be dressed in the regalia of the Second Order. This ritual is an elaborated form of the Consecration of the Lotus Wand given in Regardie's *The Golden Dawn*.

Find the position of the East.

Prepare an invocation of the Forces of the Zodiac.

Place the Altar in the center of the room. Arrange upon it, the Cross and Triangle. Place the incense and rose in the East above the Cross and Triangle. Candle in the South. Cup in the West. Salt in the North.

Light the candle and incense.

Stand west of the Altar, holding the new wand by the black portion and say: "HEKAS! HEKAS! ESTE BEBELOI!"

Go to the East and perform the LBRP. (When tracing the pentagrams hold the Wand by the white portion and point with the black. For the Qabalistic Cross, hold the Wand by the white portion and keep the flower always pointed upwards.)

Take up the cup and purify the room with water, starting in the East. (Trace the Cross and Invoking Water Triangle in all quarters.) As you do so, repeat, "So therefore, first, the Priest who governeth the works of Fire, must sprinkle with the lustral water of the loud resounding sea."

Take up the candle and consecrate the room with Fire, starting in the East. (Trace the Cross and Invoking Fire Triangle in all quarters.) As you do so, repeat, "And when after all the Phantoms are banished, thou shalt see that Holy and Formless Fire, that Fire which darts and flashes through the hidden depths of the Universe. Hear thou the Voice of Fire!"

Take up the wand again, by the white portion. Circumambulate the Temple three times and, at the end, repeat the Adoration of the Lord of the Universe as in the Ritual of the 0=0 Grade, saluting at each adoration with the Projection Sign, and at the word "Darkness" giving the Sign of Silence.

"Holy art Thou, Lord of the Universe!"
"Holy art Thou, whom Nature hath not formed!"
"Holy art Thou, the Vast and the Mighty One!"
"Lord of the Light and of the Darkness!"

Perform the Supreme Invoking Ritual of the Pentagram at the Four Quarters of the room.

Stand east of the Altar and face east. Hold the Lotus Wand by the white portion, and give the Adeptus Minor Signs. Look upward, holding the Wand high and say:

"O Harpocrates, Lord of Silence, Who art enthroned upon the Lotus. Twenty-Six are the Petals of the Lotus, Flower of thy Wand. O Lord of Creation, they are the Number of Thy Name. In the name of Yod He Vav He, let the Divine Light descend!"

Facing consecutively the quarter where each Sign is according to the Horary Figure for the time of working, repeat in each of the 12 directions the invocation which follows, using the appropriate Divine and Angelic names and Letters for each. Begin with Aries. (Remember that the symbols are to be set out on the floor COUNTERCLOCKWISE around the room, just as a Zodiacal chart going from Aries to Pisces would be. You will have to walk CLOCKWISE around the room however, to walk from one sign to the next.) Hold the Wand by the appropriate colored band, (pointing with the flower end) and in the left hand the Element from off the Altar, which is referred to the particular Sign.

(For *ARIES*) Take up the candle in left hand. Hold the red band and trace over the Zodiacal symbol the Invoking Pentagram of Spirit Active. Say the appropriate names. Give the LVX Signs. Trace the Invoking Pentagram of Fire. Draw the sigil of Aries in the center. Vibrate the appropriate names for the Element of Fire and give the appropriate Grade Sign (which in this case is that of Philosophus.) Then say:

The Heaven is above and the Earth is beneath. And betwixt the Light and the Darkness, the colors vibrate. I supplicate the Powers and Forces governing the Nature, Place, and Authority of the Sign, ARIES, by the Majesty of the Divine Name, YOD HEH VAV HEH, with which, in Earth life and language, I ascribe the letter HEH, to which is allotted the symbolic Tribe of GAD and over which is the Angel MELCHIDAEL, to bestow this present day and hour, and confirm their mystic and potent influence upon the RED Band of this Lotus Wand, which I hereby dedicate to purity and to Occult Work, and may its grasp strengthen me in the work of the character of ARIES and its attributes.

(For *TAURUS*) Take up the salt in left hand. Hold the red-orange band and trace over the Zodiacal symbol the Invoking Pentagram of Spirit Passive. Say the appropriate names. Give the LVX Signs. Trace the Invoking Pentagram of Earth. Draw the sigil of Taurus in the center. Vibrate the appropriate Earth names and give the appropriate Grade Sign (which in this case is that of Zelator.) Then say:

The Heaven is above and the Earth is beneath. And betwixt the Light and the Darkness, the colors vibrate. I supplicate the Powers and Forces governing the Nature, Place, and Authority of the Sign, TAURUS, by the Majesty of the Divine Name, YOD HEH HEH VAV, with which, in Earth life and language, I ascribe the letter VAV, to which is allotted the symbolic Tribe of EPHRAIM and over which is the Angel ASMODEL, to bestow this present day and hour, and confirm their mystic and potent influence upon the RED-ORANGE Band of this Lotus Wand, which I hereby dedicate to purity and to Occult Work, and may its grasp strengthen me in the work of the character of TAURUS and its attributes.

(For GEMINI) Rose in left hand. Hold the orange band. Trace Invoking Pentagram of Spirit Active. Vibrate the appropriate names. Give the LVX Signs. Trace the Invoking Pentagram of Air. Draw the sigil of Gemini in the center. Say the appropriate Air names and give the Sign of Theoricus. Then say:

The Heaven is above and the Earth is beneath. And betwixt the Light and the Darkness, the colors vibrate. I supplicate the Powers and Forces governing the Nature, Place, and Authority of the Sign, GEMINI, by the Majesty of the Divine Name, YOD

VAV HEH HEH, with which, in Earth life and language, I ascribe the letter ZAYIN, to which is allotted the symbolic Tribe of MANASSEH and over which is the Angel AMBRIEL, to bestow this present day and hour, and confirm their mystic and potent influence upon the ORANGE Band of this Lotus Wand, which I hereby dedicate to purity and to Occult Work, and may its grasp strengthen me in the work of the character of GEMINI and its attributes.

(For *CANCER*) Cup in left hand. Hold the yellow-orange band. Trace Invoking Pentagram of Spirit Passive. Intone the appropriate names. Give the LVX Signs. Trace the Invoking Pentagram of Water. Draw the sigil of Cancer in the center. Vibrate the appropriate Water names and give the Sign of Practicus. Then say:

The Heaven is above and the Earth is beneath. And betwixt the Light and the Darkness, the colors vibrate. I supplicate the Powers and Forces governing the Nature, Place, and Authority of the Sign, CANCER, by the Majesty of the Divine Name, HEH VAV HEH YOD, with which, in Earth life and language, I ascribe the letter CHETH, to which is allotted the symbolic Tribe of ISSACHAR and over which is the Angel MURIEL, to bestow this present day and hour, and confirm their mystic and potent influence upon the YELLOW-ORANGE Band of this Lotus Wand, which I hereby dedicate to purity and to Occult Work, and may its grasp strengthen me in the work of the character of CANCER and its attributes.

(For *LEO*) Candle in left hand. Hold the yellow band. Trace Invoking Pentagram of Spirit Active. Vibrate the appropriate names. Give the LVX Signs. Trace the Invoking Pentagram of Fire. Draw the sigil of Cancer in the center. Say the appropriate Fire names and give the Sign of Philosophus. Then say:

The Heaven is above and the Earth is beneath. And betwixt the Light and the Darkness, the colors vibrate. I supplicate the Powers and Forces governing the Nature, Place, and Authority of the Sign, LEO, by the Majesty of the Divine Name, HEH VAV YOD HEH, with which, in Earth life and language, I ascribe the letter TETH, to which is allotted the symbolic Tribe of JUDAH and over which is the Angel VERCHIEL, to bestow this present day and hour, and confirm their mystic and potent influence upon the YELLOW Band of this Lotus Wand, which I hereby dedicate to purity and to Occult Work, and may its grasp strengthen me in the work of the character of LEO and its attributes.

(For *VIRGO*) Salt in left hand. Hold the yellow-green band. Trace Invoking Pentagram of Spirit Passive. Say the appropriate names. Give the LVX Signs. Trace the Invoking Pentagram of Earth. Draw the sigil of Virgo in the center. Intone the appropriate Earth names and give the Sign of Zelator. Then say:

The Heaven is above and the Earth is beneath. And betwixt the Light and the Darkness, the colors vibrate. I supplicate the Powers and Forces governing the Nature, Place, and Authority of the Sign, VIRGO, by the Majesty of the Divine Name, HEH HEH YOD VAV, with which, in Earth life and language, I ascribe the letter YOD, to which is allotted the symbolic Tribe of NAPHTHALI and over which is the Angel HAMALIEL, to bestow this present day and hour, and confirm their mystic and potent influence upon the YELLOW-GREEN Band of this Lotus Wand, which I hereby dedicate to purity and to Occult Work, and may its grasp strengthen me in the work of the character of VIRGO and its attributes.

(For *LIBRA*) Rose in left hand. Hold the green band. Trace Invoking Pentagram of Spirit Active. Intone the appropriate names. Give the LVX Signs. Trace the Invoking Pentagram of Air. Draw the sigil of Libra in the center. Say the appropriate Air names and give the Sign of Theoricus. Then say:

The Heaven is above and the Earth is beneath. And betwixt the Light and the Darkness, the colors vibrate. I supplicate the Powers and Forces governing the Nature, Place, and Authority of the Sign, LIBRA, by the Majesty of the Divine Name, VAV HEH YOD HEH, with which, in Earth life and language, I ascribe the letter LAMED, to which is allotted the symbolic Tribe of ASSHUR and over which is the Angel ZURIEL, to bestow this present day and hour, and confirm their mystic and potent influence upon the GREEN Band of this Lotus Wand, which I hereby dedicate to purity and to Occult Work, and may its grasp strengthen me in the work of the character of LIBRA and its attributes.

(For *SCORPIO*) Cup in left hand. Hold the blue-green band. Trace Invoking Pentagram of Spirit Passive. Say the appropriate names. Give the LVX Signs. Trace the Invoking Pentagram of Water. Draw the sigil of Scorpio in the center. Vibrate the appropriate Water names and give the Sign of Practicus. Then say:

The Heaven is above and the Earth is beneath. And betwixt the Light and the Darkness, the colors vibrate. I supplicate the Powers and Forces governing the Nature, Place, and Authority of the Sign, SCORPIO, by the Majesty of the Divine Name, VAV HEH HEH YOD, with which, in Earth life and language, I ascribe the letter NUN, to which is allotted the symbolic Tribe of DAN and over which is the Angel BARCHIEL, to bestow this present day and hour, and confirm their mystic and potent influence upon the BLUE-GREEN Band of this Lotus Wand, which I hereby dedicate to purity and to Occult Work, and may its grasp strengthen me in the work of the character of SCORPIO and its attributes.

(For SAGITTARIUS) Candle in left hand. Hold the blue band. Trace Invoking Pentagram of Spirit Active. Vibrate the appropriate names. Give the LVX Signs. Trace the Invoking Pentagram of Fire. Draw the sigil of Sagittarius in the center. Say the appropriate Fire names and give the Sign of Philosophus. Then say:

The Heaven is above and the Earth is beneath. And betwixt the Light and the Darkness, the colors vibrate. I supplicate the Powers and Forces governing the Nature, Place, and Authority of the Sign, SAGITTARIUS, by the Majesty of the Divine Name, VAV YOD HEH HEH, with which, in Earth life and language, I ascribe the letter SAMEKH, to which is allotted the symbolic Tribe of BENJAMIN and over which is the Angel ADVACHIEL, to bestow this present day and hour, and confirm their mystic and potent influence upon the BLUE Band of this Lotus Wand, which I hereby dedicate to purity and to Occult Work, and may its grasp strengthen me in the work of the character of SAGITTARIUS and its attributes.

(For *CAPRICORN*) Salt in left hand. Hold the blue-violet band. Trace Invoking Pentagram of Spirit Passive. Say the appropriate names. Give the LVX Signs. Trace the Invoking Pentagram of Earth. Draw the sigil of Capricorn in the center. Intone the appropriate Earth names and give the Sign of Zelator. Then say:

The Heaven is above and the Earth is beneath. And betwixt the Light and the Darkness, the colors vibrate. I supplicate the Powers and Forces governing the Nature, Place, and Authority of the Sign, CAPRICORN, by the Majesty of the Divine Name, HEH YOD HEH VAV, with which, in Earth life and language, I ascribe the letter AYIN, to which is allotted the symbolic Tribe of ZEBULUN and over which is the Angel HANAEL, to bestow this present day and hour, and confirm their mystic and potent influence upon the BLUE-VIOLET Band of this Lotus Wand, which I hereby dedicate to purity and to Occult Work, and may its grasp strengthen me in the work of the character of CAPRICORN and its attributes.

(For *AQUARIUS*) Rose in left hand. Hold the violet band. Trace Invoking Pentagram of Spirit Active. Intone the appropriate names. Give the LVX Signs. Trace the Invoking Pentagram of Air. Draw the sigil of Aquarius in the center. Say the appropriate Air names and give the Sign of Theoricus. Then say:

The Heaven is above and the Earth is beneath. And betwixt the Light and the Darkness, the colors vibrate. I supplicate the Powers and Forces governing the Nature, Place, and Authority of the Sign, AQUARIUS, by the Majesty of the Divine Name, HEH YOD VAV HEH, with which, in Earth life and language, I ascribe the letter TZADDI, to which is allotted the symbolic Tribe of REUBEN and over which is the Angel CAMBRIEL, to bestow this present day and hour, and confirm their mystic and potent influence upon the VIOLET Band of this Lotus Wand, which I hereby dedicate to purity and to Occult Work, and may its grasp strengthen me in the work of the character of AQUARIUS and its attributes.

(For *PISCES*) Cup in left hand. Hold the red-violet band. Trace Invoking Pentagram of Spirit Passive. Say the appropriate names. Give the LVX Signs. Trace the Invoking Pentagram of Water. Draw the sigil of Pisces in the center. Vibrate the appropriate Water names and give the Sign of Practicus. Then say:

The Heaven is above and the Earth is beneath. And betwixt the Light and the Darkness, the colors vibrate. I supplicate the Powers and Forces governing the Nature, Place, and Authority of the sign PISCES, by the Majesty of the Divine Name, HEH HEH VAV YOD, with which, in Earth life and language, I ascribe the letter QOPH, to which is allotted the symbolic Tribe of SIMEON and over which is the Angel AMNITZIEL, to bestow this present day and hour, and confirm their mystic and potent influence upon the RED-VIOLET Band of this Lotus Wand, which I hereby dedicate to purity and to Occult Work, and may its grasp strengthen me in the work of the character of PISCES and its attributes.*

Lay the wand on the Altar, Lotus end towards the East.

Stand west of the Altar, face east, raise hands and say:

O ISIS! Great Goddess of the Forces of Nature, let Thine Influence descend and consecrate this Wand which I dedicate to Thee for the performance of the works of the Magick of Light!

Wrap the wand in silk or linen.

Purify the room with Water and Fire as before.

Perform reverse circumambulation.

Stand west of the Altar and face east. Say:

I now release any spirits that may have been imprisoned by this ceremony. Go in peace with the blessings of YEHESHUAH YEHOVASHAH!

Perform the LBRP.

Say, "I now declare this Temple duly closed."

SO MOTE IT BE

Ritual for Use

An Invocation of Aries

The Lotus Wand is a powerful implement that can be used for many diverse magickal operations. It is the primary tool of the Adept. Because of its construction, the Wand is ideal for rituals which invoke Zodiacal or planetary energies. Such energies can be invoked, or called within the psyche of the Magician from without, in order to balance out unfavorable aspects in the birth chart. For example, a person who has too much Air and too little Earth in his/her birth chart could use the Lotus Wand in a ritual to invoke the stabilizing energies of Taurus. Or if a person suffers from a lack of ego and feel-

---

* In Regardie's *The Golden Dawn*, the symbolic tribes of Israel for the signs of Virgo and Pisces were mistakenly transposed.

ings of inferiority, the self-assurance of the Sign of Leo could be called upon. The ritual we present here is an Invocation of Aries, the first Sign of the Zodiac. As such, Aries is the Sign of new beginnings, new expressions, and growth. The Energy of this Sign is creative and enthusiastic. A ritual of this type would be performed in order to stimulate the creative drive of the magician, or perhaps infuse him/her with needed Arian stamina and strength. It could also be performed in order to initiate a new cycle of personal development.

(This ritual would be best performed during the day and hour of Mars—see the table of planetary hours.) The White Altar is to be set up in the Temple space. The Enochian Tablets are to be placed in their respective quarters. The Tablet of Union, Cross and Triangle, Incense and rose, candle, cup of water, and platter of salt should be on the Altar. An Iset for the Adept should be placed in the West. The position of Aries should be determined for the ritual time, and a symbol of Aries placed on the floor or hung on the wall corresponding to the direction of the Sign. The Adept should be dressed in Second Order Regalia. The consecrated Lotus Wand should be close at hand. Give the LVX signs upon entering the Temple.

Sit in the West for a period of meditation. When ready, give five knocks with the black end of the wand against the Iset. Then take up the Wand by the black end. Go to the Northeast and say, "HEKAS, HEKAS, ESTE BEBELOI! Far from this sacred place be the profane!"

Perform the LBRP. (Hold by white part of the Wand, flower always pointing upwards for the Qabalistic Cross. When tracing the pentagrams, grasp the Wand by the white portion and point with the black end.)

Perform the BRH.

Take up the Cup. Purify the Temple with water in all quarters, starting in the East, tracing Cross and Water Triangle. Say, "So therefore first the priest who governeth the works of Fire must sprinkle with the Lustral Waters of the loud resounding sea."

Take up the incense. Consecrate the room with Fire in all quarters, tracing the Cross and Fire Triangle. Say, "And when after all the phantoms are banished, thou shalt see that Holy and formless Fire, that Fire which darts and flashes through the hidden depths of the Universe. Hear Thou, the Voice of Fire!"

Take the Lotus Wand by the white portion and circumambulate the Temple three times deosil, saluting with the Neophyte Signs when passing the East. Then stand west of the Altar facing east and perform the Adoration to the Lord of the Universe.

Go to the East and perform the complete Supreme Invoking Ritual of the Pentagram (SIRP). Hold the white portion of the Lotus Wand when performing the Qabalistic Cross. Grasp the Kerubic bands of the Wand when invoking each Element: Violet—Aquarius band for Air, Yellow—Leo for Fire, Blue-green—Scorpio for Water, and Red-orange—Taurus for Earth.

Return to the East and vibrate the name "EHEIEH" four times, using the Vibratory Formula of the Middle Pillar. Then give the LVX Signs. Say, "Unto Thee Sole Wise, Sole Eternal, and Sole Merciful One, be praise and glory for ever. Who hath permitted me, who now standeth humbly before Thee, to enter thus far into the sanctuary of thy mysteries. Not unto me, Adonai, but unto Thy name be the glory, now and forever more. Let the influence of Thy Divine Ones descend upon my head, and teach me the value of self-sacrifice so that I shrink not in the hour of trial. But that thus my name my be written on high, and my Genius stand in the presence of the Holy One. In that hour when the Son of Humanity is invoked before the Lord of Spirits and his Name before the Ancient of Days."

Astrally formulate four Pillars surrounding you. Then visualize clearly a large Banner of the East. After the image is firmly within your mind, see it enveloping you as a cloak.

Perform the Qabalistic Cross. Then take the Lotus Wand by the red band and use the white end to draw with. Perform the Supreme Invoking Pentagram Ritual of Aries. (Trace the Invoking Pentagram of Spirit Active and the Invoking Pentagram of Fire in ALL FOUR Quarters, vibrating "BITOM" and "EHEIEH" for Spirit, and "OIP TEAA PEDOCE" and "ELOHIM" for Fire. Give the appropriate Signs after each pentagram. Also use the Aries sigil in the center of the Fire Pentagram instead of the Kerubic sigil.) Follow this with the Invocation of the Four Archangels and repeat the Qabalistic Cross.

Perform the Lesser Invoking Hexagram Ritual of Mars, commencing with the Qabalistic Cross. Then draw the four Lesser

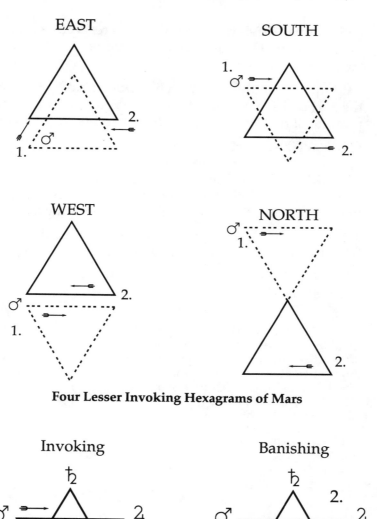

EAST

SOUTH

WEST

NORTH

Four Lesser Invoking Hexagrams of Mars

Invoking

Banishing

The Greater Hexagram of Mars

Hexagrams of Mars (four forms) in their respective quarters, intoning "ARARITA" as each is traced. Follow this with the Analysis of the Keyword.

Take up the Candle in your left hand. Still holding the Wand by the red band, face the direction where you have determined the position of the Sign of Aries to be at the time of the working.

In front of the Aries Sigil, trace the Greater Invoking Hexagram of Mars (the ruling planet of Aries). Vibrate the name "ARARITA" while drawing the Hexagram. Intone "ELOHIM GIBOR" when tracing the Mars sigil in the center. Trace the Hebrew letter "ALEPH" and intone the name of the letter.

Then trace the sigil of Aries in the center of the figure and vibrate the permutation of the Divine Name attributed to Aries, "YOD HEH VAV HEH."

Say the following:

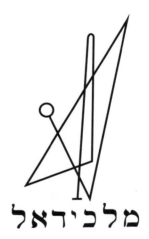

MELCHIDAEL

In the First Permutation of the unutterable name of the God the Vast One, Thee I invoke! O Powers of the Sign of the Ram! Prince of the Zodiac! Leader of the Celestial Signs! Thee I invoke! Lord of the Head! ARIES! Sacred One of Amon-Ra! Harbinger of Spring, Thee I invoke! Thou who leadeth the Tribe of GAD! Thou Golden-fleeced One who art Ruler over the letter HEH (draw letter) and the Red band of the Wand I grasp! Thee I invoke! Thou whose Mighty archangel is MELCHIDAEL! (Draw sigil) Thee I invoke!

O Thou whose Names are many: BARA! ASWINI! ALHAMAL! AJA! MESHA! TELI! AMRU! KUZI! ARIETE! ARIES! I invoke Thee, Lord of Valor who dost kindle within the soul, the ardent Fires of vitality and courage! Initiator of growth and inspiration! Grant unto me your stamina and strength! Bestow upon me your bold creativity and enthusiasm! Thus will I go forward with the resolve of the Ram beating within my breast; ever forward to prosper and attain. Ever forward with the Life-giving Waters of Spring in my Soul, and the Fiery Ram of the Stars within my heart.

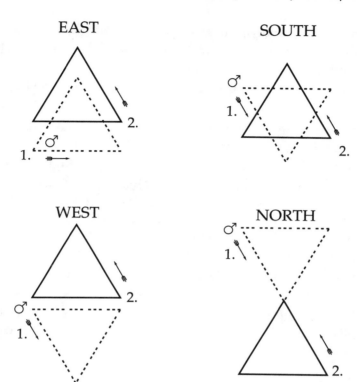

EAST   SOUTH

WEST   NORTH

Four Lesser Banishing Hexagrams of Mars

Stand in the position of the Tau Cross. Vibrate "YOD HEH VAV HEH" four times using the Vibratory Formula of the Middle Pillar. Feel a connection between the Sign of Aries and the corresponding part of your Sphere of Sensation (Aura). Breathe in and imagine the energy of Aries entering your right nostril as you do so. Breathe out imagining the energy passing through the left nostril, equilibriating the Fiery martial energy with Venusian compassion. Feel an influx of Divine White Light tempering all energies within you. Continue to contemplate the Light for as long as you wish. Then replace the candle upon the Altar.

Go to the west of the Altar and face east. Hold the Lotus Wand by the white band. Raise your hands and say, "Not unto my name, O Adonai, but to Thine be ascribed the Kingdom, the Power and Glory, now and forever more! Amen!" Give the LVX Signs.

Purify and consecrate the Temple with Water and Fire as in the beginning.

Perform the reverse circumambulation, three times widdershins. Perform again the Adoration to the Lord of the Universe.

Return to the position of Aries in the Temple. Hold the Wand by the red band and draw with the black end. Trace the Greater Banishing Hexagram of Mars in that direction, vibrating the names of "ARARITA", "ELOHIM GIBOR" and "ALEPH" Also trace the sigil of Aries and intone "YHVH."

Perform the Lesser Banishing Hexagram Ritual of Mars (the four forms in their respective quarters). Begin with the Qabalistic Cross and end with the Analysis of the Keyword.

Still holding the Wand by the red band and pointing with the black, trace the Banishing Pentagram of Fire (with Aries sigil in center) in ALL FOUR QUARTERS.

Grasp the Wand by the white band and point with the black end of the Wand, Perform the LBRP and the BRH.

Return to the East and say, "I now release any spirits that may have been imprisoned by this ceremony. Depart in peace to your abodes and habitations. Go with the blessings of YEHESHUAH YEHOVASHAH." Trace the Rose and Cross.

Give five knocks as in the beginning.

Say "I now declare this Temple duly closed."

SO MOTE IT BE

The Rose Cross Lamen

Use and Symbolism

The Rose Cross Lamen is to be made by each Adept alone, and consecrated—never touched by any other person—and wrapped in white silk or linen when not in use. The motto of the owner is painted on the reverse side, and it is to be worn suspended from a yellow collarette at all meetings of Adepts.

It is a complete synthesis of the Masculine, Positive or Rainbow scale of color attributions, which is also called "The Scale of the King."

The four ends of the Cross belong to the four elements and are colored accordingly. The white portion belongs to the Holy Spirit and the Planets.

The 22 petals of the Rose refer to the 22 Paths. It is the Cross in Tiphareth, the receptacle and the center of the Forces of the Sephiroth and the Paths.

The extreme center of the Rose is white, the reflected Spiritual brightness of Kether, bearing upon it the Red Rose of Five Petals and the Golden Cross of Six squares; four green Rays issuant around the Angles of the Cross, from which the Second Order takes its name. They are the symbols of the Receiving Force.

Upon the white portion of the symbol, below the Rose, is placed the Hexagram, with the Planets in the order which is the key of the Supreme Ritual of Hexagram.

Around the Pentagrams, which are placed one upon each Elemental colored arm, are drawn the symbols of the Spirit and the Four Elements, in the order which is the key to the Supreme Ritual of the Pentagram. Upon each of the floriated ends of the Cross are arranged the Three Alchemical Principles, but in a different order for each Element, and as showing their different operation therein.

The uppermost arm of the Cross, allotted to Air, is of the yellow color of Tiphareth. In it the flowing Philosophic Mercurial nature is chief and without hinderance to its mobility; hence the ever moving nature of Air. Its Sulphureous side is drawn from the part of Fire, whence its luminous and electrical qualities. Its Saline side is from the Water, whence result clouds and rain from the action of the Solar Forces.

The lowest arm of the Cross, allotted to Earth, is of the four colors of Malkuth, the Earth being of the nature of a container and receiver of the other influences. The Citrine answers to its Airy part, the Olive to the Watery, the Russet to the Fire, and the black to the lowest part, Earth. Here also is the Mercurial part chief, but hindered by the compound nature whence its faculty becomes germinative rather than mobile, while the Sulphur and the Salt are respectively from the sides of Water and Fire, which almost neutralize their natural operation and bring about the fixedness and immobility of Earth.

The extremity allotted to Fire is of the scarlet color of Geburah, and in it the Suphureous nature is chief, whence its powers of heat and burning. The Salt is from the side of Earth, whence the necessity for a constant substantial pabulum whereon to act, and the Mercury is from the side of Air, whence the leaping, lambent motion of flame especially when acted upon by wind.

The extremity allotted to Water is of the blue color of Chesed, and in it the Saline side is chief as exemplified in the salt water of the Ocean, to which all waters go; and from whence also is derived the nature of always preserving the horizontal line. The Mercurial part is from Earth, whence the weight and force of its flux and reflux. Its Sulphuric part is from the Air whence the effect of waves and storms. So that the disposition of these Three Principles forms the key of their Alchemic operation in the Elements.

The white rays issuing from behind the Rose at the inner angles between the Arms are the Rays of the Divine Light issuing and coruscating from the Reflected Light of Kether in its center; and the letters and symbols on them refer to the analysis of the Key Word of an Adeptus Minor, I.N.R.I. by which the opening of the Vault is accomplished.

The twelve letters of the twelve outer petals follow the Order of the Signs of the Zodiac. Uppermost is Heh, the letter of Aries, followed by Vav, Zayin, Cheth, Teth, Yod, while the letter of Libra, which is Lamed in lowermost. Ascending are Nun, Samekh, Ayin, Tzaddi, Qoph.

The Seven Double Letters of the middle row are allotted to the Planets in the order of their Exaltations, the Planets being Wanderers; the Stars are fixed with respect to the Earth. These letters are Peh, Resh, Beth, with Daleth exactly over Libra, followed by Gimel, Tau, Caph.*

The Three Mother letters are allotted to the Elements and are so arranged that the Petal of Air should be beneath the arm of the Cross allotted to Air, while those of Fire and Water are on counterchanged sides, so that the forces of the Arms of the Cross should not too much override the Planetary and Zodiacal forces in the Rose, which might otherwise be the case were the petal of Fire placed on the same side as the arm of Fire and that of Water on the side of Water.

---

* In all editions of Regardie's The Golden Dawn, the Hebrew letters Tau and Kaph are shown incorrectly transposed on the second ring of petals. In the accompanying diagram of the Rose Cross Lamen shown here, these letters are shown in their proper positions.

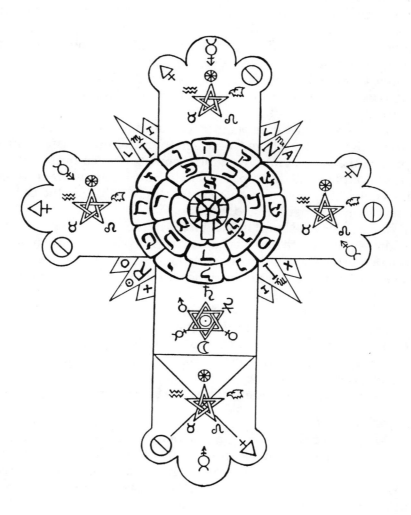

The Rose Cross Lamen
(front)

The Rose is also a glyph of the entire manifest Universe. This symbol when properly painted should resemble a perfect color wheel. Any error in the pigments will be readily apparent to an artist. (The Hermetic Order of the Golden Dawn developed a method of drawing sigils from the Rose in which a name was broken down into its Hebrew letters. A continuous line is drawn from one Hebrew letter to the next. Sigils drawn from the Rose are more practical to use than those drawn from traditional Kameas or Magickal Squares.)

The back of the Cross bears inscriptions in Latin: "The Master Jesus Christ, God and Man," between four Maltese Crosses which represent the Four Pyramids of the Elements opened out.

This is placed at the uppermost part because therein is affirmed a Descent of the Divine Force into Tiphareth, which is the central point between Supernals and Inferiors.

But at the lowest part is written the motto of the Zelator Adeptus Minor, because therein is the affirmation of the elevation of the Human into the Divine. But this is impossible without the assistance of the Divine Spirit from Kether, whence the space above Malkuth is white upon the front aspect of the Cross, white being the Symbol of the Spiritual rescued from the Material.

In the center is written in Latin between the Symbols of the Alchemical Principles, of which the outermost is Sulphur, the Purgatorial Fire of Suffering and Self-Sacrifice, "Blessed be the Lord our God who hath given us the Symbol Signum." And this is a word of six letters, representing the six Creative Periods in the Universe.

Materials Needed

Many Magicians make this lamen out of heavy cardboard which is then painted in the appropriate colors. However, we have always preferred lamens which have a sculptured, three-dimensional appearance. The Rose Cross described here has the feel and solidity of a truly powerful magickal implement. The colors must be clear and brilliant. If they are not, the symbol is useless either as a symbol or insignium. This is another reason why the exact acrylic colors listed in the introduction should be used.

One 6" square piece of pine, bass or plywood that is 1/2" or 3/8" thick
One small piece of 1/8" thick basswood
Yellow carpenter's glue
Wood putty
Gesso

Acrylic paints: red, orange, yellow, green, blue, blue-violet, violet,
    red-violet, black, white, iridescent gold
Sealant: clear lacquer finish

Tools Needed
    Jigsaw or scroll saw
    Craft knife with wood carving blade
    Sandpaper—medium and fine
    Artist's brushes—medium to very fine

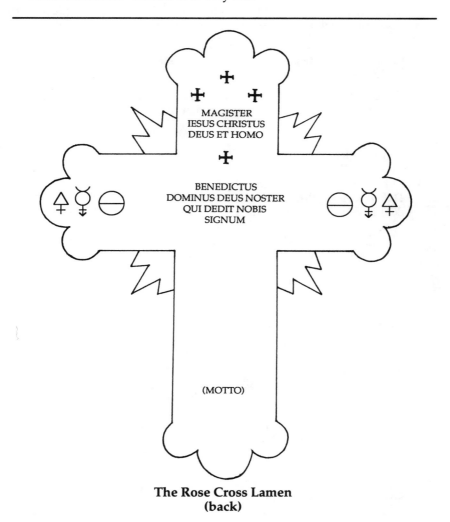

The Rose Cross Lamen
(back)

Construction

1) Trace the Cross portion of the Lamen onto the 6" sq. piece of pine or plywood. Make it slightly larger than the Cross shown in the diagram. Trace the four glories separately on the 1/8" basswood. Trace the circle for the rose on the 1/8" basswood.

2) Cut out all sections of the Lamen.

3) Glue the four glories to the cross at the junction of the arms. Let dry. Fill in any gaps with wood putty. Sand, apply a coat of gesso and allow to dry. Sand and add another coat if needed.

4) Trace three rows of petals onto the circular rose section. (Be sure to draw the small rose cross in the center as well.)

5) Using the knife with carving blade, gouge out a slight depression in the center of each rose petal. (When finished the rose section should have a 3-dimensional look.)

6) Cover the front part of the rose with a coat of gesso. Let dry. Apply glue to the back of the rose and attach to the Cross. Allow to dry.

Finishing Steps

7) Paint the Rose Cross in the following colors:
   RIGHT ARM—blue with orange symbols
   LEFT ARM—red with green symbols
   TOP ARM—yellow with violet symbols
   BOTTOM ARM—top part: white with black symbols, bottom
       part: Citrine, Olive, Russet, and black with white symbols.
   CENTER OF THE ROSE: Gold Cross with green glories and a
       red rose of five petals in the center. Background circle of
       white.
   THE PETALS OF THE ROSE:
   ALEPH—yellow ground, violet letter
   BETH—yellow ground, violet letter
   GIMEL—blue ground, orange letter
   DALETH—-green ground, red letter
   HEH—red ground, green letter
   VAV—red-orange ground, blue-green letter
   ZAYIN—orange ground, blue letter
   CHETH—yellow-orange ground, blue-violet letter
   TETH—yellow ground, violet letter
   YOD—yellow-green ground, red-violet letter
   KAPH—violet ground, yellow letter
   LAMED—green ground, red letter
   MEM—blue ground, orange letter
   NUN—blue-green ground, red-orange letter
   SAMEKH—blue ground, orange letter
   AYIN—blue-violet ground, yellow-orange letter

PEH—red ground, green letter
TZADDI—violet ground, yellow letter
QOPH—red-violet ground, yellow-green letter
RESH—orange ground, blue letter
SHIN—red ground, green letter
TAU—blue-violet ground, yellow-orange letter

8) The back of the Cross, as well as the four glories, are to be painted white with black letters. The sides of the lamen may be painted either gold or the colors of the arms.

9) Once the painted Rose Cross is dry, apply a coat of sealant for protection. When completely dry, a small piece of velcro can be glued to the back of the Cross which will attach to a yellow collar similar to the one described in chapter 1.

Ritual for Use

Consecration of the Rose Cross

Arrange a central Altar draped in black. Place upon it the Triangle and Cross as in the Neophyte Grade. Also place on the Altar the rose, cup, salt and fire; but place the cup between Cross and Triangle as in the Repast of the Four Elements from the 0=0 grade. The Adept should be dressed in the regalia of the Second Order. Incense and a second cup of water should be placed in the South and North part of the Temple respectively. The consecrated Lotus Wand should be near at hand. This ritual is an elaborated version of the Consecration of the Rose Cross given in Regardie's *The Golden Dawn*.

Place the new Rose Cross upon the Triangle.

Take up the Lotus Wand by the black band. Go to the Northeast of the Temple and say, "HEKAS, HEKAS, ESTI BEBELOI!"

Perform the LBRP. (Hold the white portion and keep the flower upright for the Qabalistic Cross. When tracing the pentagrams, grasp the Wand by the white band and point with the black end.)

Perform the BRH.

Place the wand upon the Altar, Lotus facing east.

Purify the chamber with water in the four quarters, tracing the Cross and the Invoking Water Triangle. Repeat the words: "So therefore first the Priest who governeth the Works of Fire must sprinkle with the Lustral Waters of the loud resounding Sea."

Consecrate the chamber with Fire in the four quarters, tracing the Cross and the Invoking Fire Triangle. Repeat the words: "And when after all the phantoms are banished, thou shalt see that Holy and Formless Fire, that Fire which darts and flashes through the hidden depths of the Universe, hear thou the voice of Fire."

Take up the wand by the white band. Circumambulate deosil three times.

Return to the west of the Altar and repeat the Adoration to the Lord of the Universe:

"Holy art Thou, Lord of the Universe!"
"Holy art Thou, whom Nature hath not formed."
"Holy art Thou, the Vast and the Mighty One."
"Lord of the Light and of the Darkness."

Give the Projection Sign at each adoration, and the Sign of Silence at the close.

Go the East and perform the complete Supreme Invoking Ritual of the Pentagram. Hold the white portion of the Lotus Wand when performing the Qabalistic Cross. Grasp the Kerubic bands of the Wand when invoking each Element: Violet—Aquarius band for Air, Yellow—Leo for Fire, Blue-green—Scorpio for Water, and Red-orange—Taurus for Earth.

Go to the west of the Altar and stand facing east. Hold the Lotus Wand by the white band. Make over the Rose Cross in the Air as if standing on the center of the Rose, the symbol of the Circle and Cross. Invoke all the Divine and Angelic Names of Tiphareth by one or the other of the following passages:

O Thou most sublime Majesty on High, who art at certain seasons worthily represented by the glorious Sun of Tiphareth, I beseech Thee to bestow upon this symbol of the Rose and the Cross, which I have formed to Thy honor, and for the furtherance of the Great Work, in a spirit of purity and love, the most excellent virtues, by the Divine Name of YHVH, and the great name of YHVH

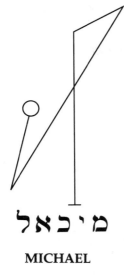

MICHAEL

ELOAH VE DAATH. Deign I beseech Thee to grant that the Great Archangel RAPHAEL, and the Mighty Angel MICHAEL may strengthen this emblem, and through the sphere of the splendid Orb of Shemesh may confer upon it such Power and Virtue, as to lead me by it towards the solution of the Great Secret.

(Alternative:) O Thou Most Glorious Light which lighteneth every being who cometh into the world. Thou who art in due season shadowed forth by Tiphareth, the Sun of Beauty, I implore Thee to direct Thy Light upon this symbol of the Rose and Cross which I have fashioned in Thine Honor and for the furtherance of the Great Work. By the Divine Name YHVH, by Thy Name of Wisdom YHVH ELOAH VE DAATH, permit I beseech Thee Thy shining Archangel RAPHAEL, and Thy Strong Angel MICHAEL, so to influence this emblem that it may be mighty for all good so that through the glorious sphere of Shemesh they may bestow upon it such power that in wearing it, I may at length lose and so find myself in that Ineffable Light which I most humbly seek.

Raise the hands and eyes skyward during the prayer, lowering them as you finish it.

Repeat from Genesis, "And a River, Nahar, went forth out of Eden to water the Garden, and from thence it was parted and came into four heads."

Describe over the white portion of the Rose Cross a circle and then the Greater Invoking Hexagrams of the Planets, as if standing upon it, repeating the necessary names, holding the Wand by the portion representing either the day or night house of the planet.

(Note: Begin with the Hexagram of Saturn holding the wand by either violet—Aquarius [day house] or blue-violet—Capricorn [night house] vibrating "ARARITA," "YHVH ELOHIM" and "ALEPH.") Then follow:

Jupiter: "ARARITA," "EL" and "RESH" (Sagittarius—day or Pisces—night)

Mars: "ARARITA," "ELOHIM GIBOR" and "ALEPH" (Aries—day or Scorpio—night)

Venus: "ARARITA," "YHVH TZABAOTH," and "YOD" (Libra—day or Taurus—night)

Mercury: "ARARITA," "ELOHIM TZABAOTH," and "TAU" (Gemini—day or Virgo—night)

Luna: "ARARITA," "SHADDI EL CHAI" and "ALEPH" (Hold Wand by Cancer band only)

For Sol trace the six Invoking Hexagrams as before, but hold the Wand by the yellow (Leo) band and draw the solar symbol in the center of each. Intone the names: "ARARITA," "YHVH ELOAH VE DAATH" and "RESH."

Hold the Lotus Wand by the white portion. Describe the Equilibriating Pentagrams of Spirit Active and Spirit Passive along with their Spirit symbols: First trace a circle over the Lamen. Then draw the Invoking Pentagram of Spirit Active, vibrating "EXARP" and "EHEIEH." Trace the Invoking Pentagram of Spirit Passive and intone "HCOMA" and "AGLA." Draw the

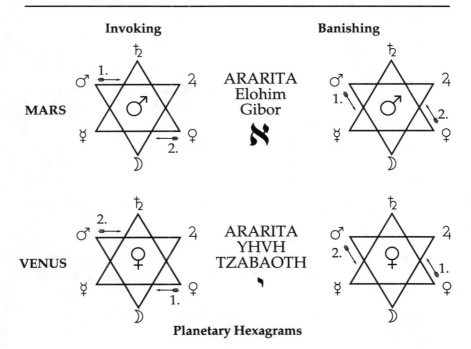

Planetary Hexagrams

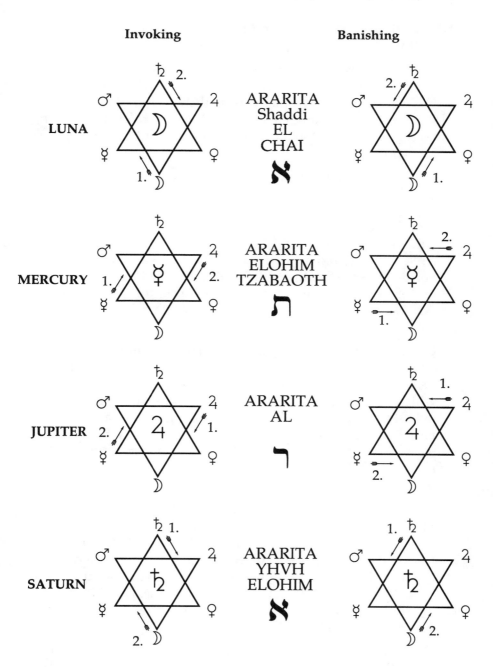

Invoking   **Banishing**

LUNA

ARARITA
Shaddi
EL
CHAI

א

MERCURY

ARARITA
ELOHIM
TZABAOTH

ה

JUPITER

ARARITA
AL

ר

SATURN

ARARITA
YHVH
ELOHIM

א

Planetary Hexagrams

same figure again and vibrate "NANTA" and "AGLA." Trace the Invoking Pentagram of Spirit Active and vibrate "BITOM" and "EHEIEH."

Then over the four colored arms in turn describe the Invoking Pentagrams of each Element, using the words and grade signs. Repeat the verse from Genesis II, 13, 14, 15, referring to each, holding the Lotus Wand by the Kerubic band of the Element (as follows):

Grasp the wand by the yellow (Leo) band and hold the flower end over the red Fire arm of the Cross. Say: "And the Name of the First River is Pison, it is that which compasseth the whole land of Havilah, where there is gold. And the gold of that land is good. There is Bdellium and the Onyx stone." Trace a circle over the red arm and draw the Invoking Pentagram of Spirit Active, vibrating "BITOM" and "EHEIEH." Give the LVX Signs. Trace the Invoking Pentagram of Fire, vibrating "OIP TEAA PEDOCE" and "ELOHIM." Give the Philosophus Sign.

Grasp the wand by the blue-green (Scorpio) band and hold the flower end of the Wand over the blue arm of the Cross. Say: "And the Name of the Second River is Gihon, the same as that which compasseth the whole land of Ethiopia." Trace a circle over the blue arm and draw the Invoking Pentagram of Spirit Passive, vibrating "HCOMA" and "AGLA." Give the LVX Signs. Trace the Invoking Pentagram of Water, vibrating the names "EMPEH ARSEL GAIOL" and "AL." Give the Practicus Sign.

Grasp the wand by the violet (Aquarius) band and hold the Lotus flower over the yellow arm of the cross. Say: "And the Name of the Third River is Hiddekel, that is it which goeth forth to the East of Assyria." Trace a circle over the yellow arm and draw the Invoking Pentagram of Spirit Active, vibrating the names "EXARP" and "EHEIEH." Give the LVX Signs. Trace the Invoking Pentagram of Air, intoning the names, "ORO IBAH AOZPI" and "YHVH." Give the Theoricus Sign.

Grasp the wand by the red-orange (Taurus) band and hold the Lotus flower over the dark Earthy arm of the Cross. Say: "And the Fourth River is Euphrates." Trace a circle over the arm and draw the Invoking Pentagram of Spirit Passive, vibrating the names, "NANTA" and "AGLA." Give the LVX Signs. Trace the Invoking Pentagram of Earth, intoning the names, "EMOR DIAL HECTEGA" and "ADONAI." Give the Zelator Sign.

Hold the wand by the white part and trace a circle from left to right over the outermost Twelve Petals of the Rose, and vibrate the name, "ADONAI."

Trace a circle over the seven middle Petals of the Rose and intone "ARARITA."

Trace a circle over the Three innermost Petals and vibrate, "YHVH."

Draw a perpendicular line from top to bottom and say: "EHEIEH."

Trace a horizontal line from left to right and say: "ELOHIM."

Wrap the newly consecrated Rose Cross in white silk or linen.

Purify and consecrate the Temple with Water and Fire as in the beginning.

Perform the Reverse Circumambulation three times counter-clockwise.

Stand west of the Altar and face east. Say, "I now release any Spirits that may have been imprisoned by this ceremony. Depart in peace to your abodes and habitations. Go with the blessings of YEHESHUAH YEHOVASHAH."

Perform the LBRP.

Perform the BRH.

Say, "I now declare this Temple duly closed."

SO MOTE IT BE

A Ritual for Use

A Rite of Healing

This ritual employs the healing qualities of Tiphareth as embodied in the Rose Cross Lamen, in order to restore the health and vitality of another person.

The Temple should be arranged in accordance with the Neophyte Hall. Water and Fire (incense) should be placed in the North and South. The Adept should be dressed in the regalia of the Second Order, and should wear his/her newly consecrated Rose Cross Lamen.

Relax. When ready to begin, give five knocks.

Take up the Lotus Wand by the black end. Go to the Northeast and proclaim, "HEKAS, HEKAS, ESTE BEBELOI! Far from this sacred place be the profane!"

Go to the East. Grasp the Lotus Wand by the white portion and point with the black. Perform the LBRP.

Take up the cup. Purify the Temple with Water in all quarters, starting in the East by drawing the Cross and Invoking Water Triangle. Say: "The Rivers have raised, O Tetragrammaton! The Rivers have raised their sound. The Rivers keep raising their pounding. Above the sounds of vast waters, the majestic breaking waves of the sea, AL is majestic in the Height!"

Replace the cup. Take up the incense. Consecrate the Temple with Fire in all quarters, by tracing the Cross and the Invoking Fire Triangle. Say, "Adonai hath built his chambers with beams in the very Waters. Making the clouds his chariot, walking upon the wings of the Wind. Making his angels spirits, His ministers a devouring Fire!"

Replace incense. Circumambulate the Temple three times with Sol, saluting with the Neophyte Signs when passing the East.

Stand west of the Altar and face east. Perform the Adoration to the Lord of the Universe.

Perform the Rose Cross Ritual (described in chapter 6). After you have established the six crosses in the room, do not immediately perform the Analysis of the Keyword, but instead project an astral image of the person you intend to heal in the center of the room. Send a healing thought ray from your Tiphareth Center, through the Rose Cross Lamen, to the image of the person. Bring forth a red ray from Geburah to Tiphareth through the Lamen, and project it at the source of ailment or infection. Visualize this ray purging the illness from the body of the stricken individual. When this is accomplished, project a healing rose pink ray from Tiphareth itself, to mend and restore the person to good health.

Give the Projection Sign at the Astral figure and intone "EHEIEH" employing the Vibratory Formula of the Middle Pillar. As you do so imagine the petal of the Hebrew Letter Kaph being sent forth from the Rose on your lamen. Empowered by the rose ray of Tiphareth it ascends to the Kether Center of the Astral form. Once this happens the sphere turns brilliant white. Give the Sign of Silence.

Again give the Sign of the Enterer at the figure and intone "YHVH ELOHIM" using the Vibratory Formula. Visualize the petal of the Hebrew letter Beth going forth from your lamen on the rose ray of Tiphareth. See it enter the Daath center of the Astral Form. Once this occurs, the sphere becomes white-grey. Give the Sign of Silence.

Project again at the figure, and intone the name "YHVH ELOAH VE-DAATH." See the petal of the Hebrew letter Tau rise from the lamen and travel along the rose pink ray. Imagine it being absorbed into the Tiphareth center of the astral figure. Once this happens, the sphere becomes golden-yellow. Give the Sign of Silence.

Project again at the figure, and vibrate the name, "SHADDAI EL CHAI." See the Yod-petal lift off your lamen to journey along the rose pink ray until it is absorbed into the Yesod Center of the figure. When thiscoccurs, the sphere changes to bright violet. Give the Sign of Silence.

Project for the last time, and intone the name, "ADONAI HA-ARETZ." Visualize the petal of the letter Mem traversing the rose ray to the Malkuth Center of the Astral form. When this happens, the sphere takes on the four colors of Malkuth. Give the Sign of Silence.

Imagine the astral form of the person completely cured and revitalized by the healing energies of the Reconciling Pillar you have invoked. See the form as strong, active and full of life. Visualize the shining Archangel Raphael standing over the person, holding the Caduceus Wand over the crown of the individual's head. At this point withdraw the rose pink ray back into your Tiphareth center.

Finally perform the Analysis of the Keyword as given at the end of the Rose Cross Ritual. At the words, "Let the Divine Light Descend!" visualize the brilliant white Supernal Light bathing the astral form of the person, providing a spiritual healing as well as a physical one. Repeat the invocation: "Come Thou, in the Power of Light! Come Thou, in the Light of Wisdom! Come Thou, in the Mercy of the Light! The Light hath Healing in its Wings!" Contemplate the healing Light about the figure for a some time, circulating the pure energy in ribbons and spiral bands which serve to strengthen the aura of the person.

When finished, say to the figure, "Go thou to the living being of whom thou art a reflection. Take with thee strength, vitality and health. Return with the blessings of YEHESHUAH YEHOVASHAH!" Trace the Rose Cross before the figure and send it to the individual. Perform the Qabalistic Cross.

Purify and consecrate the Temple as before.

Perform the reverse circumambulation, three times widdershins.

Perform the LBRP.

Say, "In the name of YEHESHUAH I now set free any spirits that may have been imprisoned by this ceremony."

Give five knocks as in the beginning.

Say, "I now declare this Temple duly closed."

SO MOTE IT BE

The Magick Sword

Use and Symbolism

The Magick Sword of the Z.A.M. is to be used in all cases where great force and strength are to be used and are required, but principally for banishing and for defence against evil forces. For this reason it is under the Presidency of Geburah and of Mars, whose Names and Forces are to be invoked at its consecration, which should take palace in the day and hour of Mars, or else during the course of the Fiery Tattwa.

Any convenient sword may be adapted to this use, but the handle, hilt, and guard must be such as to offer surfaces for inscriptions. It should be of medium length and weight.

The motto of the Adept should be engraved upon it, or upon the hilt in letters of green, in addition to the mystic devices and names. The hilt, pommel and guard are to be colored a flame red. The blade should be clean and bright. Pentagrams should be painted on salient portions, because this is the lineal figure of Geburah. The Divine and Angelic Names related to Geburah are then to be added in green, and also their sigils taken from the Rose. The Sword must be consecrated in due form.

Here again let the Zelator Adeptus Minor remember his Obligation never to use his knowledge of practical magick for purposes of Evil, and let him be well assured that if he do this, notwithstanding his pledge, the evil he endeavors to bring about will re-act on himself. He will experience in his own person and affairs that very thing he has endeavoured to bring about for another.

The sword is to be used with great respect only for banishings, protection and certain rituals (such as consecrations and evocations) where the Force of Geburah is needed to bar and to threaten.

Materials Needed

One 1-1/2" wide piece of flat steel that is 4' long and 1/8" thick
One 3/4" thick piece of pine or basswood approx. 9" x 6"
Three 1-1/2" wooden balls
Masking tape
A strong epoxy
Yellow carpenter's glue
A smooth piece of red leather
Gesso
Acrylic paint: red, green
Clear butyrate lacquer

Tools Needed
Vise
Jigsaw or hacksaw with metal cutting blade
Electric drill with 1/8" bit
Electric grinder (or drill with grinding wheel)
Coarse and fine emery paper
File
Coarse and fine Sandpaper
Craft knife
Artist's brushes—medium to fine

Construction: The Blade

1) Secure the flat steel in a vice. Using a jigsaw or hacksaw, cut one end of the piece of steel into a shank that is 1/4" wide and 4" long.

2) Using a grinding wheel with course emery paper, grind the other end of the steel down until both edges taper down to a point. Grind both edges of the blade as well (the edges do not have to be extremely sharp). Use a finer emery cloth for smoothing the steel where you have ground it down. Polish the blade and remove any rust spots. Apply a coat of clear butyrate lacquer to protect the steel and prevent rusting. Put aside to dry fully.

Construction: The Hilt

3) Take the 3/4" piece of wood and draw the pattern for the two pieces which comprise the handle, the guard and the grip. The guard should be 9" long and 1" wide at the center. (The double tips should flare out 2" tip to tip on either end.) The grip will be 6" long and 1" wide at the middle. Only one end has double tips which flare out 2".

4) Cut the two handle pieces out with the jigsaw.

5) Use coarse sandpaper to sand down all six tips on the ends of the two pieces until they are tapered points. (The guard of the sword is based upon two crescents placed back-to-back.)

6) Find the center of the top of the guard (on the 3/4" side—NOT the 1' front.) Mark with a pencil. Mark the center of the bottom as well. (This will be the side that butts up against the top of the blade.)

7) Secure the guard in a vise. Using a 1/8" bit, drill a hole through the mark you have drawn. You should now have a guard piece with a hole that runs through the center from top to bottom. Drill two holes close together in a straight line lengthwise from this hole in order to widen the original hole. (The extended hole should be wide enough to run the shank of the blade through it.) Use a small file inside the widened hole to even it out. Sand the entire piece with fine sandpaper.

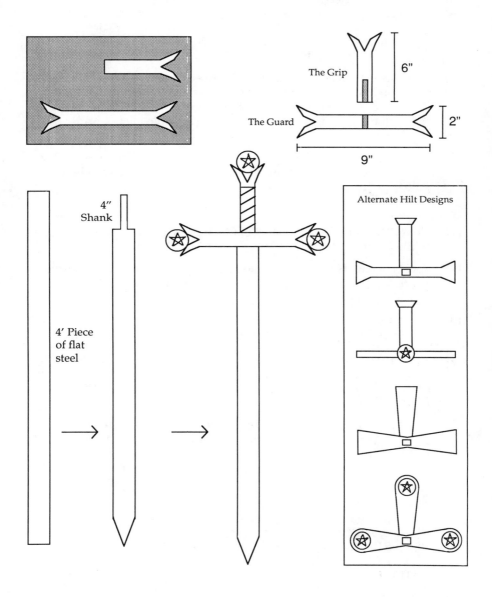

The Grip

The Guard

6"

2"

9"

4" Shank

4' Piece of flat steel

Alternate Hilt Designs

The Magick Sword

8) Secure the grip in the vise. Find the center of the end which has no tips. Drill a straight 1/8" hole into the end which is 4" deep. Drill a couple more holes as before to widen the original hole in order to fit the blade shank. Sand the entire piece with fine sandpaper.

9) Assemble the blade, guard and grip to see if all pieces fit well and are not crooked. Make adjustments if necessary. Then fill the holes of both handle pieces with a strong epoxy. Attach the shank of the blade through the guard piece and into the grip. Hold pieces firmly until the epoxy sets. Allow to dry fully.

10) Take one of the wooden balls and epoxy it into place between one set of double tips on the handle. Repeat with the other two wooden balls. Allow to dry.

Finishing Steps

11) Cover the top end of the steel blade with masking tape to protect it while painting the handle.

12) Apply a coat of gesso to the handle. Let dry. Sand. Apply another coat if needed. (Leave about 4" of the grip unpainted from the guard to just below the double tips . . . this part will be covered by leather.)

13) Paint the gesso-covered areas, including the wooden balls with acrylic red paint. Allow to dry. A second coat may be needed.

14) Cut the piece of red leather into a long strip that is 1-1/4" wide. Apply carpenter's glue to the unpainted area of the grip. Wrap the leather in an even spiral around the grip. Trim off excess leather with the craft knife. Allow to dry.

15) Paint pentagrams on both sides of the wooden balls in green. Also paint in green the following Hebrew names and sigils on all sides of the guard:

GOD NAME: Elohim Gibor (ALHIM GBOR)
ARCHANGEL: Kamael (KMAL)
ANGELS: Seraphim (ShRPhIM)
PLANET: Madim (MDIM) Mars
PLANETARY ANGEL: Zamael (ZMAL)
PLANETARY INTELLIGENCE: Graphiel (GRAPhIAL)
PLANETARY SPIRIT: Bartzabel (BRTzBAL)
MOTTO

16) After all paint has dried, coat the handle with a clear lacquer finish for protection. Let dry. Remove masking tape from blade.

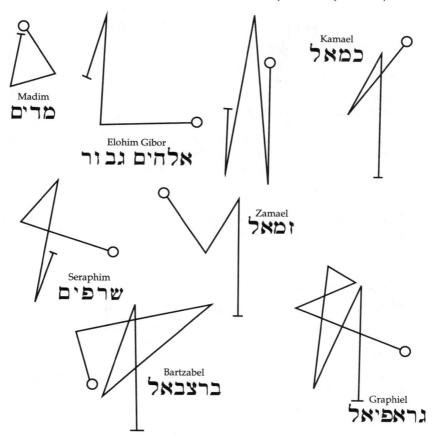

Sigils and Hebrew Names for Construction of the Magick Sword

A Ritual for Use

Consecration Ritual of the Sword

The Temple is to be arranged in accordance with the Neophyte Hall. Upon the black Altar are to be placed the Red Cross and the White Triangle, rose and incense, cup and water, candle, platter of salt. The position of Mars is to be determined for the time of the ritual. The Adept is to be dressed in the regalia of the Second Order and should also wear the consecrated Rose Cross. The Magician might also choose to wear a red cloak/tabard and a red lamen. The Lotus Wand and the newly made sword should be close at hand. (This ritual is also found in Regardie's *The Golden Dawn*.)

Place the sword upon the Altar, hilt to the East near the incense, point toward the West near Water.

Take up the Lotus Wand by the black end.

Go to the Northeast of the Temple and say "HEKAS! HEKAS! ESTE BEBELOI!" Go the East.

Perform the LBRP. (When tracing the pentagrams grasp the wand by the white portion and point with the black. Keep the flower end upright for the Qabalistic Cross.)

Perform the BRH.

Take up the cup of water and purify the Temple in all four quarters (starting in the East) by tracing the Cross and the Invoking Water Triangle. Say, "So therefore first the Priest who governeth the works of Fire must sprinkle with the Lustral Waters of the loud, resounding sea."

Replace the cup. Take up the incense. Consecrate the Temple by tracing the Cross and the Invoking Fire Triangle in each quarter. Say, "And when after all the Phantoms are banished, thou shalt see that holy and formless Fire, that Fire which darts and flashes through the hidden depths of the Universe. Hear thou, the Voice of Fire!"

Replace the incense. Take up the wand by the white portion. Circumambulate with Sol three times, saluting in the East with the Neophyte Signs.

Return to the West and face east. Perform the Adoration to the Lord of the Universe:

"Holy art Thou, Lord of the Universe!"
"Holy art Thou, Whom Nature hath not formed!"
"Holy art Thou, the Vast and the Mighty One!"
"Lord of the Light and of the Darkness!"

Perform the Lesser Invoking Ritual of the Hexagram of Mars. (Hold the Wand by the white portion when giving the Qabalistic Cross—keeping the Lotus flower always upright. Then trace the four forms of the Lesser Mars Hexagram by holding either the red band [Aries—day house] or the blue-green band [Scorpio—night house]. Grasp the white portion of the wand when performing the Analysis of the Keyword.) (The Mars Hexagrams are shown in the section which describes the ritual of "An Invocation of Aries.")

Return to the west of the Altar.

Turn to face the direction in which you have found Mars to be— standing so that the Altar is between yourself and Mars.

Grasp the wand by the band that is attributed to the sign that Mars is in. Describe in the air the Invoking Pentagram of the sign that Mars happens to be in at the time of the ritual. (Trace the Invoking Pentagram of Spirit Active or Passive, depending upon the elemental affiliation of the sign. Point with the Flower end of the wand. Say the appropriate names and give the LVX signs.) Trace the Invoking Pentagram of the sign (determined by its elemental affinity), but instead of the Kerubic sigil in the center, trace the symbol of the sign itself. Say the appropriate names and give the grade sign.

Then trace the Invoking Hexagram of Mars (Greater form) holding the wand by the white band and pointing with the Lotus flower. Vibrate the names, "ARARITA," "ELO-HIM GIBOR" and "ALEPH" as you trace the figure and sigil.

Recite the following Invocation to the Powers of Geburah and the Forces of Mars, tracing the sigil of each as you read it:

O Mighty Power who governeth Geburah, Thou strong and terrible Divine ELOHIM GIBOR, I beseech Thee to bestow upon this Magick Sword Power and Might to slay the evil and weakness I may encounter. In the Fiery Sphere of MADIM, may it be welded and tempered to unswerving strength and fidelity. May Thy Great Archangel KAMAEL bestow upon me courage wherewith to use it aright and may The Powerful Angels of the Order of SERAPHIM scorch with their flames the feebleness of purpose which would hinder my search for the True Light."

Hold the wand by the white portion and point with the flower end. Then trace in the air, slowly above the sword, and as if standing upon it, a circle going from left to right. Then draw the Greater Invoking Hexagram of Mars and vibrate the appropriate Names.

Next trace over the sword the letters of the names used in the invocation and their several sigils. Put down the wand.

Take up the cup and purify the new sword with water, making

the Cross and Triangle over it.

Replace the cup and take up the incense. Consecrate the sword, making the Cross and Triangle over it.

Take up the new sword and perform with it the Lesser Invoking Ritual of the Hexagram of Mars (four forms).

Perform with the sword the Supreme Invoking Ritual of the Hexagram of Mars (the Greater Hexagram of Mars in all four quarters), vibrating "ARARITA" "ELOHIM GIBOR" and "ALEPH."

Lay the sword on the Altar.

Purify and consecrate the Temple as before.

Perform the Reverse circumambulation three times widdershins.

Go to the East and say, "I now release any spirits that may have been imprisoned by this ceremony. Go in peace to your abodes and habitations with the blessings of YEHESHUAH YEHOVASHAH."

Perform with the sword the BRH.

Perform the LBRP, concluding with the Qabalistic Prayer.

Wrap the sword in white or scarlet silk or linen. Let no other person touch it.

Say, "I now declare this Temple duly closed."

SO MOTE IT BE

Rituals for Use

Appropriate Rituals to perform with the Magick Sword would be the Lesser Banishing Ritual of the Pentagram, the Supreme Banishing Ritual of the Pentagram, and the Lesser Banishing Ritual of the Hexagram.

THE FOUR ELEMENTAL WEAPONS

These are the Tarot Symbols of the letters of the Divine Name YHVH, and of the elements, and have a certain bond and sympathy between them. So that even if only one is to be used, the others should be also present, even as each of the Four Elemental Tablets is divided in itself unto Four Lesser Angles representing the other three Elements bound together therewith in the same Tablet. Therefore also let the Z.A.M. remember that when he works with these forces he is as it were dealing with the Forces of the Letters of the Divine Name.

Each implement must be consecrated, and when this has been done, no one else must touch it.

The Earth Pentacle

Use and Symbolism

The pentacle is used by the Adept in all magickal workings of the nature of Earth, and is under the presidency of Heh Final, and of the "Pentacle of the Tarot." The Z.A.M. uses it in rituals where the spirits of the element of Earth are invoked.

The four quarters of the pentacle are painted in the Briah (Queen Scale) colors of Malkuth, alluding to the sub-quarters or sub-elements that exist within the make-up of the Tenth Sephirah. The Citrine Quarter is the Airy Part of Earth, formed from the mixture of orange and green (Hod and Netzach). Russet is the Fiery Part of Earth, formed from the mixture of orange and violet (Hod and Yesod). Olive is the Watery part of Earth, created from combining green and violet (Netzach and Yesod). Black is coarse, Earth of Earth, a combination of all the colors grounding in Malkuth. (Note: the colors of Malkuth in the Queen Scale have perplexed many people. Oftentimes citrine has been depicted in many books as being nearly yellow. However, if one follows the rules given above, orange and green will rarely yield the color yellow.)

The white edge and border of the pentacle allude to the necessity of Spirit which must ever guide the actions of Matter. The white Hexagram is a symbol of the Divine Union of opposites, the marriage of Fire and Water. It represents perfection, harmony, and reconciliation. Here it symbolizes the Divine Spirit equilibriating and binding together all four elements of Malkuth.

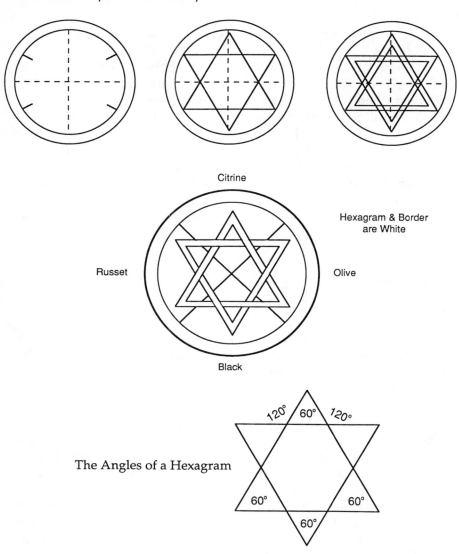

Citrine

Hexagram & Border
are White

Russet

Olive

Black

120° 60° 120°

The Angles of a Hexagram

60°   60°

60°

The Earth Pentacle

Materials Needed
A piece of soft wood (pine or bass) 1/2" thick and at least 5" x 5" wide
Wood putty
Gesso
Acrylic paint: white, black, orange, green, violet
Sealant: clear lacquer finish

Tools Needed
    Electric jigsaw or coping saw
    Compass, pencil and straightedge
    Artist's brushes—fine and medium sizes
    File or rasp
    Fine sandpaper

Construction
1) Using the compass, draw a 4-1/2"–5" circle on the piece of wood. Cut out circle with saw.

2) If disk has jagged edges, file them smooth. If there are any gaps or holes, fill them with wood putty.

3) Sand the disk until it is smooth. Paint entire disk with gesso. Let dry. Sand. Apply a second coat if needed, let dry and sand again.

Drawing the Hexagram
4) Find the center hole created by the compass point and draw a second, smaller circle 1/2" inside the edge of the disk. Lightly draw a cross from the center of the circle which divides it into four equal portions.

5) Divide the circle into six equal parts beginning at the intersection of the top of the circle and the vertical line of the cross. Draw lines which connect these points, forming the hexagram.

6) Draw a second set of lines approximately 1/4" inside the first. Divide the quarters created by the cross in half, thus creating a second diagonal cross which is to be painted in the Queen Scale colors of Malkuth.

7) Repeat steps 4-6 on the other side of the disk. (Try to align the hexagrams to matching positions on both sides.)

Applying the Colors
8) Using the medium and small artist's brushes, paint the pentacle, one side at a time, as follows:

    THE EDGE AND BORDER: White
    THE TOP QUARTER: Citrine—a mixture of orange & green
    THE LEFT QUARTER: Russet—a mixture of orange & violet
    THE RIGHT QUARTER: Olive—a mixture of green & violet
    THE BOTTOM QUARTER: Black
    THE HEXAGRAM: White

9) Allow the paint to dry thoroughly.

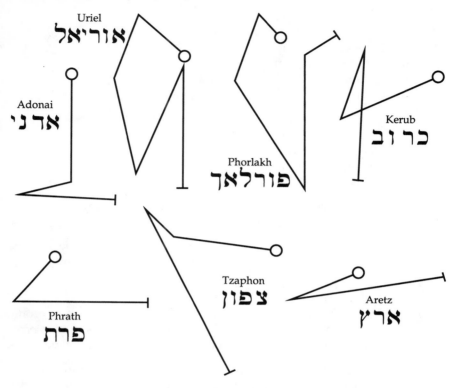

The Pentacle Inscriptions

Finishing Steps: The Inscriptions

10) Lightly trace with a pencil two circular guidelines on the white outer band. (These can be removed later with a kneaded eraser.) Within these guidelines trace the necessary inscriptions in Hebrew followed by the appropriate sigils.

GOD NAME: Adonai (ADNI)
ARCHANGEL: Uriel (AURIAL)
ANGEL: Phorlakh (PhORLAK)
RULER: Kerub (KRUB)
RIVER OF PARADISE: Phrath (PhRTh)
CARDINAL POINT: Tzaphon (TzPhON)—North
ELEMENT: Aretz (ARTz)—Earth
MOTTO:—Magician's Magickal Name

Using a fine-tipped brush, paint all these inscriptions in black on both sides of the pentacle. Allow to dry.

11) Spray or brush on a sealant to protect the finished pentacle.

The Air Dagger

The Air Dagger

Use and Symbolism

The Air Dagger is to be used by the Adept in all magickal workings of the element of Air, and under the presidency of Vav, and the "Sword of the Tarot."

Let there be no confusion between the Magick Sword and the Air Dagger. The Magick Sword is under Geburah and is for strength and defence. The Air Dagger is for Air, for Vav of YHVH, and is to be used with the three other Elemental Implements. They belong to different planes and any substitution of one for the other is harmful. In addition, the Air Dagger of the Z.A.M. is not to be used in rituals that call for a plain dagger, such as the Lesser Banishing Ritual of the Pentagram. For this, a dagger of no special design is required.

The dagger handle is yellow, the color assigned to elemental Air. The dagger can be likened to the tip of the spear, cast through the Air to hit its target.

Construction

For the Air Dagger of the Z.A.M. it is necessary to purchase a dagger with a 4"-6" long blade. For this implement the most important thing is that the handle be wide enough to paint the appropriate names and sigils on. However, if such a dagger is not forthcoming it is possible to re-work a short-handled dagger to the needed specifications.

If your dagger has a metal handle, use emery cloth or sandpaper on it to "rough up" the surface of the metal enough to hold the primer coat of paint. Also cover the blade with masking tape before you begin painting. Spray the handle with a primer coat. You may use yellow enamel paint only if it approximates the color of acrylic paint described in the introduction. When dry, remove the masking tape and allow the dagger to dry overnight.

One way of extending the handle of the dagger to a more appropriate size and shape is to use oven-hardening clay. Simply mold the clay over the handle into the desired shape and bake it in the oven following the directions for hardening the clay. (The Air Dagger with the T-shaped handle pictured in this book was constructed in this fashion.)

Another way to extend the handle is to remove the blade entirely from the old handle and mount it on a new one. Many inexpensive daggers are sold in flea markets for anywhere between

$4-$10. These daggers usually have a wooden grip between a brass guard and pommel. Secure the wooden shaft of the dagger in a pair of vice grips. Then take another pair of vise-grips or pliers and unscrew the brass pommel until it comes off. All the parts of the handle should come off once the pommel is removed, although you may require a hammer to loosen the various parts. All that will remain is the dagger blade with a metal shank sticking out the back. This entire operation should take no more than five minutes. A wooden handle like that of the Magick Sword (only smaller) can then be constructed and attached to the dagger blade.

　　Whichever of these methods you choose is unimportant. Once the prime coat or gesso has dried and been sanded, the entire handle should be painted with acrylic yellow.

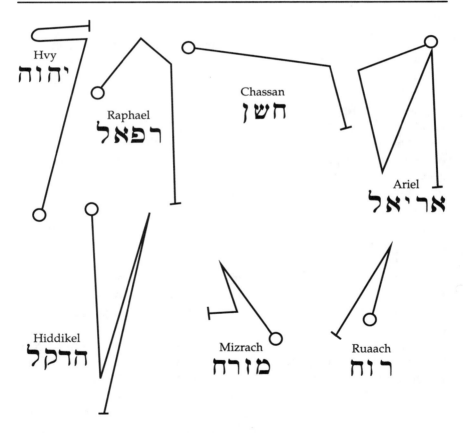

Sigils for the Air Dagger

Finishing Steps: The Inscriptions
Pencil in and then paint the following names in Hebrew along with their sigils upon the handle of the Air Dagger. Use acrylic violet paint for these names. (Note: In this case the yellow is the "ground" color, while the violet is the "charge.")

The names and sigils to be painted on the handle of the Air Dagger are as follows:

DIVINE NAME: YHVH (YHVH)
ARCHANGEL: Raphael (RPhAL)
ANGEL: Chassan (ChShN)
RULER: Ariel (ARIAL)
RIVER OF PARADISE: Hiddikel (HDQL)
CARDINAL POINT: Mizrach (MZRCh)—East
ELEMENT: RUACH (RUCh)—Air
MOTTO: —————————

When finished, let the paint dry. Then spray or brush on a sealant for protection of the paint.

The Water Cup
Use and Symbolism
The Water Cup is used by the Adept in all magickal workings of the nature of Water, and under the presidency of the letter Heh, and the "Cup of the Tarot."

This cup should not be confused with a separate chalice required for the Repast of the Four Elements. A plain chalice of this sort is symbolic of the heart center of Osiris (Tiphareth). The elaborate Water Cup of the Z.A.M. is to be used in rituals involving the elements.

Since the design of the Water Cup presented here is based upon the Cup of Stolistes, as referred to in the Practicus Grade, it partakes of the same symbolism. (Refer to the Admission Badge of the Grade of 3=8 in chapter 2.)

The Water Cup of the Z.A.M. is one implement whose construction seems to vary with the ingenuity of the magician making it. The Golden Dawn instructions suggest that any glass cup with a stem can be used, and paper petals attached. Although this method is the least satisfying, it appears to have been the most common method used to create the Cup. In our time there seem to be a large number of Magicians who are also talented artists and craftsmen.

Some have produced highly creative elemental weapons, which no doubt would have made 19th century magicians envious. One of the most beautiful implements made today is the traditional Water Cup formed from melted or slumped stained glass in the photo below.

Many Magicians have a way of finding a metal, ceramic or wooden cup that will work nicely for the elemental tool. (The top of the Cup should flare outward like a crocus flower.) One of the Water Cups shown in this book was made from a single piece of wood cut out on a lathe.

If a metal cup is used, smooth the surface to be painted with an emery cloth. The petals can be etched in using an electric cutting tool with a fine bit. Files and emery cloth with varying coarseness made be used. Apply masking tape over all areas of the Cup except the petals. Then spray the petals with a metal primer coat. Let the primer dry, then paint the petals with a brilliant enamel blue.

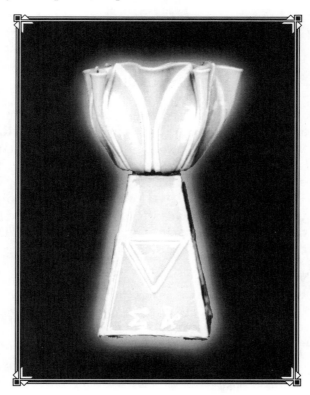

A Stained Glass Water Cup

A Water Chalice

If a suitable wooden cup is found, take off any varnish with a paint remover. The lines of the petals can be carved into the surface of the cup using a rotary tool and gouging bit. The entire cup should be painted with a prime coat of gesso and allowed to dry, before being painted with acrylic paint.

The type of cup that we have found most satisfactory for this implement is based upon the Cup of Stolistes as described in the 3=8 grade of Practicus. This form of the Cup is not as difficult to make as it might first appear.

Materials Needed

A plain wooden bowl, such as a sugar bowl, approx. 3-1/2" wide and 3" in height

One 8" square piece of basswood, 1/4" thick

3" square piece of basswood, 3/4" thick

One 1-1/2" wooden ball

Quick-setting epoxy

Grout or plaster of Paris

Wood putty

Gesso

Acrylic paints: blue and orange
Spar urethane for water-proofing

Tools Needed
Scroll saw or coping saw
Rotary power tool with carving wheel and gouging bit
Sandpaper—coarse and fine grained
Small chisel
Artist's brushes—medium and fine

Construction: The Bowl (Crescent)

1) Remove any varnish or finish from the bowl with paint remover.

2) If the bottom of the bowl is too shallow, cut a small circular piece of the 3/4" basswood to fit just over the bottom side of the bowl. (Optional) Make one side of it concave with the rotary tool.

3) Glue the concave side to the bottom of the bowl. Let dry. Sand the added-on piece of wood until it is rounded enough to look like the natural base of the bowl.

4) With the rotary tool and carving wheel, carve eight equal petals into the bowl so that the petals look as if they are raised off the surface of the vessel. (You may instead opt for gluing on petals that have been cut out of poster-board or cardboard.)

Construction: The Triangular Base

5) Take the 1/4" thick bass wood and cut out three triangles which are 3-3/4" wide at the base and 3" in height. (Note: the base needs to be wider than the height for support.)

6) On one side of all three triangles, sand the two edges (not the base) at an angle inward, giving you two mitred edges on the same side of each triangle.

7) Glue the mitred edges of all three triangles together to form a three-sided pyramid. (The mitred edges on the inside of the pyramid will insure that the figure will have three perfect seams.) Let the glue dry. Fill any gaps with wood putty.

Construction: The Ball (Circle)

8) Take the wooden ball and gouge out the top of it to form a concave area that will fit snugly against the base of the bowl. In the bottom of the wooden ball, chisel out a triangular hole that will fit snugly over the apex of the pyramid base.

9) Using a quick-setting epoxy, glue the ball onto the top of the pyramid. Be sure it is centered. Allow glue to harden.

10) Glue the bowl to the top of the ball. Be sure it is centered (Walk around the implement to check its straightness—the pyramidal base often causes optical illusions of bending.) Hold the bowl in place until the epoxy sets. Allow glue to harden.

11) Turn the cup upside-down and fill the pyramidal base with grout or plaster of Paris. This gives the bottom of the cup weight, to help balance the unusual design of the Implement. Let dry.

Finishing Steps
12) Paint the entire cup, inside and out with gesso. Let dry. Sand until smooth. Add a second coat if needed.

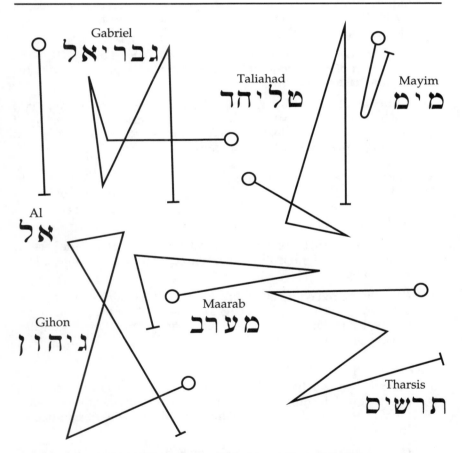

Sigils and Hebrew Letters for a Water Chalice

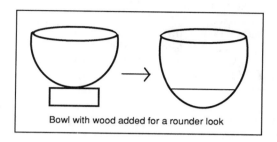

Bowl with wood added for a rounder look

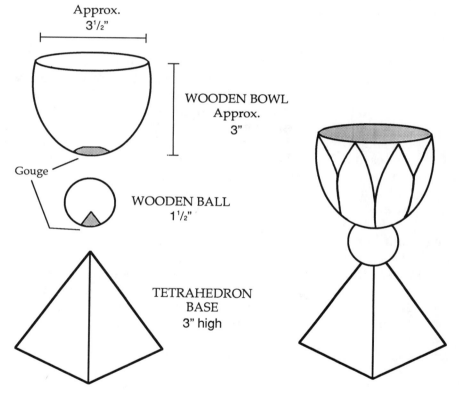

Approx.
3¹/₂"

WOODEN BOWL
Approx.
3"

Gouge

WOODEN BALL
1¹/₂"

TETRAHEDRON
BASE
3" high

The Water Cup

13)   Paint the petals of the cup with acrylic blue. The ball, base and inside
of the cup can be of a lighter blue. The edges of the petals, the Hebrew
names and sigils should be painted in orange. The inscriptions for the
Water Cup are as follows:

DIVINE NAME: EL (AL)
ARCHANGEL: Gabriel (GBRIAL)
ANGEL: Taliahad (TLIHD)
RULER: Tharsis (ThRShIS)
RIVER OF PARADISE: Gihon (GIHON)
CARDINAL POINT: Maarab (MAaRB)—West
ELEMENT: Mayim (MIM)—Water
MOTTO: ——————————————————

14) After all paint has dried, cover the entire cup with Spar Urethane to protect and water-proof the cup. Make certain that the inside of the cup is well coated. Allow to dry thoroughly.

The Fire Wand

Use and Symbolism

The Fire Wand of the Z.A.M. is used in all magickal workings of the nature of Fire and under the presidency of Yod and of the "Wand of the Tarot." It should not be used in anything other than a ritual which involves the elements.

The shape of the Wand is phallic—a cone mounted on a shaft. Cirlot states that the symbolism of the cone may be derived from the association of the circle with the triangle or pyramid. Some writers have stated that it is a solar symbol. In any event, the flaming yods painted around the cone firmly establish its Father/Fire energy. Since the Hebrew letter Yod also represents a sperm, the inseminating qualities of Fire are also stressed on this implement.

The Fire Wand is the most challenging of all the Elemental Weapons to construct. The problem it presents is that a magnetic wire must run through its center, end to end. The Golden Dawn manuscripts suggest making the Wand out of cane, which has a natural hollow running through it. The Wand shown in the photo was cut entirely on a lathe. Nowadays, it is possible to find a drill bit which is slender and twelve inches in length. Of course, drilling a hole straight through the center of a 10" long dowel is a feat worthy of a master craftsman. The dowel could be cut into three sections to make drilling easier, but it is still difficult. What is presented here is a far easier alternative.

Materials Needed

One 3/4" dowel that is 12" in length
One 1/16" diameter steel wire that is 15-3/4" in length
One 3" x 2" piece of soft wood (pine or bass)
Epoxy

Yellow carpenter's glue
Gesso
Acrylic paints: red, yellow, green
Wood putty
A 3" x 1" piece of leather that is approx. 1/8" or more in thickness
Sealant: clear lacquer finish

Tools Needed

Table saw
Two pieces of wood long enough to guide the dowel during cutting
Vise
Electric drill with 3/4" bit
Straight edge and craft knife
A strong magnet
File or rasp
Artist's brushes
Sandpaper

Construction: The Shaft

1) Set up the table saw so that only 3/8" of the blade is exposed. Set up the protective fence of the saw so that it is 3/8" away from the blade.

2) THIS IS IMPORTANT: Use the two pieces of wood to guide the dowel through the saw—never get your hands close to the saw blade. Use one piece to push the dowel from the bottom end lengthwise over the blade slowly. Use the other piece of wood to hold the dowel (from the side) against fence to guide it. DO NOT RUSH! Safety is the most important consideration here. You can always buy another dowel if your first effort is not satisfactory.

3) Using the wood, push the dowel lengthwise across the saw blade. The end result should be a dowel which has a 3/8" deep cut running its entire length.

Construction: The Cone

4) Reset the table saw so that the blade protrudes 1". Take the 3" x 2" long piece of soft wood and run it across the blade lengthwise using the two pieces of wood to guide it as before. You will end up with a piece of wood that has a 1" cut running through its 3" length.

5) Secure the piece of wood in a vice. At the exact center point of one end (easily found by the cut just made) drill a shallow hole approx. 1/8" deep using a 3/4" drill bit. (The end of the shaft will later fit snugly into this slight depression.)

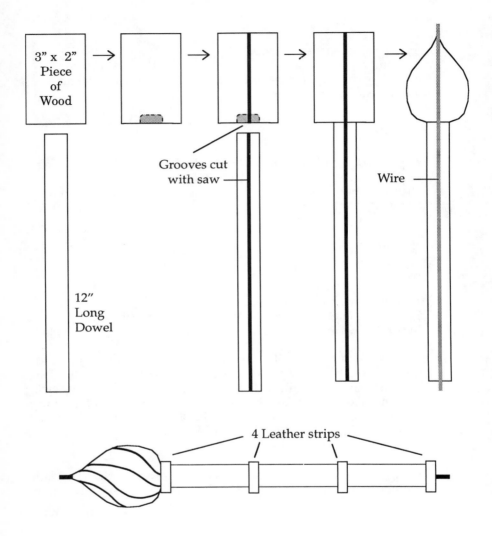

3" x 2"
Piece
of
Wood

12"
Long
Dowel

Grooves cut
with saw

Wire

4 Leather strips

The Fire Wand

6) With the wood still in the vice, shape its top end into the desired cone-shape using a rasp or file and sandpaper. Then turn the piece around so that you can round-off the bottom of the cone.

Construction: The Wire

7) Take the wire and repeatedly move a strong magnet across it in one direction only. When the wire is effectively magnetized, it should be

able to pick up a pin. The end which attracts the pin will be the end that sticks out of the cone-shaped head of the Wand.

8) Apply glue to one end of the shaft and secure into the 3/4" hole drilled into the bottom of the cone. Make sure that the grooves cut into both pieces are perfectly aligned. Let dry completely.

9) Place the wire into the groove of the shaft and cone so that the magnetized end of wire sticks out about 1/16" from the point of the cone. The wire should also stick out 1/16" from the bottom of the shaft.

10) Fill in the groove with wood putty. Let dry, then sand smooth so that the Wand appears never to have been cut at all.

Construction: The Bands

11) Take the piece of leather and cut it into four strips which are 3" long and 1/4" wide, using a straight edge and a craft knife.

12) Glue the underside of each strip and wrap around the wand shaft at intervals of approx. 3-5/8". (Trim off excess leather with the knife.)

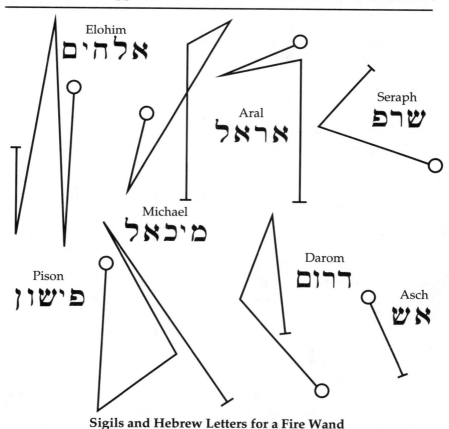

Sigils and Hebrew Letters for a Fire Wand

One strip will be directly under the cone, two will be in the central area of the shaft, and the fourth will be placed at the very bottom of the shaft. (Note: Construct wooden rings if desired, following the procedures given earlier in this book, though on a smaller scale.)

Finishing Steps

13) Fill in gaps with wood putty and let dry. Sand if needed. Cover entire wand with gesso and let dry. Sand, and add a second coat if needed.

14) Draw three wavy flame-shaped Yods at even lengths around the cone. Paint these Yods and the four bands in yellow.

15) Paint the remaining part of the cone and the shaft with red. Paint the following inscriptions on the red parts of the Wand (cone and shaft) in green. When all paint is dry, spray or brush on sealant.

> DIVINE NAME: Elohim (ALHIM)
> ARCHANGEL: Michael (MIKAL)
> ANGEL: Aral (ARAL)
> RULER: Seraph (ShRPh)
> RIVER OF PARADISE: Pison (PIShON)
> CARDINAL POINT: Darom (DROM) -South
> ELEMENT: Asch (ASh)—Fire
> MOTTO: —————————————

A Ritual for Use

Consecration Ritual for the Four Elemental Weapons

Part 1: The Opening

The Adept is to be dressed in the regalia of the Second Order. The Temple is to be arranged as in the 0=0 grade. On hand should be the Lotus Wand, Rose Cross Lamen and Magick Sword. All four newly made Elemental weapons should be on the Altar in their respective quarters, in addition to the Cross, Triangle, Tablet of Union, rose and incense, candle, cup of water, and platter of salt. The four Elemental tablets should be placed in their proper position around the room.

Each implement can be consecrated on different days or consecutively after 24-minute intervals between each consecration. Each weapon should be consecrated when the Tattwa of its specific Element is in course. (To find the Course of a Tattwa, note the time of Sunrise. Akasha always begins with sunrise and lasts 24 minutes, followed by Vayu—24 minutes, Tejas—24 minutes, Apas—24 minutes, and Prithivi—24 minutes.)

Each Elemental consecration is a separate ritual, although they may be done successively. The opening and closing of the ceremony do not have to be done more than once if all are consecrated on one occasion.

Prepare an Invocation to the King and Six Seniors of the Enochian Tablets for each Element. (Note: This Consecration Ritual is based upon the final version of the Tablets revealed to Dee and Kelly which are described in chapter 3. If you are using Enochian Tablets based upon the those described in the Stella Matutina manuscripts, use the Enochian Names provided in the Consecration Ceremony given in Regardie's, *The Golden Dawn*.)

Take up the Lotus Wand by the black portion. Go to the Northeast of the Temple and say: "HEKAS! HEKAS! ESTE BEBELOI!"

Put down the wand and take up the Magick Sword. Return to the East and perform the LBRP.

Lay down the sword and take up the cup. Purify the Temple in all quarters by tracing a cross and sprinkling thrice in the form of a Water Triangle. Say: "So therefore first the Priest who governeth the works of Fire must sprinkle with the Lustral Waters of the loud resounding sea!"

Replace the cup. Take up the incense. Consecrate the four quarters by tracing a cross and waving the incense thrice in the form of the Fire Triangle. Say: "And when after all the Phantoms are banished, thou shalt see that Holy and formless Fire, that Fire which darts and flashes through the hidden depths of the Universe. Hear thou, the Voice of Fire!"

Replace the incense. Take up the Lotus Wand by the white portion. Circumambulate with the Sun three times, giving the Neophyte Signs when passing the East.

Go to the west of the Altar and face East. Repeat the Adoration to the Lord of the Universe:

"Holy art Thou, Lord of the Universe!"
"Holy art Thou, whom Nature hath not formed!"
"Holy art Thou, the Vast and the Mighty One!"
"Lord of the Light and of the Darkness!"

Part 2: The Rite of Consecration

Varying with each implement on different days, or with 24-minute intervals between each commencement, according to Tattwas, perform the Supreme Invoking Ritual of the Pentagram (of the specific elemental required) with the Lotus Wand, holding it by the appropriate band of the Kerubic Figure: Red-orange Taurus for Earth, violet Aquarius band for Air, blue-green Scorpio for Water and yellow Leo band for Fire. (If the first implement is the pentacle, trace the Invoking Pentagram of Spirit Passive along with the Invoking Pentagram of Earth in ALL four quarters. The same rule applies to the other implements, all in accordance with the element required.) Be sure to always commence and close with the Qabalistic Cross, holding the wand by the white part.

Stand facing the Altar AND the quarter of the Element whose implement you are consecrating. Hold the wand by the appropriate Kerubic band as before. Trace in the Air over the implement, as if standing upon it, a circle followed by the appropriate Invoking Spirit Pentagram and the Invoking Pentagram of the Element.

Invoke by the following speech, the Divine and Angelic Names already painted upon the implement, making their Hebrew letters and sigils in the Air, over the Implement with the Lotus Wand:

FOR THE PENTACLE

O Thou, Who art from everlasting, Thou Who hast created all things, and doth clothe Thyself with the Forces of Nature as with a garment, by Thy Holy and Divine Name ADONAI whereby Thou art known especially in that quarter we name TZAPHON, the North. I beseech Thee to grant unto me strength and insight for my search after the Hidden Light and Wisdom."

I entreat Thee to cause Thy Wonderful Archangel URIEL, who governeth the works of Earth to guide me in the Pathway: and furthermore to direct Thine Angel PHORLAKH to watch over my footsteps therein. May the Ruler of Earth, the powerful Prince KERUB by the gracious permission of the Infinite Supreme, increase and strengthen the hidden forces and occult virtues of this Earth Pentacle, so that I may be enabled with it to perform aright those Magickal operations, for which it has been fashioned. For which purpose I now perform this mystic rite of Consecration in the Divine Presence of ADONAI!

Lay aside the Lotus Wand. Take up the sword and read the Invocation to the King, tracing in the Air the Invoking Pentagram of Earth. Say:

In the Three Great Secret Holy Names of God borne upon the Banners of the North, EMOR DIAL HECTEGA, I summon Thee, Thou Great King of the North, IC ZOD HEH CHAL, to attend upon this ceremony and by Thy presence increase its effect, whereby I do now consecrate this Magickal Pentacle. Confer upon it the utmost occult might and virtue of which Thou mayest judge it to be capable in all works of the nature of Earth so that in it I may find a strong defence and a powerful weapon wherewith to rule and direct the Spirits of the Elements.

Still with the sword, trace over the implement the Hexagram of Saturn, and read the Invocation to the Six Seniors:

Ye Mighty Princes of the Great Northern Quadrangle, I invoke you who art known to me by the honorable title, and position of rank, of Seniors. Hear my petition, oh ye mighty Princes, the Six Seniors of the Northern quarter of the Earth who bear the names of: LAIDROM. ALHCTGA. ACZINOR. AHMLICV. LZINOPO. LIIANSA. (Lah-ee-dah-roh-mee. Ah-el-heck-tay-gah. Ah-kah-zod-ee-noh-ray. Ah-hay-mee-lee-coh-vah. El-zod-ee-noh-poh. Lee-ee-ah-noo-sah.) And be this day present with me. Bestow upon this Earth Pentacle the Strength and purity whereof ye are Masters in the Elemental Forces which ye control; that its outward and material form may remain a true symbol of the inward and spiritual force.

Then read the Invocations of the Angels governing the Four Lesser angles of the Earth Tablet. (Note: we have found it highly effective to hold the implement in front of the Lesser Angle as it is being invoked.) For EACH angle, trace a circle, followed by an Invoking Spirit Passive Pentagram. Say the appropriate names and give the LVX Signs. Then draw the Invoking Pentagram of Earth. Say the appropriate names and give the Zelator Sign.

FOR THE LESSER ANGLE OF FIRE: Take up the Fire Wand and say: "O Thou Glorious Angel, NASMT (En-ah-ess-mee-tay), Thou who governest the Fiery essences of Earth, I invoke to Thee to bestow upon this Pentacle the Magick Powers of which thou art Sovereign, that by its help I may govern the Spirits of Whom Thou art Lord, in all seriousness and steadfastness." With the Fire Wand over the russet quarter of the pentacle, trace the circle and pentagrams mentioned above.

FOR THE LESSER ANGLE OF WATER: Take up the Water Cup and say: "O Thou Glorious Angel, NPHRA (En-pay-hay-rah), Thou who governest the moist and fluid essences of Earth, I invoke Thee to bestow upon this Pentacle the Magick Powers of which Thou art Sovereign that by its help I may govern the Spirits, of whom Thou art Lord, in all seriousness and steadfastness." With the Cup over the olive quarter of the pentacle, trace the circle, Invoking Spirit Passive, and Invoking Earth Pentagram as before.

FOR THE LESSER ANGLE OF AIR: Take up the Air Dagger and say: "O Thou Glorious Angel, NBOZA (En-boh-zod-ah), Thou who governest the Airy and Delicate Essence of the Earth, I invoke Thee to bestow upon this Pentacle the Magick Powers of which Thou art Master, that with its help I may govern the spirits of whom Thou art Lord, in all seriousness and steadfastness." With the Dagger over the citrine quarter, trace the figures mentioned above.

FOR THE LESSER ANGLE OF EARTH: Take up the Sword and say: "O Thou Glorious angel, NOCNC (En-oh-coh-noo-cah), Thou who governest the dense and solid Earth, I invoke Thee to bestow upon this Pentacle the Magick Powers of which Thou art Master, that with its help I may govern the spirits of whom Thou art Lord, in all seriousness and steadfastness." With the Sword over the black quarter, trace the figures mentioned above.

Take up the newly consecrated implement and perform with it the Supreme Invoking Ritual of the Pentagram of its Element in all four quarters. (Commence with the Qabalistic Cross, then trace the Invoking Spirit Passive Pentagram followed by the Invoking Earth Pentagram, while saying the appropriate names and giving the proper Signs. Draw these same figures in the East, South, West and North. Return to the East and invoke the Archangels. Finish with the Qabalistic Cross.) You may wish to recite the Prayer of the Gnomes (chapter 2).

FOR THE AIR DAGGER

O Thou, Who art from everlasting, Thou Who hast created all things, and doth clothe Thyself with the Forces of Nature as with a garment, by Thy Holy and Divine Name YHVH whereby Thou art known especially in that quarter we name MIZRACH, the East. I beseech Thee to grant unto me strength and insight for my search after the Hidden Light and Wisdom."

I entreat Thee to cause Thy Wonderful Archangel RAPHAEL, who governeth the works of Air to guide me in the Pathway: and furthermore to direct Thine Angel CHASSAN to watch over my footsteps therein. May the Ruler of Air, the powerful Prince ARIEL by the gracious permission of the Infinite Supreme, increase and strengthen the hidden forces and occult virtues of this Air Dagger, so that I may be enabled with it to perform aright those Magickal operations, for which it has been fashioned. For which purpose I now perform this mystic rite of Consecration in the Divine Presence of YHVH!

Lay aside the Lotus Wand. Take up the sword and read the Invocation to the King, tracing in the Air the Invoking Pentagram of Air. Say:

In the Three Great Secret Holy Names of God borne upon the Banners of the East, ORO IBAH AOZPI, I summon Thee, Thou Great King of the East, BATAIVAH, to attend upon this ceremony and by Thy presence increase its effect, whereby I do now consecrate this Magickal Dagger. Confer upon it the utmost occult might and virtue of which Thou mayest judge it to be capable in all works of the nature of Air so that in it I may find a strong defence and a powerful weapon wherewith to rule and direct the Spirits of the Elements.

Still with the sword, trace over the implement the Hexagram of Saturn, and read the Invocation to the Six Seniors:

Ye Mighty Princes of the Great Eastern Quadrangle, I invoke you who art known to me by the honorable title, and position of rank, of Seniors. Hear my petition, oh ye mighty Princes, the Six Seniors of the Eastern quarter of the Earth who bear the names of: HABIORO. AHAOZPI. AAOZAIF. AVTOTAR. HTMORDA. HIPOTGA. (Hah-bee-oh-roh. Ah-hah-oh-zoad-pee. Ah-ah-oh-zoad-ah-eef. Ah-vah-toh-tah-ray. Hay-tay-moh-ar-dah. Hay-ee-poh-tay-gah.) And be this day resent with me. Bestow upon this Air Dagger the Strength and purity whereof ye are Masters in the Elemental Forces which ye control; that its outward and material form may remain a true symbol of the inward and spiritual force.

Then read the Invocations of the Angels governing the Four Lesser angles of the Air Tablet. For EACH angle, trace a circle, followed by an Invoking Spirit Active Pentagram. Say the appropriate names and give the LVX Signs. Then draw the Invoking Pentagram of Air. Say the appropriate Air names and give the Theoricus Sign.

FOR THE LESSER ANGLE OF FIRE: Take up the Fire Wand and say: "O Thou Resplendent Angel, EXGSD (Ex-gee-ess-dah), Thou who governest the Fiery Realms of Air, I conjure Thee to confer upon this Dagger, Thy Mysterious and Magickal Powers, that I thereby may control the Spirits who serve Thee for such purposes as be pure and upright." With Fire Wand over the Dagger, trace the circle and pentagrams mentioned above.

FOR THE LESSER ANGLE OF WATER: Take up the Water Cup and say: "O Thou Resplendent Angel, EYTPA (Ay-ee-tay-pay-ah), Thou who governest the Realms of fluid Air, I conjure Thee to confer upon this Dagger Thy Mysterious Powers, that by its aid I may control the Spirits who serve Thee for such purposes as be pure and upright." With the Cup over the Dagger, trace the circle, Invoking Spirit Active, and Invoking Air Pentagram as before.

FOR THE LESSER ANGLE OF AIR: Take up the Sword and say: "O Thou Resplendent Angel, ERZLA (Ay-ray-zoad-lah), Thou who rulest the Realms of Pure and Permeating Air, I conjure Thee to confer upon this Dagger the Magick Powers of which Thou art Master, whereby I may control the Spirits who serve Thee, for such purposes as be pure and upright." With the Sword over the Dagger, trace the figures mentioned above.

FOR THE LESSER ANGLE OF EARTH: Take up the Pentacle and say: "O Thou Resplendent angel, ETNBR (Ay-tay-noo-bay-ray), Thou who rulest the Denser Realms of Air symbolized by the Lesser Angle of Earth, I conjure Thee to confer upon this Dagger the Magick Powers of which Thou art Master, whereby I may control the spirits who serve Thee, for such purposes as be pure and upright." With the Pentacle over the Dagger, trace the figures mentioned above.

Take up the newly consecrated implement and perform with it the Supreme Invoking Ritual of the Pentagram of its Element in all four quarters. (Commence with the Qabalistic Cross, then trace the Invoking Spirit Active Pentagram followed by the Invoking Air Pentagram, while saying the appropriate names and giving the proper Signs. Draw these same figures in the East, South, West and North. Return to the East and invoke the Archangels. Finish with the Qabalistic Cross.) You may choose to recite the Prayer of the Sylphs (chapter 2).

FOR THE WATER CUP

O Thou, Who art from everlasting, Thou Who hast created all things, and doth clothe Thyself with the Forces of Nature as with a garment, by Thy Holy and Divine Name EL whereby Thou art known especially in that quarter we name MAARAB, the West. I beseech Thee to grant unto me strength and insight for my search after the Hidden Light and Wisdom."

I entreat Thee to cause Thy Wonderful Archangel GABRIEL, who governeth the works of Air to guide me in the Pathway: and furthermore to direct Thine Angel TALIAHAD to watch over my footsteps therein. May the Ruler of Water, the powerful Prince THARSIS by the gracious permission of the Infinite Supreme, increase and strengthen the hidden forces and occult virtues of this Water Cup, so that I may be enabled with it to perform aright those Magickal operations, for which it has been fashioned. For which purpose I now perform this mystic rite of Consecration in the Divine Presence of EL!

Lay aside the Lotus Wand. Take up the sword and read the Invocation to the King, tracing in the Air the Invoking Pentagram of Water. Say:

In the Three Great Secret Holy Names of God borne upon the Banners of the West, EMPEH ARSEL GAIOL, I summon Thee, Thou Great King of the West, RA AGIOSEL, to attend upon this ceremony and by Thy presence increase its effect, whereby I do now consecrate this Magickal Chalice. Confer upon it the utmost occult might and virtue of which Thou mayest judge it to be capable in all works of the nature of Water so that in it I may find a strong defence and a powerful weapon wherewith to rule and direct the Spirits of the Elements.

Still with the sword, trace over the implement the Hexagram of Saturn, and read the Invocation to the Six Seniors:

Ye Mighty Princes of the Great Western Quadrangle, I invoke you who art known to me by the honorable title, and position of rank, of Seniors. Hear my petition, oh ye mighty Princes, the Six Seniors of the Western quarter of the Earth who bear the names of: LSRAHPM. SLGAIOL. SAIINOV. SONIZNT. LAOAXRP. LIGDISA. (El-ess-rah-hay-pay-mee. Ess-el-gah-ee-ol. Sah-ee-ee-noh-vah. Soh-nee-zoad-noo-tay. Lah-oh-ahx-ar-pay.) And be this day present with me. Bestow upon this Water Cup the Strength and purity whereof ye are Masters in the Elemental Forces which ye control; that its outward and material form may remain a true symbol of the inward and spiritual force."

Then read the Invocations of the Angels governing the Four Lesser angles of the Water Tablet. For EACH angle, trace a circle, followed by an Invoking Spirit Passive Pentagram. Say the appropriate names and give the LVX Signs. Then draw the Invoking Pentagram of Water. Say the appropriate Water names and give the Practicus Sign.

FOR THE LESSER ANGLE OF FIRE: Take up the Fire Wand and say: "O Thou Powerful Angel, HNLRX (Hay-noo-el-rex), Thou who art Lord and Ruler over the Fiery Waters, I beseech Thee to endue this Cup with the Magick Powers of which Thou art Lord, that I may with its aid direct the Spirits who serve Thee in purity and singleness of aim." With Fire Wand over the Chalice, trace the circle and pentagrams mentioned above.

FOR THE LESSER ANGLE OF WATER: Take up the Sword and say: "O Thou Powerful Angel, HTDIM (Hay-tay-dee-mee), Thou who art Lord and Ruler over the pure and fluid Element of Water, I beseech Thee to endue this Cup with the Magick Powers of which Thou art Lord, that I may with its aid direct the Spirits who serve Thee in purity and singleness of aim." With the Sword over the Cup, trace the circle, Invoking Spirit Passive, and Invoking Water Pentagram as before.

FOR THE LESSER ANGLE OF AIR: Take up the Air Dagger and say: "O Thou Powerful Angel, HTAAD (Hay-tay-ah-ah-dah), Thou who art Lord and Ruler of the Etheric and Airy qualities of Water, I beseech Thee to endue this Cup with the Magick Powers of which Thou art Lord, that I may with its aid direct the Spirits who serve Thee in purity and singleness of aim." With the Dagger over the Chalice, trace the figures mentioned above.

FOR THE LESSER ANGLE OF EARTH: Take up the Pentacle and say: "O Thou Powerful angel, HMAGL (Hay-mah-gee-el), Thou who art Lord and Ruler of the more dense and solid qualities of Water, I beseech Thee to endue this Cup with the Magick Powers of which Thou art Lord, that with its aid I may direct the Spirits who serve Thee in purity and singleness of aim." With the Pentacle over the Chalice, trace the figures mentioned above.

Take up the newly consecrated implement and perform with it the Supreme Invoking Ritual of the Pentagram of its Element in all four quarters. (Commence with the Qabalistic Cross, then trace the Invoking Spirit Passive Pentagram followed by the Invoking Water Pentagram, while saying the appropriate names and giving the proper Signs. Draw these same figures in the East, South, West and North. Return to the East and invoke the Archangels. Finish with the Qabalistic Cross.) You may choose to recite the Prayer of the Undines (chapter 2).

FOR THE FIRE WAND

O Thou, Who art from everlasting, Thou Who hast created all things, and doth clothe Thyself with the Forces of Nature as with a garment, by Thy Holy and Divine Name ELOHIM whereby Thou art known especially in that quarter we name DAROM, the South. I beseech Thee to grant unto me strength and insight for my search after the Hidden Light and Wisdom.

I entreat Thee to cause Thy Wonderful Archangel

MICHAEL, who governeth the works of Fire, to guide me in the Pathway: and furthermore to direct Thine Angel ARAL to watch over my footsteps therein. May the Ruler of Fire, the powerful Prince SERAPH by the gracious permission of the Infinite Supreme, increase and strengthen the hidden forces and occult virtues of this Fire Wand, so that I may be enabled with it to perform aright those Magickal operations, for which it has been fashioned. For which purpose I now perform this mystic rite of Consecration in the Divine Presence of ELOHIM!

Lay aside the Lotus Wand. Take up the sword and read the Invocation to the King, tracing in the Air the Invoking Pentagram of Fire. Say:

In the Three Great Secret Holy Names of God borne upon the Banners of the South, OIP TEAA PEDOCE, I summon Thee, Thou Great King of the South, EDEL PERNAA, to attend upon this ceremony and by Thy presence increase its effect, whereby I do now consecrate this Magickal Fire Wand. Confer upon it the utmost occult might and virtue of which Thou mayest judge it to be capable in all works of the nature of Fire so that in it I may find a strong defense and a powerful weapon wherewith to rule and direct the Spirits of the Elements.

Still with the sword, trace over the implement the Hexagram of Saturn, and read the Invocation to the Six Seniors:

Ye Mighty Princes of the Great Southern Quadrangle, I invoke you who art known to me by the honorable title, and position of rank, of Seniors. Hear my petition, oh ye mighty Princes, the Six Seniors of the Southern quarter of the Earth who bear the names of: AAETPIO. AAPDOCE. ADOEOET. ANODOIN. ALND-VOD. ARINNAP. (Ah-ah-ay-tay-pay-ee-oh. Ah-ah-pay-doh-kay. Ah-doh-ay-oh-ay-tay. Ah-noh-doh-ee-noo. Ahl-noo-dah-voh-dah. Ah-roh-ee-noo-nah-peh.) And be this day present with me. Bestow upon this Fire Wand the Strength and purity whereof ye are Masters in the Elemental Forces which ye control; that its outward and material form may remain a true symbol of the inward and spiritual force.

Then read the Invocations of the Angels governing the Four Lesser angles of the Fire Tablet. For EACH angle, trace a circle, followed by an Invoking Spirit Active Pentagram. Say the appropriate names and give the LVX Signs. Then draw the Invoking Pentagram of Fire. Say the appropriate names and give the Philosophus Sign.

FOR THE LESSER ANGLE OF FIRE: Take up the Sword and say: "O Thou Mighty Angel, BZIZA (Bah-zoad-ee-zoad-ah), Thou who art

Lord and President over the Four Angels of the Fiery Lesser Quadrangle of Fire, I invoke Thee to impress into this weapon the force and fiery energy of Thy Kingdom and Servants, that by it I may control them for all just and righteous purposes." With Sword over the Fire Wand, trace the circle and pentagrams mentioned above.

FOR THE LESSER ANGLE OF WATER: Take up the Cup and say: "O Thou Mighty Angel, BANAA (Bah-ahn-ah-ah), Thou who art Lord and President over the Four Angels of Fluid Fire, I beseech Thee to impress into this weapon Thy Magick Power that by it I may control the Spirits who serve Thee for all just and righteous purposes." With the Cup over the Wand, trace the circle, Invoking Spirit Active, and Invoking Fire Pentagram as before.

FOR THE LESSER ANGLE OF AIR: Take up the Air Dagger and say: "O Thou Mighty Angel, BDOPA (Bay-doh-pah), Thou who art Lord and President over the Four Angels and Governors of the subtle and aspiring Etheric Fire, I beseech Thee to bestow upon this weapon Thy strength and fiery steadfastness, that with it I may control the Spirits of Thy Realm for all just and righteous purposes." With the Dagger over the Wand, trace the figures mentioned above.

FOR THE LESSER ANGLE OF EARTH: Take up the Pentacle and say: O Thou Mighty angel, BPSAC (Bay-pay-sah-cah), Thou who art Lord and President over the Four Angels of the denser Fire of Earth, I beseech Thee to bestow upon this weapon Thy strength and fiery steadfastness that with it I may control the Spirits of Thy Realm for all just and righteous purposes." With the Pentacle over the Wand, trace the figures mentioned above.

Take up the newly consecrated implement and perform with it the Supreme Invoking Ritual of the Pentagram of its Element in all four quarters. (Commence with the Qabalistic Cross, then trace the Invoking Spirit Active Pentagram followed by the Invoking Fire Pentagram, while saying the appropriate names and giving the proper Signs. Draw these same figures in the East, South, West and North. Return to the East and invoke the Archangels. Finish with the Qabalistic Cross.) You may wish to recite the Prayer of the Salamanders (chapter 2).

Part 3: The Closing

When completed, each Elemental weapon is to be wrapped in silk or linen which is either white or the color of the implement.

Purify the Temple with water, exactly as in the beginning.

Consecrate the Temple with Fire, as at the Opening.

Perform the Reverse Circumambulation three times counter-clockwise.

Stand West of the Altar, facing East and say: "I now release any Spirits that may have been imprisoned by this ceremony. Depart in peace to your abodes and habitations. Go with the Blessings of YEHESHUAH YEHOVASHAH!"

Perform the LBRP. (Note: If you prefer, perform the Supreme Banishing Ritual of a specific element, if not all implements have been consecrated at the same ceremony.)

Say, "I now declare this Temple duly closed."

SO MOTE IT BE

Rituals for Use with the Four Elemental Weapons

The Pentacle: Invoking The Powers Of Earth

Part 1: The Opening

For this ritual, the Z.A.M. will need to arrange the hall according to the portal Temple, complete with Enochian tablets. Upon the Altar should be a rose, incense, candle, cup of water, platter of salt, and the Tablet of Union. In addition to this, the Elemental weapons should all be placed upon the Altar in their proper quarter. The Adept should be dressed in the full regalia of the Second Order, complete with Rose Cross lamen. The Magician will also need the Lotus Wand and the Magick Sword.

Relax for a short period of meditation.

Give five knocks.

Take up the Sword. Go to the Northwest of the Temple and say:

"HEKAS! HEKAS! ESTE BEBELOI!"

Perform with the sword the LBRP.

Take up the Cup of Water. Purify the Temple with Water by tracing the Cross and invoking Water Triangle in all quarters, starting in the East. Say, "Tetragrammaton has described a circle upon the face of the Waters." Replace the Chalice upon the Altar.

Take up the incense. Consecrate the Temple with Fire by tracing the Cross and Invoking Fire Triangle in all quarters, saying: "The Voice of Tetragrammaton draws out flames of Fire. From the heavens, Tetragrammaton spoke, that we might hear and receive illumination. And upon the Earth Tetragrammaton displayed unto us his great Fire. The Words of the Elohim were heard in the Fire." Replace the incense upon the Altar.

Take up the Lotus Wand. Perform with it the SIRP, holding the Kerubic band appropriate to each quarter.

Return to the West of the Altar and face East. Hold the Lotus Wand by the white portion and describe in the Air above the Tablet of Union as if standing upon it, a white circle. Then draw each of the Spirit Pentagrams of the four quarters along with their Spirit sigils and vibrate the Appropriate words: "EX-ARP—EHEIEH. HCOMA—AGLA. NANTA—AGLA. BITOM—EHEIEH." Then say, "In the names and letters of the mystical Tablet of Union, I invoke ye, ye Divine Forces of the Spirit of Life."

Make the sign of the Rending of the Veil: clasp hands together as if praying, then thrust them forward. Take a step forward with the left foot and separate the hands as if opening a curtain. Visualize the Veil as you step through it.

Remain west of the Altar, holding the white portion of the Lotus Wand. Trace a circle over the Tablet of Union as you repeat the First Enochian Key:

"Ol Sonuf Vorsag Goho Iad Balt. Lonsh Claz Vonpho Sobra Z-Ol Ror I Ta Nazps Od Graa Ta Malprg Ds Hol-Q Qaa Nothoa Zimz Od Commah Ta Nobloh Zien Soba Thil Gnonp Prge Aldi Ds Vrbs Oboleh G Rsam: Casarm Ohorela Taba Pir Ds Zonrensg Cab Erm Iadnah Pilah Farzm Znrza Adna Gono Iadpil Ds Hom Od Toh Saba Ipam Lu

Ipamis Ds Loholo Vep Zomd Poamal Od Bogpa Aai Ta Piap Piamol Od Vaoan. Zacare Eca Od Zamran: Odo Cicle Qaa Zorge Lap Zirdo Noco Mad Hoath Iaida."

Phonetic: (Oh-el Soh-noof Vay-oh-air-sah-jee Goh-hoh Ee-ah-dah Bal-tah, El-on-shee Kahl-zoad Von-pay-hoh: Soh-bay-rah Zoad-oh-lah Roh-ray Ee Tah Nan-zoad-pay-ess, Oh-dah Jee-rah-ah Tah Mahl-peer-jee: Dah-ess Hoh-el-koh Kah-ah No-thoh-ah Zoad-ee-mah-zoad Oh-dah Koh-mah-mah-kay Tah Noh-bloh-hay Zoad-ee-ay-noo So-bah Tah-hee-lah jee-noh-noo-pay Peer-jee Ahl-dee Dah-ess Ur-bass Oh-boh-lay Jee Rah-sah-may: Cahs-ar-may Oh-hor-ray-lah Tah-bah Peer Dah-es Zoad-oh-noo-ray-noo-sah-jee Kah-bah Air-may Ee-ad-nah. Pee-lah-hay Far-zoad-mee Zoad-noo-ray-zoad-ah Ahd-nah Goh-noh Ee-ah-dah-pee-el Oh-dah Vay-oh-ah-noo. Zoad-a-kah-ray Ay-kah Oh-dah Zoad-a-mer-ah-noo. Oh-dah Kee-clay Kah-ah. Zoad-or-jee Lah-pay Zoad-ee-ray-doh Noh-koh Mah-dah, Hoh-ah-tah-hay Ee-ah-ee-dah.)

(This translates as: "I reign over you Saith the God of Justice. In power exalted above the firmament of Wrath. In Whose hands the Sun is as a sword and the Moon as through-thrusting fire: Who measureth your garments in midst of my vestures and trussed you together as the palms of my hands: Whose seats I garnished with the fire of gathering: Who beautified your garments with admiration: To whom I made a law to govern the Holy Ones: Who delivered you a rod with the Ark of Knowledge. Moreover Ye lifted up your voices and swear obedience and faith to Him that liveth and triumpheth: Whose beginning is not nor end cannot be: which shineth as a flame in the midst of your palaces and reigneth amongst you as the balance of righteousness and truth. Move therefore and show yourselves: open the mysteries of your creation. Be friendly unto me. For I am the servant of the same your God, the true worshipper of the Highest.")

Trace a circle over the first letter "N" in the the third line of the Tablet as you repeat the Second Enochian Key:

"Adgt V Paah Zong Om Faaip Sald Vi-I-V-L Sobam Ial-Prg I-Za-Zaz Pi-Adph: Casarma Abramg Ta Talho Paracleda Q Ta Lorslq Turbs Ooge Baltoh. Givi Chis Lusd Orri Od Micalp Chis Bia Ozongon. Lap Noan Trof Cors Ta Ge O Q Manin Ia-Idon. Torzu Gohe L Zacar Eca C Noqod. Zamran Micalzo Od Ozazm Vrelp Lap Zir Io-Iad."

Phonetic: (Ahd-gee-tay Vah-pah-hay Zoad-oh-noo-jee Oh-mah Fah-ah-ee-pay, Vee-ee-vee-el Soh-bah-may Ee-ahl-peer-jee Ee-zoad-ah-zoad-ah-zoad Pee-ahd-pay-hay: Cah-sar-mah Ah-brahn-jee Tah-hoh Para-clay-dah, Koh-Tah Lor-es-sel-koh Toor-bay-ess Oh-oh-jee Bal-toh-hah. Jee-vee Kah-hee-sah Loos-dah Ohr-ree Oh-dah Mee-cal-pah Kah-hees-ah Bee-ah Oh-zoad-oh-noo-goh-noo. Lah-pay Noh-ah-noo Tro-eff Cor-say Tah Jee Oh Koh Mah-nee-no Ee-ah-ee-doh-noo. Tohr-zoad-oo Goh-hay El. Zoad-ah-kah-ray Ay-kah Kah Noh-Kwoh-dah. Zoad-ah-mer-ah-noo. Me-kah-el-zoad-oh Oh-dah Oh-zoad-ah-zoad-may Vod-rel-pay, Lah-pay Zoad-ee-ray Ee-oh Ee-ah-dah.)

(This translates as: "Can the Wings of the Wind Understand your voices of Wonder, O You the Second of the First, Whom the burning flames have framed within the depth of my jaws: Whom I have prepared as cups for a wedding or as the flowers in their beauty for the chamber of the Righteous. Stronger are your feet than the barren stone and mightier are your voices than the manifold winds. For ye are become a building such as is not save in the mind of the All-Powerful. Arise, saith the First. Move, therefore, unto thy servants. Show yourselves in power and make me a strong seer of things, for I am of Him that liveth forever.")

Say, "I invoke ye, ye Angelic guardians of the stellar Realms! Ye whose abode lies beyond the domain of the Visible Kingdom! Just as Ye are the stewards of the gates of the Universe, be ye also the defenders of this Magick Circle of Art! Protect this consecrated Temple from the profane and the unbalanced! Grant unto me the Strength, the Will and the Knowledge to perform this ceremony aright, that I might not degrade this sacred sphere. Let me prove myself to be a worthy vessel for the mysteries of the Spirit Divine! Anoint me with the Brilliant Light!"

Take up the Lotus Wand by the white part. Circumambulate the Temple thrice following the course of the Sun. Give the Neophyte Signs when passing the East.

Go to the west of the Altar and face east. Perform the Adoration to the Lord of the Universe:

"Holy art Thou, Lord of the Universe!"
"Holy art Thou, Whom Nature hath not formed!"
"Holy art Thou, the Vast and the Mighty One!"
"Lord of the Light and of the Darkness!"

Part 2: Invoking the Powers of Earth
Take up the Earth Pentacle. Go the East and raise the implement high. Say: "I adore Thee, Lord and King of Earth. ADONAI HA-ARETZ! ADONAI MELEKH! Unto Thee" (touch pentacle to the crown of the head) "...be ascribed the Kingdom" (touch the breast) "and the Power" (touch right shoulder) "and the glory" (touch left shoulder). "Malkuth, Geburah, Gedulah." (Trace the

circle and Cross toward the East at the word, Malkuth.) "The Rose of Sharon and the Lily of the Valley, Amen." Give the Zelator Sign.

Go to the North and face the Elemental Tablet there. With the pentacle, trace a circle in front of the Tablet. Then trace the Invoking Pentagram of Spirit Passive and vibrate the names "NANTA" and "AGLA." Give the LVX Signs. Trace the Invoking Pentagram of Earth and vibrate "EMOR DIAL HECTEGA" and "ADONAI." Give the Sign of the Zelator.

Say: "And the Elohim said, 'Let us make Adam in our Image, after our likeness and let them have dominion over the fish of the sea and over the fowl of the air and over every creeping thing that creepeth over the Earth.' And the Elohim created Eth ha-Adam in their own Image, in the Image of the Elohim created they them. In the name of Adonai Melekh and of the Bride and the Queen of the Kingdom, Spirits of Earth adore Adonai!"

Trace the sigil of Taurus in front of the Tablet with the Pentacle. Say, "In the Name of URIEL, the Great Archangel of Earth, and by the sign of the Head of the Ox, Spirits of Earth, adore Adonai!"

Trace a Cross and say, "In the Names and Letters of the Great Northern Quadrangle, and by the Three Great Secret Names of God, borne upon the Banners of the North—EMOR DIAL HEC-TEGA—Spirits of Earth, adore Adonai!"

Trace the Sigil of the Whirl and say, "In the name of IC ZOD HEH CHAL, Great King of the North, Spirits of Earth, adore Adonai!"

Recite the Fifth Enochian Key:

"Sapah Zimmi D U-I-V Od Noas Ta Qanis Adroch Dorphal Caosg Od Faonts Piripsol Ta Blior. Casarm A-M-Ipzi Nazarth AF Od Dlugar Zizop Zlida Caosgi Tol Torgi: Od Z Chis E Siasch L Ta-Vi-U Od Iaod Thild Ds Hubar P E O A L Soba Cormfa Chis Ta La Vls Od Q Cocasb. Eca Niis Od Darbs Qaas F Etharzi Od Bliora. Ia-Ial Ed-Nas Cicles. Bagle? Ge-Iad I L."

Phonetic: (Sah-pah-hay Zoad-ee-mee-ee Doo-ee-vay Oh-dah Noh-ahs Tay-ah Kah-nees Ah-droh-kay, Dor-pay-hal Kah-ohs-gah Oh-dah Fah-ohn-tay-ess Pee-reep-sol Tay-ah Blee-ohr. Kah-sar-may Ah-mee-eep-zoad-ee Nah-zoad-arth Ah-eff Oh-dah Dah-loo-gahr Zoad-

ee-zoad-oh-pay Zoad-lee-dah Kah-ohs-jee Toh Tor-jee: Oh-dah Zoad
Kah-hee-sah Ay See-ahs-kay Ayl Tah vee-oo Od-dah Ee-ah-oh-dah
Tay-heel-dah Dah-ess Hoo-bar Pay Ay Oh Ah El, Soh-bah Kohr-em-
fah Kah-hee-sah Tay-ah El-ah Vah-less Oh-dah Koh Koh-kahs-bay.
Ay-kah Nee-ee-sah Oh-dah Dahr-bay-ess Kah-ah-sah Eff Ay-thar-
zoad-ee Oh-dah Blee-ohr-ah. Ee-ah-ee-al-el Ehd-nahs Kee-klay-sah.
Bah-glay? Jee-ee-ah-dah Ee-el.)

(This translates as: "The mighty sounds have entered in the Third
Angle And are become as Olives in the Olive Mount, Looking with
gladness upon the Earth, and dwelling in the Brightness of the Heavens as continual comforters. Unto Whom I fastened 19 Pillars of Gladness and gave them Vessels to water the Earth with all her creatures:
And they are the brothers of the First and the Second, and the beginning of their own Seats which are garnished with 69636 continual
burning Lamps, whose numbers are as the First, the Ends, and the
Contents of Time. Therefore come ye and obey your creation. Visit us
in peace and comfort. Conclude us Receivers of your Mysteries, For
why? Our Lord and Master is the All One.")

Vibrate the name of "ADONAI" four times, using the Vibratory
Formula of the Middle Pillar.

Trace a Cross and Circle (Rose Cross) in front of the tablet with
the pentacle. Recite the following, making certain to vibrate the
Divine names and trace their sigils in the air with the pentacle:

In and by the name of ADONAI HA-ARETZ! ADONAI
MELEKH! And under the authority of URIEL, Great archangel
of the element of Earth, I command ye beings of the of the Great
Northern Quadrangle, from the quarter known as TZAPHON! I
summon all ye Archangels, Angels, Kings, Rulers and Elementals to be present at this ceremony. Grant unto me your powers
of solidity, completion and materialization! Grant that my
earthly and secular environment may be a stable one, devoid of
poverty, oppression and hardship that would cause any inter-
ference in my pursuit of the Hidden Wisdom, and my completion of the Great Work. To this end make manifest . . ." (Clearly
state here the purpose of the ritual—such as a project you wish
to see completed, etc.) "This I ask in all sincerity for such purposes as be pure and upright, and in compliance with my aspiration to the Divine."

Visualize your stated purpose or project reaching full manifestation, as if it had already materialized and you were merely
observing it. Take as much time as you need to complete the
meditation.

Part 3: The Closing

Go to the East of the Altar and perform the Qabalistic Cross. Repeat the words also in English saying: "Unto Thee, O Tetragrammaton, be ascribed the Kingdom, the Power and the Glory, now and forever more, Amen."

Perform the Reverse circumambulation three times counterclockwise.

Return to the quarter you have invoked and trace with the Elemental implement the appropriate Banishing Pentagrams, with proper names and Grade Signs. Return the implement to the Altar.

Take up the Lotus Wand by the white portion and trace the Banishing Pentagrams of Spirit Active and Spirit Passive over the Tablet of Union.

Perform the Supreme Banishing Ritual of the Pentagram using either the Magick Sword or the Lotus Wand (holding the appropriate Kerubic band for each quarter and pointing with the black end.)

Perform with the sword the Lesser Banishing Ritual of the Pentagram.

Say: "I now release any spirits that may have been imprisoned by this ceremony. Depart in peace to your abodes and habitations. Go with the blessing of YEHESHUAH YEHOVASHAH."

Give five knocks as in the beginning.

Say, "I now declare this Temple duly closed."

SO MOTE IT BE

A Ritual for Use with the Air Dagger

Invoking the Powers of Air

Part 1: The Opening

For this part of the ritual, follow the instructions given in the previous ritual, but trace a circle around the letter "E" of the first line of the Tablet of Union as you recite the Second Enochian Key.)

Part 2: Invoking the Powers of Air

Take up the Air Dagger. Go the East and raise the implement high. Say: "I adore Thee, Lord and King of Air! SHADDAI EL CHAI, Almighty and Everlasting—Ever-Living be Thy Name, Ever Magnified in the Life of All. Amen." Give the Theoricus Sign.

Face the Elemental Tablet of the East. With the Dagger, trace a circle in front of the Tablet. Then trace the Invoking Pentagram of Spirit Active and vibrate the names "EXARP" and "EHEIEH." Give the LVX Signs. Trace the Invoking Pentagram of Air and vibrate "ORO IBAH AOZPI" and "YHVH" Give the Sign of the Theoricus.

Say: "And the Elohim said, 'Let us make Adam in our Image, after our likeness and let them have dominion over the fowl of the Air.' In the Great Divine Name of YOD HEH VAV HEH and of SHADDAI EL CHAI, Spirits of Air, adore your Creator!"

Trace the sigil of Aquarius in front of the Tablet with the Dagger. Say, "In the Name of RAPHAEL, the Great Archangel of Air, and by the sign of the Head of the Man, Spirits of Air, adore your Creator!"

Trace a Cross and say, "In the Names and Letters of the Great Eastern Quadrangle, revealed unto Enoch by the Great Angel, AVE, Spirits of Air, adore your Creator!" (Hold the Dagger high) "And by the Three Great Secret Names of God, borne upon the Banners of the East—ORO IBAH AOZPI—Spirits of Air, adore your Creator!"

Trace a Spiral and say, "In the name of BATAIVAH, Great King of the East, Spirits of Air, adore your Creator!"

Recite the Third Enochian Key:

"Micma Goho Mad Zir Comselha Zien Biah Os Londah. Norz Chis Othil Gigipah Vnd-L Chis ta Pu-Im Q Mospleh Teloch Qui-I-N Toltorg Chis I Chis-Ge In Ozien Ds T Brgdo Od Torzul. I Li E Ol Balzarg Od Aala Thiln Os Netaab Dluga Vonsarg Lonsa Cap-Mi-Ali Vors CLA Homil Cocasb Fafen Izizop Od Miinoag De Gnetaab Vaun Na-Na-E-El Panpir Malpirg Pild Caosg Noan Vnalah Balt Od Vaoan. Do-O-I-A p Mad Goholor Gohus Amiran Micma Iehusoz Ca-Cacom Od Do-O-A-In Noar Mica-Olz A-Ai-Om Casarmg Gohia Zacar Vniglag Od Im-Va-Mar Pugo Plapli Ananael Qa-A-An."

Phonetic: (Meek-mah! Goh-hoh Mah-dah. Zoad-ee-ray Kohm-sel-hah Zoad-ee-ay-noo Bee-ah-hay Oh-ess Lon-doh-hah. Nohr-zoad Kah-hee-sah Oh-thee-lah Jee-jee-pay-hay, Oon-dah-lah Kah-hee-sah Tah Poo-eem Kwo-Mohs-play Tay-lohk-hay, kwee-ee-noo Tohl-tor-jee, Kah-hees Ee Kah-hees-jee Ee-noo Oh-zoad-ee-ay-noo, Day-ess Tay Bray-jee-dah Oh-dah Tor-zoad-oo-lah. Ee-Lee Ay Oh-Lah Bahl-zoad-ahr-jee Oh-dah Ah-ah-lah, Tay-heel-noo Oh-ess Nay-tah-ah-bay, Dah-loo-gahr Vohn-sar-jee Lohn-sah Cah-pee-mee-ah-lee Vor-sah Cah El Ah, Hoh-meel Koh-kahs-bay; Fah-fay-noo Ee-zoad-ee-zoad-oh-pay Oh Dah Mee-ee-noh-ah-jee Day Jee-nay-tah-ah-bah Vah-oo-noo Nah-nah-ay-el; Pahn-peer-Mahl-peer-jee Pee-el-dah Kah-ohs-gah. Noh-ah-noo Oo-nah-lah Bal-tah Oh-dah Vay-oh-ah-noo. Doo-oh-ee-ah-pay Mah-dah, Go-hoh-lor Goh-hoos Ah-mee-rah-noo. Meek-mah Yeh-hoo-soh-zoad Kah-kah-coh-mah Oh-dah Doh-oh-ah-ee-noo Noh-ahr Mee-kah-ohl-zoad Ah-ah-ee-oh-mah, Kah-sarm-jee Go-hee-ah; Zoad-dah-kah-ray Oo-nee-glah-jee Oh-dah Eem-vah-mar Poo-joh, Plah-plee Ah-nah-nah-el Kah-ah-noo.)

(This translates as: "Behold saith your God. I am a Circle on whose hands stand Twelve Kingdoms. Six are the seats of Living Breath, the rest are as sharp sickles or the horns of Death, wherein the creatures of Earth are and are not, except Mine own hands which also sleep and shall rise. In the first I made you stewards and placed you in the seats Twelve of Government, giving unto every one of you power successively over Four, Five and Six, the true Ages of Time: to the intent that from the highest Vessels and the corners of your governments ye might work My power: Pouring down the Fires of Life and increase continually upon the Earth. Thus ye are become the Skirts of Justice and Truth. In the Name of the same your God lift up, I say yourselves. Behold, his mercies flourish and his name is become mighty amongst us, in Whom we say: Move, Descend and apply yourselves unto us, as unto the Partakers of the Secret Wisdom of your creation.)

Vibrate the name of "YOD HEH VAV HEH" four times, using the Vibratory Formula of the Middle Pillar.

Trace a Cross and Circle (Rose Cross) in front of the tablet with the Dagger. Recite the following, making certain to vibrate the Divine names and trace their sigils in the air with the pentacle:

In and by the name of SHADDAI EL CHAI and in the concealed Name of YHVH! And under the authority of RAPHAEL, Great archangel of the element of Air, I command ye beings of the Great Eastern Quadrangle, from the quarter known as MIZRACH! I summon all ye archangels, angels, Kings, Rulers and Elementals to be present at this ceremony. Grant unto me your powers of intellect, of healing, and communication! Grant unto me good health, safe travel, freedom from strife and quarrels, as well as the mental skills needed for the working of true Magick and for communication with my Higher Genius." (Clearly state here the purpose of the ritual—such as an illness you seek to heal; a quarrel you wish to reconcile, or a puzzle you seek to solve through the powers of intellect, etc.) "This I ask in all sincerity for such purposes as be pure and upright, and in compliance with my aspiration to complete the Great Work.

Visualize your stated purpose for the ritual as if your goal had already been reached. Take as much time as you need to complete the meditation.

Part 3: The Closing
Perform this part of the ritual exactly as in the ritual of Invoking the Powers of Earth.

A Ritual for Use with the Water Cup

Invoking the Powers of Water

Part 1: The Opening
For this part of the ritual, follow the instructions given in the ritual for Invoking the Powers of Earth, but trace a circle around the letter "H" of the second line of the Tablet of Union as you recite the Second Enochian Key.)

Part 2: Invoking the Powers of Water
Take up the Water Cup. Go the East and raise the implement high. Say: "I adore Thee, Lord and King of Water! ELOHIM TZABAOTH—Elohim of Hosts! Glory be unto the RUACH ELOHIM who moved upon the face of the Waters of Creation, Amen." Give the Practicus Sign.

Go to the West and face the Elemental Tablet. With the Cup, trace a circle in front of the Tablet. Then trace the Invoking Pentagram of Spirit Passive and vibrate the names "HCOMA" and "AGLA." Give the LVX Signs. Trace the Invoking Pentagram of Water and vibrate "EMPEH ARSEL GAIOL" and "Aleph Lamed, AL" Give the Sign of the Practicus.

Say: "And the Elohim said, 'Let us make Adam in our Image, after our likeness and let them have dominion over the fish of the Sea.' In the Great Divine Name of AL, strong and powerful and in the name of ELOHIM TZABAOTH, Spirits of Water, adore your Creator!"

Trace the sigil of the Eagle in front of the Tablet with the Cup. Say, "In the Name of GABRIEL, the Great Archangel of Water, and by the sign of the Head of the Eagle, Spirits of Water, adore your Creator!"

Trace a Cross and say, "In the Names and Letters of the Great Western Quadrangle, revealed unto Enoch by the Great Angel, AVE, Spirits of Water, adore your Creator!" (Hold the Cup high) "And by the Three Great Secret Names of God, borne upon the Banners of the West—EMPEH ARSEL GAIOL—Spirits of Water, adore your Creator!"

Trace The sigil of the Whirl and say, "In the name of RA-AGIOSEL, Great King of the West, Spirits of Water, adore your Creator!"

Recite the Fourth Enochian Key:

"Othil Lusdi Babage Od Dorpha Gohol G-Chis-Ge Avavago Cormp P D Ds Sonf Vi-Vi-Iv Casarmi Oali MAPM Sobam Ag Cormpo Crp L Casarmg Cro-Od-Zi Chis Od Vgeg Ds T Capimali Chis Capimaom Od Lonshin Chis Ta L-O CLA Torzu Nor-Quasahi Od F Caosga: Bagle Zire Mad Ds I Od Apila. Do-O-A-Ip Qaal Zacar Od Zamran Obelisong Rest-El Aaf Nor-Molap."

Phonetic: (Oh-thee-lah Loos-dee Bah-bah-jee Oh-dah Dor-pay-hah Goh-hoh-lah: Jee-kah-hees-jee Ah-vah-vah-goh Kohr-em-pay Pay-Dah Dah-ess Son-noof Vee-vee-ee-vah Kas-ahrm-ee Oh-al-lee Em-Ah-Pay-Em Soh-bah-mah Ah-gee-Kohr-em-poh Kah-ar-pay El: Kah-sarm-jee Kroh-oh-dah-zoad-ee Kah-hee-sah Oh-dah Lon-shee-noo Kah-hee-sah Tay-ah Elo-oh Kay-El-Ah. Tor-zoad-oo Nohr-kwah-sah-hee, Oh-dah Eff Kah-ohs-gah; Bah-glay Zoad-ee-ray Mah-dah Dah-ess Ee Oh-dah Ah-pee-lah. Doo-ah-ee-pay Kah-ah-lah, Zoad-a Kar-ah Oh-dah Zoad-ah-mer-ah-noo Oh-bay-lee-son-jee, Ray-stel-ah Ah-ah-eff Nohr-moh-lah-pay.)

(This translates as: "I have set my feet in the South and have looked about me saying: Are not the Thunders of Increase numbered thirty-three which reign in the Second Angle? Under Whom I have placed Nine Six Three Nine, Whom None hath yet numbered but One: In whom the Second Beginning of things are and wax strong, which also successively are the numbers of Time, and their powers are as the first. Arise ye Sons of Pleasure and visit the Earth: For I am the Lord your God which is and liveth for ever. In the Name of the Creator, move and show yourselves as pleasant deliverers that you may praise Him amongst the Sons of Men.")

Vibrate the name of "AL" twice, using the Vibratory Formula of the Middle Pillar.

Trace a Cross and Circle (Rose Cross) in front of the tablet with the Cup. Recite the following, making certain to vibrate the Divine names and trace their sigils in the air with the Cup:

"In and by the name of ELOHIM TZABAOTH and in the Divine and most powerful Name of AL! And under the authority of GABRIEL, Great archangel of the element of Water, I command ye beings of the Great Western Quadrangle, from the quarter known as MAARAB! I summon all ye archangels, angels, Kings, Rulers and Elementals to be present at this ceremony. Grant unto me your feminine powers of creativity, fertility, and pleasure! Grant unto me your imaginative spark; Inspire me with your sensual imagery! Let my hand, heart and mind be as artistic tools for the inventive Genius of the Higher. Let my Soul be as the canvas painted by the brilliance of the Light Divine in the colors of the Chameleon." (Clearly state here the purpose of the ritual—such as the conception of a creative idea, productivity in a certain endeavor, or happiness in marriage, etc.) "This I ask in all sincerity for such purposes as be pure and upright, and in compliance with my aspiration to complete the Great Work."

Visualize your stated purpose for the ritual as if your goal had already been reached. Take as much time as you need to complete the meditation.

Part 3: The Closing
Perform this part of the ritual exactly as in the rite of Invoking the Powers of Earth.

A Ritual for Use with the Fire Wand

Invoking the Powers of Fire

Part 1: The Opening
For this part of the ritual, follow the instructions given in the ritual for Invoking the Powers of Earth, but trace a circle around the letter "B" of the Fourth line of the Tablet of Union as you recite the Second Enochian Key.)

Part 2: Invoking the Powers of Fire
Take up the Fire Wand. Go the East and raise the implement

high. Say: "I adore Thee, Lord and King of Fire! YHVH TZABAOTH—Blessed be Thou—Leader of Armies is Thy Name, Amen." Give the Philosophus Sign.

Go to the South and face the Elemental Tablet. With the Fire Wand, trace a circle in front of the Tablet. Then trace the Invoking Pentagram of Spirit Passive and vibrate the names "BITOM" and "EHEIEH." Give the LVX Signs. Trace the Invoking Pentagram of Fire and vibrate "OIP TEAA PEDOCE" and "ELOHIM." Give the Sign of the Philosophus.

Say: "And the Elohim said, 'Let us make Adam in our Image, after our likeness and let them have dominion.' In the Name of ELOHIM, Mighty and Ruling, and in the Name of YHVH TZABAOTH, Spirits of Fire, adore your Creator!"

Trace the sigil of Leo in front of the Tablet with the Wand. Say, "In the Name of MICHAEL, the Great Archangel of Fire, and by the sign of the Lion, Spirits of Fire, adore your Creator!"

Trace a Cross and say, "In the Names and Letters of the Great Southern Quadrangle, revealed unto Enoch by the Great Angel, AVE, Spirits of Fire, adore your Creator!" (Hold the Wand high) "And by the Three Great Secret Names of God, borne upon the Banners of the South—OIP TEAA PEDOCE—Spirits of Fire, adore your Creator!"

Trace a Whirl sigil and say, "In the name of EDELPERNA, Great King of the South, Spirits of Fire, adore your Creator!"

Recite the Sixth Enochian Key:

"Gah S Diu Chis Em Micalzo Pil-Zin Sobam El Harg Mir Babalon Od obloc Samvelg Dlugar Malprg Ar Caosgi Od A C A M Canal Sobol Zar F Bliard Caosgi Od Chisa Netaab Od Miam Ta Viv Od D Darsar Solpeth Bi-En B-Ri-Ta Od Zacam G-Micalza Sobol Ath Trian Lu-Ia He Od Ecrin Mad Qaa-On."

(Gah-hay Ess Dee-oo Kah-hee-sah Ay-em, Mee-kahl-zoad-oh Peel-zoad-ee-noo; Soh-bah-may El Har-jee Meer Bah-bah-loh-noo Oh-dah Oh-bloh-kah Sahm-vay-lan-jee: Dah-loo-gar Mah-lah-peer-jee Ah-ray Kah-ohs-jee, Oh-dah Ah Kah Ah Em Kah-nahl So-bo-loh Zoad-ah-ray Eff Blee-ahr-dah Kah-ohs-jee, Oh-dah Kah-hee-say Nay-tah-ah-bay Oh-dah Mee-ah may Tay-ah Vee-ee-vah Oh-dah Dah. Dahr-sahr Sohl-pet-hay Bee-ay-noo. Bay-ree-tah Oh-dah Zoad-ah-kah-may Jee-mee-kah-el-zoad-ah So-boh-lah Aht-hay Tre-ah-noo Loo-ee-ah Hay Oh-dah Ay-kree-noo Mah-dah Kah-ah-noo.)

(This translates as: "The Spirits of the Fourth Angle are Nine, mighty in the firmament of the waters: Whom the first hath planted a torment to the wicked and a garland to the Righteous: Giving unto them fiery darts to Vanne the Earth, and 7699 Continual workmen whose courses visit with comfort the Earth, and are in governement and continuance as the Second and the Third. Wherefore, hearken unto my voice. I have talked of you and I move you in power and presence; Whose works shall be a Song of Honour and the Praise of your God in your Creation.")

Vibrate the name of "ELOHIM" four times, using the Vibratory Formula of the Middle Pillar.

Trace a Cross and Circle (Rose Cross) in front of the tablet with the Fire Wand. Recite the following, making certain to vibrate the Divine names and trace their sigils in the air with the Wand:

In and by the name of YHVH TZABAOTH and in the Divine and most powerful Name of ELOHIM! And under the authority of MICHAEL, Great archangel of the element of Fire, I command ye beings of the Great Southern Quadrangle, from the quarter known as DAROM! I summon all ye archangels, angels, Kings, Rulers and Elementals to be present at this ceremony. Grant unto me your masculine powers of creation, of great energy, and strength. Grant unto me the vitality, tenacity and steadfast resolution I require as Seeker on the Path of Light! Give me dominion and authority to command the spirits of all the Elements—only for true and just purposes. May my soul be like unto an athanor which contains a fiery passion for the Knowledge of the Light Divine."

(Clearly state here the purpose of the ritual—such as the desire for the strength to finish an endeavor which has already been started, or the energy necessary to be assertive in a specific situation, etc.) "This I ask in all sincerity for such purposes as be pure and upright, and in compliance with my aspiration to complete the Great Work."

Visualize your stated purpose for the ritual as if your goal had already been reached. Take as much time as you need to complete the meditation.

Part 3: The Closing
Perform this part of the ritual exactly as in the rite of Invoking the Powers of Earth.

CHAPTER SIX

Nontraditional Implements

On occasion new implements have been designed by Inner Order members for the purpose of introducing to Outer Order members the practical techniques of ceremonial magick. The creation of such tools was inspired by recent changes in the curriculum of the Golden Dawn, for previously ritual work was not begun by the student until he/she had advanced to the Second Order. However, in recognition of the fact that the wide availability of occult material in various publications had caused students to be better prepared to begin practical work, the modern incarnation of the Golden Dawn has incorporated some practical ritual techniques and implements into the curriculum of the Outer Order. The Outer Wand of Double Power is an example of this kind of implement.

Other implements described in this chapter are new tools which have been created for use in rituals which are based on the traditional ceremonial techniques of the Golden Dawn. Many more such implements can be devised by the creative Magician.

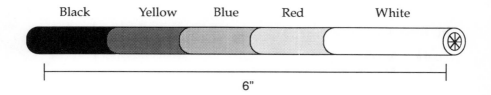

The Outer Wand of Double Power

The Outer Wand of Double Power

Use and Symbolism

   The Outer Wand of Double Power is a simple wand that is employed in the basic Golden Dawn techniques of invoking and banishing.

Materials Needed

   One 3/4" thick wooden dowel approx. 20" in length
   Gesso
   Acrylic paint: white and black
   Sealant: clear lacquer finish

Tools Needed

   Sandpaper (fine grained)
   Artist's brushes (medium)
   Masking tape

Construction

   1)   Cover the dowel with a coat of gesso. Allow to dry. Sand lightly until smooth. Apply a second coat if needed.

   2)   Mark the dowel into two sections, each of which is 10" in length. Paint half of the wand black and the other half white. (Use masking tape to paint a straight line separating the two halves of the wand.)

   3)   When all paint is dry apply a coat of sealant for protection.

Rituals for Use

   This wand is especially designed to be used in the Lesser Banishing Ritual of the Pentagram. In addition, all of the rituals given in chapter 2 are performed using this implement. In banishing, the black end of the wand is used to point and trace figures with. For invokings, the white end is utilized.

The Rose Cross Wand

Materials Needed

   One 3/4" thick dowel between 20" to 24" in length
   One 3/4" thick piece of pine or bass approx. 6" long and 6" wide
   One 1/4" wooden dowel or peg 1" in length
   Wood putty
   Gesso
   Acrylic paints: white, gold, red, yellow, orange
   Sealant: clear lacquer finish

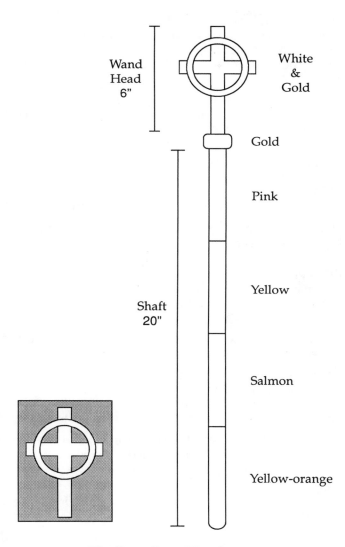

Wand
Head
6"

White
&
Gold

Gold

Pink

Yellow

Shaft
20"

Salmon

Yellow-orange

The Rose Cross Wand

Tools Needed
    Scroll saw or coping saw
    Electric drill with 1/4" and 3/4" bits
    Sandpaper (coarse, medium and fine)
    An index card
    Artist's brushes (large, medium and fine)

Construction: The Rose Cross Head

1) Draw the circled cross shown in the diagram with proper dimensions on the 6" x 6" piece of wood. (The shaft of the cross will be 6" in length while the arms will be 4".) With the saw, cut out the outer shape of the circled cross.

2) Drill four holes, one inside each of the shaded (negative space) areas of the wand head. (Remember: it is important to use a drill bit that is wider than your saw blade.)

3) With your saw unplugged, detach the blade from the saw. Stick the blade through one of the holes you have drilled and re-attach the blade to the saw. Plug the saw back in and begin cutting out the shaded area of wood. Repeat this process for all four drilled holes until all the waste area of wood has been cut out.

4) Drill a hole 1/2" deep and 1/4" wide in the center of the bottom side of the wand head.

Construction: The Shaft

5) From a leftover piece of the 3/4" thick pine wood, draw one 1-1/2" circle. In the center, drill a 3/4" diameter hole. You will end up with a donut-shaped ring of wood.

6) Take the long dowel (shaft) and drill a hole 1/2" deep and 1/4" in diameter into one end of it.

7) Glue the 1" wooden peg into the hole you have just drilled so that half of the peg is embedded into the end of the dowel and half of it sticks out. Apply glue to the inside of the ring. Slide it over the top end of the shaft. (If the ring is too tight, sand inside its center hole.)

8) Pour some glue into the hole you drilled into the bottom end of the wand head and attach the cross to the wand shaft. Let dry.

Finishing Steps

9) Fill in any gaps with wood putty. Sand the entire surface of the wand so that it is smooth.

10) With a paint brush, cover the wand with a coat of gesso. Allow to dry.

11) Sand the painted surface (especially the shaft) lightly until smooth. Apply a second coat if needed.

12) Measure and mark the shaft into four equal sections. Use an index card wrapped around the shaft to draw a straight line around the dowel. Paint the wand as follows:

THE CROSS—White front and back with gold sides
THE RING—Gold
TOP QUARTER OF SHAFT—Rose pink (mix red and white)

SECOND QUARTER OF SHAFT—Yellow
THIRD QUARTER—Salmon (mix pink and yellow)
BOTTOM QUARTER—Yellow-orange

13)   Paint or spray on a sealant to protect the painted wand. Allow to dry.

Use and Symbolism

The Rose Cross Wand was designed specifically for use in the Traditional Rose Cross Ritual of the Second Order. The symbolism of the Rose and Cross has been previously described in chapter 5.

The Rose Cross is one of the emblems associated with the Sixth Sephirah of Tiphareth, the sphere of beauty and equilibrium. The color of the head of the wand denotes the illumination of LVX, the Divine Light of the Cross. The Cross stands upon a single golden ring which alludes to Tiphareth. The shaft of the wand is divided into the colors of Tiphareth in each of the Four Worlds of the Qabalah in descending order: Tiphareth in Atziluth—pink, Tiphareth in Briah—yellow, Tiphareth in Yetzirah—Salmon, Tiphareth in Assiah—Yellow-orange. Grasping the wand by any of these four bands in performance of the Rose Cross Ritual (or any meditation on Tiphareth) can help the Magician explore the Sixth Sephirah in these specific Qabalistic Worlds.

Ritual for Use

The Ritual of the Rose Cross

Uses of the Rose Cross Ritual

The Rose Cross Ritual is more of a blessing than a banishing. It is like a veil, enclosing the aura with a protection against outside influences. Whereas the Lesser Banishing Ritual of the Pentagrams protect, they also light up the astral and make entities aware of you. Use the pentagrams to banish and the Rose Cross to maintain peace.

The RCR is a call to another mode of your consciousness. It is a good preparation for meditation, and, when combined with the Analysis of the Keyword, is a form of invocation of Higher Wisdom which is helpful when solving problems or trying to maintain inner calm.

When you are quite familiar with the ritual, it can be done in the imagination while resting or lying down. Used with rhythmic breathing, it will withdraw the mind from pain and release you for sleep.

The ritual can be done to help others in pain or difficulty. For this purpose, build up an astral image of the person in the center of the room, and, after surrounding the person with six crosses, call down the light upon him or her.

The RCR can be used as protection against psychic invasion from the thoughts of others or from disturbed psychic conditions.

The Ritual of the Rose Cross

The Adept should be dressed in the regalia of the Second Order. The room should be clear of any obstructions (the altar should be moved aside). The only implement needed will be the Rose Cross Wand (substituted for the incense stick suggested in Regardie's book, *The Golden Dawn*).

> Stand in the center of the room for a few moments in meditation, while performing the exercise of the Four-fold Breath. Hold the wand head directly in front of your Tiphareth center as you do so.

> Grasp the wand by the rose pink band. Go to the southeast corner of the room and face outward. Trace a large cross and circle there with the head of the wand. As you draw the cross, visualize it in a golden light. The circle should be imagined as flaming red. While tracing this symbol, vibrate the name, "YEHESHUAH." On the last syllable, thrust through the center of the circled cross with the head of the wand.

> Keep the tip of the wand at the level of the center of the cross and walk to the southwest corner of the room. Draw the cross and circle, or Rose Cross, as before and thrust the wand through the center of the figure intoning, "YEHESHUAH."

> Move to the northwest and repeat this process.

> Move to the northeast and repeat.

> Return to the southeast and complete the circle. Touch the head of the wand to the cross already drawn there, but do not re-trace or intone the name.

> Now move diagonally across the room toward the northwest, but stop in the center of the Temple and make the Rose Cross

above your head. Intone the name as before. With the wand head held straight up in the air, walk to the northwest corner of the room. Touch the tip of the wand to the center of the cross already formulated there. Do not retrace the cross or say the name.

Move diagonally across the room again toward the southeast but stop in the center of the Temple. Trace the Rose Cross below you and vibrate the name. Keep the tip of the wand held down and continue to walk to the southeast corner. Touch the tip of the wand to the center of the Rose Cross already traced there. Do not re-trace or intone.

Move deosil to the southwest and touch the head of the wand to the cross already traced there.

Walk diagonally toward the northeast but stop in the middle of the room to touch the center of the cross above your head. Intone the name. Continue on to the northeast and touch the wand to the center of the cross formulated there.

Move diagonally across the room toward the southwest but stop in the middle of the Temple to touch the cross below you. Intone the name. Continue on to the southwest corner and touch the center of the cross already there.

Move clockwise and link up with all the crosses by touching their centers with the wand (northwest, northeast). No need to intone as you do so.

Upon returning to the southeast, the site of the first cross, touch the center and pause. Then retrace the golden cross over the original, only much larger. Vibrate, "YEHESHUAH." Trace a larger red circle over the original and intone, "YEHOVASHAH."

Walk deosil to the center of the room. Observe all six Rose Crosses surrounding you, all connected by ribbons of light.

Still holding the wand by the Atziluth band, perform the Analysis of the Keyword. End the Analysis by vibrating the four Tablet of Union names to equilibrate the Light: "EXARP.

HCOMA. NANTA. BITOM."* Then aspire to the Light and draw it down over your head to your feet. Say, "Let the Divine Light Descend!"

THIS ENDS THE RITE

The Box for Geomantic Divination

Based on an implement suggested by Israel Regardie
and constructed by Bill Allen

Geomancy is an ancient form of divination associated with the element of Earth. It was originally performed by poking holes into dirt or sand to obtain different symbols and figures. These geomantic figures were then used to obtain answers to particular questions. Although nowadays this procedure can be done entirely using pen and paper, there is an advantage to using earth in that it helps to formulate the magickal link between the diviner and the planetary Genii summoned.

The Golden Dawn made the study of geomancy a part of its curriculum, along with the tarot, astrology, and the tattwas. The art of Geomancy is described in Israel Regardie's *The Golden Dawn*, but his discussion is limited in that most of the tables list only a narrow set of fixed responses to proposed questions (for instance: evil, good, medium, sometimes evil). These stock answers are not well suited to accommodate the types of questions the modern geomancer asks. However, by reading between the lines of furnished answers and consulting a good book on astrology, the outcome of the divination may be accurately determined for any questions.

Since it isn't always convenient to step outside and poke holes in the ground to obtain an answer to a question, a box can be made to hold consecrated soil, and a geomantic divination can be done at your convenience.

Materials Needed
One piece of 3/4" thick plywood that is approx. 1' x 4'
One 1/4" thick piece of plywood that is 10-1/2" square
One 1/4" thick dowel that is approx. 12" long
One 3/4" x 1/2" piece of basswood (model strut) that is at least 31" long
Wood glue
Wood putty

---

* These four names would not be pronounced if the Adept were working in the Vault.

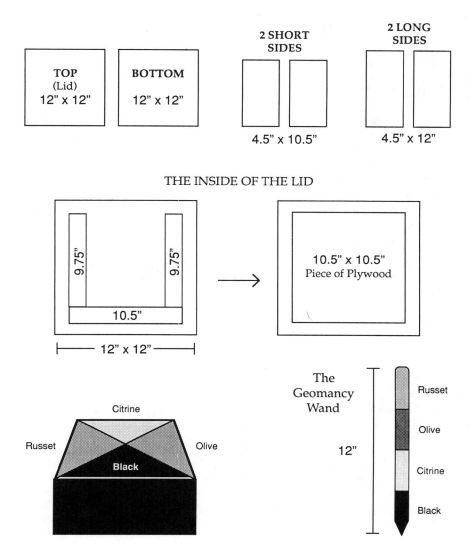

The Box for Geomantic Divination

1-1/2" long finishing nails
Gesso
Acrylic paints: black, white, violet, orange, green
Sealant: clear lacquer finish

Tools Needed
Table saw or jigsaw
Hammer
Nail punch
Sandpaper
Artist's brushes

Construction: The Box
1) Cut the 3/4" plywood into six pieces as follows:
THE TOP—One 12" x 12" piece
THE BOTTOM—One 12" x 12" piece
TWO SHORT SIDES—both pieces 4-1/2" x 10-1/2"
TWO LONG SIDES—both pieces 4-1/2" x 12"

2) Nail the four side pieces together, end to end, as in the diagram. (The 12" long piece will be directly opposite its twin, with the shorter pieces separating them. Be sure to apply glue to the edges before nailing.) Glue and nail the bottom piece to the four side pieces. Fill in any gaps with wood putty and sand smooth.

Construction: The Lid
3) Take the 3/4" x 1/2" model strut and cut it into three pieces: One 10-1/2" long piece, and two 9-3/4" long pieces.

4) Glue these three pieces onto the inside of the lid piece, so that they are all 3/4" from the edge on three sides. (See the diagram.)

5) Nail the 1/4" thick piece of plywood to the inside of the lid over the three pieces of wood. The lid should fit snugly in place over the box. If it is too tight, sand the inside pieces of the lid.

Finishing Steps
6) Cover the box with a coat of gesso.

7) Mark the top of the box into four sections, corner to corner. Paint the sections in the appropriate Malkuth colors: citrine, olive, russet and black. Paint the sides of the box accordingly. Paint the bottom and inside of the box black.

8) Paint the underside of the lid white. On this white field paint in black a list of the geomantic figures and sigils shown in the diagram. This diagram will be a handy reference in an actual divination. (Sigils as-

sociated with the element of earth can also be painted on the inside of the lid. See the sigils of the Earth Pentacle in chapter 5.)

The Geomancy Wand

9) Take the 12" long slender dowel and sharpen one end of it. Measure the wand off into four equal sections. Paint the wand either black or in the four colors of Malkuth in the following order: russet, olive, citrine and black. (The pointed end should be black.) The wand can be stored in the hollow space inside the lid under the 1/4" plywood.

10) Apply a coat of sealant to the box, inside and out. Apply sealant to the wand as well.

11) The box should be filled with dry black earth. Sand does not yield the best results. The soil can be taken from a special or sacred place to help reinforce a strong spiritual bond between the earth and the geomancer. The wand is used to poke holes into the consecrated soil. Once the box is completed and filled with earth, it should be consecrated with the following ritual:

Ritual for Use

Consecration of the Geomancy Box

Items needed: salt, a black or green candle, Dittany of Crete incense if available, a copy of the Prayer of the Gnomes from the Zelator Ceremony. The geomancy box should be placed on the Altar.

Take a ritual bath, robe up and do a relaxation ritual or earth meditation.

Perform the LBRP. Possibly the BRH as well.

Perform the Supreme Invoking Ritual of Pentagram for Earth. (Draw the Invoking Spirit Passive Pentagram and the Invoking Earth Pentagram in all quarters, vibrating "NANTA, AGLA" and "EMOR DIAL HECTEGA, ADONAI.")

Take the box from the Altar and place it in the northern quarter. Trace a circle around it. Inside of this circle trace the Invoking Pentagram of Earth. Vibrate the name "ADONAI HA ARETZ" and light the candle nearby. Use a stick of incense or index finger to trace the Taurus symbol over the box.

Then facing north, stand in the 1=10 grade sign of Zelator and say, "In the divine name ADONAI HA ARETZ, I invoke the great and mighty Archangel, URIEL, to bestow upon this box the power of truth. I call and invoke the Ashim, the Souls of Fire, to make this earthen box a true and faithful tool for divination."

Sprinkle some salt over the box and in the soil while visualizing it surrounded by white light.

Recite the Prayer of the Gnomes from the Zelator ritual. Visualize the gnomes assisting you in this consecration. Then charge the box with the Sign of the Enterer ten times using the full force of your Will each time you thrust forward. Finish with the Sign of Silence.

Perform the LBRP and if necessary, the BRH as well.

How to Use the Geomancy Box

The following is meant only to supplement crucial reading on Geomancy found in Regardie's *The Golden Dawn*. Essential charts and diagrams from that book should be referred to.

Formulate and state a question you wish to have answered in the divination.

Using the wand as a drawing tool, trace within the soil contained in the box a circle and an Invoking Pentagram of Earth. In the center of the pentagram draw the sigil of the planetary ruler who pertains to your question (i.e., the ruler of the planet whose energy would be most helpful in the matter).

Create the sixteen figures required for judging the outcome by counting sixteen lines of dots or holes poked into the soil. Determine each line to have either an odd or even number of dots. If a line has an even number it is assigned two dots. If the number is odd, it receives one dot. The sixteen lines produce four MOTHERS (figures 1-4). Each Mother is a figure formed from four of the sixteen lines.

Then come the four DAUGHTERS (figures 5-8) formed from the heads, necks, bodies and feet of the Mothers. (All the heads of the Mothers form the first Daughter, all the necks form the second Daughter, etc.)

The next group of four figures is known as the NEPHEWS, sometimes called the RESULTANTS (figures 9-12). The first

THE GEOMANTIC FIGURES AND THEIR GENII
(To be painted on the inside of the Geomancy Box)

Geomantic Figure	Zodiacal Attribution	Name of Figure	Ruling Planet	Sigil of Genii	Ruler (Genii)	Geomantic Figure	Zodiacal Attribution	Name of Figure	Ruling Planet	Sigil of Genii	Ruler (Genii)
• • • • •	♈	Puer	♂		Bartzabel	• • • • •	♎	Puella	♀		Kedemel
• • • • • •	♉	Amissio	♀		Kedemel	• • • • • • •	♏	Rubeus	♂		Bartzabel
• • • • • • •	♊	Albus	☿		Taphthartharath	• • • • • •	♐	Acquisitio	♃		Hismael
• • • • • • • •	♋	Populus	☽		Chasmodai	• • • • • •	♑	Carcer	♄		Zazel
• • • •	♋	Via	☽		Chasmodai	• • • • • • •	♒	Tristitia	♄		Zazel
• • • • • •	♌	Fortuna Major	☉		Sorath	• • • • • • •	♓	Laetitia	♃		Hismael
• • • • • •	♌	Fortuna Minor	☉		Sorath	• • • • •	☊	Caput Draconis	♀ ♃		Hismael & Kedemel
• • • • • •	♍	Conjunctio	☿		Taphthartharath	• • • • •	☋	Cauda Draconis	♂ ♄		Zazel & Bartzabel

nephew is formed by adding Mothers 1 and 2, the Second Nephew is created by adding Mothers 3 and 4, the third Nephew is formed by adding the first two Daughters (figures 5 and 6). The last Nephew is formed by combining the final two daughters (figures 7 and 8).

Check to see if the Rubeus or Cauda Draconis are in the first house. If they are, destroy the chart and wait at least two hours before asking the question again.

Form the RIGHT WITNESS (figure 13) by adding the first two Nephews (figures 9 and 10). Form the LEFT WITNESS (figure 14) by adding the final two Nephews (figures 11 and 12).

Form the JUDGE (figure 15) by adding together the two witnesses.

a) Assess the general nature of the figure.
b) Interpret the figure in light of the zodiacal house to which the question pertains.
c) Interpret the Judge and the two Witnesses:

A good Judge made of two good Witnesses is good.

A bad Judge made of two bad Witnesses is bad.

A good Judge made of mixed good and bad Witnesses means success, but delay and vexation.

Two good Witnesses and a bad Judge, the result will be unfortunate in the end.

First Witness is good and the second bad, the success will be very doubtful.

First Witness bad and the second good, unfortunate beginning will take a good turn.

Check to see if the same geomantic figure as the Judge actually turns up anywhere else.
d) Calculate the PART OF FORTUNE (especially helpful in questions of money). It is calculated by adding together all the points of the first twelve figures, then dividing this number by 12. The remaining number will indicate the house to which the Part of Fortune is allocated. Having found the house, the figure will provide, in context of its house, details concerning the querent's financial position.

A GEOMANCY CHART

Divination No. _____   Date _____   Time _____

Aspects _____   Day of _____   Hour of _____

_____

QUESTION: _____

_____

House _____   Planet _____   Genius _____

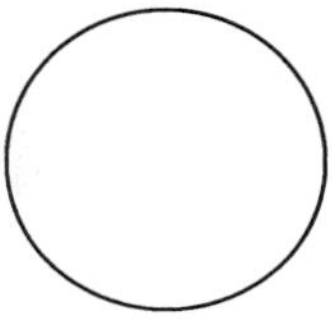

1	5	9
2	6	10
3	7	11
4	8	12

LW	RW	Judge	Rec.

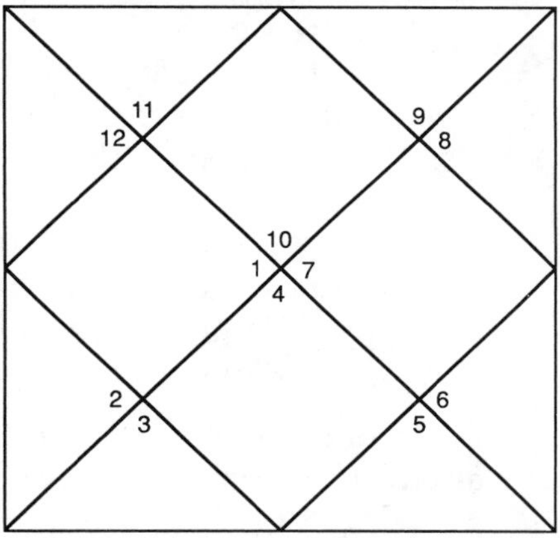

Significator _____

Trines _____

Squares _____

Sextiles _____

Opp. _____

4th House _____

INTERPRETATION: _____

_____

_____

_____

_____

_____

_____

Lay out the first 12 figures (Mothers, Daughters, and Nephews) on the square chart provided for interpretation of houses. (This is to give greater detail of a complex question. A simple "yes/ no" question will have been answered by this point.) The figures are placed as follows:

Figure 1 goes in the 10th House.
Figure 2 goes in the 1st House.
Figure 3 goes in the 4th House.
Figure 4 goes in the 7th House.
Figure 5 goes in the 11th House.
Figure 6 goes in the 2nd House.
Figure 7 goes in the 5th House.
Figure 8 goes in the 8th House.
Figure 9 goes in the 12th House.
Figure 10 goes in the 3rd House.
Figure 11 goes in the 6th House.
Figure 12 goes in the 9th House.

Determine which particular house relates to the question being asked. This figure will have great significance to the reading.

Write down the Zodiacal attributions of each figure in each house. (If the First House contains the figure of Amissio, which relates to Taurus, then the first house starts with and is Taurus. The rest of the houses follow in order, so that Figure 6 in the 2nd House is in the House of Gemini, even if the Figure happens to be Fortuna Minor, which relates to Leo. Thus as in astrology, the planet of Leo, the Sun, is in Gemini.)

Determine the planets, which is simply the ruling planet of the sign in each house, i.e. Puer equals Mars. (A normal Zodiacal chart showing the 12 houses in the circular or wheel form might be useful to write this information on.)

Also determine the balance of elements (Fire, Water, Air, Earth) in the chart. See if an imbalance of elemental forces is apparent.

Estimate the essential dignity of the figure. (Essential dignity of a figure in a particular house is a measure of its strength and the degree to which it will influence the judgment.) A figure is STRONGEST when in what is called its house, VERY STRONG when in its exaltation, STRONG in its triplicity, VERY WEAK in its fall; WEAKEST of all in its detriment. A figure is in its fall when in a house opposite to that of its exaltation, and in its detriment when opposite to its own house.

Consider the ASPECTS of the figure: OPPOSITION would be the house directly opposite the house in question. The house in question is known as the SIGNIFICATOR.

SQUARE—count four houses from and including the Significator in both directions. Both Opposition and Square are stressful.

SEXTILE—count three houses from and including the Significator in both directions. This is a mildly benevolent aspect.

TRINE—count five houses from and including the Significator in both directions. Both Sextile and Trine ease the situation.

The directions are known as DEXTER (clockwise) and SINISTER (counterclockwise). Dexter is the more powerful of the two.

After all is looked at, check the figure in the 4th House, which denotes the conclusion or outcome of the matter in question.

If you are still unsure at this point, construct the 16th and final figure of the RECONCILER, by adding the 1st Mother and the Judge. This will give a final reading.

The Spirit Wand

Use and Symbolism
  The Hebrew letter Shin, when painted white, represents the fifth element of Spirit. (When red it becomes the Shin of Fire.) This letter has the numerical value of 300, which has the same Qabalaistic value as Ruach Elohim, a Hebrew phrase meaning *The Spirit of the Living God*. Shin consists of three Yods, or flaming tongues of light. The letter symbolizes the highest aspirations of the soul, and indeed the three Yods seem to point toward the omnipresence of the Supernal Triad.
  The Wand is divided into five sections, one for each letter of the Pentagramaton, the five-lettered name of Yeheshuah, and the Five Elements. The colors on the shaft represent the five sub-elements of Eth: White—Spirit of Spirit, Pale Yellow—Air of Spirit, Grey—Earth of Spirit, Pink—Fire of Spirit, and Pale Blue—Water of Spirit.

Materials Needed
    One 3/4" thick dowel between 20" to 24" in length
    One 3/4" thick piece of pine or bass approx. 6" long and 6" wide
    One 1/4" wooden dowel or peg 1" in length
    Wood putty
    Gesso
    Acrylic paints: white, gray, red, yellow, blue
    Sealant: clear lacquer finish

Tools Needed
    Dremel scroll saw
    Electric drill with 1/4" and 3/4" bits
    Sandpaper (coarse, medium and fine)
    An index card
    Artist's brushes (large medium and fine)

Construction: The Head
1) Draw the Hebrew letter Shin shown in the diagram with proper dimensions on the 6" x 6" piece of wood. (The letter should be no more than 4" x 4".) With the saw, cut out the shape of the letter.

2) Drill a hole 1/2" deep and 1/4" wide in the center of the bottom side of the letter.

Construction: The Shaft
3) From a left over piece of the 3/4" thick pine wood, draw one 1-1/2" circle. In the center, drill a 3/4" diameter hole. You will end up with a donut-shaped ring of wood.

4) Take the long dowel (shaft) and drill a hole 1/2" deep and 1/4" in diameter into one end of it. Glue the 1" wooden peg into the hole you have just drilled so that half of the peg is embedded into the end of the dowel and half of it sticks out.

5) Apply glue to the inside of the ring. Slide it over the top end of the shaft. (If the ring is too tight, sand inside its center hole.) Pour some glue into the hole you drilled into the bottom end of the wand head and attach the Shin to the wand shaft. Let dry.

Finishing Steps
6) Fill in any gaps with wood putty. Sand the entire surface of the wand so that it is smooth.With a paint brush, cover the wand with a coat of gesso. Allow to dry.

7) Sand the painted surface (especially the shaft) lightly until smooth. Apply a second coat if needed.

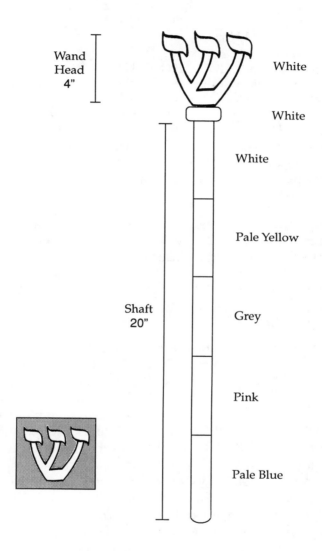

Wand
Head
4"

White

White

White

Pale Yellow

Shaft
20"

Grey

Pink

Pale Blue

The Spirit Wand

8) Measure and mark the shaft into five equal sections. (Use an index card wrapped around the shaft as a guide to draw a straight line around the dowel.) Paint the wand as follows:

THE WAND HEAD—White
THE RING—White
THE UPPER SECTION OF THE SHAFT—White
THE SECOND SECTION—Pale yellow (yellow and white)
THE THIRD SECTION—Gray
THE FOURTH SECTION—Pink (red and white)
THE FIFTH SECTION—Pale blue (blue and white)

9) Paint or spray on a sealant to protect the painted wand. Allow to dry.

(Note: An alternative version of the Spirit Wand could be made utilizing the Spirit Wheel as the wand head in place of the Shin.)

Ritual for Use
The Spirit Wand could be employed in any ritual where the element of Spirit is invoked. The Supreme Invocation of Eth given in chapter 4 can be adapted for use with this wand.

The Sephirotic Wand

Use and Symbolism
The Sephirotic Wands are each naturally aligned by their geometric heads to a particular Sephirah. The shafts are divided into the color scales of the Four Worlds of the Qabalah: Atziluth, Briah, Yetzirah and Assiah. For example, the Binah Wand with the triangular head has its shaft divided into the colors of: Binah in Atziluth (red), Binah in Briah (black), Binah in Yetzirah (dark brown) and Binah in Assiah (gray-flecked pink). The head of the wand is always white. (This is adapted from the Lotus Wand, which is grasped by the white band to invoke any of the Sephiroth.) These wands can be used in a ritual/meditation to invoke and explore the energies of a particular Sephirah in any of the Four Worlds.

(Note: An ambitious Magician could make a series of wands allotted to the 22 paths of the Tarot, using the same methods given here. The head of such a wand would be fashioned in the shape of one of the twenty-two letters of the Hebrew alphabet (Teth for the Path of Strength, Mem for the Hanged Man, and so forth). The shaft would likewise be divided into four sections and painted as the Path colors in the Four Color scales. See Regardie's *The Golden Dawn* for a list of these color scales.)

Materials Needed

One 3/4" thick dowel between 20" to 24" in length
One 3/4" thick piece of pine or bass approx. 8" long and 8" wide
One 1/4" wooden dowel or peg 1" in length
Wood putty
Gesso
Acrylic paints: white, black, gray, red, yellow, blue, green, orange,
   violet, blue-violet, red-violet.
Sealant: clear lacquer finish

Tools Needed

Scroll saw
Electric drill with 1/4" and 3/4" bits
Sandpaper (coarse, medium and fine)
An index card
Artist's brushes (large, medium and fine)

Construction: The Head

1) Draw the geometric designs shown in the diagram with proper dimensions on the 8" x 8" piece of wood. (The wand head should be no more than 4" x 4".)

2) With the saw, cut out the shape of the letter. (Follow directions given earlier in this book for cutting out the shaded [waste areas] of wood. For the more complex designs such as the enneangle and dekangle, you might wish to cut out just the outside shape of the form and simply paint the shaded [waste] areas with a neutral gray or black.)

3) Drill a hole 1/2" deep and 1/4" wide in the center of the bottom side of the wand head.

Construction: The Shaft

(Note: Follow steps 3–5 as given for the construction of the Spirit Wand in this Chapter.)

Finishing Steps

6) Fill in any gaps with wood putty. Sand the entire surface of the wand so that it is smooth.

7) With a paint brush, cover the wand with a coat of gesso. Allow to dry. Sand the painted surface (especially the shaft) lightly until smooth. Apply a second coat if needed.

8) Measure and mark the shaft into four equal sections. (Use an index card wrapped around the shaft as a guide to draw a straight line around the dowel.)

9) Paint the wand as follows, depending upon which Sephirah the wand is attributed to:

KETHER: The Point and Ring—iridescent white. The Top Section—iridescent white. The Second Section—white brilliance (white covered by a coat of iridescent white.) The Third Section—white brilliance. The Final Section—white-flecked gold.

CHOKMAH: The Line and Ring—white. The First Section—soft blue (blue mixed with a small amount of white). The Second Section—gray. The Third Section—bluish Mother of Pearl (blue mixed with iridescent white). The Final Section—white-flecked red, blue, and yellow.

BINAH: The Triangle and Ring—white. The First Section—red. The Second Section—black. The Third Section—dark brown (red and black mixed). The Final Section—gray-flecked pink.

CHESED: The Square and Ring—white. The First Section—violet. The Second Section—blue. The Third Section—deep violet (violet and blue mixed). The Final Section—deep blue-flecked yellow.

GEBURAH: The Pentagram and Ring—white. The First Section—orange. The Second Section—red. The Third Section—red-orange. The Final Section—red-flecked black.

TIPHARETH: The Hexagram and Ring—white. The First Section—Pink. The Second Section—yellow. The Third Section—Salmon (pink and yellow mixed). The Final Section—yellow-orange.

NETZACH: The Heptagram and Ring—white. The First Section—yellow-orange. The Second Section—green. The Third Section—yellow-green. The Final Section—olive-flecked gold.

HOD: The Octagram and Ring—white. The First Section—violet. The Second Section—orange. The Third Section—russet. The Final Section—yellow-brown flecked white.

YESOD: The Enneagram and Ring—white. The First Section—blue-violet. The Second Section—violet. The Third Section—dark violet (violet mixed with a touch of black). The Final Section—citrine-flecked blue.

MALKUTH: The Enneagram and Ring—white. The First Section—yellow. The Second Section—citrine, russet, olive, black. The Third Section—citrine, russet, olive, black-flecked gold. The Final Section—black-rayed yellow.

10) Paint or spray on a sealant to protect the painted wand. Allow to dry.

THE BINAH WAND

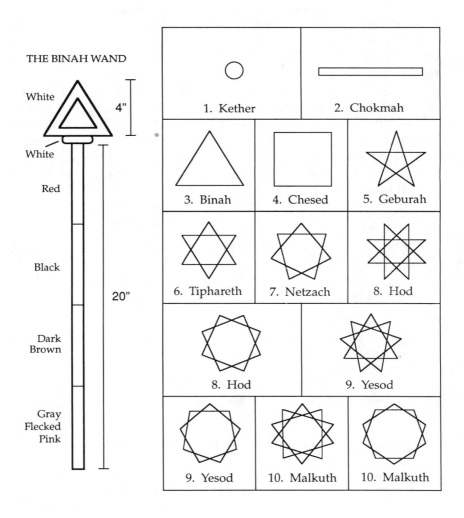

White

4"

White

Red

Black

20"

Dark
Brown

Gray
Flecked
Pink

1. Kether

2. Chokmah

3. Binah

4. Chesed

5. Geburah

6. Tiphareth

7. Netzach

8. Hod

8. Hod

9. Yesod

9. Yesod

10. Malkuth

10. Malkuth

The Sephirotic Wand

Ritual for Use

An Invocation of Binah

(This Ritual would be best performed during the day and hour of Saturn—see the Table of Planetary Hours.) The White Altar is to be set up in the Temple space. The Enochian Tablets are to be placed in their respective quarters. The Tablet of Union, the Cross and Triangle, incense and rose, candle, cup of water and platter of salt should be on the Altar. An Iset for the Adept should be placed in the West. The sword for banishing should be close at hand. The position of Saturn should be determined for the time of the ritual, and a symbol of Saturn should be placed on the floor or hung on the wall corresponding to the direction of the Planet. Next to the sigil should be placed four cards from *The New Golden Dawn Ritual Tarot Deck*; the four threes of the Minor Arcana. The Adept should be dressed in Second Order Regalia. The Binah Wand should be close at hand.

Sit in the West for a period of meditation. When ready, give five knocks against the Iset or Altar. Then take up the sword. Go to the Northeast and say, "HEKAS, HEKAS, ESTE BEBELOI! Far from this sacred place be the profane!"

Perform the LBRP.

Perform the BRH.

Take up the cup. Purify the Temple with water in all quarters, starting in the East, tracing Cross and Water Triangle. Say, "So therefore first the priest who governeth the works of Fire must sprinkle with the Lustral Waters of the loud resounding sea."

Take up the incense. Consecrate the room with Fire in all quarters, tracing the Cross and Fire Triangle. Say, "And when after all the phantoms are banished, thou shalt see that Holy and formless Fire, that Fire which darts and flashes through the hidden depths of the Universe. Hear Thou, the Voice of Fire!"

Circumambulate the Temple three times deosil, saluting with the Neophyte Signs when passing the East. Then stand west of the Altar facing East and perform the Adoration to the Lord of the Universe:

"Holy art Thou, Lord of the Universe."
"Holy art Thou, whom Nature hath not formed."

"Holy art Thou, the Vast and the Mighty One."
"Lord of the Light and of the Darkness."

Go the East and perform the complete Supreme Invoking Ritual of the Pentagram (SIRP).

Return to the East and vibrate the name "EHEIEH" four times, using the Vibratory Formula of the Middle Pillar. Then give the LVX Signs. Say, "Unto Thee Sole Wise, Sole Eternal, and Sole Merciful One, be praise and glory for ever. Who hath permitted me, who now standeth humbly before Thee, to enter thus far into the sanctuary of thy mysteries. Not unto me, Adonai, but unto Thy name be the glory, now and forever more. Let the influence of Thy Divine Ones descend upon my head, and teach me the value of self-sacrifice so that I shrink not in the hour of trial. But that thus my name may be written on high, and my Genius stand in the presence of the Holy One. In that hour when the Son of Humanity is invoked before the Lord of Spirits and his Name before the Ancient of Days."

Astrally formulate four Pillars surrounding you. Then visualize clearly a large Banner of the East. After the image is firmly within your mind, see it enveloping you as a cloak.

Perform the Qabalistic Cross. Then take the Binah Wand by the red band and perform the Lesser Invoking Hexagram Ritual of Saturn. (Commence with the Qabalistic Cross. Trace the four lesser forms of the Invoking Hexagram of Saturn in their respective quarters, vibrating "ARARITA" as you draw each hexagram. Follow this with the Analysis of the Keyword.)

Take up the candle in your left hand. Still holding the wand by the red band, face the direction where you have determined the position of the Saturn to be at the time of the working. In front of the Saturn sigil, trace the Supreme Invoking Hexagram of Saturn. Vibrate "ARARITA," "YHVH ELOHIM" and "ALEPH."

Say the following:

In the Divine name of YHVH ELOHIM, I invoke the Third Intelligence known as BINAH!" Trace the letters, Beth, Yod, Nun and Heh. "I call upon the powers of Understanding which reside in the Third Emanation. AMA! The dark sterile Mother. AIMA! the bright fertile Mother. Thou who art enthroned at the head of the Pillar of Severity in the Supernal Triangle. Thee I invoke! Thou art the Sanctifying Intelligence and the Fountain of Primordial Wisdom. Thee I invoke! Thou whose roots are in Amen! Thou who art the parent of faith and from whom faith emanates. Thee I invoke! Thou who are the Eternal Matron, MARAH, the great sea! KHORSIA, the royal Throne! Thee I invoke! Thou whose archangel is the mighty TZAPHKIEL, the Beholder of God, and whose angelic choir is the ARALIM, the Thrones! Thou whose physical representation is the sphere of SHABBATHAI! Thee I invoke!

None shall reach the Father save by the Mother! Grant unto me your aspects of infinite patience, and the capacity for understanding the Hidden Knowledge. Teach me the virtue of silence and the properties of organization and discipline. Thou Divine Mother who hast been called by many names: ISIS. RHEA. HERA. DEMETER. FRIGGA. MARY. STELLA MARIS, the Star of the Sea! O thou archetype eternal of Maternity and Love! Grant unto me your stability and strength. Completion of the Supernal Realm! Bathe me in Thy Holy Spirit! Thus may I at length restore the Garden and bridge the Abyss, so that humanity may once again gaze upon the splendors of Eden through my eyes. Thus may I at length look upon Thee, AIMA ELOHIM, Great Goddess clothed with the Sun, with the Moon under thy feet, and the Crown of twelve stars upon thy head.

Grasp the Binah Wand by the red Atziluth band. Vibrate the name of "YHVH ELOHIM" while tracing its sigil over the Three of Wands from the Tarot. Meditate upon the color of Binah in the King Scale. Visualize a swirling mass of red clouds. This is Binah at its most archetypal level. The color red indicates the harmony that exists between the Great Feminine Principle and the masculine Element of Fire at this elevation on the Tree. Binah in Atziluth is a cauldron into which the dynamic Fire energy of Chokmah is funneled and captured.

Grasp the Binah Wand by the black Briah band. Vibrate the name of "TZAPHKIEL" while tracing the sigil of the archangel over the Three of Cups from the Tarot. Meditate upon the color of Binah in the Queen Scale. Imagine that the red clouds of Binah in Atziluth have stopped their swirling motion. Binah at this level is dark like the inside of a womb ... you can almost hear the heartbeat of the Great Goddess. Black is the result of all colors being absorbed into the sea of Binah. It is the pregnant and form-building aspect of the Eternal Mother.

Grasp the wand by the dark brown Yetzirah band. Vibrate the name of "ARALIM" while tracing the sigil of the order of angels over the Three of Swords from the Tarot. Meditate upon the color of Binah in the Prince Scale. Visualize this level of Binah as the Dark Mother in her restrictive, form-destroying mode. The color of the womb here is dark brown, the color resulting from the mixture of red and black. It signifies the menstrual blood of the Goddess.

Grasp the wand by the Assiah band (gray-flecked pink). Vibrate the name of "SHABBATHAI" while tracing its sigil over the Three of Pentacles from the Tarot. Meditate on the color of Binah in the Princess Scale:

Grey is the color of the "child" resulting from the mating of Spirit (white) and Matter (black). It is the completion of the pregnancy—the manifested progeny of Chokmah and Binah. Pink is the other color of the child which identifies it as the Son of the Father and the Mother—the King who rules in Tiphareth.

Contemplate for as long as you wish any of the four colors attributed to Binah in the different Qabalistic Worlds. Then go to the west of the Altar and face East. Hold the Binah Wand by the red band. Raise your hands and say, "Not unto my name, O Tetragrammaton, but to Thine be ascribed the Kingdom, the Power and Glory, now and forever more! Amen!" Give the LVX Signs.

Purify and consecrate the temple with Water and Fire as in the beginning.

Perform the Reverse Circumambulation, three times widdershins. Perform again the Adoration to the Lord of the Universe.

Return to the position of Saturn in the temple. Holding the Wand by the red band, trace the Greater Banishing Hexagram of Saturn in that direction, vibrating the names of "ARARITA", "YHVH ELOHIM" and "ALEPH".

Perform the Lesser Banishing Hexagram Ritual of Saturn (the four forms in their respective quarters). Begin with the Qabalistic Cross and end with the Analysis of the Keyword.

Put the Binah Wand aside and take up the sword. Perform the LBRP and the BRH.

Return to the East and say, "I now release any spirits that may have been imprisoned by this ceremony. Depart in peace to your abodes and habitations. Go with the sanction of YHVH ELOHIM and the blessings of YEHESHUAH YEHOVA-SHAH."

Give five knocks as in the beginning.

Say "I now declare this Temple duly closed."

SO MOTE IT BE.

The Wand for Tarot Divination

Use and Symbolism

This wand is used to charge and give added strength to any divination using the Tarot. The wand is small enough to carry anywhere along with a deck of Tarot cards.

A formula which is useful in assisting concentration, and formulating a link between the Diviner and the intelligences referred to the Tarot, is to take the pack in the left and with the right hand hold the Tarot Wand. Trace a circle over the deck and say: "In the divine name IAO, I invoke Thee thou great Angel HRU (Her-oo) who art set over the operations of this Secret Wisdom. Lay thine hand invisibly on these consecrated cards of art, that thereby I may obtain true knowledge of hidden things, to the glory of the ineffable Name. Amen."

The divination can now continue, using whatever particular card spread you prefer.

Materials Needed

One 3/8" dowel approx. 6"–8" in length
Gesso
Acrylic paints: white, black, red, blue, yellow, green, orange, violet
Sealant: clear lacquer finish

Tools Needed

Sandpaper—fine grained
Artist's brushes

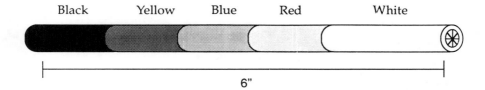

Black   Yellow   Blue   Red   White

6"

The Tarot Wand

Construction

1) For this simple little wand you will need to cover the dowel with a coat of gesso. let dry. Sand lightly.

2) Divide the shaft into five sections, one long section and four shorter sections. Paint the longest section white. This is the top of the wand. Paint the shorter sections in descending order as follows: red, blue, yellow and black.

Finishing Steps

3) On the white end, paint the symbol of a wheel with twelve spokes in black. (You may wish to paint the wheel on the very tip of the wand.) Also on the white band, paint the sigil of the angel HRU, the word ROTA, and your own magickal motto.

4) On the red band paint the letters and sigil of the word ATZILUTH in green.

5) On the blue band paint the letters and sigil of the word BRIAH in orange.

6) On the yellow section, paint the letters and sigil of the word YET-ZIRAH in violet.

7) On the black band, paint the letters and sigil of the word ASSIAH in white.

8) Apply a coat of sealant for protection.

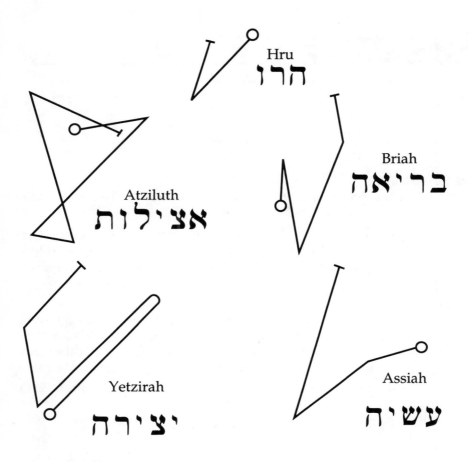

Hru
הרו

Briah
בריאה

Atziluth
אצילות

Yetzirah
יצירה

Assiah
עשיה

Sigils and Symbols used on the Tarot Wand

Afterword

by Donald Michael Kraig

By the time you get to this afterword, most of you will have either read this book or at least looked through it. When you decide to use it, however, you will truly take a step away from those dilettantes who claim to be magicians but who, in reality, are what Israel Regardie used to refer to as the "inepti."

To the best of my knowledge, two books were published over a decade ago which gave cursory (and sometimes incorrect) explanations on how to build a small selection of the tools described in this book, along with some generic magickal tools. As of this writing neither of the two are in print. The book you hold in your hands, however, is quite different from them—they explained how to build objects; this explains how to use the tools you construct in the transformational alchemy which will lead to your further spiritual development. It is this growth which is the true goal of ceremonial magic and of groups such as the Hermetic Order of the Golden Dawn.

If you think that this is overstating the issue, good! You are on your way to becoming a true magician by not simply taking somebody's word for it. True magicians are thinkers and experimenters, not blind followers of personalities who died decades or centuries ago. But I am not overstating the issue. Building the tools and working with the rituals as described in this book will make a difference in your life. The only way you will know this for sure, of course, is when you try them out for yourself.

Some people who are not ceremonial magicians have pointed out to me that the magickal tools are only that—tools. A true magician, they claim, does not need to have daggers, wands, etc. They proudly say that they can do all the magic they desire with a few well-chosen words or a snap of the fingers.

While it is partly true that the tools are an extension of the magician (the proper consecration, charging and use of magical tools also makes them into powerful talismans of collected magical energy), such a claim misses the point. The various tools can be used as aids for learning how to direct magical energies, just as learning to read aloud precedes learning to read silently.

Any ritual can be successfully performed with the fingers, and understanding of the ritual and the proper visualizations and vocalizations. I have found, however, that the tools reinforce and enhance my own magical abilities. The tools do not give me added powers, but they do allow me to use my abilities to my fullest capacity. They enhance my ritual work and my life as a magician. They make every aspect of my life more magical. Let me describe some of my experiences in this.

The first tool I created and used was a robe. I owned a sewing machine—I used it primarily for patching up clothes—but I had never attempted a sewing project of this complexity. I had never even used a pattern.

I followed the instructions which I had been given for making the robe to the letter. (I think I may have used too many pins to hold the material in place while I was sewing it, however. Dropped pins turned up in bare feet for months after I was finished!) Sometimes the pieces of cloth in front of me made no logical sense. Finally, It started to take shape. When it was finished I marveled at what I had created. The pieces of material had become a Tau robe. This certainly was an alchemical change.

No, there was no shaking of hands or tense anticipation as I put on the robe for the first time. It was, after all, just a piece of cloth. I knew that there would be no "poof" of smoke, leaving me surrounded by women, gold and jewels, as a result of donning what I had made. I was wrong.

After I put it on I discovered that something did change—me. I had never worn a robe like this before. It felt good on me; like it was a part of me. I felt special. The first ritual I performed in it, the Lesser Banishing Ritual of the Pentagram, felt different: more effective, more powerful.

Perhaps it was a psychological lift, perhaps it was an objective change. I have no doubt, however, that when I wore the robe my rituals improved in quality, intensity, and effect. As a result of working with that one simple tool I was accelerating my evolution into something more than I was—I was truly becoming a magician.

The next tool I made was an altar. I am not great with woodworking, but the design was simple. I spent a great deal of time getting a smooth coat of paint on the altar. As a finishing fillip I decoupaged a large painting of a pentagram (which I hand-colored) on the top and one of the Tree of Life on the front.

Using an altar—one specifically designed for doing ritual, not merely an extra table—made a difference in my rituals. The altar forms a central focal point around which the ritual circle is created. I discovered that it was an important addition to making a magical circle even though it was at the center and not the circumference.

I have long-since gifted both that robe and my altar to my good friend and teacher Cris Monnastre. It is my sincere hope that they continue to serve her, and those who work with her, well.

As I slowly created or changed various items into magical tools I found that my own abilities and spirituality were growing. Each new tool added to the power and effectiveness of my ritual work.

To my great surprise I discovered that when I was ready to use a tool which I did not have, it would either come to me or I would develop the skills to create it. I remember a "chance" occurrence which took place around 1980. I was walking around an area in San Diego where there were several used book stores, wondering how I would ever find a sword that I could adapt for magical use. I happened to walk past an Oriental herb store where martial arts classes were also taught. Something drew me inside and I saw a sword hanging on the wall which would have been perfect for my purposes. I asked if it was for sale and the one person in the store said I would have to ask the owner, as it was his personal sword. The owner, I was told, would be back in an hour.

During that hour I walked around with my head spinning. It was too perfect. It was the ideal shape. But had it been used for fighting? If so I would have to cleanse it very thoroughly. If it had ever drawn blood I didn't want it at all. Worst of all, I did not have a great deal of money. Going over my finances in my head I realized that I could only afford to pay $35.00 for any sword. I had already looked at many swords and most went from $55.00 to many hundreds of dollars. Still I knew I would never be content if I didn't find out the entire story of this sword.

After an hour had passed I went back into the store. The man whom I had talked with was gone and an older person was there. I asked him if he was the owner. When he told me he was I asked how much he wanted for the sword.

He gazed up at the sword with a look in his eye as if he had forgotten about it entirely. "Gee," he explained, "I had never thought of selling it. I bought it from the maker when I was in Japan and I personally brought it over by boat. I was going to use it for [martial arts] practice but I never did. I'm sorry," he added, "but I couldn't sell it for less than $35.00."

Needless to say, after some minor physical alterations, appropriate painting and magical consecration and charging, I still have it as one of my prime magical tools.

I think that using the tools of magic is important for practitioners. People in Western society today are different from those who lived 100-2,000 years ago. We now have blasting stereos and brilliant colors as found on everything from television screens to shoelaces. Our lives are filled with an intensity of sensation—visual, aural, etc.—which might have inundated our predecessors. Those who have avoided society, who live in rural areas and who have eliminated the intensity of city living from their lives may find that a simple dagger and branch from a tree may be enough to use. I, however, grew up in a large city, and for many purposes find that I want more to help excite my senses and enhance my magic. For me there is a difference in performing rituals with specially created (or modified) and charged tools, as opposed to using no tools or items that are simply found. You will discover those differences, too.

I have worked with the Golden Dawn system of Magick as outlined in Israel Regardie's *The Golden Dawn* for many years and found my rituals to be enhanced by the tools I made and used. In turn, my work affected my psyche and helped to make me a more magical person. As I have written many times, "Magick is not something you do, magick is something you are." I have spent thousands of hours over the last two-and-a-half decades in the trial and error of building tools. If I had possessed this book 25 years ago I would have saved myself a great deal of time and effort. In a sense I envy those who are starting out in the study of ceremonial magic and the Golden Dawn system. Many of the things I had to learn through meditation, study of rare books, and trial and error are now easily available.

The magical current which is the source of the real power of the Golden Dawn can be tapped into by anyone. You do not need to be a member of any particular group. With diligence, practice and study of works such as this one and those of Israel Regardie you can link with the Golden Dawn's magical current and become a magician in the Golden Dawn tradition.

Recently a person asked me, "If you were a member of a magical order, what grade would you be in?"

"That's easy," I replied. "I'd be a neophyte. I'm still learning new things every day. Sometimes I find a teacher in the strangest places."

Yes, I do believe in the old statement that when the student is ready the teacher will appear.

This book can be your teacher if you are ready.

Epilogue

by Adam P. Forrest

This Fall, I was very pleased to learn that another book by Chic and Tabatha Cicero—the one you have just read—was being prepared for publication, and I was also very honored when they asked me to prepare this outline of the modern history and Work of the Golden Dawn to serve as an epilogue.

The Hermetic Order of the Golden Dawn manifested in Britain at a time when many Britons were seeking a more vital, stimulating, alternative to the exoteric spirituality offered by the established churches of England, and at a time when there was a desire for spiritual growth in England and abroad. It was at this point that America took an early step toward the manifestation of the New Aeon by exporting to Britain and all of Europe first Spiritualism, then Theosophy. Spiritualism provoked a huge excitement because it provided a direct experience of the Spiritual, but its limitations were great. It seemed to offer contact with only the lowest levels of the spiritual world; it was also perceived to be intellectually unsophisticated, since there was no intellectual tradition supporting it. Then came Theosophy. Its point of contact with the spiritual world was not through recently deceased relatives, but with enlightened Masters. It also offered a more satisfying intellectual content, as well as an intriguing claim to represent an ancient Secret Tradition.

The Theosophical Society was founded in New York City in 1875 by a group of Spiritualists, Qabalists, Freemasons, and Rosicrucians. There was not a single representative of the Eastern Tradition among the founders. At this initial stage, Madame Blavatsky identified her Inner contacts, her Masters or Secret Chiefs as Serapis Bey, Polydorus Isurenus, and Robert More—three Masters from an Egyptian Order carrying on the work of Zoroaster and Solomon. Even the notorious Mahatma Letters which Blavatsky's associates supposedly received from the Masters were originally signed "Serapis" (that is, the name under which Osiris was worshipped most widely in the Graeco-Roman world). In other words, the Theosophical Society was founded as a Western Esoteric Society. It was several years later, when Blavatsky and Olcott converted to Buddhism, that the Society decisively shifted to an Eastern orientation, and Blavatsky traded in her three Occidental Masters for the Asians "Koot Hoomi," "Morya," and "Djwal Khul."

It is entirely possible that if the Theosophical Society had held to its original course, there might never have been a Golden Dawn, because neither the spiritual seekers who were drawn together to form an esoteric group nor the Inner sources which inspired its foundation, would have needed a Golden Dawn. But the Theosophical Society did turn to the East, and a vital task was left undone.

In 1875, a group of Spiritualists, Qabalists, Freemasons, and Rosicrucians foundeded the Theosophical Society; thirteen years later, it was a group of Theosophists, Qabalists, Freemasons, and Rosicrucians who founded the Hermetic Order of the Golden Dawn to carry out the Work abandoned by the Theosophical Society. For the tasks which the Golden Dawn was called to undertake were to serve as Guardians of the *Western* Esoteric Tradition and to initiate, educate, and nurture those individuals called to carry on the Great Work.

The Order succeeded to an amazing degree, as the founders of the G.:D.: had been well-suited to their task. Greatly Honored Frater Non Omnis Moriar (Wescott) was a high-Grade Mason who had both the esoteric scholarship and the managerial abilities required to bring the organization together. Frater Deo Duce Comite Ferro (Mathers) was not only an occult scholar and gifted ritualist, but also the true Magician of the Order. He was responsible for establishing the Inner contacts with the Secret Chiefs which made the Golden Dawn a legitimate Magical and Initiatory Order rather than merely a ritualized antiquarian fraternity like the Societas Rosicruciana in Anglia.

The Fraters and Sorores who came after them included many teachers still well-known today and still teaching posthumously through their published works; such people as Dion Fortune, A.E.

Waite, Aleister Crowley, Paul Foster Case, and Francis Israel Regardie.

It seems that there are Adepts in every generation who are called to dedicate themselves completely to the Work, in a way that is not possible or probably even desirable for the majority of Initiates. These Adepts who offer themselves to the Work in this special way are not all great Adepts, though the greatest of Adepts are usually to be found among them. In retrospect it is clear that the late Francis Israel Regardie, our truly Very Honored Frater Ad Majorem Adonai Gloriam, was one of those who offered himself to the Work in this special way. Though I cannot personally count him among the great Adepts of our Order, I see him as one of the committed few who was called to a special task. In Regardie's case, along with numberless smaller services, I perceive two vital tasks which he accomplished for our Work.

The first of these was when, in 1937, fearing the collapse of the weakened structure of the Order in the hands of the ill-trained Stella Matutina Chiefs, he published the basic curriculum of the Golden Dawn. In the next few years, the remnant of the S.:M.: (with the exception of an isolated off-shoot Temple in New Zealand) ceased group Work. Although this was largely a result of their inability to adapt to the results of Regardie's action, i.e., their inability to deal with a very different approach to the idea of secrecy (which was called for now that much of their curriculum was in the public domain), still, it was also the case that the S.:M.: had never truly established contact with the Inner sources behind the Golden Dawn, and for this reason were unable to draw upon those resources to move on to a new phase of the work. Thus Regardie, by his publication of the Golden Dawn's curriculum and rituals, had fulfilled the principle original task of the Order—to preserve the Western Esoteric Tradition from extinction.*

The appropriateness of Regardie's decision to publish the Order's documents has been a subject of debate in magical circles for 50 years. As I have already stated, I believe he was carrying out the Work of the Order when he did so, and I am eternally grateful that he did. I was a teenager when I bought my first copy of The Golden Dawn, seeking with the passion and determination of youth for a

---

* For with the basic curriculum of the Golden Dawn now readily available in libraries and bookstores throughout the Western hemisphere, the Western Esoteric Tradition will survive in some form so long as a literate humankind survives.—APF

valid and consistent system to tie together the disparate Magical material I had been studying for several years. Within an hour of opening the book, I knew—with a deep and satisfying sense of homecoming—that I had found my system. In the years since that day, I have met many Magicians who owe Regardie an immeasurable debt for the same experience. Of course, it is not just individuals but also organizations which have been enriched by the ready availability of the G.:D.: material. The curricula of such outstanding Western Exoteric Orders as the Aurum Solis and the Servants of the Light clearly show the incorporation and adaptation of much Golden Dawn material. I have seen many Wiccans and other Neopagans employing the Pentagram system of the Golden Dawn, often unaware of its source; and I have even seen the Middle Pillar taught in a "New Age" self-help manual. The vitalizing influence of the Order has spread far and wide through the alternative spiritual community in the West.

Of course, another important change wrought by Regardie's publication was the transformation of the nature of secrecy necessary within viable manifestations of the Order. Total secrecy is healthy within the formative stages of a Magical Order, rather as one may begin to grow a flower in the controlled environment of the greenhouse before transplanting it to the garden. Furthermore, privacy and limited secrecy is sometimes necessary, due both to the delicate nature of Magical Work and to protect the right of individual members to pursue their spiritual Path free from intrusions and persecution. However, the arguments for total secrecy are unconvincing and archaic at best, and egotistical and petty at worst. In the final analysis, all such arguments eventually boil down to the notion that the Inner secrets of the Initiatic Traditions are so potent that only Initiates may be trusted with them. First, I know many Initiates and non-Initiates, and I have encountered as many good, wise, and reliable people outside the circle of Initiation as within it. Second, most of the curriculum of the Golden Dawn through the Subgrade of Zelator Adeptus Minor has been publicly available for half a century, and none of the problems of the modern world are even remotely connected with the release of that knowledge. Third, I know much of what remains unpublished of the Order Teachings, and while there is certainly power in those teachings, it is not a dangerous power; the Mysteries entrusted to the Order are concerned with spiritual growth and evolution, and the last thing from which

Western civilization needs to be protected is spiritual growth and evolution.

The second significant task carried out by Regardie was, as an Adept, to bring a valid branch of the initiatory lineage of the Golden Dawn to America* the alchemical melting pot where the New Age was incubating.** Such tasks are not always easy. A.M.A.G. waited here four decades until the threads of the pattern came together. Then, in one of those graceful synchronicities which often play mid-wife to significant Magical events, a couple in Georgia were inspired—at that time scarcely aware of what they were undertaking—to build a Rosicrucian Vault, the powerful ritual chamber required to pass on the Adept Initiation, at precisely the time when two Magicians (one on the east coast of the United States and one on the west coast), unknown to each other or to the Georgia couple, came to be ready to receive that Initiation. And A.M.A.G., with the right to confer the Initiation in such a Vault, was the connecting link among them. And so, in one remarkable weekend, Regardie presided over two Initiations into the Inner Order, the first and the last which he ever performed; and the Lamp of the Keryx was passed into American hands.

In the intervening years, those first two Initiates of the Inner Order have been joined by an ever-growing college of brother and sister Adepts, enough to assure the continuation of the Order. With the twin tasks of preserving the Western Mystery Tradition and of maintaining the initiatory lineage of the Golden Dawn accomplished, there remains only the continuing responsibility of the Order to train and prepare the next generations of aspirants for eventual Adeptship and to nourish them in their quest for spiritual evolution, the centerpiece of which, in the developmental schema of the Golden Dawn, is the Attainment of the Augoeides, the Epiphany of Adonai, or—in the well-known phrase of Abramelin—the Knowledge and Conversation of the Holy Guardian Angel. In other words,

---

* There had been earlier G.˙.D.˙.: Temples in America warranted by DDCF, at least one of which had a period of institutional vitality, but these had died out without a strong connection to their Initiatory source. Paul Foster Case, a scion of that early vital Temple, went on to found the still-existing Builders of the Adytum.—APF

** For, contrary to the claims of Crowley and some of his Thelemic successors, the Order of the Golden Dawn—as its name clearly signifies—is not a relic of an expiring Aeon, but a harbinger of the New Aeon of Aquarius, synthesizing the best of our spiritual heritage from preceding Aeons with the fresh insights and dynamic evolutionary Current of the Age dawning about us.—APF. Trans. William Law, 1784.—APF

the Order is designed to be in itself one valid answer to the essential question of the pilgrim on the Path of the Western Mysteries, a question well-put by the Silesian mystic Jakob Boehme:

> How am I to wait for the rising of this glorious Sun, and how am I to seek in the Centre this Foundation of Light which may enlighten me throughout and bring all my properties into perfect Harmony? I am in Nature, as I said before; and which Way shall I pass through Nature and the Light thereof so that I may come into the Supernal and Supersensual Ground whence this true Light, which is the Light of Minds, doth arise: and this without the destruction of my Nature, or quenching the Light of it, which is my Reason?

We can all be grateful that there continue to be teachers like Chic and Tabatha Cicero willing to take pen in hand and continue the ongoing answer of the Tradition to this question. So if you are a seeker on this Quest—as I assume you are by your study of this book—I offer you my sincere congratulations on having found the Ciceros, for I can assure you on the basis of long personal experience that they are excellent companions to have by your side on this Path.

—Adam Forrest
Sandalphon House
Winter Solstice 1991

BIBLIOGRAPHY

Ashcroft-Nowicki, Dolores. *The Shining Paths*. Wellingborough, Northamptonshire: The Aquarian Press, 1983.

Budge, E. A. Wallis. *The Gods of the Egyptians*, Vol. 1 & 2. New York: Dover Publications, Inc., 1969.

Budge, E.A. Wallis. *The Book of the Dead*. London: Routledge & Kegan Paul Ltd., 1969.

Case, Paul Foster. *The Book of Tokens*. 10th ed. Los Angeles: Builders of the Adytum, 1983.

Cirlot, J. E. *A Dictionary of Symbols*. 2nd ed. New York: Philosophical Library, 1983.

Colquhoun, Ithell. *Sword of Wisdom*. New York: G. P. Putnam's Sons, 1975.

Crowley, Aleister. *777*. York Beach, ME: Samuel Weiser, Inc., 1973.

Divine Pymander of Hermes Mercurius Trismegistus. Des Plaines, IL: Yogi Publication Society.

Fortune, Dion. *The Mystical Qabalah*. New York: Ibis Books, 1981.

Gilbert, R. A. *The Golden Dawn Companion*. Wellingborough, Northamptonshire: The Aquarian Press, 1986.

Gilbert, R. A. *The Sorcerer and His Apprentice*. Wellingborough, Northamptonshire: The Aquarian Press, 1983.

Godwin, David. *Godwin's Cabalistic Encyclopedia*. 2nd ed. St. Paul, MN: Llewellyn Publications, 1989.

Gray, William G. *The Ladder of Lights*. York Beach, ME: Samuel Weiser, Inc., 1981.

Hall, Manly P. *The Secret Teachings of All Ages*. Los Angeles: The Philosophical Research Society, Inc., 1977.

James, Geoffrey. *The Enochian Evocation of Dr. John Dee.* Gillette, New Jersey: Heptangle Books, 1984.

Knight, Gareth. *A Practical Guide to Qabalistic Symbolism.* New York: Samuel Weiser, Inc. 1983.

Kraig, Donald Michael. *Modern Magick.* St. Paul, MN: Llewellyn Publications, 1988.

McLean, Adam. *The Alchemical Mandala.* Grand Rapids, MI: Phanes Press, 1989.

Olcott, William Tyler. *Star Lore of All Ages.* New York: G. P. Putnam's Sons – The Knickerbocker Press, 1911.

Parachemy, Journal of Hermetic Arts and Sciences. Summer 1979, Vol. VII, Number 3.

Parachemy, Journal of Hermetic Arts and Sciences. Summer 1977, Vol. V, Number 3.

Regardie, Israel. *Ceremonial Magic.* Wellingborough, Northamptonshire: The Aquarian Press, 1982.

Regardie, Israel. *The Complete Golden Dawn System of Magic.* Phoenix, Arizona: Falcon Press, 1984.

Regardie, Israel. *Foundations of Practical Magic.* 2nd ed. Wellingborough, Northamptonshire: The Aquarian Press, 1983.

Regardie, Israel. *The Golden Dawn.* 4th ed. St. Paul, MN: Llewellyn Publications, 1982.

Regardie, Israel. *The Middle Pillar.* 2nd ed. St. Paul, MN: Llewellyn Publications, 1985.

Regardie, Israel. *The Tree of Life.* York Beach, ME: Samuel Weiser, Inc., 1972.

Stanley, Thomas. *The Chaldaean Oracles.* Gillette, New Jersey: Heptangle Books, 1989.

Torrens, R. G. *The Secret Rituals of the Golden Dawn.* New York: Samuel Weiser, Inc. 1973.

Wang, Robert. *The Qabalistic Tarot.* York Beach, ME: Samuel Weiser, Inc., 1983.

Wang, Robert. *The Secret Temple.* New York: Samuel Weiser, Inc., 1980.

STAY IN TOUCH

On the following pages you will find listed, with their current prices, some of the books and tapes now available on related subjects. Your book dealer stocks most of these, and will stock new titles in the Llewellyn series as they become available. We urge your patronage. However, to obtain our full catalog, to keep informed of new titles as they are released and to benefit from informative articles and helpful news, you are invited to write for our bi-monthly news magazine/catalog. A sample copy is free, and it will continue coming to you at no cost as long as you are an active mail customer. Or you may keep it coming for a full year with a donation of just $7.00 in U.S.A. and Canada ($20.00 overseas, first class mail). Many bookstores also have *The Llewellyn New Times* available to their customers. Ask for it.

Stay in touch! In *The Llewellyn New Times'* pages you will find news and reviews of new books, tapes and services, announcements of meetings and seminars, articles helpful to our readers, news of authors, advertising of products and services, special money-making opportunities, and much more.

The Llewellyn New Times
P.O. Box 64383-Dept. 150, St. Paul, MN 55164-0383, U.S.A.

• • •

TO ORDER BOOKS AND TAPES

If your book dealer does not have the books and tapes described on the following pages readily available, you may order them direct from the publisher by sending full price in U.S. funds, plus $3.00 for postage and handling for orders *under* $10.00; $4.00 for orders *over* $10.00. There are no postage and handling charges for orders over $50.00. UPS Delivery: We ship UPS whenever possible. Delivery guaranteed. Provide your street address as UPS does not deliver to P.O. Boxes. UPS to Canada requires a $50.00 minimum order. Allow 4-6 weeks for delivery. Orders outside the U.S.A. and Canada: Airmail—add retail price of book; add $5.00 for each non-book item (tapes, etc.); add $1.00 per item for surface mail.

FOR GROUP STUDY AND PURCHASE

Because there is a great deal of interest in group discussion and study of the subject matter of this book, we feel that we should encourage the adoption and use of this particular book by such groups by offering a special "quantity" price to group leaders or "agents."

Our Special Quantity Price for a minimum order of five copies of *Secrets of a Golden Dawn Temple* is $59.85 cash-with-order. This price includes postage and handling within the United States. Minnesota residents must add 6.5% sales tax. For additional quantities, please order in multiples of five. For Canadian and foreign orders, add postage and handling charges as above. Credit card (VISA, Master Card, American Express) orders are accepted. Charge card orders only may be phoned free ($15.00 minimum order) within the U.S.A. or Canada by dialing 1-800-THE-MOON. Customer service calls dial 1-612-291-1970. Mail Orders to:

LLEWELLYN PUBLICATIONS
P.O. Box 64383, Dept. 150, St. Paul, MN 55164-0383, U.S.A.

Prices subject to change without notice.

THE NEW GOLDEN DAWN RITUAL TAROT
Keys to the Rituals, Symbolism, Magic & Divination
by Chic Cicero & Sandra Tabatha Cicero

This is the indispensable companion to Llewellyn's New Golden Dawn Ritual Tarot Deck. It provides a card-by-card analysis of the deck's intricate symbolism, an introduction to the Qabalah, and a section on the use of the deck for practical rituals, meditations and divination procedures. The Tarot newcomer as well as the advanced magician will benefit from this groundbreaking work.

The highlight of the book is the section on rituals. Instructions are included for: ritual baths, Lesser Banishing Ritual of the Pentagram, Tarot deck consecration ritual, using the Tarot for talismans, scrying with the Tarot, dream work with the Tarot, the Golden Dawn method of Tarot divination, and much, much more.

The Golden Dawn is experiencing a widespread revival among New Agers, Wiccans, mystics and ceremonial magicians. This book and companion deck are just what people are looking for: traditional Golden Dawn knowledge with new rituals written by authors with "magickal credentials."

0-87542-139-3, 256 pgs., 6 x 9, illus.,   **$10.95**

THE NEW GOLDEN DAWN RITUAL TAROT DECK
by Sandra Tabatha Cicero

The original Tarot deck of the Hermetic Order of the Golden Dawn has been copied and interpreted many times. While each deck has its own special flair, The New Golden Dawn Ritual Tarot Deck may well be the most important new Tarot deck for the 1990s and beyond.

From its inception 100 years ago, the Golden Dawn continues to be the authority on the initiatory and meditative teachings of the Tarot. The Golden Dawn used certain cards in their initiation rituals. Now, for the first time ever, a deck incorporates not only the traditional Tarot images but also all of the temple symbolism needed for use in the Golden Dawn rituals. This is the first deck that is perfect both for divination and for ritual work. Meditation on the Major Arcana cards can lead to a lightning flash of enlightenment and spiritual understanding in the Western magickal tradition. The New Golden Dawn Ritual Tarot Deck was encouraged by the late Israel Regardie, and it is for anyone who wants a reliable Tarot deck that follows the Western magickal tradition.

0-87542-138-5, boxed set: 79-card deck with booklet   **$19.95**

THE GOLDEN DAWN
The Original Account of the Teachings, Rites & Ceremonies of the Hermetic Order
As revealed by Israel Regardie
Complete in one volume with further revision, expansion, and additional notes by Regardie, Cris Monnastre, and others. Expanded with an index of more than 100 pages!

Originally published in four bulky volumes of some 1,200 pages, this 6th Revised and Enlarged Edition has been entirely reset in modern, less space-consuming type, in half the pages (while retaining the original pagination in marginal notation for reference) for greater ease and use.

Corrections of typographical errors perpetuated in the original and subsequent editions have been made, with further revision and additional text and notes by noted scholars and by actual practitioners of the Golden Dawn system of Magick, with an Introduction by the only student ever accepted for personal training by Regardie.

Also included are Initiation Ceremonies, important rituals for consecration and invocation, methods of meditation and magical working based on the Enochian Tablets, studies in the Tarot, and the system of Qabalistic Correspondences that unite the World's religions and magical traditions into a comprehensive and practical whole.

This volume is designed as a study and practice curriculum suited to both group and private practice. Meditation upon, and following with the Active Imagination, the Initiation Ceremonies are fully experiential without need of participation in group or lodge. A very complete reference encyclopedia of Western Magick.
0-87542-663-8, 840 pgs., 6 x 9, illus., softcover   **$19.95**

A GARDEN OF POMEGRANATES
by Israel Regardie
What is the Tree of Life? It's the ground plan of the Qabalistic system—a set of symbols used since ancient times to study the Universe. The Tree of Life is a geometrical arrangement of ten sephiroth, or spheres, each of which is associated with a different archetypal idea, and 22 paths which connect the spheres.This system of primal correspondences has been found the most efficient plan ever devised to classify and organize the characteristics of the self. Israel Regardie has written one of the best and most lucid introductions to the Qabalah. *A Garden of Pomegranates* combines Regardie's own studies with his notes on the works of Aleister Crowley, A. E. Waite, Eliphas Levi and D. H. Lawrence. No longer is the wisdom of the Qabalah to be held secret! The needs of today place the burden of growth upon each and every person . . . each has to undertake the Path as his or her own responsibility, but every help is given in the most ancient and yet most modern teaching here known to humankind.
0-87542-690-5, 160 pgs., 5 1/4 x 8, softcover   **$8.95**

THE MIDDLE PILLAR
by Israel Regardie

Between the two outer pillars of the Qabalistic Tree of Life, the extremes of Mercy and Severity, stands *The Middle Pillar*, signifying one who has achieved equilibrium in his or her own self.

Integration of the human personality is vital to the continuance of creative life. Without it, man lives as an outsider to his own true self. By combining Magic and Psychology in the Middle Pillar Ritual/Exercise (a magical meditation technique), we bring into balance the opposing elements of the psyche while yet holding within their essence and allowing full expression of man's entire being.

In this book, and with this practice, you will learn to: understand the psyche through its correspondences of the Tree of Life; expand self-awareness, thereby intensifying the inner growth process; activate creative and intuitive potentials; understand the individual thought patterns which control every facet of personal behavior; and regain the sense of balance and peace of mind—the equilibrium that everyone needs for physical and psychic health.

0-87542-658-1, 176 pgs., 5-1/4x8, softcover   **$8.95**

MODERN MAGICK
Eleven Lessons in the High Magickal Arts
by Donald Michael Kraig

Modern Magick is the most comprehensive step-by-step introduction to the art of ceremonial magic ever offered. The eleven lessons in this book will guide you from the easiest of rituals and the construction of your magickal tools through the highest forms of magick: designing your own rituals and doing pathworking. Along the way you will learn the secrets of the Kabbalah in a clear and easy-to-understand manner. You will also discover the true secrets of invocation (channeling) and evocation, and the missing information that will finally make the ancient grimoires, such as the "Keys of Solomon," not only comprehensible, but usable. *Modern Magick* is designed so anyone can use it, and it is the perfect guidebook for students and classes. It will also help to round out the knowledge of long-time practitioners of the magickal arts.

0-87542-324-8, 592 pgs., 6 x 9, illus., index, softcover   **$14.95**

GODWIN'S CABALISTIC ENCYCLOPEDIA
A Complete Guide to Cabalistic Magick
by David Godwin

This is the most complete correlation of Hebrew and English ideas ever offered. It is a dictionary of Cabalism arranged, with definitions, alphabetically in Hebrew and numerically. With this book, the practicing Cabalist or student no longer needs access to a large number of books on mysticism, magic and the occult in order to trace down the basic meanings, Hebrew spellings, and enumerations of the hundreds of terms, words, and names that are included in this book.

This book includes: all of the two-letter root words found in Biblical Hebrew, the many names of God, the Planets, the Astrological Signs, Numerous Angels, the Shem ha-Mephorash, the Spirits of the *Goetia*, the correspondences of the 32 Paths, a comparison of the Tarot and the Cabala, a guide to Hebrew Pronunciation, and a complete edition of Aleister Crowley's valuable book *Sepher Sephiroth*.

Here is a book that is a must for the shelf of all Magicians, Cabalists, Astrologers, Tarot students, Thelemites, and those with any interest at all in the spiritual aspects of our universe.

0-87542-292-6, 528 pgs., 6 x 9   **$15.00**

MAGIC AND THE WESTERN MIND
Ancient Knowledge and the Transformation of Consciousness
by Gareth Knight

Magic and the Western Mind explains why intelligent and responsible people are turning to magic and the occult as a radical and important way to find meaning in modern life, as well as a means of survival for themselves and the planet.

First published in 1978 as *A History of White Magic*, this book illustrates, in a wide historical survey, how the higher imagination has been used to aid the evolution of consciousness—from the ancient mystery religions, through alchemy, Renaissance magic, the Rosicrucian Manifestoes, Freemasonry, 19th-century magic fraternities, up to psychoanalysis and the current occult revival. Plus it offers some surprising insights into the little-known interests of famous people.The Western mind developed magic originally as one of the noblest of arts and sciences. Now, with the help of this book, anyone can defend a belief in magic in convincing terms.

0-87542-374-4, 336 pgs., 6 x 9, illus., softcover   **$12.95**